# *Community Psychology*

## LINKING INDIVIDUALS AND COMMUNITIES

**JAMES H. DALTON**
*Bloomsburg University*

**MAURICE J. ELIAS**
*Rutgers University*

**ABRAHAM WANDERSMAN**
*University of South Carolina*

**Wadsworth**
Thomson Learning

*Australia • Canada • Mexico • Singapore • Spain • United Kingdom • United States*

Psychology Editor: Marianne Taflinger
Editorial Assistant: Suzanne Wood
Marketing Manager: Mark Linsenman
Project Editor: Debby Kramer
Print Buyer: Mary Noel
Permissions Editor: Bob Kauser
Production Service: Thomas E. Dorsaneo

Text Designer: Adrianne Bosworth
Copy Editor: Mike Cannon
Illustrator: TBH Typecast, Inc.
Cover Designer: Jennifer Dunn
Compositor: TBH Typecast, Inc.
Printer: R. R. Donnelley & Sons

For more information, contact
Wadsworth/Thomson Learning
10 Davis Drive
Belmont, CA 94002-3098 USA
http://www.wadsworth.com

**International Headquarters**
Thomson Learning
International Division
290 Harbor Drive, 2nd Floor
Stamford, CT 06902-7477
USA

**UK/Europe/Middle East/South Africa**
Thomson Learning
Berkshire House
168-173 High Holborn
London WC1V 7AA
United Kingdom

**Asia**
Thomson Learning
60 Albert Street, #15-01
Albert Complex
Singapore 189969

**Canada**
Nelson Thomson Learning
1120 Birchmount Road
Toronto, Ontario M1K 5G4
Canada

**Library of Congress Cataloging-in-Publication Data**

Dalton, James H.
    Community psychology : linking individuals and communities / James H. Dalton,
Maurice J. Elias, Abraham Wandersman.
        p.   cm.
    Includes bibliographical references and index.
    ISBN 0-534-16128-6
    1. Community psychology  2. Community mental health services.    I. Elias, Maurice J.
II. Wandersman, Abraham.    III. Title.

RA790.5 .D35  2000
362.2—dc21                                                                      00-024485

*To my wife Carolyn, whose companionship, love, and wisdom sustain me daily; to my sister Mary Hannah, who exemplifies courage; and to the memory of Heath and Sally Dalton, who taught by example the integration of faith and action.*

J.H.D.

*To my wife Ellen, with gratitude for her unwavering and cherished support always; and to Agnes and Sol Elias, whose unwavering support has served as the springboard for my accomplishments.*

M.J.E.

*To my wife Lois, whose love and wisdom make me happy and wiser; and to my father Irving Wandersman and in memory of my mother Hadassah Wandersman, who saw great things in me and nurtured me.*

A.W.

# Brief Contents

# CONTENTS

CHAPTER 2

# How Did Community Psychology Develop?   26

## PART TWO

# COMMUNITY RESEARCH   59

CHAPTER 3

# *The Aims of Community Research*   *60*

CHAPTER 4

## The Methods of Community Research   87

PART THREE

# UNDERSTANDING COMMUNITIES    119

CHAPTER 5

## *Understanding Ecology    120*

CHAPTER 6

## *Understanding Human Diversity*   *152*

CHAPTER 7

# Understanding Sense of Community   186

CHAPTER 8

## Understanding Coping and Social Support   218

PART FOUR

# PREVENTING PROBLEM BEHAVIOR AND PROMOTING SOCIAL COMPETENCE    257

CHAPTER 9

## *Prevention and Promotion: Key Concepts    258*

CHAPTER 10

## Prevention and Promotion: Current and Future Applications 284

CHAPTER 11

## Prevention and Promotion: Implementing Programs 309

PART FIVE

# COMMUNITY AND SOCIAL CHANGE    339

CHAPTER 12

## *Citizen Participation and Empowerment*    *340*

CHAPTER 13

## *Organizing for Community and Social Change    371*

CHAPTER 14

## *Program Evaluation and Program Development*   **403**

CHAPTER 15

## Looking Back, Looking Ahead    435

# PREFACE

## TO EVERY READER

We invite you to join us for this book's journey through the exciting field of community psychology. We seek to help you appreciate how psychology cannot understand individuals without considering the communities in which we live. Humans are community-seeking animals. Relationships with others are at the center of our lives. Individual lives and community life are intertwined, and this book illuminates many of the ways in which that intertwining occurs.

Our writing is influenced by our points of view (on some issues, we hold at least one per author). Throughout the book, we strive to be comprehensive and to discuss alternative views fairly. Yet our writing is inevitably the result of our experiences and perspectives, which means that those with different experiences and perspectives may view things differently. We respect that. This book is designed to lead to discussions, enabling you to develop and express your own views, and to understand those of others. That is what the ideal of respect for human diversity is about.

To enliven the journey and to engage you actively in learning, we have included a number of exercises, questions and examples to stimulate your thinking about communities in your own life, and to help you apply the concepts of community psychology. We encourage you to use these resources extensively.

The three of us were drawn to community psychology because it engaged our interests, passions, voices, values, and hopes for the individuals and communities in our lives. We invite you to join us in exploring this exciting field.

## TO INSTRUCTORS

We intend this book to be useful for upper-level undergraduate students and graduate students in psychology and related fields. Our perspective on community psychology generated distinctive chapters and content.

- Chapter 6, "Understanding Human Diversity", is the first such chapter in a community psychology textbook. We describe three conceptual frameworks for understanding diversity in community psychology, and consider what cultural competence and sensitivity mean for community psychologists. In addition, every chapter in the textbook includes examples of research and action that address human diversity.
- Chapter 7, "Understanding Sense of Community" is the first chapter-length discussion of this important concept. We describe conceptions of the psychological sense

of community and apply them to self-help organizations, neighborhoods, and religious/spiritual communities.

- Chapter 11, "Prevention and Promotion: Implementing Programs", is also the first of its kind. Innovative, effective community programs are increasingly being developed, yet not always transferred with fidelity or effectiveness to settings beyond their original context. Community psychology will not effectively extend the reach and impact of prevention/promotion programs until our students understand this critical issue. Maurice Elias is the primary author of this chapter.
- Chapter 14, "Program Evaluation and Program Development", is the first to integrate these two elements of effective community programs. Often separated, they can be integrated wisely to provide information that enriches program planning and implementation. Our chapter contains many real-life examples and applications. Abraham Wandersman is the primary author of this chapter.
- Chapters 12 and 13 explore the intertwining of citizen participation, empowerment, and sense of community, and how they influence community and social change. We also offer many practical examples and steps for those planning community change efforts. These conceptual and action issues have become key themes in community psychology.
- Chapter 11 (described above) is part of a three-chapter unit on "Preventing Problem Behavior and Promoting Social Competence". To paraphrase Buzz Lightyear, we "go to prevention and beyond": we focus on strengthening protective factors such as social competence, as well as taking an international perspective on prevention/promotion. Maurice Elias is the primary author of these chapters.
- Our perspective on the importance of religion and spirituality in community life is reflected in our chapters on human diversity, sense of community, coping and social support, citizen participation, and community change.
- Chapters 3–4 on the aims and methods of community research reflects the increasing importance of contextualist epistemology, researcher-community partnerships, and qualitative research methods, while also including innovative quantitative methods. (This unit may be used as it is placed, or following Chapter 8, or near the book's end, preceding or following Chapter 14.)
- Chapter 8, "Understanding Coping and Social Support" emphasizes social context and resources in coping, especially social support.

For a comprehensive overview of our chapters, we refer you to the complete Table of Contents and to the overview of the book given at the conclusion of Chapter 1.

The three authors wrote all of our chapters as joint products, with extensive feedback and revision among ourselves. Nonetheless, each chapter had a primary author whose perspective shaped it the most. James Dalton was primary author for Chapters 1–8, 12, 13 and 15; Maurice Elias for Chapters 9-11; Abraham Wandersman for Chapter 14. Jean Ann Linney collaborated in writing Chapter 5.

**Pedagogy**    Our perspective also generated a distinctive approach to pedagogy and writing.

- We begin each chapter with an exercise, story, or set of real-life examples, to illustrate what is to come. Our purpose is engage readers' thinking about communities in their own lives. Often, we continue this process through the chapter.

- Following each chapter are exercises, *addressed to the student*, which apply selected concepts from the chapter. Some of these make useful homework exercises, alone or with a classmate or friend. Others can be used in class as the basis of discussion.
- After certain sets of chapters (following Chapters 5, 8, 11, 13 and 14) we have provided Interchapter Exercises. These are longer and in more depth than chapter exercises, allowing the student or team of students to apply concepts from the preceding chapter(s) to a community environment or dilemma drawn from *their* experience. Interchapter Exercises include assessing a community environment, mapping your social support network, reading critically about prevention/promotion programs, and planning the development of a community coalition and a community program.
- Recommended Readings and World Wide Web sites also follow the chapters. We have shared our favorites and those that have been helpful to our students.
- Many journal articles in our Recommended Readings and in our references are available through *InfoTrac:* a fully searchable, online library of journals that students can access from their computer, if the instructor adopts the InfoTrac service. Two of the journals we cite most often are available in InfoTrac: the *American Journal of Community Psychology,* and the *Journal of Social Issues,* as well as other journals relevant to community psychology.
- We have included several study aids in every chapter: detailed chapter outlines, tables containing key concepts, figures that illustrate relationships among concepts, and chapter summaries.

## ACKNOWLEDGMENTS

This book would never have been conceived or written without the support of the communities in which its authors live and work, and of many individuals.

First, we thank Jean Ann Linney, who initiated our collaborative efforts in planning this text, but whose professional commitments later precluded her continuing with it. Jean Ann collaborated on chapter 5, reviewed chapter 14, and has been gracious and supportive throughout. We also thank Marianne Taflinger, our editor at Wadsworth, whose skillful mix of persistence and forbearance helped to finish this project and to do it well. In addition, we thank Jim Kelly and Beth Shinn for writing forewords and for helping each of us in many ways. We also thankfully acknowledge the influence of authors of prior textbooks in community psychology, especially Kenneth Heller, Richard Price, Shulamit Reinharz, Stephanie Riger, Murray Levine, David Perkins, and Julian Rappaport.

Jim Dalton wishes to thank special mentors and friends whose counsel and caring made possible his pursuing a vocation in community psychology, and helped shape many of the ideals that underlie this text. They are George Baxter, Thomas Peake, George Allen, Bill Iverson, Jack Chinsky, Maurice Elias, and George Howe.

Maurice Elias has drawn inspiration from many colleagues in community psychology. Those who provided special encouragement at early and difficult times are Jim Kelly, George Spivack, Myrna Shure, Emory Cowen, George Howe, Steve Larcen, Beth Shinn, Ed Trickett, Tom Gullotta, Cary Cherniss, John Rosado and Roger Weissberg.

Abe Wandersman would like to acknowledge his teachers who have expanded and enriched his view of the world, including his Cornell professors William Lambert, Edward Devereux, Urie Bronfenbrenner, Leonard Reissman, and Frank Becker. They spent many hours engaged in discussing ideas, ideals, and realities. His wife Lois also fulfilled this role at Cornell and sustains it now. Abe also acknowledges his many colleagues who collaborated in the research described in this book. They include (retrospectively) Pam Imm, Matt Chinman, Bob Goodman, David Fettterman, Margaret Dugan, Shakeh Kaftarian, Bill Hallman, Richard Rich, Doug Perkins, John Prestby, Donald Unger, David Chavis, Paul Florin and many others.

Our reviewers' support and critiques genuinely shaped the content and style of this book. We are expecially grateful to them: Douglas Perkins, Steve Davis, and Joseph Hughey field-tested drafts of this text in their classes; their feedback similarly shaped our revisions. A number of colleagues answered our questions, provided materials that greatly helped us, or granted permission to quote or adapt their works. These include David Altman, Eileen Astor-Stetson, Bill Berkowitz, Anne Brodsky, Kambon Camara, David Chavis, Paul Dokecki, Kevin Everhart, Steve Fawcett, David Fetterman, Mark Fondacaro, Pennie Foster-Fishman, Shelly Harrell, Kelly Hazel, Kenneth Heller, Jean Hill, Stevan Hobfoll, Keith Humphreys, Leonard Jason, Patricia Kamarinos, James Kelly, Christopher Keys, Donald Klein, Bret Kloos, Jeffrey Kress, Ed Madara, Frank Masterpasqua, Kenneth Maton, Greg Meissen, Thom Moore, Anne Mulvey, Cliff O'Donnell, Emily Ozer, Isaac Prilleltensky, Julian Rappaport, Marybeth Shinn, Christopher Sonn, Paul Speer, Debra Srebnik, Mary Ann Thomen, David Todd, Paul Toro, Edison Trickett, Richard Walsh-Bowers, Tom Wolff, and Marc Zimmerman. We especially thank our many recent students who read drafts, wrote responses, tested exercises, endured our mistakes, and otherwise helped improve this book.

We would also like to thank the reviewers who graciously agreed to review our work anonymously for the publisher. Now that we know who they are, we'd like to extend our warm appreciation for their diligent and creative efforts. They are: Dr. Lori Barker-Hackett, Dr. De Bryant, Dr. Jim Cook, Dr. Terry Cronan, Dr. Mary Davidson, Dr. Pennie Foster-Fishman, Dr. Margaret Gibbs, Dr. Dale Johnson, Dr. James Kelly, Dr. Marguerite Kermis, Dr. Raymond Lorion, Dr. John Malarkey, Dr. Mark Matthews, Dr. Judith Primavera, Dr. Bruce Tefft, Dr. Paul Toro, and Dr. Nancy Worsham.

Finally, we deeply thank our families, whose love, patience, and support always nurture and enrich our lives; and the communities in our lives that sustain us as well.

February 2000

James H. Dalton
Maurice J. Elias
Abraham Wandersman

# About the Authors

 James H. Dalton, Jr., Ph.D. is Professor of Psychology at Blooms-burg University, in Pennsylvania. He received his doctorate from the University of Connecticut, and his B.A. from King College, in Tennessee. With Maurice Elias, he co-developed the Community Psychology Education Connection, a resource for teachers of community psychology courses. The Education Connection maintains a clearinghouse of community psychology course mate-rials, fosters exchange of teaching ideas among community psy-chology instructors, and provides a column in *The Community Psychologist* newsletter. In Bloomsburg, Dr. Dalton has played leadership roles in the Task Force on Racial Equity and other groups devoted to community and social change. Dr. Dalton is married and the father of two children, Craig and Julia. By the time you read this, he hopes to have returned to pur-suing one of his favorite hobbies: hiking in the Appalachian Mountains.

 Maurice J. Elias, Ph.D., is Professor in the Department of Psy-chology at Rutgers University. He received his doctorate from the University of Connecticut, and his B.A. from Queens College, City University of New York. He co-developed the Social Deci-sion Making-Social Problem Solving Project which received the 1988 Lela Rowland Prevention Award from the National Mental Health Association and was named as a Model Program by the National Educational Goals Panel. Dr. Elias is also a member of the Leadership Team of the Collaborative to Advance Social and Emotional Learning (CASEL) and a Trustee of the Association for Children of New Jersey and the Hope Foundation. With colleagues at CASEL, Dr. Elias was senior author of *Promoting Social and Emotional Learning: Guidelines for Educators*, published by the Association for Supervision and

Curriculum Development and circulated to over 100,000 educational leaders in the U.S. and internationally. He also is a member of the expert panel that advised the development of the NASP/CECP *Early Warning Signs, Timely Response* book on violence prevention and subsequent materials, and he is the author of numerous books and articles on prevention. Dr. Elias has served in various capacities for the Society for Community Research and Action/APA Div. 27, most recently working as part of a team establishing a practice journal for the field. He also is a Contributing Faculty member at the Bildner Center for the Study of Jewish Life, and Co-Director (with Jeffrey Kress), of the Jewish Adolescent Identity Development Project. Dr. Elias is married and the father of two childrenl, Sara Elizabeth and Samara Alexandra.

Abraham Wandersman, Ph.D., is a Professor of Psychology at the University of South Carolina-Columbia. He received his doctorate from Cornell University, and his B.A. from the State University of New York at Stony Brook. Dr. Wandersman has performed research on environmental issues and community responses. He also performs research and program evaluation on citizen participation in community organizations and coalitions and on interagency collaboration. Dr. Wandersman is a co-author (with Jean Ann Linney) of *Prevention Plus III* and a co-editor (with David Fetterman and Shakeh Kaftarian) of *Empowerment Evaluation: Knowledge and Tools for Self Assessment and Accountability*. In 1998 he received the Myrdal Award for Evaluation Practice from the American Evaluation Association. He is currently working with the Governor's office of South Carolina on its statewide school readiness initiative called First Steps. Dr. Wandersman is married and the father of two children, Seth Ilya and Jeffrey Pall.

## PART One

# Introducing Community Psychology

# WHAT IS COMMUNITY PSYCHOLOGY?

# OPENING EXERCISE

Before you begin reading this chapter, study Figure 1.1, often known as the nine-dot problem, and try to solve it. Keep at it for at least several minutes before consulting Figure 1.2 on a following page for the answer.

Were you surprised by the answer in Figure 1.2? Here's an account by one author of this book (James H. Dalton).

> The first time I encountered this problem (in Watzlawick, Weakland, & Fisch, 1974), I diagrammed alternative solutions for a number of minutes, then gave up. Of course, I was surprised how simple the answer was! I had committed the error that most people commit when they encounter this problem: I made an assumption that was not given in the instructions or the diagram. The $3 \times 3$ array of nine dots seemed to me to create a square box, and I tried to draw all four straight lines within that box. Not only was that assumption unnecessary, *it actually made the problem impossible to solve.*
>
> The real problem was not the arrangements of the nine dots, but my mistaken assumption about the solution (and my increasing frustration as attempted solutions within the box failed). That box was a frame through which I viewed the nine-dot array, a frame that highlighted and limited what I saw there. And of course, that frame was more powerful because I did not recognize or question it.

Community psychology is concerned with social and community problems, and with how social systems affect the lives of individuals. Those problems, of course, are considerably more complex than the nine-dot problem in Figure 1.1. Yet this simple, abstract problem contains a key message of this textbook. The assumptions that people make about problems, especially when we are unaware that we are making them, determine the ways that we approach and try to solve a problem. We attempt solutions based on our assumptions, which we often consider common sense. These assumptions come from one's cultural background, personal experiences, education, and biases (and sometimes the biases that came with one's education). However, these assumptions often limit one's thinking, and may actually prevent effective responses to the problem. When that happens, a person's assumptions become the real problem. Thus, we all need to question our assumptions about social problems and social systems, seeking to understand our assumptions as well as those systems themselves. A person, a community, or a community psychology that ignores the ways in which these problems are framed will be imprisoned by those frames.

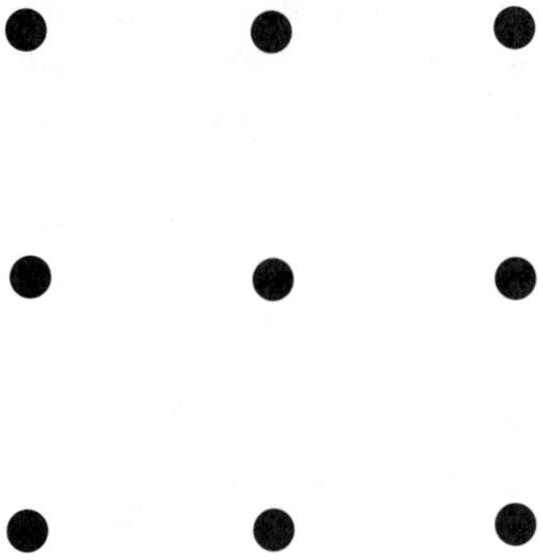

**FIGURE 1.1**

Instructions: Devise a way to draw four straight lines that pass through all nine dots, without lifting your pencil from the paper and without retracing a line. From *Change: Principles of Problem Formation and Problem Resolution* (p. 25), by P. Watzlawick, J. Weakland, and R. Fisch, 1974, New York: Norton. Reprinted with permission of the author.

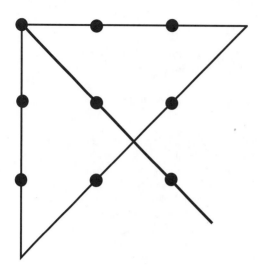

**FIGURE 1.2**

Solution to the problem presented in Figure 1.1. From *Change: Principles of Problem Formation and Problem Resolution* (p. 27), by P. Watzlawick, J. Weakland, and R. Fisch, 1974, New York: Norton. Reprinted with permission of the author.

## WHAT ARE THE KEY POINTS OF THIS CHAPTER?

In this introductory chapter we have four goals. First, we define the field of community psychology. The remainder of the chapter elaborates on that definition to deepen its meaning. Second, we illustrate how community psychology involves a shift in perspective, similar to the nine-dot problem, in thinking about individuals and communities. Third, we discuss the ecological levels of analysis that connect the individual to multiple social structures, from networks of friends to societies and cultures. Finally, we complete our introductory discussion of community psychology by defining seven core values that it represents.

## WHAT IS COMMUNITY PSYCHOLOGY? A DEFINITION

At first, the ideas of *community* and *psychology* seem contradictory. Community suggests the idea of persons coming together in some shared endeavor or at least geographic proximity, and connotes groups, neighborhoods, and larger structures. Psychology has traditionally concerned the individual: cognition, motivation, behavior, development, and related processes. In Western cultures, the nature and interests of individual and community have been considered different, often even opposing. Thus, isn't community psychology an oxymoron, a contradiction in terms (Shinn, 1990)?

A paradox exists when two seemingly contradictory ideas turn out, upon further analysis, to be interrelated, not contradictory. That is true of individual and community: They are linked in a number of ways. The concept of a community psychology offers a rich metaphor for exploring those linkages (Shinn, 1990). Keeping in mind the continuing diversity of community psychologists' interests, concepts, values, and methods, we offer this definition:

*Community psychology* concerns the relationships of the individual to communities and society. Through collaborative research and action, community psychologists seek to understand and to enhance quality of life for individuals, communities, and society.

Let's unpack this definition. Community psychology concerns the multiple relationships between the individual and communities, defining community broadly. An individual lives within many social structures that form communities, at multiple levels: networks of friends or extended family, workplace, school, voluntary association, religious congregation or spiritual community, neighborhood and wider locality, society and culture. The individual in community psychology is understood in terms of these relationships, not in isolation.

Community psychology's focus is not on the individual or on the environment alone, but on their connection. Cultural beliefs and traditions affect community or organizational characteristics, which in turn affect interpersonal relationships and individual lives. In the opposite direction, individuals acting in concert influence organizations, communities, and ultimately (in the long term) society. Community psychology also examines the influences of social structures on each other; for instance, how citizen organizations can influence the wider community. Yet that understanding is always tied in some way to how these structures affect or involve individuals.

Community psychology is committed to the development of psychologically valid knowledge, but also to making that knowledge useful in community life. In the community psychology perspective, knowledge is constructed through action. The community psychologist's role has often been described as that of a *participant–conceptualizer,* actively involved in community processes while also attempting to understand and explain them (Bennett et al., 1966, pp. 7–8). This perspective is aptly summarized in these comments:

> If you want to understand something, try to change it. (Dearborn, cited in Bronfenbrenner, 1979, p. 37)

> There is nothing so useful as a good theory. (Lewin, cited in Marrow, 1969)

> If we are afraid of testing our ideas about society by intervening in it, and if we are always detached observers of society and rarely if ever participants in it, we can only give our students ideas about society, not our experiences in it. We can tell our students about how society ought to be, but not what it is like to try to change the way things are. (S. B. Sarason, 1974, p. 266)

Community psychology's theory and concepts flow from involvement in community interventions and change, which are to be rigorously studied. Findings from research are then used both to build theory and to guide further community action. For example, a program developed in a high school setting to prevent or lessen violence represents a community action. Yet it also generates greater knowledge of the problem, the school and community setting, and prevention methods. That knowledge is useful not only for planning future programs but also for developing knowledge in psychology about adolescent development, social relations, organizational dynamics, and other topics.

Moreover, community psychology research and action are collaborative, based on partnerships with the persons or communities affected. A research project or action program developed from a community psychology perspective is planned and implemented with community members, recognizing their expertise and practical understanding of their community, and addressing their questions and aims. This is another aspect of the participant–conceptualizer role.

Finally, the aim of community psychology is the understanding and enhancement of both community and individual life. Community psychologists see these not as opposites, but as inextricable in the long term. A community that does not promote development of its members limits its collective potential, while individual growth and quality of life are enhanced when community life flowers. Consider, for instance, whether individual happiness and growth are better promoted in a neighborhood marked by indifference or conflict among neighbors or in one marked by friendships, neighborliness, and mutual respect. From another angle for instance, programs concerned with preventing drug abuse among adolescents (Botvin & Tortu, 1988) or with promoting child literacy (Cronan, Cruz, Arriaga, & Sarkin, 1996) at first may seem focused on the individual development of their participants. Yet, effectively addressing these issues in a preventive way enhances community life and reduces the shared costs of later problems.

## COMMUNITY PSYCHOLOGY: A SHIFT IN PERSPECTIVE

We can illustrate our definition of community perspective in part by showing how it leads to a shift of perspective about four real-life problems.

### Homelessness

One former U.S. president famously asserted that people become homeless "more or less by choice," which represents an individual view, focused on the characteristics of homeless persons. A different view is that homelessness can be described as a game of musical chairs (McChesney, cited in Shinn, 1990). The best predictor of the extent of homelessness in a community is (surprise!) the ratio of low-income housing units available compared to the number of persons and families seeking them. In a game of musical chairs, this is the ratio of chairs available to the number of players.

Of course, individual variables also influence who is homeless. These may include individual income, availability of family or friends who can offer temporary shelter, availability of social support for facing economic and other stressors, and individual resilience (e.g., optimism) for facing those stressors. To continue the musical chairs analogy, these factors determine who gets available seats and who is left standing, but not how many chairs are available.

A psychological study of homelessness that reveals only individual-level variables would be missing the larger reality: the supply of affordable housing units and the demand for them. Moreover, social policy that seeks to strengthen only individual and microsystem variables (better individual coping skills, improved job-interviewing skills, enhanced social support, or increased optimism) may reshuffle which musical-chairs players are left standing, yet do nothing about the number of available chairs.

### System Dependence

This chapter's primary author (James H. Dalton) once supervised a student intern in a crisis intervention center. She described some persons who called the center phone line frequently as "system-dependent" (a term she learned from her local clinical supervisor). System-dependent individuals seemed to need the social support of talking to center staff, often daily, and sought hospitalization frequently. The concept of system-dependence located the causes of this problem within the individual person. The phone line staff tried to resist these "manipulations" by clients in order to help the client to learn to live independently. Their efforts were only somewhat successful.

A different view might result from asking these questions: What family, friendship, or other sources of support are missing from this caller's life, such that he or she seeks so ardently a conversation with a stranger or the security of a hospital? Does this person have supportive family or friendship ties, and does the mental health system include or relate to those family or friends? Does a mutual help group exist locally that this person could join? What is this person's housing situation and how can it be improved to make support more accessible? What are the sources of meaning or purpose (for instance, friendship, work or community service, or spirituality) in this person's life? How can those sources of meaning be strengthened? All of these questions make primary the life experiences and the environment of the person (Riger, 1990).

## Self-Reliance

This is a core value of the dominant U.S. culture and a theme in many cultures influenced by global capitalism and by individualism (which we discuss in chaps. 2 and 6 in detail). In its most individualistic form, it involves taking care of oneself, making decisions independently, and avoiding dependence on others. Yet the reality of everyday life, in any culture, is that almost every individual is dependent on others in a myriad of ways, while others also depend on that person. Consider this example from a community psychology study of coping with life-threatening pulmonary disease:

> One woman was propping her ill husband's pillow, serving him lunch, adjusting his oxygen, giving him medication, reminding him of our appointment, and casually straightening the room with few wasted motions, while her husband boldly told the interviewer, 'I don't receive much help from others. I believe you should get things done on your own.' (Hobfoll, 1998, p. 131).

Individuals exist in a web of relationships with others. Community psychology focuses on the individual in that web, not on the individual alone.

## Professional Worldviews

For a final instance of a shift of perspective, consider this comment by a community psychologist:

> Our professional traditions tell us to attend to symptoms of depressed affect, such as the number of days when it was hard to get up in the morning, and to ignore signs of political apathy, such as the number of years of not registering to vote. We ask about queasy stomachs, sleepless nights, and family conflicts, but not about feeling safe in the streets, the number of persons on our block that we know by first name, or the availability of recreational centers for teens. We ask our teenagers about their

experiences with drugs, alcohol, and sex, but do not ask them about their hopes for the future, the community attributes they value, or whether they believe that they can make a personal impact upon the way they or others will live 10 years from now. . . . My point is fairly straightforward: not asking about community structures reflects our theoretical biases which, in turn, defines the domain of relevant inquiry. . . . The study of community structures will become part of our professional agenda only when we expand the conceptual templates through which we view the world, and we come to believe that community structures are modifiable and worth our collective effort. (Heller, 1989, p. 12).

Do you see the distinction Heller (1989) described? The professional traditions of clinical psychology, from which community psychology originally sprang in the United States, direct attention to internal processes (e.g., mood, queasy stomachs, or sleepless-ness) and to individual behavior (e.g., drug use). This largely overlooks the relationship of individuals to their communities: knowing neighbors, feeling safe, having a recreational space, and helping to determine their community's future. Yet these individual–community relationships often are crucial for individual and community well-being.

## First-Order and Second-Order Change

A shift of perspective is also involved in how community psychologists view the process of change in communities. A distinction can be made between *first-order change* and *second-order change* (Watzlawick et al., 1974). In attempting to solve a problem, one may alter, rearrange, or substitute the individual members of a group. That is first-order change, and although it may resolve some aspects of the problem, it often leads in the long run to the same problems with a new or rearranged cast of characters. It leads to the conclusion that the more things change, the more they remain the same.

Attempting to resolve homelessness by altering the homeless individuals without addressing the supply of affordable housing is an example of first-order change. Attempt-ing to change system-dependent individuals without attention to their life situation and experiences is also an example of first-order change. First-order change may be effective for some purposes, but it is limited because it does not address the linkages between indi-vidual and community.

To get a better idea of first-order change, try a thought experiment suggested by com-munity psychologist Seymour Sarason (1972) to analyze the educational system. Criticisms of schools, at least in the United States, often focus blame on individuals or collections of individuals, such as incompetent teachers, unmotivated or unprepared students, or unin-volved parents, administrators, or board members. To analyze these criticisms, imagine changing every individual person in the school: firing all teachers and staff and hiring replacements, obtaining a new student population, and changing every individual from the school board to the classroom, yet leaving intact the structure of role relationships and policies about how the school is to be run. How long do you think it will be before the same issues and criticisms return? If your answer is "not long," you are seeing the limita-tions of first-order change.

A group is not just a collection of individuals; it is also a set of explicit or implicit assumptions about relations between members. Changing these assumptions (thus chang-ing the system) is an example of second-order change.

For community problems, second-order change alters the role relationships among persons in a setting (Linney, 1990; Seidman, 1988). Role relationships are based on explicit or implicit assumptions about how the group or setting should function. An example is that in most classrooms, teachers ask most of the questions. This has more to do with the teacher-student role relationship than with the personalities of teacher and students (S. B. Sarason, 1995; Seidman, 1988).

How does second-order change alter role relationships? Instead of preserving rigid lines between bosses who make decisions and workers who carry them out, it involves collaborative decision making. Instead of preserving rigid lines of expertise between mental health professionals and their patients, it involves finding ways that persons with disorders may help each other, or ways that persons with disorders may be enabled to assume greater autonomy in managing their lives. In a classroom marked by inequality and conflict between students of different races, second-order change involves creating collaborative group exercises and making sure all students are treated as equals (Aronson, Stephan, Sikes, Blaney & Snapp, 1978).

Second-order change is often the focus of community psychology. It requires attention to social systems or structures beyond the individual. That requires a set of concepts for describing those structures, which community psychologists term *ecological levels of analysis.*

# ECOLOGICAL LEVELS OF ANALYSIS IN COMMUNITY PSYCHOLOGY

What are ecological levels of analysis? This discussion begins with an example of their importance.

## Child Maltreatment: Ecological Levels of Analysis

Maltreatment (abuse and neglect) of children represents a major social problem in the United States and in other countries. In a review of the research literature on its causes, a developmental psychologist (Belsky, 1993) noted that child maltreatment has no single cause or simple set of causes; rather, multiple processes at multiple levels contribute to make it more or less likely in a particular situation.

The research Belsky (1993) reviewed indicates that maltreatment is partly a result of individual parental factors. For instance, parents are more likely to abuse or neglect their child if they are less able to manage negative emotions, have a troubled childhood history of their own, and rely on punitive control and physical punishment. Yet these individual factors do not explain child maltreatment fully. For instance, many parents with troubled histories, even a history of having been abused, do not abuse or neglect their children. The broader context must be taken into account (Belsky, 1993).

One contextual factor is social support for parents, including both aid or advice in parenting and emotional support. Parents who maltreat their children tend to be socially isolated, lacking support from family or friends (Belsky, 1993). That isolation often is partly a result of their own actions, but also is influenced by community factors. A study of Chicago neighborhoods, all similar in socioeconomic status, compared those in which reported child maltreatment rates were higher with those in which the rates were lower (Garbarino & Kostelny, 1992). The neighborhoods with less reported abuse had more neighborly ties, stronger community organizations and leadership, and higher reported quality of neighborhood life. Another contextual factor influencing the likelihood of maltreatment is level of unemployment in a community (Belsky, 1980). Finally, nations (such as the United States) with greater public condoning of violence as a means of parental control and for resolving disputes also have higher rates of child maltreatment (Belsky, 1993).

To summarize, child maltreatment involves not only individual-parental factors, but also characteristics of support networks, neighborhoods, economic factors such as unemployment, and cultural forces such as support for violence (Belsky, 1980, 1993). It provides an example of the value of taking multiple levels of factors into account, both for understanding and for planning action. The community psychology perspective is defined in part by its insistence on multiple levels of analysis.

## A Metaphor for Ecological Levels

Ecological levels of analysis are usefully illustrated with a metaphor suggested by Bronfenbrenner (1979): the Russian nesting doll. A nesting doll is round or egg-shaped and contains a succession of smaller dolls, each inside the other. Each doll, when opened, reveals a smaller doll inside, until the smallest one appears. As a metaphor, the nesting doll calls attention to how the smallest doll exists within layers of larger dolls, just as each individual exists within layers of social relationships: family, friendship network, organizations, neighborhoods, and cultures and societies. However, the nesting doll metaphor is incomplete: Not only is each individual nested within larger units, but individual life is strongly influenced by those layers of relationships and in turn influences them as well. Individuals, societies, and the layers of relationships between them are interdependent. Indeed, the field of community psychology is based on that interdependence.

Figure 1.3 illustrates the concept of ecological levels of analysis in community psychology.

**Individuals**    Consider the smallest nesting doll to be the individual person, nested within a set of interdependent layers of relationships. The person chooses his or her relationships or environments to some extent, and influences them in many ways; likewise, they influence the person's choices. Much research in community psychology concerns individuals, although not in terms of personality differences or internal processes. Rather, individuals are studied in terms of their relationships to the environments in their lives. For example, overcoming alcohol abuse has been studied in relation to changes in employment and to mutual help group involvement (Dooley & Prause, 1997; Humphreys, Finney, & Moos, 1994).

Much research and action in community psychology involves the ecological transitions (Bronfenbrenner, 1979) made by individuals undergoing changes in social relationships, such as entering or leaving school, marrying, divorcing, becoming a new parent, losing a job, or bereavement. Many community psychology action programs attempt to strengthen individuals' skills for coping with such transitions, or for relating well to others (Albee & Gullotta, 1997).

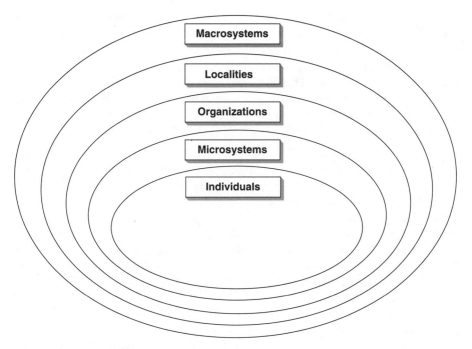

FIGURE **1.3**

Levels of analysis for community psychology.

*Microsystems*    In our nesting doll metaphor, the first encapsulating doll represents the level of analysis just beyond the individual: microsystems. Microsystems are environments in which the person engages in direct, personal interaction with others over time (Bronfenbrenner, 1979, p. 22). They include families (nuclear and extended), classrooms, friendship networks, scout troops, athletic teams, residence hall wings, small businesses, self-help groups, and similar groups, as long as these are small enough to provide face-to-face, influential, personal relationships. Many small workplaces and community organizations, and small religious congregations are microsystems. The connection between individuals and microsystems occurs through the creating of interpersonal relationships, assuming of social roles, and performing of shared tasks (Maton & Salem, 1995).

*Organizations*    The next larger encapsulating doll represents the *organizational level of analysis*. Organizations consist of sets of microsystems, such as classes, staff, and board making up a school; departments and other units making up a university; or departments, shifts, or work teams making up a factory. Larger religious congregations are usually composed of smaller microsystems such as choirs, religious classes, or prayer groups; larger volunteer community organizations usually work through committees or subgroups. Individuals participate in organizations and often feel a loyalty to them, sometimes even to quite large ones, but that participation is usually enacted through a microsystem of the larger organization.

Community psychology is concerned with organizations, both with their relationships to smaller microsystems and individual members, and with their relationships with the larger community and society. Organizations studied by community psychologists include human service organizations, treatment programs, corporations, neighborhood associations, cooperative housing units, religious congregations, and citizen community organizations. Much of the extensive research on community interventions designed to prevent problems in living or to promote wellness involves organizations, chiefly schools and health care settings (Durlak & Wells, 1997).

**Localities**    The *locality level of analysis* is represented by the next encapsulating doll. Although the term *community* has meanings at many levels of analysis, one prominent meaning refers to geographic localities, including rural counties, small towns, urban blocks or neighborhoods, and entire cities. Individuals participate in the life of their shared locality mainly through community organizations or institutions. Even in small towns, individuals seldom influence the wider community unless they work alongside other citizens in an organization or are part of an influential microsystem that spans several organizations. Thus, localities may be understood as sets of organizations or of microsystems.

Some of the factors associated with greater levels of child maltreatment mentioned earlier are locality-level variables. The Garbarino and Kostelny (1992) study is one example: In Chicago neighborhoods with lower rates of child maltreatment, neighboring, community organizations, and a positive sense of community were stronger. Moreover, families in which maltreatment occurs are more likely than others to be isolated from such community support (Belsky, 1993).

An example of the linkage between organizations and wider localities is the recent emergence of community coalitions, comprised of representatives of various community groups and organizations, formed to address wider community issues such as drug abuse or health concerns. The psychological sense of community and citizen participation and empowerment in communities also have been extensively studied.

**Macrosystems**    Finally, beyond the locality in scope, and represented by the largest nesting doll, are macrosystems (Bronfenbrenner, 1979). These include societies (usually understood as nations) and cultures, as well as governmental and economic institutions beyond the local community. Bronfenbrenner restricted his usage of this term to societies and cultures, but other levels, such as regional differences within a national culture, multiple levels of government, and international corporations also influence smaller systems and individuals.

Macrosystems exercise influence not only through policies and specific governmental or economic decisions, but through ideologies and belief systems. For instance, individualism as a cultural tradition greatly influences U.S. culture and the discipline of psychology. A further example, noted above, is that cultural values and forces are related to incidence of violence (Belsky, 1993; Lipset, 1996). Macrosystems form contexts within which the other levels function, thus influencing individual, microsystem, organizational, and community life.

An important level of analysis that we will include under macrosystems is the *population level of analysis*. A population is often defined by demographic category: by gender, race or ethnicity, nationality, socioeconomic status or income, or other measurable characteristic. Depending on the focus of community research or action, being a member of a given population may be an important contextual variable. For instance, recent community psychology studies have concerned populations such as lesbian and gay communities, persons with physical disabilities, Southeast Asian immigrants to the United States, Latinos/Latinas, Black women, American Indians, homeless youth, unemployed autoworkers, and others. From a community psychology perspective, such studies seek to identify not only macrosystem stressors but also strengths and assets of populations. In addition, the diversity within a population category must be recognized; not all individuals, microsystems or communities within a population are identical, of course.

Many studies in community psychology concern more than one level of analysis. For instance, Schwarzer, Hahn, and Schroeder (1994) studied social support networks (microsystems) among residents and migrants from East Germany following a major macrosystems change, the opening of the border between East and West Germany. Community psychologists often also seek to make their work with communities and smaller units of analysis contribute to social change in macrosystems. Another example is a study of rural midwestern U.S. families that documented that economic stress on families lowered adolescents' sense of control in their lives and increased symptoms of anxiety and depression (Conger, Conger, Matthews, & Elder, 1999).

Table 1.1 gives examples of phenomena studied by community psychologists at each ecological level of analysis.

---

**TABLE 1.1**    **ECOLOGICAL LEVELS OF ANALYSIS FOR COMMUNITY PSYCHOLOGY**

| Level | Examples of research topics |
| --- | --- |
| **Individual** | Individual outcomes of community problems: e.g., depression, anxiety, drug abuse, loneliness. Community programs for strengthening individual competencies or coping skills: e.g., problem-solving, empathy, assertion (e.g., Albee & Gullotta, 1997; Durlak & Wells, 1997, 1998). |
| **Microsystem** | Families, social support networks, mutual help groups, caregiving relationships, classrooms, adolescent peer relationships (e.g., Chung & Elias, 1996; Humphreys & Noke, 1997; Latkin, Mandell, Vlahov, Oziemkowska, & Celentano, 1996; Ozer, Weinstein, Maslach, & Siegel, 1997; Roosa, Dumka, & Tein, 1996; Seidman et al., 1995; Turner & Catania, 1997). |
| **Organization** | Schools, health care settings, workplaces, religious organizations, human service organizations, citizen organizations, neighborhood associations, cooperative housing (e.g., Bond & Keys, 1993; Foster-Fishman & Keys, 1997; Kloos & Moore, in press; Perkins, Brown, & Taylor, 1996; Saegert & Winkel, 1996; Speer & Hughey, 1995; Timko, 1996). |
| **Community** | Community coalitions for drug abuse prevention, health promotion, and community change; psychological sense of community (e.g., Biglan et al., 1996; Fawcett et al., 1995; Jason, 1997; Kaniasty & Norris, 1995; McMillan et al., 1995; McMillan & Chavis, 1986; S. B. Sarason, 1974; Zimmerman & Perkins, 1995). |
| **Macrosystem** | Studies of cultural forces, of oppressed populations, and of macrosystem factors and change (e.g., Belsky, 1993; Conger et al., 1999; Mitchell & Beals, 1997; Schwarzer, Hahn, & Schroeder, 1994; Serrano-Garcia & Bond, 1994; J. Unger, Kipke, Simon, Montgomery, & Johnson, 1997). |

# SEVEN CORE VALUES IN COMMUNITY PSYCHOLOGY

To elaborate the definition of community psychology, we have described ecological levels of analysis. Now we elaborate it further by discussing the core values of the field. Community psychology is not a "value-free" science. Its core ideals guide its research and action.

What are those core values? Every community psychology research project or action initiative requires attention to its creators' answer to two questions (Prilleltensky, 1997, 1999):

- What is the good life?
- What is the good society?

Answers to these questions influence, for instance, the choice of dependent or outcome variables in research, the conditions that are hypothesized to influence those outcomes, the goals of a community program or intervention, and the methods of that intervention.

Of course, no discipline commands unanimity of values among its members, and community psychologists in particular can be a skeptical lot. Yet describing the implicit or explicit values of the field is useful. The debates among community psychologists seldom occur because a value is prized by some and rejected by others in the abstract. Instead, the complexities of community life lead to conflicting values and to differing choices about which value is most important in a given context. Values for community psychology therefore must be understood in terms of how they complement each other in practice (Prilleltensky, 1999).

Table 1.2 lists the seven core values. We begin with the value most closely linked to the individual level of analysis, then proceed to those more closely linked to community and macrosystem levels. This order is not a ranking of these values' importance. Our discussion of seven core community psychology values follows, with some exceptions, Prilleltensky's (1997, 1999) analysis.

## Individual Wellness

This value (Cowen, 1991, 1994; Prilleltensky, 1999) refers to physical and psychological health, including the presence of social–emotional coping skills to maintain that health. It also goes beyond minimal criteria of health to include personal well-being, development of identity, and attainment of personal goals such as academic achievement or pursuit of spiritual meaning (e.g., Maton, Hrabowski, & Greif, 1998; Maton & Wells, 1995). Symptoms

**TABLE 1.2    SEVEN CORE VALUES IN COMMUNITY PSYCHOLOGY**

| | |
|---|---|
| Individual wellness | Collaboration and community strengths |
| Sense of community | Respect for human diversity |
| Social justice | Empirical grounding |
| Citizen participation | |

of psychological distress, indicators of coping competence, and measures of personal well-being are often the dependent variables or outcome criteria for community psychology research and intervention.

Of course, these concerns are also the focus of clinical psychology and related fields, especially at the individual and family levels of analysis. Clinical treatment of clients provides caring and compassion. Yet enactment of that compassion is limited to the clinician's client caseload. Those who cannot afford psychotherapy, for instance, are excluded (Prilleltensky, 1997).

One of the events leading to the founding of community psychology was the recognition that clinical treatment alone would never meet all the mental health needs of a society. Albee's (1959) study found that supplying the mental health needs of the United States through psychotherapy and similar professional services would be practically impossible. (Albee's analysis of 40 years ago is even more believable now in the era of managed health care.) Clinical care is valuable, but not available to all, and often those who need it most do not have access to it. Action beyond clinical care is needed.

Applying this value in action, community psychologists have helped develop, or strengthen through research, community programs and organizations concerned with the following:

- prevention of maladaptive behavior
- developing competencies or skills for adaptive coping
- social support in coping, and self-help or mutual aid groups
- intervention programs in nonclinical settings such as schools.

Community psychologists have provided solid evidence that preventive interventions in communities are effective (Albee & Gullotta, 1997; Cowen, 1994; Durlak & Wells, 1997, 1998; Heller, 1990; Price, Cowen, Lorion, & Ramos-McKay, 1988). The range of such problems includes difficulties in the social and academic development of children, adolescent behavior problems and juvenile delinquency, adult physical health and depression, family transitions such as divorce, and family violence (Albee & Gullotta, 1997; Barton, Hopkins, McElhaney, Heigel, & Salassi, 1995; L. Bond & Compas, 1989; Price et al., 1988).

In addition, community psychologists have studied mutual aid and self-help organizations, in which people with a shared problem or situation form a community and help each other cope. Alcoholics Anonymous and other Twelve Step organizations are the best-known examples. Community psychologists and other social scientists, who are willing to respect the values and experiences of group members, have been able to study these organizations and document their effects (e.g., Borkman, 1991; Humphreys & Rappaport, 1994; L. Roberts et al., 1991; Zimmerman et al., 1991). Community psychologists have also studied coping with stress and the importance of social support from informal networks of friends and others as well (e.g., Gesten & Jason, 1987; Hobfoll & Vaux, 1993).

The concepts and methods of "prevention science" (Coie et al., 1993), social support (e.g., Hobfoll & Vaux, 1993) and psychological wellness (Cowen, 1994) have been developed in collaboration with many other disciplines, and are not the exclusive province of community psychology. They complement the approaches of clinical psychology and other fields. Moreover, some of these concepts have become mainstream within the overall field of psychology as well (Heller, 1990).

## Sense of Community

This value is explicit in the name of the field and is at the center of some definitions of it (S. B. Sarason, 1974). Sense of community refers to a perception of belongingness and mutual commitment, which links individuals in a collective unity (D. W. McMillan & Chavis, 1986; S. B. Sarason, 1974). S. B. Sarason (1974) further defined it to include "interdependence with others, a willingness to maintain this interdependence by giving to or doing for others what one expects from them, the feeling that one is part of a larger dependable and stable structure (p. 157)."

This value of community balances the value of individual wellness. The emphasis in Western cultures and in the field of psychology is on the individual, which in its worst forms can foster selfishness or indifference to others in the community (Bellah, Madsen, Sullivan, Swidler, & Tipton, 1985; Prilleltensky, 1999; Wallach & Wallach, 1983). From a community psychology perspective, strong communities benefit individuals; quality of life for the individual and for the community are intertwined (Prilleltensky, 1999).

Community psychologists apply this value in action by studying and working to strengthen communities. These communities may include neighborhoods (e.g., Wandersman & Florin, 1990), the mutual aid and self-help groups mentioned earlier, religious and spiritual communities (e.g., Kloos & Moore, 2000; Maton & Wells, 1995), and other groupings. An example is the Block Booster Project, which worked with urban block associations in New York City (Florin, Chavis, Wandersman & Rich, 1992). Block associations are citizen organizations organized for each city block that sponsor activities such as crime prevention, recreation, and youth programs, and address other neighborhood issues. Community coalitions on preventing drug abuse are another example (Fawcett et al., 1995; B. McMillan, Florin, Stevenson, Kerman, & Mitchell, 1995).

## Social Justice

Social justice has multiple meanings (Fondacaro & Weinberg, 1999). Prilleltensky (1999) defined this as fair, equitable allocation of resources, opportunities, obligations, and bargaining power in society as a whole. It is thus concerned with equality. One way for community psychologists to apply this value in action involves research that takes into account the social and economic factors that affect individual wellness (Prilleltensky, 1999). It also involves advocacy for policies that make resources for wellness available to all members of a community or society, especially its least privileged.

U.S. history has been marked by struggles for access to justice by groups excluded from it. The American constitutional ideals of justice were compromised from the very first by exclusion of many groups from pursuit of those ideals (Phillips, 1993). The groups excluded from social justice in U.S. history have included women, persons of color, the poor, immigrants, workers, gay men and lesbians, and others. The practical meanings of American ideals of justice are continually being tested, sometimes expanding and sometimes contracting, as groups gain or lose the power to pursue those ideals. Justice may be sought nationally, in local communities, or in workplaces, through laws and policies designed to limit unfair treatment. It may also be sought in personal relationships, for instance in seeking to empower, and avoid exploiting, women in those relationships.

The tradition of liberation psychology in Latin America represents one example of a psychological pursuit of social justice (Montero, 1996). Feminism's concern for social justice has had a strong effect on psychology, including community psychology. Two examples have been research on violence against women (e.g., Campbell, 1998) and methods of research that enable women to articulate their own "voice" and experiences in their own terms (Gilligan, 1982; Reinharz, 1994; Riger, 1990). A concern for justice also is closely connected to the influential concept of empowerment (Rappaport, 1981, 1987), which is discussed in later chapters.

## *Citizen Participation*

This value refers to peaceful, respectful, collaborative processes of making decisions that allow all members of a community to have meaningful involvement (Prilleltensky, 1999; Wandersman & Florin, 1990). At a higher ecological level, it also refers to the ability of a community to participate in decisions that determine its future. Both senses of the term are related to the concept of empowerment (Rappaport, 1987, 1995; Zimmerman & Perkins, 1995). The idea that communities should participate in defining the problems or issues that affect them, and in deciding how to resolve them, is fundamental to the community psychology perspective.

Examples of citizen participation in action occur at several ecological levels. Mutual aid and self-help groups represent a means of coping with or overcoming personal problems that are based on a participatory model rather than dependence on professional experts. Grassroots citizen groups and neighborhood organizations provide another example. Community-wide drug abuse prevention coalitions also promote citizen participation.

An example of this value in action is as follows: A community psychologist was engaged by a community health coalition to work with citizens in one local community to plan community health initiatives. An evening meeting open to all citizens was scheduled. In preparing for such a meeting, one might perhaps expect to discuss a community education campaign to promote healthy exercise or nutrition, or the need for a community clinic, or offering screening programs for diseases such as diabetes or hypertension, or forming self-help groups for those with particular conditions. Instead, the most important need identified by many citizens was for street signs. The community psychologist could barely contain his surprise. Yet recently in this community, several persons needing emergency medical care had been delayed, with serious consequences, because ambulances had not been able to locate residences by street address.

The community psychologist duly noted this concern, then sought to turn the conversation to other matters more in line with his preconceptions of community health issues. However, the local citizens would not have it; they wanted a plan for action on street signs. When that need had been met, they reasoned, the health coalition could be trusted to work with them on other issues. The community psychologist then shifted to working together with the citizens to get the municipality to erect better street signs (Wolff & Lee, 1997). Instead of pursuing his own ideas or agenda, he worked with citizens to accomplish their goals. His action illustrates the value of citizen participation as well as the value of collaboration, which is described next.

## Collaboration and Community Strengths

This value involves relationships between community psychologists and citizens with whom they work. It is perhaps the most distinctive value of community psychology.

Psychologists usually relate to community members as experts: researchers, clinical or educational professionals, organizational consultants, and similar roles. That sets up a hierarchical, unequal relationship of expert and client. Community psychologists certainly have expertise to share with communities, but they also seek to identify and appreciate the life experiences, wisdom, and resources (in short, the community strengths) that already exist there. They seek to create a collaborative relationship in which both psychologist and community members contribute knowledge and resources, and in which both participate in the processes of setting goals and making decisions (Kelly, 1986; Prilleltensky, 1999; Tyler, Pargament, & Gatz, 1983).

Community psychologists increasingly are emphasizing this value in their research and action. Those efforts include working with community members to determine the goals and methods of a community program, as well as using methods of research that tap the viewpoints and experiences of community members rather than just measuring variables determined by the researcher. This means, for instance, building a respectful, collaborative relationship with a community before research or action begins (Kelly, 1986). It also means careful choice of research methods and procedures that are appropriate for the community (e.g., Brydon-Miller & Tolman, 1997; K. Miller & Banyard, 1998; Seidman, Hughes, & Williams, 1993; Tolan, Keys, Chertok, & Jason, 1990).

The value of collaboration and community strengths directs attention to *how* community psychologists do their work. Thus it concerns means, not ends. It may be understood as procedural justice or fairness in methods (Fondacaro & Weinberg, 1999), whereas social justice as we have defined it refers to fairness of outcomes or ends (Prilleltensky, 1999). Work with communities requires attention to both means and ends. It also is related to the value of sense of community; community psychologists seek to build a communal relationship with community members.

## Respect for Human Diversity

This value recognizes and prizes the variety of communities and social identities, based on gender, ethnic or racial membership, sexual orientation, ability or disability, socioeconomic status, age, or other terms. It has become an important value in community psychology, at the center of some definitions of the field (Rappaport, 1977a). Understanding individuals in communities, especially in multicultural societies, requires a respect for diversity (Trickett, 1996). Concepts related to human diversity are greatly expanding the focus and enriching the depth of community research and action (Serrano-Garcia & Bond, 1994; Trickett, Watts, & Birman, 1994; Wilson, 1997). These efforts especially include studies designed to understand populations, whether defined by race–ethnicity, culture, gender, socioeconomic status, or other identity, in their own terms.

One aspect of respecting human diversity, similar to the idea of community strengths just mentioned, is searching for the strengths and resources in all cultures, and among populations often demeaned in wider society. Identifying strengths and survival skills developed among women, or members of self-help groups (Borkman, 1991) provides an example of this perspective, as does identifying African cultural traditions that promote personal growth and sense of community (L. J. Myers & Speight, 1994).

Another aspect is adapting research methods and questions to be appropriate to the culture studied. This is more than simply translating questionnaires into a language other than English. It involves a thoroughgoing reexamination of the aims, methods, and expected outcomes of research, in terms of the worldview and values of the culture to be studied (Marin, Marin, Perez-Stable, Sabogal, & Otero-Sabogal, 1990; Seidman, Hughes, & Williams, 1993).

Respect for diversity is often related to the other values we have discussed, principally sense of community, social justice and citizen participation, and collaboration and community strengths. It involves genuinely accepting diverse persons and groups as equals.

## Empirical Grounding

Since its origins, community psychology has prized the integration of research with community action. At the 1965 Swampscott conference that marked the emergence of community psychology as a separate discipline, the role of participant–conceptualizer expressed this ideal (Bennett et al., 1966). Community psychologists are impatient both with theory that lacks empirical basis in community life and with research that ignores the context and interests of the community in which it occurred. The value community psychologists place on empirical research is what makes the field different from a social movement or community action group with similar values. Community psychologists seek to define, understand, and address community problems and issues in ways that can be studied in research.

Empirical grounding as a value in community psychology no longer means solely experimental or quantitative research. In 1988, a major conference led to broadened boundaries of acceptable research methods (Tolan et al., 1990). Qualitative research methods have assumed a more important role in understanding community life, along with innovative quantitative methods adapted to community uses (see chaps. 3 and 4).

Community psychologists accept the assertion that no research is value-free, and that researchers' theory, concepts, and findings are shaped by their values and preconceptions. Drawing conclusions from research thus requires attention to those values, not simply to the data. In addition, community researchers seek to collaborate with community members in performing research. Thus, community research is often different in method and outcome from laboratory-based research in psychology. Yet empirical knowledge, from a diversity of sources, is prized in community psychology as a distinctive emphasis of the field.

## CONCLUSION: VALUES AND CONTEXT

These seven values are competing yet complementary. There are many pairings among them of related opposites that must be balanced with each other. For instance, individual wellness must be balanced with concern for the wider community. Although individual wellness and social justice are not contradictory in theory, pursuing both competently in practice is difficult for an individual community psychologist, and even for the discipline as a whole. Collaborating with local community members is a time-consuming approach that can slow the completion of research needed to provide empirical grounding. Promoting a local sense of community does not necessarily promote a wider sense of solidarity or concern for the wider society. Respect for diversity of populations within a multicultural society must be balanced with a concern for bonds of solidarity across the wider society (Prilleltensky, 1999).

Community life, and a wise community psychology, require choices and accommodations among these values rather than single-minded pursuit of one or two. Community psychologists must carefully choose among competing values, reckoning their tradeoffs and limits. Both the dilemmas and the richness of community psychology are perhaps most apparent when those choices are weighed carefully.

In the abstract, ideas like individual wellness, social justice, respect for diversity, and sense of community can mean very different things to different persons or in different contexts. The seven values we have described must be defined further in terms of the history of their use in community psychology (Riger, 1999). Otherwise, they can be (and have been) used in contradictory ways. It is to that history of ideas and action in community psychology that we turn in chapter 2.

## An Overview of This Book

This textbook is divided into five units. In this chapter, we have defined and elaborated on the meaning of community psychology. In chapter 2, we continue that elaboration by examining the history of the field.

The second unit concerns the research aims and methods of community psychology. We describe the context and purposes of community research, and how this involves a collaborative relationship with the community that hosts the research. We then examine qualitative and quantitative approaches to conducting community research. Throughout the unit, we emphasize and give examples of the intertwining of research and community action.

Our third unit covers concepts of community psychology that cut across a number of specific areas of research and community action. These are not simply theoretical; they often arise from community research and from the experiences of those in action programs. They make many aspects of community life more understandable: for example, schools, neighborhoods, social support networks, prevention/promotion programs, and grassroots community organizations. In chapter 5, we examine ecological concepts used to understand physical and social settings in terms of their relationships to individuals and communities. In chapter 6, we examine human diversity, beginning by defining some of the dimensions of diversity. We then describe three perspectives for understanding differences among populations: culture, oppression and power, and acculturation. We emphasize the connections between these concepts and individual life in communities. In chapter 7, we take up the psychological sense of community and its importance in the lives of individuals and communities. We illustrate that importance by discussing research on self-help groups, religious–spiritual communities, and neighborhoods. Finally, in chapter 8, we describe an ecological perspective on coping with stressors and adverse circumstances, especially emphasizing the resource of social support. This ties ecological and community concepts to individual living.

Our fourth unit covers a long-standing concern in community psychology: prevention of problems in living and promotion of psychosocial competence. Chapter 9 describes basic concepts for understanding the aims and approaches of prevention/promotion programs in the community, framing these in terms of risk and protective processes and the importance of social and emotional competence. Chapter 10 reviews exemplary prevention/promotion programs and emphasizes how these are continuously evolving and changing. One of our aims in that chapter is to provide you with the conceptual tools to analyze prevention/promotion needs and approaches in your own community. Chapter 11 concerns the cutting-edge issue of implementation of prevention/promotion programs in communities, especially the importance of adapting the program to local context and resources.

Our final unit concerns broader community-level initiatives and change. In chapter 12, we discuss citizen participation and personal empowerment through grassroots community organizations and involvement in community change. In chapter 13, we describe aims and methods of community change initiatives, examining how citizens can collectively address community issues and improve the quality of life in their communities. Chapter 14 discusses how community programs and initiatives can be developed and evaluated in a more planned manner, using program evaluation to improve their effectiveness. Chapter 15 summarizes themes of community psychology and future challenges for the field.

These chapters and units form an organic whole. Community psychologists, as you can see throughout this book, emphasize the intertwining and mutual influence of many things that seem to be opposites: community research and community action; individual and community life; preventing personal problems and improving the quality of community life; conceptual knowledge, empirical research, and personal experience in communities; and psychologists and community members. We note many of the interconnections among concepts, values, research, and action as we proceed. We ask that you look for them as well. We hope that you will come to share our enthusiastic interest in communities and community psychology.

## Chapter Summary

**1.** Community psychology concerns the relationships of the individual to communities and society. Through collaborative research and action, it seeks to understand and to enhance quality of life for individuals, communities and society. This definition emphasizes the linkages described above. It also emphasizes the collaborative approach of community psychology, whether in research or action. Community psychologists seek to work with community members as partners. Finally, community psychology is concerned with improving the well-being of individuals and of communities.

**2.** Compared to other psychological fields, community psychology involves a shift in perspective. That shift means that the focus of community psychology is not on the individual alone, but on the linkages between individual and social structure, including friendship networks, organizations, communities, and societies and cultures. We illustrated this shift with three examples: homelessness as a game of musical chairs, the life situations of persons labeled as system-dependent, and how professional worldviews draw psychologists' attention to individual symptoms rather than connections between individuals and community life. We introduced the concepts of first-order change and second-order change to describe how this applies to attempts to resolve community problems.

**3.** In order to understand linkages between individuals and communities and society, community psychologists study ecological levels of analysis. Individuals are nested within microsystems such as families, friendship networks, classrooms, and small groups. Microsystems often are nested within organizations such as schools and workplaces. Organizations are nested within wider localities, such as neighborhoods. Communities are nested within macrosystems such as societies, cultures, and populations defined by shared characteristics. Each of these levels affects the lives of individuals within it.

**4.** Community psychology is based on seven core values: individual wellness, sense of community, social justice, citizen participation, collaboration and community strengths, respect for human diversity, and empirical grounding. These values are interrelated and influence each other. Pursuit of one value, without consideration of the others, leads to one-sided research and action.

## BRIEF EXERCISES

**1.** On a sheet of paper, list at least ten important social problems facing your community or society. Examples might include the following: violence (in neighborhoods or families or elsewhere), poverty, child maltreatment, quality of education, crime, drug abuse, AIDS, health care, care of the elderly, homelessness, sexism, racism. (This list is illustrative, not exhaustive.)

Now that you have read about shifts of perspective and levels of analysis, suggest how each problem has causal factors at individual, microsystem, organizational, community or macrosystem levels.

**2.** Review the ecological levels of analysis in Table 1.1 or Figure 1.3. At what level of analysis are these community programs or interventions aimed? (A program may concern more than one level.)

A. A school program in which students who have conduct problems are referred by teachers or counselors to special group counseling sessions. There they learn skills in assertion, labeling and expressing emotions, resolving disputes nonviolently, and setting personal goals.

B. A school adopts an addition to the second-grade curriculum in which students learn about labeling and expressing emotions through group exercises, stories, and artwork. All second-graders are involved in this curriculum taught by their regular teachers.

C. In the wake of a sudden, disastrous flood, an elementary school devotes part of every school day for a month to group discussions of student memories and emotional difficulties, and Saturday mornings to school-organized community cleanup.

D. A foundation funds research comparing the effects on student development of various types of middle schools, which vary in faculty–student contact, curriculum, and informal student groupings. They release the findings to the press and meet with educational policy-makers in state and federal government.

E. A self-help group meets monthly for parents bereaved by the death of their child. Members discuss their bereavement and other topics of shared concern, exchanging ideas, feelings, and support.

F. Community members band together, through religious congregations, to pressure schools in their area to open their recreational and computer facilities to the public at night (Speer & Hughey, 1995).

G. A nationally televised documentary reviews the unmet developmental needs of young children, and effective programs or methods of addressing those needs.

## RECOMMENDED READINGS

Bronfenbrenner, U. (1979). *The ecology of human development.* Cambridge, MA: Harvard University Press.
> The first chapter provides a classic statement of ecological perspective and concepts.

Heller, K., Price, R. H., Reinharz, S., Riger, S., & Wandersman, A. (1984). *Psychology and community change.* Homewood, IL: Dorsey/Pacific Grove, CA: Wadsworth.

Levine, M., & Perkins, D. V. (1997). *Principles of community psychology: Perspectives and applications* (2nd ed.). New York: Oxford University Press.

Rappaport, J. (1977). Community psychology: Values, research, and action. New York: Holt, Rinehart & Winston.
> The introductory chapters of these three classic textbooks provide differing (yet converging) definitions of community psychology.

Rappaport, J., & Seidman, E. (Eds.). (2000). *Handbook of community psychology.* New York: Plenum.
> A major resource; 38 chapters on community psychology topics.

Prilleltensky, I. (1997). Values, assumptions, and practices: Assessing the moral implications of psychological discourse and action. *American Psychologist, 52,* 517–535.
> An analysis of values for psychology as a discipline, from a critical psychology perspective.

Shinn, M. (1990). Mixing and matching: Levels of conceptualization, measurement, and statistical analysis in community research. In P. Tolan, C. Keys, F. Chertok, & L. Jason, (Eds.), *Researching community psychology* (pp. 111–126). Washington, DC: American Psychological Association.
> A review of conceptual and methodological issues regarding levels of analysis in research.

## JOURNALS RELEVANT TO COMMUNITY PSYCHOLOGY

We asked members of the on-line listserve group of the Society for Community Research and Action, the principal professional body in community psychology, to suggest journals relevant to community psychology for this table. The listserve has over 500 subscribers including community psychologists, students, and others. Here are their suggestions.

AIDS Quarterly
American Journal of Community Psychology°
American Journal of Evaluation
American Journal of Orthopsychiatry
American Journal of Preventive Medicine
American Journal of Public Health
American Psychologist
Applied and Preventive Psychology
Canadian Journal of Community Mental
    Health
Canadian Journal of Evaluation
Child Development
Community Development Journal
Community Mental Health Journal
Community, Work and Family
Cultural Diversity and Ethnic Minority
    Psychology
Educational Leadership°
Environment and Behavior
Evaluation
Evaluation and Program Planning
Evaluation Review
Feminism and Psychology
Gender & Society
Health Education and Behavior
International Journal of Community
    Development
Journal of Applied Behavioral Science
Journal of Applied Social Psychology
Journal of Community Discourse (on-line)
Journal of Community Practice
Journal of Community Psychology

Journal of Community and Applied Social
    Psychology
Journal of Consulting and Clinical
    Psychology
Journal of Educational and Psychological
    Consultation
Journal of Environmental Psychology
Journal of Health and Social Behavior
Journal of Human Ecology
Journal of Interpersonal Violence
Journal of Prevention and Intervention
    in the Community
Journal of Primary Prevention
Journal of Research on Adolescence
Journal of Rural Community Psychology
Journal of Social Issues°
Law and Human Behavior
New Directions in Evaluation
Prevention Science
Psychology, Public Policy and Law
Psychiatric Rehabilitation Journal
Psychiatric Services (formerly Hospital
    and Community Psychiatry)
Psychology of Women Quarterly
Public Health Policy
Rural Sociology
Social Policy°
Social Problems°
Social Science and Medicine
The Community Psychologist
Tobacco Control
Violence Against Women

°These journals appear in the InfoTrac College Edition Online Library, available from Wadsworth Publishing.

# RECOMMENDED WEBSITES

Here and in later chapters we provide addresses for Internet websites that provide especially useful resources for information relevant to each chapter. We have visited each site to determine its utility, and provide brief comments. Of course, our choices are only some of the many websites relevant to community psychology!

The Community Psychology Network
(http://www.cmmtypsych.net)
    The Community Psychology Network contains many kinds of information about community psychology. It uses the metaphor of a college campus to organize its holdings: an

admissions office for graduate school information, a student lounge for student topics and comments, a lecture hall that compiles course materials for instructors, a bookstore, a library, a suggested reading list on community psychology, a career planning center, and other sites. The site also links to a number of other community psychology sites, including sign-ups for e-mail-based listserve discussion groups. This is an excellent site, useful for folks all the way from undergraduate students just learning about the field to professional community psychologists.

Society for Community Research and Action
(http://www.apa.org/divisions/div27)

The Website of the Society for Community Research and Action (SCRA), the international professional body of community psychology, which is also a division of the American Psychological Association. It contains information on SCRA mission and goals, membership benefits, activities, and conferences. The site also summarizes information on committees and interest groups within the SCRA, which include groups on aging, children and youth, community health, disabilities, prevention/promotion, rural issues, schools, self help and mutual support, stress and coping, cultural and racial affairs, women, and social policy. Information on graduate schools and job opportunities in community psychology is available as well.

For Websites related to child abuse and neglect, discussed in this chapter, see Recommended Websites for chapter 9.

# How Did Community Psychology Develop?

# INTRODUCTION

- One hundred years ago, U.S. society faced alarming problems of urban poverty, poor housing, family stressors, issues of sexuality and pregnancy, drug abuse, and juvenile crime. Community initiatives emerged that were surprisingly similar to today's community psychology.
- Then as now, women were at the forefront of many community initiatives, including settlement houses and the struggle for birth control and maternal health services.
- Then as now, U.S. society faced the challenges posed by the differences between waves of new immigrants, indigenous Native Americans and African Americans, and the dominant American culture. Cultural diversity is not a new issue.
- African Americans, including social scientist W. E. B. DuBois and journalist Ida B. Wells, promoted the empowerment of their people through community research and advocacy.
- The Second World War and its lingering effects on soldiers directed the birth and rapid growth of the profession of clinical psychology in the United States. The profession thus oriented itself primarily to treating adults who were already experiencing problems, not to children and families or to preventing problems. That left open a niche for the development of community psychology.
- During that postwar period, in Wellesley, Massachusetts, a group of free-thinking psychiatrists, psychologists, and others sought to prevent psychological problems by identifying the strengths of the community and by finding ways to make these useful to individuals and families in crisis throughout the community.
- Community psychology in Latin America arose not from clinical psychology as in the United States, but from the transformation of social psychology to promote social justice.
- Conceptions of community problems and what to do about them do not comprise a simple story of scientific progress, but ebb and flow with changes in social and historical forces.

These are some of the stories discussed in this chapter. To understand community psychology in depth, it is important to study the history of communities and of psychology in the 20th century. We must place community psychology in a historical narrative, a progression of events that forms a story. That narrative will have settings, characters, and turns of plot. One of its themes, for instance, is that individual and community quality of life are intertwined; pursuit of one requires the other. To understand the concepts of community psychology that we introduced in chapter 1, one needs to learn about that story. It concerns questions such as the following.

- How did community psychology develop its emphasis on the connections between social forces and individual quality of life?
- How did it become oriented to preventing psychological problems and promoting strengths in individuals and communities?
- How did it develop research in communities rather than the laboratory?
- How did it come to be distinct from clinical and social psychology and other psychological fields?
- How did it develop its core values?

Community psychology is usually considered to have originated at a conference of psychologists held in Swampscott, Massachusetts in 1965. Yet the story does not start there. The Swampscott Conference did not occur in a vacuum—it was nested in the historical and cultural context of mid-20th-century U.S. society and psychology. In fact, community psychology in the United States was evolving before Swampscott, and it has continued to evolve since. Moreover, community psychology in other countries sprang from different roots than in the United States. To understand the development of community psychology, one must go back "before the beginning" (S. B. Sarason, 1974) to analyze the history of communities and psychology throughout the 20th century.

## What Are The Key Points Of This Chapter?

In this chapter, our focus is mainly the history of community psychology in the United States, although we do consider some international issues. First, we describe individualism as an ideology and its impact on U.S. society and the field of psychology. Second, we discuss a hypothesis concerning how shifts of historical forces influence views of social problems in the United States. Third, we examine changes in views of social problems in the United States early in the 20th century that illustrate such a historical shift and that also reveal some important predecessors of community psychology. Fourth, we describe how forces in the United States after the Second World War led to the emergence of community psychology there. Fifth, we describe how community psychology diverged from community mental health and became a distinct field. Finally, we describe the social context of community psychology today, after another shift in historical forces, and in international perspective. We hope to convince you that understanding where community psychology came from is essential to understanding what it is today and where it may be heading tomorrow.

## Individualism in U.S. Culture and Psychology

To introduce the history of community psychology, we now describe the perspective of individualism and its influence on U.S. culture and on psychology as a discipline. It is important to understand individualism and its limitations, because awareness of those limitations by some psychologists led to the founding of community psychology.

Our analysis of individualism focuses on U.S. society and history. Although community psychology is an international discipline, it has strong roots in U.S. culture and psychology. Its concepts and practices have been influenced by the forces and unrecognized assumptions of Western cultures. Those forces operate in their most individualistic form in U.S. culture (Lipset, 1996). Moreover, the dominant international presence of Western economies makes some experience with individualistic thinking and behavior almost inevitable worldwide. If you live in a society that shares at least some of the individualism of Western cultures, you probably will recognize the themes we emphasize here.

Even within the United States, no single "American culture" exists. However, community psychologists and other scholars have identified dominant forces, ideals, and assumptions operating in U.S. society that, although not endorsed by all of its communities or citizens, exert significant influence on public opinion and on psychological research and practice. These forces create an "American worldview" (S. B. Sarason, 1994), and a "dominant cultural narrative" (Rappaport, 1995). That worldview provides frames for picturing ourselves, the discipline of psychology, and our communities and society. The dominant cultural narrative provides story lines for understanding our experiences and history. Unless we are aware of those frames, they can imprison us and prevent us from seeing alternative worldviews.

## Individualism as a Worldview

In their volume, *Habits of the Heart*, Bellah and colleagues described *individualism* as the "first language" of U.S. society (Bellah, Madsen, Sullivan, Swidler, & Tipton, 1985, p. 20). Individualism takes many forms, and its expression is channeled to some extent by a diversity of "second languages," or alternative sets of values. Nonetheless, when U.S. citizens converse in public about actions that individuals, communities, or the nation should take, the ideas, assumptions, and language of individualism dominate the conversation.

Individualism is related to the historical ideal of political freedom. However, it primarily concerns economic and personal freedom from restraint, not freedom that results from involvement in a supportive community. Alexis de Tocqueville (1835/1987), whose impressions of the United States in 1835 are still recognized for their insight into American character, described it thus:

> Individualism is a calm and considered feeling which disposes each citizen to isolate himself from the mass of his fellows and withdraw into a circle of family and friends; with this little society formed to his taste, he gladly leaves the greater society to look after itself.... They form the habit of thinking of themselves in isolation and imagine that their whole destiny is in their hands. (p. 11)

Such a lifestyle, Tocqueville (1835/1987) noted, separates individual and family from community and society. The individualistic adult does emerge from the private sphere of family and friends into the public spheres of work and marketplace, but only to pursue private ends, and withdraws once these ends are achieved (Bellah, Madsen, Sullivan, Swidler, & Tipton, 1991). Tocqueville believed that individualism easily leads to uncaring selfishness, and ultimately to tyranny, as citizens withdraw from shared governance of their communities and society.

**Utilitarian Individualism**    Bellah et al. (1985) identified two forms of individualism in contemporary U.S. society. Utilitarian individualism is concerned with material success and security for the individual or family. The personal qualities of initiative, hard work, and self-reliance, and a society that provides economic opportunity and freedom to get ahead on one's own, characterize this orientation. Individual ability and effort are assumed to be the major (often only) causes of success or failure in a competitive society. Utilitarian individualism is succinctly expressed in Benjamin Franklin's *Poor Richard's Almanac* (Bellah et al., 1985) and in contemporary self-help books on success.

**Expressive Individualism**    This tradition is a reaction against the utilitarian philosophy, but it is still individualistic in focus. One's concern lies with personal happiness, self-discovery, and self-expression rather than material success. "Finding oneself,"

self-actualization, and individual happiness become personal ends, and a society is desired that allows such self-discovery. Expressive individualism is expressed lyrically in Whitman's *Song of Myself* (Bellah et al., 1985), in some forms of psychology, or often on MTV. Such a lifestyle may be very different than one based on individualism's utilitarian form, but nonetheless it is self-focused. Moreover, it usually requires at least minimal economic prosperity and security, and historically often follows periods of concern with utilitarian success.

*Critiques of Individualism*    In both versions of individualism, it is assumed that as long as laws prohibit the worst forms of selfishness, the pursuit of individual interests will eventually lead to emergence of what is best for society as well. The individual's right to choose is paramount. It is also assumed that the individual's characteristics (talent, effort, personality), not cooperation with others or one's access to resources, determine one's fate in life (recall Tocqueville's 1835/1987, comment that individualists regard their destiny as being in their own hands).

Psychologist William Ryan (1971, 1981, 1994) provided examples of the worldview of individualism applied to social problems. In individualistic thinking, these problems lie within the biological, psychological, or moral makeup of the individual. Thus, psychological maladjustment, drug abuse, crime, educational difficulties, or poverty are interpreted only as individual deficits to be remedied by changes in the individuals themselves. Social factors (e.g., unemployment, discrimination, deficient schools, exposure to violence) that also contribute greatly to such problems are ignored and left unaddressed (Mirowsky & Ross, 1989). Ryan (1971), coining a now-popular term, called this process "blaming the victim." Persons who are victimized by social forces are blamed for their problems when their personal characteristics are assumed to be the causes. Victim-blaming is likely when one's thinking is caught within an individualistic framework; the shift of perspective, described earlier in this chapter, has not occurred.

The evidence reviewed by Lipset (1996) indicates that individualism is a double-edged sword for U.S. society. He argued that the tradition of emphasis on individual rights, while providing the basis for many political and economic freedoms and for a strong sense of personal responsibility and initiative, is inextricably associated with less desirable outcomes. These include—when compared with Canada, Western Europe, and Japan—higher rates of crime and of civil suits, of drug use, and of divorce, less spending and support for the poor and more negative views of the poor, and less voter participation in elections. Each of these, Lipset argued, is partly rooted in the individualistic worldview described by Tocqueville (1835/1987), in which individuals insist on their own rights, act for what they see as their interests (utilitarian or expressive), withdraw from concern with larger society, and assume that when problems occur, other individuals are at fault. Less spending for the poor and more negative views of them as a group represent forms of blaming the victim.

A liberal, enlightened version of individualism would include a concern for the rights and needs of others, because a reciprocal concern could in return be expected from others (Phillips, 1993). As we noted above, individual quality of life often improves when community life also flowers. Yet such social concern is often weak or missing in individualistic views and practices (Bellah et al., 1985, 1991), particularly those in which the economic market is the model for social relationships.

## Alternatives to Individualism

*Citizen Participation; Religion and Spirituality*  Bellah et al. (1985, 1991) argued that individualism is the first language of U.S. society, but not its only language. Second languages also influence the culture and the thinking of its citizens. The tradition of individual involvement in government and in community affairs is one second language (Bellah et al., 1985). Bellah et al. (1985) termed this "civic republicanism"; community psychologists use the term "citizen participation" for the same idea. It is exemplified in the New England town meeting, in block associations and neighborhood organizations in cities, in local school boards, and in participation of citizens in nonprofit community organizations and charities.

Religious beliefs and institutions, and personal spirituality, provide another second language in U.S. culture (Bellah et al., 1985). A connection between religious transcendence and human community has been a long-standing historical theme (S. B. Sarason, 1993), and survey data indicate that religion and spirituality still play a major role in the lives of many Americans (Lipset, 1996; Pargament & Maton, in press).

The traditions of citizen participation and religion and spirituality often represent a concern with the individual's "psychological sense of community" with others beyond self and family (S. B. Sarason, 1974). In both traditions, individualistic interests and desires must be balanced with the good of the society as a whole. Both traditions also offer a conception of individuals joining together in communities that is missing in many individualistic accounts (Bellah et al., 1985, 1991). Both emphasize cooperation and connectedness in relationships, and assume that part of being human is a need for such ties. Both traditions have historically been misused for a variety of purposes, as when religious belief has been used to justify slavery, subjugate women, or attack other religions or worldviews. Yet they also offer values that can counter extreme individualism.

Themes of connectedness are often considered a particular concern of women (Gilligan, 1982) and oppressed or subordinate groups (Gaines & Reed, 1995; Riger, 1993). Such a concern with connectedness is also a characteristic of societies that emphasize collectivist values, such as many Asian, African, and Native American cultures (Kim, Triandis, Kagitcibasi, Choi, & Yoon, 1994; Lipset, 1996; see also chap. 6 of this book). Even in an individualistic society such as that of the United States, these traditions can channel the forces of individualism for social good.

*Liberation*  Another alternative to individualism concerns achieving social justice and equality, and might be labeled *liberation*. As we noted in chapter 1, American history has been marked by struggles to overcome injustice. Women, persons of color, the poor, immigrants, workers, gay men and lesbians, and other groups have sought to overcome injustice. Individualistic worldviews have supported those injustices by providing individual explanations that blame the victim. Liberation movements call for social change that corrects those injustices. Advocates of liberation may speak in the languages of religion or civic participation, but their ultimate purpose is not limited to those ideals. For instance, some organizations and individuals in the civil rights movement of the 1950s and 1960s based much of their appeal in Judeo-Christian concepts, but theirs was a liberation rather than a soley religious movement.

*Fair Play, Fair Shares*    Ryan (1981, 1994) identified two definitions of the cherished American value of equality that help illustrate the traditions of individualism and its alternatives. The "fair play" definition of equality, based on utilitarian individualism, is focused on assuring rules of fairness in competition for economic and social advancement. Citizens accept great inequalities of outcome in that competition, as long as the procedures are believed to treat individuals similarly. It is assumed that these inequalities are caused by differences in individual talent and effort. This definition is consistent with individualistic conceptions of freedom as "freedom from" the interference of others in the pursuit of economic success or personal self-actualization (Bellah et al., 1985).

Ryan (1981, 1994) described an alternative perspective of "fair shares," which means concern not so much with fairness of procedure as with minimizing extreme inequalities of outcome. Adopting a fair shares perspective does not preclude fair play rules, but it goes beyond them to consider other factors. From a fair shares perspective, equality involves the commitment of a community to taking care of all of its members. For instance, equality involves limiting the accumulation of wealth so that everyone has some minimum level of economic security. Achieving absolute equality of wealth is impractical, but extreme inequalities are avoided.

In the fair shares perspective, inequalities based on socioeconomic factors can be recognized and mitigated. Inequality of role relationships (e.g., between men and women, Whites and persons of color, and employers and employees) can be altered. The fair shares perspective is consistent with the liberation tradition, and with many of the ideals of biblical religion and civic participation. It meshes with these traditions because of its emphasis on individuals coming together (and limiting pursuit of their individual interests) in the interest of the community and society.

Ryan (1981, 1994) emphasized that although both perspectives have value, fair play thinking dominates American discussions of equality. Yet fair play thinking presumes that all participants in the race for economic and social advancement begin at the same starting line, and that all that is needed is to make sure the race is conducted fairly. In fact, few citizens really believe that all share the same economic or educational resources, the same chances of employment in well-paying jobs, or the same starting lines for advancement. In the United States, a very small proportion of the population controls a very large proportion of the wealth (Lipset, 1996). This suggests that to attain truly fair play, it is necessary to create fair shares.

## Psychology and Individualism

Individualism has strongly affected the discipline of psychology as well. Psychology in the United States has traditionally defined itself as the study of the individual organism (S. B. Sarason, 1974). Even social psychologists have studied primarily the cognitions and attitudes of individuals. The tradition of behaviorism, which does emphasize the importance of environment more than individual characteristics, has seldom studied the complexity of cultural–social variables. An alternative conception of psychology as the study of the relationship of individuals to the sociocultural environment is implicit in the early works of John Dewey and William James, and later in the work of Alfred Adler and Kurt Lewin, but that potential has been largely ignored until recently (Gergen, Gulerce, Lock, & Misra, 1996; S. B. Sarason, 1974).

Psychological interventions are also primarily individualistic. The psychometric study of individual differences has long been linked to testing in schools and industry, where its uses promote utilitarian individualism. Individuals are measured, sorted, and perhaps changed, but the environments of school and work seldom receive such scrutiny.

In addition, the practice of much psychotherapy is based on the assumptions of expressive individualism (Bellah et al. 1985). In psychotherapy, the client focuses inward to find new ways of living that yield greater personal happiness. Concern for others is assumed to automatically follow from this concern for self (Wallach & Wallach, 1983). This approach is often helpful for those whose lives are in serious disarray. Yet as a general philosophy of living, it emphasizes self-fulfillment and says little about commitment to others.

Doherty (1995) posed an instructive example. Paul, a divorced client in a men's group, felt overwhelmed and dissatisfied with the child-care plan in which he was responsible for all three of his children on weekends. In one therapy session, he announced his decision that he would take only two of his children at a time, in rotation. He believed that he could do a better job of parenting this way. Doherty, the therapist, objected, pointing out that this would leave Paul's wife with no time away from parenting and would pose long-term risks to the children if she could not cope. The group rushed to Paul's defense, with the most articulate member asking, "I thought you were here to help us, the people in this room. She's not your client, we are" (Doherty, 1995, p. 51). Doherty's dilemma illustrates a choice between acting for the client's individual health and growth (at least as the client can imagine it at the time) and that of others. In this case, Doherty pursued his point that Paul should take into account the interests of his ex-wife and children. Eventually Paul and the group accepted that as a countervailing principle and began to look for other solutions to Paul's problem.

Critics of psychotherapy from within the field (Wallach & Wallach, 1983) and outside it (Bellah et al., 1985) have made similar points. Although psychotherapy holds great value in many contexts, it is not a panacea, and moral dilemmas are not avoided by a focus on individual fulfillment. Other values must be considered.

Expressive or utilitarian individualism in psychology focuses on individual change. Western societies have invested much money and other resources in efforts to resolve social problems by changing individuals, often through psychological means, yet many of those problems remain. Environmental (organizational, community, societal) change may be necessary to improve quality of life for many individuals and communities. Our point is not that individually based research, testing, and psychotherapy are never useful, but that psychology relies heavily on such individualistic tools when others are also needed.

## Creative Tensions

In reading the section, did you have the sense of partial agreement with different, even opposing points of view? Social and community issues do not have simple, correct answers (S. B. Sarason, 1978). They often involve a *creative tension* in which two opposing perspectives both contain some truth, to the extent that their proponents are intellectually honest and provide evidence for their views (Rappaport, 1981). The assumptions and limitations of both viewpoints need to be understood. Debate is healthy and to be expected. Rappaport (1981) even proposed "Rappaport's Rule": "When everyone agrees with you, worry" (p. 3).

Examples of creative tensions abound in community and social life. Individualism versus connectedness and social concern forms one such tension. Fair play versus fair shares is another. The historical focus on the individual in psychology, versus the ecological-levels viewpoint of community psychology, forms a third creative tension. Community psychologists have developed characteristic values and concerns in part because their experiences have shown the limitations of a purely individualistic point of view. That is not to deny the importance of understanding individuals, but to affirm the need to understand them in the context of social relationships and forces.

Now we turn to how forces such as individualism and alternatives to it shift in their influence on U.S. society over time.

## How Do Historical Cycles Influence Definition of Social Problems?

Levine and Levine (1992), a community psychologist and a sociologist, studied the historical relationship in the United States between social–political forces and helping services for children and families. Their analysis illustrates how forces in society at large shape public beliefs about psychological, family, community, and social problems, as well as beliefs about what interventions are appropriate to ameliorate them. Their conclusions seem to apply to helping services for adults as well as children.

Although their original work compared two periods of U.S. history in the early 20th century, their analysis also fits more recent events directly affecting community psychology. In fact, they wrote the first edition of their book (Levine & Levine, 1970) as community psychology emerged as a distinct field, because they realized that seemingly new ideas were not so new. Forms of helping and community development of a century ago surprisingly resemble community psychology today.

Levine and Levine (1992) proposed a simple hypothesis to interpret the impact of these historical forces. In times that are socially and politically progressive, human problems will be conceptualized in environmental terms. Progressive times are not necessarily associated with one political party, but are marked by optimism about the possibility of lessening social problems and improving community life. Social problems include issues as varied as poverty, drug abuse, crime, mental disturbance, and the educational and behavioral problems of children. In what seems like common sense during a progressive period, the nature and causes of such problems will be understood in terms of community life. Interventions to lessen such problems will address community factors, such as poverty, housing, lack of educational opportunity, unemployment, support for families, and lack of social ties. Interventions will focus on changing or creating community settings (e.g., neighborhoods, schools, community organizations) to promote stronger communities.

Conversely, during times that are politically conservative, the same problems will be conceptualized in terms of individual factors, biological or narrowly psychological. Conservative times are not necessarily tied to one political party, but to pessimism about whether communities can be improved or whether social problems can be lessened. Interventions will be services delivered by medical or psychological professionals, designed to change individuals (or at most families). What seems like common sense during a conservative period will find the sole roots of human problems in individual genetics or personality or character, thus making it easier to blame the victim (Ryan, 1971).

Social forces thus define what is considered a problem and how it is to be solved. The services provided to address these problems will be strongly influenced by the dominant viewpoint of the period. Those forces also define what research is considered worth doing (and funding), and how that research is interpreted and applied in practice. For instance, in conservative times biological research is more emphasized and funded; in progressive times, research emphasizing social–environmental forces receives more attention and funding.

The differences between progressive and conservative times are not absolute (Levine & Levine, 1992). Any historical period contains both perspectives. One viewpoint will become dominant, but its opposite has not been eradicated, only reduced in influence. Both perspectives also contain some truth, yet neither completely accounts for individual and social difficulties.

The swings of the sociopolitical pendulum should not be regarded as completely balanced within U.S. society. Individualism is the first language of American ideals (Bellah et al., 1985). It becomes most dominant in conservative times, yet is powerful even in progressive times. Thus the emphasis of those times on social–environmental explanations for social problems is always limited by the power of individualistic ideals.

Given this influence of social trends on the generation and use of scientific knowledge, one might argue that the best policy is to insulate psychological research as much as possible from the influence of society. However, Levine and Levine (1992) did not advocate such insulation. They regarded the influence of society on helping services and on psychology as inevitable. Thus, people need to understand historical trends and their limitations, not seek in vain to avoid them.

We now discuss a swing of the historical pendulum beginning about 100 years ago in the United States. Then we skip ahead somewhat to discuss the origins of community psychology in mid-20th-century U.S. society, and finally bring that story up to the present in the United States and internationally. Much of that discussion will reveal events consistent with the Levine and Levine (1992) hypothesis.

## A Progressive Period: 1890–1914

Levine and Levine (1992) initially studied services for children and families between 1890 and 1914, usually considered the "Progressive" period in U.S. political history. Many modern organizations for children and adults originated during this comparatively short period of reform. The list of innovations includes the Boy Scouts, Girl Scouts, Camp Fire Girls, and YWCA; the first juvenile courts; the first psychological clinics, founded primarily for children and families; national public organizations for family services and for mental health; innovations in education such as the visiting teacher movement and special education; and legal reforms such as child labor laws (Levine & Levine, 1992, pp. 10 and 233). Advocacy for social reform was not limited to children's issues; this was also the era that saw the rise of settlement houses, the struggle to establish birth control services for women (Levine & Levine, 1992), and the founding of the National Association for the Advancement of Colored People (NAACP; Huggins, 1986).

These innovations were in part a response to the effects of decades of immigration, urbanization, and industrialization on U.S. society. The United States was no longer a Protestant, rural society, but an increasingly diverse, urban society with extremes of wealth and poverty. Nuclear families immigrated to cities from the country or abroad; they were removed from the support of relatives, often lived in poverty, and could not meet the demands placed on them. Neither could schools originally designed for more affluent, less diverse student populations. Economic security weakened as industrialization and an expanding labor market made individual laborers economically expendable. Drug abuse, particularly alcoholism, was widespread and widely denounced. The control of individual behavior exercised by family and neighborhood weakened, and agents of social control, such as police, became expected to replace them (M. Levine, 1981; Levine & Levine, 1992). Juvenile crime surfaced as a problem. Slavery, ended by the Civil War, had been replaced by a system of Jim Crow laws and customs that effectively kept most African Americans in poverty. Although these problems are not identical to those of today, there are parallels between social problems then and now.

However, the existence of these social problems does not completely explain the rapid innovation in social organizations and services that occurred during the Progressive period. Changes in public beliefs about the causes and appropriate responses to these problems were also involved (Levine & Levine, 1992). Four initiatives during this period particularly represent forerunners of today's community psychology. We now examine the development of the earliest psychological clinics, the settlement house movement, the movement for women's access to birth control and health services, and the emergence of the early civil rights and Black liberation movements (these are listed in Table 2.1).

***Psychological Clinics***   The best-known early examples of psychological services in the United States were Lightner Witmer's clinic in Philadelphia, primarily concerned with educational problems of children, and the clinic established by William Healy and Grace Fernald, attached to the juvenile court in Chicago (Levine & Levine, 1992). Witmer believed "the school room, the juvenile court, and the streets are a larger laboratory for psychology" (Witmer, cited in Golann & Baker, 1975, p. 1). The clinic used innovative teaching methods, provided by teachers and paraprofessionals, to enable children with a variety of learning problems to progress educationally. Witmer emphasized that every child can learn, so teaching methods must be altered to fit the needs of the child. (One of the first settings for training and research in community psychology, Sarason's Psycho-Educational Clinic, was named after Witmer's clinic). Healy and Fernald's clinic emphasized the potential skills, not the deficits, of the juvenile offenders evaluated there, and sought to rely on community interventions rather than prison or removal from the community. These also are themes of programs recently devised by community psychologists in the juvenile justice system (e.g., W. S. Davidson & Redner, 1988). These clinics created new roles for psychologists, differing from the roles of medical treatment or judicial punishment. They also altered perceptions of the individual child or adolescent from a focus on deficits to a focus on strengths or potential (Levine & Levine, 1992).

Interestingly, Alfred Adler founded clinics attached to the schools in Vienna, Austria, during the 1920s, a period of progressive reform there. Like Witmer's and Healy and Fernald's efforts, Adler stressed an environmental approach. The Vienna clinics established services for children and families that coordinated the work of teachers, parents, and men-

| TABLE 2.1 | SOCIAL INITIATIVES DURING TWO HISTORICAL PERIODS: 1890–1932 |
|---|---|
| **Period** | **Initiatives** |
| Progressive (1890–1914) | Founding of innovative community organizations<br>Early psychological clinics<br>Settlement houses<br>Movement for birth control and maternal health services<br>Early civil rights initiatives |
| Conservative (1919–1932) | Eugenics, intelligence testing |

tal health professionals. Their services emphasized early intervention in children's adjustment problems and the development of social skills, anticipating many school-based prevention programs today (Furtmuller, 1979; Gurney, 1968).

*Settlement Houses*    These settings were often founded by women (Jane Addams, Lillian Wald, and Ida B. Wells are examples) in low-income, urban, immigrant neighborhoods. They were often motivated by the values of religion and citizen participation, and by the liberation ideals of the growing feminist, civil rights and labor movements. Settlement workers moved into the neighborhoods where they would work. They were usually received with understandable initial suspicion and often had much to learn about life there, but eventually they learned to work alongside their new neighbors. Settlement houses provided health education to individual mothers and families, established educational services (e.g., some of the earliest kindergartens) and advocated for better public schools, organized community clubs that provided activities for youth, and advocated for better public services (e.g., police, sanitation, public health) as well as child labor laws and better working conditions (Levine & Levine, 1992).

Settlement houses fostered second-order change (Watzlawick et al., 1974) and altered existing role relationships. They emphasized structural changes in society, not just helping services for individuals. They were governed on egalitarian principles intended to minimize differences of socioeconomic status. Founders (often of privileged background) worked to enable neighborhood residents to assume leadership roles. Settlement workers, usually women, sought to empower women in a variety of roles. This represents early pursuit of the values of social justice and democratic participation described in chapter 1. Addams's Hull House, in Chicago, also enabled social scientists, particularly sociologists, to learn about life in low-income urban neighborhoods firsthand, from their residents. Some settlement workers, including Addams, participated directly in politics, although they were usually more successful with issues-oriented advocacy than in running for office (Levine & Levine, 1992). Settlement house workers initiated what later became the field of social work. Their efforts foreshadowed the themes of community psychology as well.

*Birth Control and Maternal Health Services*    Another innovation of the period was the struggle to make these services accessible to women (Levine & Levine, 1992). One leader of this struggle was Margaret Sanger, a labor activist and nurse to mothers in

New York City's Lower East Side. Sanger found her impoverished clients desperate for ways to prevent further pregnancies. Birth control information was practically nonexistent, and the methods most commonly taught depended heavily on the self-restraint of the male, effectively disempowering women.

Sanger developed and published materials on reproduction and birth control for women and opened a women's health clinic in Brooklyn that distributed contraceptive information. Both of these actions violated laws against providing contraceptive information, and her pamphlets were considered pornographic by authorities because they contained explicit sexual information. Sanger fled the country, then returned to contest her arrests in court, and served time in jail. Eventually she and others attracted public support and began to win greater freedom for women to obtain contraceptive and family planning information (Levine & Levine, 1992).

Sanger spoke and wrote widely on birth control, emphasizing its relationship to women's control over their bodies and lives. Her work involved second-order change, challenging existing role relationships between men and women, professionals and patients, and poor and working-class women and privileged, often male, opponents of birth control.

***Early Civil Rights Initiatives***   W. E. B. DuBois was the first African American to receive a Harvard doctoral degree (in 1895); he was a student and friend of William James there. He began a scholarly career by studying African American life in Philadelphia and in the South, using both the quantitative and ethnographic methods of early sociology. With others (including Ida B. Wells), he cofounded the NAACP in 1910 to pursue the liberation of Black Americans through social advocacy and legal action. DuBois edited *The Crisis*, the NAACP publication, and wrote extensively through other outlets (Huggins, 1986). The NAACP soon became a strident advocate for Black interests, separating itself from the often more accommodationist approach of Booker T. Washington. By midcentury, its legal advocacy of civil rights was winning court decisions and dismantling legal segregation in many spheres of U.S. life.

By then DuBois had become disenchanted with both the NAACP and the likelihood of genuine Black liberation in the United States, so he moved abroad. Yet his career provides an example of social advocacy rooted in scholarly perspective. His 1903 prophecy is well-known: "The problem of the twentieth century is the problem of the color line,—the relation of the darker to the lighter races of men" (W. E. B. DuBois, 1903/1986, p. 372).

Settlement houses, early psychological clinics, the birth control movement, and the advocacy of DuBois and the NAACP are only some examples of the initiatives of the Progressive Era. They shared an emphasis on environmental causes of problems for individuals and families. Access to education and economic opportunities and creating new social institutions and community organizations were believed to be the best ways to help individuals. These ideas and practices arose during a politically progressive time in which social institutions were under great pressure to change, especially to be more responsive to the less fortunate (M. Levine & Levine, 1992, p. 243). That was soon to change.

## A Conservative Period: 1919–1932

The First World War and its aftermath altered U.S. society and the nature of helping services (Levine & Levine, 1992). Society grew more conservative, and the values of utilitarian and expressive individualism became dominant. Business interests largely controlled government; stock market speculation and the "Roaring Twenties" ensued. The country tried Prohibition as a solution to alcohol abuse. Reactionary movements such as the Ku Klux Klan enjoyed new popularity, and anti-Semitic campaigns were led by such mainstream figures as automobile magnate Henry Ford (K. Heller, Price, Reinhard, Riger, & Wandersman, 1984). In the wake of the Russian revolution, fear of Communism gripped the country. Jane Addams and Lillian Wald, leaders of the settlement house movement, were branded as Communists by a Senate committee (Levine & Levine, 1992). An example of how this sociopolitical climate of the Twenties influenced psychology involves eugenics and Social Darwinism (see Table 2.1).

***Eugenics and Intelligence Testing***    The ideology of Social Darwinism, popular before the Progressive period, enjoyed a comeback. This view borrowed concepts from evolutionary theory, such as "struggle for existence" and "survival of the fittest" (Heller, 1984, p. 31), applying them in ways Darwin had never stated, but consistent with utilitarian individualism. Unlike the assumptions underlying the Progressive reforms, Social Darwinist thinking held that individuals who experienced problems in living were unfit for meeting the demands of existence. Aid to such individuals would perpetuate their problems, not resolve them. The problem lay within the individual's biological makeup, not the environment. Advocates of eugenics proposed and succeeded in restricting individuals to institutions, sterilizing them to prevent perpetuation of their genes, and reducing immigration by groups of "inferior" genetic stock.

Advocates of Social Darwinism and eugenics included some prominent psychologists. In the United States, early psychological tests of intelligence were used as scientific evidence of the genetic inferiority of African Americans and recent immigrant groups such as Eastern and Southern Europeans. That evidence was then used to secure laws restricting immigration from those countries (Kamin, 1974). In Britain, Pearson (developer of the Pearson *r* correlation) also argued against immigration by citing research finding Jewish immigrants inferior to native British stock in intelligence (Aronson, 1992). Eugenicists assumed that differences in performance on intelligence tests reflected differences in innate abilities, an individualistic view. Factors such as lack of familiarity with English among recent immigrants, inadequate schools, and test bias have since been shown to explain the early findings of racial–ethnic differences (Gould, 1981; Kamin, 1974). Even the idea that biologically distinct races exist among humans has been strongly questioned (Zuckerman, 1990). Yet the recent debate over *The Bell Curve* (Herrnstein & Murray, 1994) indicates that the idea of racial differences in intelligence has not disappeared.

# COMMUNITY PSYCHOLOGY EMERGES
# IN THE UNITED STATES

During the 1930s and 1940s, the United States and its allies overcame a disastrous economic depression and won the Second World War. Those events set in motion important changes in U.S. society. Social changes altered the practice of psychology and eventually led to the emergence of community psychology.

We now describe four forces that directly influenced the emergence of community psychology. (This framework is a simplification of the myriad of factors involved.) Two

|  | **FACTORS INFLUENCING THE EMERGENCE** |
|---|---|
| TABLE 2.2 | **OF COMMUNITY PSYCHOLOGY** |

| | Origin of Concern | |
|---|---|---|
| **Area of Concern** | **Academic Disciplines** | **Social Conflicts** |
| **Mental health** | Application of preventive concepts to mental health (especially Erich Lindemann) | Changes in mental health services due to war, scandal, new treatments |
| **Social issues** | Social–psychological interest in group dynamics and action research (especially Kurt Lewin) | Social change movements (e.g., civil rights, feminism, peace, environment, gay/lesbian rights) |

of these forces originated within the academic disciplines of psychology, psychiatry, and public health. Two others concerned U.S. society as a whole. Viewed from another perspective, two forces concerned the mental health system, and two others concerned broader social conflicts, chiefly concerning issues of power and intergroup relations (see Table 2.2).

## A Preventive Perspective on Problems in Living

> No disease has ever been eradicated through clinical treatment of those already suffering from the disorder. Only prevention has ever achieved such eradication. (Albee, 1995)

The first of these forces involved the development of a preventive perspective on mental health services, influenced by the concepts of the discipline of public health. Public health theory and practice is not so much concerned with the treatment of existing illness as with its prevention. Prevention may take a variety of forms, ranging from sanitation to education to early treatment of contagious diseases, to control their spread. Moreover, public health takes a population perspective, focusing on control or prevention of disease within a community, state, or society, not merely within the individual. Applied to the area of mental health services by psychiatrist Erich Lindemann and his colleagues, a public health perspective emphasized environmental factors in mental disorder, early intervention in psychological problems, community-based services rather than isolation in hospital settings, and using community and individual strengths to prevent problems in living (G. Caplan, 1961, Klein & Lindemann, 1961; Lindemann, 1957).

The public health, preventive perspective was strengthened by several large-scale studies that demonstrated the influence of social and economic factors in the causation and treatment of mental disorders (Hollingshead & Redlich, 1958; Spaulding & Balch, 1983; Stanton & Schwartz, 1954). These studies were part of a larger sociological and anthropological literature that by the mid-1950s had clearly established that illness (physical or mental) was not solely the result of individual vulnerability, but also the consequence of social structure (Paul, 1955). Consistent with the Levine and Levine (1992) hypothesis, as the United States became more politically progressive, environmental explanations of human problems became more credible.

This led to renewed interest in prevention of psychological problems, not emphasized since the Progressive Era. Erich Lindemann (1944, 1957) emphasized the importance of life crises and transitions as the points of intervention for mental health services. His best-known study (Lindemann, 1944) concerned coping with bereavement among family survivors of those who died in a nightclub fire. Rather than waiting for full-blown disorders to develop, Lindemann advocated education about coping and support for dealing with specific crises, to have a preventive effect (Spaulding & Balch, 1983). Moreover, such intervention would be directed at strengthening and supporting existing community resources, not replacing them (Klein, 1995). Through the work of Lindemann and his successor, Gerald Caplan (1961), and others, the field of preventive psychiatry attracted interest and funding during the 1950s and 1960s.

The public health concepts of prevention were demonstrated in several service settings. At the request of community leaders, Lindemann in 1948 helped to found the Human Relations Service in Wellesley, Massachusetts, which provided consultation with parents and teachers, educational workshops, support groups, crisis intervention, and short-term therapy (recall the early psychological clinics). All this was done in a context that emphasized collaboration between Service staff, citizens, and community leaders such as clergy and school officials (Klein & Lindemann, 1961; Lindemann, 1957). This represents the value of collaboration and participation (see chap. 1), and embodies the altering of role relationships that is associated with second-order change.

An early director of the Human Relations Service, Donald Klein, was a psychologist who was later instrumental in the emergence of community psychology. The Service also provided a setting for research by psychologists, sociologists, and anthropologists interested in mental health and public health (Felsinger & Klein, 1957; Kelly, 1984; Klein, 1984; Naegele, 1955).

In 1953, psychologist John Glidewell, working with a public health department in St. Louis County, Missouri, established programs in schools and with parents designed to prevent behavior disorders in children (Glidewell, 1994; Glidewell, Gildea, & Kaufman, 1973; Spaulding & Balch, 1983). In 1958, Emory Cowen and colleagues implemented the Primary Mental Health Project in the elementary schools of Rochester, New York, seeking to detect early indicators of school maladjustment in students and intervene before full-blown problems appeared (Spaulding & Balch, 1983).

Although not working within a public health framework, two other early programs also are noteworthy. Seymour Sarason and colleagues at the Yale Psycho-Educational Clinic (named for Lightner Witmer's first clinic) began collaborating with schools and other institutions for youth in 1962. Their work concerned a number of projects to improve the responsiveness of these settings to the youth and to the communities that the settings were designed to serve (S. B. Sarason, 1988). In the 1950s, George W. Fairweather and colleagues at a Palo Alto, California, Veterans Administration hospital began developing and evaluating innovative, peer-group-based treatments for adult men with chronic mental disorders, at first within the hospital and later in the community (Fairweather, 1979, 1994; Fairweather, Sanders, Cressler & Maynard, 1969). As at the Human Relations Service, many of these innovative programs were marked by an atmosphere of collaboration with community members that helped to initiate second-order change. Many also evaluated their efforts with empirical research (e.g., Fairweather, 1979).

Interest in community services and prevention among psychologists resulted in a conference held in 1955 at Stanford University (Strother, 1957), where Lindemann, Klein, and others described their work and suggested future possibilities for psychologists in a field called "community mental health" (Felsinger & Klein, 1957). However, the conferees underestimated the sharp resistance to prevention concepts and services by advocates of traditional clinical care (Strother, 1987). Neither community mental health services nor prevention represented the mainstream of either psychiatry or clinical psychology. That tension would continue to influence the development of community mental health and community psychology.

## Reforms in the Mental Health System

> The war changed everything and everyone. (S. B. Sarason, 1995)

The second force leading to the emergence of community psychology involved sweeping changes in the U.S. system of mental health care, which began with the Second World War and continued into the 1960s (Humphreys, 1996; M. Levine, 1981; S. B. Sarason, 1988). After the war, the Veterans Administration (VA) was created to care for the unprecedented numbers of veterans with medical (including mental) disorders. In addition, the National Institute of Mental Health (NIMH) was established to coordinate funding for mental health research and training. Both of these federal administrations decided to rely heavily on psychologists and to fund their training.

These events led to the emergence of a specialty of clinical psychology separate from the rest of the discipline. Under the influence of the VA and NIMH, clinical psychology training expanded exponentially, becoming a specialized program with equal emphasis on scientific and clinical skills, the latter often learned in medical settings. Clinical psychology as it is today is thus largely the product of a particular historical period, the Second World War and its aftermath (Humphreys, 1996; S. B. Sarason, 1988). In particular, its emphasis on individual psychotherapy with adults is a product of the needs of the VA and the treatment orientation of a medical model. The child–family focus and environmental perspective of the Progressive-Era psychological clinics, another possible pathway for the new field, was largely overlooked (S. B. Sarason, 1974). An exception was that Robert Felix, head of NIMH during its early years, supported the development of preventive interventions and research, including Glidewell's programs in schools and the Human Relations Service (Felix, 1957; Goldston, 1994; Spaulding & Balch, 1983).

Also emerging in the postwar society was a movement for reform in the quality of mental health care (Levine, 1981; S. B. Sarason, 1974; Spaulding & Balch, 1983). By the 1950s, inhumane care in mental hospitals had gained the attention of society, as it has periodically during U.S. history (M. Levine, 1981; Rappaport, 1977a), and propelled calls for treatment of mental disorders outside the hospital. Journalistic accounts and films documented inhumane conditions within psychiatric hospitals, and citizen groups such as the National Association for Mental Health advocated reform. Advances in psychotropic medication also made prolonged hospitalization less necessary (Levine, 1981), strengthening reform efforts.

In 1961, the federally sponsored Joint Commission on Mental Illness and Mental Health, founded to respond to the calls for reform, recommended sweeping changes in mental health care (Joint Commission, 1961). In one of the Commission's studies, psychologist George Albee (1959) reviewed recent research that documented surprisingly high rates of mental disorders, compared this with the costs of training clinical professionals, and concluded that the United States could never afford to train enough professionals to provide clinical care for all who needed it. Albee and others called for an emphasis on prevention. However, most of the members of the Joint Commission remained committed to professional models of diagnosis and treatment (M. Levine, 1981).

As a response to the Joint Commission report, the NIMH proposed a system of community mental health centers (CMHCs; Goldston, 1994; M. Levine, 1981). With the support of President Kennedy, who was personally interested in mental health and retardation, and through timely advocacy by members of Congress, the NIMH, and the National Mental Health Association, Congress passed the Community Mental Health Centers Act in 1963. CMHCs were given a different mandate than traditional psychiatric hospitals, including not only care for persons with mental disorders in the community, but also crisis intervention, consultation with other community agencies, and prevention (Levine, 1981).

## Group Dynamics and Action Research

> Kurt Lewin was not concerned with research topics considered 'proper' within psychology, but with understanding interesting situations. (Zander, 1995)

The third force influencing the development of community psychology originated in the discipline of psychology. That force comprised the group dynamics and action research traditions that began with Kurt Lewin (Marrow, 1969).

Lewin spent much of his career attempting to demonstrate to laboratory-based psychologists and to citizens that social action and research could be integrated in a way that enriches both. He is known for asserting that "there is nothing so practical as a good theory" (Marrow, 1969). During the 1940s Lewin, a refugee from Germany, became interested in how the study of group dynamics (a developing field of research within social psychology) could be used to generate knowledge about social and community problems.

Significantly, the first community problem with which the Lewin action research team became involved was not primarily a mental health issue. The team was asked to help develop methods to reduce anti-Semitism in local communities (Marrow, 1969, pp. 210–211). The efforts of the Lewin team led to the creation of training groups in group dynamics (T-groups; Bradford, Gibb, & Benne, 1964). After Lewin's death, his students and others founded the National Training Laboratories (NTL) in Bethel, Maine, a center for professionals and citizens to learn about the dynamics within and between groups that influence the lives of individuals and communities (Marrow, 1969; Zander, 1995). The NTL workshops (still offered today) focus on the development of participant skills for working in groups and communities. They are not therapy groups or support groups and are not clinical in orientation. Instead, they embody social–psychological concern with group dynamics. Moreover, the Lewinian approach emphasized a collaborative partnership of professionals and community members (Marrow, 1969).

Several early community psychologists worked with NTL. These included Donald Klein and John Glidewell, who thus linked the innovations in community mental health discussed earlier with the NTL group dynamics and action research tradition (Glidewell, 1994; Klein, 1987, 1995). However, those involved in NTL eventually diverged from the more research-oriented social psychologists studying group dynamics (Zander, 1995). The action research tradition never represented the mainstream of social psychology. A new field was needed to express a developing set of concepts, values, and roles.

## Movements for Social Change

The fourth force influencing the development of community psychology involves movements for social change and liberation that gained attention in the United States in the 1960s, particularly the movements for civil rights (and later, Black power), feminism, peace, the environment, and gay/lesbian rights. These movements are associated in the popular mindset with the 1960s, although all had much longer historical roots (recall the discussion of Sanger and DuBois, for instance). The movements reached a crescendo during the 1960s and brought their grievances and ideals to national attention. That crescendo often coincided with conflicts such as civil-rights demonstrations, urban riots, and opposition to the Vietnam war.

The ideals of these movements were interdependent, often involving similar changes in society (Kelly, 1990). Indeed, one commonality was the challenging of hierarchical, unequal role relationships between Whites and people of color, men and women, experts and citizens, persons of heterosexual and homosexual orientations, and the powerful and the oppressed. Moreover, the young often assumed leadership: College students sat in at segregated lunch counters, organized Freedom Rides through the segregated South (J. Lewis, 1998), led antiwar protests, and organized the first Earth Day. Values common to all five movements match well with some core values of community psychology: social justice, democratic participation, and respect for diversity.

Another commonality of the five movements was that they sought to link social action at the local and national levels. Advocates in each movement pursued change in local communities and nationally. "Think globally, act locally" became a motto. The issues raised by the five social movements of the 1960s could not have been addressed solely at the local level. For instance, dismantling legalized racial segregation required both local activism and (often reluctant) intervention by national government (Lewis, 1998; Payne, 1997). Neither local nor national action alone was sufficient. This is consistent with an ecological view of levels of analysis.

The five movements have much in common with a community psychology perspective. Feminism, for example, shares many aims with community psychology (Mulvey, 1988). Both perspectives criticize the blaming of victims. Further, one of the key insights of feminism is that "the personal is political": even personal relationships are influenced by power dynamics and societal beliefs that oppress women. Again, this is consistent with an ecological emphasis on levels of analysis. Both feminism and community psychology call attention to inequalities in role relationships, such as professional–client or male–female. Both perspectives emphasize peer support and organizing members of a community as methods of change, while also recognizing the need for advocacy at macrosystem levels. Of course, there are differences, principally that feminism arose as a social movement whereas community psychology originated as an academic discipline. Yet the ideals of feminism and similar social movements helped to create the context in which community psychology emerged.

In that context, many psychologists were convinced that citizen and community action was necessary to bring about social change and that psychology had a role to play (Walsh, 1987). This perspective had been bolstered in 1954, when the Supreme Court cited psychological research findings as part of its rationale for overturning segregated schools in the *Brown v. Board of Education of Topeka* case. A further impetus was that in the last year of his life, Martin Luther King Jr. addressed the American Psychological Association, calling for them to study and promote citizen leadership and social action, especially among African Americans (King, 1968). A social climate existed in which the need for a community psychology was acknowledged (Bennett et al., 1966; Kelly, 1990; S. B. Sarason, 1974).

## The Undercurrent of Optimism

> We had just won a huge war, the biggest ever. And we had started from way back— we had been about to get whipped. If we could do this, we could do anything, including solving all the social problems of the U.S.: race relations, poverty. . . . There was a sense of optimism . . . a messianic zeal. . . . We believed that we could change the world, and we felt that we had just done it.
>
> Solving social problems is sobering, [for example] if you want to prevent behavior problems in schools. . . .To win wars, you kill people and destroy things. To solve social problems, you must build things, create things." (Glidewell, 1994)

Glidewell's remark illustrates an underlying support for all four forces we have described in the postwar, midcentury period: optimism about the solution of social problems (Kelly, 1990; S. B. Sarason, 1994). That optimism is very American in nature (Lipset, 1996; S. B. Sarason, 1994), and especially strong in progressive times. The 20-year postwar period saw economic expansion and a generally progressive public mood, despite Cold War tensions and changes in political control of the Federal government. In accordance with the Levine and Levine (1992) hypothesis, this underlying optimism supported community initiatives to address social problems. The four forces we have described were rooted in that optimism and progressive context.

Federal funders of new and innovative human services looked to the social sciences, including psychology, as a source of scientific solutions to social problems. A community psychology could provide important concepts and research for mental health reform and broader community change (Kelly, 1990). This attitude grew, in part, out of a very American faith in science and technology, based on society's experiences in the Second World War and the Cold War (S. B. Sarason, 1994) and gaining clearest expression in the space program. That faith in science, including social science, has since been replaced by a more sober sense of the real but limited utility of social science for social reform (Kelly, 1990), reflected in Glidewell's (1994) remarks above.

## The Swampscott Conference

> The excitement of Swampscott is with me still. (Klein, 1995, 30 years after the Swampscott conference)

In May, 1965, 39 psychologists gathered at the seaside resort of Swampscott, Massachusetts to discuss graduate training of psychologists for new roles in the new CMHC system (Goldston, 1994; Klein, 1987; Walsh, 1987). As was typical of psychology and most sciences and professions at the time, the conferees were White and male (J. G. Kelly, personal communication June, 1995; Walsh, 1987). Yet most of the group described themselves as atypical psychologists, because their involvement in community work had transformed their interests and skills (Bennett et al., 1966). Many of them were forging new connections between academic researchers, community mental health professionals, and citizens.

At Swampscott, a call emerged for a new field, to be named community psychology. It would concern "psychological processes that link social systems with individual behavior in complex interaction" (Bennett et al., 1966, p. 7). Community psychology would not be limited to mental health issues or settings. It thus would be distinct from community mental health, although the two would overlap.

Conferees agreed on the concept of community psychologist as "participant–conceptualizer" (Bennett et al., 1966, p. 7) who would act as a change agent in communities as well as conduct research on the effectiveness of those change efforts. They discussed new roles for community psychologists: developing prevention programs, consulting with schools and community agencies, advocating for community change, and collaborating with citizens. Conferees also called for interdisciplinary collaboration in research and action, and humility in the face of complex community dynamics (Bennett et al., 1966). Many of its themes still mark today's community psychology.

# Community Psychology Develops as a Distinctive Field

After Swampscott, community psychology developed a distinctive identity, separate from community mental health. Four trends were important in that development, and another conference played an important role.

## Changes in Community Mental Health

The community mental health movement burgeoned at first in the 1960s. A number of community-oriented psychologists began working in CMHCs. They consulted with human services and schools, performed evaluation research, directed prevention programs, and usually also provided clinical services. However, community mental health quickly became largely clinical-medical in nature (M. Levine, 1981; S. B. Sarason, 1974).

A trend of deinstitutionalization accelerated, in which persons with severe mental disorders were discharged from psychiatric institutions into communities. Continuing advances in psychotropic medications and the progressive sociopolitical climate supported this trend, but less humane reasons were also involved. Deinstitutionalization enabled governments to cut costs, but led to dumping of persons with severe mental disorders into communities without adequate services for their care (M. Levine, 1981; Linney, 1990). In essence, U.S. society has taken money out of mental hospitals but has not shifted enough of that money to community mental health services (see Winerip, 1999, for a current account of this process). A few exemplary community mental health treatment programs have survived, such as Assertive Community Treatment (G. Bond et al., 1990), but the funding climate has not been friendly.

## The Limitations of Government-Funded Social Change

Another U.S. social–political trend lessened public support for community innovation and social change. The early optimism of community psychology and the Johnson administration's War on Poverty arose from some similar roots. By 1970, the limits of some War on Poverty efforts had been recognized (K. Heller et al., 1984; Moynihan, 1969). Some programs lacked clear objectives and thus pursued a number of sometimes contradictory aims. In addition, the Federal government mandated participation by the poor in planning and decision making (based on the values of democratic participation and self-determination). However, few groups had experience in doing this, and in many settings it led to unresolved conflicts that challenged local political elites who then found ways to weaken or eliminate programs.

Other trends also played a role. The Federal government could not fund both the Vietnam War and the War on Poverty. In addition, political rhetoric about erasing poverty had raised public expectations unrealistically high; when obstacles were encountered and hopes of quick "victories" in the "war" on poverty diminished, so did public support.

However, the War on Poverty also had lasting positive effects. For instance, two educationally oriented programs, Head Start for young children and their families, and Upward Bound for adolescents, have endured despite enduring funding cutbacks. One reason for the staying power of Head Start is that it could point to research findings documenting their effectiveness (Zigler, 1994). This indicates the practicality of community psychology's core value of empirical grounding.

## The Search for an Identity for Community Psychology

These trends, and the limitations of community mental health services and roles, led to an identity problem for community psychology. Despite efforts begun at Swampscott to distinguish community mental health and community psychology, the two remained closely intertwined for over a decade (Goodstein & Sandler, 1978). The CMHCs brought psychologists and other mental health professionals into the "community," yet that term was defined so loosely that it meant almost any setting outside traditional mental hospitals. The individualistic functions of clinical assessment and treatment were transferred from the psychiatric institution to the CMHC without substantial alteration, while innovative community-oriented functions such as consultation and prevention proved more difficult to establish and fund in the climate of cost-cutting and deinstitutionalization.

Cowen's (1973) *Annual Review of Psychology* article, "Social and Community Interventions" (the first devoted to this topic) was both an indication of the importance of community psychology and of the difficulty in defining it. Reviewing scholarly articles concerned with community mental health, he found less than 3% with a prevention focus and noted little in common among many community interventions. Nonetheless, he identified a number of interventions, principally dealing with child or youth development and often focused on disadvantaged populations and collaborating with local citizens. Cowen also called for more emphasis on primary prevention. His advocacy helped move community psychology away from the community mental health focus.

In 1974, S. B. Sarason published a critique of the field, in which he proposed that community psychology should abandon its individualistic focus on mental health services in favor of a broader concern with the "psychological sense of community." Community psychologists could then conceptualize and intervene in what Sarason saw as the defining problem of an individualistic society, the individual's disconnection from others. Sarason argued that studying and attempting to enhance the psychological sense of community would build a community psychology more focused on the relationships between individuals and their communities, rather than just on the psychological adjustment of individuals. It would also be less constrained by changes in mental health practices and funding and by the traditional concepts and research methods of psychology.

## Community Psychology Develops in Latin America

At about the same time as community psychology sought to develop a distinctive identity in North America, a community psychology perspective was developing among psychologists throughout Latin America, largely independent of North American trends (Comas-Diaz, Lykes, & Alarcon, 1998; Montero, 1996). The Latin American movements for community psychology and liberation psychology grew largely out of social psychology, rather than from clinical psychology. In some countries (e.g., Chile, Guatemala), these trends were a response to repressive government regimes and overt conflict. These developments were also influenced by liberation theology, which blended many values of Christianity and Latin American liberation struggles. At the community level, liberation theology and psychology emphasized empowerment of citizens and struggle against injustice. Another influence was the approach of Brazilian educator and activist Paulo Friere (1970/1993), who focused on education as a means of raising consciousness of the individual effects of social conditions and ideologies. Like practitioners of community psychology, Freire focused on practical, local initiatives for social change.

Latin American community psychology thus came to emphasize values of democratic participation, social justice, and local community, and concepts of power and ideology. It pursued second-order change in social structure. Community psychology established a presence in Puerto Rico, Venezuela, Brazil, Mexico, and other countries (Montero, 1996).

## The Austin Conference

During the 10 years following the Swampscott conference, community psychology generated both great interest and a concern over its identity. In April 1975, over 100 community psychologists and students from the United States and Puerto Rico gathered at the University of Texas in Austin for a conference on training. This time, the title and focus clearly concerned community psychology (Iscoe, Bloom, & Spielberger, 1977).

The issues discussed at the conference foreshadowed important changes to come in community psychology. These discussions accelerated the divergence of the field from the clinical concerns of community mental health (Glidewell, 1977; Kelly, 1977; Rappaport, 1977b; Rieff, 1977; S. B. Sarason, 1977). Although psychological well-being of individuals remained an important concern, the means of fostering that well-being were no longer limited to mental health services, but increasingly included microsystem, organizational, and community development efforts. Prevention of psychological problems and promotion of social competence, especially in schools, represented one important theme. A second theme concerned social action and advocacy to address issues such as social justice, poverty, racism, and sexism.

The Austin conference roster of participants was more diverse than that of Swampscott, and reflected a third theme, the emergence of respect for diversity as a core value. The perspectives of women and persons of color began to be heard, although these groups were concentrated among students and junior professionals, not among senior professionals. Reports from working groups of Black, Hispanic, and women participants emphasized the importance of translating the core values of the field into tangible changes in training, research, and community action (Iscoe et al., 1977).

# Four Current Trends in Community Psychology

In the 25 years since the Austin Conference, four overarching trends have emerged in community psychology. Each trend represents a pathway that is still incomplete, with much to be done before the ideals often articulated by community psychologists are actualized. The four trends concern the following:

- prevention and competence promotion
- community-building, citizen participation, and empowerment
- understanding human and cultural diversity
- developing "adventuresome" research methods to match the complexity of community phenomena

## *Prevention and Competence Promotion*

Community psychology has developed a distinctive body of knowledge regarding prevention of problems in living. Its approach often involves elements of competence promotion and education in skills for healthy living, which then provide a preventive effect. It most directly reflects the core values of individual wellness (Cowen, 1994; Prilleltensky, 1999) and empirical grounding described in chapter 1.

This approach is now substantiated by sound research and effective interventions (Albee & Gullotta, 1997; Cowen, 1994; Durlak & Wells, 1997, 1998; Heller, 1990; Price, Cowen, Lorion, & Ramos-McKay, 1988). As we noted in chapter 1, prevention programs now effectively address problems such as difficulties in children's social and academic development; adolescent behavior problems, drug use, and juvenile delinquency; adult physical health and depression; HIV/AIDS prevention; and family issues such as divorce and family violence (Albee & Gullotta, 1997; Barton, Hopkins, McElhaney, Heigel, & Salassi, 1995; L. Bond & Compas, 1989; Peterson, 1998; Price et al., 1988). To mental health professionals and others skeptical of the utility of prevention, community psychologists can now offer solid evidence of effectiveness.

The concepts and methods of "prevention science" (Coie et al., 1993) involve community psychology, clinical psychology, public health, developmental psychology, and other fields (Kelly, 1990). This, of course, was a primary concern of Erich Lindemann and other pioneers of community mental health, and provides one measure of the impact of community psychology.

## Community-Building, Citizen Participation, and Empowerment

Community psychology also has developed concepts, research, and interventions that go well beyond a focus on individual wellness to a concern with the relationship between individuals and their communities. This trend most directly concerns the core values of sense of community, citizen participation, social justice, and collaboration and community strengths.

Two origins of this theme were S. B. Sarason's (1974) concern with the psychological sense of community and Rappaport's (1981, 1987) call for a focus on empowerment (we discuss these in detail in later chapters). Another root was Shinn's (1987) call for an expansion of the settings for community research and action, beyond mental health settings to work sites, religious settings, voluntary associations, government, and other settings.

Community psychologists now study and collaborate with work organizations (M. Bond & Keys, 1993; Keys & Frank, 1987; Shinn, 1987), mutual help groups (Borkman, 1991), citizen organizations (Speer & Hughey, 1995; Wandersman & Florin, 1990; Zimmerman & Perkins, 1995), and other community settings (Heller, 1989; Jason, 1991). They seek to study, change, or create an organizational or community system. Rather than influence individual wellness directly, their aim is to enhance quality of life for the entire community, and thus individual wellness indirectly. Their perspective is that individual and community well-being are intertwined.

Elias (1987) integrated the two trends of prevention and community by calling for attention in preventive interventions to creating environments that promote competence and help prevent problems. That involves second-order change, a change in the relationships and practices of a setting, not just change in its individual members.

## Human Diversity

Community psychology is reaching out to include a greater diversity of persons and groups in its work, in accordance with its core value of respect for diversity. The demographic makeup of the field has begun to change as more women and persons of color have become community psychologists, for instance, and as more international interrelationships have developed. The current picture within community psychology is one of increasing awareness of the importance of human diversity for community psychology. However, that potential is still in the process of being realized in action (Mulvey, 1988; Serrano-Garcia & Bond, 1994; Suarez-Balcazar, Durlak, & Smith, 1994).

Community psychologists have begun to examine in more depth the characteristics and dynamics of communities and populations on the basis of their gender, race, ethnicity, age, sexual orientation, socioeconomic status, cultural background, and other variables (e.g., Harper & Schneider, 1999; Harrell, Taylor, & Burke, 1999; Potts, 1999; Serrano-Garcia & Bond, 1994; Trickett, Watts, & Birman, 1994). To understand that diversity, community psychologists must consider the impact of culture as well as social injustice and oppression (Watts, 1994). Addressing these issues also requires innovation in research methods to be appropriate to the culture studied (Seidman, Hughes, & Williams, 1993).

In addition, community psychology is an international field. Once largely North American, community psychology training programs and practitioners now exist in a number of countries. As we have described, community psychology in Latin America has developed a distinctive perspective (Montero, 1996), and training programs exist in several Latin American countries. Community psychologists in several European countries, South Africa, New Zealand, and Australia have developed research, intervention, and training programs. Opportunities are expanding steadily for studying problems such as homelessness, in international perspective (Toro & Rojansky, 1990). Internationally, community psychologists are often very aware of the political context in which they work (e.g., Lazarus & Prinsloo, 1995; Montero, 1996; Serrano-Garcia, 1984). This awareness strengthens their local work and increases understanding of such factors in all societies.

## Adventuresome Research

Empirical grounding is a distinctive core value of community psychology, and the field has always sought to base its concepts and action in research. The gap between the experimental-laboratory research tradition of psychology and the complex phenomena studied by community psychologists has led to development of innovative research methods (Tolan et al., 1990). Early reviews of articles in community psychology journals found that research was almost always conducted at the individual level of analysis and concerned with individual adjustment, whereas study of communities was neglected (Lounsbury, Leader, Meares, & Cook, 1980; McClure et al., 1980; Novaco & Monahan, 1980). A later review, covering articles up to 1988, revealed increased study of communities and somewhat more diversity of participants. Still, a disparity remained between the concepts and the research methods used by community psychologists (Speer et al., 1992; see also Kelly, 1990).

These forces led to a major conference in research methods in community psychology, held in Chicago, Illinois in 1988. The report of that conference (Tolan et al., 1990) called for "adventuresome research" that goes beyond traditional methods to develop research that portrays the complexity of communities and individuals' lives in them. It also advocated greater use of qualitative and ethnographic research methods that are more sensitive to the ways that research participants think about the phenomena being studied, rather than just using measurement instruments based on researchers' preconceptions (see Brydon-Miller & Tolman, 1997; Miller & Banyard, 1998). Feminist scholars, for instance, have developed methods for research that emphasize understanding of cultural–social context and situation, and studying peoples' lives in relation to those contexts (Riger, 1990; Reinharz, 1994). In addition, community psychologists are developing culturally appropriate approaches to research (Harrell et al., 1999; Seidman et al., 1993) and ways to conduct research that enable community members to become collaborators, not merely research participants (Brydon-Miller & Tolman, 1997; Tandon, Azelton, Kelly, & Strickland, 1998). These developments blend the core value of respect for diversity with adventuresome research. We examine these issues in depth in chapters 3–4.

The concern of prevention and promotion researchers with describing, measuring, and understanding the processes of change in preventive interventions has led to innovations in prevention research (Jansen & Johnson, 1993; Linney & Wandersman, 1991). Examples of long-term action research projects have become common, in which interventions are directly influenced by research findings, and research is designed to document the impact of interventions (Price et al., 1988). This continues the action research tradition pioneered by Lewin and his associates (Kelly, 1990).

Finally, adventuresome research also involves interdisciplinary collaboration. Community psychologists are interested in community and social problems that spill over disciplinary boundaries. The field originated amidst interdisciplinary collaboration. Founders of the field worked with colleagues in public health, community psychiatry, education, and related fields in settings like the Wellesley Human Relations Service. In 1987, the principal professional organization of the field changed its name to the Society for Community Research and Action (SCRA), to emphasize its interdisciplinary perspective. Today the field is linked to anthropology, community development, government, political science, and other fields. Within psychology, community psychologists work with developmental, environmental, social, and clinical psychologists (e.g., Leadbeater, Maton, & Schellenbach, 1999).

# COMMUNITY PSYCHOLOGY AND ITS CURRENT SOCIAL CONTEXT

As it developed a distinctive identity, community psychology also coped with changing social and political contexts. During the 1970s and 1980s, U.S. society became more conservative; this trend also occurred to some extent in other countries with active fields of community psychology, including Britain, Canada, Australia, and New Zealand. In the United States, political leaders and citizens questioned many of the ideals and programs of the 1960s and even of the New Deal of the 1930s. As M. Levine and Levine (1970) had forecast, this affected viewpoints and government policies regarding social problems. The environmental perspective that had led to community psychology was supplanted by a strongly biomedical perspective. To some extent this change was propelled by genuine advances in biomedical research and treatment, particularly for the more severe mental disorders. However, much of the pendulum swing was the result of social forces. Funding agencies explicitly called for psychological research on biomedical, not social, causes of mental disorders, and researchers' interests and studies followed suit (Humphreys & Rappaport, 1993).

In addition, Federal attention shifted from mental health to substance abuse. Drug abuse was a social issue not defined or dominated by progressives, and thus was available for conservative activism (Humphreys & Rappaport, 1993). Under President Reagan, conservatives declared a War on Drugs. It focused on causal factors within the individual, such as genes, illness, and personal moral weakness, that are characteristically emphasized in a conservative period (M. Levine & Levine, 1992). It also greatly expanded the use of police and prisons. The Federal prison population doubled during the Reagan administration; most of the increase was in drug offenders (Humphreys & Rappaport, 1993).

Federally funded psychological research was focused on individual-level (biological or narrowly psychological) factors. Psychological journals for the years 1981–1992 contained 170 articles for *drug addiction and personality* and only 3 references for *drug addiction and poverty*; similar findings appear if similar index terms (e.g., *drug abuse, alcoholism, socioeconomic status*) are searched (Humphreys & Rappaport, 1993). A telling indicator of how research on social problems is affected by political trends is that during the 1980s, primary funding for research on the problem of homelessness was provided by the federal Alcohol, Drug Abuse and Mental Health Administration, not the Department of Housing and Urban Development (Humphreys & Rappaport, 1993). Homelessness was thus defined in terms of individual problems, and research focused on the subgroup of homeless persons with substance abuse and mental disorders, rather than on access to affordable housing and employment, which were issues affecting all homeless persons (Humphreys & Rappaport, 1993; Shinn, 1992). These individualistic views of social problems are consistent with the M. Levine and Levine (1992) hypothesis about conservative periods.

In the United States at least, this conservative period has moderated, yet generally persisted, through the political changes of the 1990s. Individualistic explanations of poverty, crime, and many other problems continue to dominate discussion of public issues.

## Community Psychology Responses to the Social Context

Opportunities for community research and action do exist in conservative times. S. B. Sarason (1976) articulated the "anarchist insight" (with which many conservatives agree) that government interventions for social problems may undermine the psychological sense of community and feelings of responsibility to other community members. Mann (1998) asserted that many progressive efforts for social change "have foundered from a failure to take the local context into account," while that local context is precisely what community psychologists study (S. B. Sarason, 1974; Heller 1989; Kelly, 1990). Lappe and DuBois (1994) and Wolff (1994) asserted that across the U.S. political spectrum, agreement is increasing that social problems must be addressed at the community level. An emphasis on local initiative fits conservative and progressive views as well as the tradition of citizen participation (Bellah et al., 1985).

Linney (1990) delineated three trends that offer windows of opportunity for community psychology in the United States during conservative times. Her advice is still timely. First, the shift in power from federal to state and local governments affords community psychologists easier access to legislators, executive agencies, and policy making. Second, distrust in government, characteristic of a conservative period, has helped create a number of grassroots movements at the community level, consistent with the community psychology core values of citizen participation and sense of community.

Third, the budget-cutting cost consciousness of conservative governments may paradoxically open opportunities for preventive and nontraditional innovations, if they can show the reduced cost of their programs compared to traditional approaches. This is especially true in the areas of health and mental health, where highly professionalized medical treatments have been very expensive. Prevention programs and peer self-help groups often provide lower cost alternatives. Humphreys (1996) argued that the pressures for cost containment in medicine and mental health care today will force clinical psychology to reconsider its emphasis on psychotherapy. That trend could lead to a focus on preventive services concerning health as well as mental health, and to collaboration between clinical, community, and health psychology.

An example of the fiscal benefits of a preventive program is provided by longitudinal follow-up evaluations of the High/Scope Perry Preschool program, one of the models for Head Start (Schweinhart & Weikert, 1988). These studies included cost–benefit analyses that demonstrated long-term benefits to taxpayers of $23,000 for every year that a child was enrolled in this high-quality preschool for economically disadvantaged children. Compared with controls, graduates of the program were less likely to use special education services in their school years, less likely to need welfare assistance as adults, less likely to be imprisoned, and paid more taxes as adults. Thus, a program that may appear at first to be a costly means of addressing poverty actually saved money in the long run.

Finally, even the emphasis on biological factors in psychology, characteristic of conservative periods, does not always preclude a concern for community and preventive intervention. The current resurgence of behavior–genetic and temperament viewpoints in psychology offers interesting possibilities for community psychology. For instance, temperamental differences among individuals do not determine behavior alone, but interact with environments (Buss, 1995; Kagan, 1994). Community psychologists may study how environments (e.g., classrooms and teaching methods) may be altered to accommodate individuals of differing temperaments. (Recall the insistence of Lightner Witmer that every child can learn, if given the appropriate environment.)

It would be heedless of history to forget that the dominant public views of a conservative period are often associated with narrowly individualistic perspectives and often emphasize victim-blaming views of social problems. In the United States at least, they also often fail to understand or appreciate the diversity of society and keep money and other resources in affluent communities rather than using them where they are needed most. For instance, as we have described, cost cutting without regard for program quality in the U.S. mental health system has resulted in the dumping of persons with serious mental disorders on the streets. Yet these issues often are better addressed at local and state levels than nationally.

Community psychologists who are explicit about their values, able to support their claims with relevant research findings, and willing to find common ground with those who differ can continue to work with communities in a number of ways during conservative times. Community psychology has made substantive contributions to psychological knowledge and to society during this conservative period (Heller, 1990). In fact, Kelly (1990) argued that the absence of generous external funding makes it easier for the field to determine its own direction now than at its creation in the 1960s, when community mental health funding influenced the focus of the field.

## Conclusion: A Distinctive Community Psychology

In 1990, Heller summarized the development of community psychology during its first 25 years as a shift from "unbridled optimism and unsubstantiated rhetoric" in the 1960s to "solid accomplishment in theory construction and well-controlled demonstration projects" (pp. 142–143). However, Heller (1990, p. 143) noted that community psychologists have encountered realistic limitations to social and community change and need to increase their understanding of the complex processes of integrating community action and research. Kelly (1990) noted the same themes of accomplishment in community-based research coupled with the need to understand more fully the communities in which community psychologists work.

These conclusions are still timely. Community psychology is maturing as a field and broadening its membership and focus. Yet much remains to be done in order to understand the relationships of communities and individuals and strengthen their quality of life. Even the most experienced community psychologist is still a student of the relationship of individual and community life. Every generation of those students builds on the experiences of prior generations, yet re-invents community psychology to reflect the social contexts it currently faces.

Some of the most distinctive tools that community psychology possesses for these tasks are its approaches to community research. Being participant–conceptualizers means actively integrating community action with research. The aims and methods of community research also comprise some of the most rapidly changing areas of the field, as community psychologists explore the challenges of adventuresome research. In the next two chapters, we turn to discussion of those challenges in conducting community research.

## CHAPTER SUMMARY

**1.** Although it is an international discipline, community psychology has strong roots in U.S. culture. That culture is influenced by *individualism,* which elevates the individual (and sometimes immediate family) as primary and generally discounts involvement in and responsibility for wider communities or society. It has two forms: *utilitarian* and *expressive.* Individualism has a number of advantages and drawbacks. One important drawback is that it leads to *blaming the victim,* which reflects an exclusive focus on individual causes of personal problems or poverty.

**2.** In U.S. society, individualism has been moderated by other traditions. These buffer the impact of individualism on society, and provide alternatives to purely individualistic thinking. Three such traditions have been *citizen participation, religion and spirituality,* and *liberation.* One way of understanding individualism and these alternatives is Ryan's (1994) distinction between *fair play* and *fair shares* orientations.

**3.** Individualism has influenced the perspective of psychology in many ways, chiefly by narrowing its focus to the individual rather than the individual in social context.

**4.** Historical understanding of the field requires understanding the *Levine and Levine hypothesis* of social–political changes in U.S. society and how they influence beliefs about social problems and actions to address those problems. In *progressive* times, *environmental* explanations of social problems will be favored, and changes in community environments will be initiated. In *conservative* times, *individualistic* explanations of social problems will be favored, and individuals will be the focus of change efforts.

**5.** The period 1890–1914 was a progressive time, although the social problems of that time seem similar to those of today. Community initiatives to address those problems included settlement houses, early psychological clinics, the birth control and maternal health movement, and early civil rights initiatives. These constitute forerunners of many community psychology concepts and practices.

**6.** The period 1919–1932 was a conservative time. Social problems were defined and addressed in individual terms; examples included the eugenics movement and intelligence testing.

**7.** The progressive period after the Second World War led to the emergence of community psychology. Among the many forces that led to this development, we identified four forces for special attention: the rise of a *preventive perspective* on psychological disorders and problems in living, the *reforms in mental health care* due to the impact of the war and of scandals in mental institutions on the practice of psychology and other mental health professions, the rise of *action research and group dynamics,* and the impact of widespread *movements for social change* such as the civil rights, feminist, environmental and gay/lesbian rights movements.

**8.** Community psychology was generally recognized as a field at the *Swampscott Conference* in 1965, where the concept of community psychologist as *participant–conceptualizer* was proposed.

**9.** During the 1960s and 1970s, community psychology in the United States diverged from community mental health. The limitations of government-funded social change became apparent. Community psychology developed in Latin America with a distinctive concern for social justice. The field began to assume a distinctive identity after the *Austin Conference* in 1975.

**10.** Four current trends exist in community psychology: prevention and competence promotion; community-building, citizen participation, and empowerment; human diversity; and adventuresome research.

**11.** Recently, in many countries, including the United States, community psychology has worked within a conservative social context. In the United States, the changes from the progressive period of its founding to its current conservative context parallel the Levine and Levine analysis of earlier periods. Yet these times also provide opportunities for community psychology to grow, chiefly through involvement in local communities.

# BRIEF EXERCISES

**1.** Obtain and read the reports on the Swampscott and/or Austin conferences (see Recommended Readings). List indicators of the seven core values of community psychology or explicit mention of specific levels of analysis beyond the individual (see chap. 1). In addition, note other comments that illustrate the historical context of the developing field of community psychology. Could you have predicted, from reading these reports, where community psychology is today? Compare your findings with those of a classmate.

**2.** Read an empirical article and/or a conceptual article appearing in a community psychology journal. Describe which core values (see chap. 1) and current trends of community psychology (see this chapter) it addresses.

**3.** One tangible result of the feminist movement in the United States has been Federal Title IX, which mandates that schools and colleges receiving Federal funds must spend equally on women's and men's sports. Interview at least one woman who attended high school before 1970, asking about her opportunities for involvement in athletics in school (and in college if she attended one), whether she would have liked more, what the positive and negative outcomes of athletic involvement might be, and about differences (if any) between the influence of sports on women and men, as she sees them. Compare her views with yours, and compare athletic opportunities for women then with those available today. Discuss your findings with a friend or classmate.

**4.** Interview your instructor or another person in community psychology about his or her personal history of involvement in community psychology. Ask about influential teachers, readings, and experiences. Ask about what energized your instructor to enter the field and about his or her related interests outside the field.

# RECOMMENDED READINGS

Bellah, R., Madsen, R., Sullivan, W., Swidler, A., & Tipton, S. (1985). *Habits of the heart: Individualism and commitment in American life.* New York: Harper & Row.
>    A historical–sociological critique of individualism and alternative values in U.S. society, with many narratives of personal lives as illustrations. A classic, although limited by its middle-class research sample and lack of attention to social conflict. See also critiques in *The Nation* (1985, December 28), pp. 717–723.

Ryan, W. (1971). *Blaming the victim* New York: Random House.

Ryan, W. (1994). Many cooks, brave men, apples, and oranges: How people think about equality. *American Journal of Community Psychology, 22,* 25–36.
>    Either of these sources is a succinct statement of Ryan's insightful critique of individualistic thinking as applied to human and social problems. *Blaming the Victim* is a classic.

Levine, M., & Levine, A. (1992). *Helping children: A social history.* New York: Oxford University Press.
>    Presents the Levine and Levine hypothesis about historical change and helping services, and describes the society and social innovations of the Progressive Era. Profiles many of the innovations and leaders described in that portion of our chapter.

Bennett, C., Anderson, L., Cooper, S., Hassol, L., Klein, D., & Rosenblum, G. (1966). *Community psychology.* Boston: Boston University and South Shore Mental Health Center.

Iscoe, I., Bloom, B., & Spielberger, C. (Eds.). (1977). *Community psychology in transition: Proceedings of the national conference on training in community psychology.* Washington, DC: Hemisphere.
>    These are the reports on the Swampscott and Austin conferences. Both reports are interesting writings in which to search for early statements of community psychology themes and core values.

Sarason, S. (1974). *The psychological sense of community: Prospects for a community psychology.* San Francisco: Jossey-Bass.
>    Historically important in defining the divergence between community psychology and community mental health. Chapters 2–5 describe the historical origins of community psychology and provide a critique of American psychology.

Glidewell, J. C. (Ed.) (1984). A tribute to Erich Lindemann (special section). *American Journal of Community Psychology, 12,* 511–536.

Kelly, J. G. (Ed.). (1987). Special issue: Swampscott anniversary symposium. *American Journal of Community Psychology, 15,* 511–632.
     Two journal special issues giving retrospective accounts of Lindemann and of the Swampscott Conference.

Elias, M. J. (1987). Establishing enduring prevention programs: Advancing the legacy of Swampscott. *American Journal of Community Psychology, 15,* 539–554.

Shinn, M. (1987). Expanding community psychology's domain. *American Journal of Community Psychology, 15,* 555–574.

Snowden, L. R. (1987). The peculiar successes of community psychology: Service delivery to ethnic minorities and the poor. *American Journal of Community Psychology, 15,* 575–586.
     Three assessments of community psychology, 30 years after Swampscott. Still timely.

Heller., K. (1990). Social and community intervention. *Annual Review of Psychology, 41,* 141–168.

Kelly, J. G. (1990). Changing contexts and the field of community psychology. *American Journal of Community Psychology, 18,* 769–792.

Linney, J. A. (1990). Community psychology into the 1990s: Capitalizing opportunity and promoting innovation. *American Journal of Community Psychology, 18,* 1–17.
     Three perspectives on the history and future of community psychology. Still timely.

## PART two

# COMMUNITY
# RESEARCH

# THE AIMS OF COMMUNITY RESEARCH

# INTRODUCTION

> My department colleagues asked me, 'Where have you been? We haven't seen you in three days!' I told them I had been out collecting data. 'Oh? In whose laboratory?' [they asked]. 'In St. Louis County,' I said. 'It's a great laboratory.' (Glidewell, 1994)

John Glidewell developed one of the first preventive mental health interventions in schools during the 1950s, in St. Louis County, Missouri. His account above of a conversation with his psychology department colleagues during that time still rings true today. Although psychology is not as strongly based in laboratory research today, many students (and psychologists) still imagine community research only with difficulty. Yet communities offer rich opportunities for research, whether generating knowledge of the community as it exists or studying the effectiveness of efforts to improve the quality of community life.

Community research does involve giving up at least a portion of what makes the laboratory such a useful setting for research: control. The laboratory psychologist largely or completely controls the choice of phenomena to study, the perspective from which to study it, methodology, treatment of participants during the procedure, format in which those participants provide data, analysis of data, interpretation of findings, and reporting of results. That control promotes clarity of hypotheses and conclusions, and the production of some forms of knowledge. Of course, the researcher must make all these choices within accepted ethical limits. Yet the degree of control granted the psychological researcher in the laboratory is great.

However, although many individuals (especially students taking introductory psychology) are willing to give up enough control to briefly participate in a laboratory experiment, few citizens are willing to cede control in the settings where they and their families live every day: for instance, school, work, family, neighborhood, mutual help group. Thus the settings that are most significant for community psychology research are also most important to their inhabitants.

In this chapter, we present a different view of control: *sharing* control with community members can *enrich* the knowledge gained from community research. Well-designed community research, conducted within a collaborative relationship with a community, can yield insights not available in the laboratory. Those insights are based on immersion in community life and provide knowledge useful to both the community and the researcher. In this chapter, you will learn about possibilities for sharing control with the community regarding every step of research listed above.

Sharing control does not mean giving it up. A collaborative relationship means a partnership in which both community and researchers plan and implement research. Our goal is for you to become better informed about the tradeoffs involved in each decision and to understand and respect the interests of communities as well as the methods of psychological research. This chapter is constructed around five questions concerning these issues. By its end, we hope that you understand that community research, instead of being less valid because it is less experimentally controlled, can actually become richer by embracing the complexities of community life and seeking to understand them through careful inquiry.

## WHAT ARE THE KEY POINTS OF THIS CHAPTER?

In this chapter, we discuss the aims and purposes of community research and how that involves a partnership between researchers and community members. We structure that discussion in terms of five questions that community researchers must ask themselves before and during a community research project. Those questions concern the phenomena to be studied, the theory and values of the researchers, the ecological level(s) of analysis and cultural setting(s) of the study, and the nature of the partnership between researchers and citizens. Throughout, we give examples and guidelines for applying these ideas in community research. We conclude with five principles for conducting community research. This chapter provides the basis for chapter 4, in which we discuss specific community research methods.

## FIVE QUESTIONS FOR COMMUNITY RESEARCH

S. B. Sarason (1972) spoke of the period "before the beginning" of a community organization, institution, or initiative. In that period, the persons involved become aware of a problem or challenge to be addressed, and often struggle to make sense of it and of what to do about it. This concept also fits well with the early stages of a research project, well before a design is chosen and data collected (Rappaport, 1990). It occurs as researchers answer five questions that actually involve a number of decisions about the research. These questions concern issues that arise before the beginning, but run throughout the research project (see Table 3.1). The first two are as follows:

### 1. What Phenomenon (i.e., Issue, Topic, Process) Will We Study?

### 2. From What Perspective of Theory and Values Will We Study It?

Recall the nine-dot problem in chapter 1. In that problem, unrecognized assumptions often prevent successful resolution of the problem. Similarly, unrecognized assumptions influence researchers' choices of phenomenon and perspective. Those assumptions can concern one's most basic ideas of what constitutes social-scientific knowledge.

| TABLE 3.1 | QUESTIONS FOR COMMUNITY RESEARCHERS |
| --- | --- |

1. What phenonenon will we study?
2. From what perspective of theory and values will we study it?
3. At what level of analysis will we conduct this research?
4. Within what cultural context will we conduct this research, and how will we understand that context?
5. Within what relationship with a community will we conduct this research?

## Positivist and Contextualist Epistemologies

One source of unrecognized assumptions is one's *epistemology*. Epistemology refers to a theory of knowledge: what constitutes trustworthy knowledge, what evidence is accepted as trustworthy, what methods are acceptable for generating knowledge. In psychology, the dominant epistemology has been *positivism*, which underlies the historically dominant theoretical schools such as behaviorism and cognitivism. Positivism has assumed many forms, but a few common elements important in psychology are these: pursuit of objectivity and value-free neutrality in research, an ultimate goal of understanding cause and effect relationships, hypothesis testing and control of extraneous factors as methods of gaining that understanding, and measurement as a source of data. Positivism also emphasizes value-free, objective inquiry and seeks to construct generalizable laws or principles applicable in many circumstances. Pursuit of these aims requires control over the setting and methods of inquiry, and it is no accident that positivistic inquiry in psychology has occurred mainly in laboratories and other settings controlled by researchers.

This vision of research (admittedly oversimplified here for purposes of exposition) has come under increasing scrutiny. As Gergen (1973) and others showed, no observer is value-free; one is always a member of a culture and influenced by it. Moreover, Gergen (1973) argued, the general laws that are a goal of positivism are limited in applicability by the particular qualities of cultures, historical circumstances, and situations in which individuals live. Feminist researchers (Belenky, Clinchy, Goldberger, & Tarule, 1986; Gilligan, 1982; Reinharz, 1994; Riger, 1990) argued that psychological research methods and findings have reflected the worldview of men more than women. Bronfenbrenner (1979), in developmental psychology, and Kelly (1986), in community psychology, have advocated ecological approaches to research in community settings. From these and other sources, a number of alternatives have arisen to respond to the limitations of positivistic inquiry.

One approach adapts the methods of experimental, positivistic inquiry to the realities of community settings. Thus, quasi-experimental designs and statistical (rather than experimental) controls are used if setting practicalities preclude random assignment to experimental conditions (Cook & Campbell, 1979; Judd & Kenny, 1981; Rapkin & Mulvey, 1990). Standardized questionnaires with established reliability and validity enable study of many community phenomena in which experimentation is impossible. Quantitative methods such as multivariate analyses make it possible to include or control many extraneous variables and to study multiple dependent variables. Researchers also have recognized the methodological and theoretical challenges posed by ecological levels of analysis (Rapkin & Mulvey, 1990; Shinn, 1990).

Another approach involves a *contextualist* epistemology (Kingry-Westergaard & Kelly, 1990). A similar term is *constructivist* epistemology (Riger, 1990). Contextualism is focused on deeper understanding of a local and particular context rather than broad, general laws. It seeks to be grounded (Strauss, 1987) in a particular setting and time. Instead of pursuing the ideal of value-free objectivity, a contextualist epistemology assumes that knowing occurs in a relationship and is a product of a social connection between researcher and research participant. This emphasis on knowing through connection, collaboration, and mutual understanding is a particular emphasis of feminist researchers (e.g., Belenky et al., 1986). Knowledge is not built through objective, impersonal research, but rather an understanding that is constructed out of the sharing of experiences between persons (Riger, 1990). Contextualist research proceeds through a collaborative partnership of researchers with the people who will participate in that research. Because knowledge is an understanding of a context and is constructed within a relationship, measurement and hypothesis-testing recede in importance. Contextualist approaches are concerned with understanding the meaning of an event to the people who experience it, more than with the causes of their behaviors or cognitions. For these purposes, qualitative research methods, such as ethnography and interviewing, usually provide the best techniques.

"Before the beginning" of community research, a contextualist epistemology has different aims than a positivist approach. Contextualist concerns include finding a setting or community in which to ground one's research, developing a collaborative relationship with its members, gaining a cultural understanding of that community, and learning from the persons there. These are useful aims to have, even for researchers who otherwise adopt a positivist epistemology.

It is difficult to pursue community research within a rigorously positivist epistemology. However, much useful community research has had positivistic features, especially use of measurement and experimentation modified to fit community settings. Contextualist epistemology has become increasingly influential in community psychology in the last two decades. For instance, its emphasis on the researcher–community relationship has become a theme of community research in general. Both provide valuable insights for understanding and changing communities. Our point here is to advocate that community researchers make explicit choices about epistemology while recognizing the tradeoffs involved, and be able to modify one's epistemology to adapt to community settings.

## Social Issues and Research: Technological and Dialectical Perspectives

In addition to deciding on a more positivistic or contextualist perspective, community researchers must also decide how their research will relate to the community or social issues they study. Price (1989) identified two approaches to that question that can be labeled *technological* and *dialectical* (see Table 3.2).

Technological community research involves performing research relevant to social problems, from a stance as value-neutral as possible, in a way that seeks concrete problems for research and attempts to find concrete, pragmatic answers to these problems (Price,

| TABLE 3.2 | PERSPECTIVES FOR COMMUNITY RESEARCH |
|---|---|
| Epistemology | Approach to social issues |
| Positivist | Technological |
| Contextualist | Dialectical |
| | Stating premises boldly and explicitly |
| | Attending to unheard voices |
| | Strengths perspective |

1989). Much social science research assumes this stance, which dominated the early development of community psychology and is still useful today. How does a nation or a community prevent the spread of AIDS, reduce its rate of adolescent pregnancy, reduce the proportion of children growing up in poverty, or reduce violence in its schools? Technological community research attempts to define these issues, identify their causes, develop programs to address those factors, and then evaluate the effectiveness of those programs. It applies (with modifications) the scientific methods and findings of psychology to society.

The usefulness of technological research depends on social consensus in definition of problems, causes, and programs (Price, 1989). Without that consensus, no reasonably objective approach may be possible. However, even with public health problems that can be identified with precision and for which causal factors are understood (e.g., the diagnosis and transmission of AIDS, the effects of tobacco use), there is often great controversy in a community about prevention programs (e.g., needle exchange, efforts to curb smoking through taxation). Such conflicts mushroom when community members cannot even agree on the definition of the problem and its causes, as with issues of sexuality, child and family stressors, and many forms of drug abuse, for instance. A research team may use what they believe are commonsensical or empirically sound definitions of problems, causes, and measurements, only to find their findings rejected by those who disagree with their premises. For instance, Price (1989) described his own experience in testifying before Congress about exemplary community programs for those coping with marital separation, teen pregnancy, or child abuse, only to receive the response that such programs undermined the institution of marriage and family values. Thus, Price (1989, p. 157) argued that many social dilemmas are better understood as social conflicts than as social "problems" to be "solved."

Does such lack of consensus on social issues mean empirical research in communities is useless? Price (1989) said no. A second approach recognizes the inevitability of social conflict yet advocates the usefulness of community research. We label it the dialectical perspective (see Rappaport, 1981). Dialectical research involves three qualities: stating premises boldly and explicitly, attending to unheard voices, and assuming a strengths perspective.

Researchers who take a dialectical perspective assume that social issues involve two (or perhaps more) opposing positions, each with different value assumptions as well as different definitions and theories of the problem. Both also generate empirical findings that reflect their perspectives. Dialectical researchers join this process of conflict by *stating their premises boldly and explicitly.* They take sides in debates involving value stances as well as empirical findings and bear witness when their findings are relevant to those debates (Price, 1989). Their stances often involve professional and political risk. Once made, however, these stances clarify decisions about what is to be studied and often how to study it. Bold stating of basic premises, for instance, led feminist researchers and advocates to conduct research that has clarified the nature of domestic violence and sexual assault (Russo & Dabul, 1994).

How can a community researcher know what side to take in such a debate? One's own social values provide a guide. A more general guideline was suggested by Price (1989), Rappaport (1981, 1990), and Riger (1990). They argued that conflicts about social issues are dominated by the powerful, who define the problem and set the terms of debate. The ideas of the powerful become the conventional wisdom about the problem. When debate is dominated by the powerful, an important role of community researchers is to identify a perspective or group that is being ignored and to perform research that helps bring attention to it. This research will provide knowledge that defines the limits of prevailing views and puts that research in a broader context. It also provides opportunities for expression to less powerful persons or communities, whose ideas and experiences are being ignored. This approach might be labeled *attending to unheard voices.*

The metaphor of voice comes most directly from some feminist thinkers (Belenky et al., 1986; Gilligan, 1982; Reinharz, 1994; Riger, 1990) who advocated that research methods and findings reflect closely the experiences, worldviews, and knowledge of research participants. Traditional psychological methods and theories have, in their view, obscured and distorted the experiences and knowledge of women. Part of that obscuring has occurred because the voices—the words, intuitions, and insights—of women have not been clearly heard or understood. This obscuring of voices has also happened to other groups not well-represented among researchers (Trickett et al., 1994). Reinharz (1994) noted that researchers cannot "give" voice to excluded groups or individuals; voice is something one develops oneself. Yet researchers can create ways to listen to and learn from voices of persons not well-represented in the knowledge base of psychology.

Attending to unheard voices involves beginning research from the standpoint of the lives and experiences of the least powerful individuals within social systems. That starting point for community psychology was advocated by Reinharz (1994) and Riger (1990), writing from a feminist viewpoint, by Rappaport (1990), writing from an empowerment viewpoint; and by Montero (1998) and Serrano-Garcia (1990), representing the community psychology of Latin America and the Caribbean. Attending to unheard voices means studying the experiences of people who are most affected by the practices of a system but who have the least control over those practices: the most isolated, marginal, or least powerful. Study their worldview and experiences to understand not only them, but the systems that affect them. That knowledge can then be used to advocate for those populations and for social change (Montero, 1998; Rappaport, 1990).

For instance, clinical research on treatment for persons with serious mental illness often focuses on evaluating services provided by professionals and agencies, measured in terms of psychological criteria chosen by the researchers. By focusing on the effectiveness of services, a way of thinking is created in which professionals act (choose and implement treatments) and clients are acted upon (treated). One gains a different perspective by studying the everyday life experiences of persons with serious mental illness themselves (Riger, 1990) or by studying mutual help groups (Rappaport, 1993; see chap. 7). Persons who experience the illness become central to the research. It concerns how they make everyday choices (including economic, vocational, and housing ones), as well as how they help each other. Both perspectives are valuable, yet evaluation of professional treatment has been pursued with more academic support and funding than study of everyday coping and mutual help among persons with serious mental illness (Toro, 1990).

A dialectical stance also often involves taking a *strengths perspective*. This involves research that identifies the strengths of individuals and groups whose problems or limitations are usually emphasized (and often demeaned). Some questions about strengths proposed and studied by community researchers include the following. How do homeless single mothers cope effectively with the economic and parenting challenges in their lives (Banyard, 1995)? What protective factors are associated with abstinence from alcohol use among early adolescents (Spoth, Redmond, Hockaday, & Yoo, 1996)? What factors lead to resilience among young urban children under major life stress (Wyman, Cowen, Work, & Parker, 1991)? A strengths perspective also means identifying assets of communities, not dwelling on their needs (Kretzmann & McKnight, 1993). What resources of ideas, skills, and mutual support exist in a low-income urban neighborhood or rural area? What values and resources exist within the traditions of African and African-American culture for the development of African-American young men (Watts, 1993)? A strengths perspective is not Pollyanna-ish. It does not mean that challenges and needs must be ignored, but it does mean that researchers also account for resources and strengths in individuals or communities. Thus, the strengths perspective avoids victim-blaming.

To summarize, a dialectical perspective for community research involves recognizing a debate involving social or community issues, being explicit about one's values in that debate, and conducting research consistent with one's values that contributes knowledge to that debate. Further, it involves attending to unheard voices of the less powerful and taking a strengths perspective. Taking sides in a dialectical perspective involves truth-telling (Price, 1989), not sloppiness or inattention to one's biases, or intellectual dishonesty. Methods of data collection and analysis still must be defensible (Riger, 1990).

Some community psychologists adopt a more technological role, others a more dialectical one. As with the choice of a more positivist or more contextualist epistemology, the technological–dialectical choice is largely philosophical. Price (1989) listed limitations of each approach. The principal drawback of the technological approach is its assumption of objectivity when in fact it may reflect the ideas and experiences of only part of society; this leads to overlooking one's own values and biases. Explicit discussion of premises and concepts, especially with those who will be affected by the research, helps to reduce this. One principal drawback of the dialectical perspective is that assuming an advocacy stance may oversimplify complex social issues. Recognition of the rationale and evidence for opposing views helps to reduce this. In addition, well-intentioned advocacy may not necessarily benefit those it is intended to help or the community as a whole. Careful consideration of likely consequences, and study of actual consequences, helps to reduce this limitation.

The complexity of communities demands a body of community research that includes both approaches. However, whether the researcher assumes a dialectical or a technological stance, boldly and explicitly stating one's values and assumptions tends to improve community research. It clarifies the reasoning behind the researcher's choice of phenomena and perspective, the first two questions involved "before the beginning." In addition, whichever approach is chosen, collaboration with community members, listening carefully to their perspectives, and looking for community strengths express core values of community psychology and are often adopted by researchers pursuing either technological or dialectical approaches.

# ECOLOGICAL LEVELS OF ANALYSIS IN COMMUNITY RESEARCH

A third question follows soon after the questions of phenomenon and perspective:

## 3. At What Ecological Level(s) of Analysis Will We Conduct This Research?

Researchers must choose a level (or sometimes multiple levels) on which to focus their concepts, measurement, and (if they choose) intervention. Will they measure individuals, microsystems, organizations, localities, populations, or macrosystems? At what level might they attempt to intervene, for instance to develop a prevention program?

These questions are actively debated in community psychology even among experienced researchers. Perhaps the most essential point is that multiple levels do exist and that theoretical perspective and empirical research depend in part on the level of analysis chosen. The level most associated with psychology, study of individuals, is only one choice available to community researchers. From an ecological point of view, research at different levels (for instance, individual and microsystem) provides different lenses through which to understand the same phenomenon. Let's consider some examples of this change of perspective.

**Social Support Networks**   Do senior citizens receive support from individuals only, or do microsystems and organizations also provide support beyond that from individuals? Felton and Berry (1992) conducted a study of social support networks among senior citizens at a hospital geriatric clinic. Their interview questions, following standardized, often-used procedures, asked respondents to name or give initials of individuals who provided important support in their lives. Yet Felton and Berry's respondents provided some initially puzzling answers. Although asked for individuals, many gave answers like "all my nieces and nephews," "my grandchildren," and "the people at my senior center." Almost one-third of the respondents named such groups, not an individual, at least once. In total, about 10% of the support sources listed were groups. When interviewers asked for clarification, most respondents insisted that they meant a group, and that it was the group as a whole, not particular individuals, who provided support. (Notice that Felton & Berry, 1992, then listened to and reported the "unheard voices" of these respondents, whose ideas did not neatly fit the measurement procedure.)

What do we make of this finding? Social support has usually been understood and measured as a process occurring between two individuals. This has kept much of the research on social support at the individual level (Felton & Shinn, 1992). Yet clearly social support also occurs in groups (Maton, 1989), especially in microsystems. Those groups provide support and a sense of community even when the individual members change. Maton (1989) found that highly supportive religious congregations, mutual help groups, and senior centers provided significant aid to members facing a variety of stressors. In fact, the sense of belonging within such an organization or microsystem (social integration) may be as important as social support from individuals (Felton & Shinn, 1992).

**Neighborhood Citizen Participation**   What determines actual citizen participation in neighborhood associations? D. D. Perkins, Florin, Rich, Wandersman, and Chavis (1990) analyzed predictors of citizen participation as part of the Block Booster Project, an action research project conducted in urban neighborhoods. They focused on city blocks and block associations formed by residents. When Perkins et al. compared individuals' extent of participation in block associations, those who owned their homes (vs. renting), who had lived longer on the block, and who had higher incomes participated more (this is consistent with prior research). Then Perkins et al. computed means for the three residential and income variables for each block and compared blocks, not individuals, on the extent of their residents' participation. In that block-level analysis, none of the three income/residence factors were associated with participation.

What does this mean? D. D. Perkins et al. (1990, p. 106) interpreted it this way. Within a block, the individuals most likely to participate were long-time residents, homeowners, and those with higher incomes. Yet blocks with few long-term, homeowning, or higher income residents still mustered as much citizen participation overall as blocks with many of these residents. In their study, this appeared to be because the sense of community among residents of the block as a whole was more important for participation than the individual characteristics of its residents.

If D. D. Perkins et al. (1990) had not compared blocks as well as individuals, they would have concluded that owning a home, having a higher income, and being a long-term resident are the most important factors in citizen participation. These variables are difficult to change, and would give dispiriting news to residents of lower income neighborhoods attempting to improve the quality of neighborhood life. Instead, the more accurate picture emerges that these demographic factors make a difference within a block, but they are not as important as other factors, and blocks without these resources can mobilize other resources (e.g., sense of community) to increase participation. Their analysis revealed not only differences by level of analysis, but also suggested community strengths for lower income neighborhoods.

The metaphor of homelessness as a game of musical chairs, which we presented in chapter 1, provides another example of the importance of ecological levels of analysis.

## Levels of Analysis and Scope of Research

Level of analysis makes a difference before the beginning in determining the scope of the study, and later in the choice of measurement strategies. The scope of the study concerns the social unit(s) to be studied. Is a prevention program to be implemented in one classroom and perhaps compared with a similar classroom in the same school as a control (microsystem level)? Is it instead to be implemented in one school or school district, compared with similar other schools (organizational or perhaps locality level)? Will it be studied in an international or cross-cultural context? For a study of adolescent drug use, what variables should be included as protective factors that lead to resisting drug use? Individual personality traits? Microsystem factors, such as family and peer influences? Neighborhood characteristics? Are protective factors provided differently in different racial or ethnic populations, or at different socioeconomic levels? Shall a study of neighborhood empowerment focus on the effects of a block association on its individual members, or focus on the functioning of the block association as an organization, or focus on its effects on the quality of life in the neighborhood as a whole? The challenge for a community psychology is addressing the interrelationships among these differing levels of analysis, not just studying individual variables in isolation.

***How Can Settings Be Studied?***    How can researchers study the characteristics of levels beyond the individual, such as microsystems, organizations, and communities?

In chapter 5 we describe the idea of measuring the social climate of a setting (Moos, 1984, 1994). In a number of studies, Moos and associates measured the psychological characteristics of environments such as classrooms and mental health treatment settings. They did this by using questionnaires to ask individuals about their perceptions of qualities of the environment, which are summed to measure constructs such as supportiveness of relationships among setting members, how task-oriented the setting is, and how clear the goals and rules of the organization are. These are subjective ratings, based on individual judgments. When scores are aggregated for a number of individuals, however, the means on these variables can provide a measure of setting characteristics compared with other settings. The variability of these measures among individuals in a setting indicates their degree of agreement about setting characteristics.

More objective measures of a small group or organization can be provided by independent outside observers (Shinn, 1990). L. Roberts et al. (1991, 1999) used trained, independent observers to conduct behavioral observations of a self-help group. Their studies yielded important findings about social support exchanged in such groups.

An intermediate approach uses key informants, persons connected in some way to group members but who still provide an outside perspective. B. McMillan et al. (1995) studied Rhode Island community drug abuse prevention coalitions. They asked local government leaders, school superintendents, and chiefs of police to rate the effectiveness of these coalitions.

Another approach is to identify and count events or changes in a community or an organization as a whole. Fawcett and his associates have developed a variety of such measures, for instance concerning advocacy for persons with disabilities (Fawcett et al., 1994) and drug abuse prevention coalitions (Fawcett et al., 1995). Examples of such community changes include a new high school peer-helping program to reduce drug abuse, a new radio station policy prohibiting glamorization of drug use, and training courses for clergy in drug abuse prevention efforts for their congregations (Fawcett et al., 1995). Speer, Hughey, Gensheimer, and Adams-Leavitt (1995) used archival data to measure the impact of community advocacy organizations. Over a 3-year period, they counted the number of stories in major metropolitan newspapers on two such organizations and the number of ideas emphasized by each group's outreach that appeared in these stories. Such measures are especially useful in longitudinal studies of one community over time.

# UNDERSTANDING THE CULTURAL CONTEXT OF RESEARCH

Community psychology places high value on understanding human diversity. However, the extent of published research that uses culturally diverse samples or concerns issues of cultural diversity has lagged behind those espoused values (Bernal & Enchantegui-de-Jesus, 1994; Loo, Fong, & Iwamasa, 1988). Recently, special journal issues (e.g., Seidman et al., 1993; Serrano-Garcia & Bond, 1994; Wilson, 1997) and books (e.g., Trickett et al., 1994) have helped to stimulate more research on diversity issues. Community researchers are recognizing what has been true all along—that one question to be answered before the beginning of research is this:

## 4.   Within What Cultural Context Will We Conduct This Research, and How Will We Understand That Context?

All research, of course, occurs within a culture, and perhaps within more than one. Even a controlled laboratory study of college sophomores in the United States, occurs within the culture of college life in the United States., as well as within the particular culture of that college. However, understanding diverse cultures, populations, and settings is central to community psychology. Thus, it is especially important that community researchers study a variety of cultures and communities. They also need to understand how they themselves are affected by culture, as well as how research participants are. Choices made by researchers about phenomena to study, perspective, research design, measurement, and data collection are based in cultural assumptions. Three important issues arise when these choices are made in community research.

***Assumptions of Population Homogeneity***    First is the issue of challenging one's own image of another culture, especially understanding the diversity within every culture. An assumption of population homogeneity (Sasao & Sue, 1993) categorizes all members of a cultural group as alike and overlooks differences among them. Research in social categorization (cited by Kelly, Azelton, Burzette, & Mock, 1994) suggested that this results from the cognitive tendency to think about members of one's cultural ingroup in more detail than persons outside it. Thus, people understand members of their own culture in complex ways, as individuals and as members of various groups or categories. Yet people think more simplistically about members of other cultures or communities, tend to categorize them in more general terms, and think of them all as members of a general category. This is ethnocentrism, although often inadvertent. It also reflects lack of detailed knowledge and experience with phenomena we wish to understand, in the communities where they occur. Forming a collaborative relationship with community members helps to counteract assumptions of population homogeneity.

Examples of this diversity within a population include differences in life experiences and worldview between Puerto Ricans, Cuban Americans, Mexican Americans, and other groups grouped in the Latino/Latina category. Also important are differences between generations of immigrant groups (e.g., first generation immigrants from Mexico, third generation Mexican-Americans), as well as socioeconomic or other differences within ethnic or racial categories (Hughes, Seidman & Williams, 1993; Sasao & Sue, 1993). In studies of alcohol use among Americans of Japanese ancestry, findings from samples in Hawaii did not generalize even to Americans of Japanese ancestry on the mainland (Sasao & Sue, 1993). At the individual level, some members of an ethnic population consider their ethnicity a very important aspect of their personal identity, whereas others do not (we describe this issue of acculturation in chap. 6).

***Assumptions of Methodological Equivalence***    The second issue encountered in research concerns equivalence of research methods across cultures (Hughes et al., 1993). Such assumptions can occur even when cultural differences are not the topic of research or recognized by researchers. Linguistic equivalence of questionnaires or other measurement instruments is the simplest example. Tanaka-Matsumi and Marsella (cited in Hughes et al., 1993) found that the English clinical term *depression* and the closest Japanese translation *yuutsu* were not equivalent. When asked to define them, U.S. citizens described internal states such as "sad" and "lonely," whereas Japanese described external states such as "dark" and "rain." Careful checks on translation can reduce but not eliminate problems of lack of linguistic equivalence.

Issues of scale equivalence refers to whether choices on questionnaires or other measures mean the same thing across cultures. Hughes et al. (1993) cited studies finding that African-American and Hispanic participants were more likely to use the extremes of Likert scales, whereas White respondents were more likely to use the intermediate areas of such scales. Task equivalence refers to the research setting; Bronfenbrenner (1979, p. 111) argued that social class differences in parenting style found in some U.S. studies (based on assessment of parenting in a laboratory task) may reflect greater familiarity and comfort of middle-class parents with the lab setting than genuine differences in parenting at home. Vega (1992) criticized studies of health interventions that expected extensive time commitments from participants inconsistent with their cultural practices. Finally, the quantitative, objective approach of Western science and psychology are inappropriate for understanding many cultures, where impersonal inquiry, measurement of abstract conceptions, and self-disclosure to strangers are rare.

***Between-Group and Within-Group Designs***    The third issue encountered in research concerns whether to compare two or more cultures or populations, or study one in detail. This involves the classic *emic–etic* distinction (Zane & Sue, 1986). A between-group, etic, design compares two or more cultural groups, for instance African Americans and Latinos/Latinas, on variables specified by the researchers. Its strength is that such comparison can yield knowledge of differences that leads to better understanding of both cultures. One drawback is that the researchers' own cultures will affect their design, assessment, and interpretation of differences in potentially ethnocentric ways. In addition, the equivalence of procedures, setting, and assessment in both cultures must be assured. Finally, without a deep understanding of both cultures, it is difficult to avoid interpreting differences as a deficit or weakness in one of the cultural groups (Hughes et al., 1993).

Researchers using a within-group, emic, design study a cultural group, for instance Puerto Ricans, in more depth, on its own terms. Comparisons and differences between cultures are not the focus, and understanding the "why" of cultural practices is often easier. In addition, subgroups within the culture (e.g., based on socioeconomic status) can be understood more clearly (Hughes et al., 1993). Population-specific psychologies, such as the study of psychological aspects of Mexican, Polish or Filipino culture have recently been studied (Kim & Berry, 1993). This study often can precede and inform etic comparisons of two or more populations, but a deeper understanding of many cultures is needed first, in the near future.

# GUIDELINES FOR UNDERSTANDING CULTURAL CONTEXT IN COMMUNITY RESEARCH

What can researchers do to recognize these issues and respond to them? A number of community psychologists have recently presented guidelines for recognizing and studying cultural issues in community research (Hughes et al., 1993; Kelly et al., 1994; Sasao & Sue,

1993; Trickett, 1996; Vega, 1992). Some of the most basic follow; we refer you to the original sources for more detail. These are guidelines; exceptions or practical compromises may be crafted in specific contexts.

1.   Create collaborative partnerships between researchers and members of cultural communities involved in or affected by research. Encourage participation in decisions about all aspects of the research design and implementation, especially conceptualizing the questions to be studied, assuring equivalence of procedures and assessment instruments, and interpretation of findings.

We discuss such partnerships later in this chapter, but here are two examples of their value in understanding cultural differences. Kelly and his associates (Kelly et al., 1994; Tandon et al., 1998) have pursued a long-term research project on the nature of leadership in an African-American community in the United States, and developed a partnership with a panel of community leaders there. Those local leaders, with the support of the researchers, actually designed the interview used in the research. The researchers' original conceptions of leadership focused on personal qualities of individual leaders (Kelly et al., 1994, p. 433). However, the leaders on the panel articulated a different, more collective definition of leadership, based on their experiences in working together. Those leaders used the metaphor of making soup to describe the importance of both individual contributions and group experiences. The research team's perspective, based in the individualism of psychology, was expanded by this encounter with different cultural assumptions.

A second example comes from the same project. When individual members of the panel missed a meeting, the chief researcher would call them very soon to communicate the date of the next meeting. This inadvertently undermined the efforts of the local community leader of the panel and also was not consistent with the social norms of the community about how best to remind members of their commitments. The researcher and panel leader shared their concerns, learned about each other's personal styles and cultural etiquette, and decided how best to encourage panel members to participate.

2.   Define cultural groups in terms that they use themselves, and use their definitions for determining membership in that group. Avoid use of easily observed markers such as skin color or surname or nationality unless members of a cultural community agree.

3.   Seek to understand the diversity within a cultural group or community and the factors that create these differences. Seek understanding not only of the overall culture and population, but also of the specific setting where the research takes place (e.g., school, neighborhood, organization). If possible, sample more than one setting within the culture.

4.   *Consider qualitative research methods* (discussed in the next chapter), or use qualitative findings from prior studies. These allow richer understanding of cultural practices and fuller interaction between researcher and participant, and can reduce ethnocentric procedures and interpretations. If appropriate, useful ways may then be found to use quantitative measurement as well (Hughes et al., 1993).

5.   Given the current lack of knowledge of many cultural factors relevant to the concerns of community psychology, *consider avoiding comparisons between cultural groups* unless methodological equivalence has been established and comparisons can be fully understood (Hughes et al., 1993). Consider assuming a *strengths perspective* to describe cultures (Snowden, 1987).

6. *Expect to modify everything* that worked in one cultural community for use in another: theoretical assumptions, measurement techniques, interview methods, data-analytic and statistical procedures, and methods of reporting findings. Value these experiences as enriching and extending knowledge.

In this section, we have focused on a few representative, specific issues for conducting research. We have left for chapter 6 a larger analysis of cultural and other concepts for understanding human diversity. We conclude that chapter with further concepts and issues to consider for conducting culturally sensitive research.

## COMMUNITY RESEARCH AS A COLLABORATIVE PARTNERSHIP

> The first time I ever did research, I'll never forget it. . . . I went through eleven organizations; they all turned me down. So Baake called some guy . . . and said will you be kind to Chris Argyris and let him come into your bank and interview some people. . . . So I went in and interviewed fifty people, did my study. . . . And I went and gave the people some feedback, and they said 'We like this. Would you come in now and do a total bank study?' Which I did. . . . I got almost diametrically opposed data. And I had interviewed twenty-five of the same people that I interviewed before. . . . I had nineteen of them come into a room, and I said 'You can tell me what's going on. They said 'Professor, it ain't so difficult. Four weeks ago, it was be-kind-to-Chris week. So some of us answered the questions in a way, who cares, and some said what the hell, it's not threatening, tell the truth. Now you come back as a consultant/researcher. Those of us who are now frightened distort the data, and those who think they might get some help give you the truth.' (Argyris, quoted in Kelly, 1986, p. 583)

It is clear from this anecdote that the quality and usefulness of research data depends on the context in which it is collected, and especially on the relationship between researcher and research participants. When the researcher's position, power, and purposes changed, so did the nature of what employees told him. In this anecdote, Argyris was performing organizational research, but similar issues pervade community psychology research. They involve the cultural issues just discussed, and more. Thus, before the beginning, community research involves a fifth question:

## 5.  *Within What Relationship with a Community Will We Conduct This Research?*

One metaphor for the researcher–community relationship is that of guest and host (Robinson, 1990). Research is conducted by guests in the host community; among the good manners that might be expected of such guests are full disclosure of their intent and methods, seeking permission for their activities, respect for host wishes and views, and meaningful thanks for hospitality. Reciprocating gifts is good manners for guests; the researchers receive the gift of cooperation by the community in providing data, while reciprocation might involve providing some product of that research in a form useful to the community. Another metaphor for the researcher–community relationship is a partnership, with both parties having some degree of choice and control, and with open, honest communication, compromise, and respect regarding those choices. As in most partnerships, each partner brings unique resources to the shared work (Tyler et al., 1983). In a third metaphor, the researcher becomes an ally with the community in its struggle against more powerful force. This metaphor is reflected in participatory action research (Brydon-Miller & Tolman, 1997; Yeich, 1996) and in the idea of attending to unheard voices described earlier in this chapter. Although the role of the researcher differs in these three metaphors, all imply a concern for the long-term well-being of the community, rather than a short-term exchange that benefits the researcher more than the community.

Research and action actually are "inseparable and simultaneous" (Serrano-Garcia, 1990, p. 172). To make any community decision, citizens analyze their community in some way. Moreover, any research project conducted in the community affects it in many ways. Data collection alone makes an impact in the community, as citizens provide time for interviews or questionnaires, or access to records or meetings. In addition, merely thinking about interview questions regarding one's neighborhood may alter one's view of it. Moreover, many groups have been exploited by research (Santiago-Rivera, Morse, Hunt, & Lickers, 1998). The intertwining of action and research raises challenges, yet also gives opportunities for community members and researchers to teach each other and to enhance each others' work.

Integrating research and action, through collaborating with communities as partners, addresses core values of community psychology: empirical grounding, collaboration and community strengths, citizen participation, social justice, and respect for diversity. These are themes of participatory action research (Brydon-Miller, 1997), Serrano-Garcia's (1990) intervention within research, feminist approaches (Reinharz, 1994; Riger, 1990), empowerment research (Rappaport, 1990), and the ecological, collaborative approach advocated by Kelly and associates (Kelly et al., 1994; Tandon et al., 1998).

These issues become even more important if the partnership involves a preventive intervention as well as research on its effectiveness. The problem to be addressed or prevented, the specific objectives of a preventive program (in schools or through home visits, for instance), the procedures by which it is to be carried out and by whom, and the nature of research or evaluation of the program's effects, are all issues to be determined in partnership with the community or setting where the program is to occur. It is imperative that researchers commit themselves to long-term work with the community as the program (if effective) is incorporated into the everyday life of the community or setting (Elias, 1987). Chapters 11 and 14 discuss these issues in detail.

In this section, we review specific approaches to facilitating researcher–community partnership at each stage of community research: before the beginning, defining the topic, collecting data, interpreting and reporting findings, and taking action based on findings. At each step, we present approaches that maximize participation by community members. We do not advocate that these are useful or appropriate in every context or that they are endorsed in entirety by every community psychologist. Moreover, use of these methods does not magically erase the power differential usually present between researcher and community (M. Bond, 1990; E. Burman, 1997). However, the best way to begin to understand the community–researcher relationship is to present collaborative–participatory methods in ways that clarify the value issues and practical tradeoffs involved. Researchers and communities often craft compromises in specific contexts.

***Partnership "Before the Beginning"***   How can researchers involve community members "before the beginning?" This begins with entry of researchers into the community (Chataway, 1997; Kelly, 1986; Serrano-Garcia, 1990). Some issues might include the following. Are researchers invited into the community? By whom, and under what terms? If they gain entry by seeking permission for research or by offering a program, with whom do they communicate? Are the persons or organizations with whom a relationship is built representative of the community? Do they represent one side of a controversy? If so, is that position consistent with the researchers' values? Do several groups exist within the community with competing views of research (Chataway, 1997)? Are the community members in a position that is vulnerable if the research becomes controversial? Who will benefit from research in this community (Rappaport, 1990)? Researchers need to provide the community with as much information as possible, as early as possible, about themselves and their purposes (Serrano-Garcia, 1990).

One way to build a community–researcher partnership is to form a community research panel (Tandon et al., 1998) or dialogue group (Chataway, 1997) that includes representatives of community organizations and/or other citizens. This allows researchers to communicate and negotiate with community members most involved in the research and through them with the wider community (Serrano-Garcia, 1990; Tandon et al., 1998). It also improves the ability of researchers to understand the cultural characteristics of the community (Chataway, 1997; Hughes et al., 1993; Kelly et al., 1994; Santiago-Rivera et al., 1998). This may involve some demystifying of the images many citizens hold of the objectivity, complexity, and authority of research (Chavis, Stucky, & Wandersman, 1983), thus helping them to understand that they have real contributions to make. To promote effective communication within the team, researchers must be willing to find a vocabulary that is commonsensical yet not condescending (W. L. Robinson, 1990). In addition, researchers need to communicate that community members' experiential, "insider" knowledge-for-living is useful in research, and to solicit it from citizens. Recall the "making soup" metaphor for community leadership, suggested by citizens (Kelly et al., 1994).

Kelly et al. (1994) emphasized social–ecological aspects of forming the community-researcher partnership. First, interdependence of researchers and citizens must be built through interpersonal relationships. That involves plenty of face-to-face contact, in informal ways that allow getting to know each other and learning about each other, without the barriers of expertise and titles. Second, that relationship-building promotes seeing each other as having resources or talents that can be shared and celebrated and that cement group ties. Those resources exist among both researchers and community members. Resources include different forms of knowledge and skills, as well as personal commitment to the community and networks of relationships. Creating opportunities for community members to explain their community and culture to researchers, in an atmosphere of learning and respect, builds appreciation of those resources. Researchers also must respect the host community culture, vocabulary, and folkways.

***Research Decisions***   Once formed, the community research panel can begin to negotiate and plan the carrying out of research. What specific phenomena will they study? How can the perspectives, the voices, of community members be elicited about these? How can questionnaires, interviews, or other research methods be designed that reflect the experiences of community members, not just the preconceptions of researchers? Some examples of issues for the research team to negotiate include whether to use a no-treatment control group in the evaluation of a program (Swift, 1990), multiple observers of mutual help group meetings (L. Roberts et al., 1991), and the format and questions for questionnaires (Chataway, 1997; Kelly et al., 1994; Serrano-Garcia, 1990). In addition, where will original data be kept, and how can its confidentiality best be assured (Santiago-Rivera et al., 1998)?

These and similar decisions have tradeoffs. For instance, lack of a control group will greatly limit the evaluation of a program's effectiveness. Open-ended items make it more difficult to develop standardized, highly reliable, valid measurement instruments and use a large sample. Negotiating methodological or practical decisions with the community takes time and involves compromise. Yet the traditional psychological paradigm, in which researchers make these and other choices in the interest of experimental control, is also limited. Many phenomena of interest to communities and community researchers simply cannot be studied with such standardization. Moreover, genuine collaboration with community members can increase the validity of measurement, as research participants take more seriously their provision of data to researchers. (Have you ever completed a survey hurriedly because you had no investment in the results?) Creating a positive relationship with a community affords returning there for future studies. The tradeoffs must be considered in each study and community.

Kelly and associates (Kelly et al., 1994; Tandon et al., 1998) studied the development of community leadership among members of an African-American neighborhood in Chicago. The researchers developed a working relationship with a community group, the Developing Communities Project (DCP). Staff of the DCP chose members of a community research panel to work with the researchers. This panel developed a set of criteria for research methods: that they must provide personal contact and dialogue, must make it possible for participants to describe their experiences in their own words, and must be anchored to the experiences of the participants. Through a series of 19 meetings, the researchers and the panel agreed on a semistructured interview technique, including wording of questions. This promoted trust between the panel and researchers, and eventually between interviewers and participants.

Another step in the community–researcher partnership is interpretation of results. Community researchers have presented results to community members and asked them to suggest their own interpretations (Chataway, 1997; Chavis et al., 1983; Kieffer, 1984; Santiago-Rivera et al., 1998). Chavis et al. embedded this within a workshop in which citizen leaders defined issues in their neighborhoods, as well as heard about the research results. To interpret results, researchers and citizens can consider questions such as the following (Serrano-Garcia, 1990). Are these results surprising? Why? If they contradict citizen views, is that due to measurement methods, type of questions asked, sampling bias, differences in perspective due to social context (social class, race, gender, or other group differences)? How can these results be useful to the community? What assumptions are required to apply these findings to the wider community?

**Outcomes of Research**    Final issues concern the products of research and the actions they generate. What reports or other products of research will be produced, and for what purposes? Will researchers provide reports, workshops, or other products that help the community to understand itself better and to address its concerns? Will research help the community to obtain outside resources it may need to tackle those concerns? Will community members be given credit for their contributions to research? Who will review the final reports of the research?

Chavis et al. (1983) and a citizens' panel developed a set of workshops for leaders of block associations. Community members led these workshops. The researchers discussed their research methods in common-sense terms, presented their results on predictors of participation in block associations, and asked for feedback and interpretations by the citizens. Participants broke into small groups, listed priority problems for their neighborhood, and devised action plans. The workshops enriched the researchers' understanding of their results and facilitated action by the community.

Chataway (1997) conducted participatory action research with the Kahnawake Mohawk community near Montreal. After research that dealt with questions defined by the community, she wrote a preliminary summary of results and presented it to several focus groups of 5–25 community members each. The focus groups offered feedback, and suggested that Chataway bring together representatives of five competing groups within the community to discuss her research and their differences. She then wrote a summary of that dialogue, with input from group members, for publication within the community.

## A Collaborative Research Partnership: The Akwesasne Study

Santiago-Rivera et al. (1998) reported on the process of building a collaborative partnership between university-based researchers and the Akwesasne Mohawk community, located along the St. Lawrence River between the United States and Canada (near the Kahnawake community but separate from it). Their work illustrates many aspects of the participatory approach. Santiago-Rivera et al. described it as based on the values of respect for the knowledge of community members as well as researchers, equity in the use of resources, and empowerment of community members through participation in the research planning and implementation.

The Mohawk community at Akwesasne faces serious environmental contamination stemming from industrial plants in the area that dumped pollutants (e.g., fluorides, cyanide, PCBs) into the land, water, and air. Ms. Katsi Cook, a Mohawk midwife and community leader, headed efforts to obtain support for research that would document these problems and help gain resources for mitigating them. Santiago-Rivera et al. (1998) became involved as part of a study, funded by an external grant, of the effect of PCB exposure on physical and psychological health of Akwesasne citizens.

To conduct research based on the values of respect, equity, and empowerment, Santiago-Rivera et al. (1998) and their Mohawk hosts worked through a process that had been developed by the Akwesasne Task Force on the Environment, a Mohawk community group. First, the academic researchers found that they had to adapt their communication style to facilitate dialogue on an equal basis with community members. They spent much time listening to the experiences and views of many community members. They worked to lower barriers such as the use of scientific vocabulary that would limit that dialogue. In addition, the research team sought education in Mohawk culture: beliefs, customs, language and the history of the community. These might affect the research in many ways. Mohawk beliefs about their spiritual relationship with the land made environmental contamination a deeply emotional and spiritual matter. Customs regarding interpersonal relationships affected every aspect of data collection and research planning. The researchers had to learn Mohawk culture sufficiently to gain the trust of their community partners.

These steps of relationship building led to information gathering. Scientists who had performed earlier environmental studies of the PCB pollution presented their findings, and Mohawk Nation members responded with their concerns about the effects of that contamination on their lives and community. In addition, the community members had many questions for the Santiago-Rivera research team about their psychological study: How will this benefit us? How will you assure confidentiality of data? Will you follow a research protocol and methods that we approve? Who will own and keep the data? Who will be employed with the research grant money?

The negotiation of these and other decisions constituted the next step, establishing a research agenda. Researchers and the Akwesasne Task Force worked together to assess the cultural appropriateness of all measurements and materials and to field-test all methods and materials in a small pilot study with Mohawk citizens. These participants not only completed all measurements, but also discussed their concerns with the research team and suggested changes. The pilot study also involved continuing to listen and learn about Mohawk culture. It was critical to gaining acceptance within the whole community for the larger study to be performed. Finally, the researchers and task force negotiated roles for carrying out research. This included hiring and training Mohawk staff for data collection and supervisory responsibilities. They also decided that all original data would remain in the Akwesasne community, an Akwesasne committee would review all research to assure that it had followed agreed-on procedures, and an Akwesasne Task Force member would be co-author of any published reports.

Obviously, the researchers and community could not obtain this degree of collaboration without a workable means of resolving disagreements. The Mohawk method is to do this by discussion and consensus. The researchers had to adjust their schedules and styles to participate in this approach; balancing the time needed for consensus and the reporting deadlines of the granting agency was a problem. However, the commitment of both the Akwesasne and the researchers led to successful resolutions of these issues and completion of research that benefited both parties.

## Contributions and Limitations of a Collaborative Approach

Participatory action research and other forms of genuine community collaboration can enhance the validity and richness of findings and provide research useful to communities. The participatory approach is especially appropriate and promising in communities or with populations that have been exploited and misrepresented by past research. Examples include women, the poor, and persons of color (Tandon et al., 1998). It also offers several potential bases for integrating research and community action (e.g., Chavis et al. 1983).

Serrano-Garcia (1990) and others have listed several drawbacks of involving community members fully in the conduct of research. First, it is time-consuming for citizens and researchers. Citizens ordinarily must master a new role, which empowers them but which can take time, effort, and skill development. The extent of that commitment should be chosen by the citizens and respected by the researchers (Serrano-Garcia, 1990). Second, participation in the design of research opens citizens to criticism by other community members displeased by the methods or findings. Researchers must respect the wishes of community panel members for private rather than public involvement if necessary (Chataway, 1997). Third, the university environment presents obstacles to participatory research by faculty and students. Graduate programs need to develop more training for the sensitivity, communication, and negotiation that conducting research with full citizen participation involves. Moreover, universities often demand research products (e.g., publications) more quickly than such community research may allow, and in a form not useful to communities. Fourth, even participatory research may have unintended consequences for the community, perhaps extending a history of exploitation of oppressed groups (E. Burman, 1997).

Serrano-Garcia (1990) advocated leveling the traditionally hierarchical, unequal relationship between researcher and participant or community member. The Akwesasne and Kahnawake Mohawk studies (Chataway, 1997; Santiago-Rivera et al., 1998) did that to a great degree, as have others (e.g., Tandon et al., 1998; Yeich, 1996). However, M. Bond (1990) and Chataway (1997) argued that some hierarchy may be inevitable, inherent in the research enterprise or because of past misuse of research. Bond and Chataway both advocated recognizing power differences where they occur in the community–researcher relationship, finding ways to discuss and lessen these, and promoting respect for the knowledge and resources provided by both researchers and community members. Each community may require a different "fit" of researcher and citizen roles (M. Bond, 1990; Chavis et al., 1983).

# FIVE PRINCIPLES OF COMMUNITY RESEARCH PARTNERSHIPS

However researchers and citizens develop their relationship, the community research that we advocate involves principles articulated by Price and Cherniss (1977); Heller, Price, Reinharz, Riger, and Wandersman (1984, pp. 56–58); and Kelly (1986). In the section below, we closely follow these analyses (see also Table 3.3).

## Community Research Is Stimulated by Community Needs

Community research addresses issues and challenges faced by communities, whether or not these fit neatly into the theories and concepts of the discipline of psychology. Theory often can provide a perspective for interpreting community issues, and a researcher needs to choose an issue for research consistent with one's values, but these alone are not sufficient bases for community research. The researcher also must consider community needs and interests. A community facing increased violence in its schools will expect research and recommended action, perhaps a prevention program, to address that problem. Moreover, because that community will probably not have consensus on how to define that problem or resolve it, the community researcher may be taking sides by choosing to work with one community group and not another or to advocate one means of prevention and not another.

## Community Research Is an Exchange of Resources

Kelly (1986, p. 581; Kelly et al., 1994) proposed that research be considered an exchange of resources: Researchers and participants each have knowledge, values, and skills that

| TABLE 3.3 | FIVE PRINCIPLES OF COMMUNITY RESEARCH PARTNERSHIPS |
|-----------|---------------------------------------------------|

1. Community research is stimulated by community needs.
2. Community research is an exchange of resources.
3. Community research is a tool for social action.
4. Evaluation of social action is an ethical imperative.
5. Community research yields products useful to the community.

they prize and can share. Community participants have experiential knowledge of their communities and culture that is critical to understanding them. That knowledge also educates researchers. The process of research may reveal patterns of which citizens are not aware or information they can use in practical ways. Creating a collaborative relationship enables both citizens and researchers to share these resources and to enrich each others' efforts. In Kelly's (1986) view, community psychology research involves a commitment to establishing a relationship in which that exchange occurs, and in which those resources are recognized and celebrated. Researchers and citizens become interdependent and create a greater sense of community by working together.

## Community Research Is a Tool for Social Action

As Heller et al. (1984) noted, community research provides information for community decisions. It becomes a means of influencing them. When communicated in useful terms, research findings can help shape community perceptions and decisions on issues such as neighborhood crime, school violence, drug abuse, or health care for the aging. Findings can influence skeptical listeners and counter opposing arguments. Prevention initiatives often are based on local research findings as well as on reviews of wider research. Research findings are seldom as influential on community decisions as factors such as community tradition, interpersonal networks, and other social forces, but they can play an important role. That potential influence strengthens the ethical imperative that one's research be valid and honest.

## Evaluation of Social Action Is an Ethical Imperative

Research evaluating the outcomes of community decisions and programs is ethically imperative. It documents the consequences of decisions and provides a feedback loop for further decisions. That ethical imperative is even stronger for the researcher if one's research actually influences a decision. It also is stronger if the research is part of a preventive intervention or community initiative.

## Community Research Yields Products Useful to the Community

Academic research typically generates journal articles, presentations, and other reports for academic readers. These products build knowledge for the long run but do not satisfy the immediate decision-making needs of communities. Those needs must be met through communicating with different audiences: legislative committees, community groups, consumers of the mass media, government or private leaders, voters, jurors, and others. Not all of these audiences will have the time or patience to consider threats to validity, all complexities of an issue, or the need to test their assumptions empirically. They have decisions to make. Moreover, their values may not be the same as the researcher's on the issue at hand. Community researchers must find ways to communicate their findings in ways that respect the knowledge and values of diverse community audiences. They also must be able to admit what they do not know and what their findings cannot indicate (Price, 1989).

Heller et al. (1984) noted that community research following these principles is likely to take longer than laboratory studies. It demands skills not usually taught in graduate programs, such as communicating findings to community audiences. It may mean making difficult, controversial choices about which community group to work with. Finally, for a researcher in academia, it does not necessarily bring respect from advocates of more laboratory-based research, illustrated by John Glidewell's (1994) story cited at the outset of this chapter.

Yet, as Glidewell (1994) also asserted, community research is also very rewarding. It stimulates endless questions for study. It affords learning from community members who view things differently, and enriches the interpretation of one's findings. It leads to the development of new skills. Perhaps most important, community research invigorates researchers and citizens through immersion in community life.

## CONCLUSION

Our format of five questions for community research provides structure for this chapter. However, it has one limitation: It may be read as implying that the choices of phenomenon, perspective, level(s) of analysis, cultural context and community relationship occur in a sequence, and that each follows from the prior choice in the list. That is not true. These choices are interdependent and influence each other. It is not unusual for an existing partnership with a community organization to influence the researcher's choice of phenomenon, perspective and level of analysis for a study. Alternatively, a researcher may study his or her own culture or population, often within an existing relationship with a specific community. Other pathways of influence among the five questions also exist.

What is certain, however, is that all five questions are involved in community research, whether explicitly chosen by the researcher or implicitly assumed without reflection. Community research always occurs within a culture and a community, always has a level of analysis, and always concerns a particular phenomenon understood from a particular perspective. Our purpose in this chapter has been to make you aware of these questions, and thus capable of making explicit, reasoned choices in performing community research.

## CHAPTER SUMMARY

**1.** Communities provide useful settings for research. Community research means sharing with citizens some aspects of control that the laboratory grants to the researcher. Yet the gains from community research outweigh this limitation.

**2.** Conducting community research involves explicitly answering five questions. The first two questions are: *What phenomenon will we study? From what perspective of theory and values will we study it?*

**3.** Community research is directed by the researcher's epistemology or theory of knowledge. What is knowledge, and how is it gained? What evidence is trustworthy, and how is it obtained? Two epistemologies dominate community research. *Positivist* views emphasize objectivity, measurement, experimentation, and hypothesis-testing to discover cause and effect, and discovery of general laws applicable in many settings. *Contextualist* views emphasize a connection between researcher and participant, and understanding of the particular setting where research occurs rather than general laws. They are also concerned with understanding the meaning of an event to the people who experience it, more than with the causes of their behaviors or cognitions.

**4.** Social issues also affect community research. Community research may be conducted from a *technological* perspective, in which social problems are defined in terms consensually agreed on, and solutions are sought and tested in research. A problem with this is that social issues are often conflicts between competing perspectives offering different definitions of the issue.

**5.** A *dialectical* perspective in community research assumes a viewpoint on one side of a contested issue, *stating premises boldly and explicitly.* It involves conducting research that is honest and credible, but that is pursued within one set of assumptions. *Attending to unheard voices,* persons who are affected by social issues and policies but who hold little power, is also characteristic of the dialectical approach. Examples include research on the views of women and persons with serious mental illness. This approach also involves taking a *strengths perspective* on the participants or communities being researched, for instance identifying existing competencies and protective factors. A problem with the dialectical approach is that it may oversimplify complex issues.

**6.** Question 3 is: *At what level of analysis will we conduct this research?* Levels of analysis in community research include individuals, microsystems, organizations, localities, populations, and macrosystems. We reviewed how thinking in levels-of-analysis terms helps to clarify confusing findings on social support networks and neighborhood citizen participation. Thinking in levels-of-analysis terms may involve studying the social climate, group dynamics, or community impact of settings rather than individual characteristics.

**7.** Question 4 is: *Within what cultural context will we conduct this research, and how will we understand that context?* Two common assumptions must be confronted to conduct culturally meaningful community research. First is the assumption of *population homogeneity,* which discounts differences among individuals or subgroups within a culture. Second is the assumption of *methodological equivalence,* which overlooks differences in the meaning and validity of research instruments and methods in differing cultures.

**8.** A third cultural research issue is whether to conduct an *etic,* or *between-group,* study (which compares populations or cultures) or an *emic* or *within-group,* study (which studies phenomena within a population). A drawback of a between-group study is that the comparisons may be based on incomplete understanding of one or both cultures, and thus unfair or premature. A within-group study provides deeper knowledge of a particular cultural group, but its generalizability is limited to that culture.

**9.** Guidelines for conducting culturally sensitive community research include establishing a collaborative partnership with the community, defining cultural groups in terms they use themselves, understanding the diversity within a cultural group, beginning with qualitative methods and within-group designs, and expecting to modify methodological procedures and assumptions. The reward for these steps is culturally sensitive research that deepens knowledge of diverse cultural groups.

**10.** Question 5 is: *Within what relationship with a community will we conduct this research?* We advocate community research that develops a collaborative relationship with members of the community and that takes their interests into account.

**11.** We described participatory approaches in detail to help define the issues involved in a community research partnership. These include developing an understanding of the community and learning from its citizens. Developing a community research panel allows researchers to involve citizens in helping to make decisions about research objectives, questions for interviews/questionnaires, decisions about confidentiality and ownership of data, interpretation of findings, and use of findings. Products of community research for the community can include workshops for community members and planning of initiatives for action by community members. Involving community members in research to this extent involves tradeoffs. Each researcher–community partnership will have its own level of appropriate involvement.

**12.** Five principles summarize the basic elements of community research partnerships. These are shown in Table 3.3.

# BRIEF EXERCISES

**1.** List what you believe are the advantages and limitations of positivist and contextualist epistemologies for *community* research. Do the same for technological and dialectical approaches to research on social issues. Don't limit your imagination to what appears explicitly in the chapter! For best results, arrange with a classmate for each of you to assume opposing positions (positivist vs. contextualist; technological vs. dialectical) and debate the merits of each perspective.

**2.** At what level of analysis (individual, microsystem, organization, locality, population, macrosystem) do you think the following questions are best researched?

    (a) Will an intervention to restrict youth access to tobacco products work equally well in four different towns? (Biglan et al., 1996)

    (b) Is a segment devoted to specific advice on how to quit smoking, broadcast during local television news shows, effective in helping individuals quit smoking? (Jason, 1998)

    (c) Are the academic and social experiences of African-American women athletes in college similar to those of White women athletes, Black women nonathletes, or Black men athletes? (Sellers, Kuperminc, & Damas, 1997)

    (d) Is an intervention in fifth-grade classrooms to teach students to resolve disagreements before they escalate into violence effective in increasing behavioral skills and in reducing violence in the school? (Consider that these skills, if learned, are used in the hallway, lunch period, and recess when students are not segregated by classroom.)

**3.** Imagine yourself as a resident of a neighborhood about to be studied by community psychologists interested in citizen participation. Alternatively, imagine yourself as a school board member of a school system about to agree to implement and evaluate an innovative drug abuse prevention program in the middle school. For either of these scenarios, what voice or control would you wish to have regarding these research decisions:

- What hypotheses or topics will be researched?
- School scenario only: What will be taught in the drug abuse program?
- What questions will be asked in questionnaires or interviews?
- Who will be asked these questions?
- Will community members be asked to provide their interpretations of research findings?
- Will the actual data be stored in the community or with the researchers, and how will confidentiality be assured?
- How will research findings be reported to the community?
- What written products will the research generate?
- Will there be followup contact by researchers to help the community use the findings in practical ways?

**4.** Explain the five principles of community research partnerships in your own words to someone who hasn't read this chapter.

## RECOMMENDED READINGS

Tolan, P., Keys, C., Chertok, F., & Jason, L. (Eds.). (1990). *Researching community psychology.* Washington, DC: American Psychological Association.

> The product of a major conference on community research, this is the best single volume on community psychology research. It contains both articles reflecting a single point of view and committee reports reporting the discussion of specific topics at the conference. In preparing this chapter, we relied especially on the following chapters:

> Kingry-Westergaard, C. & Kelly, J. *A contextualist epistemology for community psychology.* (pp. 23–31)

> Riger, S. *Ways of knowing and organizational approaches to community research.* (pp. 42–50)

> Rappaport, J. *Research methods and the empowerment social agenda.* (pp. 51–63)

> Shinn, M. *Mixing and matching: Levels of conceptualization, measurement, and statistical analysis in community research.* (pp. 111–126)

> Serrano-Garcia, I. *Implementing research: Putting our values to work.* (pp. 171–182)

> Bond, M. *Defining the research relationship: Maximizing participation in an unequal world.* (pp. 183–185)

Trickett, E., Watts, R., & Birman, D. (Eds.). (1994). *Human diversity: Perspectives on people in context.* San Francisco: Jossey-Bass.

> The following chapters are particularly useful concerning contexts of research:

> Russo, N. F., & Dabul, A. *Feminism and psychology: A dynamic interaction* (pp. 81–100).

Reinharz, S. *Toward an ethnography of "voice" and "silence"* (pp. 178–200).

Kelly, J. G. et al, *Creating settings for diversity: An ecological thesis* (pp. 424–451).

Seidman, E., Hughes, D., & Williams, N. (Eds.). (1993). Culturally anchored methodology. [Special issue]. *American Journal of Community Psychology, 21*(6).

Santiago-Rivera, A., Morse, G.S., Hunt, A., & Lickers, H. (1998). Building a community-based research partnership: Lessons from the Mohawk Nation of Akwesasne. *Journal of Community Psychology, 26,* 163–174.

We relied heavily on these two sources in discussing cultural issues in community research.

# THE METHODS OF COMMUNITY RESEARCH

Having answered the five questions for community research in the previous chapter, what methods do researchers use to conduct community research? That question is our concern in this chapter.

# WHAT ARE THE KEY POINTS OF THIS CHAPTER?

We divide our discussion into sections on qualitative and quantitative methods, to help you understand each approach in its own terms. In each section, we discuss in detail a small number of important methods or research designs useful in community research. For each of those, we include examples of actual studies and a summary of the strengths and limitations of that method. Our overarching themes are that different methods yield different forms of knowledge, that choice of methods must depend on the questions to be answered in the research, and that community psychology as a field is best served by a diversity of forms of knowledge and methods of research.

## Comparing Qualitative and Quantitative Methods

In part, the differences between qualitative and quantitative methods arise from differences in fundamental epistemology that we described in the previous chapter. Qualitative methods are usually based in contextualist perspective, in which a central goal is to understand the meaning of a phenomenon for persons who experience it. Quantitative methods are based in positivism, which seeks understanding of cause–effect relationships through testing of hypotheses. In psychology, quantitative methods have long been considered "research," and numbers, not words, true "data." Qualitative methods often have been considered unscientific or useful only as preliminary research, despite the important contributions of qualitative studies to the discipline. Qualitative methods are now enjoying a renaissance in psychology, in part due to critiques of the limitations of quantitative methods. That renaissance is becoming especially important in community psychology (Tolan et al., 1990).

However, qualitative and quantitative approaches can complement each other. The limitations of one are often the strengths of the other. No approach to research provides the only or royal road to knowledge. Community researchers would be wise to respect and know how to use both types of methods. Ideally, the nature of the research question to be studied would play an important role in choosing methods. In some studies, both qualitative and quantitative methods can be used in the same study (Maton, 1993). We do not expect every community researcher to be equally competent in qualitative and quantitative methods. Specialization is to be expected in complex procedures of data collection and analysis. Yet the student of community psychology and community research needs to be familiar with both approaches to knowing.

Both types of methods can be used within the collaborative partnership with community members that we defined in the previous chapter. Qualitative methods do involve more explicit attention to building a relationship with the participants in research than quantitative approaches. The constructivist epistemology on which much qualitative work is now based emphasizes knowing within a relationship or conversation (Riger, 1990).

Quantitative methods are historically based in a positivist epistemology that emphasizes objectivity rather than relatedness. Yet quantitative methods can be, and are, used in collaborative research. Genuine commitment to participatory decision making and to empowerment of the community marks the collaborative partnership, not the specific choice of methodology.

## Cross-Sectional and Longitudinal Designs

One other distinction is important in our discussion: *cross-sectional* versus *longitudinal* designs. Cross-sectional designs are used to study a phenomenon at one point in time, when researchers seek to describe it and perhaps to understand its causes and effects at that time. Cross-sectional research may be conducted with attention to historical influences on that phenomenon, but data collection and interpretation are focused on one point in time. Longitudinal research is used to follow individuals or communities over time. It involves repeated contacts with participants and analysis of change. As with the qualitative–quantitative distinction, each approach complements the other and provides knowledge that the other cannot provide. However, particularly with quantitative methods, we highlight longitudinal designs, because the understanding of change is central to community psychology.

# QUALITATIVE METHODS

Qualitative methods have a long history in psychology. The clinical case history is one forerunner of the qualitative methods described below. In social psychology, many early examples also exist (Marecek, Fine, & Kidder, 1997). These include Dollard's (1937) study, *Caste and Class in a Southern Town;* Festinger, Riecken, and Schachter's (1956) study of cognitive dissonance among members of a doomsday sect, *When Prophecy Fails;* and Rosenhan's (1973) infiltration of psychiatric units by pseudopatients, "On Being Sane in Insane Places." Feminist psychologists have emphasized qualitative methods. The best-known of these are Gilligan's (1982) *In a Different Voice* and Belenky, Clinchy, Goldberger, and Tarule's (1986) *Women's Ways of Knowing.* Recent articles by community psychologists on feminist qualitative methods include Reinharz (1994) and Riger (1990).

## Common Features of Qualitative Methods

Qualitative research includes a diversity of methods. Despite this diversity, most of them share some common features, which are listed below (adapted from Miles & Huberman, 1994, pp. 6–7; and Rappaport, 1990).

1. Intensive contact with a field setting or sample of individuals, providing an in-depth sample of life experiences in that setting or for those persons. In general, qualitative methods work within the context of a local and particular setting, for data analysis and interpretation. The particular qualities of the sample or setting are important in qualitative research.

2. The researcher relies on a sample of informants to provide accounts of the setting or phenomenon studied. This sample of persons is usually small to facilitate the level of detail needed. Researchers may also rely on their own experiences as sources of information.

3. As much as possible, the researcher sets aside (brackets) preconceptions and attempts to understand the persons or setting on their terms, in their language and context. Attentiveness, asking open-ended questions, and providing freedom for interviewees to structure their own responses and ideas are thus preferred over standardized questionnaires (which reflect the preconceptions of the researcher).

4. Qualitative data in psychology usually are words. The researcher seeks specific *thick description* of personal experiences, detailed enough to provide convincing evidence of realism. This also affords later checking for significant details and patterns. Other researchers can also use these detailed notes or transcripts to check the validity of analysis and interpretation.

5. The aim of research is to understand a phenomenon "from the inside," from the perspective of the persons studied. This includes understanding how they perceive and explain these experiences in the context studied. Explanation is largely equated with understanding the meaning of the setting for those persons.

6. The processes of data collection, data analysis, and interpretation overlap, and the researcher moves back and forth among them frequently. (In quantitative research, these steps are usually separate and conducted in order.) Analysis often consists of identifying (coding) repeating themes or patterns (of actions, feelings, ideas) or separating and comparing distinct categories or stages. For instance, a researcher may use a question-ordered matrix (Sonn & Fisher, 1996, p. 421), in which questions form the columns, individual interviewees the rows, and answers by each participant the entries in each cell. This framework promotes comparison of responses. Themes or categories are usually tested by collecting and analyzing more data. Using multiple coders and interrater reliability checks during analysis strengthens reliability. Computer software enhances this verbal data analysis.

7. Usually after several rounds of refinement through data collection and analysis, the researcher may check themes and interpretations by presenting them to informants or other community members for correction, clarification, or other feedback.

8. It is possible to have multiple interpretations or accounts of a setting or phenomenon studied, based on different viewpoints. However, an account should be internally consistent and compelling in terms of its realism and thick description.

9. In community psychology and other action-oriented disciplines, an additional aim may be to use the process and findings of research to work with community members to plan preventive interventions or community change.

Qualitative methods have a number of advantages. They are very useful for developing an understanding of a culture or community. Moreover, in some cultures and communities quantitative science is not familiar or has been an instrument of oppression (recall the Akwesasne study in the previous chapter). Qualitative methods may be the only way to gain the cooperation of citizen participants. As such, they are very useful for attending to unheard voices of groups not often studied or understood in social science. In addition, they are useful for describing a phenomenon of interest, and in refining categories or techniques for later development of quantitative measurement. Perhaps most important, they are useful in understanding the personal experience of members of a community and for understanding the interplay of multiple factors in community life. They yield "insider" knowledge that is deep, rich, and contextual, concerning many interrelated variables, which is especially useful for understanding particular cultures, situations, and populations.

Qualitative methods also have limitations. An important one is that generalizability is difficult when samples are small and data collection procedures are not standardized. Comparison of results across studies, or of differences between groups, is often more difficult than with quantitative studies. Abstract generalizations from multiple empirical studies are thus more difficult, as is testing of causal hypotheses. Of course, these are not the major purposes of contextual inquiry and most qualitative studies. Again, the researchers' purposes shape choices of methods.

## *Reliability, Validity, and Generalizability*

Students often question the reliability, validity, generalizability, and subjectivity of qualitative methods (Rabinowitz & Weseen, 1997). However, qualitative methods are concerned with different purposes than quantitative research. Explanation in a qualitative study involves understanding the meaning of complex settings or processes for the persons who experience them. Knowing for certain the causes of these experiences is less important than understanding what they mean in the life of the research participant. This represents *insider knowledge.* Explanation in quantitative terms usually means measuring or manipulating the variables of interest to the researcher, as objectively as possible, guided by prior knowledge and theory. The goal is causal inference by an observer, understanding of cause–effect relationships through hypothesis testing. This represents *outsider knowledge,* gathered from a distance and not necessarily reflecting the meaning of a situation for those who experience it.

Reliability for quantitative methods involves use of standardized measurements with established reliability and validity. For qualitative methods, it is usually a matter of inter-rater reliability among multiple readers who are coding or categorizing verbal data. Moreover, the connection of researcher and participant in qualitative studies allows clarifying of what those participants mean by their responses to questions, an issue of reliability and validity that is overlooked in standardized questionnaires.

Qualitative studies study a small sample intensively, in depth. Generalizability of findings is more limited with these small samples than with larger quantitative studies. However, qualitative methods afford in-depth analysis of subgroups that are often overlooked in quantitative analyses of larger samples. In addition, the thick description generated by qualitative research allows other researchers to compare in depth the nature of the context and persons studied with other samples.

Issues of validity in qualitative research are addressed in part by *triangulation,* the use of different methods to understand the same phenomenon. These can be interviews and personal observation, use of several informants who can be expected to have different viewpoints, use of multiple interviewers, or even use of some quantitative measures along with qualitative data. Triangulation in qualitative studies is analogous to use of multiple measures of a variable in quantitative research. In addition, the thick, detailed description of experiences in qualitative research provides convincing realism and level of detail that allows judgment of validity.

Bias affects both qualitative and quantitative methods (Marecek, Fine & Kidder, 1998). Qualitative researchers may subtly and unknowingly select or remember informants, events, or verbal comments that confirm their preconceptions or personal values. Their analyses of verbal data may produce themes or interpretations with which others disagree. Yet these problems exist in different forms for quantitative researchers. The use of measurement instruments developed by researchers also reflects one's preconceptions, and can produce results that confirm them. Quantitative data analysis is often a matter of choices of statistical methods and of how to deal with outliers, nonnormal distributions, and other anomalies. All of these are choices in which one's preconceptions play a role. Moreover, a prolonged engagement with a setting and sample of individuals is characteristic of qualitative research. This depth of experience lends credibility to its findings.

Finally, choices of what to study and of how to interpret findings are matters of theory and values, whatever the method. "Whether numbers or words, data do not speak for themselves" (Marecek et al., 1998, p. 632). In fact, explicit statements of the researcher's perspective or values help to clarify the interpretation (and potential bias) involved in any study. In addition, qualitative analyses are often based in a constructivist epistemology in which multiple interpretations are expected to arise from different viewpoints regarding complex phenomena. Control to eliminate competing explanations is not the goal. Instead, the goal is describing and understanding the many forms of personal and community experience. See Table 4.1 for a simplified comparison of qualitative and quantitative methods.

We discuss four general categories of qualitative methods: participant observation, interviews, focus groups, and organizational/community case studies. These do not exhaust the variety of qualitative methods. However, the descriptions below attempt to communicate the essence of qualitative inquiry.

## *Participant Observation*

Many community researchers, especially if they conduct participatory action research, conduct at least some participant observation. For the purposes of some studies, it is the primary method. Both words in its title are important. Participant observation involves careful, detailed *observation,* with written notes and conceptual interpretation, not just a description or a memoir. Yet it is also *participation,* as the researcher becomes a member of a community or a collaborator in its efforts, an actor in community life. This provides at least some of the experiential insider knowledge of community members, while the researcher also strives to maintain an outsider perspective.

The participant observer lives in a locality or joins an organization or microsystem, cultivating face-to-face relationships with community members. By minimizing the distance between researcher and community, yet also conducting systematic inquiry, the participant observer hopes to understand the complexity of a community. This method also embodies the feminist idea that knowing takes place within a relationship and is experiential (Riger, 1990), not merely intellectual or distant.

In some ways, participant observation resembles a clinical case study. However, participant observation in community research usually involves less of a status difference between researcher and community members than exists between therapist and client.

| TABLE 4.1 | A SIMPLIFIED COMPARISION OF QUALITATIVE AND QUANTITATIVE METHODS | |
|---|---|---|
| **Criterion** | **Qualitative Methods** | **Quantitative Methods** |
| Epistemology | Contextualism | Positivism |
| Purpose | Understanding the meaning of setting or life experience; "insider" knowledge | Causal inference through hypothesis-testing; "outsider" knowledge |
| Nature of data | Words | Numbers |
| Reliability | Interrater reliability among coders of verbal material | Use of standardized measurement instruments and procedures |
| Validity | Thick, detailed description allows understanding of context; triangulation of sources | Experimental or statistical control of confounding factors allows clarity of interpretation; multiple measures of variables |
| Generalizability | Intensive study of smaller samples; thick, verbal description permits comparison with other samples | Extensive study of larger samples; quantified description of sample permits comparison with other samples |

Note: Miles and Huberman (1994) and Rappaport (1990) were especially helpful in constructing this table.

Participant observation also is distinct from being a consultant, because consulting also involves a status differential. (Recall from the previous chapter Argyris's account of eliciting different responses from the same bank employees when he became a consultant.) To some extent, the collaborative research relationship in the previous chapter also involves some participant observation. However, as a research method, participant observation goes well beyond gaining basic cultural understanding and building a relationship.

***Strengths and Limitations*** Participant observation is the method of choice for a researcher seeking maximum insider knowledge and depth of experience in a community. The participant observer knows the setting thoroughly and can communicate its essence vividly. This method also maximizes the researcher–community relationship, and affords thick description of many aspects of community life. All these provide contextual understanding of the community.

However, that depth of knowledge comes at a price. First, the focus on one setting necessarily means that generalizability to other settings is a problem. This can be mitigated by visiting other settings, usually in less depth but long enough to discern the applicability of one's findings.

A second issue concerns the validity of the participant observer's understanding of the setting. The participant observer usually has to rely on field notes as data, rather than the detailed information available from other qualitative methods such as interviews. The researcher's notes, analysis and interpretation can be affected by selective observation, selective memory, and selective interpretations. Findings can also be affected by an unrepresentative sample of informants or an unrepresentative sample of situations studied (observations of formal meetings but not informal caucuses or personal contacts, for instance). Researchers need to report explicitly their value commitments relevant to the study, and whether they took sides in a controversy, so that readers can judge the effects of these choices on data collection and interpretation.

Another problem is that the researcher is influencing (at least weakly, but perhaps strongly) the phenomena or community under study. Field notes and interpretations should explicitly indicate the extent of the researcher's influence on the actions of others so that the impact of the researcher's participation can be assessed (Bell & Newby, 1971; Heller, Price, Reinharz, Riger, & Wandersman, 1984).

A final limitation of the participant observation is the role conflict created by playing both participant and observer roles (Wicker & Sommer, 1993). An ethical and personal problem concerns what the researcher tells the members of the community about the research. For instance, the more forthrightly the researcher speaks of taking field notes, the more suspicious or less revealing the community members may be. On the other hand, both the interests of collaborative research and the norms of neighborliness require that some explanation of one's research intent and methods be made and that outright deception be avoided. Striking a balance between these is an important part of gaining entry and forming a relationship.

Playing a role that is both an insider and a researcher can be stressful for the researcher (Wicker & Sommer, 1993). Becoming an insider makes it more difficult to mention unpopular observations about the community. However, these issues can be minimized when researcher and community agree to a collaborative partnership, in which findings can be honestly discussed, and when the research has clear, tangible benefits for the community.

**Exemplary Study**    Kroeker (1995, 1996) used participant observation to study the community functioning of peasant agricultural cooperatives in Nicaragua.

> The main portion of the research was done through 7 months of participant observation in one agricultural cooperative in Nicaragua, and four follow-up visits. I lived in the cooperative, observing formal and informal meetings. I shared their living conditions and food, in exchange for assisting in the education of the children and in a peer adult education program. By living among them, I was able to integrate, listen, engage in many conversations, ask questions, and determine subtle feelings and meanings. The notes of the cooperative's meetings, conversations and observations were supplemented by documents and observations of processes and interactions in the village and in the town close to the cooperative. The research also included a general study of other cooperatives in Nicaragua through a literature review, interviews of key informants, and visits to 15 cooperatives around the country (Kroeker, 1995, p. 754)

These sources of data provided thick description of the cooperative as a community. To analyze her data, Kroeker (p. 754) categorized the information she had collected, identified patterns and causal links, and developed interpretations of the meaning of these. This was a reiterative process involving several repetitions of data collection and analysis. She identified alternative interpretations of her findings and weighed the evidence for each interpretation.

Kroeker's (1995, 1996) reports presented the history of the cooperative movement in Nicaragua, then her findings from one cooperative. She clearly identified with the cooperative community and presented her findings from that viewpoint. Themes she identified included the importance of consciousness-raising and development of skills in citizen participation, and the difficulties of strengthening these in a context where such citizen leadership has not been possible before and where many outsiders do not believe it workable now. One of her principal findings was the importance of "accompaniment," a process of mentoring and support for emerging leadership skills that Kroeker herself was able to provide to the cooperative members. This role involved encouraging local leaders rather than assuming leadership herself. Kroeker describes its emotional and practical meaning from the viewpoint of an outsider who has become a committed yet observant insider.

> My presence in LVR [the cooperative] was a constant intervention. Besides the education work, my influence was indirect, as they observed everything I did, and I accompanied them during critical moments in and out of the coop [cooperative]. Since I was present and available among the members and willing to listen, several members (including most of the coop women) felt free to share their feelings and frustrations with me, to ask for explanations, and to request my presence when they met with outsiders. It was a situation of interchange. My background gave me a number of resources, including knowledge, from which they were particularly eager to benefit. My presence was thus a bridge between them and the rest of the world. At the same time, I was learning many things from them, such as agricultural methods, which gave them pride. (Kroeker, 1996, pp. 133–134)

Kroeker's (1995, 1996) collaborative approach and willingness to work in empowering ways with the cooperative members fits the ideas of participatory action research and a collaborative partnership discussed in the previous chapter. These go beyond participant observation to provide benefits for the cooperative, as well as enrich her findings.

## Qualitative Interviewing

Interviewing a sample of individuals has become a popular qualitative research format. The interview is often open-ended or minimally structured, to promote participants' describing their experiences in their words. Samples are usually small to facilitate interviewing and analysis in depth. The researcher is not a participant in the phenomenon or community under study, but usually does assume a role of collaboration and often extended conversations or contacts with interviewees.

**Strengths and Limitations**    Qualitative interviewing allows flexible exploration of the phenomenon of interest and discovery of aspects not anticipated by the researcher. It affords a strong relationship between researcher and research participant. If provides contextual understanding of the life experiences of a community, culture or population.

Interviewing has several advantages over participant observation. First, the conditions of data collection can be more standardized, limiting biases of selective perception, memory and interpretation. With participants' permission, interviews can be recorded and transcripts prepared so that analysis can be based on their actual words. Second, that analysis can also be standardized and performed by multiple, independent raters, not just the interviewer, which increases reliability and validity. Third, the interviewer can develop a relationship with the setting and participants that is mutual and trusting, yet with fewer of the stresses of being a participant and insider. Of course, all these also mean that the insights developed from interviews are less direct than those from participant observation.

At the same time, qualitative interviewing provides thick description, attending to the voices and perspectives of participants, and discovery of viewpoints different from the researcher's preconceptions. However, these require a focus on intensive study of a small sample, which means that generalizability of findings is an issue.

***Exemplary Studies***     What are the developmental stages of personal empowerment among community activists? Kieffer's (1984) study of this question provides a good example of the use of qualitative interviewing methods. Kieffer used a small sample, interviewed at length, to generate a model of four stages in the development of personal empowerment among these activists. That model, however, was not solely Kieffer's idea; it emerged from a process of unstructured interviewing and repeated checking of his ideas with his participants (Kieffer, 1984, pp. 13–15).

Kieffer (1984) began by identifying, through a number of referral sources, 15 persons who had become citizen activist-leaders in their communities in the late 1970s in the United States. This sample is small and limited in many ways, but was drawn from diverse geographical regions and types of community work. Kieffer interviewed participants in their communities, tape-recording the interviews. His interviews were open-ended, with the aim of prompting participants to describe in their own words the story of their personal transition from uninvolved citizen to activist. Kieffer sent each participant a transcript of the interview and asked for any further thoughts or corrections. He then reviewed the transcripts and responses to transcripts to develop preliminary interpretations.

Several months later, Kieffer (1984) re-interviewed 10 participants (logistical problems precluded interviewing the other 5). Kieffer discussed his preliminary interpretations, and asked participants to react to them and to extend or clarify their earlier comments. He wrote a comprehensive "portrait" (Kieffer, 1984, p. 14) of each individual on the basis of the themes identified in each interview. He then reviewed the portraits of all participants and identified themes of personal development that were applicable to all participants. (Note that his analysis sought to identify similarities shared by all participants, whereas experimental techniques typically seek to identify differences between two or more groups.) These themes comprised the stages of personal empowerment that Kieffer reported.

What stressors do homeless mothers face, and how do they cope with them? Banyard (1995) studied these questions through qualitative interviewing. Banyard prepared herself to study this population by working in a shelter for homeless families for an extended period. To conduct the study, Banyard and three associates interviewed 64 homeless mothers who were living with their children under age 12 in homeless shelters in the U.S. Midwest. Interviewers asked participants to describe a "difficult situation that you faced in the past week and how you dealt with it" ( Banyard, 1995, pp. 875–876). Participants were encouraged to describe their experience in their own words. Follow-up questions were asked to clarify feelings about the situation and support provided by others. Interviewers then repeated this procedure for a "difficult situation that had to do with your children" and "that had to do with money" (p. 876). This eliciting of narratives about three situations provided a form of triangulation. All interviews were tape-recorded and transcribed.

For analysis, Banyard (1995) divided answers given by the women into sections concerning what they coped with and how they coped. Next she developed categories of types of stress faced by the women and the types of coping strategies they used, based as much as possible on their actual words. Banyard then refined the initial categories to form a smaller set of more general categories for interpretation and reporting. "Negative cases," or responses that did not fit the categories, were reexamined to refine and extend categories. Throughout the analysis, she consulted with a woman who had been homeless and who remained closely connected with homeless mothers. This consultant provided reviews of the transcripts and critiques of categories and interpretations. This provided a way to check Banyard's interpretations, because it was not possible for her to follow up with the actual interviewees. The categories of types of stress and methods of coping formed the principal findings of Banyard's report.

## Focus Groups

An alternative to interviewing individuals is a focus group discussion. This is an interview with a group, conducted along lines somewhat similar to an individual interview, to generate thick description and qualitative information in response to questions or discussion topics. Thus, a focus group discussion is an interview with multiple persons who form an interdependent group. It helps researchers to assess similarities and differences among individuals directly and allows focus group participants to elaborate on ideas and themes by reacting to each other, not just to an interviewer. Hughes and DuMont (1993) offered an introduction to the use of focus group research methods in community psychology.

In focus group research, the group, not the individual, is the unit of analysis: The sample size is one for each group. Individual comments are not independent of other group members; indeed, one of the purposes of the focus group is to elicit discussion. Each group is usually composed of 6–12 participants who share some characteristic of concern to the researchers: for example, the same race, gender, culture, or age, similar occupations, or the same health problem. This homogeneity helps to promote free discussion and ability of participants to be able to identify with each others' experiences. A group of strangers is preferred to minimize the effects of prior personal contacts (Hughes & DuMont, 1993).

Because the group is the unit of analysis, multiple focus groups are needed to provide more generalizable information about the population studied and to compare groups with different characteristics (husbands vs. wives, for example). However, as with qualitative interviewing, samples are seldom representative of a large population. The data that qualitative interviews and focus groups yield is a deep, rich understanding that is tied to particular contexts.

The focus group is conducted by a moderator. The moderator's responsibilities include creating an environment conducive to free discussion, speaking in language comfortable to all participants, ensuring that all members participate, eliciting both agreement and disagreement, and balancing between being nondirective and covering all topics of interest to the researchers. The moderator uses a discussion guide that includes topics or questions to be discussed and that moves from general topics to specific phenomena relevant to the research (Hughes & DuMont, 1993).

Analysis of focus group data is similar to the process of analyzing individual qualitative interviews, but more complex. Participants use words differently, and the moderator has less control than an interviewer of individuals to ask for elaboration of what is meant by a remark or to control changes of topic. However, methods, including computer software, exist to analyze focus group data.

***Strengths and Limitations***    Focus groups have several advantages over other qualitative methods. They allow greater access to shared knowledge and language among participants, because this is often cued by mutual discussion more than in individual interviews. They also allow researchers to observe social interaction among group participants, perhaps revealing behavioral patterns unavailable in individual interviews. Researchers can structure discussion and learn about topics of interest and personal experiences of others more easily than with participant observation. Thus, focus groups may improve researchers' understanding of a culture or community, illuminate social processes difficult to study in other ways, provide early exploration of a topic prior to quantitative studies, or test interview questions or questionnaires to be used later with a larger sample (Dumka, Gonzales, Wood, & Formoso, 1998; Hughes & DuMont, 1993).

***Exemplary Studies***    Hughes and DuMont (1993) used focus group methods to initiate a set of studies on whether experiences with racism at work influenced how African American parents socialized their children to deal with racism. They created six focus groups of African American working parents, three in blue-collar occupations and three in white-collar jobs, because one focus of their study was to discover if experiences differed by job type. The researchers coded and analyzed focus group participant statements describing work conditions and racism, stories of particular incidents, and conclusions that participants themselves had drawn from their experiences. The researchers also pilot-tested a questionnaire for investigating these topics.

The focus groups suggested a number of specific incidents and patterns of discrimination not anticipated by the researchers. For instance, the discrimination reported by blue-collar workers was more overt and openly expressed; for white-collar workers it was indirect and difficult to pin on one person. In addition, the effects of neighborhood and other out-of-work experiences had not been part of the original research plans, but the focus groups made it clear that these would have to be studied as well.

Dumka et al. (1998) initiated a series of studies on parenting stress and adolescent mental health among low-income families by using both individual qualitative interviews and focus groups. They convened 12 focus groups in a 3 × 4 design. This included one group each for single mothers, mothers in two-parent families, and fathers in two-parent families, among four ethnic–racial groups: African Americans, European Americans, Mexican Americans, and Mexican immigrants. The groups contributed important ideas and feedback about stressors faced by parents of adolescents in each ethnic population. These enhanced the development of a culturally sensitive questionnaire measuring parenting stress for each group. Their ideas also were useful in designing prevention interventions to promote parenting skills for dealing with the issues of adolescence in each culture.

## Organizational and Community Case Studies

The case study method, usually conducted on individuals in clinical psychology, can be applied to different levels of analysis: organizations and localities. Organizational or community case studies tend to rely on qualitative data, especially interviews and observation, but perhaps participant observation. Researchers may also use archival sources and quantatitive measurements. Examples of archival sources (i.e., from organizational archives) include meeting minutes, memos, policy manuals, and records of task accomplishment. A case study of a community may use newspaper stories or other archival sources.

A case study is typically longitudinal in focus, one of its usual purposes being to describe change over time. One study we describe below (M. Bond & Keys, 1993) was based on an 8-year relationship between researchers and an organization; the scope of the study covered events before then, spanning decades. The organizational or community case study usually concerns a process of development or change that takes months or years. When available, quantitative data also can be used in time-series format to measure such changes (Fawcett et al., 1995; Zimmerman et al., 1991). We describe such quantitative methods later in this chapter.

An organizational case study also often concerns organizational structure. Foster-Fishman and Keys (1997), for instance, analyzed the different meanings of an empowerment initiative in a statewide organization for its top executives, middle managers, and staff workers. M. Bond and Keys (1993) studied subgroups within a community organization: directors, board, and volunteers. Gruber and Trickett (1987) studied the relationships among teachers, students, and parents on the board of an alternative school. When community psychologists study organizational structure, however, they are typically interested in its effects on individuals, especially those who have little control within that structure.

The clinical case study method involves a status differential between therapist and client. A similar differential may occur in an organizational or community case study, between consultant and client organization, or the relationship may be more collaborative. An organizational or community case study also may involve the conflicts between insider–participant and outsider–observer roles mentioned earlier.

***Strengths and Limitations***   Like other methods that focus on one setting (e.g., participant observation), the strengths of the case study concern its ability to understand in depth a single setting. Researchers can use a variety of data sources to understand the organization's functioning, formal and informal. By using multiple data sources, subjective biases can be checked. The longitudinal focus of most case studies is also a strength for understanding change and causal relationships. Although case-study researchers cannot study the latter with experimental control, they can identify complex patterns of causation in natural settings.

The principal limitation for case study methods (like participant observation) is that the focus on a single organization or community means that generalizability of findings to other settings is uncertain. Of course, this can be mitigated by including multiple case studies in one analysis, but that may undermine some of the strengths described above.

The use of archival data presents both advantages and problems. Written records can provide information on meetings or other events not attended by the researcher and remembered imperfectly by interview informants. Archival records also can document observable events significant to an organization, such as the opening of a new facility or establishment of mutual help groups in new areas. However, few organizational archives are kept for the same purposes as those of a researcher. Thus, researchers who review archival data often cannot discover the events or processes that they are most interested in, such as the conflict and compromise preceding a decision that was sparingly reported in meeting minutes.

***Exemplary Study*** M. Bond and Keys (1993) conducted a case study of interrelation-ships among board members at Midwest ARC, an advocacy organization and service pro-vider for persons with developmental disabilities. The authors had already established a relationship with Midwest ARC in which they provided training. They studied this organi-zation because it seemed to have strong board–staff–volunteer relations (reflecting a strengths perspective).

The case study involved use of several data sources. The researchers reviewed organi-zational documents covering over 20 years, including board meeting agendas and minutes, year-end reports, by-laws and policy manuals, and organizational charts. They interviewed 16 individuals currently or previously involved with the organization, and observed four board meetings. Particularly in the interviews and documents, the researchers sought information on changing relationships among board, staff, and volunteers over time. By using multiple data sources, they could lessen subjective biases by analyzing events and meanings agreed on by several interviewees or other sources. They presented their find-ings to the two chief staff members and the board, soliciting their corrections and in-terpretations (M. Bond & Keys, 1993, pp. 41–43). As we describe in detail in chapter 12, M. Bond and Keys found a history of conflict among these subgroups, not surprising in a community organization. They also identified several means by which these conflicts had been resolved.

## Narratives as Qualitative Data

Qualitative methods often tap narratives: stories that participants tell. Narratives have a plot, a sequence of events understandable in roughly chronological order, and characters who are meaningful in the storyteller's life. They may be autobiographical or stories or myths epitomizing the participant's culture. They often reflect psychological themes about everyday life, and thus offer insights into behaviors, personal experiences, and social rela-tionships. Short narratives include descriptions of situations in their lives such as those that Banyard's (1995) participants provided. Longer narratives include life history interviewing or autobiographies (Dollard, 1937; Runyan, 1982) that focus on one's life in general or tes-timonies such as might be provided in a twelve-step mutual help group (Rappaport, 1993). Kieffer's (1984) participants told narratives of their personal development that were inter-mediate in length. A case study of an organization or community is also a narrative. Narra-tives may be solicited in interviews and focus groups. They are a research focus in several social sciences, including anthropology, sociology, and cognitive, personality and develop-mental psychology (Hughes & DuMont, 1993; Rappaport, 1993, 1995; Tappan, 1997).

Important for qualitative understanding is that the narrative is told in a form deter-mined by the participant, not by the interviewer's questions. Depending on the purposes of the research, it may not be important that all events in a narrative be verifiable facts, and some important cultural narratives are myths and legends. Qualitative understanding is concerned with the meaning that participants make of the narrative for their lives. Narra-tives can be recorded and analyzed for descriptive statements (e.g., events) and abstract themes (Hughes & DuMont, 1993). Narratives are one of the best ways to attend to unheard voices, and to form an understanding of a culture or community.

# Quantitative Methods

We now turn to methods that emphasize measurement, statistical analysis, and experimental or statistical control. Although these methods are associated with the psychological laboratory, they have great value in community research. These methods are valuable for different purposes than the qualitative methods we have discussed thus far.

Quantitative methods are based in a positivist epistemology, as we described earlier in this chapter. However, that does not mean that quantitative community researchers assume that they hold a position of value-free neutrality. As with qualitative research, quantitative investigators need to be explicit about their preconceptions and their relationship with the providers of data, and need to attend to how these shape their choices in data collection, analysis, and interpretation (Rapkin & Mulvey, 1990).

## Common Features of Quantitative Methods

A great diversity of quantitative methods exists. However, most quantitative methods in community research share some common features. We don't wish to repeat all of what you may have learned in previous methodology courses, so the list below focuses on features that offer clear contrasts with qualitative methods and with laboratory experimentation.

1. Measurement is paramount. Although some constructs can only be categorized (e.g., gender, or two conditions to be compared in an experiment), the purpose is almost always to study their relationship to measured variables. Data are numbers.
2. Standardized measurement instruments with known psychometric properties are preferred, to ensure reliable, valid measurement. The flexibility and contextual sensitivity of qualitative methods are lost, but comparability of findings across studies and control of extraneous variables are increased.
3. An important objective is understanding cause and effect relationships. This can then lead to prediction of effects and to social action to promote desirable effects. Even in correlational, epidemiological, or other types of nonexperimental quantitative studies, the purpose is usually to identify empirical relationships that could eventually yield cause–effect knowledge.
4. Hypothesis testing is the best way to advance understanding of cause and effect. Hypotheses require preexisting theory or knowledge to select variables for study and to propose testable statements about their probable relationships.
5. The clearest way to test a cause–effect hypothesis and interpret the results is the "true" experiment, in which participants (individuals, classrooms, or other units) are randomly assigned to experimental and control conditions and other variables are controlled. If this level of control cannot be gained, approximations to it (e.g., quasi-experiments, statistical controls) are useful.
6. Experimental community research is usually "experimental social innovation" (Fairweather, 1967), in which social action programs or initiatives are tested for whether they attain their goals, with the most rigorous experimental controls possible, often in comparison to an alternative or existing program or policy.

7. The ultimate purpose is to derive general, predictable statements that are true across contexts, settings, and communities. (For example, empirical findings show a program to prevent adolescent drug abuse is effective for attaining its goals, in many communities.)

Quantitative methods thus possess many advantages. Their use of measurement enables detailed comparisons across groups that were measured with standardized methods or instruments (such as questionnaires). The efficiency of standardized instruments means that samples can be larger and more representative of a population. This enhances generalizability of findings. Researchers can more easily replicate or extend other researchers' findings and conduct controlled testing of hypotheses about cause and effect. Quantitative studies yield knowledge that is broad, generalized, and less subjective than qualitative studies—in short, outsider knowledge.

Quantitative methods also have limitations. Because standardized instruments are based on prior theory and research, they leave little opportunity for learning about the freely expressed conceptions of the participants in a study in progress. Researchers usually will only learn about the variables that they chose to study, not about others they overlooked. Thus, their standardization may not be sensitive to cultural, community, or other differences in psychological phenomena or in the ways that participants understand those phenomena. Moreover, quantitative findings often have breadth of generalizability, but not as much depth of understanding of context. Thus, their findings may be difficult to apply to a particular context or community, especially when application involves additional factors or variables not addressed in the research. Again, researchers' purposes shape the choices of research methods.

Next, we discuss the most common forms of quantitative studies in community psychology research: quantitative observation and experimental social innovation.

## Quantitative Observation

Quantitative observation methods include a variety of designs and procedures. A researcher may sample a number of persons, measuring statistical relationships between continuous variables such as socioeconomic status and fear of crime. Another researcher may compare naturally occurring groups (women and men; or urban, suburban, and rural residents), in terms of their fear of crime. In addition, these methods include *quantified naturalistic observational studies*. For instance, studies of GROW, a mutual help group for persons with serious mental illness, used quantified behavioral observation of its meetings (Luke, Rappaport, & Seidman, 1991; L. Roberts et al., 1991). Another type of quantitative observation involves time-series studies. For instance, Dooley and Prause (1997) studied the relationship over time of employment change and alcohol abuse among U.S. youth. A final example of quantitative observation methods is *epidemiological studies* (to be described later). What we are labeling quantitative observation methods are also known as nonexperimental methods or methods of passive observation (Cook & Campbell, 1979; Linney & Reppucci, 1982).

The number of variables in quantitative observation studies, and their interrelationships, may be few and simple or many and complex. Statistical analyses may include correlation, multiple regression, path analysis and structural modeling, and even *t* tests and analyses of variance to compare naturally occurring groups. Data are collected primarily by means of questionnaires or structured interviews but may also include behavioral observation or other methods. Epidemiological methods, for instance, may use archival records of a diagnosed disorder.

**Common Features**    Despite this diversity, quantitative observation methods usually share some common features.

1. They rely on previous knowledge and/or exploratory research to determine which variables to study and how to measure them, and to select a population to sample. Qualitative research is useful for obtaining such knowledge.
2. They use selected, measurable variables, typically standardized instruments with established reliability and validity.
3. They typically employ larger samples than qualitative or experimental studies to facilitate statistical analysis and increase generalizability of findings.
4. They are used to identify relationships among variables and to generate hypotheses. They can also be used to test cause–effect hypotheses under some conditions (Cook & Campbell, 1979; see below).
5. They are nonexperimental methods, because they do not involve planned, systematic attempts to change settings or persons (i.e., manipulation of an independent variable).
6. They can be used in either cross-sectional or longitudinal designs. Although cross-sectional uses are probably more common, longitudinal data sets afford closer study of potential cause–effect relationships.

**Correlation and Causation**    Early undergraduate education in psychology typically contrasts correlation and causation. Just because two factors are associated statistically, you learned, does not mean that one causes another. The causation could just as easily run in the opposite direction than what you think ("reverse causation": B causes A rather than A causing B). Or the causal factor may be a "third variable" that determines both correlated variables (C causes both A and B).

Under some conditions, however, nonexperimental designs can be used to identify causal patterns and test causal hypotheses. The simplest case involves precedence in time: If change in A is correlated with change in B, yet A consistently precedes B, a causal interpretation (A causes B) is more warranted (although not certain: another variable may cause these changes in a sequential order). A theoretical model, based on prior knowledge of relationships among A, B, C, and other related variables, strengthens causal inference from nonexperimental data (Cook & Campbell, 1979). Such causal inference thus relies on multivariate statistical methods (e.g., multiple regression, path analysis, structural modeling) that analyze relationships among multiple variables. These rely on statistical control of extraneous variables, not experimental control.

We have avoided the term correlational methods in this section, to distinguish clearly between design and statistical analysis. Correlational statistics, whether univariate or multiple regression, can be used to analyze either experimental or nonexperimental data sets. Conversely, statistics traditionally associated with experimental designs, such as analysis of variance, can be used to analyze naturally occurring group differences (e.g., social class differences) in nonexperimental data sets. Both types of statistical analysis are derived from the same general linear statistical model (Cook & Campbell, 1979, p. 295).

*Epidemiology*   This category of quantitative observation methods deserves special note for community research concerned with health and mental health. Epidemiology is the study of the frequency and distribution of physical and mental disorders and of risk and protective factors for these. It is usually a precursor to more experimental studies of causal factors of these disorders and is essential to practical planning of prevention and treatment. Epidemiology is most often used in the discipline of public health, but is increasingly used in the social sciences (Linney & Reppucci, 1982).

Two basic epidemiological concepts are *incidence* and *prevalence*. Incidence is the rate of new occurrences of a disorder in a population within a specific time period (usually a year). It is thus a measure of the frequency of the onset of a disorder, or at least of it first being reported to a health professional. Prevalence is the rate of existing occurrences of a disorder in a population within a time period. It includes both new cases and continuing cases of the disorder that began before the time period studied. Both concepts are usually expressed as rates (e.g., the number of cases per thousand persons in the population).

The incidence–prevalence distinction is important for community psychology. Prevention by definition is more concerned with incidence and with risk and protective factors for it; these provide a road map for prevention efforts. In contrast, prevalence is more relevant to studies of mutual help, which is focused not only on persons newly experiencing a disorder but also on those living with it over time.

When incidence and prevalence rates have been determined for a population, epidemiological research is focused on identifying risk and protective factors. Quantified variables and large samples are used to identify the factors associated with increased likelihood of a disorder (*risk factors*). These may be causes of the disorder or simply correlated with it. *Protective factors* are associated with lesser likelihood of a disorder; they may counteract or buffer the effects of the disorder's causes or simply be correlated with other factors that do so. Identifying these helps to design preventive programs that weaken risk factors and promote protective factors.

*Strengths and Limitations*   Quantitative observation methods have a number of strengths. First, measurement of observation variables affords statistical analysis of the strength and significance of relationships among variables. This cannot be directly addressed in qualitative studies. Second, they can be used to study variables that cannot be manipulated in an experiment. An example would be differences associated with naturally occurring populations based on social class, race, gender, or age. Third, by focusing on a selected set of quantified variables, these methods facilitate study of large samples, thus providing greater generalizability than most qualitative and experimental designs. Fourth, epidemiological research on the incidence of disorder can be used to evaluate the outcome of preventive efforts.

Finally, quantitative observation studies often identify factors that can be targeted for social or community change, even without experimental knowledge of specific causes and effects. In everyday life, factors often influence each other in a mutual relationship: A increases B, which then leads to an increase in A, and so on. In such a situation, correlational knowledge is often sufficient to initiate change. One need not know all the cause–effect relationships for youth violence, for instance, in order to identify risk and protective factors, and to initiate change efforts.

However, quantitative observation methods have several limitations. They rely on prior knowledge to select and measure variables and populations. In addition, the knowledge provided by quantitative observation studies is usually "decontextualized," gathered from individuals across a number of settings. This increases potential generalizability of findings, yet limits in-depth knowledge of particular settings or cultures. Finally, causal inference and testing of causal hypotheses is limited in these designs, as we have discussed.

The focus of epidemiological research on disorders also limits its utility for community psychology (Linney & Reppucci, 1982). Community psychology is concerned with overall psychological well-being, including but not limited to disorders. Its focus on promotion of strengths or competencies for living goes beyond identifying protective factors for disorders. In addition, if mental disorder is studied, difficulties of accurate diagnosis and measurement make its epidemiology more difficult than that of physical disease.

***Exemplary Studies***    Can the processes of helping in mutual help groups be studied quantitatively? L. Roberts et al. (1991, 1999) developed a quantitative system for measuring behaviors in meetings of GROW, a mutual help group for persons with serious mental illness. Their system used three instruments: Behavioral Interaction Codes (BICs) completed during meetings by a trained observer, Observer Rating Forms that the observer completed after the meeting to record overall qualities of the meeting, and Participant Rating Forms, completed by group members after the meeting. All were developed with the input and permission of GROW, which also limited the number of observers to one per meeting to minimize disruption. Behaviors coded on BICs included support, interpretation of others' comments, direct guidance, questions, self-disclosure, and request for help or feedback (L. Roberts et al., 1991).

Ten observers studied 15 different GROW chapters over a 2-year period, for a total of 527 meetings. BIC measures correlated with participant ratings of overall meeting quality, providing evidence of validity. L. Roberts et al. (1991) found that supportive comments (including support, interpretation, guidance, and other behaviors) were very common in GROW groups, seven times more common than negative comments. Members who most often provided help to others (measured by the BIC) improved the most in social adjustment (L. Roberts et al., 1999). The BIC and related measures contributed important empirical knowledge of the actual processes of mutual help.

Mason, Chapman, and Scott (1999) applied epidemiological methods to identify variables at or near birth that were risk factors for severe emotional disturbances (SEDs) in adolescence. They linked birth records for children born in Florida in 1979–1980 with Florida public school records of those classified as having a severe emotional disturbance at age 13 (a prevalence indicator). Although cause–effect relationships cannot be determined, this longitudinal time frame helps to clarify potential causes and effects. Two early risk factors emerged as strong predictors of SEDs: being male, and whether the mother had not attained a high school degree at time of birth. Boys were over four times more likely than girls to be classified as having an SED, and those whose mothers had less than a high school education were also more than four times more likely to be classified with SED than those whose mothers had more education. Low birth weight, infrequent prenatal care, and having an unmarried mother less than age 18 were also significant predictors, but were weaker than the first two factors.

This study illustrated the potential of using epidemiological data to identify risk factors, as well as the unanswered questions that epidemiological studies may raise. The data set included only children who were both born in Florida and were in public school there 13 years later. As Mason et al. (1999) pointed out, this omitted immigrants to the state, such as those from the Caribbean and Central and South America for whom the risk factors may be very different. It concerned only risk factors measurable at birth, and thus focused on health status and maternal variables. Economic, school, neighborhood, family dynamics, and even paternal variables could not be studied directly in these data as either risk or protective factors. For instance, the third variable behind many of the factors listed above could have been poverty and associated economic stress. The gender difference may have reflected causal factors varying in level of analysis from biological to cultural. However, no study can address all such factors at once. The Mason et al. study did suggest that education, prenatal health care, and other initiatives for young mothers could have a preventive effect on SED among their children. Its findings point to future research and possible early preventive interventions for an important adolescent problem.

Most studies of risk and protective factors for adolescent behavior problems, however, use correlational rather than epidemiological methods. For instance, Allison et al. (1999) summarized correlational studies that indicated that adolescent drug use (including tobacco and alcohol) is more likely if family members (parents or others) use drugs, parents fail to monitor their adolescent children's associates or behavior closely, or parents do not maintain close, supportive relationships with children. Adolescent drug use is also more likely if peer behavior and attitudes support or model drug use, and if teens believe that drug use is normal or frequent among their peers (all peers, not just friends). Untangling the causal pathways among these factors is difficult, and those pathways probably differ by cultural, community, and family context (see also Seidman, 1991). However, untangling all causal pathways may not be necessary to develop workable prevention programs that address these and other risk and protective factors. Such a focus on action is the hallmark of the next class of quantitative methods in community research: experimental social innovation methods.

## Experimental Social Innovation

> If you want to understand something, try to change it. (Dearborn, cited in Bronfenbrenner, 1979, p. 37).

Fairweather's (1967) concept of experimental social innovation is the community research approach closest to the classic laboratory experiment (Linney & Reppucci, 1982). Yet it involves the gritty world of community action as well. It epitomizes Dearborn's insight quoted above.

Experimental social innovation involves two roles: social planner or activist involved in designing innovative responses to social problems, and scientific evaluator of the effectiveness of those innovations (Linney & Reppucci, 1982). (The same person or team need not play both roles.) In experimental terminology, the independent variable is the social innovation (program, policy, or practice), compared to a control condition. That program may, for instance, be designed to prevent a specific problem behavior. Dependent variables are measurements of the goals of the program or of the social problem it addresses. This research method addresses the ethical imperative that the effects of social actions be evaluated (recall this from chap. 3).

Experimental social innovation is based on careful groundwork before an innovation is implemented and tested (Linney, 1989; Linney & Reppucci, 1982). A collaborative partnership with the community setting(s) affected by the innovation is central to the concept. In addition, careful definition of the problem(s) to be addressed, of the goals of an innovation and how these address the target problem, and of the nature of the innovation itself are necessary. For instance, questions like the following may be asked about adolescent tobacco use: How, when, where, and with whom do teens most often use tobacco products? How is this use initiated, and what types of teens are most vulnerable? How is tobacco obtained? Is education likely to alter these patterns? Is making tobacco more difficult to obtain likely to alter them? Thus, experimental social innovation is usually best done after preliminary fact-finding and is based on an understanding of the context (setting, community, or culture) in which the innovation will be implemented. The best way to gain this understanding is often to perform qualitative research.

Once the experimental social innovation is designed, community researchers conduct a study in which it is implemented and compared with some form of control or comparison condition (Linney, 1989). Outcomes of the innovation versus the control are measured and statistically compared. Conclusions can then be drawn about the effectiveness of the innovation, because confounding factors have been controlled to a great extent.

## Randomized Field Experiments

This is the most rigorous form of experimental social innovation. It applies the pretest–posttest control group experimental design (Campbell & Stanley, 1963) to community settings. Experimental and control groups are compared at a pretest before the implementation of the social innovation, at which they are expected to be equal on measures of dependent variables. They are compared again at posttest, when they are expected to differ.

The experimental social innovation represents the experimental condition. The control condition can often be "treatment as usual" under existing policy or practices. For example, in Fairweather's Community Lodge study (Fairweather, Sanders, Cressler, & Maynard, 1969), persons in a psychiatric hospital were assigned to either the Community Lodge program in the hospital and afterward, or to the usual treatment and aftercare procedures for the hospital. (The Community Lodge involved group treatment in the hospital and being released as a group to a residence where participants lived and worked as a self-governing community.) In other cases, two different innovations are available and can be compared with each other (Linney, 1989), such as two contrasting prevention programs in a school. Dependent variables measure the goals of the innovation or the social problem being addressed. The chief dependent variables in the Community Lodge study, for instance, concerned relapse rates among persons in the Community Lodge versus the control condition.

A key issue is the method of assignment to experimental and control conditions. If this is random, many confounding variables are controlled (Campbell & Stanley, 1963). These include individual differences in personality, coping skills, social support networks, and life experiences that may affect their responses to the innovation. Confounds also include differences between groups in demographics such as gender, age, race, and family income. In the laboratory, random assignment is taken for granted, but in the community it must be achieved by negotiation through collaborative relationships with stakeholders. Nonetheless, Fairweather (1979) argued that it can often be achieved, as he did with the Community Lodge study. When random assignment is used, a true control condition is created with which to compare the innovation.

**Strengths and Limitations**    Randomized field experiments are unsurpassed for clarity of interpretation in testing a social innovation. With greater control over confounding factors, researchers can make more confident interpretations of its effects. Moreover, if experimental studies demonstrate the effectiveness of a social innovation, advocacy for it can be more effective. Randomized field experiments have helped to document the effects of many preventive interventions in community psychology and increase the credibility of prevention efforts generally (Albee & Gullotta, 1997; Price et al., 1988).

However, experiments require substantial prior knowledge of the context, which is needed to propose hypotheses or social innovations worth testing. They are not the first studies to conduct on a new social issue or in a seldom-studied setting. A useful sequence is often to conduct qualitative studies to understand the context, correlational or similar studies to identify key variables, and only then experiments to test causal hypotheses or experimental social innovations.

Experiments also require substantial control over a setting. That control includes permission to collect quantitative data (often in multiple waves), and random assignment to experimental conditions. That degree of control must be negotiated with the stakeholders in the setting, after forming a collaborative relationship and clearly explaining the advantages and procedures of experimental control and measurement. If the goals and methods of experimental inquiry fit reasonably well with the interests of the setting, a happy convergence of research and community goals exists.

**Exemplary Study**    Florin et al. (1992) used a randomized experimental design to evaluate the effects of the Block Booster Project, a training program for leaders in neighborhood block associations in New York City. Their evaluation is a good example of a community-level experiment.

The Block Booster Project worked with local block associations. Each association is formed for a city block, encompassing the area of both sides of one street, one block long. Enhancing the functioning of those citizen participation associations is critical to their viability; many such associations start up, then become inactive within a year or two. The Block Booster staff worked with 27 block associations. For all of these, staff conducted a survey of block residents to assess each block association's organizational strengths and limitations, and developed a profile of strengths and weaknesses for each association.

Block Booster staff then randomly assigned 18 block associations to an experimental condition. Two leaders from each association participated in a workshop on strengthening block associations, and participated in ongoing meetings and consultations with Block

Booster staff. Nine other associations were assigned to a control condition, which had only a written report and some telephone technical assistance, not the workshops and other consultation. (Note that this study uses associations, not individuals, as the unit of analysis.)

When contacted 10 months after the workshops, 44% of control associations had already become inactive, whereas only 22% of associations in the experimental condition had become inactive. The Block Booster Project thus cut the attrition rate in half. In a context where many associations become inactive quickly, this provides sound evidence of effectiveness (Florin et al., 1992).

There is one caveat: This finding leaves open the question of what exactly caused the better performance of the experimental group. It may have been due simply to having been selected for a workshop and monitored afterward or to having met and formed supportive relationships with other association leaders. However, in follow-up interviews, leaders in the experimental group remembered specific findings about their association from the profiles and reported using their workshop learning and materials (Florin et al., 1992). These data support the conclusion that the workshops and consultations were effective. The Block Booster Project as a whole is an effective social innovation, whatever the exact mechanisms of its effect.

## Nonequivalent Comparison Group Designs

For a variety of reasons, many settings simply cannot support random assignment to experimental and control conditions. For instance, seldom can a school randomly assign some children to an innovative classroom and others to a control classroom; even if they did, the students may mix at lunch or recess so much that experimental control is lost. Providing the innovation to all students in a grade and comparing their outcomes to another school or to students in a previous year means, of course, that random assignment and assurance of equivalence between groups is lost. Comparing a sample of schools rather than a sample of individuals (making the unit of analysis the school, not the individual) may be prohibitively expensive.

Yet many of the strengths of the experiment can be retained if researchers are creative about working around such obstacles. There are many quasi-experimental ways to do that. Using a nonequivalent comparison group is one of the most common.

Nonequivalent comparison group designs are used whenever assignment to experimental or comparison condition is something other than random (Judd & Kenny, 1981). For instance, different classrooms within a school or different schools within a region may serve as experimental and comparison conditions. Assignment to classroom or choice of school is not random, but the classes or schools may be similar. The choice of comparison group is critical to generating interpretable results (Cook & Campbell, 1979; Judd & Kenny, 1981; Linney & Reppucci, 1982). Variables to equate as much as possible include socioeconomic status, race, gender, age, and other demographic factors. In schools, for example, such variables include student and teacher demographics as well as school size and curriculum (Linney & Reppucci, 1982).

**Strengths and Limitations**    These are much the same as for randomized field experiments. However, the control of confounding factors is much weaker, and clarity of interpretation and confidence in conclusions is decreased. Researchers in this situation must collect as much data as possible on factors that may confound the comparison. This allows them to document the similarity of the two conditions or to use those variables as statistical controls. For instance, researchers may be able to show that the social class makeup of the experimental and control conditions was similar even when random assignment was not possible. Alternatively, the researchers may be able to control effects of social class statistically as a covariate or as an additional variable in a causal model. The ultimate goal is to weaken or eliminate plausible competing explanations for experimental results. If significant differences occur between innovation and comparison groups, what factors other than the innovation may account for this difference? How can researchers collect evidence that such factors did not affect this study? The Block Booster Project evaluation described above illustrates the use of follow-up survey data to weaken plausible alternative explanations of results.

## Interrupted Time-Series Designs

Another approach to experimental control when random assignment is impossible is the use of time-series designs. These are often used in *single-case experiments,* involving repeated measurement of one participant over time. Data are collected in a baseline period before implementation of an experimental manipulation and then compared to data collected during and after the implementation. Thus these are known as interrupted time-series designs, because the manipulation interrupts the series of measurements. Quantitative case studies of individual psychotherapy clients follow this design, using observable measures of symptoms before and after treatment. Substitute a single community or organization for the individual participant, and you have a useful design for small-scale experimental social innovation.

***Strengths and Limitations***    In single-case experiments, the advantages of repeated measurement of key variables can be combined with the intensive study of individual persons or communities in context (Biglan et al., 1996). They can be combined with qualitative methods in organizational case studies (e.g., Fawcett et al., 1995; Zimmerman et al., 1991), for instance. A time-series format can even be used in a randomized experiment or a nonequivalent comparison group design, comparing an experimental and a control/comparison group over many repeated measurements. This is stronger for drawing conclusions than either method alone (Linney & Reppucci, 1982). The principal strength of time-series designs is their longitudinal perspective for studying change.

However, time-series designs in community research are open to a number of external confounds (Linney & Reppucci, 1982). These include seasonal or cyclical fluctuations in the variables measured. An example is that the number of college students who seek counseling rises as final exams approach. If seeking counseling is used as a dependent variable in a time-series study, researchers must take this seasonal rise into account. A further confound concerns historical events that affect the variables measured. An example is negative national publicity about tobacco use at the same time as implementation of a local antitobacco prevention program for youth. If youth tobacco use drops, the publicity may have been the real cause, not the prevention program. Finally, studies of a single case or community, even over a long time period, have questionable generalizability to other communities.

A key issue for time-series designs is the number of measurements in the baseline and experimental periods (Linney & Reppucci, 1982). Instead of measuring a larger number of individuals for one or two time periods, time-series designs measure one individual (or a small number of them) over a larger number of repeated times. Thus, a question to ask is the following: How large and representative is the sample of times measured? Social innovations may have gradual or delayed effects difficult to detect in a short time-series design (Cook & Campbell, 1979). Seasonal or cyclical fluctuations in the dependent variable may be detected if the time series is long enough.

***Multiple-Baseline Designs***   This variation of times-series design provides one approach to reducing the problems of external confounds and generalizability. Think of this design as a set of time-series studies, each conducted in a different community to provide greater generalizability. The experimental social innovation is implemented at a different time in each community so that effects of an external historical factor (happening at the same time for all communities, such as publicity about tobacco use) will not be confounded with the innovation. If the dependent variable measures show a change soon after the implementation of the innovation, at a different date in each community, confidence can be stronger that the innovation (not some confound) caused this effect. In effect, the design tests whether findings from one community can be replicated in other communities, within a single study (Biglan et al. 1996).

The multiple-baseline design reduces but does not eliminate the problems of a time-series design. The multiple communities studied are still nonequivalent (assignment of individuals to them is not random), and differences among them still exist that complicate interpretation (see Cook & Campbell, 1979, pp. 225–230). However, it is a useful way to combine the elements of repeated measurement, intensive study of a single community, and replication across communities.

***Exemplary Study***   Can use of behavioral techniques reduce the willingness of merchants to sell tobacco products to adolescents? That was the question studied by Biglan and colleagues (Biglan et al., 1995, 1996). They studied whole communities, not just individuals or retail stores, combining multiple-baseline and time-series methods. Their findings as well as their research methods are important for drug abuse prevention, health promotion, and community change initiatives.

Biglan et al. (1996) and colleagues empirically evaluated an intervention to reduce teen use of tobacco products in rural Oregon communities. It focused on sales of tobacco to youth by retail merchants, which are illegal but seldom punished. Biglan et al. (1996) analyzed the antecedents and consequences of those sales from a behavioral perspective and devised a five-part intervention to prevent them.

The intervention mobilized community support by organizing a community proclamation opposing tobacco sales to minors. Then each merchant was visited to remind them of the proclamation and was given a description of the law and signs about it for posting. The key element was *intervention* visits to merchants by teen volunteers seeking to purchase tobacco products. If the clerk asked for identification or refused to sell, the volunteer handed the clerk a thank you letter and a gift certificate donated by a local business (positive reinforcement). If the clerk was willing to sell, the volunteer declined to buy and gave the clerk a reminder statement about the law and proclamation. The researchers periodically provided feedback to merchants about their clerks' behavior in general (but not about individual clerks). In addition, they publicly praised clerks and stores who had refused to sell, in newspaper articles, ads, and circulars (again providing reinforcement).

Measurement of intervention effectiveness was conducted with additional *assessment* visits to stores by teens seeking to purchase tobacco. These measurement visits were separate from the intervention visits, and did not provide reinforcement of refusals to sell or reminders of the law. Teens asked to buy tobacco, then declined to buy if a clerk was willing to sell. Over 200 volunteer youth, ranging in age from 14 to 17, participated as testers. Males sought to purchase cigarettes or smokeless tobacco, females only cigarettes. Attempts to buy were balanced by gender. Willingness or refusal to sell during these visits were used to construct the dependent variable in the research design.

Researchers measured effectiveness of the intervention by community, not by individual store, because they had implemented a community intervention. The dependent variable was the proportion of stores in a community willing to sell tobacco to youth during each assessment period, which were 3 weeks apart. The researchers used repeated assessments, up to a total of 16 periods. In two studies (Biglan et al., 1995, 1996), researchers studied eight communities in rural Oregon. All were smaller than 6,000 in population, with predominantly White populations, and economically relying mainly on agriculture and timber.

Biglan et al. (1995, 1996) used time-series techniques by collecting baseline assessments in each community before implementing the intervention, then comparing those data to assessments during and after the intervention. They used multiple-baseline techniques by conducting the intervention at different times in different communities. If willingness to sell decreased only after the intervention, conducted at different times in different communities, it is more likely that the intervention (not an extraneous factor) was the cause of those declines. One way of thinking about the Biglan et al. (1995, 1996) design is as eight quantitative case studies, each of a different community, involving time-series measurement, with the intervention implemented at different times in different cases (the multiple baseline element).

Biglan et al. (1996) reported results for four communities. In two communities, clerks' willingness to sell during assessment visits clearly dropped following the intervention. These differences were statistically significant. The intervention occurred at different times in these two communities, so one can be more confident that the intervention caused the reduction. In a third community, the intervention apparently took longer to become effective. In a fourth, baseline (pre-intervention) willingness to sell was somewhat lower, and the intervention did not make a significant difference. These contextual differences illustrate how local community factors can influence the intervention's effectiveness.

In a further analysis, Biglan et al. (1996) averaged results across all eight communities in the Biglan et al. (1995, 1996) studies. Willingness to sell after the intervention, averaged across communities, was significantly lower than during baseline measurements.

The generalizability of these findings may be limited, because the sample was only eight relatively similar communities. In addition, as with the Block Booster Project, exactly what element of the intervention accounted for its success (e.g., community proclamation, reinforcement of clerk refusals to sell, feedback to merchants, or the combination of these) is not clear. Yet the intervention package, in most communities, was effective in reducing retail clerks' willingness to sell tobacco to youth. As Biglan et al. (1996) pointed out, preventing sales in one community does not necessarily mean youth will not use tobacco, because they may obtain it from adults or in other communities. However, both behavioral analysis and common sense suggest that the more difficult it is to obtain tobacco, the less likely that youth will begin to use it.

## CONCLUSIONS

Table 4.2 summarizes the distinctive features, strengths, and limitations of the qualitative and quantitative methods described in this chapter.

We emphasize two themes that run through the methods we have covered. First, qualitative and quantitative methods complement each other. Much can be gained by conducting research that uses both or that synthesizes the knowledge provided by each approach. For instance, the study of citizen participation and empowerment has benefited both from Kieffer's (1984) qualitative study of developmental stages and from the Block Booster Project quantitative studies (Florin et al., 1992).

Second, a longitudinal perspective greatly enhances community research. Studying changes over time reveals the workings of communities in ways not available in cross-sectional analysis. Understanding the dynamics of communities, and individuals' relationships to them ultimately requires a historical perspective and an analysis of change, especially of community and individual development. In choosing exemplary studies for this chapter, we have tried to highlight whenever possible those that attend to the history of their context or to change over time in persons or communities (e.g., Biglan et al., 1996; M. Bond & Keys, 1993; Florin et al., 1992; Kieffer, 1984).

Gaining historical–cultural understanding and conducting longitudinal research both are costly in time, money, and effort. A longitudinal design is not the best way to study every research question. Yet historical and longitudinal approaches are good, often the best, ways to enact a commitment to a collaborative partnership with a community, and to provide knowledge useful to that community and to the world beyond it.

## CHAPTER SUMMARY

**1.** Community research methods can be divided into qualitative and quantitative methods on the basis of whether the data studied are in verbal or numerical form. Each method has characteristic strengths and limitations. Table 4.1 summarizes the purposes and approaches of each class of methods. Qualitative methods provide *insider knowledge* of what a psychological or community phenomenon means to those who experience it. Quantitative methods provide *outsider knowledge* that is more useful in making comparisons and testing causal hypotheses.

| | TABLE 4.2 COMPARISON OF COMMUNITY RESEARCH METHODS | | |
|---|---|---|---|
| **Method** | **Distinctive Features** | **Strengths** | **Limitations** |
| ***Qualitative Methods*** | | | |
| Participant observation | Researcher "joins" community, assumes insider and outsider perspectives, lives/ works alongside informants | Maximum insider knowledge, thick description, maximum relationship with community, contextual understanding | Generalizability; selective observation, memory; informant sampling; influencing phenomenon of study; role conflict |
| Qualitative interviewing of individuals | Collaborative approach, open-ended questioning to elicit participant language and experiences, intensive study of small sample | Flexible exploration of topics not antici-pated by researcher, thick description, more standardized than participant observation, relationship with partici-pants, contextual understanding | Generalizability, less direct experience than participant observation, less stan-dardization than qualitative methods |
| Focus group interviewing | Similar to qualitative interviews, but conducted with a group to elicit shared views | Similar to qualitative interviews, but allows group elaboration; observation of group dynamics | Similar to qualitative interviews; less depth of understanding of individual than qualitative interviewing of individuals |
| Organizational/ community case study | Study of single organization or community over time | Understanding setting in depth, under-standing changes in setting, thick description, contextual, understanding | Generalizability; limitations of archival data and retrospective interviews |
| ***Quantitative Methods*** | | | |
| Quantitative observation, epidemiology | Measurement and statistical analysis of standardized data from large samples, studied without experimental intervention | Standardized methods, estimating strength of relationships among variables, study of variables that cannot be experimentally manipulated, generalizability, practicality | Reliance on prior knowledge, causal inference limited, often decontextualized, epidemiological focus on disorder |
| Randomized field experiments | Evaluation of social innovation with control group and standardized measurement | Standardized methods, control of confounding factors, causal inference | Reliance on prior knowledge, requires control of setting, generalizability |
| Nonequivalent comparison group designs | Much the same as field experiments, without random assignment to conditions | Standardized methods, some control of confounds, practicality | Reliance on prior knowledge, comparability of groups, requires some control of setting, generalizability |
| Interrupted time-series designs | Longitudinal measurement of one or a few settings before and after an interven-tion; may use multiple-baseline design | Measurement with contextual perspec-tive, practicality, longitudinal perspective, replication in multiple baseline | Reliance on prior knowledge, external confounds in time series, requires some control of setting, generalizability |

**2.** *Cross-sectional* research studies a phenomenon at one point in time. *Longitudinal* research concerns change over time, and can be used to study community or individual change.

**3.** Qualitative methods involve intensive study of a setting and/or smaller samples of individuals. The goal is to understand the meaning of a setting or experience for the individuals studied, applicable mainly in that context. The researcher seeks to put aside preconceptions and learn about the setting and research participants in their own terms. Open-ended questions and attending carefully to their language are examples of ways to do this. The researcher seeks *thick description* of the experiences of participants.

**4.** Collection, analysis, and interpretation of qualitative data often overlap as the researcher develops a better understanding of the phenomenon. Analysis typically involves identifying themes or separating and comparing distinct categories. These are then tested by analyzing more data and by using multiple coders. After several rounds of refinement, the researcher often checks the analysis and interpretation by having participants review them.

**5.** Quantitative research emphasizes measurement, experimentation, and hypothesis testing. Standardized measurements with established reliability and validity are preferred. Statistical analysis of numerical data is the dominant method of analysis. Methods may involve quantitative observation of existing phenomena or experimental studies that seek to alter phenomena in order to understand causality.

**6.** An important objective of quantitative methods is understanding cause–effect relationships. The clearest way to study these is by testing hypotheses, and the most certain tests of hypotheses are experiments. The ultimate objective is general knowledge in the form of generalizations applicable across many contexts or settings.

**7.** In community research, an important use of experiments and similar methods is *experimental social innovation,* in which social innovations are tested for effectiveness.

**8.** Table 4.2 summarizes the distinctive features, strengths, and limitations of eight specific qualitative and quantitative methods often used in community research.

# BRIEF EXERCISES

**1.** Individually or in a small group, review an exemplary study described in this chapter. If possible, read the original source. Imagine that you have been asked to plan a follow-up study on the same topic, *using a different methodology discussed in this chapter,* in the same setting or in another setting.

For instance, for the Biglan et al. (1996) study of youth access to tobacco in Oregon towns, plan a follow-up study concerning the same topic. You may use the same four towns or a different sample of towns, including outside Oregon. You may focus on particular stores instead of entire towns, or on chains of stores in a region. You may study intensively the interactions or personal experiences of store clerks and teen customers. However, you cannot use a multiple-baseline, interrupted time-series design; you must choose one of the other seven types of designs described in this chapter or a different design of your own devising.

Some exemplary studies described in the chapter that are useful for this exercise (see references) are as follows:

- Kieffer (1984): Stages of empowerment among community activists
- Banyard (1995): Coping among homeless mothers
- M. Bond & Keys (1993): Organizational case study of Midwest ARC
- L. Roberts et al. (1991): Behavioral observation of GROW meetings
- Mason et al. (1999): Early risk factors for severe emotional disturbance
- Florin et al. (1992): Block Booster Project experiment
- Biglan et al. (1996): Restricting sales of tobacco to youth.

**2.** Individually or as a team, choose a topic or question for community research and propose a study using one of the eight types of designs described in this chapter. Be able to discuss the strengths and limitations of your choice.

**3.** Classify the following examples of studies as one (in some cases, more than one) of the eight types of methodological designs described in this chapter.

(a) A prevention program is implemented for all seventh-grade students in one school. The program is designed to increase skills in making decisions. Performance of these students on questionnaire and behavioral measures of decision making will be compared before and after the intervention. Performance will also be compared with seventh-grade students in another school, similar in size and in socioeconomic and racial makeup.

(b) Latino and Latina students entering a predominantly European American university are interviewed before beginning classes, at the midpoint and at the end of their first semester, and again during their second semester. Interviews concern students' own descriptions of their experiences and ways of coping with college life. One goal of the research is to identify common themes among their experiences.

(c) A community organizer is hired to help residents of a low-income urban neighborhood initiate their own strategies for community economic development and crime prevention. She decides to live in the neighborhood and cultivates a relationship with the neighborhood community association that involves research as well as action. Data collection in this case means keeping systematic notes on her experiences and contacts.

(d) A state law mandates that all school districts in the state implement some type of program designed to reduce school violence. In a decision that stuns yet pleases the project evaluation research team, 66 districts, varying in demographic makeup and size, agree to use the same program involving training in conflict resolution skills. Of these 66 districts, half will implement the program in the next year and half the year after. In the latter group, current policies will be used in the first year. Measures of conflict and violence will be collected in all schools throughout these two years, and for two more years thereafter. In another stunning decision, the 66 district superintendents agree to be randomly assigned to which year their districts will receive the program.

(e) An additional research team is hired to study the school violence intervention above. They will study three districts that implement the program in its first year.

By meeting with and questioning students, parents, teachers, and administrators, they hope to focus on how the program actually operates and what difference it makes, if any, in school life.

**4.** Write a brief essay to yourself on this topic: In general, are qualitative or quantitative methods more appealing to me as methods for studying individuals and communities? (Make a clear choice in your essay, even if you recognize the merits of both approaches.)

To fill out your essay, ask yourself these questions. What does my choice tell me about my own epistemology: my own sense of what knowledge is, how it can be gained, what methods and findings are trustworthy; my own sense of how individuals and communities are best understood? Would I like to learn to use particular methods in this chapter in research of my own?

When finished, share your essay with a classmate, and discuss your choices.

**5.** Arrange a debate between advocates of qualitative and quantitative methods for community research. Emphasize the different purposes, features, strengths, and limitations of the different approaches.

## RECOMMENDED READINGS

Denzin, N., & Lincoln, Y. (Eds.). (1994). *Handbook of qualitative research.* Thousand Oaks, CA: Sage.

Miles, M., & Huberman, A. (1994). *Qualitative data analysis* (2nd ed.). Thousand Oaks, CA: Sage.
  Guides to collecting and analyzing qualitative data.

Cook, T., & Campbell, D. (1979). *Quasi-experimentation: Design and analysis for field settings.* Chicago: Rand McNally.

Linney, J. A. (1989). Optimizing research strategies in the schools. In L. A. Bond & B. E. Compas (Eds.), *Primary prevention in the schools* (pp. 50–76). Newbury Park, CA: Sage Publications.

Linney, J. A., & Reppucci, N. D. (1982). Research design and methods in community psychology. In P. Kendall & J. Butcher (Eds.), *Handbook of research methods in clinical psychology* (pp. 535-566). New York: Wiley.
  Guides to quantitative methods of community research.

Brydon-Miller, M., & Tolman, D. (Eds.). (1997). Transforming psychology: Interpretive and participatory research methods [Special issue]. *Journal of Social Issues, 53* (4).

Miller, K., & Banyard, V. (Eds.) (1998). Qualitative research in community psychology [Special issue]. *American Journal of Community Psychology, 26* (4).
  Special issues concerning methods and examples of research.

Banyard, V. (1995). "Taking another route": Daily survival narratives from mothers who are homeless. *American Journal of Community Psychology, 23,* 871–892.

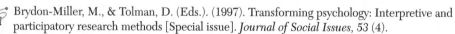

These articles appear in journals in the InfoTrac College Edition on-line library available from Wadsworth.

Biglan, A., Ary, D., Koehn, V., Levings, D., Smith, S., Wright, Z., James L., & Henderson, J. (1996). Mobilizing positive reinforcement in communities to reduce youth access to tobacco. *American Journal of Community Psychology, 24,* 625–638.

Foster-Fishman, P., Salem, D., Chibnall, S., Legler, R., & Yapchai, C. (1998). Empirical support for the critical assumptions of empowerment theory. *American Journal of Community Psychology, 26,* 507–536.

Kroeker, C. (1995). Individual, organizational, and societal empowerment: A study of the processes of a Nicaraguan agricultural cooperative. *American Journal of Community Psychology, 23,* 749–764.
> Specific recent studies illustrating diverse methods, that are readable for undergraduate students and useful for graduate students.

## PART three

# UNDERSTANDING
# COMMUNITIES

# UNDERSTANDING ECOLOGY

## Individuals within Environments*

*This chapter was written in collaboration with Jean Ann Linney.

# OPENING EXERCISE AND INTRODUCTION

Take a moment to remember, as fully as you can, your first visit to the college or university you now attend (or one you attended earlier). What do you recall about the college as a *setting*—about its atmosphere, its "feel" for you as an individual? Was it a quiet, tree-lined campus, or did it reflect the excitement of an urban university? Did you feel welcomed? Did you feel that you could ask anyone for directions or help, or did most people seem busy? Were places for social gathering quickly obvious? Did you sense that people like you live, study, or work here, or did you feel different in some important way? Write a few notes on these memories.

Now take a longer view. How has this college environment affected you as an individual? How have your experiences in this environment shaped your learning, personal development, network of friends, vocational aspirations, and personal well-being? What skills for effective coping have you learned in this environment? What values have you developed or strengthened? Write down the changes you have experienced.

How well do you know your classmates other than your immediate friends? How well do you know the faculty and staff? What help do you provide to or receive from each of these groups? Can you identify the following resources on your campus: a place where you like to socialize? A quiet place to study? A place and person you would seek for help with a personal-emotional problem? A place where scholarly discussion happens outside of class? A place for group study? A place to exercise? A place for commuter students to meet? Access to parking or to public transportation? Other resources you use or need? Write down your ideas about these issues.

Finally, assume a critical stance. What changes would you suggest to improve your college or university environment? That includes changes in the physical campus, the education and other services the college offers, its policies and rules, its staff or student makeup, or anything else you suggest. Write down your suggestions.

These questions reflect the concepts community psychologists and others have developed to understand the interaction of environments (of which a college is one example) and persons in everyday life. This study of persons in ecological context has been a central theme for community psychology. The report from the 1965 Swampscott meeting identified "the reciprocal relationships between individuals and the social systems with which they interact" (Bennett et al. 1966, p. 7) as an essential focus of community psychology. Much of the thinking in community psychology is rooted in the fundamental assumption that the behavior of individuals cannot be understood without consideration of *ecological context*. By that term, we mean the settings or surroundings that impinge on an individual. These include physical or architectural environments, and the social occasions that occur within these environments, such as classes or meetings, friends eating lunch together, or shopping for groceries. The ecological context of an individual's actions or experiences involves social relationships at each level of analysis described in chapter 1. Our focus in this chapter is chiefly on microsystems, organizations, and communities, although we also consider how these are affected by macrosystems.

For a century, ecological context has been implicitly recognized as an important force in understanding human behavior. At the turn of the 20th century, Lightner Witmer and the staff of the early child development clinics did their work in the settings where children lived and went to school. They recognized that to improve behavior or learning required working in those settings and changing them to some extent. Kurt Lewin (1935;

Marrow, 1969) argued that "B = f(P, E)," that behavior is a function of person *and* environment. Theories of personality proposed by Murray (1938), Rotter (1954), and Bandura (1986) emphasized the interaction of person and situation, although applications of their concepts in research and practice have focused on individual factors. The field of environmental psychology arose at about the same time and from similar conceptual roots as community psychology, to investigate the effect of physical (usually built) environments on behavior. Even advocates of genetic, temperament, and other biological perspectives argue that environments interact with individual factors (e.g., Buss, 1995; Kagan, 1994). However, the specific ways that contextual and individual variables interact are not well understood. In part that is because measurement and theory for studying individual variables have long been the focus of psychology, whereas less attention has been devoted to measuring contextual factors.

Examples of the interplay of individual and environment are all around us. How did you select a university to attend? Financial considerations? Academic offerings or reputation? Social atmosphere? Distance from home? All of these are contextual factors interacting with your needs or preferences. For a further example, think about how the decor, music, and seating arrangements contribute to the ambiance of a restaurant. In a musical ensemble, a workplace, or a family, an individual may stand out at a given moment, but to understand that individual's actions, one must understand his or her relationship to the group, in context.

Kelly's (1979a) work on the social ecology of two U.S. high schools documented what has been termed *person–environment fit*. Kelly and associates measured individual differences among high school boys in exploratory personal style: how much the individual takes risks in exploring and participating in school activities (academic and otherwise) (Kelly, 1979a, pp. 82–83). "High explorers" became involved in many activities and were more active and assertive there, compared to "low explorers." The researchers also compared a high school marked by higher turnover of students (almost 19% of one's class membership changed annually) with a similar school with lower turnover (8%). In general, high explorers were more closely involved with peers in the higher turnover school, whereas low explorers were more involved with peers at the lower turnover school (e.g., Kelly, 1979, p. 142 and 192). Thus, for an individual student, whether exploring is effective in making friends and being involved with others depends in part on the school context. Exploring is adaptive in the higher turnover setting, where there is more need to make new friends yearly. It is not as adaptive in the low-turnover school, where there is more continuity. These differences could be even greater if schools with higher turnover rates were sampled.

# What Are the Key Points of This Chapter?

In this chapter, we examine concepts and community research regarding ecological context. First, we describe five broad conceptual perspectives for describing ecological context and explaining its impact on individuals. These perspectives range in focus from microsystems to organizations to communities. Second, for a more specific example of the importance of context, we review research on the influence of urban neighborhoods on individual behavior and development. We summarize this research in terms of specific models of the neighborhood–individual relationship. Finally, we highlight three exemplary community programs that actually altered ecological contexts to improve the quality of individuals' lives.

# CONCEPTUAL MODELS OF ECOLOGICAL CONTEXT

In this section, we describe five ecological models used in community psychology to describe environments and their impact on individuals. As you read about each one, keep in mind the levels of analysis that we introduced in chapter 1: microsystem, organization, community, macrosystem. Some of the models can be used at multiple levels, others fit one or two levels best.

## *Barker: Ecological Psychology and Behavior Settings*

In 1947, Barker and colleagues began studying the lives of children in a town referred to as "Midwest" (actually Oskaloosa, Kansas). In this small town, they aimed to understand children's lives in context (Barker, 1968; Barker & Wright, 1955; Barker & Associates, 1978). They understood that everyday contexts cannot be comprehensively studied in a laboratory, or by questionnaire or even interviews, because all of these depend on what questions the researcher chooses to ask. The Barker family moved to Midwest to live, and with their colleagues opened a research office. After gaining the trust and cooperation of Midwest residents, they and their associates began careful, systematic, naturalistic observations of children's everyday lives. Barker (1978, p. 3) termed this studying the "stream of behavior," rather than breaking that stream into bits and choosing only some bits to understand apart from the whole. They soon discovered that they could not study children's lives in context without including nearly the whole town.

> The truth is that we soon became overwhelmed with individual behavior. We estimated that the 119 children of Midwest engaged in about one hundred thousand behavior episodes daily. . . . We sampled behavior in such divergent places as the drugstore, the Sunday School classes, the 4-H Club meeting, and the football games. . . . At this point, we stopped focusing exclusively on the behavior of individuals and saw for the first time a thing that is obvious to the inhabitants of Midwest, namely, that behavior comes in extraindividual wave patterns that are as visible and invariant as the pools and rapids of Slough Creek, west of town. The Presbyterian worship services, the high school basketball games, and the post office, for example, persist year after year with their unique configurations of behavior, despite constant changes in the persons involved. These persisting, extraindividual behavior phenomena we have called the *standing behavior patterns* of Midwest." (Barker & Wright, 1978, pp. 24–25)

Ecological psychology, the theory and methodology developed in Midwest, is an important basis of both environmental and community psychology. Barker and colleagues studied Midwest, and eventually a similar English town ("Yoredale") and other settings, by observing physical and social environments where community life was created and sustained. They were interested not in individual personalities, but in the standing patterns of behavior that were characteristic of a behavior setting regardless of which individuals were there (Barker, 1965, 1968; Barker & Associates, 1978; Barker & Schoggen, 1973; Barker & Wright, 1955). Their early work laid much of the groundwork for ecological concepts in this chapter. It has been extended by Schoggen (1989), Wicker (1979) and others.

***Behavior Settings***    Barker (1968) developed this concept as the primary unit of analysis for his approach. A behavior setting is defined by its time and space boundaries, and by a *standing pattern of behavior.* Thus, the behavior setting of a third-grade class in Midwest met weekdays in one classroom at the school, proceeding through a program involving predictable teacher and student behavior, largely regardless of which individuals were present. The drugstore behavior setting had wider time boundaries and more turnover of "inhabitants" (customers and staff), but occurred in a single place and involved standing behavior patterns regardless of which individual customers and staff were present. It included three areas that were not independent enough to be considered separate settings: soda fountain, pharmacy, and variety department. Some behavior settings were embedded within larger behavior settings, such as classes within a school. Others stood alone, such as a service station. Some occurred only yearly, such as a talent show, whereas others were daily events. Barker (1968, p. 106) and colleagues identified 884 behavior settings in Midwest in 1963–1964; almost all could be grouped into five categories: government, business, educational, religious, and voluntary association, as illustrated in Table 5.1.

A behavior setting is not simply a physical place, but is a place, time, *and* a standing behavior pattern. The sanctuary of the Methodist church in Midwest is a physical setting, but not a behavior setting. Instead, several behavior settings occur within it, such as worship services, choir practices, and weddings. In contrast, many small businesses comprise both a physical setting and a behavior setting; the drug store is an example. The physical setting and the behavior setting are synomorphic or matched in their structure. The seats in a lecture hall face the speaker, for example, while the podium faces the audience (Barker, 1968). This makes possible the standing behavior pattern.

Classic behavior setting theory stipulates that the persons in a setting are largely interchangeable; the same patterns of behavior occur irrespective of the specific individuals

| TABLE 5.1 | BEHAVIOR SETTINGS IN "MIDWEST" |
|---|---|
| **Category** | **Examples of Behavior Settings** |
| Business | Attorneys' office, bank, beauty shop, barber shop, construction business, drugstore, music lessons, tavern |
| Education | Sixth grade math class, basketball game, dance, girls' locker room, parent–teacher conferences, senior class box social |
| Government | County treasurer's office, court session, election polling place |
| Religion | Worship service, choir practice, religious class, religious fellowship meeting, wedding |
| Voluntary association | 4-H club banquet, 4-H club regular meeting, Scout troop meeting, women's club meeting |

Note: Taken from Barker (1968, pp. 36 and 110–116).

(Barker, 1968). Barker further hypothesized that behavior settings have a set of rules, implicit or explicit, that maintain the standing behavior pattern (Barker, 1968, pp. 167–171). These rules can be seen in specific behavior patterns.

- *Program circuits*, such as an agenda for a meeting, structure the overall standing behavior pattern.
- *Goal circuits* satisfy goals of individuals, such as a customer purchasing an item or a member participating in a worship service.

The rules also incorporate control mechanisms to limit behavior that would threaten the program and setting.

- *Deviation-countering circuits* involve correction of inhabitants' behavior and training them in desired actions.
- *Vetoing circuits* occur when individuals are excluded from the behavior setting.

The purpose of ecological psychology is to identify behavior settings and to understand the physical features and social circuits that maintain them.

A baseball game provides an illustration of the heuristic value of this approach (Barker, 1968). The game is a behavior setting, a standing pattern of behavior, occurring within a given time and place. The field defines the physical environment alone, but reveals little about the game. Similarly, we would not be able to understand the game or individual players' acts by focusing on each player in isolation (the common individual-level focus of psychological research). Imagine, for example, a videotape showing the first base player alone, without the context of the field or of plays not involving the first baseman. Very little could be learned about what this player is doing and why, and it would be quite difficult to predict that player's behavior. By observing the context of the entire behavior setting, the program circuits or rules become more comprehensible. So do the relationships among players, at least as they concern the conduct of the game. Barker (1968) suggested that it is the combination of the physical field, game time, and the standing patterns of behavior among players (and fans) that constitute the behavior setting of a baseball game.

Identifying behavior settings, as initially performed in Midwest, was an exceedingly lengthy process, especially in the days before computerized data analysis. Barker and colleagues spent over a year in an exhaustive description of the behavior settings in Midwest (Barker & Wright, 1955). Behavior setting methodology has been applied in schools (Barker & Gump, 1964; Schoggen & Schoggen, 1988), churches (Wicker, 1969), residential treatment facilities (Linney, Webb, & Rosenberg, 1985), mutual help groups (Luke et al., 1991), and work settings (Oxley & Barrera, 1984). These applications often have involved smaller systems (e.g., a group home) or specific types of behavior settings and thus require less time. Wicker (1979) suggested methods of sampling to streamline the procedure.

***Underpopulated Settings*** A second contribution of Barker's ecological approach has been the study of "manning" theory (Barker, 1968). (Wicker [1979, p. 756]) suggested the more inclusive term "staffing" theory, and Schoggen (1989) suggested the terms "underpopulated" and "optimally populated" settings. We use the latter terms.)

In a classic study, *Big School, Small School,* Barker and Gump (1964) compared involvement of students in extracurricular activities (one form of behavior settings) in large and small high schools in Kansas (enrollments ranged from 35 to over 2,000). In the smaller schools, they found greater levels of student involvement in performances and in leadership roles, and higher levels of student satisfaction and attachment to school. There existed a slightly greater number of opportunities for involvement in larger schools. Yet students in smaller schools were twice as likely to participate in active ways, and on average participated in a wider variety of activities.

Barker and Gump (1964) also found that students in smaller schools perceived more responsibility to volunteer for activities. They often reported a sense that even if they weren't talented in a particular activity, their help was needed. The larger schools had higher rates of uninvolved, "marginal" students with little sense of commitment to the school or social connection with school peers or staff. In chapter 9, we take up some implications of these ideas for prevention programs in schools.

Studies in a variety of settings have established that the critical factor is the ratio of the number of roles available in a behavior setting, compared to the number of individuals available to play those roles (Wicker, 1979, 1987). An *optimally populated setting* has as many or more players than roles. Settings easily recruit enough members to fill their roles; other students are marginalized or left out. In fact, Barker (1968, p. 181) theorized that vetoing circuits (behaviors that screen out potential members) would be especially common in these settings, because there are plenty of replacements available. A large school will probably have tryouts or auditions for athletic teams, musical groups, dramatic productions, and so on; only the most talented will be able to participate. Barker and Gump (1964) found that larger schools contained more optimally populated settings.

An *underpopulated setting* has more roles than members. That increases member sense of responsibility for maintaining the setting and offers them the chance to develop skills they otherwise might not have learned. It may also increase the diversity of persons participating in the setting, attracting unused resources. For example, a shy person who otherwise would not try out for a school play is pressed into service, developing social skills or perhaps revealing hidden talents. In addition, members of an underpopulated behavior setting would engage in deviation-countering circuits rather than vetoing circuits. That is, they would invest time and effort in teaching the skills needed for a role in the setting (and correcting errors in performance), rather than excluding the person. This strategy makes sense if members are needed to play roles necessary for maintaining the setting. Barker and Gump (1964) found that smaller schools contained more underpopulated settings. Of course, members in an extremely underpopulated setting will "burn out"; the setting may even be disbanded. Yet moderate understaffing may lead to positive outcomes for individuals (greater skill or personal development) and setting (greater commitment among members).

These concepts fit the organizational strategies of GROW, a mutual help organization for persons with serious mental illness. GROW deliberately limits the size of local chapters, creates leadership roles for all members, and maximizes member sense of responsibility for group functioning. These methods promote member personal development and mutual commitment and illustrate practical benefits of an underpopulated behavior setting (Luke et al., 1991; Zimmerman et al., 1991).

***Contributions and Limitations***   Ecological psychology is an important perspective in community psychology. The concept of behavior setting and theory of underpopulated settings represent two major contributions to how community psychologists think about context.

We have mentioned one limitation: the laborious naturalistic observation of behavior settings, unless sampling techniques are adopted. A second limitation is that behavior setting theory focuses on how behavior settings perpetuate themselves and mold the behavior of individuals. This is one side of the picture, but it underplays how settings are created and changed, and how individuals influence settings (D. V. Perkins, Burns, Perry, & Nielsen, 1988). Having originally been developed in a small-town setting, this emphasis on stability rather than change is understandable, yet limited in scope. Third, the effects of underpopulated and optimally populated settings have not always been replicated in later studies, and their relationship to individual adjustment and behavior appear more complicated than behavior setting theory suggests (D. V. Perkins et al., 1988). (See Schoggen, 1988, for a defense of behavior setting concepts on these points.)

Despite these limitations, ecological psychology provides an important perspective for community psychology. By focusing on settings and behavior, ecological psychology has generated an enduring body of concepts and research and influenced the development of other ecological perspectives.

## Kelly: Four Ecological Principles

Adapting concepts from the biological field of ecology, Kelly and colleagues postulated four ecological principles as a framework for community psychology: interdependence, cycling of resources, adaptation, and succession (Kelly, 1966, 1970, 1979a; Trickett, Kelly, & Todd, 1972; Trickett, Kelly, & Vincent, 1985; Vincent & Trickett, 1983). These concepts have been very influential in understanding ecological context. You should understand them as characteristics of settings, not of individuals. Workplaces, for instance, differ in the extent of interdependence among workers, in what resources are cycled, and in what individual skills are needed to adapt to the setting. Of course, these setting factors influence individual life greatly in schools, families, workplaces, and other settings.

***Interdependence***   This fundamental axiom of any ecosystem recognizes that the system has multiple, related parts; change in one affects the others (Trickett, Kelly & Todd, 1972). The components of any ecological system thus are interdependent. For a public school, interdependent components include students, teachers, administrators and other staff, parents, board members, and district taxpayers. For a business firm, they include stockholders, board members, executives, employees, their families, and even suppliers and customers.

Consider the ecology of a family for example. If one family member gets the flu, everyone else is affected in one way or another. If a young child is sick, an older member of the family will likely miss work or school to stay at home with the sick child. Others in the family may also become ill in turn. If the primary caregiver gets the flu, meal preparation, washing, transportation, and a host of other daily operations for every other member of the family are affected. The change may be temporary, with the system returning to its previous state after a few days. Some changes in one member are not temporary, however. Think about the implications for your family system of having an ailing grandparent join the household, for instance.

A corollary of the principle of interdependence is that any change in a system will have multiple consequences, some of them unanticipated and perhaps unwanted. Similarly, change efforts within a system may be thwarted because interdependent components of the system are not addressed. For instance, cooperative learning efforts in a classroom may fail if the administrators or parents strongly endorse individual competition in education.

**Cycling of Resources**     Kelly's second principle is closely related to interdependence. It specifies that any system can be understood by examining how resources are defined, used, created, conserved and transformed (Trickett, Kelly & Todd, 1972). In a garden ecology for example, resources like water, sunlight, plants, and soil nutrients cycle through predictable processes resulting in fruits and vegetables consumed by insects, humans, and other animals.

Social ecologies can also be described and understood by the cycling of resources. What might be the resources important for a family ecology? Time, nurturance, attention, emotional support, money, and other tangible goods might all be resources cycled by families. By examining the cycling of resources, one can begin to characterize family priorities and connections. Similarly, what resources (especially intangible ones) are cycled among students at your university? Information is exchanged in many forms, such as advice on courses, professors, social life, job possibilities. Emotional support, practical assistance, and tutoring also are resources often exchanged.

The principle of resource cycling also concerns how resources are recognized and conserved. You may not recognize how family members represent resources useful to you until you encounter a stressful life event they have lived through and can advise you about. An acquaintance who is a physics major may mean little to you until you take a physics course. An implication of Kelly's approach is to search any environment (family, organization, neighborhood) for resources (tangible or intangible) that may contribute to individual or system well-being. A second implication is to create or strengthen resources in that system.

Stack's (1974) classic study of a low-income African American midwestern community highlighted patterns of resource sharing. In The Flats (a public housing community with limited financial resources), residents shared furniture, child care, food stamps, and money beyond their own families. For example, a member of the community loaned furniture to a neighbor for an extended period of time, and that neighbor had previously cared for her child while she was looking for work out of town. To an outsider, this exchange of resources may seem risky for families with little money, but it made sense to those within the system. Resources were allocated to those who needed them, and today's provider may be tomorrow's recipient. Stack's detailed study of this system documented an ecology in which the interdependence of the members can be understood by charting the cycling of resources.

**Adaptation**     The third ecological principle concerns person-environment fit or match. Individuals cope with the constraints or demands of an environment using resources available there (Trickett, Kelly & Todd, 1972). If you can, recall how you adapted to the demands of your first job. In addition, environments are dynamic systems that develop in response to changes among their members. Think about the changes in a family precipitated by events such as the birth of a child, a teen getting a driver's license, or a mother entering college. These changes reflect how settings adapt to individuals, as well as reflect interdependence among family members. Individual adaptation to the demands or norms of an environment is necessary to remain there. Alternatively, an overly restrictive environment may find it difficult to attract new members or retain member involvement.

For an illustration of the adaptation principle, list the skills or competencies you have needed for effective coping in the college environment. Examples of necessary skills may include good note-taking, knowing how to study for an essay versus for a multiple-choice test, making conversation and new friends, resolving roommate conflicts, time management, money budgeting, resilience after setbacks, and asking for help. Whether you possessed them before entering college, or have learned them here, these skills indicate the adaptive demands made by the college environment. If you do not possess these skills, it is likely you will not stay in college and graduate. In addition, a college that does not offer ways of learning these skills may experience difficulty in retaining students.

Adaptation involves values as well as skills. The values prized within a setting are shaped by ecological forces and are reflected in environmental demands and adaptive efforts by individuals. A class that values individual competition, for instance, will require different forms of adaptation for its students than one that prizes cooperation.

Learning adaptive skills also often involves interdependence with others and cycling of resources such as information and emotional support. A further implication of the adaptation principle is that every environment is different. Skills demanded for students are different from those for factory workers or homemakers or police officers.

**Succession**     The fourth ecological principle specifies that ecologies change over time, and that understanding the other three principles must be understood in terms of that pattern of change (Trickett, Kelly & Todd, 1972). Returning to the garden ecology, we know that in the absence of tending to that garden, the continued presence of light and water will fuel the ecology, but in time it will change in predictable ways. Some plants (often "weeds") will crowd out other plants, and the taller varieties will reduce the sunlight available to shorter ones. Over time, a largely or completely different array of plants will exist there.

The principle of succession is equally applicable to the ecology of the family or the community. How many times have you heard that "you have to work at keeping a marriage healthy"? Like the garden, over time the patterns of interdependence, the cycling of resources such as emotional support, and adaptive actions between married persons can become routine. The nature of the relationship may change, perhaps with the partners drifting apart. At the cultural level, the forms of marriage have been changing in Western societies over the last century, another process of succession that affects individual life. Divorce and living together while unmarried are more frequent. Single parenting and same-gender partnering are increasingly accepted. These changes in forms of marriage are influenced by larger social and cultural forces, and in turn influence individual choices about marriage.

An implication of succession, especially related to interdependence and cycling of resources, is that before psychologists plan an intervention in a system, they need to understand that system's history. They should carefully study whether their goals are being met in some way (however incompletely) within the system as it exists. In a school responding to a crisis such as a student suicide, for instance, providing additional professional counseling for students by adults may be less effective than strengthening existing means of peer helping already exchanged among students.

The rise of mutual help groups among persons with a variety of psychological and medical problems, largely without professional planning or intervention, provides a further example. Mutual help involves all four ecological principles. The group's primary purpose is to strengthen individual adaptation of its members; discussion focuses on that. Interdependence is encouraged, often including individual contacts and encouragement outside the group meetings. Social support, information, and other resources are exchanged. Persons who have been encouraged elsewhere to think of themselves as needing resources have the uplifting experience of providing resources to others. The historical development of a local self-help group, a national organization, or the self-help movement as a whole illustrates succession. For instance, a local group is usually founded by a few pioneers, but its effects are limited unless it continues after those founders have moved on.

**Contributions and Limitations**   Kelly's four principles provide distinctive, useful concepts for describing the dynamics of social environments. They address aspects not emphasized in other approaches, such as resources and succession.

In addition, Kelly, Trickett, and associates (e.g., Kelly, 1979b, 1986; Kingry-Westergaard & Kelly, 1990; Tandon et al., 1998; Vincent & Trickett, 1983) have applied the ecological principles to the conduct of research and psychological intervention in the community. This includes establishing an interdependent relationship between researchers and host community, identifying and cultivating community members who can be resources for the research, and anticipating unintended effects of research or intervention. The writings of Kelly and associates eloquently express values of genuine interdependence with community members and appreciation of community resources. This perspective underlies many of the aims of community research discussed in chapter 3.

Kelly's concepts do not specify causal relationships among variables; they are intended as general concepts rather than as a causal model (Kelly, 1970; Trickett, Kelly & Todd, 1972). Moreover, they are not associated with a characteristic method of observation or measurement; in fact, their implication is that those should depend on the unique ecology of each setting (Kingry-Westergaard & Kelly, 1990; Tandon et al., 1998). Yet the continuing use of Kelly's concepts indicates their ongoing importance for both research and action in community psychology (e.g., Speer & Hughey, 1995).

## Moos: Social Climate Dimensions

Murray's (1938) early theory of personality posited person–environment interaction: that individuals seek to satisfy needs in environments, but those environments also provide opportunities or constraints on satisfying those needs. Murray termed the latter process the "press" of the environment. One measure of press is whether the persons in a situation share common perceptions of that environment. Based in part on this conceptual framework, Moos and colleagues developed the Social Climate Scales to assess the shared perceptions of a setting among its members (e.g., Moos, 1973, 1979, 1994). The social climate concept also fits within more general models of individual adaptation and well-being

(Holahan & Moos, 1994; Holahan, Moos & Bonin, 1997; Moos, 1984, 1996; Moos & Lemke, 1996).

Social climate scales exist for microsystem and organizational settings including workplaces, families, university residence halls, psychiatric inpatient settings, correctional settings, community treatment settings, supported community living facilities, military units, and classrooms (Moos, 1994). They have been used in a number of countries and languages (e.g., Moos & Trickett, 1987). The Social Climate Scales are based on three primary dimensions to characterize any setting; each of these has subscales depending on the type of setting measured (Moos, 1984, 1994).

The *Relationship* dimension concerns mutual supportiveness, involvement and cohesion of members (Moos, 1994). The Classroom Environment Scale, for instance, is used to measure high school classroom environments (Moos & Trickett, 1987). It contains subscales on the extent to which students are involved in and participate in class, the extent of affiliation or friendship they report among classmates, and the amount of support they perceive from the teacher (Moos & Trickett, 1987). The Family Environment Scale (Moos & Moos, 1986), in contrast, includes subscales on how cohesive and how expressive the members perceive their family to be, and the extent of conflict they perceive. These constructs also are conceptually related to Kelly's principles of interdependence and cycling of resources (Trickett, Kelly & Todd, 1972).

The *Personal Development* dimension concerns the extent to which individual autonomy, growth, and skill development are fostered in the setting (Moos, 1994). The Classroom Environment Scale contains a subscale concerning the amount of emphasis on planned activities and staying on task and a subscale on competition among students (Moos & Trickett, 1987). The Family Environment Scale (Moos & Moos, 1986) includes subscales concerning the independence accorded individual family members and the family's emphasis on achievement, intellectual–cultural pursuits, recreation, and moral–religious concerns. These environmental demands also are related to Kelly's principle of adaptation.

The *System Maintenance and Change* dimension concerns the emphasis in the setting on order, clarity of rules and expectations, and control of behavior (Moos, 1994). The Classroom Environment Scale contains subscales concerning the extent to which class activities are organized and orderly, the clarity of rules and consequences, the strictness of the teacher, and the extent to which innovative activities and thinking are welcomed in the classroom (Moos & Trickett, 1987). The Family Environment Scale (Moos & Moos, 1986) includes scales on the extent of organization in the family and control exerted by parents. These are conceptually related to Barker's (1968) behavior setting programs, especially deviation-countering and vetoing circuits, and again to adaptation in Kelly's framework (Trickett, Kelly & Todd, 1972).

Moos' Social Climate Scales include items constructed to reflect each of these dimensions. Persons in the setting complete these items to report their perception of that setting. Each social climate measure yields a profile of scores based on the aggregated responses (usually a mean) of the setting members for each dimension. Thus, the profiles quantify shared perceptions of the environment (Moos, 1994).

Social climate scales are useful in consultation and program development (Moos, 1984). A consultant may have setting members complete a social climate scale twice, once to report the setting characteristics ("real" setting), and again to report how they desire the setting to be ("ideal" setting). The consultant then presents the aggregated group scores on both real and ideal perceptions of the environment. The group then discusses how to change the environment to become more like the shared ideal profile.

**Research on Social Climates**    Social climate scales are widely used measures of microsystem and organizational environments. Social climate scores have been statistically related to measures of individual well-being such as job satisfaction and psychological adjustment (Repetti & Cosmas, 1991). Specific findings include the following examples. High school classrooms that emphasize competition and teacher control, but not teacher support and student involvement, have greater absenteeism (Moos, 1984). School class-rooms perceived as structured, task-oriented, and yet supportive showed greater gains in standardized test scores than other classrooms (Moos, 1984). Children in well-organized families tend to be more socially and emotionally adjusted, whereas those in rigid, strict families tend to be less secure and have less self-control (Moos, 1984). Juvenile delinquent treatment programs higher on support, autonomy, and clarity of expectations have lower rates of recidivism (Moos, 1975). Treatment settings perceived as less supportive by clients and/or staff, and that lack clear rules and procedures, have higher dropout rates (Moos, 1984).

**Contributions and Limitations**    Social climate scales measure important but intangible aspects of settings, such as supportiveness, rule clarity, and individual autonomy. Measuring these qualities relies on individual cognitions, and connects those with setting characteristics in a way that behavior setting theory, for instance, does not. The conceptual value and ease of use of social climate scales has fostered research and practical applications in a variety of settings, generating a rich literature of empirical findings. In that literature, social climate concepts have been used to measure distinctive setting characteristics and to predict important individual outcomes.

The chief limitation of social climate scales is that individuals or subgroups within the setting may see its social climate differently. For instance, Raviv, Raviv, and Reisel (1990) reported differences between teachers and students in the same classroom, and Trickett, Trickett, Castro, and Schaffner (1982) found differences between students and independent observers. These discrepancies suggest social climate measures are influenced by one's personality and social role or subgroup in the setting, not just by the setting's overall characteristics. For instance, if the mean score (for a sample of setting members) is midway on a social climate scale (e.g., supportiveness), it could mean at least two things. It may indicate unanimous perceptions of medium supportiveness, or it may reflect two polarized camps of setting members, one group perceiving a very supportive setting while the other perceives a very unsupportive setting. The same environment may generate quite different perceptions among women and men, for example. Thus, social climate scores should be examined carefully for variation among individuals or subgroups in the setting (Moos, 1996; Shinn, 1990). However, due to the contributions mentioned above, the social climate approach has greatly enriched both research and practice in community psychology and other fields.

## Seidman: Social Regularities

S. B. Sarason (e.g., 1974, 1982, 1995) has often described how settings function by creating predictable relationships among their members, and how those qualities persist over time despite attempts to change the setting. Drawing in part on that approach, Seidman (1988, 1990) proposed that settings be understood in terms of *social regularities*, defined as the routine patterns of social relations among the elements (e.g., persons) within a setting, over time (Seidman, 1988, pp. 9–10; 1990, pp. 92–93). Seidman's focus is not on individual personalities, but on relationships between individuals. (Recall how solving the nine-dot problem in chap. 1 involved changing assumptions about relationships among dots, not the dots themselves. In addition, second-order change, also discussed in chap. 1, involves changing relationships among members of a group, not changing the individual members themselves.)

The social regularities perspective thus searches for patterns of behavior that reveal relationships among the setting members. Understanding roles played by setting members aids that search (Goffman, 1959; Sarbin, 1970). Regularities in social settings are often defined by role relationships: teacher–student, therapist–client, employer–employee, parent–child. Roles are enacted in a specific setting (similar to Barker's (1968) behavior setting and standing pattern of behavior). However, the social regularity perspective goes beyond behavior setting theory in attending to what role relationships reveal about power, resources, and inequalities in a setting (Seidman, 1988).

Think back over your schooling for a moment. Who asks most of the questions in the school or college classroom? If your answer is the teacher, you've noticed a social regularity based on role. In most classrooms, teachers ask most questions (S. B. Sarason, 1982; Seidman, 1988). Why is this so predictable, despite the diversity of teachers and students and levels of education? The informal analyses one hears in hallways and at lunch focus on attributes of persons or populations (teachers are boring, so students aren't interested learning more; students are lazy, and must be quizzed to spur effort). Instead, might this regularity have to do with implicit assumptions (of both teachers and students) about who can think for themselves and generate questions? Or about what can be gained from the class, and how it ought to be conducted? In other words, about role relationships in the setting? Moreover, although blaming teachers or students seldom leads to constructive change in schools, a focus on the learning relationship has led to innovations such as cooperative learning methods.

Another social regularity in schools concerns racial desegregation (Linney, 1986; Seidman, 1988). A historical social regularity is that U.S. schools have been a sorting mechanism for separating students by achievement or test scores, then preparing them for different roles in society. A second regularity has been widespread sorting of students by race and also by income. When the courts mandated that separate schools for African Americans were illegal, communities brought Black and White students into the same schools. Yet a study in a Midwestern city revealed a new form of sorting on a different plane. On the basis of (mainly White) staff perceptions of their abilities, Black students were assigned disproportionately to classes and curricula that limited their ability to apply for college and their future attainments (Linney, 1986). By sorting on this basis, the school system continued (in modified form) the social regularity of racial separation. The new form of sorting may have been unintentional rather than segregation by law. Nonetheless, it affected the students' lives (Linney, 1986).

A final example of a social regularity concerns professional psychotherapy and mutual help for persons with mental disorders (Seidman, 1988). In a professionally conducted group, members may fall into more passive "patient behavior," even when the professional seeks to promote mutual help (Toro et al., 1988). By contrast, in a mutual help group conducted by members, all of whom who have experienced the focal problem that is the concern of the group, members exchange helping. In studies comparing the social climates of professionally conducted groups with peer-led groups, members of peer-led groups rated their groups as more cohesive, and as fostering more independence (Toro, Rappaport, & Seidman, 1987; Toro et al., 1988). These differences are best understood as social regularities involving behavior of both therapists and members, not simply as the responsibility of one or the other.

***Contributions and Limitations***     The concept of social regularity draws attention to role relationships, and is perhaps more easily connected to individual behavior and psychological concerns than other ecological concepts. It also offers a way of understanding why it often seems that the more things change in a setting, the more they remain the same. Often, attempts to change a setting, such as a school or health care setting, are undermined by social regularities, especially role relationships, that were not changed. Only if those social regularities are altered is the system itself changed (Linney, 1986; Seidman, 1988).

The concept of social regularities complements the systems of Barker, Kelly and Moos, by calling attention to role relationships and to power. However, identifying social regularities requires rich understanding of a setting. Methods for doing this include naturalistic observation, case study, and ethnographic approaches. Once regularities are identified, quantitative methods may also be used. However they are studied, analyzing social regularities is important for understanding ecological context.

## Environmental Psychology

Environmental psychology, and interdisciplinary studies of environment and behavior, examine the influence of physical characteristics of a setting (especially built environments) on behavior (Saegert & Winkel, 1990; Stokols & Altman, 1987; Sundstrom, Bell, Busby, & Asmus, 1996; Timko, 1996). Environmental psychology in the United States arose at about the same historical time as community psychology. Its founders, unlike community psychology's, were primarily social psychologists interested in the physical environment and behavior. Yet both fields emphasize a shift of perspective from individual to individual-in-environment, and they overlap in several ways. The ecological psychology of Barker and colleagues is one example. Studies of the psychological effects of stressful environmental conditions, such as neighborhood noise, are another (Wandersman & Nation, 1998). Both fields emphasize research conducted in field settings and application of their concepts to social action. Shinn (1996a) and others have noted an increased interest in the physical environment in community psychology.

A major focus of environmental psychology is the study of proximity to environmental stressors, such as noise, air pollution, and crowded housing (Saegert & Winkel, 1990; Sundstrom et al., 1996). A community-level topic of research, of interest to both environmental and community psychologists, concerns the psychological effects of living near toxic disaster or waste sites. For instance, the psychological effects of two notable incidents from the late 1970s have been researched intensively and longitudinally. At Love Canal, near Niagara Falls, New York, residents discovered in 1977 that they were living above a chemical waste dump when birth defects began appearing. The effects of that disaster, and of citizen activism in response, were studied by A. Levine and associates (A. Levine, 1982; Stone & Levine, 1985). The Three Mile Island nuclear plant near Harrisburg, Pennsylvania, had a serious accident in which radiation was released in 1979; the stressful effects of this accident on nearby residents have been studied over time (Baum, 1987; Baum & Fleming, 1993). In both cases, uncertainty about the levels of actual exposure to radiation or toxic substances and inconsistencies in public statements by industry and government officials exacerbated the stressful effects of the event (see also Wandersman & Hallman, 1993). After the Three Mile Island incident, blood pressure remained elevated, immune-system functioning depressed, and symptoms of posttraumatic stress more common among nearby residents than in comparison samples. These effects did not dissipate for nearly 10 years (Baum & Fleming, 1993). Citizen response to technological disasters has become an area of convergence between environmental and community psychology (Rich, Edelstein, Hallman, & Wandersman, 1995).

Environmental psychologists also study the microsystem and individual effects of architectural features. Examples include studies of enclosed work spaces, windows, and aspects of housing design (Sundstrom et al., 1996), as well as the design of theme parks. For a personal example, consider arrangement of furniture in indoor spaces on your campus or in your workplace. The psychology department of one of the authors recently remodeled common space in the department offices, to redirect traffic flow and conversation areas away from the staff working. Students and faculty responded by regularly moving chairs to resemble the old arrangement, presumably to recreate the social spaces. In the department of another author, a common area for students has some seats in a circle, a few student carrels, snack machines and faculty mailboxes nearby, and is located between the hallway and psychology department offices. This creates a popular social space in which faculty and students can encounter each other outside of class, as well as a corner for study when the space is quiet. Yet the competition for space on campus is keen, and periodically this social space must be vigorously defended against administrative attempts to use it for offices or a classroom. These examples illustrate the relationships among microsystem, organizational, and physical factors, especially conflicts between work and social contact.

Environmental psychology is also becoming concerned with the interaction of physical, sociocultural and community variables. An example is the Community Household Model action research of Saegert and colleagues (Saegert & Winkel, 1990, 1996). These psychologists studied urban housing that had been abandoned by absentee landlords. The residents, mostly low-income women of color, pioneered an affordable approach to cooperative ownership. Effective citizen leaders emerged, particularly among women and elderly residents. Their efforts were energized by the importance of housing and of attachment to place (home and neighborhood) for women and families, which was documented in the research. The work of Kuo, Sullivan, Coley, and Brunson (1998) and Saegert and associates represents a convergence of ideas from environmental and community psychology.

***Contributions and Limitations***    By emphasizing the importance of the physical environment, environmental psychology complements the more social perspective of the other approaches. This perspective is useful at microsystem, neighborhood, and community levels. Although the focus of environmental psychology is distinct from that of community psychology, there are significant areas of overlap. We review further examples of these, concerning neighborhoods and stress, shortly.

## Comparing the Perspectives: An Example

To compare these five perspectives, consider a play to be performed by students in a high school setting. Each of the perspectives focuses on particular aspects of the production and suggests different ways to promote its artistic, social, or educational goals.

Imagine a high school play as a behavior setting. It has boundaries of time (for practices and performances) and space (an auditorium or theater). It has a standing pattern of behavior: During the performances, actors, audience, and others behave in predictable ways and locate themselves in predictable places. These behavior patterns indicate the program circuit or agenda: to perform a certain play to entertain an audience. The behavior setting is not necessarily tied to one physical place; it is a *behavior* setting.

If the setting is underpopulated, having fewer participants than roles or functions to be filled, the principles of ecological psychology would predict that setting members (director, cast, and crew) would seek to recruit additional help, and be likely to take on extra roles or tasks. They would engage in more deviation-countering circuits, teaching needed skills and keeping members involved. A person with no acting experience may be pressed to join the cast, developing new skills or revealing hidden talents. If, in contrast, the setting is optimally populated, vetoing circuits are likely; a member who cannot learn a role or task can be replaced easily. There will be auditions for parts, and only the best actors will be accepted. Other students will become marginalized.

If many students seek to be involved in the play, the staff could create the benefits of underpopulated settings by having two casts of different actors perform the play on alternate nights or stage a second production with different actors (Wicker, 1973).

How could the high school play be described in terms of Kelly's (Trickett, Kelly & Todd, 1972) ecological principles? By working together, the students are likely to build interdependent ties among themselves and with the director. This interdependence provides a basis for exchange of resources such as encouragement, instruction (especially from the director), and socializing. In addition, the play has interdependent relationships with other settings within the school. Its existence allows students who are not outstanding in other areas (e.g., academics, athletics) to feel connected with others, contribute to school life, and perhaps to shine, becoming recognized for their work (Elias, 1987). Having multiple casts (see above) would increase these interdependencies even more. The play is also a way for the school to connect with and be recognized in the community, as when community members attend performances.

Resources may be cycled between the play and the school as a whole. In a school in which drama is prized, money, facilities, student interest, and overall support will be plentiful; in one that does not prize drama, the play will receive little of these. Availability of resources also depends on the strength of interdependent relationships built between the drama faculty and administration, parents, school board members, and others. In turn, the play may generate a flow of resources from the community to the school. For instance, families, friends, and businesses may contribute resources such as props, costumes, food for intermission, and encouragement.

Adaptation for students involved in the play will involve learning skills in performance, set design, lighting, and so on. All members may have to help in publicizing and managing the production. These skills may also have adaptive value in the larger environments of school or community, for instance in future employment. In addition, the play will occur within a pattern of succession. It may be the first such production or the latest in a line of successful, well-attended productions; the latter may have more resources available, but also place higher expectations on the cast and crew. There may be a number of students who appeared in previous productions (low turnover) or everyone may be a neophyte (high turnover); this will affect many aspects of the play's production.

Kelly's ecological principles focus on resources in the setting, how these are created and exchanged, and how they are related to interdependent relationships, individual adaptation, and the history of the setting. To use these concepts, the director and students could discuss how to identify and obtain needed resources, and promote healthy interdependence and individual adaptation.

How could a high school play be assessed in terms of Moos' (1984; 1996) social climate dimensions? Members of the production (including director, actors, and crew) would complete questionnaires about their perceptions of the production environment. If they generally agree that play members were actively involved and supported each other well, and believe the director was supportive, scores will be high on Relationship dimension scales. Questions on that dimension might also assess conflict among members. The Personal Development dimension would concern whether participating in the play provided them opportunities to develop skills or experience personal growth. System Maintenance and Change items would measure their perceptions about how organized the production was, how much control the director exerted, the clarity of expectations for members' performance, and how much creativity was valued.

Moos' social climate concepts offer a measurable approach to understanding and changing the social dynamics of the production, including both its artistic task and social relationships. Widely shared perceptions, based on group scores, probably indicate qualities of the environment. Different perceptions among subgroups (director vs. actors; men vs. women) would indicate a need to understand what aspects of the play as a setting led to those differences. Conclusions about social climate could be used in planning the next production.

What social regularities (Seidman, 1988) and role relationships are involved here? One concerns the roles of director and actors. The director, usually a faculty member, will assume a powerful role. Choosing the play, making casting decisions, coaching actors, and assuming responsibility for the quality of performance are all functions that the director may perform. With inexperienced actors, that assumption of power may make sense. However, each of these functions could be shared with experienced actors to promote their skill development and personal growth. Such altering of social regularities could also mobilize resources such as hidden leadership talents among the students. It changes the usual role relationship in schools but promotes the educational and perhaps artistic value of the production. (Indeed, using students as directors and in other authority roles seems more common in drama than in other areas of many schools.) The concept of social regularities calls

| TABLE 5.2 | KEY ECOLOGICAL CHARACTERISTICS OF SOCIAL ENVIRONMENTS |
| --- | --- |

**Barker: Behavior Setting Theory**
  Behavior setting (time, place, program); Optimally populated, underpopulated settings

**Kelly: Ecological Principles**
  Interdependence; Cycling of resources; Adaptation; Succession

**Moos: Social Climate Dimensions**
  Relationship; Personal development; System maintenance and change

**Seidman: Social Regularities**
  Role relationships

**Environmental Psychology**
  Environmental stressors; Architectural features; Interaction of physical features and community factors

attention to power and resources predictably invested in social roles in the setting, and how these may be changed to promote the development of individuals or settings.

Finally, an environmental psychologist would examine the physical setting and how it strengthens or interferes with the performance. This might concern temperature, seating, acoustics, and sight lines from audience to stage. The design of the stage set and lighting involves similar concerns. If the play is unlikely to draw a large crowd or is best performed with greater audience involvement, a small space would be preferred to large auditorium. Audience participation, if desired, could be promoted by altering the room or seating. Actors in character could meet patrons at the door and create an atmosphere of immersion in the play and its setting. An environmental psychology perspective focuses on how aspects of the physical environment structure and limit behavior, and how these could be manipulated to promote the social or artistic goals of the play.

Key concepts from the ecological frameworks of Barker, Kelly, Moos, Seidman and the environmental psychology perspective are listed in Table 5.2.

# LINKING NEIGHBORHOOD CONTEXT WITH PSYCHOLOGICAL OUTCOMES

Understanding ecological context is often made easier by focusing on one level of analysis. In this section, we turn to empirical research on linkages between neighborhood and individual life. How do neighborhood environmental stressors affect individual development and functioning?

Wandersman and Nation (1998) reviewed research on urban neighborhood stressors and individual mental health. They described three conceptual models that illustrate ways of thinking about how neighborhood ecology affects individuals negatively: structural characteristics, neighborhood disorder, and environmental stressors. Each model identifies

| TABLE 5.3 | MODELS LINKING ECOLOGICAL CONTEXT AND INDIVIDUAL OUTCOMES | | |

| Model | Examples of Contextual Factors | Examples of Mediating Processes | Examples of Outcome |
| --- | --- | --- | --- |
| Structural characteristics (social) | Socioeconomic status, residential turnover | Neighborhood social ties, support; personal, social coping resources | Child maltreatment, delinquency, and mental disorders |
| Neighborhood disorder | Physical and social incivilities | Defensible space | Fear of crime, anxiety, and depression |
| Environmental stressors (physical) | Noise, crowding | Coping, habituation | Academic, personal problems |

Note: Sources were Belsky (1993), Simons et al. (1996), and Wandersman and Nation (1998).

stressful aspects of neighborhood context, individual outcomes that are affected by that context, and mediating processes that connect context and individual adjustment. One note to remember: This research has focused on the negative effects of urban neighborhoods, not on their strengths (Wandersman & Nation, 1998). Urban neighborhoods also have strengths that need to be understood, as we discuss later.

Table 5.3 summarizes the three models.

## Structural Characteristics Model

This model concerns contextual factors based on societal or neighborhood social structure. It is grounded in correlations between social–structural characteristics of neighborhoods (such as average socioeconomic status or proportion of single-parent families) and the prevalence of mental health problems there (Wandersman & Nation, 1998). Another structural finding is that in neighborhoods with high residential turnover, juvenile delinquency is more common (Wandersman & Nation, 1998). This research has a long history, going back to the Chicago school of ecological sociology (cf. Bernard, 1973; S. B. Sarason, 1974). In contemporary psychological versions of this approach, neighborhood characteristics are hypothesized to affect mental health status through *mediating processes* such as increased psychological stress, limited resources, and breakdowns in neighborhood social organization and support. For instance, low income families by definition have fewer economic resources and thus are more likely to be adversely affected by economically stressful events such as job loss, illness, or unexpected expenses. If neighborhood support is also limited, these stressors have greater effects.

Structural factors are not limited to cities. In one rural study, community disadvantage (computed from community rates of unemployment, receiving of government assistance, and proportion of population with less than high school education) predicted rates of conduct problems among adolescent boys, while the proportion of single-parent households in the community predicted conduct problems among adolescent girls (Simons, Johnson, Beaman, Conger, & Whitbeck, 1996).

## Mediating Processes

Obviously, not everyone facing socioeconomic or other disadvantages, or living in a neighborhood where many others do, develops mental health problems. Studies of neighborhood structural variables also show that mediating factors are important. For instance, in low-income urban neighborhoods where social ties and support among residents are stronger, child maltreatment is less common than in socioeconomically similar neighborhoods where these supports are weaker (Garbarino & Kostelny, 1992). In chapter 8, we describe resources, individual and social, that can lessen the effect of macrosystem, socioeconomic, and community risk factors. Families, peers, and religious–spiritual resources are examples of such mediating factors.

A mediating process identified in environmental psychology is the attractiveness of common or public spaces in urban neighborhoods or elsewhere. Kuo et al. (1998), in a study of a large public housing project in Chicago, found that greenness, the presence of trees and other vegetation, in public spaces was statistically associated with use of these common spaces and with formation of social ties among residents. Moreover, greenness and neighborhood social ties were positively associated with sense of safety and adjustment to the neighborhood.

## Neighborhood Disorder Model

The second conceptual model (Wandersman & Nation, 1998) focuses on *incivilities:* physical and social signs of neighborhood disruption. It has been applied mainly to the study of crime-related outcomes. Physical incivilities include abandoned or dilapidated buildings, litter, vandalism, and graffiti. Social incivilities include public drunkenness, gang activities, and drug trade. The Block Environment Inventory (D. D. Perkins & Taylor, 1996) measures physical and social incivilities. Trained observers complete the inventory by visiting a city block to observe incivilities. According to the neighborhood model, incivilities threaten residents' sense of defensible (safe) space for themselves or their families. Threats to defensible space, in turn, increase citizen fear of crime and other psychological symptoms. Thus perception of defensible space and fear of crime are mediating processes between neighborhood disorder and individual mental health.

D. D. Perkins and Taylor (1996; Taylor & Perkins, 1989) reported data supporting this model from studies of urban neighborhoods. Residents of city blocks with greater signs of disorder (especially physical incivilities) tended to have greater fear of crime, more depression, and more anxiety than those with fewer signs of disorder. Fear of crime also represented an important mediating process between these neighborhood characteristics and mental health. It was associated with elevated depression and anxiety even when stressful life events and daily hassles were controlled (Taylor & Perkins, 1989).

## Environmental Stress Model

This model focuses on the neighborhood physical environment, rather than the social–structural variables emphasized in the structural characteristics model. A sizable body of research in environmental psychology demonstrates how ambient, ongoing, environmental stressors such as overcrowding, noise, and exposure to pollution affect individual mental health and development (Wandersman & Nation, 1998). Chronic noise, for example, has been shown to be associated with lower levels of academic performance among children in a school adjacent to train tracks (Bronzaft & McCarthy, 1975). Saegert (1982) reported that children living in high-density, large apartment buildings had more behavior problems, higher levels of anxiety and hyperactivity, and lower academic achievement than similar-income children living in less dense and smaller buildings. Residents habituate to the stimulus and/or learn to cope with the ambient stressor, but they still experience its long-term effects.

## Strengthening Neighborhoods and Families

Wandersman and Nation (1998) also reviewed a number of strategies shown to be effective ways for communities and families to limit the negative effects of neighborhood context. These include promoting the existing strengths of the community, such as encouraging informal neighboring and strengthening existing social support systems for residents (e.g., parents). Clinical interventions that link family therapy with community resources of jobs, child care, and other resources are also helpful. Interventions designed to prevent problems are also promising (see chaps. 9–11). Working with community organizations such as block associations can help address neighborhood problems and improve neighborhood life (see chaps. 12–13).

## Contributions and Limitations

The structural characteristics, neighborhood disorder, and environmental stress models were developed to address different research questions and purposes. Yet they converge to illustrate the powerful effects of neighborhood context on individual lives. These three models emphasize the negative, stressful effects of some urban neighborhoods more than the strengths there (Wandersman & Nation, 1998). Yet physical features (e.g., greenery that attracts people to public spaces), neighborhood organizations, and informal social ties can provide positive community strengths in urban neighborhoods (Belsky, 1993; Kuo et al., 1998; Wandersman & Nation, 1998). A challenge for future research is to study strengths in urban and other neighborhoods in more depth (e.g., Saegert & Winkel, 1996).

# CHANGING THE ECOLOGICAL CONTEXT

Can environments be created or altered to enhance their members' quality of life? In this section, we describe three different instances for which the answer has been affirmative: an alternative community setting for persons with mental illness, an innovative approach to easing stressful school transitions, and a planned town.

## The Community Lodge: Creating an Alternative Setting

Changing existing settings is usually not easy, even when one can identify the contextual variables that need to be addressed. Settings, social systems, and individuals within them generally resist change and try to preserve the status quo. The concepts of interdependence, adaptation, and social regularities suggest some ways in which this happens. Another approach to improving quality of life for individuals is to create a new setting, which community psychologists term an *alternative setting*.

The Community Lodge (Fairweather, 1979, 1994; Fairweather et al., 1969) was an early influence on community psychology and community mental health. Yet some of its principal elements have never been widely adopted in the mental health system, at least in the United States. Those elements happen to be the aspects that pose the most interesting challenges to social regularities of mental health care. Thus, the Community Lodge movement exemplifies alternative settings.

The Community Lodge idea began in the psychiatric hospital setting of the 1950s. After working in psychiatric hospital care for some time, Fairweather and others recognized that the context and demands of the hospital did not promote the aim of independent community living for persons with serious mental illness. In hospital settings, the patient has few opportunities for decision making and autonomy. "Good behavior" usually means following orders. In contrast, once discharged the individual needs to take initiative, make independent decisions, keep track of time, and form supportive relationships with others. The social regularities are different.

Fairweather's group developed inpatient group treatments that promoted the ability of persons with even the most serious mental disorders to make decisions with the help of peers and to prepare for living outside the hospital. However, even those treatments were not enough; those persons, once released, still returned to the hospital at too high a rate after too short a period in the community. The problem, Fairweather and associates realized, was that there was no community setting, set of roles, or adequate support for the person when released from the hospital. Altering regularities within the hospital was not enough.

Fairweather and associates thus created an alternative community setting based on a different set of role relationships among professional staff and patients. The Community Lodge is based on supportive peer relationships that make community living possible even for those coping with serious mental illness. Community Lodges have several distinctive features. The most important and surprising one is that Lodge residents govern themselves. Professionals serve only as consultants and eventually phase out of professional contact. Lodge members assume responsibility for monitoring each other for taking medication, behaving responsibly within and outside the Lodge, and related issues. Lodges decide for themselves, as a group, whether to admit new members or to dismiss members (which seldom happens). Lodges often have an associated business, so that they can offer suitable work for residents and be self-supporting (Fairweather, 1979, 1994).

The first Community Lodge was a group of men released from a Veterans' Administration psychiatric hospital in California. Their experiences offer some insight into the process of creating an alternative setting (Fairweather, 1979, pp. 316–322 and 327–333). An old motel was leased and refurbished for their Lodge. After visiting the new Lodge several times, the members were discharged from the hospital and moved in. After several trial and error experiences, Lodge members became self-governing. They developed Lodge rules that, for instance, made it acceptable to discuss symptoms of mental illness with other Lodge members, but not with neighbors. The researchers were surprised that some of the previously most seriously ill persons became active members of the community.

With consultation, Lodge members established a janitorial and gardening business, and eventually became economically self-supporting. Finally, they felt confident enough that they ended their professional relationship with Fairweather, although infrequent social contacts continued (Fairweather, 1994). A number of Community Lodges now exist in the United States.

In controlled studies using volunteers randomly assigned to a Lodge or to ordinary psychiatric aftercare, Fairweather (1979) and Fairweather et al. (1969) demonstrated that Lodge members, although similar to the control group on background variables, relapsed less often, spent fewer days in the hospital when they did, and spent more days employed than the controls. These differences persisted for 5 years of follow-up studies. Moreover, the Community Lodge method was less expensive than traditional community aftercare.

By demonstrating the effectiveness of community-based housing and economic ventures, the Community Lodge studies have contributed to the expansion of mental health care in communities since the 1960s. Yet their key element, self-government by Lodge members, has seldom been adopted (Fairweather, 1979). Perhaps that is because it undermines a social regularity many professionals believe is essential for helping persons with mental illness: professional supervision and control. As Fairweather often has pointed out, the Community Lodge findings indicate otherwise. Although professionals are involved in the founding of a Lodge, their involvement is defined as consultation and phased out over time.

## STEP: Altering Social Regularities in School

Think back to your first day of high school. Did you have these concerns: finding classes and your locker, getting lost, worrying about academic requirements and demanding teachers, staying in contact with your old friends in a bigger and more complicated setting, making new friends, avoid hazing or harassment from older students, and finding a way to "fit in" in this new environment?

The School Transitional Environment Program (STEP; Felner & Adan, 1988) was designed to address issues such as these. STEP specifically alters key social regularities characteristic of American public junior and senior high schools. These school transitions are clearly difficult. For most students, academic performance, involvement in school activities, social support from school staff, and self-esteem drop during these transitions (Reyes, Gillock, & Kobus, 1994; Seidman, Allen, Aber, Mitchell, & Feinman, 1994).

The STEP program has two essential components: "(a) reorganizing the regularities of the school environment to reduce the degree of flux and complexity of the social and physical setting that the student confronts; and (b) restructuring the roles of homeroom teachers and guidance personnel" (Felner & Adan, 1988, p. 114). To address the first component, the STEP program clusters students in groups that are assigned to take many of their primary academic subjects and homeroom together. These academic subjects are offered in locations in close proximity to the homerooms and by a core group of teachers who work together as a team. These simple modifications facilitate forming multiple new peer relationships. They also facilitate students' sense of comfort with the school environment. These effects are especially salient in large school buildings with multiple feeder schools.

The second component of the STEP program involves redefinition of roles for the homeroom teacher. STEP homeroom teachers serve as the primary link between the school and the student's family. The STEP homeroom teacher assumes many tasks and responsibilities of the guidance counselor (e.g., contacting the family if the student is absent, meeting with parents, and serving as a central referral point for a range of issues affecting the student).

In the initial experimental trial of the STEP program, a randomly selected group of ninth graders participating in the STEP program were compared with a matched comparison sample of students in the same school. Felner and Adan (1988) reported significantly lower school absentee rates and higher grades for STEP program students at the end of the ninth grade. STEP students felt more positively about the school environment, considering it to be more stable, supportive, organized, and understandable. STEP students' self-concept scores remained stable over the year, while those of students not in STEP declined. STEP teachers also reported higher levels of satisfaction with teaching. By the end of 10th grade, fewer STEP students had dropped out of school.

Replications of the STEP program in junior high and middle schools, with suburban and rural samples, showed similar results (Felner & Adan, 1988). Thus STEP seems to reduce the stressful effects of school transition, at several different grade levels and in varying locales.

## Seaside: A Planned Town

Seaside, Florida, is a planned seasonal–residential community that has been widely recognized for its physical features designed to increase residents' neighboring and sense of community (Plas & Lewis, 1996). For instance, town codes require front porches and low picket fences for each house, and town design emphasizes walkways to the town center and beach while strictly limiting automobile use. Businesses are accessible on foot from anywhere in the community. The code encourages diversity of architecture as long as features encouraging neighboring are maintained. These features were based on study of older, established communities with a strong sense of community (Plas & Lewis, 1996).

Plas and Lewis (1996) studied Seaside to determine if the architectural and town-planning features were related to neighboring and sense of community. They conducted naturalistic observation of physical features and neighboring behavior. They also interviewed residents and visitors (mainly White, relatively affluent families) and employees of town businesses (more representative of the U.S. population in race and income). Both groups praised Seaside's neighborliness and sense of community and considered these to be related to its physical environmental features. This occurs despite the fact that most of Seaside's residents are seasonal, and suggests the strength of the physical features in encouraging forming of neighborly ties even with relative strangers.

Seaside has quickly become so popular that owning a home there is economically out of reach for most of the U.S. population, and its seasonal nature is not representative of most communities. Yet many of its physical features (e.g., front porches) are based on traditional designs, and others, such as limitations on auto traffic and creating pedestrian walkways, can be adopted widely. Seaside's architecture creates shared public spaces that many neighborhoods, even urban blocks, already have in some form. (The urban greenery studied by Kuo et al. (1998) represents one example.) These physical features represent promising ideas for building cohesive communities in the future.

## CONCLUDING THEMES

Three themes run through much of the theory, research, and action we have described in this chapter. Two of these themes are related concepts: interdependence and resources. These are, of course, explicit in Kelly's ecological perspective (Trickett, Kelly & Todd, 1972) but are implicit in other views. Interdependence concerns the ways in which individuals in a group, setting, or community are related to, and even dependent on, each other. The concept of resources involves a search for existing material and social strengths in a setting, and understanding how these are or can be exchanged to promote the well-being of individuals and the setting. A recognition of social interdependence and of local resources is an undercurrent in the descriptions of life in Midwest by Barker (1968) and colleagues, who seemed to delight in small-town life. Moos' (1994) social climate scales measure relationships and support among setting inhabitants. Environmental psychology draws attention to the interdependence of physical and social environments, and to the ways in which physical environments can provide resources for social interdependence (e.g., when urban greenery promotes neighboring) or threaten resources (e.g., natural or technological disasters). Seidman's (1988) social regularity concept concerns interdependence in role relationships and how these shape access to resources and power. The empirical models of how neighborhood characteristics influence individual functioning (Wandersman & Nation, 1998) also indicate the importance of interdependence. Neighborhoods provide not only stressors but also resources for neighborhood life and individual well-being. The concepts of interdependence and resources lie at the core of the ways that community psychologists think about ecological context.

The final theme reflects the role for community psychologists proposed at the Swampscott conference: the participant–conceptualizer in community life (Bennett et al., 1966). In this chapter, we first introduced five conceptual models that can be used to describe or analyze settings at many levels of analysis. Then we reviewed empirical research on neighborhood influences on individual life. These concepts and research findings represent the conceptualizer side of the Swampscott vision. Finally, we reviewed three examples of community initiatives that actually altered environments to promote individual quality of life, in contexts ranging from classrooms to communities. Those examples represent participation in communities while also documenting program effects through qualitative and quantitative community research.

The concept of ecological context is central to community psychology. In many ways, the entire field is about understanding how contexts influence individuals, and about how to alter contexts to enhance individuals' lives. In that sense, most of the remaining chapters of this text elaborate on or extend this one. That will become apparent as we take up concepts of diversity, community, and coping in the next three chapters, as well as when we consider prevention and promotion and community change in later chapters.

# CHAPTER SUMMARY

**1.** *Ecological context* consists of the physical and social aspects of environments that influence individual behavior, well-being, and development. Examples of this include the impact of neighborhood, school climate, and family.

**2.** Community psychologists seek to understand the interplay of ecological context and individual life, including *person–environment fit,* and to find ways to alter contexts to enhance individuals' quality of life.

**3.** Barker's *ecological psychology* was developed to study social behavior in everyday context. Barker and associates proposed the concept of *behavior setting,* comprised of a physical place, time, and program or standing pattern of behavior.

**4.** Barker and associates also proposed the idea that individual behavior is influenced by the ratio of the number of available roles and the number of persons in a behavior setting. *Optimally populated settings* engage only some persons, leaving others marginal. Somewhat *underpopulated settings* require participation from all inhabitants to fill needed roles, and thus contribute to greater skill development and mutual commitment among inhabitants.

**5.** Kelly proposed four ecological principles for describing contexts in community psychology. *Interdependence* refers to the extent of interconnection among persons. *Cycling of resources* calls attention to how tangible and intangible resources are defined, created, exchanged, and conserved. *Adaptation* refers to the demands made on individuals by the setting, and how individuals cope with those demands. *Succession* refers to how settings are created, maintained, and changed over time.

**6.** Moos developed the idea of measuring the *social climate* of environments, through the perceptions of their members. In Moos's approach, social climates have three basic dimensions: Relationship, Personal Development, and System Maintenance and Change. Social climate scales have been related in research to many measures of individual behavior and well-being.

**7.** Seidman developed the concept of a *social regularity,* a predictable pattern of social behavior in a setting, often a role relationship such as teacher–student.

**8.** *Environmental psychology* concerns the relationships between the physical environment and individual or social behavior. Topics related to community psychology include environmental stress, architectural features and behavior, and the relationship of these to community factors.

**9.** Wandersman and Nation reviewed research on neighborhood contexts and individual functioning. They defined three models that have dominated research on how these are related. The *structural characteristics* model emphasizes demographic characteristics of neighborhoods such as socioeconomic status. *Mediating factors* such as social support buffer the relationship between these variables and individual functioning. The *neighborhood disorder* model focuses on neighborhood physical and social incivilities and fear of crime. The *environmental stressor* model emphasizes ongoing, ambient stressors in the environment such as noise and crowding.

**10.** Community psychologists are especially concerned with how ecological contexts can be altered to improve individuals' quality of life. The concept of *alternative setting* is important, in which those dissatisfied with an existing setting work together to create a new setting that provides a different ecological context. We described three examples of interventions to alter ecological context: the Community Lodge as an alternative setting for persons with serious mental illness, the STEP program that altered social regularities of schools to enhance student academic achievement, and Seaside, a planned town that enhanced neighbor interaction.

**11.** Three themes that run through the chapter are the concepts of interdependence and resources, and the community psychologist's role of participant–conceptualizer.

# BRIEF EXERCISES

**1.** Choose two classes you have taken (at any level of education), one that you enjoyed and one you did not. Try to choose classes that are at similar levels of difficulty.

Describe how these two classes differed as behavior settings. List as many differences as you can, then list the variables these differences represent (e.g., reliance on lecture vs. group activities, competition vs. cooperation among students, differences in physical classroom or size of class, skills needed for effective adaptation, vetoing vs. deviation-countering circuits, social regularities).

Explain your variables to a classmate, to check the clarity of your reasoning. Find the Classroom Environment Scale (CES; Moos & Trickett, 1987), or use the description of those scales in the chapter, and compare your variables with those on the CES.

Finally, consider that different students learn best in different types of class environments. For the two classes you described, suggest the types of students who might learn well in each class.

**2.** Think back over your life experiences, and choose an optimally populated behavior setting, in which members equaled or outnumbered available roles, and an underpopulated setting, in which roles outnumbered members. (If you have no immediate ideas, start by analyzing your high school along the lines of Barker and Gump [1964], *Big school, small school.*) Describe the two settings, especially their differences. Then answer the questions below.

- Did the optimally populated setting generate more marginal members who were not involved or committed to the setting (as Barker and Gump would predict)? Were vetoing circuits common?
- Did the underpopulated setting "pull" its members into roles through which they developed new skills, or greater self-esteem? Did it generate a greater sense of involvement or commitment among members? Were deviation-countering circuits common?
- Which setting was more enjoyable for you as a member? Why?

**3.** Review the two articles on physical environment and neighborly contact cited in the chapter: the planned town of Seaside (Plas & Lewis, 1996), and the study of greenery in an urban setting (Kuo et al., 1998).

Walk through a residential neighborhood (at home, or elsewhere). The best time to do this is early evenings in warm weather. Look for the features that Seaside emulated: front porches where people sit, pedestrian walkways and sidewalks, and streets with little traffic. Do these features encourage saying hello, conversation, or other neighborly contacts, even with people you don't know? Does the lack of them discourage such contact? Are there other features that encourage contact?

Visit common spaces such as parks or playgrounds, no matter how small. Do they have vegetation such as grass and trees? Does the greenery encourage neighborly contacts? Are there other features that do so?

# RECOMMENDED READINGS

Barker, R. (1968). *Ecological psychology.* Stanford, CA: Stanford University Press. Revised and extended in Schoggen, P. (1989). *Behavior settings.* Stanford, CA: Stanford University Press.

Barker, R. and Associates. (1978). *Habitats, environments, and human behavior.* San Francisco: Jossey-Bass.

Wicker, A. (1979). Ecological psychology: Some recent and prospective developments. *American Psychologist, 34,* 755–765.

> These are classic sources on ecological psychology. Chapters in Barker and Associates (1978) give an overview.

Trickett, E. J., Kelly, J. G., & Todd, D. M. (1972). The social environment of the school: Guidelines for individual change and organizational redevelopment. In S. Golann & C. Eisdorfer (Eds.), *Handbook of community mental health* (pp. 331–406). New York: Appleton-Century-Crofts. (See especially pp. 391–400.)

Vincent, T., & Trickett, E. (1983). Preventive intervention and the human context: Ecological approaches to environmental assessment and change. In R. Felner, L. Jason, J. Moritsugu & S. Farber, (Eds.), *Preventive psychology: Theory, research and practice* (pp. 67–86). New York: Pergamon.

> Each describes Kelly's ecological concepts and their applications to community psychology.

Moos, R. (1984). Context and coping: Toward a unifying conceptual framework. *American Journal of Community Psychology, 12,* 5–25.

> This is a classic, succinct overview of social climate concepts and how they are related to individual well-being.

Seidman, E. (1988). Back to the future, community psychology: Unfolding a theory of social intervention. *American Journal of Community Psychology, 16,* 3–24.

> This article describes the derivation and examples of the social regularity concept.

Shinn, M. (Ed). (1996b). Ecological assessment. *American Journal of Community Psychology* [Special issue], *24* (1).

Wandersman, A., & Nation, M. (1998). Urban neighborhoods and mental health: Psychological contributions to understanding toxicity, resilience and interventions. *American Psychologist, 53,* 647–656.

> A review of research on neighborhoods and individual well-being.

This article appears in journals in the InfoTrac College Edition on-line library available from Wadsworth.

# ECOLOGICAL ANALYSIS
## Analyzing a Setting

Chapter 5 presents ecological concepts and research at a number of levels of analysis. In this exercise, you will analyze a setting at the microsystem or organization level.

To begin, choose a behavior setting. As defined by Barker and associates, a behavior setting must have:

- a physical time and place,
- clear boundaries of space or time to separate it from other settings,
- a standing pattern of behavior.

This may involve a microsystem or organization; choose a behavior setting other than your immediate family. Choose a setting carefully: one that you know well from personal experience, preferably one that you can observe now. You may choose a setting from your past experience if you remember it very well. Choose one that involves at least 10 people (an arbitrary rule of thumb to ensure enough roles and members to analyze). Some examples include a class, student organization, playground, residence hall wing or unit, small workplace, social club, or religious congregation (or group within it such as a choir or class).

Analyze the setting in terms of each section below. Observing the setting again is a good idea. Doing this with a friend is often more fun.

**Physical Setting**   Describe the setting's natural, architectural, and furnishing features: its location, size, boundaries, arrangement of space, furniture (and whether it is movable), pathways of travel, greenery (if outdoors). At what times is it used? Is it ever crowded, or empty? Can you describe its "atmosphere" as a physical setting?

Can you suggest useful changes in the physical features of the setting?

**Behavior Setting**   This part uses concepts drawn from Barker's theory of behavior settings.

Describe the setting's program or standing pattern(s) of behavior. Be as detailed as you can. How many persons are involved? Is there high turnover of persons (e.g., a retail store, playground) or low turnover (e.g., first-grade class)?

Define the goal circuits of the setting. That is, describe the most common goals that a person might pursue in this setting. Another way to think about this: What reinforcements do persons seek in this setting?

Finally, consider how this setting is related to other behavior settings. Is it part of a larger organization? Does it relate directly to other behavior settings?

***Underpopulated and Optimally Populated Settings***    Does the setting seem optimally populated or underpopulated? Slightly or very much so?

If the setting seems optimally populated, does it exclude a number of persons who would otherwise be likely to participate (vetoing circuits)? Does it tend to involve individuals only in specialized roles?

If the setting seems underpopulated, does it involve persons in a variety of roles? Does anyone play two or more roles? Are roles left unfilled? How actively does it recruit participants? Do persons in the setting take time to teach members how to play their roles (deviation-countering circuits)? How strong is the commitment of setting participants to this setting?

Can you suggest useful changes in these practices to create more of the benefits of underpopulated settings?

***Population/Structural Characteristics***    Describe setting participants in demographic terms, by gender, race, age, or other categories. How do these demographic characteristics influence how the setting works? For instance, if members of the setting are mainly persons of a certain age, or of one gender, how does that affect the atmosphere of the setting?

***Social Regularities***    Can you identify one social regularity or predictable pattern of behavior to analyze (recall the example of teachers asking questions more than students). What role relationships does the regularity involve? (For instance, consider the interlocking roles of teacher–student, boss–employee, organization officer–member, staff member–patient.) Are there differences in power based on this regularity?

Can you suggest changes in social regularities to pursue the setting's mission or purpose better?

***Social Climate***    If your setting is one for which Moos (1994) and associates have developed a social climate scale (see your instructor about this), complete the scale. If you can, find other setting members to complete it as well, and compute the mean and range of scores for each of the subscales. If a scale is not available, review the discussion in the chapter and decide on social climate concepts that can be used to describe the setting.

What changes would you suggest to improve the setting's social climate?

***Ecological Principles***    This section concerns Kelly's ecological principles. You may be able to use information from other sections here.

How are setting participants interdependent? How frequently do they interact? (See your answers on social climate relationship dimensions above.) How could interdependence be enhanced in this setting? Would that be desirable?

What resources, tangible or intangible, exist in the setting? Intangible examples might include knowledge, skills, emotional support, time, energy, commitment, vision for the future, and rituals or traditions of the setting. How are these resources cycled or exchanged in the setting? How could resources be better cultivated or used in the setting?

What demands does this setting place on participants (adaptation)? What skills are needed for participants to adapt to this setting? How can these skills be learned? How could the setting promote learning of these skills?

How has this setting changed over time (succession)? What characteristics of this setting have remained stable over time? What do you foresee for the future of this setting?

***Summary***    Which of the sections above generates the most interesting information about the setting? Are there important things about the setting that are not covered in these questions and concepts? What are the most important things you have learned through this exercise?

# UNDERSTANDING HUMAN DIVERSITY

## OPENING EXERCISE

What is human diversity? Let's begin by performing a simple exercise to place yourself in the "diversity of contexts" (Trickett, 1996) in your life. Describing these contexts will not reflect all of what makes you a unique individual, but it will help you to understand some of the cultural and social forces that influence you every day. If some of the influences that we discuss seem trivial to you, remember the nine-dot diagram in chapter 1. The assumptions that operate outside our awareness are often the most powerful.

*Are you a woman or man?* How does this influence, for instance, your everyday behavior, your life and career planning, or your approach to friendships or intimate relationships? Does your gender, for instance, make it easier or more difficult to discern your own emotions and express them to others? Does it affect your ideas of the importance of relationships in your life?

*What is your nationality or culture? What is your first language?* How do these factors affect your values, life and career planning, family relationships, friendships? If you had to describe your culture in a dozen words, what words would you choose, and why? How much experience have you had with other cultures?

*How would you describe your race and ethnicity?* How does it influence your life, interactions with strangers or friends, language and speech, life and career planning, choice of college, friendships? How many meaningful relationships do you have with others of a different race or ethnicity? What are the most important contributions that your racial or ethnic group has made to your society? (It's OK if your answers here overlap with those to the question above.)

*How do socioeconomic factors affect your life?* How did they affect the nature and quality of education in your home community? Your choice of college, or experiences in college? Has your education been affected by greater or lesser access at home to books, computers, travel, or other educational advantages? Has a need to hold a time-consuming job, or another economic stressor, interfered with your schooling? How many of your friends come from socioeconomic circumstances different from yours?

*What is your age?* How does it affect your everyday life, friendships, life and career planning, and other choices?

*What is your sexual orientation?* Have you ever thought of having a sexual orientation? Has understanding your orientation ever been difficult for you? How does your orientation affect your everyday life, friendships, life and career planning, and other choices?

*Do you have a religious or spiritual belief, practice or background?* If so, how does your personal spirituality influence your values, daily life, and relationships with others? Are you a member of an organized religion or congregation? If so, what role does that faith community play in your life? Have your life and career plans, or choice of college, been influenced by your spirituality or religion? Even if you are not actively religious or spiritual, do you have a religious background that still influences you?

153

We could write similar paragraphs about physical or mental ability/disability, rural/suburban/urban background, or other forms of diversity that influence individual's everyday lives.

We ask these questions to indicate some themes of this chapter, and to "shift the center" (Andersen & Collins, 1998) of your thinking. We sometimes encounter among students and others the assumption that "diversity" means the study of people other than a European American, middle class, heterosexual norm. Yet everyone has a culture, a race, a gender, a sexual orientation, and a place somewhere on each dimension of human diversity. One goal of this chapter is for you to be able to understand dimensions of human diversity, and to understand your place, and others' places, on each dimension.

Moreover, "shifting the center" involves releasing the idea that one group represents the norm on any dimension. Community psychology takes the perspective of *pluralism,* that no culture represents a norm or superior position. This perspective does not define a difference as a deficit, but searches for cultural, community, and human strengths revealed in human diversity (Trickett et al., 1994). That is part of what the value of respect for diversity means in community psychology.

## WHAT ARE THE KEY POINTS OF THIS CHAPTER?

How do we address issues of human diversity in this chapter? First, we describe important dimensions of diversity for community research and action. Second, we discuss differences between individualistic and collectivistic cultures of the world. *Culture* does not simply mean customs or language. It involves fundamentally different ways of defining ourselves and our relations to others.

However, many forms of diversity are not simply cultural. They also involve issues of social power; some forms of diversity are respected and others demeaned or even targeted for violence. We discuss these issues in terms of oppression. Next, we discuss how individuals adapt to cultural and oppressive forces and how they define themselves in relation to society. Finally, we consider how these issues are related to community research and action, including what cultural competence means for community psychologists.

Throughout this chapter, we emphasize the theme that understanding human diversity means studying the lives of others and ourselves from a pluralistic perspective while recognizing how our own values affect our perspective (see Box 6.1).

The meaning of this chapter is dependent on one's context and experiences. As a team of authors, we invite you then to read on, sample the ideas here, measure their meaning against your own experiences, and seek broader experiences that educate you further in issues of human diversity.

## KEY DIMENSIONS OF HUMAN DIVERSITY FOR COMMUNITY PSYCHOLOGY

We now describe the most important dimensions of human diversity for community psychology. The nine dimensions we emphasize here certainly do not exhaust all the forms of

## 6.1  *The Perspective of This Chapter's Primary Author*

To the reader it may seem ironic at best to learn that the primary author of this chapter on human diversity is a White heterosexual man, a university professor who has enjoyed a privileged life in many ways and who has lived almost all his life in rural U.S. (mostly Appalachian) towns. Having come to write this chapter by a mixture of circumstance and choice, that irony is not lost on me. Yet I have had good teachers on issues of diversity, many of them not in academia. I have lived for short periods in multiethnic cities, including an inner-city neighborhood. I have a viewpoint on issues of human diversity, particularly oppression, that is based in my experiences, and on participation in efforts to dismantle forms of oppression.

A limitation of my perspective is that most of my experience with racism, for instance, has concerned two groups: European Americans and African Americans. My life experience is centered in the United States, a further limitation in understanding world cultures. My perspective on human diversity is still developing, and has strengths, drawbacks, and omissions. However, that perspective is supplemented by those of my co-authors and of the reviewers of our prepublication drafts. All of these sources have broadened and deepened this chapter.—James H. Dalton

---

human diversity, but they do represent dimensions frequently addressed in community psychology research and action. The nine dimensions are listed in Table 6.1.

## Culture

"*Cultural diversity*" has become a buzzword as the world's societies have become more interdependent. The term *culture* has been stretched to refer to nation-states, ethnic and religious groups, and even social institutions such as schools and corporations. The concept of culture also is often used interchangeably with terms such as *race, ethnicity,* and *nationality* (Betancourt & Lopez, 1993, p. 630).

What, then, is *culture,* and how are cultures diverse? After decades of debate, anthropologists and other social scientists have not settled on a single definition of culture, but certain key elements are identifiable (Lonner, 1994). It does not explain anything to say that "Astrid behaves in a certain way because she is Swedish" (Lonner, 1994, p. 234). To understand cultural influences on Astrid's actions in a certain situation, we need to specify a Swedish cultural element that shapes her actions in that situation. The importance of that element must be reflected in other aspects of Swedish culture. These might include a behavioral norm taught to children, a tradition reflected in literature or in religious or political documents, a concept for which Swedish language has a word, a folk saying, or other cultural expression. Shared language, social roles and norms, values, and attitudes are particularly important to psychologists (Triandis, 1994). As a rule of thumb, culture is often expressed in what the society or group seeks to transmit (e.g., by education or example) to younger generations or to immigrants.

| TABLE 6.1 | KEY DIMENSIONS OF HUMAN DIVERSITY FOR COMMUNITY PSYCHOLOGY |
|---|---|

| | |
|---|---|
| Culture | Ability/Disability |
| Race | Age |
| Ethnicity | Socioeconomic Status, Social Class |
| Gender | Religion and Spirituality |
| Sexual Orientation | |

Note: This list is not exhaustive, but represents a limited number of dimensions often studied by community psychologists.

For relatively isolated human groups (e.g., a tribal culture in New Guinea) and nations with a largely homogeneous population (e.g., Japan), cultural boundaries are fairly clear and distinctive cultural elements more easily identified. In multicultural societies with heterogeneous populations (e.g., Canada, Brazil, United States), boundaries between cultural groupings within the society are more fluid, and identifying distinctive cultural components is more difficult.

## Race

Susie Guillory Phipps, a white-skinned person of almost totally European ancestry, has one Black ancestor: a slave in the 18th century who bore a child to her White slaveowner. Phipps thus is legally considered "colored" in her state of Louisiana. In the 1980s, she went to court to have that status changed to "White," but lost. Her experience illustrates both the biological dilemmas and the continuing social significance of racial concepts in the United States (Feagin & Feagin, 1999).

Race has long occupied a "quasi-biological" status in European and American psychological thought (Zuckerman, 1990). That quasi-biological definition of race has provided an intellectual basis for assumptions of White superiority. The damage done to human lives by thinking of race in biological terms makes it doubly important to define race carefully.

Although debate continues in anthropology concerning the origins of human "racial" variations, most psychologists have concluded that race as a biological variable is not a meaningful concept for psychology today (Betancourt & Lopez, 1993; Helms, 1994; Zuckerman, 1990). Variation in behavior and abilities among individuals within the three traditional racial categories (Negroid, Mongoloid, Caucasoid) far outweighs variation between groups. The races are biologically much more alike than different. When racial differences appear, as in IQ scores, differences are attributable to social and economic variables, not race per se (Zuckerman, 1990).

Yet race does have psychological and social meaning in many societies—as a socially constructed set of categories related to inequalities of status and power. Race is important because racism makes it so. In the United States, Whites often need pay little attention to race, because most seldom encounter racial prejudice. However, persons of color are often made acutely aware of their race by others. That difference in life experience and perspective reflects a powerful set of social dynamics important in community psychology. Racial distinctions in U.S. life are based on a history of slavery and segregation and the assumptions of White supremacy that were used to justify them. Today's differences in sociopolitical and economic power are maintained by persistent (often unrecognized) versions of those assumptions of superiority (Hacker, 1992; Helms, 1994).

Race is more than simply ethnicity (Frable, 1997; Helms, 1994; J. M. Jones, 1991). Race is "socially defined on the basis of *physical* criteria" (Van den Berghe, cited in J. M. Jones, 1991, p. 454). That is, people make racial distinctions based on assumptions about observable physical qualities such as skin color. Ethnicity is "socially defined on the basis of *cultural* criteria" (Van den Berghe, cited in J. M. Jones, 1991, p. 454), such as language, national origin, customs, and values, having little to do with physical appearance (Feagin & Feagin, 1999).

An example of the significance of race for those of different ethnic or national backgrounds is that in the United States, persons of largely African ancestry include at least three groups: African Americans with long ancestries in the United States, recent immigrants from Africa, and Black persons of Caribbean background. Yet all share experiences associated with Black life and racism in the United States.

No terminology is entirely satisfactory to describe the racial diversity of U.S. and many other societies, as recent debates over U.S. census categories has illustrated. When discussing race in this chapter in U.S. context, we use general racial category terms (e.g., Latino/Latina, European American) when necessary to refer to broad groupings defined by racial criteria rather than by specific ethnicity. We recognize that such terms often cover a very great diversity of ethnic groups; thus, where possible, we discuss specific ethnic groups (e.g., Puerto Ricans, Japanese Americans). We use other racial terms if used by authors whose works we are describing. When we use the terms Black and White, primarily for brevity, we capitalize them to remind you to think of these categories as socially constructed categories rather than biological races. Finally, when needed we use *persons of color* to refer to all persons of ancestry other than European. This term sometimes is necessary to discuss the effects of racism that targets multiple groups. In other nations, different categories and terms will be necessary.

Use of almost any terminology and definition of race can perpetuate the history of racial oppression in some way (see Andersen & Collins, 1998, p. xiv). Yet community psychology, at least in the United States, cannot ignore race, despite the drawbacks of our vocabulary for discussing it (Suarez-Balcazar, 1998; Trickett et al., 1994).

## *Ethnicity*

Ethnicity can be defined as a social identity, based on one's ancestry or culture of origin, as modified by the culture in which one currently resides (Helms, 1994, p. 293). The term is related to the Greek *ethnos* referring to tribe or nationality. Ethnicity is defined by language, customs, values, social ties, and other aspects of subjective culture, not by physical appearance (Feagin & Feagin, 1999). Religion may be an important aspect of ethnicity, but many major religions are multiethnic. Within broad racial groups in the United States, important ethnic groups exist, such as the differences among Puerto Ricans, Mexican Americans, and Cuban Americans (Feagin & Feagin, 1999), or among Asian Americans of Japanese, Chinese, Indian, or Vietnamese ancestry.

Ethnicity is not based on a single culture, but on the interaction of at least two cultures. It is defined in terms of both ancestry and experiences in the society in which one lives. Being Chinese American is not simply being Chinese, but is defined by the interaction (including conflict) of Chinese and U.S. cultures (Sasao & Sue, 1993).

## Gender

As with race, the biological differences between females and males provide a distinction, usually observable, that has been the basis of socially constructed concepts and definitions of "sexual" differences. Thus it is useful to distinguish between *sex*, referring to biological differences between males and females, and *gender*, referring to socially constructed assumptions, attitudes, roles, and social institutions that assume differences between women and men (Deaux, 1985; R. K. Unger & Crawford, 1992). Gender concepts are rooted in culture or society, not in biological differences but in how those differences are interpreted and used.

Gender is a better concept than sex for describing, for instance, conceptions of femininity and masculinity, division of labor between wife and husband in a traditional family, the importance of personal relationships in one's life, issues such as sexual assault and harassment, or income differences between men and women (R. K. Unger & Crawford, 1992). It represents an important variable for community psychology (Mulvey, 1988; Reinharz, 1994; Russo & Dabul, 1994).

## Sexual Orientation

This dimension refers to sexual or romantic attraction to one or both genders. It is best understood as a continuum from exclusively heterosexual to exclusively homosexual, with many areas between (e.g., predominantly homosexual, predominantly heterosexual, bisexual). Sexual orientation refers to attraction, emotions, and self-concept. It is not necessarily expressed in behavior. Choice of sexual partners is influenced by many factors and social pressures as well as by underlying orientation (Gonsiorek & Weinrich, 1991). Sexual orientation also is distinct from *gender identity,* one's sense of being psychologically male or female, and from *gender role,* one's adherence to social norms for masculinity and femininity.

Sexual orientation has been socially defined in ways that often create stereotypes; lead to victimization of lesbians, gay men, and bisexual persons (Pilkington & D'Augelli, 1995; Waldo, Hesson-McInnis, & D'Augelli, 1998); and powerfully influence identity development (Garnets & D'Augelli, 1994). Transgendered persons, who alter their outward gender to reflect their underlying psychological gender identity, are similarly victimized, and may join lesbian–gay–bisexual communities or groups although they are not dealing with issues of sexual orientation.

## Ability/Disability

A further human diversity dimension concerns the human experience of physical or mental disabilities. The occurrence of a disability of either type creates life experiences different from those of fully "able" persons. Moreover, issues of stigma, exclusion, and justice arise regarding treatment of persons with disabilities (e.g., Fawcett et al., 1994). This dimension is important in part because many, perhaps most, persons will experience a disability at some time in their lives. Because of its historical roots in community mental health, community psychology has especially focused on community issues concerning persons with mental disabilities or illnesses (e.g., L. Roberts et al., 1991). However, physical disability is also an area of interest (Fawcett et al., 1994).

## Age

Children, adolescents, and younger and older adults differ in psychological concerns, developmental transitions, and community involvement. The process of aging also brings changes in relationships to families, communities, and social institutions such as work and health care. Community psychology research and practice must, therefore, concern itself with age and aging (Gatz & Cotton, 1994).

## Socioeconomic Status/Social Class

However conceptualized, this comprises a central dimension for sociology that has seldom received enough attention in psychology. Yet in the everyday world of communities, differences of social class hold great psychological import, influencing identity and self-conceptions, interpersonal relationships, socialization, well-being, living environment, educational opportunities, and many other psychological issues. As with other dimensions of diversity, social class is not merely a matter of different cultural characteristics, but of differences in power, especially economic resources and opportunities. Moreover, issues of social class also often involve race, ethnicity, and gender in U.S. society; the poor are disproportionately women and persons of color.

## Religion and Spirituality

These topics comprise an area of growing interest in community psychology. Both concern the "search for significance" or meaning in living (Pargament, 1997) and the importance of transcendence, of being involved in something greater than oneself and one's immediate time (S. B. Sarason, 1993). Religion and spirituality concern community psychology because of their importance for personal development, coping, and well-being, as well as the importance of religious institutions in community life (Kloos & Moore, 2000; Maton & Wells, 1995; Pargament & Maton, 2000; S. B. Sarason, 1993).

We adopt a common viewpoint concerning concepts of religion and spirituality (J. L. Hill, 2000). Religion concerns involvement in a faith community (religious congregation or similar group) with a particular set of beliefs and practices. Personal spirituality concerns individual experiences of transcendence, a sense of unity with the universe through a power that is beyond our comprehension (Hill, 2000), whether this experience is connected to a faith community or not. We discuss these issues in more detail in chapter 7.

Spirituality and religion interrelate with culture and ethnicity. For instance, spirituality and religious practices have been crucial for the collective survival of African Americans (Myers & Speight, 1994; Watts, 1993) and North American Indians and Alaska Natives (Hazel & Mohatt, in press; Walsh-Bowers, 2000). It is impossible to understand many cultures without understanding their religious institutions and spiritual practices. Yet religion and spirituality are not simply contained in our cultural dimension above; differences among religious groups within a culture or society are important for community psychology as well.

These nine dimensions, while important for community psychology, are only some of the dimensions of human diversity. For instance, we have not included differences in community life among rural, suburban, and urban communities (Muehrer, 1997), nationality, or generational differences in immigrant families. In any given situation, many forms of diversity may be psychologically important.

# INDIVIDUALISM–COLLECTIVISM: A CROSS-CULTURAL DIMENSION

> To increase employee productivity, a Texas corporation told its employees to look in the mirror and say "I'm beautiful" 100 times before coming to work. For much the same purpose, a Japanese supermarket in New Jersey told its employees to begin each work day by telling another employee that he or she is beautiful. In North America, "the squeaky wheel gets the grease." In Japan, "the nail that stands out gets pounded down." (Markus & Kitayama, 1991, p. 224)

Scientific study of cultural differences such as these has popularized the field of *cross-cultural psychology*, which is concerned with understanding the impact of culture on individual lives. For instance, Gergen (1973, p. 312) argued that in cross-cultural perspective, many concepts of social and personality psychology would look much different. High self-esteem, prized in Western cultures, could be considered an excessive focus on oneself. Seeking to control the events in one's life might communicate a lack of respect for others. Social conformity could be viewed as behavior cementing the solidarity of an important group.

One of the most influential concepts in cross-cultural psychology in the last two decades has been the distinction between *individualistic* and *collectivistic* cultures (Hofstede, 1980; Kagitçibasi, 1997; Kim et al., 1994; Triandis, 1994). The individualism–collectivism dimension provides a broad concept that helps to compare individual actions and social customs across a number of cultures. As a broad concept, it has many exceptions in specific contexts, and provides only a beginning for understanding a specific culture.

Cross-cultural psychological findings have consistently indicated a dimension or spectrum of core cultural values of individualism–collectivism. In the more individualistic societies, citizens tend to endorse values of individual self-reliance, assertion, competition, and achievement most highly. Individual freedom is paramount in life decisions such as career and marriage, in beliefs, and in work behavior. The most individualistic country, by a variety of measures, is the United States (Hofstede, 1980; Lipset, 1996). Other countries with dominant cultural traditions rooted in Northern Europe are also more individualistic (e.g., Australia, Britain, Canada, the Netherlands, and New Zealand in Hofstede's, 1980, study).

In collectivistic countries, individuals tend to value cooperation, harmony within work groups, and putting group interests and group achievement first. In those cultures, individual achievement is believed to be attained through group success. The interests of the individual (properly understood) and the group are considered identical. The group may be the extended family, work group, ethnic group or (more rarely) nation. (Note that collectivistic values here concern cultural forces, not political systems such as communism.) Nations in Asia, South America and Africa tend to score as the most collectivistic. Much of the recent research literature has compared U.S. samples with Japanese, Indian, or Chinese (often Hong Kong) samples (Kagitçibasi, 1997). The notion of collectivism also is consistent, for instance, with Afrocentric concepts (Nobles, 1991) and ideals rooted in Mexican culture such as the overriding importance of family and community (Gloria, 1999).

The individualism–collectivism dimension refers to differences in cultural perspective and values, not to individual traits. Even in so individualistic a society as the United States, women (Gilligan, 1982), African American communities (Stack, 1974; Watts, 1993), religious communities such as the Amish, and other groups exemplify collectivistic values to some extent. Many collectivistic cultures also are incorporating more individualistic themes, particularly in work settings as global capitalism grows. Yet significant statistical differences in individualistic and collectivistic values do exist between national samples (Hofstede, 1980; Kagitçibasi, 1997).

Individualism–collectivism can be understood in terms of cultural norms. We list these in Table 6.2 and discuss each level below.

## Independent Self and Interdependent Self

The psychological meaning of individualism–collectivism partly involves the *independent self* and the *interdependent self* (Markus & Kitiyama, 1991). This distinction has also been termed "separated" versus "related" selves (Kagitçibasi, 1997). Individualistic cultures promote the development of an independent self, clearly separated from others in terms of emotions, attitudes, and identity. That self is based on a sharp, clear boundary between the individual and others. Finding and expressing your unique identity is emphasized in Western societies (recall expressive individualism in chap. 1; Bellah et al., 1985).

In collectivistic cultures, an interdependent self is cultivated and valued. It is based on a fluid, permeable boundary between self and others. One's identity is defined in terms of relationships to others; emotions, attitudes, and actions that sustain those relationships are valued. The interdependent self is related to Afrocentric ideas of the extended self (Nobles, 1991) and feminist conceptions of relatedness (Gilligan, 1982). For instance, in a study in which U.S. and Chinese students in a U.S. university were asked to define themselves in their own terms, U.S. students described themselves mainly in terms of personality traits such as *shy*, whereas the Chinese students tended to describe their group affiliations, such as *college student* (Trafimow, Triandis & Goto, 1991).

In individualistic cultures, expression of ego-focused emotions such as anger, frustration, and pride is more common and accepted. These are related to the attainment or blocking of individualistic goals. Confrontation and conflict also are more accepted. Such emotions and conflicts are less expressed in collectivistic cultures. In contrast, the interdependent self attends more to other-focused feelings, such as sympathy, shared shame due to failure, and feelings of connection or communion with others. Markus and Kitayama (1991) listed 11 emotional states recognized in the Japanese language but not in English; many of these concern other-focused feelings of connection, respect, and dependence on others.

| TABLE 6.2 | INDIVIDUALISTIC AND COLLECTIVISTIC CULTURES |
|---|---|
| **Individualistic Culture** | **Collective Culture** |
| *Primary values* | |
| Individual autonomy, choice | Ingroup harmony, loyalty |
| Competition with others | Cooperation with ingroup |
| *Conception of self* | |
| Independent self | Interdependent self |
| Strong self–others boundary | Fluid self–others boundary |
| Self-reliance valued | Connection to ingroup valued |
| Individual uniqueness emphasized | Ingroup similarity emphasized |
| *Emotion, motivation* | |
| Attention to ego-focused emotion (e.g., anger, pride) | Attention to shared emotion (e.g., communion, shame) |
| Confrontation is acceptable | Confrontation (in ingroup) avoided |
| Assertion valued | Self-effacement, humility valued |
| Primary control emphasized | Secondary control emphasized |
| Dependence avoided | Ostracism avoided |
| *Work-related variables* | |
| Individual achievement valued | Ingroup achievement valued |
| Success attributed to self | Success attributed to group |
| *Group dynamics* | |
| Ingroup–outgroup boundary fluid | Ingroup–outgroup boundary strong |
| Less commitment among ingroup members | More commitment among ingroup members |
| Inequality common, accepted | Equality fostered, in ingroup |
| Reciprocity is voluntary | Reciprocity is obligatory |

Note: The individualism–collectivism concept is a dimension, not a dichotomy. We use a dichotomy format here for simplicity.

Sources: Kagitçibasi (1997), Markus and Kitayama (1991), Triandis (1994, especially pp. 167–172).

In motivational terms, individualistic cultures foster active attempts to control one's environment (primary control), and individual achievement. Collectivistic cultures foster accommodation to external and social circumstances through self-control (secondary control). Group achievement is prized and seen as the route for individual advancement (Markus & Kitayama, 1991). Dependence on others is avoided in individualistic cultures; ostracism is avoided in collectivistic cultures.

## Ingroup and Outgroup

An important element of a collectivistic culture is the concept of *ingroup* (Triandis, 1994). All cultures have ingroup–outgroup distinctions to some extent (Brewer, 1997). The ingroup is particularly important in collectivistic cultures. Although the self is considered interdependent, individuals do not consider themselves interdependent with all other persons, but rather with the key groups in one's life: for example, extended family, classmates, work team, community, or even nation, depending on the context. In many collectivistic cultures, ingroups are based on ascribed characteristics determined at birth (e.g., family, clan, caste, ethnicity). There is a sense of connection and mutual commitment among members of the ingroup that is not granted to others, who are members of *outgroups*. Thus the sharp boundary in collectivistic cultures is drawn between ingroup and outgroup, whereas in individualistic cultures it is drawn between the individual and all others. That makes the ingroup weaker in individualistic cultures.

The ingroup–outgroup boundary creates security and interdependence among ingroup members, but indifference, ethnocentrism, or even hostility may be expressed toward outgroups. "Collectivism is not altruism, but ingroup egoism. In a collectivistic society, a poor relative can expect to be helped, but not a poor stranger" (Hofstede, 1994, p. xiii).

Behavior in work settings illustrates the importance of ingroups in collectivistic cultures. Success is more often attributed to oneself in individualistic cultures, and individual competition is expected. In collectivistic cultures, the interdependent self seeks advancement through and for the ingroup, success is attributed to the group or the situation, self-effacement and modesty are prized, and cooperation is promoted. Interestingly, "social loafing," in which individuals work with less effort in a group than alone, is common in individualistic cultures but not in collectivistic cultures (Kagitçibasi, 1997).

Inequality of resources or outcomes is common and accepted in individualistic cultures as an outgrowth of competition among independent selves. Recall our discussion of fair play values in chapter 1 (Ryan, 1994). In a collectivistic culture, equality among ingroup members is prized and rewards are shared (Kagitçibasi, 1997). Recall our discussion of fair shares values (Ryan, 1994). Helping another, or returning a favor done for you, are considered desirable but voluntary in individualistic cultures. They are obligatory in collectivistic cultures, where ingroup members consider themselves interdependent.

However, there are limits on the extent of equality and sharing in collectivistic cultures. Many collectivistic cultures also prize traditional sources of authority, such as elders, men, chieftains, religious leaders, or members of higher castes. Especially within an ingroup such authority figures hold more power and resources. Triandis (1994) distinguishes between "hierarchical" collectivists who honor such authority ranking, and "horizontal" collectivists who allocate resources more equally. The extent of authority ranking also varies within individualistic cultures, although not necessarily based on the same traditions.

## *Contributions and Limitations of the Individualism–Collectivism Concept*

Concepts of individualism and collectivism illuminate general psychological differences between cultures, especially for those with experience in only one culture. However, they have several limitations. First, globalization and cross-cultural contact is decreasing the psychological distance between cultures (Hermans & Kempen, 1998). Individualistic and collectivistic cultures now influence each other. Second, considerable diversity exists among collectivistic cultures. For instance, the interdependent self as described above (based mainly on studies from East Asia) is emotionally restrained, whereas emotional expressiveness is characteristic of African cultures (Butler, 1992).

Finally, these concepts do not illuminate any specific culture very well (Watts, 1994). The anthropological concepts of *emic* and *etic* study apply here (Zane & Sue, 1986). Cross-cultural psychology takes an etic perspective, which compares cultures in universal terms along dimensions such as individualism–collectivism. In an emic study, researchers seek to understand one culture "from the inside," in its own terms, with as little reference to other cultures' concepts as possible. This does not yield cross-cultural comparisons, but does build deeper understanding on which later comparisons may be built.

The emic study of *indigenous* or *population-specific* psychologies (Kim & Berry, 1993; Watts, 1994) has arisen to study specific cultures. Examples include Black psychology (R.L. Jones, 1991) and Mexican, Polish, Filipino, and other psychologies (Kim & Berry, 1993). Psychological descriptions of African American culture, for instance, have emphasized themes characteristic of its African roots (e.g., J. M. Jones, 1991; Nobles, 1991; Watts, 1993).

For many students, your next step in cultural study might well be emic study of a specific culture. Most community research and action occurs in a specific community and cultural context. Knowledge and appreciation of that context is the most important cultural prerequisite for that work. However, to fully understand human diversity, we next must take up another aspect of community life, beyond that of culture.

## THE OPPRESSION PERSPECTIVE ON HUMAN DIVERSITY

> Whenever you feel like criticizing anyone, he told me, just remember that all the people in this world haven't had the advantages that you've had. (Fitzgerald, 1925/1995, p. 5)

Consider these differences in U.S. society:

- Among full-time employees in the United States, women average about 70% of the income of men (Hacker, 1992, p. 94).
- Black men in the United States average about 60% of the income of White men. Black women average about 80% as much as White women (Hacker, 1992, pp. 94–95). (One reason that racial income disparity among women is smaller than among men is that women make less than men overall.)
- Similar disparities appear between Whites and Mexican Americans, Native Americans, Puerto Ricans, and Cuban Americans (Feagin & Feagin, 1999).
- Observational studies and police records have revealed that White and Black drivers on the turnpikes of two U.S. states were equally likely to exceed the speed limit and equally likely, if stopped by police, to possess illegal drugs. Yet Black drivers were more likely to be stopped by police, to be searched, and thus more likely to be arrested for drug offenses (Lamberth, 1998). This pattern has been labeled "police profiling" because officers are taught a profile of the typical drug offender, believed to be African American.

These differences among men and women and among racial and ethnic groups do not result from cultural factors. Rates of crime, school dropouts, teen pregnancies, and other social problems sometimes are blamed on cultural factors, yet are better understood as individual attempts to cope with realities of economic resources and social power. Blaming the culture can be just another way of blaming the victims.

To understand such differences, a viewpoint is required that takes account of inequalities in social and economic *power* in ways that cultural concepts cannot. Oppression theory does that, and we describe it in this section to complement our earlier coverage of cultural differences. Understanding and working in many communities requires both perspectives. Some phenomena of community life are better understood in cultural terms, some in terms of power.

## Oppression: Initial Definitions

Oppression occurs when an *asymmetry* or unequal relationship is used unjustly to grant power and resources to one group and withhold them from another (Prilleltensky & Gonick, 1994; Tatum, 1997; Watts, 1994; Watts, Griffith, & Abdul-Adil, 1999). The more powerful group is termed the *dominant* or *privileged* group; the less powerful is the *targeted* or *subordinated* group (J. B. Miller, 1976; Tatum, 1997). One's status in this asymmetry is based on the content of the oppressive system. Human differences that have been exploited by oppressive systems include all the dimensions of human diversity we named earlier. Oppressive asymmetries are often based on *ascribed* characteristics determined at birth or otherwise outside personal control. For instance, the oppressive system of racism in the United States creates a privileged group of White persons, and a subordinate group of all others: African Americans, Latinos/Latinas, Asian Americans, and Native Americans. Sexism creates privileges for men and subordinates women.

Resources controlled by a dominant or privileged group may include economic or other tangible resources, status and influence, sociopolitical power, interpersonal connections among elites, the power to frame discussion of issues and conflicts (often exerted through the media and the educational system), and representation in political offices and corporate boardrooms. Perhaps most insidious is the use of cultural and educational forces to convince members of the subordinated group that they actually are inferior and do not deserve treatment as equals. This sense of inferiority is termed *internalized oppression* (Prilleltensky & Gonick, 1994; Watts et al., 1999).

Members of the privileged group are granted resources, power, and freedom from subordination by the oppressive system, not by their own efforts (McIntosh, 1998; J. B. Miller, 1976; Prilleltensky & Gonick, 1994). Members of this privileged class may not recognize or consent to this, yet they are granted the privileges anyway. Not every U.S. White person supports racism, or exhibits overt racial prejudice, but they are privileged by systems that operate in racist ways regardless. Similar statements apply to individuals in other privileged groups (see Box 6.2).

The subordinated class are denied access to power and resources, without their consent. However, they are not powerless. In fact, they will resist the inequality of power in many ways, direct and indirect. The strengths of their cultural heritage may provide resources for doing so, as both spirituality and mutual assistance have for African Americans. The subordinated group may also develop ways of coping with the oppressive inequality and of indirectly protecting themselves. Women who are victims of battering often learn to interpret the nuances of their partners' moods (Tatum, 1997). The subordinated group may comply overtly with oppressors, yet create personal identities revealed only with other members of their group, as "Coloured" South Africans did under apartheid (Sonn & Fisher, 1998).

Oppressive systems have long historical roots. Those systems, not individuals currently living within them, are the source of asymmetry (Prilleltensky & Gonick, 1994; Freire, 1970/1993). For instance, to dismantle sexism, patriarchy (the system of unearned male power) is the opponent, not individual men. Dismantling oppression liberates both the privileged and the oppressed from a system that dehumanizes them both (Friere, 1970/1993). Thus, oppression theory is consistent with the emphasis in community psychology on analyzing social systems.

Box 6.2 illustrates asymmetries or inequalities of power and resources characteristic of oppressive social systems.

## Multiple Forms of Oppression

In most if not all societies, multiple forms of oppression exist. Steele (1997) summarized evidence that in the United States, even the best African American students are affected by racist stereotypes, and even the most mathematically talented women are similarly affected by stereotypes about women's mathematical ability. Moreover, the same individual can be privileged by one oppression while subordinated by another. In the United States, Black men are oppressed by racism and privileged by sexism; White women are oppressed by sexism and privileged by racism; working-class and low-income White men are oppressed by socioeconomic classism, while privileged by racism and sexism.

Recognizing multiple forms of oppression does not mean that all are equally vicious in any given context. However, it is so difficult to compare different forms of oppression that attempts to determine "whose oppression is worst" are fruitless, even destructive. Community psychologists need to attend to multiple realities and to the ways in which multiple oppressions interact (Wilson, 1997).

## Oppression: Multiple Levels of Analysis

If it is so unjust, how is an oppressive system of social arrangements sustained? Consistent with a community psychology perspective, answers can be found at macrosystem, locality, institutional, interpersonal, and individual levels of analysis. All create inequalities of power.

***Breathing "Smog": Cultural Myths***    Asymmetry of power and resources is sustained in part by widely accepted cultural myths that rationalize it (Freire, 1970/1993; Prilleltensky & Gonick, 1994; Ryan, 1971; Watts, 1994). As a result, members of the dominant group and even the subordinated group may not even realize the system of oppression exists. They often believe that the injustices created by oppression are natural. Tatum (1997) likened this process to "breathing smog": After a while, one doesn't notice it and the air seems natural. Hess (1997) described disparities in income between his father and the plant managers (see Box 6.2). To those managers (and to their superiors and their stockholders), those inequalities no doubt seemed to be the natural order of economic life.

One example of "smog" can be a false reading of individual effort. In an individualistic society, members attribute successes and failures to individual characteristics and

## 6.2   *Two Accounts of Subordination and Privilege*

The following personal statements discuss asymmetries based on systems of oppression.

### *From* Class and Me *(Hess, 1997)*

I was raised in a very poor, working-class family. Very poor means being raised in a cold, cramped, unhealthy house (our only heat was unventilated gas stoves, and I had pneumonia every winter), not having dental care, having very limited medical care, two pairs of pants, shirts, etc., one pair of shoes, and a high starch diet with meat once a week. There were no books in our house and only a radio until I was 15. . . . On my own as a child I observed that Dad worked as hard as the plant overseers, who made many times his pay. My mother was a good manager, cooked from scratch, and canned 300 quarts of berries, tomatoes, peaches, and vegetables each year. When I was 15, a union was organized at the plant where Dad worked, and after a six-month strike wages began to increase until, by the time I graduated from high school, my parents were able to buy and rehab the old house we lived in, which didn't even have a bathroom.

I grew up in a very class-conscious school system, where I was put in the slow learner's class in first grade on the basis of a test where the teacher had each student stand before the class and recite the ABC's. I'd never heard of the ABC's. I taught myself to read in third grade, as I was unable to use the phonics system we were taught. In sixth grade my reading skills tested on a third year of college level. Although I was a good student in academic courses, I was not selected by teachers for yearbook, school newspaper, or any of the other middle-class honors. I received a full scholarship to attend college (this was before federal financial aid).

In short, I know firsthand there is a class system in the United States that has little to do with merit. I was the only one in my family to go to college, although my sisters had the intelligence to go. Middle-class families with much less ability had all their children in college. Culturally, I'm a hillbilly. . . . My becoming middle class was painful. I had no social graces but made a fool of myself in social situations. My college instructors laughed at me for the way I pronounced words I knew from reading but had never heard.

I have to believe, if a lower-class person can become familiar with middle-class life, certainly middle-class persons can become sensitive to those who are different: the poor, blacks, ethnic minorities (Hess, 1997, p. 7).

In the wealthiest nation in the world, Hess grew up in an oppressed class, with great disadvantages of housing, nutrition, health care, and other resources, based on inequalities of pay and wealth. (Consistent with the oppression theory, those were not addressed until workers acted collectively.) The economic injustices were complemented by social exclusion: The educational system from first grade to college made it clear that Hess was an outsider. His experiences illustrate asymmetries of economic, social status, and political power.

*(continued)*

## Oppression and Unearned Privilege

My wife and I work in the same building at the same university. When I need to work late, I do so without reservations about my personal safety. For men, our campus is safe even late at night. I don't think about whether anyone else is on my floor, or who has access to the building. When I walk to my car, I don't need to be alert. However, if she works late, my wife thinks about all of these things, for personal safety. In this society we tolerate a great deal of men's violence toward women, of which sexual assault is but one example. It is clear that I (and other men) have a privilege that my wife (and other women) do not share.

Consider a second form of privilege. When my wife and I wish to hold each other's hand or embrace in public, we do so without concern for our safety. As a teenager and college student, I was free to talk with friends about whom I was dating or wished to date. No one told crude jokes about persons of my heterosexual orientation. I did not have to agonize about what my sexual orientation was, or about whether to tell my parents about it.

This privilege is not available to one of my closest friends, who is a lesbian. She has been harassed. If she is open about her sexuality, she is excluded from some of the major institutions of society: many religious congregations, marriage, adopting a child, careers involving working with children. If she hides her sexuality, she must deal with the personal cost to her integrity and well-being. Finally, the danger of murderous violence is always there for her, at some level of awareness.

Consider a third form of privilege. Many of my Black friends and colleagues have noted that almost every day, in some way large or small, they are reminded of their race in an unpleasant way. While these reminders may be indirect, even unintentional, their effects are nonetheless real. Moreover, I have learned that the direct, intimidating incidents of racism are more common than I had realized. These incidents also create privilege for Whites, who may go for weeks or years without being confronted with the meaning of our racial status. Whites are freer (if we wish) to pursue our education, career aspirations, and leisure time almost solely in the company of people of our race. When a conflict occurs, and one needs to assert oneself with a superior at work, the manager of a retail business, or the teacher of one's children at school, or when one must call the police, Whites can be much more confident that we will be dealing with a person of our race. Whites also can much more easily arrange to protect our children from adults who may not like them, or worse, on the basis of their race (McIntosh, 1998).

A fourth form of privilege is illustrated by comparing the economic, educational, and personal advantages of middle-class life to Hess's (1997) earlier description of his childhood.

These privileges are not earned. Moreover, the privileges that, for instance, accrue to being male are not something I (or many other men) support; I would much rather live in a society in which women are safe and as privileged as men. Life in such a society would be freer for both women and men. The same is true regarding other forms of oppression. It seems to me and many others that those of us who are members of privileged groups, while we did not create these forms of oppression, have a responsibility to work to dismantle them.—James H. Dalton choices (Ryan, 1971). Oppressive systems mean that some persons' efforts are rewarded while others' are devalued. Especially for members of the privileged group, recognizing that asymmetry would create cognitive dissonance and call cherished beliefs into question. Thus, when differences occur in educational attainment, income, or other outcomes, they are motivated to explain them in terms of individual ability or effort.

In fact, an oppressive system often works best when a few members of an oppressed group break through to enjoy the privileges of the dominant group. They may be tokens, or perhaps the best at assimilating the values and behaviors of the dominant class. They may, for instance, be women who are praised by men for "thinking like a man" (J. B. Miller, 1976). The success of a few seems to offer a lesson about the value of individual effort alone. Yet even for tokens, the reality of social myths and stereotypes often means having to prove their competence repeatedly while members of the privileged group do not (Steele, 1997).

*Social Myths: The Role of Mass Media*   Print media, television, movies, radio, and the Internet comprise a very influential macrosystem. The presence and status of women, persons of color, and other oppressed groups have increased in U.S. mass media in the last half-century, especially in some select roles (e.g., sports, music, comedy). Yet many areas of the media continue to provide misleading images of oppressed populations.

Gilens (1996) investigated major U.S. news magazines and network television news shows to document some of these inaccuracies and their impact on public opinion. For instance, in coverage of poverty, African Americans comprised 60% of persons in photographs and video footage, although only 29% of the poor are African American. Every person pictured in news magazine stories about the "underclass" was African American. This coverage has real effects: Public opinion polls cited by Gilens show that U.S. citizens consistently overestimate the proportion of the poor who are Black. In addition, poll data show that Whites who believe that most of the poor are African Americans also are more likely to blame the poor for their poverty and to favor drastic cuts in welfare.

Media distortions also show up in other television genres and for other oppressed populations. A study of U.S. television dramas revealed that the proportion of Latino/Latina characters has declined since the 1950s, from 3% of all characters to 1%. Moreover, Latino/Latina characters are disproportionately portrayed as criminals. Reality-based shows featuring videotaped accounts of actual crimes also disproportionately portray Latinos/Latinas as criminals (Feagin & Feagin, 1999, p. 303).

*Neighborhood Racial "Tipping Point"*   Oppression can also exist at the neighborhood level. Hacker (1992, pp. 35–38) reviewed research on the racial "tipping point" in U.S. residential neighborhoods, especially involving White and Black residents. Surveys indicate that Black Americans prefer living in racially integrated neighborhoods more than Whites. Behaviorally, most White residents will remain in a racially mixed neighborhood only if the proportion of persons of color remains below a certain point, usually about 8%. Once that tipping point is passed, a predictable sequence occurs. White residents move out, often quickly, and no Whites move in. Blacks, often seeking an integrated neighborhood, move in only to find the area becoming all-Black or nearly so. What makes this more than simply a matter of individual prejudice is the predictable tipping point of about 8%, a surprisingly uniform figure across the nation and well below the proportion of Blacks or other persons of color in the general population.

***Institutional Oppression***     Organizations and social institutions can also contribute to oppression (J. M. Jones, 1997a). In the introduction to this section, we mentioned police profiling as an example of institutional oppression. Norton and Fox (1997) described how corporations can shunt rising executives who are women or persons of color into positions unrelated to their training, often with lesser chances of further promotion than Whites or men. As a further example, reliance on entrance examination scores for determining admission to a university can have the effect of excluding many African Americans, members of other ethnic groups, and economically disadvantaged students. A final example of institutionalized oppression is that until 1973, the mental health professions officially defined homosexuality as a mental disorder.

***Interpersonal Relationships***     These also can reveal the psychological workings of oppressive systems. The power relationships of the larger society are often mirrored in the power relationships among members of microsystems such as families and work teams (Alderfer, 1994; Friere, 1970/1993, chap. 1; J. B. Miller, 1976; Watts, 1994). The feminist slogan "The personal is political" applies here.

Goodwin, Operario, and Fiske (1998) reported studies that document how persons who hold power in a variety of laboratory situations, or who are motivated to seek such control, frequently stereotype and exclude subordinates. Sometimes these acts are intentional, sometimes they occur without the awareness of the more powerful person. Research on racism indicates that many individuals who believe themselves free of prejudice nonetheless behave in discriminatory ways (J. M. Jones, 1997a).

In his autobiography, Frederick Douglass (1845/1995) provided a classic description of oppression in personal relationships. In the 1820s, Douglass, born in slavery on Maryland's Eastern Shore, was brought to Baltimore to become a house servant. Mr. Auld, his new master, was an experienced slaveowner; Mrs. Auld was not. Thus as Douglass was learning the role of servant, Mrs. Auld was learning the role of oppressor.

> My new mistress proved to be all that she appeared when I first met her at the door—a woman of the kindest heart and feelings. . . . I scarcely knew how to behave in her presence. . . . The crouching servility, usually so acceptable a quality in a slave, did not answer when manifested toward her. Her favor was not gained by it; she seemed disturbed by it. She did not deem it impudent or unmannerly for a slave to look her in the face. . . . in the simplicity of her soul, she commenced, when I first went to live with her, to treat me as she supposed one human being ought to treat another. . . .
>
> But alas! this kind heart had but a short time to remain such. The fatal poison of irresponsible power was already in her hands, and soon commenced its infernal work. . . . she very kindly commenced to teach me the A,B,C. . . . Mr. Auld found out what was going on, and at once forbade Mrs. Auld to instruct me further, telling her, among other things, that it was unlawful, as well as unsafe, to teach a slave to read. . . .
>
> She now commenced to practise her husband's precepts. She finally became even more violent in her opposition than her husband himself. She was not satisfied with doing as well as he had commanded; she seemed anxious to do better. Nothing seemed to make her more angry than to see me with a newspaper. . . . I have had her rush up to me all of a fury, and snatch from me a newspaper, in a manner that fully revealed her apprehension (Douglass, 1845/1995, pp. 19–22).

The system of slavery dehumanized both Douglass and the Aulds, reducing their humanity to prescribed social roles (see Friere, 1970/1993). Social myths and even legal restrictions supported the inequality. Moreover, two forms of oppression exist here. The transformation in Mrs. Auld's behavior illustrates not only the morally destructive effect of slavery on the slaveowner, but also her subordination to her husband.

This passage by Douglass also illustrates a further point: Members of the subordinated group usually understand the oppression better than those who are privileged by it. Frequent participation in oppressive inequalities in relationships dulls the awareness of the privileged person, making such injustices seem natural. Yet the same encounters can lead to insights by the subordinated.

***Intergroup Relations and Individual Prejudices***    If you have taken a course in social psychology, you have no doubt learned the ways in which individual stereotypes and prejudices are developed and sustained. In an individualistic society, we often think of oppressions at a solely individual level: Racism, for instance, is limited to prejudiced individuals (hooded Klansmen and the like). From the oppression perspective, however, many other levels are involved, which interlock with individual prejudices.

Intergroup theory in social psychology holds that a distinction between ingroup and outgroup (whether in individualistic or collectivistic societies) provides one basis of stereotypes and prejudices (Brewer, 1997; Dovidio, Maruyama, & Alexander, 1997). As humans, we often hold positive attitudes about our ingroup, while stereotyping and holding prejudices about outgroup members, at least to some extent. Members of both dominant and subordinate groups thus may hold stereotypes and prejudices about the other group; all are human.

However, intergroup theory alone does not account for differences in power between groups. Oppression theory adds that the prejudices of those in the dominant group have more effect in the society and community because of the dominant status and influence of that group. Members of the subordinated group are not free of prejudice, but theirs are less powerful because of their subordinated status. For instance, in U.S. society, both Whites and persons of color are likely to hold at least some stereotypes and prejudices toward the other. Yet White persons as a group dominate economic, political, and social resources (e.g., access to employment, housing, educational advantage, mortgages, and loans). The prejudices of more powerful Whites become part of an interlocking set of social arrangements that perpetuate this control of resources and reinforce widespread beliefs in White superiority; in short, a system of racism. All Whites, regardless of their level of prejudices, benefit from this system; they are privileged by it. Similar dynamics perpetuate socioeconomic classism, sexism, and other forms of oppression.

## Oppression Theory: A Call to Action

Oppression theory is not just an intellectual analysis, it is a call to action (Freire, 1970/1993; Prilleltensky & Gonick, 1994; Serrano-Garcia, 1984). For members of subordinated groups, it provides a theory that explains their experiences and names an opponent: the oppressive system. The aim is to change the system, to liberate both oppressor and oppressed (Friere, 1970/1993).

Recall the distinction between first-order change and second-order change in chapter 1. First-order change in this context would mean the currently oppressed group simply replaces the currently privileged group as the "top dog," a reshuffling within the oppressive system. Second-order change, which involves changes in role relationships, dismantles the oppressive system and the privileged–subordinate distinctions it creates. That is the aim of oppression theory. It is thus consistent with the community psychology values of social justice, collaboration, and citizen participation (Prilleltensky & Gonick, 1994).

Oppression theory (e.g., Friere, 1970/1993) holds that three prerequisites are needed for dismantling of oppression. The first is critical awareness and understanding of the oppressive system. Second is the involvement, indeed leadership, of the subordinated group. Third is collective action; solely individual actions accomplish little against entrenched opposition. Table 6.3 summarizes key points of oppression theory.

## Contributions and Limitations of Oppression Theory

Oppression theory calls attention to the workings of power not addressed in the cultural perspective. Thus, it complements the cultural perspective, furthering understanding of

---

**TABLE 6.3    ASSUMPTIONS AND CONCEPTS OF THE OPPRESSION PERSPECTIVE**

1. Oppression involves a set of asymmetric or unequal relationships used unjustly to grant power and resources to one group and withhold them from another.

2. The more powerful group is the *dominant* or *privileged* group; the less powerful is the *oppressed* or *subordinated* group. One's group membership is often determined by birth or other factors beyond one's personal control.

3. Resources controlled by a dominant group may include economic or other tangible resources, status and influence, sociopolitical power, interpersonal connections, and the power to frame discussion of issues.

4. The oppressive system grants unearned *privileges* to members of the dominant group, whether or not they recognize or consent to them.

5. The oppressed group resists oppression, directly or indirectly, with the power they have.

6. Systems of oppression, not individuals, are the focus of the oppression perspective.

7. Multiple forms of oppression exist. An individual may be privileged by one form of oppression and subordinated by another.

8. Oppression can be understood at multiple levels of analysis: macrosystems, localities, organizations and institutions, interpersonal relationships, and individual prejudices.

9. Social myths and stereotypes rationalize an oppressive system. Tatum (1997) likened this process to "breathing smog": After a while, the workings of the oppressive system seem natural.

10. Oppressive systems create prejudice, and in turn are bolstered by the strengths of commonly accepted prejudices. All individuals may have prejudices, but those of the dominant group are more damaging because they interlock with systems of oppression.

11. Oppression theory is a call to action, to work collectively to dismantle oppressive systems.

12. Oppression dehumanizes both oppressor and oppressed. To truly dismantle it, those who oppose it must aim to liberate both oppressor and oppressed.

---

Note: Sources are Feagin and Feagin (1999), Freire (1993), J. B. Miller (1976), Olsson, Powell, and Steuhling (1998), Prilleltensky and Gonick (1994), Tatum (1997), Watts (1994).

human diversity. It also provides an action stance for social change that is lacking in the cultural perspective.

A limitation of oppression theory is that in its emphasis on social systems, it may lead to ignoring or underestimating the diversity within privileged and subordinated groups. Differences within those groups are important, whether based on power, culture, or other characteristics. A second limitation is that oppression theory can portray members of subordinated groups merely as victims, unless their cultural strengths and resistance to oppression are explicitly recognized.

A third limitation can arise when oppression theory is used in action. Oppression theory in large part concerns conflict between dominant and subordinated groups. That conflict often is based on real, undeniable injustices. Yet the ideal of liberating both the oppressor and the oppressed may be difficult to sustain in the heat of that conflict. Discussion may be dominated by blaming of individuals or groups, rather than blaming social myths and practices. For instance, Norton and Fox (1997) described how some forms of diversity training in business organizations, by emphasizing differences and ignoring shared goals, contribute to a climate of conflict and mistrust. Research on intergroup theory has shown clearly that avoiding such an outcome requires commitment to shared goals as well as to addressing injustice (J. M. Jones, 1997b; Pettigrew, 1998). The long-term value of oppression concepts may lie in how they lead to articulating and enacting Friere's (1970/1993) vision of liberating both oppressor and oppressed.

# ACCULTURATION

> One ever feels his two-ness,—an American, a Negro; two souls, two thoughts, two unreconciled strivings; two warring ideals in one dark body, whose dogged strength alone keeps it from being torn asunder.
>
> The history of the American Negro is the history of this strife,—this longing to attain self-conscious manhood, to merge his double self into a better and truer self. In this merging he wishes neither of the older selves to be lost. . . . He simply wishes to make it possible for a man to be both a Negro and an American. (DuBois, 1903/1986, p. 365)

In this famous passage, DuBois addresses a conflict of two identities that cannot be easily merged. His African ancestry and American experience promise mutual enrichment, yet forces of oppression prohibit their merging. Still, the individual must find a way to live with the two identities.

Neither the cultural nor the oppression perspectives fully address how individuals resolve such questions. A third perspective is needed. The process of *psychological acculturation* occurs when an individual member of one culture changes through contact with (usually living within) another culture (Berry & Sam, 1997). It connects concepts of culture and oppression with individual psychological functioning.

## *Acculturative Strategies*

- A family leaves civil war in their home country and immigrates to Canada.
- A student leaves his native Korea to attend graduate school in the United States.

- An American Indian student leaves his community to attend a large, predominantly European American state university.
- An Australian takes a job requiring several years' commitment in Japan.

These examples pose two questions. To what extent do persons continue to identify or maintain relationships with their culture of origin? To what extent do they identify or maintain relationships with the new or dominant culture?

Berry (Berry & Sam, 1997) proposed four strategies of psychological acculturation, to describe how individuals respond to these two questions. Originally proposed to describe experiences of immigrants adjusting to a new culture, it has been usefully applied to groups long resident within a dominant culture (e.g., African Americans, French-speaking Canadians) and indigenous peoples existing within a society dominated by a different culture (e.g., American Indians; Berry & Sam, 1997).

Identification with a culture may be behaviorally expressed in choices of language, religion, clothing, food, gender roles, child-rearing strategies, and so on. It may also be internally expressed: one's personal identity, values, emotions, aspirations, and spirituality are grounded in culture. Berry's model assumes that in acculturation the individual identifies to some extent with one or the other culture, with both, or with neither. This leads to the four strategies listed in Table 6.4 and described below (Berry & Sam, 1997).

**Separation**    If individuals identify with their culture of origin, live primarily within communities of that culture, and interact with the dominant culture only in limited ways (e.g., work or other economic exchanges), they are pursuing a strategy of separation. (If members of the dominant culture act in this way, while reserving political, economic, and social power for their group, *segregation* is the appropriate term.) Separation has been a recurrent theme (and one adaptive strategy) in the histories of African Americans and French-speaking Canadians, for instance. It also may be adopted by immigrants who live in their own ethnic community.

**Assimilation**    On the other hand, if individuals give up identifying with their culture of origin to pursue identification with the dominant culture, they are assimilating. Assimilation is a common acculturation strategy for immigrants, refugees, and similar groups in a new culture. The idea of the "melting pot" for immigrants to the United States has usually meant assimilation to the dominant Anglo-American culture in public behavior, economic activity, education, and other areas of life. The assimilation may be strong yet not total; cultural expressions such as meals within the home may reflect the culture of origin even if other attitudes and behavior are assimilated.

Some form of assimilation may be the only strategy available under powerful systems of oppression. In such circumstances, members of a subordinated population may "pass" as a member of the dominant group. Passing involves behavioral assimilation in public coupled with a different cultural identification in private. Many lesbians and gay men, especially in adolescence, respond to heterosexist oppression by passing. However, passing can exact a psychic price for maintaining a divided identity.

Assimilation may be limited for individuals and groups who differ from the dominant cultural group in obvious ways such as skin color. In a society marked by strong discrimination, even the most sincere and thorough attempts at assimilation by members of such

| TABLE 6.4 | BERRY AND SAM'S (1997) FOUR ACCULTURATIVE STRATEGIES | |
|---|---|---|
| | *Identification With Culture of Origin* | |
| *Identification with Dominant Culture* | **Stronger** | **Weaker** |
| **Stronger** | Integration (Biculturality) | Assimilation |
| **Weaker** | Separation | Marginalization |

Source: From Berry and Sam (1997).

groups may be rebuffed. After all, their most noticeable features are still the same. Attempts at assimilation into the dominant Anglo-American culture by African Americans, Native Americans, and many Latinos/Latinas have often been thwarted by the dominant culture's focus on racial characteristics (LaFromboise, Coleman, & Gerton, 1993).

***Marginalization***    This occurs if individuals do not or cannot identify with either their culture of origin or with the dominant culture (Berry & Sam, 1997, p. 267). This strategy may not be chosen, but can result from loss of contact with one's culture of origin combined with exclusion from the dominant culture. It appears to be the strategy usually associated with the greatest psychological distress (Berry & Sam, 1997; LaFromboise et al., 1993).

***Integration, biculturality***    If individuals seek to identify in meaningful ways with both their culture of origin and the dominant culture, they are using the integration or bicultural strategy (Berry & Sam, 1997; Birman, 1994; LaFromboise et al., 1993). An important outgrowth of the Berry model has been study of the bicultural strategy and its outcome: bicultural competence.

A terminological note: Some researchers define acculturation not as the process defined here, but as the extent to which a member of an ethnic group has developed competence in, or identified with, the dominant culture or language. That could reflect either assimilation or biculturality. In addition, the term *enculturation* used in many contexts refers to immersion in one's culture of origin, not to relations with the dominant culture.

## *Bicultural Competence*

LaFromboise et al., (1993) reviewed studies of psychological acculturation and defined six characteristics of bicultural competence. These are summarized in Table 6.5. They provide a useful overview of what it means to be bicultural.

LaFromboise et al. (1993, pp. 402–403) described two prerequisites to bicultural competence. Possessing a *strong cultural identity*, based on integration with one's culture of origin, is the first. This identification with one's cultural roots is a resource for (rather than an obstacle to) development of bicultural competence. It provides a secure base from which to explore and learn about the second culture.

Another secure base is provided by a strong *personal identity* (LaFromboise et al., 1993, p. 402). This involves self-awareness and an ability to distinguish between oneself and the society or peer group.

TABLE 6.5    CHARACTERISTICS OF BICULTURAL COMPETENCE

| Cognitive/Affective Factors | Social/Behavioral Factors |
| --- | --- |
| Knowledge of both cultures | Communication competency in both cultures |
| Positive attitude toward both cultures | Role repertoire in both cultures |
| Sense of bicultural efficacy | Social support ("groundedness") in both cultures |

Note: These characteristics have as a prerequisite identification with culture of origin.
Source: LaFromboise et al. (1993).

The first of the LaFromboise et al. (1993) six characteristics of bicultural competence involves sufficient *knowledge of both cultures.* This knowledge covers primary cultural values and beliefs, institutions and rituals, and everyday social norms. When the two cultures conflict, creating stressful challenges, knowledge of both is needed. The individual may find ways to integrate differing values or need to know how and when to conform one's behavior to one culture or the other. Also essential to bicultural competence is possessing *positive attitudes about both cultures,* being able to recognize strengths in each, and holding both in positive regard. Drawing on Bandura's (1986) theory of personality, LaFromboise et al. further proposed that bicultural competence requires *bicultural efficacy,* the belief or confidence that one can live satisfactorily within both cultures without compromising one's cultural and personal identity.

LaFromboise et al. (1993) cited studies showing that many American Indian children developed greater knowledge of the dominant Anglo-American culture as they moved through school, while also maintaining allegiance to tribal interpersonal norms. In universities in which Anglo-American norms were dominant, bicultural American Indian students knew more about strategies for academic achievement than American Indian peers immersed mainly in their tribal culture. Yet the bicultural students were also more likely to enroll in courses and participate in cultural activities based on American Indian cultures.

These three cognitive and affective qualities of bicultural competence are complemented by three social/behavioral factors. *Communication competency* in the languages of both cultures is critical. More broadly, possessing a wide *repertoire of social skills in both cultures* is necessary. For instance, studies of Latino/Latina and American Indian college students in the United States indicate that possessing academic and social skills for both the dominant culture and the culture of origin promoted personal adjustment to college (LaFromboise et al., 1993).

Finally, LaFromboise et al. (1993) proposed a quality they termed *groundedness,* the cultivation of social support and friendship networks within both cultures. The persons in these networks may identify with only one culture, but the overall network represents both. Social networks promote learning bicultural skills and attitudes and provide emotional support for persisting in the face of cultural conflicts and obstacles. LaFromboise et al. cited evidence that such networks are stronger if they include not only close ties to family and friends, but also a larger network of acquaintances who can provide information and contacts.

LaFromboise et al. (1993, p. 403) suggested that alternation is an adaptive strategy for developing bicultural competence. Instead of trying to integrate both cultures fully in everything one does, alternation involves preserving the skills, values, and social relationships of one's culture of origin for use in that culture (e.g., within family and ethnic community), while cultivating skills and attitudes of the second culture, and relationships with its members, in settings where that culture dominates (e.g., work, school, marketplace). This ability to discern and respond to cultural differences in settings has also been termed *code-switching.*

## Contributions and Limitations of Bicultural Competence

The LaFromboise et al. (1993) review of the value of bicultural competence chiefly covered studies among Native Americans, Latinos/Latinas, and African Americans in the United States. Berry and Sam (1997) reviewed international evidence that supported the adaptive value of a bicultural approach.

However, the most adaptive acculturation strategy depends on many contextual factors (Birman, 1994; LaFromboise et al., 1993; Trickett, 1996). Bicultural strategies are not necessarily common or adaptive. For instance, in a study of adolescents whose families had immigrated from Latin America to Washington, D.C., biculturalism was not correlated with perceptions of self-worth (Birman, 1998). In a study of Chinese Americans in San Francisco, bicultural individuals reported greater psychological well-being in general, but other orientations were more adaptive on some measures (Ying, 1995). A study of New York City residents of Puerto Rican ancestry (Cortes, Rogler, & Malgady, 1994) found that only about one fourth of respondents were bicultural. About one third were predominantly involved in Puerto Rican culture (separation), one fourth were involved predominantly in U.S. culture (assimilation), and the remainder uninvolved in either culture (marginalization).

Furthermore, an individual pursuing acculturation is influenced not only by culture, but also by other aspects of ecological context. These include gender, social class, sexual orientation, and religiosity (Hurtado, 1997; Sasao, 1999; Wink, 1997). In addition, the existence of a viable ethnic community is required for bicultural groundedness. For instance, Chinese Americans living in San Francisco will find biculturality or separation easier than Chinese Americans living in a small predominantly White town, for whom assimilation may be more adaptive (Ying, 1995).

A limitation of the alternation strategy in particular is that the person might learn behavioral skills and roles in both cultures, yet lack a deeper sense of identification with either (Birman, 1994). That resembles marginalization more than integration, and may increase the stress of acculturation rather than lessen it. For instance, Sasao (1999) developed two programs for promoting bicultural competence and preventing drug use among high-risk Asian American youth in California. One approach focused solely on behavioral skill training; the other defined and promoted biculturality in terms of cognitions and emotions as well as behaviors. The cognitive–emotional–behavioral program was more effective in preventing drug use among these youth. This suggests the importance of developing bicultural competence in multiple domains.

As memorable examples of the need for a contextual viewpoint, Birman (1994, p. 281; see also Trickett, 1996) cited two ancient stories from Jewish tradition. These illustrate the value of acculturation strategies other than biculturalism for a small cultural group within a powerful, oppressive society. Joseph, a Jew sold into slavery in Egypt by his brothers, assimilated to Egyptian society, and became by a twist of fate the instrument for preserving Jewish culture in a time of famine. Years later, Moses, a Jew reared by Egyptian royalty with little knowledge of his cultural heritage, learned of that heritage, then led a separatist movement and exodus from Egypt. His action preserved the culture that Joseph had earlier helped to preserve by assimilation.

# Implications for Community Psychologists

The concepts in this chapter have a number of implications for community psychology. In chapter 3, we discussed implications for conducting community research. Here, we focus on personal cultural competence among community psychologists, and on cultural appropriateness of community programs.

## *Cultural Competence*

Community psychologists are participant conceptualizers: We seek to understand communities by working within them. That role often requires cultural competence akin to bicultural competence in personal life. Such issues arise not only in cross-cultural efforts but also in working across lines of difference such as race, gender, or social class.

Definitions and descriptions of cultural competence for community researchers and practitioners vary (e.g., Canning, 1999; Mock, 1999; Orlandi, 1992; Resnicow, Braithwaite, Ahluwahlia, & Baranowski, 1999; Sasao, 1999) but often contain the following elements (note that several elements parallel the six characteristics in the LaFromboise et al., 1993, description of bicultural competence):

- knowledge of the characteristics, experiences, beliefs, values, and norms of the cultural group with whom one is working
- respect for these cultural elements without assumptions of superiority or inferiority
- interpersonal-behavioral skills for working within the culture
- supportive relationships within the culture with whom one is working, and in one's own culture
- "a professional stance of informed naiveté, curiosity, and humility" (Mock, 1999, p. 40), involving awareness of one's limited knowledge and a commitment to learn
- awareness of how one's own culture and experiences have shaped one's worldview
- a viewpoint that development of cultural competence is an ongoing process, not a simple achievement.

These qualities involve not only cognitive knowledge and behavioral skills, but also attitudes. Those include a curiosity about and genuine respect for the strengths of a cultural tradition, and a willingness to address differences in privilege and personal experiences with power.

# Designing Culturally Sensitive Community Programs

Imagine yourself as a community psychologist facing each of the following challenges.

- You have received a grant to offer smoking cessation services in a Hispanic community in San Francisco. This population is not reached well by existing public health programs on smoking cessation.
- As a member of an African American community, you seek to develop a program to promote positive personal development and community involvement among African American young men.

Culturally sensitive or appropriate community programs such as those above must address many aspects of the culture for which they are designed. These are best developed in genuine collaboration with members of the local culture and community in which they will be presented. Writing from a health promotion perspective, Resnicow et al. (1999) proposed a useful distinction, borrowed from linguistics: the *surface structure* and *deep structure* of a community program.

Surface structure involves the most observable aspects of a program. These include the race, ethnicity, or gender of its staff; the language used to communicate orally or in writing; the choice of cultural elements such as clothing, food, or music in program content; and the setting (e.g., a religious setting would be appropriate in some cultures, but not others). With the collaboration of community members in program design and staffing, health promotion programs often are culturally sensitive in terms of surface structure (Resnicow et al., 1999).

However, addressing surface structure may not be enough to make a community program effective. For instance, Sasao (1999) found that simply having Asian American staff in a clinical service for Asian Americans (an element of surface structure) did not resolve all cultural differences between therapists and clients.

Deep structure, in contrast, involves core cultural beliefs, values, and practices. Addressing the deep structure of a culture requires historical, psychological, and social knowledge of the culture. For instance, some Latino/Latina and African cultural beliefs emphasize supernatural causes for illness as well as natural causes (Resnicow et al., 1999). These multiple explanations of illness will affect willingness to report symptoms, choice of indigenous healers or Western health professionals, and many health-related behaviors. Design and evaluation of a health promotion outreach program must address these differences.

Addressing cultural or racial differences in the magnitude and type of stressors faced by individuals is another aspect of deep structure. In many ways, African American adolescents experience different stressors than European Americans. The former are more likely to be the victim of or witness to gun violence, to experience the death of a parent or sibling, and to encounter racial prejudice personally (Resnicow et al., 1999).

Next we present three examples of community programs that address issues of culture, in both surface and deep structure.

### Smoking Cessation in a Hispanic Community
Marin et al., (1990) developed community smoking cessation programs, and outreach awareness campaigns to publicize them, in a Hispanic neighborhood in San Francisco. Residents of the neighborhood were

mostly of Central American and Mexican ancestry. Many spoke primarily Spanish and relied mainly on Spanish-language media.

Research by Marin et al. (1990) had shown several differences in attitudes and norms between Hispanic and non-Hispanic White smokers. Hispanic smokers were more concerned about the negative effects of smoking on their families and children (e.g., second-hand smoke, setting a bad example for children). This reflects a cultural emphasis on family relationships shared by many Hispanic ethnic groups. Hispanic smokers also were more concerned about the immediate social effects of smoking (e.g., bad smell). Finally, the Hispanic value of *respeto* suggested that confrontational antismoking efforts were likely to fail, whereas efforts that maintained smooth social relations were more consistent with the culture (Marin et al., 1990).

The Marin et al. (1990) community program combined two parts. It presented information about the negative consequences of smoking through a variety of media: television and radio announcements, a radio talk show, posters, billboards and bus placards, presentations at community meetings and activities, and telephone contacts by program staff. This campaign also publicized the existence of culturally focused, Spanish-language, community smoking cessation clinics, and a self-help manual. The Spanish-language manual included personal testimonials, illustrations, and other features to maximize personal impact. All of these program elements used the prior research findings to address the issues of core Hispanic values and cultural deep structure.

Outcome research indicated that the program increased awareness of information on smoking and health among current smokers. It also increased awareness of the Hispanic smoking cessation programs, particularly among the community residents who were most immersed in Spanish-language media, and least likely to use services conducted in English. Addressing both surface structure (e.g., language) and deep structure (core cultural values) increased the program's visibility in the community.

***Manhood Development Among African American Adolescents***     Watts (1993) surveyed 40 manhood development programs for African American adolescent males in the United States. Conducted by African American men, these programs are designed to promote healthy psychological development and community involvement. They use deep structure elements from African and African American culture to promote a positive sense of self and concern for family and community.

Although many differences existed among the programs, Watts (1993) identified themes that characterize most or all of them, involving education in African and African American cultural traditions. Cultural elements usually included a Black consciousness or Afrocentric approach that identifies core culture values such as *Nguzu Saba* (Seven Principles of Blackness), celebration of African holidays and rites of passage, and study of African American history and culture. Several related themes are based on these traditions, and provide examples of a collectivistic cultural viewpoint. One was a concern for positive family relationships and commitment, while stressing ties among individual, family, and community. The ancient African proverb "It takes a whole village to raise a child" exemplifies these connections (Watts, 1993). Another emphasized the value of "giving back": personal career or economic advancement means one has a responsibility for returning resources to the community. A third theme concerned an African spiritual focus and the importance of a higher power in one's life. Finally, program leaders often spoke of building self-esteem, personal development, and community and economic empowerment, emphasizing how these are linked. "Self" represented not only the individual but also the family and community; recall the concept of an interdependent or extended self (Nobles, 1991) in collectivistic cultures.

These deep-structure cultural themes emphasize linkages of individual, family, and community. Watts (1993) noted that many of these ideals are shared in other cultures, including European American traditions. Although the surface structure of rituals, writings, and symbols differ across cultures, some underlying values (a deeper deep structure, perhaps) resemble each other: Individual responsibility to family and community, and a spiritual perspective, for instance, occur in many cultures. However, they are expressed here in a distinctively African way.

The manhood development programs described here take a cultural rather than oppression perspective. Watts (1993) noted that these programs do not address social change. Their response to racist oppression is not to challenge it directly, but to encourage individual development and community solidarity among African Americans. Watts et al. (1999) developed a program for this population that seeks to broaden this focus, promoting personal, spiritual, and sociopolitical development. It draws on African cultural and spiritual themes, as well as concepts of oppression theory, to expand the aims of manhood development to include critical thinking about wider society.

Further examples of culturally based programs in African American communities, for instance, include establishing a council of elders to re-affirm their status in the culture, rites of passage programs for adolescents based on Afrocentric themes, a quilting group for women and teens, identifying children's books with cultural themes, and celebration of Kwanzaa (Taylor & Brinkley-Kennedy, 1999; Watts et al., 1999; West-Olatunji & Watson, (1999). These initiatives place psychological development within a distinctive context of cultural values. As with manhood development, these programs were developed by members of African American communities, not imposed from the outside.

***Alaska Native Spirituality and Sobriety***    Alaska Native indigenous communities are using their cultural heritages to create community climates of sobriety, helping individuals and communities prevent and promote recovery from substance abuse (Hazel & Mohatt, in press). The diversity of Alaska Native peoples share some common cultural elements, especially spiritual perspectives, and these are key aspects of the Native sobriety movement. Common spiritual elements include beliefs in a Creator, the spirituality of all living beings, the intermingling of the spiritual and material worlds, and the importance of personal awareness of spiritual forces.

Native leaders summarized cultural elements related to sobriety in four interrelated realms of living: physical, emotional, cognitive, and spiritual. Sobriety can be promoted in the physical realm by use of Native healing and traditional foods; by participation in Native cleansing rituals, dancing, singing, and other arts; and by subsistence gathering and hunting. In the emotional realm, sobriety can be strengthened by allowing oneself to recognize and experience joyful and painful emotions, connecting emotionally with family and community, and practicing forgiveness. In the cognitive realm, sobriety is promoted by learning and taking pride in cultural legends, history, and practices; by learning the culture's language, and by taking responsibility for self, family, and community. Sobriety in the spiritual realm involves opening one's eyes to the spiritual world, connecting with ancestors, meditation, prayer, and using dreams and visions as guides (Hazel & Mohatt, in press). Promoting sobriety involves all four realms and includes both individual development and strengthening family and community bonds. Again, these cultural and spiritual elements have both culture-specific and more universal themes.

## Contributions and Limitations

Culturally sensitive programs address individuals in communities by making the program more in tune with the community's culture. They reflect the core community psychology values of respect for diversity, collaboration and community strengths, and citizen participation, even in programs mainly devoted to wellness or other aims.

Designing community programs to address deep structure may be complicated in multicultural societies, where individual members of a cultural (e.g., racial or ethnic) group differ in the extent to which they identify with the ethnic culture and/or the dominant culture. A community program designed in terms of core values and practices of an ethnic culture is likely to appeal to those who identify most with that culture (Resnicow et al., 1999), that is, those pursuing separation or bicultural strategies of acculturation. It may not engage those pursuing assimilation or who are marginalized.

As with other community programs, the effectiveness of culturally sensitive programs needs to be evaluated in research (Resnicow et al., 1999). That research could study, with methods sensitive to the culture, whether a program attains its aims, what program elements are necessary or especially effective, and which members of the cultural population are reached by the program.

## CONCLUSION

Two important questions remain for the pluralistic view that we have presented. First, does assuming a pluralistic perspective lead to endorsing all value systems (e.g., including Nazism) as equally morally compelling?

Simply put, no. Such a view is a misunderstanding of pluralism, which is concerned with understanding human diversity in context. Pluralism involves bracketing one's own values, as much as possible, and understanding other persons and cultures in their own terms. A useful byproduct of this understanding is that it often heightens awareness of one's own assumptions and values and leads to deeper understanding of both others and oneself. Only with such pluralistic, contextual understanding can principled moral stances on human social problems be constructed on the basis of knowledge, not ignorance.

Second, with all this emphasis on how humans differ across cultural, racial, ethnic, gender, and other boundaries, how can we understand what humans have in common? On what shared basis can multiracial, multicultural, or other diverse communities or societies be constructed and sustained? Is a multicultural, pluralistic society viable?

This question is more difficult and requires some historical perspective. The question may presuppose the desirability of returning to earlier times that seemed harmonious to members of privileged groups, because members of subordinated groups "knew their place." It is also important to note that Western social scientists often have assumed that their concepts and perspective were universal, and later found those ideas were ethnocentric. A multicultural community or society would foster genuine respect for all its cultural groups, while sustaining mutual commitment to shared, overarching values endorsed by all groups (J. M. Jones, 1997b).

Certainly there is much that is universal in human experience, but we can understand it only after we have learned how others view that experience differently. Perhaps it is fitting to close with a statement by one of psychology's founders, William James: "There is very little difference between one person and another, but what little difference there is, is very important" (cited in Hall, 1997, p. 650).

## CHAPTER SUMMARY

**1.** Important dimensions of human diversity for community psychology include culture, race, ethnicity, gender, sexual orientation, age, ability/disability, socioeconomic status or social class, and religion and spirituality. It is important to keep these dimensions separate conceptually, although they may converge in community life. *Pluralism* involves the assumption that everyone has a position somewhere on these dimensions and that no position is considered superior.

**2.** One important dimension of cultural diversity is *individualism–collectivism,* a topic of much research in cross-cultural psychology. Individualistic and collectivistic cultures differ in a number of ways, including *independent* and *interdependent* conceptions of self and the importance of the *ingroup.* These are summarized in Table 6.2.

**3.** Limitations of the cross-cultural perspective include the following: (a) cultures are now influencing each other, (b) diversity of collectivistic cultures, and (c) population-specific study of each culture on its own terms is needed.

**4.** Not all human diversity is the result of cultural forces. Power (economic, social, political) is an important dimension that creates group differences. The oppression perspective concerns these differences.

**5.** Oppression creates an inequality between a *dominant, privileged* group and a *subordinated, oppressed* group, often on grounds such as gender or race that cannot be changed. Key elements of *oppression theory* are summarized in Table 6.3.

**6.** Limitations of oppression theory include the following: (a) its systems focus may underestimate diversity within dominant or subordinated groups, (b) the oppressed group may be portrayed merely as victims, and (c) it may emphasize differences and conflict between groups to the exclusion of shared goals.

**7.** The *acculturation* perspective concerns individual adaptation to the interaction of two cultures or groups. Four acculturative strategies can be identified: *separation, assimilation, marginalization,* and *integration* (or *biculturality*).

**8.** *Bicultural competence* refers to skills and conditions needed for effective adaptation to a second or dominant culture while retaining identification with one's culture of origin. Its six factors are summarized in Table 6.5.

**9.** Although evidence supports the value of the bicultural strategy in many circumstances, it is not always the wisest acculturative strategy. It is not feasible or adaptive in some contexts.

**10.** *Cultural competence* for community psychologists consists of qualities that promote genuine understanding and collaboration with members of a culture. Culturally sensitive community programs address both the *surface structure* and *deep structure* of a culture.

## BRIEF EXERCISES

**1.** Experiential learning about human diversity is best done with other people, especially those who are different from you in race, gender, social class, sexual orientation, or other dimension of diversity. In addition, experiences that bridge cultural, racial, or other boundaries often involve emotions that must be understood and preconceptions that can be difficult to recognize at first. For those reasons, we recommend that you seek experiences at your campus multicultural center or other setting (on or off campus) for learning about dimensions of human diversity.

Make time for this. It's potentially one of the most meaningful parts of your education. Visit the setting, and attend lectures, workshops, or other presentations. Talk with staff or students there and indicate your interest in learning, and listen to learn. Be patient; don't try to become an instant expert. Be persistent; don't be discouraged by an initial experience that doesn't happen as you wanted it to. Recognize that students there may be interested in talking with you, but they also have other commitments. Of course, the best learning often occurs in personal relationships where trust is built and understanding unfolds over time. Cultivating these across boundaries of diverse groups can be an important part of your education.

**2.** Write your responses to the exercise that begins this chapter, and discuss them with classmates or friends. The more diverse the group for discussion, the better. The first site in the list of recommended Websites has some similar exercises that may work better for you.

## RECOMMENDED READINGS

Freire, P. (1993). *Pedagogy of the oppressed.* New York: Continuum. (Original work published 1970)
>    Classic source on the oppression perspective and educating for community change.

Hacker, A. (1992). *Two nations: Black and White, separate, hostile, unequal.* New York: Ballatine.
>    Empirical overview of race and racism in the U.S. today.

Jones, J. M. (1997a). *Prejudice and racism* (2nd ed.). New York: McGraw-Hill.
>    Classic source on forms and levels of racism in the U.S., by a social psychologist.

LaFromboise, T., Coleman, H. L. K., & Gerton, J. (1993). Psychological impact of biculturalism: Evidence and theory. *Psychological Bulletin, 114,* 395–412.
>    Review of research and model of bicultural competence.

Tatum, B. D. (1997). *Why are all the Black kids sitting together in the cafeteria?* New York: Basic Books.
>    Readable overview of oppression concepts and racial identity development, enriched with many daily examples.

Trickett, E. J. (1996). A future for community psychology: The contexts of diversity and the diversity of contexts. *American Journal of Community Psychology, 24,* 209–235.
Interprets diversity concepts from a contextual, community-oriented viewpoint.

Trickett, E. J., Watts, R. J., & Birman, D. (Eds.). (1994). *Human diversity: Perspectives on people in context.* San Francisco: Jossey-Bass.
Comprehensive introduction to diversity for community psychology.

## INFOTRAC KEYWORDS

*acculturation, bicultural(ity), culture(al), diversity;* or listing any dimension of diversity from the chapter, e.g., *aging,* or any category term, e.g., *women* or *Japanese.*

## RECOMMENDED WEBSITES

http://curry.edschool.virginia.edu/go/multicultural/home.html
The "Multicultural Pavilion" at this site offers an introduction to multicultural issues and links to hundreds of related sites. The Pavilion offers awareness activities and helpful introductory material. The links include sites for many dimensions of human diversity, for discussion groups, research resources, and information on topics as diverse as current events, food and music, and historical overviews.

http://www.magenta.nl/crosspoint/
The Crosspoint has an international focus, providing links to sites concerning human rights, antiracism issues, refugees and migrants, women's issues, and Jewish organizations, listed by country (mainly in Europe) or by subject.

http://www.apa.org/pi/programs.html
Part of the larger American Psychological Association site, this is the APA Public Interest (PI) Directorate address. This site has information on PI Directorate program areas on psychological aspects of these topics: AIDS; aging; children, youth and families; disability issues; ethnic minority affairs; lesbian, gay and bisexual concerns; public policy; urban initiatives, and women's programs.

# UNDERSTANDING SENSE OF COMMUNITY

CHAPTER

7

# OPENING EXERCISE: LISTING COMMUNITIES IN YOUR LIFE

> I have never met anyone—young or old, rich or poor, black or white, male or female, educated or not—to whom I have had any great difficulty explaining what I meant by the psychological sense of community. (S. B. Sarason, 1974, p. 1)

Let's begin with an exercise. After some reflection, write down the important communities in your life. What is a community? Well, let's not be too restrictive at first. For the sake of simplicity, let's exclude from the list your immediate family and your network of friends. You may include any of the following that are important in your life:

- your extended family, beyond your immediate nuclear family
- a campus organization, club, or team
- a workplace
- a group of students taking the same class(es)
- the block or neighborhood where you live or once lived
- your hometown and/or the locality where you live now
- a religious congregation or group
- a self-help or other support group you attend
- a recreational club, team, or league
- a voluntary association such as a civic club, political party, or group working for community improvement or change
- the college or university you are attending
- an Internet chat room or other electronic group you "visit" regularly
- any other group, organization, or community that is significant to you.

When you have finished your list, briefly write why each community is important to you. Lists composed during this exercise may be very diverse. Volunteer fire departments, campus organizations, neighborhoods, city blocks, small towns, Internet discussion groups, athletic teams, mutual help groups, extended families, religious congregations, classes of students in a graduate program, work groups, schools, and many other groupings can fit people's intuitive conceptions of community and play a significant role in their lives. Yet common meanings exist in such lists—a sense of sharing an emotional bond, of "being in this together," often a sense of trusting and caring. Community psychologists and others term this the *sense of community.*

However, discussion of lists such as these easily turns to a concern that communities and sense of community may be declining. In the United States, Harris polls have found that individual reports of sense of alienation from their communities are at the highest levels ever measured, while reported trust in others is at the lowest levels ever measured. Charitable contributions have leveled off, and levels of volunteerism in some mainline organizations (e.g., Red Cross, Boy Scouts) may be declining, at a time when government services to the poor are being slashed (Berkowitz, 1996; Putnam, 1995). Many indicators of citizens' participation in government have declined, such as voter turnout and the percentage who volunteer for a political party (Putnam, 1995). However, the news is not all bad: Socializing with neighbors has declined, yet socializing with nonneighbor friends has increased; overall use of bowling lanes has increased whereas membership in bowling leagues has declined (Putnam, 1995). Participation in self-help groups has increased sharply (Kessler, Mickelson, & Zhao, 1997). New forms of community are emerging (see Jason, 1997, chap. 5).

What do these trends mean? Is there a decline in community ties or simply a redirection of the forms of community in which citizens participate? Putnam (1995) asserted that individuals in the United States are bowling less often in leagues and more often alone, but the data he cited may indicate that they are bowling more often in informal groups, not alone. Perhaps the loss of community is only a concern for those in the upper middle class, who change their residences more often, not a concern shared by the less affluent (Hunter & Riger, 1986). Participation in traditional forms of political life (voting, party membership) clearly is dropping, yet attention to the quality of local community life seems to be

---

**TABLE 7.1    A CONVERSATION ABOUT COMMUNITY**

The following are postings to an email listserve group for community psychology. As you will see below, communication on a listserve is more like a spontaneous conversation than formal writing. The first posting below raised the topic of the meaning of communities in the U.S. today, the other postings are responses to it and to each other. As you read the postings, try analyzing them in terms of the levels of analysis described in chapter 1: Is this writer thinking of *community* as a microsystem, organization, neighborhood, city, or macrosystem?

---

To: SCRA-L@LISTSERV.UIC.EDU:

From: Frank Masterpasqua

In a recent TV interview Michael Lerner, editor of Tikkun Magazine, suggested that people (in the USA at least) are no longer likely to look to their communities for "meaning." Clearly, meaning is not easily operationalized but I take it he meant values, standards, norms, some context larger than one's self. Instead, meanings have become more individualized and personalized, probably in some part at least to the greater heterogeneity within communities. His idea resonated with me and troubled me. What, in fact, might it mean if people expect little from their communities? What if they have no expectations? Is this necessarily bad? Can it/must it change? Can community psychology play a role? What do you think?

From: Donald Klein

I don't know what the writer meant by "meaning," but it suggests something like the concept of "significance." By significance I mean having a sense of counting for something in other people's eyes. I believe that most people's sense of significance is derived from relationships to individuals and groups within the framework of their geographic and functional communities. I suspect that for us in community psychology a concept like significance is more powerful and meaningful than the more trendy self-esteem.

From: Anne Mulvey

Yes, I think we can play a role. That's what drew me to this field! Last week I hosted a meeting with graduate students in a course I teach. Women in the Community is its title and focus. We had worked with a number of community projects. 70 people came for a meeting on the topic of "Cultivating Community for Women & Girls"! Their reactions: many participants feel disconnected from community, but want "connection." We played a "stepping stones to safe communities" game & everybody loved it. We had fun, but that also took time away from focused discussion & problem-solving. Somehow, I believe the "fun" & meaning must go with the problem-solving if we are to develop healthy communities.

From: David Chavis

I think that the demise of community has been highly overrated. A similar crisis was predicted by sociologists earlier this century (e.g. Marx and Durkheim and the notions of Mass Society as the source of community). I think this analysis is a matter of class and culture. The intelligentsia is lonely and alienated. They should get involved in their neighborhood. Studies and polls have shown different trends among middle to low income groups and the growing

growing (Lappe & Dubois, 1994). See Table 7.1 for a selection of postings on an Internet listserve for community psychologists regarding the issue of what communities mean to individuals today.

Concern about the nature and sustainability of community ties is not solely a U.S. issue. A recent special issue of the international *Journal of Community and Applied Social Psychology* was devoted to cross-national studies of the relationship between individual and community. For instance, adults in Scotland had more positive conceptions of their localities and linked locality more directly with their personal identities than adults in

---

**TABLE 7.1** *(continued)*

---

ethnic and immigrant communities. I do think that Frank's questions are still very relevant, but we need to define what community we are talking about. While the importance of the neighborhood or residential community now varies, new forms of community have been developed and some old forms (e.g. faith communities) have seen growth.

From: Debra Srebnik

I'd have to agree with David here—Michael Lerner (and his book The Politics of Meaning) have spawned POM groups all over the country—I was in one for a while—pretty middle/upper middle class and white which was interesting in and of itself. I think how people define "community" is key—from ethnic to religious/spiritual, to political, to neighborhood/geographic, to common interest/issue (parents, sports, other recreation, disability, disorder such as AA/NA groups, etc.)—all can be forms of community.

From: Keith Humphreys

The data I am aware of show a decline in community based on geography (e.g., people know their neighbors less) and "forced" economic interaction (e.g., the guy at the gas station who has turned into a computer, the people at your favorite store in town, but now you shop by mail), but an increase in ties based on choice. For example, the self-help group movement has grown sharply in the last decade to 10.5 million people visiting groups a year. Or, for a personal example, I have an active collaboration and friendship with an Israeli social worker I "met" over the Internet. We've been friends for several years, but have never seen each other. He and I have more projects going together than the professor three doors down from me.

From: Paul Toro

I agree with David and Debra on this. I'd add that, even among the professional class (like most of us responding to this listserv), "community" may be more "alive and well" than we think. The nature of "community" has just become much more complex, with various "professional" and "electronic" communities (such as that represented by this listserv) playing bigger roles and people often being parts of "multiple communities." In the "old days," your community was primarily defined by geography (an actual place) and family ties, whereas now there are additional ways to define community.

From: Emily J. Ozer

When does having a large degree of "shared meaning" and strong sense of community feel oppressive or constraining to those in the minority? The main feedback I get about meaning and values of my geographical community is through the electoral process, in which all kinds of funding decisions are now being determined by referendum, so that we learn about the civic priorities of fellow citizens by what they are willing to pay for. Major battles in my city recently have been over paying to restore museums, paying to restore schools, building new ballparks. These raise big issues about the "meaning," for example, of being a town with a professional sports team, or a town without a major art museum, which are meaningful for some but certainly not for others.

Slovakia, where the concept of local community appeared to have lost much of its meaning under communism (Moodie, Markova, Farr, & Plichtova, 1997). In contrast, a comparison of Czech, Hungarian, and U.S. college students found they valued citizen participation in democratic decision making (one element of community involvement) almost equally highly (Klicperova, Feierbend, & Hofstetter, 1997).

Discussion of these issues is complicated by the variety of meanings of the term *community*. Its emotional connotations grant it power as a metaphor yet make it difficult to define in operational terms for research. It refers to varying levels of analysis: microsystems (e.g., classrooms, small groups), organizations (e.g., workplaces, schools), and localities (e.g., neighborhoods or cities). Yet community and sense of community are central ideas in *community* psychology (D. W. McMillan & Chavis, 1986; S. B. Sarason, 1974, 1986).

## WHAT ARE THE KEY POINTS OF THIS CHAPTER?

In this chapter we discuss some of the various meanings of *community*, describing types and levels of communities. We describe the basic elements of the psychological *sense of community*, a key term in community psychology. We illustrate the importance of sense of community by describing self-help groups and organizations, the role of religion and spirituality in community life, and sense of community in neighborhoods. Finally, we critique current concepts and research regarding sense of community in community psychology.

## WHAT IS A COMMUNITY?

Seymour Sarason's (1974) volume, *The Psychological Sense of Community,* set the tone for how community psychologists think about the relationships between individuals and communities. Sarason (1974) defined community as "a readily available, mutually supportive network of relationships on which one could depend" (p. 1). A strong sense of community involvement provides the antidote to what Sarason and others consider the defining problem of Western societies, the loneliness and alienation resulting from individualism (recall our discussion of individualism in chaps. 1 and 2). Sarason (1974) argued that the "absence or dilution of the psychological sense of community is the most destructive dynamic in the lives of people in our society." Its development and maintenance is "the keystone value" for a community psychology.

Sarason used the term *community* in many ways, in terms of localities, community institutions, and smaller networks of individuals (S. B. Sarason, 1974, p. 131). He included families, street gangs, friends, neighbors, religious and fraternal bodies, and even national professional organizations as forms of community (p. 153). Thus, his concept of psychological sense of community involved several levels of analysis (e.g., microsystem, institution or organization, locality, national organization). This diversity of usage and meaning reflects the diversity of definitions of community in sociology (Puddifoot, 1996) and common language (also reflected in Table 7.1). Moreover, Sarason's emphasis on the yearning for community by lonely individuals reflected only one perspective from which sociologists and other social scientists have studied community (Bernard, 1973; Hunter & Riger, 1986).

| TABLE 7.2 | **Types and Levels of Communities** |
|---|---|

| Types | Levels |
|---|---|
| Locality | Microsystem (e.g., mutual help group, classroom) |
| Relational | Organization (e.g., community group, religious congregation, workplace) |
|   Social groupings | |
|   Task-oriented organizations | Locality (e.g., block; neighborhood; town, city, or rural county) |
|     Workplaces, educational settings | |
|   Collective power structures | |

What conceptions of community are relevant to community psychology? Table 7.2 summarizes the principal concepts of types and levels of communities.

## Types of Communities

Definitions of community in sociology (e.g., Bernard, 1973) and in community psychology (e.g., K. Heller, 1989) distinguish between two meanings of the term: community as locality and community as a relational group.

**Locality**    This is the traditional conception of community. It includes city blocks, neighborhoods, small towns, and even cities and rural regions. Interpersonal ties exist among community members (residents); they are based on proximity, not necessarily choice. When residents of a locality share a strong sense of community, loyalty to place is strong and individuals often identify themselves by referring to their locality. Friends are often neighbors. Even if sense of community is not strong, political representation, public school districts, and other forms of social organization often are formed by locality. Attachment to place remains a key element of some forms of sense of community (Chavis & Pretty, 1999).

**Relational Community**    Communities may also be *relational* (K. Heller, 1989, p. 6), defined by interpersonal relationships and a sense of community but not limited by geography. Internet discussion groups provide an example of communities completely without face-to-face contact; geographic limits are irrelevant. Mutual help groups are relational communities not necessarily bounded by locality. Student clubs and organizations provide campus examples. Religious congregations, labor unions, political parties, professional associations, and other voluntary associations are usually not bounded by locality and are defined mainly or solely by their relational bonds.

Although relational communities may be based only on friendships or recreation (e.g., country club, bowling league, or sorority), many are organizations bound by a common task. A workplace or a larger corporation are examples. Bernard (1973), for instance, described seatmates on an airplane introducing themselves by their corporate employers, not by their residences. A university, although seated in a locality, is defined mainly by its educational purpose; its students often are only temporary residents of that locality.

Some organizations represent a *collective power structure* (K. Heller, 1989, p. 7). Women's or environmental advocacy organizations, chambers of commerce, and labor unions are examples. In societies, and often in localities, such a collective organization is required for citizens to influence decision making that affects their communities (whether locality or relational).

The impact of relational communities is illustrated by a trend cited earlier: In the United States at least, socializing with neighbors is decreasing while socializing with non-neighbor friends is increasing (Putnam, 1995). Thus, although the sense of community in localities may have waned in Western societies, individuals are increasingly involved in relational communities (Hunter & Riger, 1986).

However, as you may have noted above, many examples of relational communities are seated in a locality and may contribute to the sense of community there. A religious congregation and its locality may strengthen each other's sense of community. Thus, the concepts of locality and relational communities are not completely mutually exclusive; whether a community is more relational or locality-based is a matter of degree. An Internet discussion group may anchor the purely relational pole of the continuum, whereas a town or urban neighborhood with a strong sense of community among residents may represent the opposite locality pole.

## Levels of Communities

Individuals belong to many communities. In urbanized societies, or anywhere that contacts beyond the locality are easy and frequent, the individual easily becomes a member of many communities that have little relationship to each other (Hunter & Riger, 1986). This membership in multiple communities represents multiple resources for the individual, or can pose a problem of competing commitments. Have you ever had a conflict between two organizations, both of which were important to you?

This multiplicity of communities in one's life leads to conceiving of communities as existing at different levels. At present in community psychology, usage of the terms *community* and *sense of community* may involve any of several such levels. It's helpful to conceive of these in terms of the levels of analysis described in chapter 1: microsystems, organizations, localities, macrosystems. Sometimes in this chapter and in later ones you will encounter a microsystem, such as a classroom or a mutual help group, described as a community. You will also encounter references to the sense of community in an organization, such as a workplace, religious congregation, or advocacy group. Most often, and perhaps most clearly, you will encounter community defined as a locality: city block or neighborhood, or larger unit such as town, city, or rural county. Even macrosystems are sometimes termed communities: for example the business community, the religious community. (That usage is usually too general for our purposes here.) We label as clearly as possible the level of analysis when the idea of community is used. Table 7.1 reveals a diversity of levels in conceptions of community among community psychologists.

If communities exist at different levels, where is the lower boundary of the concept? What is the smallest group that can be usefully called a community? Couldn't your immediate family or your network of friends be considered a community? Certainly these have some of the psychological qualities of communities.

S. B. Sarason's (1974) original, wide-ranging discussion of the psychological sense of community certainly included such microsystems. In a recent review of research on sense of community, however, J. L. Hill (1996, p. 434) argued that for conceptual clarity, families and networks of social support or friendship should be considered social networks, not communities. J. L. Hill's view is that a community is best defined as a larger grouping of individuals who may not know all of the other members, or who have little contact with them, yet who share some sense of mutual commitment. In this chapter, we exclude immediate families and friendship/social networks from our discussion of communities, while including microsystems that meet regularly and admit new members who share the group's purposes, such as mutual help groups.

***Mediating Structures*** Some groups and organizations connect individuals with a larger organization, locality, or society. Joining them provides a sense of community for the individual and also provides a practical way to participate in the larger community or society. Thus, these intermediate communities are termed mediating structures (Berger & Neuhaus, 1977). For instance, religious congregations, civic clubs, and neighborhood associations in a locality all offer ways to become involved in the community and can give collective voice to their members' views about community issues. Thus, they mediate between individuals and the wider community. In a university that is too large for an individual student to feel much personal involvement with the whole, student clubs, athletic teams, residence hall organizations, student government or other groups provide pathways for individual involvement and shared community. They also are mediating structures. Collective power structures, discussed earlier as a type of relational community, also are mediating structures.

# SENSE OF COMMUNITY: THE McMILLAN–CHAVIS MODEL

Whether a community defines its boundaries in locality or relational terms is less important to community psychologists than the strength of bonding among its members. That bond may be termed the *psychological sense of community*. As S. B. Sarason (1974) noted, it is a rather subjective concept, yet widely recognized. He defined it as

> the perception of similarity to others, an acknowledged interdependence with others, a willingness to maintain this interdependence by giving to or doing for others what one expects from them, the feeling that one is part of a larger dependable and stable structure. (p. 157)

D. W. McMillan and Chavis (1986) reviewed research in sociology and social psychology on the sense of community and group cohesion. Their summary definition of the sense of community was similar to Sarason's (1974):

> a feeling that members have of belonging, a feeling that members matter to one another and to the group, and a shared faith that members' needs will be met through their commitment to be together. (McMillan & Chavis, 1986, p. 9)

What are the specific qualities of sense of community? McMillan and Chavis (1986) identified four major elements: membership, influence, integration and fulfillment of needs, and shared emotional connection. All four elements must be present to define a sense of community. These elements translate the overarching theme of a sense of community, which characterizes Sarason's (1974) volume, into measurable constructs for

| TABLE 7.3 | ELEMENTS OF THE PSYCHOLOGICAL SENSE OF COMMUNITY |
|---|---|

1. Membership
   The sense of having invested part of oneself in the community, and of belonging to it. It has five attributes.
   a. boundaries
   b. common symbol system
   c. emotional safety
   d. sense of belonging and identification with the community
   e. personal investment

2. Influence
   The power that members exercise over the group, and the reciprocal power that group dynamics exert on members.

3. Integration and Fulfillment of Needs
   Shared values among members, as well as the exchange of resources and satisfaction of individual needs among community members.

4. Shared Emotional Connection
   A "spiritual bond" based on a shared history among members of the community; this represents the "definitive element for true community." Several processes strengthen it, especially events that emphasize shared values and history.

Note: Based on D. W. McMillan and Chavis (1986) and D. W. McMillan (1996).

research and specific objectives for action. These elements may be applied to localities and to relational communities, at microsystem, organizational, and locality levels. Our description of these elements is based primarily on McMillan and Chavis (1986) and McMillan (1996; see Table 7.3).

## Membership

This is the sense among community members of having invested part of themselves in the community, and of belonging to it (D. W. McMillan & Chavis, 1986, p. 9). It has five attributes. The first attribute of *boundaries* refers to the necessity of defining the territory or qualities that include members and exclude nonmembers. For a locality, this involves geographic boundaries; for a relational community, it may involve similarity in interests or personalities. For an organization, boundaries involve shared purpose and goals. Boundaries may be clearly or obscurely marked, and they may be rigid or permeable. They are necessary for the community to define itself and to offer the other qualities of community to its members (D. W. McMillan & Chavis, 1986).

A *common symbol system* is a related attribute of membership. Common symbols help define membership boundaries as well as strengthen the sense of integration among members. Examples include the use of Greek letters among campus sororities, colors and symbols among youth gangs and sports teams, religious imagery, university decals on automobiles, and national flags and anthems. Symbols can be used to identify community members as well as to identify physical settings or territory.

In a community with clear boundaries, members experience *emotional safety*. Ecologically, this could mean a sense of safety from crime in a neighborhood. Relationally, it could mean a secure place to make friends. In a collective power structure its meaning may involve shared values. D. W. McMillan (1996) emphasized how emotional safety involves self-disclosure and group acceptance; this seems especially characteristic of relational communities.

A member who feels safe is likely to make *personal investment* in the community. D. W. McMillan (1996) refers to the latter as "paying dues," although it is often not monetary. Investment indicates long-term commitment to a community, such as home ownership in a neighborhood, membership in a religious congregation, or devotion of time to a charity organization. It can also involve taking emotional risks for the group. These acts not only serve as symbols of commitment, but also generate additional involvement (D. W. McMillan & Chavis, 1986).

These acts deepen a member's *sense of belonging and identification* with the community. The individual is accepted by other community members, and defines personal identity partly in terms of membership in the community. Individuals may identify with being a resident of a neighborhood, adherent of a religion, member of a profession or trade, student in a university, or member of an ethnic group. All five attributes of membership strengthen the sense of community or bond between individual members and the overall group.

## Influence

The second element refers both to the power that members exercise over the group and to the reciprocal power that group dynamics exert on members. McMillan and Chavis (1986, pp. 11–12) based their discussion of influence in part on the group cohesiveness literature in social psychology. This research supports several conclusions about the mutuality of influence in a group. Members are more attracted to a group in which they feel influential. The most influential members in the group are often those to whom the needs and values of others matter most. Those who seek to dominate or exercise power too strongly often are isolated. In addition, the more cohesive the group, the greater is its pressure for conformity. However, this is rooted in the shared commitments of each individual to the group, not simply imposed on the individual.

Thus, the individual influences the wider group or community, and that community influences the views and actions of the person, forming a feedback loop. Members who share a strong sense of community both influence others and are influenced by them. At a more general level, organizations within a community exert influence on the whole community, and are in turn influenced by it (D. W. McMillan & Chavis, 1986). K. Heller's (1989) conception of community as a collective political power structure, intended to influence larger units of government, provides an example of this influence.

## Integration and Fulfillment of Needs

Although influence often concerns vertical relations between individuals and the overall community, integration often concerns horizontal relations among members. This element of the McMillan and Chavis (1986) definition refers to two related concepts. First is the idea of *shared values*. This goes beyond the visible signs of community boundaries and symbols; it refers to deeper shared ideals that can be pursued through community involvement. Faith and service may be shared values of a religious community, while improving educational quality may be the shared value of a group of school parents.

The second concept refers to *satisfying needs and exchanging resources* among community members. D. W. McMillan (1996) referred to this as a "community economy." Individuals participate in communities in part because their individual needs are met there; these needs may be physical needs (e.g., for safety) or psychosocial needs (e.g., for learning new skills, attaining a personal goal through teamwork, socializing and making friends, or exercising leadership). Those needs are met though connecting with other members. This element is similar to the concepts of interdependence and cycling of resources in Kelly's (1970) ecological perspective (see chap. 5).

## Shared Emotional Connection

McMillan and Chavis (1986) considered this the "definitive element for true community" (p. 14). It involves a "spiritual bond": not necessarily religious-transcendent, and not easily defined, yet recognizable to those who share it. "Soul" among African-Americans is an example (D. W. McMillan & Chavis, 1986). Members of a community may recognize a shared bond through behavior, speech, or other cues. The bond itself is deeper, however, not merely a matter of behavior.

Social processes that appear to enhance shared emotional connection include positive contact among members, sharing important experiences, investment by members in the community, and honoring of members by the group. D. W. McMillan (1996) added the notion of shared dramatic moments that form the basis of this element. Rappaport (1993, 1995) and Berkowitz (1996) also emphasized the importance of shared celebrations and rituals involving community narratives or stories; these strengthen members' sense of connection.

## Summary of Elements

These four elements exist in mutual relationship; none is the root cause of the others, and all strengthen each other. McMillan and Chavis (1986) originally listed four examples of communities in terms of these elements: universities, youth gangs, neighborhoods, and the Israeli kibbutz. (Note that all are based in a locality, but these elements also fit purely relational communities.) They argued that sense of community is a powerful force, increasing individual quality of life. However, its power is not always for good; sense of community may be strong in communities that scapegoat and victimize outsiders, or in privileged communities that act to exclude outsiders and deny problems of poverty and injustice. McMillan and Chavis concluded that the challenge for community psychology is to build communities based on "faith, hope, and tolerance" and that foster "understanding and cooperation" (p. 20). Essential to those tasks is an understanding of the dynamics of the sense of community.

How is sense of community expressed in real-life settings? We now turn to detailed analysis of sense of community involving three examples: self-help groups, religious and spiritual communities, and neighborhoods. These examples involve microsystems, organizations, and localities, in the context of cultural beliefs and practices.

# SENSE OF COMMUNITY IN SELF-HELP GROUPS

Self-help or mutual aid groups represent one example of the importance of a sense of community to individuals. A generic definition of such groups is "voluntary associations of persons who share some status that results in difficulties with which the group tries to deal" (Humphreys & Rappaport, 1994, p. 218). Examples include an Alcoholics Anonymous meeting, a group for persons who have the same disability or illness (or for their family members), and a group for bereaved persons.

The terms *self-help* and *mutual aid* refer to two intertwined processes that occur in these groups (Borkman, 1991a). Mutual aid denotes the exchange of aid among peers in the group, each providing and receiving help. Self-help refers to individuals taking personal responsibility for their recovery or coping, usually with the aid of a group, but without professional treatment or going beyond that treatment. For simplicity, and to respect the language most often used by group members, we use the latter term. In addition, self-help groups are chapters of wider (often worldwide) organizations (e.g., Alcoholics Anonymous), not isolated microsystems (Borkman, 1991a). We use the term *groups,* again for simplicity and also to emphasize the helping process at the microsystem level.

Self-help groups have mushroomed in the United States and other countries. In just over 50 years, the first widely recognized self-help organization, Alcoholics Anonymous, has grown from two founders to a worldwide organization with thousands of local groups. Its Twelve Step approach has been adopted by many similar groups. Estimates based on a representative sample of U.S. citizens suggested that 10.5 million citizens attended a self-help group within the past year, and 25 million have done so within their lifetimes (Kessler et al., 1997). The proportion of the adult population in self-help groups appears equal to that engaged in psychotherapy (Borkman, 1990). In Wuthnow's (1994) representative sample of U.S. adults, fully 40% reported involvement in a group that "meets regularly and provides caring and support for its members" (Wuthnow, 1994, p. 47), a definition that included mutual aid groups, small religious groups, and others. Internet chat rooms and other on-line forms of mutual aid may expand participation even further, especially for those reluctant or unable to attend a face-to-face group (Dunham et al., 1998; Salem, Bogat, & Reid, 1997). Obviously, many people seek the sense of community that self-help groups provide.

## *What Are the Distinctive Features of Self-Help Groups?*

Self-help groups have four distinctive features (Borkman, 1991a; Riessman, 1990):

- a *focal concern:* a problem, life crisis, or issue affecting all members
- *peer relationships* among all members, rather than an unequal, professional–client relationship
- *reciprocity* of helping, so that each member both receives and provides help
- an emphasis on *experiential knowledge* rather than professional expertise.

The last three of these are the critical elements for understanding self-help. Self-help is based on peer relationships. It involves an exchange of helping based on interpersonal norms of reciprocity, rather than a professional service provided for a fee. It occurs among peers, each of whom sometimes provides aid and sometimes receives it. That helping has a different form than the relationship of professional and client. It can be understood in terms of the *helper therapy principle* (Riessman, 1990): Providing aid to others promotes one's own well-being. For instance, GROW, a group we describe in detail in the next section, emphasizes "If you need help, help others" (Maton & Salem, 1995, p. 641). In addition, Riessman argued, needing and receiving aid for one's problems is less stigmatizing if everyone in the group shares similar concerns and if one expects to provide aid to others as well as receive it.

The final distinctive element of self-help is the type of knowledge that is most respected and used for helping. Experiential knowledge is based on the personal experiences of group members who have coped with the focal concern, often for years. This practical "insider" knowledge is shared in self-help group meetings. Professional expertise is an intellectual understanding of the focal problem, which is valuable in many contexts, but professionals usually don't have direct, daily, personal experience with the focal problem.

In an empirical study of a variety of community groups, Schubert and Borkman (1991) distinguished between groups entirely relying on self-help and support groups with some professional involvement (see also Borkman, 1990). Twelve Step groups, of which Alcoholics Anonymous is the best-known, embody all four distinctive features of self-help. Schubert and Borkman (1991, p. 784) identified peer counseling groups in high schools, and Reach to Recovery, a group for women with breast cancer, as support groups involving significant training and supervision by professionals while also using some elements of mutual aid. Professional treatment and self-help are perhaps best understood as different forms of helping that can complement each other if mutually respected and conducted separately (Stewart, Banks, Crossman & Poel, 1994; Toro, Rappaport, & Seidman, 1987).

## What Really Happens in a Self-Help Group?

Let's look inside a group that has been extensively studied by community psychologists (Luke et al., 1991; Maton & Salem, 1995; L. Roberts et al., 1991, 1999; Zimmerman et al., 1991).

GROW is a self-help organization primarily for persons coping with serious mental illness (relatives and others are welcome at meetings). It began in Australia when members of an Alcoholics Anonymous meeting, who also experienced serious mental illness, began their own meeting. It has many similarities to Alcoholics Anonymous. GROW has become an international organization, active in Australia, New Zealand, Ireland, Great Britain, Canada, and the United States.

GROW groups meet weekly. As described by Roberts et al. (1991), "meetings open and close with group recitation of prayers and pledges" (p. 724). Two periods of group discussion of individual attenders' problems and progress follow, with a "period of objective discussion and learning of GROW literature" between. GROW meetings studied by Roberts et al. lasted 1 to 2 hours, with a mean attendance of 8 persons. Behavioral observation of these meetings documented that a high rate of helping interaction took place. Often, an individual member brought up a problem or gave a progress report on a problem discussed previously, and other members provided encouragement or advice or described a similar experience (L. Roberts et al., 1991, p. 734). Almost one third of comments in the discussion periods were helping acts or agreement with another speaker. Another one third of comments shared nonthreatening information intended to be helpful. Most of the rest involved asking questions or self-disclosure. Both negative comments (2%) and distracting small talk (4%) were rare. These findings are consistent with an emphasis on peer relationships, reciprocity, and experiential knowledge.

An important GROW objective is the fostering of a "caring and sharing community" among members (Maton & Salem, 1995, p. 648). GROW literature and practice emphasize interdependence and sense of community among members, with sayings such as "If you need help, help others" and "No matter how bad my condition, I am loved by God and a connecting link between persons" (Maton & Salem, 1995, p. 641). Practices such as contacts between pairs of members outside meetings, encouraging friendship among members, and provision of rides and other tangible assistance, build a peer-based support system among members (Maton & Salem, 1995, p. 648). This embodies mutual aid.

Within this community atmosphere, GROW encourages members to assume responsibility for their own coping and personal development. Its approach emphasizes member strengths and growth, with sayings such as "I can compel my muscles and limbs to act rightly in spite of my feelings" and "Mostly, when things go wrong they are meant to go wrong, so we can outgrow what we have to outgrow" (Maton & Salem, 1995, p. 641). This embodies self-help.

## Self-Help: Alternative Treatment or Form of Community?

Empirical evaluations of GROW programs have documented its efficacy in helping members make changes in their lives. Weekly attenders of GROW meetings have experienced more positive changes in psychological, interpersonal, and community adjustment than infrequent attenders. Compared with matched controls, GROW members spent less than half as many days in psychiatric hospitalization over a 32-month period (Rappaport, 1993; Maton & Salem, 1995, p. 635).

Studies of participants in Alcoholics Anonymous (AA) and similar Twelve Step groups have generated similar findings. For instance, Humphreys et al. (1994) followed 439 men and women with an alcohol abuse problem in the San Francisco area over 3 years. Participants varied in AA involvement, from none to intensive. Those more involved with AA over the 3-year period were more likely to develop active coping strategies, including less use of alcohol. They also developed greater friendship resources, especially support available from others committed to abstinence (see also Humphreys & Noke, 1997).

Self-help groups are not for everyone: Dropout rates are significant (as is also true in professional treatment), and self-help alone may not be enough for some especially complicated problems (Humphreys, 1997). Not everyone perceives membership as beneficial (S. Norton, Wandersman, & Goldman, 1993). Moreover, some self-help groups address social injustices underlying some personal problems, whereas others don't (Rapping, 1997). Yet they clearly are helpful for many in overcoming or coping with problems in living, including but not limited to addictions.

However, thinking of mutual aid and self-help as a form of group treatment for personal problems overlooks much of their value (Borkman, 1991a; Gidron & Chesler, 1994; Humphreys & Rappaport, 1994). Self-help is not merely receiving a defined treatment for a defined period. One joins a mutual aid or self-help group for an extended period, perhaps for life. Membership incurs responsibility not only for working on one's own concerns, but also for helping others. It often involves a transformation of one's identity. Rappaport (1993) argued that a more revealing view of such groups is that they are *normative communities,* providing a sense of belonging, identification with the group, and mutual commitment; in short, a psychological sense of community (see also Gidron & Chesler, 1994).

Mutual-aid and self-help groups share the four elements of a sense of community (D. W. McMillan & Chavis, 1986). Membership boundaries, the first element, are defined by the focal concern. Use of a common terminology is analogous to a common symbol system; for instance, GROW avoids stigmatizing diagnostic terms and focuses on terms like "recovering GROWer" instead. Discussion, self-disclosure, and group acceptance cement the sense of emotional safety. One of the most powerful emotional experiences reported by self-help group members is the sense that "I am not alone; others share my experiences"; these can be discussed without stigmatizing or self-blame.

Self-help also involves mutual influence, the second McMillan–Chavis (1986) element. As newcomers attend more meetings, they are socialized into mutual helping behaviors (L. Roberts et al., 1991) and eventually into leadership roles. GROW pursues an organizational strategy of creating "underpopulated settings" (Zimmerman et al., 1991). Recall this idea in Barker's (1968) ecological model, covered in chapter 5. A slightly underpopulated setting has a number of roles available for members to play, thus creating pressure for members to fill these roles in order for the setting to survive. As long as they are not overloaded, members thus develop their skills and identities in positive ways not possible in a more populated setting. GROW, independent of Barker's theory, developed an organizational approach that strongly encourages member participation in a variety of roles, such as organizing group meetings, leading group discussion, and recording group members' evaluations of each meeting. GROW also encourages formation of a new meeting when a meeting grows too large; this creates new roles for members. This method of developing leadership promotes individual influence and decentralizes power within the group.

Self-help group members also exchange resources such as experiential knowledge, individual mentoring, and group encouragement, involving the third McMillan–Chavis (1986) element: integration and fulfillment of needs. Finally, group rituals, such as the period of "prayers and pledges" in GROW, strengthen the emotional–spiritual connection among members, the fourth McMillan–Chavis element. In addition, most self-help groups cultivate the sense of connection to a larger community, not just the local meeting. For instance, recovering alcoholics often say they can attend any AA meeting and be accepted as part of a wider organization.

Rappaport (1993, 1995) described the importance of shared community events and shared narratives or stories for sustaining members' emotional–spiritual connection. These rituals also facilitate members' personal transformations in GROW and similar groups. The belief system, rituals, and group discussion of a self-help group provide a shared narrative. As members become involved in and committed to the group, they reinterpret their own life stories and identities in terms similar to the group narrative (Rappaport, 1993).

At microsystem and organizational levels, mutual aid and self-help groups and organizations provide a sense of community that can be powerful. They represent an important and growing form of community (Humphreys & Rappaport, 1994).

# RELIGION, SPIRITUALITY, AND COMMUNITIES

Religion and spirituality, and communities based on them, also represent an important force in community life. In the United States, for instance, poll respondents have more confidence in religious institutions than any other social institution (Pargament & Maton, 2000). Again, in the United States, over one third of volunteer activity is based in religious congregations, and congregations contribute more money to community causes than corporations (Maton & Wells, 1995). As we mentioned in chapter 6, religion and spirituality have played important roles in survival of oppressed groups (Hazel & Mohatt, in press; Moore, 1992). Spiritual and religious beliefs and practices can provide important resources for personal coping with stressors. Religious institutions and other forms of spiritual communities thus provide meaning in individual lives, comprise important forms of community in themselves, and contribute important resources to society. However, religious institutions also have negative effects on individuals and societies (cf. Brodsky, 2000; Hunsberger, 1995; Martin-Baro, 1990; Pargament, 1997; Ventis, 1995). For example, the available research indicates that some especially religious U.S. college students are more prejudiced than other students against African Americans, women, gay men, lesbians, and others (Hunsberger, 1995; Pargament, 1997, p. 352; Waldo et al., 1998).

Community psychologists increasingly are recognizing the importance of religion and spirituality in community life (Berkowitz, 1996; J. L. Hill, 1996; Kloos & Moore, 2000; Newbrough, 1995; Pargament & Maton, 2000; Pargament, Maton, & Hess, 1992). This leavening of interest was strengthened by S. B. Sarason (1993). As a theorist of sense of community, he noted that sense of community throughout history has usually been inextricably tied to a sense of the transcendent, a sense of spiritual experience beyond the immediate material world. S. B. Sarason asked whether modern forms of community could be sustained without that sense of transcendence.

In this section and throughout this book, we distinguish between *religion* as a set of beliefs and practices associated with a particular religious institution, and *spirituality* as a wider set of beliefs and practices associated with personal awareness of a transcendent power, not necessarily associated with a religious institution (J. L. Hill, 2000). In the United States, over 90% of poll respondents believe in God (Pargament & Maton, 2000), but many of them do not associate themselves with religious institutions. Further, spirituality concerns awareness of a higher or transcendent power in the universe, and a sense of unity with others and with nature in relation to that power, but it is not necessarily a theistic belief in God (Dokecki, Newbrough, & O'Gorman, in press; J. L. Hill, 2000). Examples of spirituality emphasized in communities not associated with traditional religious institutions include Afrocentric spiritual perspectives (L. J. Myers & Speight, 1994), spirituality in Alaska Native and North American Indian cultures (Hazel & Mohatt, in press; Walsh-Bowers, 2000), many forms of women's spirituality (Molock & Douglas, 1999; Mulvey, Gridley, & Gawith, in press; Walsh-Bowers, 2000), and many self-help groups (especially Twelve Step groups). Moreover, the interest in religious traditions in community psychology is not limited to Judaism and Christianity; it includes Islam (Abdul-Adil & Jason, 1991), Buddhism (Dockett, 1999), and other faiths. Both religious and more generally spiritual perspectives share an emphasis on *relationality*, including both connections among humans and with a transcendent being or power (Dokecki et al., in press). That emphasis on relationality fits with community psychology's emphasis on sense of community.

## How Are Religion and Spirituality Involved in Community Life?

Many religious and spiritual groups can be described in terms of the four elements of sense of community (D. W. McMillan & Chavis, 1986). They provide a sense of membership through common rituals and symbols, including rites of passage for membership. These rituals also foster identification with the community, as does education. Emotional safety is provided through small group and one-to-one sharing. The formation of a religious identity can be an important social identity, fostered by multiple religious contexts (Kress & Elias, 2000).

Religious communities also foster mutual influence and integration and fulfillment of individual needs among members. Religious norms and forms of mutual support provide guides for behavior that can be adaptive (Kress & Elias, 2000; Pargament & Maton, 2000). At least in small settings, shared decision making can occur. Members of a community can help meet each others' interpersonal, economic, psychological, and spiritual needs (Maton & Rappaport, 1984; Pargament & Maton, 2000). Religious and spiritual communities also can provide rich opportunities for members' participation (Maton & Salem, 1995), particularly if their behavior settings are underpopulated (recall behavior setting concepts from chap. 3). Finally, these settings foster emotional and spiritual bonds based on a shared sense of history and spiritual experience and on common rituals. Those bonds are based on a sense of spiritual transcendence as well as human community (S. B. Sarason, 1993).

Religion and spirituality serve four important community functions in Western cultures (Pargament & Maton, in press). First, they meet primary human needs for meaning and understanding. Humans "search for significance" in everyday life (Frankl, 1959/1984; Pargament, 1997), and religion and spirituality provide various forms of that significance. For instance, the Judeo-Christian concept of a vocation (a calling) structures career planning and use of time in meaningful ways. Moreover, religion and spirituality provide solace in the face of uncontrollable circumstances (Pargament, 1997) and ways of active coping with controllable ones (Pargament & Maton, 2000). (We describe the role of religion and spirituality in coping in chap. 6.) Finally, spiritual–religious perspectives provide narratives (i.e., shared stories that express important ideals) and provide a spiritual bond based on a sense of connection to the narrative (Rappaport & Simkins, 1992). The narrative of Passover and the Exodus in Jewish tradition is an example. These forms of spirituality strongly affect one's participation in communities. A willingness to respect transcendent spirituality is needed to understand and work with spiritual–religious communities.

Second, as we have described, religion and spirituality also meet primary needs for community and belonging (Coakes & Bishop, 1996; Pargament & Maton, 2000; Wuthnow, 1994). The forms of this community-building are very diverse, depending on the beliefs, practices, mission, and organizational structure of a religious congregation (Pargament & Maton, 2000). They are often fostered by small groups, such as groups for prayer or other spiritual practices, religious education classes, and even congregational committees.

Spiritual and religious communities serve two further functions (Pargament & Maton, 2000). They act as one counterbalance to the values and forces of individualism in the wider society, through concern for the public good, for the disenfranchised, and for individual altruism (cf. Bellah et al., 1985). Finally, some of them also provide meaning, community, and services especially for members of oppressed, disenfranchised populations. These have included, for instance, African Americans, gay and lesbian individuals, the economically oppressed, and women (Moore, 1992; Potts, 1999). Of course, many religious institutions and individuals do not live up to these ideals, and religion has often been used for social exclusion and oppression. Yet these four functions are important contributions of religious and spiritual communities.

## Action Examples

Spiritual and religious communities accomplish these functions in a variety of ways, as illustrated in the following examples (Maton & Wells, 1995). Religious institutions offer a number of supports for families, parents, and marital partners, including workshops, small group meetings, and counseling. Spiritually based mutual help, such as Alcoholics Anonymous and other groups, is a common and effective form of healing. Groups for prayer and spiritual support promote personal transformation and growth (Maton & Rappaport, 1984; Wuthnow, 1994). Training congregation members in basic helping skills facilitates mutual helping (Pargament & Maton, 2000; B. Roberts & Thorsheim, 1992). Mentoring programs for youth often have a spiritual base. Examples include Project RAISE, in which religious congregations and other groups provided academic and interpersonal mentoring for inner-city youth (Maton & Wells, 1995), and manhood development programs with an Afrocentric spiritual focus (Watts, 1993; described in chap. 6). In chapter 6, we also described indigenous spirituality and sobriety practices in Alaska Native communities (Hazel & Mohatt, in press).

Religious perspectives also provide important forms of social advocacy. These include public positions taken by religious institutions and councils, and community-level efforts by local congregations and related groups (Maton & Wells, 1995; Speer et al., 1995). Liberation, feminist, and womanist theologies (Balcazar, 1999; Dokecki et al., in press; Molock & Douglas, 1999) provide concepts for analyzing connections between religious–spiritual ideals and everyday injustices. Not surprisingly, they have arisen among members of oppressed populations. The U.S. civil rights movement provides historical examples of faith-based social change initiatives.

Dokecki et al. (in press) described three elements of faith-based community development. These elements are based on the concepts of liberation theology, which arose in Latin American Roman Catholicism to advocate for political and economic justice as one expression of Biblical ideals. One element, characteristic of religious–spiritual settings, is *communion,* the spiritual bonding among members that occurs through shared rituals and practices. A second is *reflection* on everyday events in the light of sacred writings, spiritual experience, and other ways of discerning spiritual meaning. This often reveals how an individual or community falls short of spiritual ideals. It also can yield a critical view of society that propels social change (Friere, 1970/1993). The third element, *service* or *ministry,* is action to promote individual or social change. Action is not taken alone but with the support of a community. These elements involve interpersonal, spiritual, cognitive, affective, and behavioral dimensions, appealing to the whole person in ways that can be difficult in other community settings.

Religious and spiritual settings provide important forms of sense of community, at microsystem, organizational, locality, and even macrosystem levels. Like mutual help groups, they offer a holistic approach to the person, involving affective, spiritual, cognitive, and social aspects of individuals' lives. Their importance is being increasingly recognized in community psychology (Kloos & Moore, 2000).

# SENSE OF COMMUNITY IN NEIGHBORHOODS AND LOCALITIES

For many individuals, an important source of a sense of community is the neighborhood. The exact definition of a *neighborhood* is somewhat difficult; it is larger than an urban block on one hand, and smaller than a city or town on the other, yet it has fluid boundaries with both concepts. A small town may have the qualities of a single neighborhood. Nevertheless, as S. B. Sarason (1974) said about the psychological sense of community, most of us have an intuitive idea of neighborhood.

Is the neighborhood really that important in the lives of individuals? Consider the findings of recent studies by Pretty and colleagues (Pretty, Andrewes, & Collett, 1994; Pretty, Conroy, Dugay, Fowler, & Williams, 1996). In their studies of Canadian adolescents, perceptions of sense of community in neighborhood or school was more strongly correlated with psychological well-being and loneliness (a negative correlation) than social support received from friends and family. In interviews for these studies, the adolescent respondents stressed the importance of obtaining aid if they needed it in the neighborhood, even from persons they did not know (Pretty et al., 1996). A sense of community in the neighborhood or school seemed to provide a secure base for adolescent life.

Consider another study indicating the importance of neighborhood in adolescence, with a very different sample and focus. Gonzales, Cauce, Friedman, and Mason (1996) studied predictors of grades in school for a sample of urban African-American adolescents whose neighborhoods varied in their degree of risk (occurrence of crime, gang activity, and violence in the neighborhood). Neighborhood risk was a stronger predictor of grades than family characteristics such as parent education, family income, number of parents living in the home, and maternal parenting style. The quality of neighborhood life made a difference in the lives of these adolescents as well.

## Types of Neighborhoods

Let's begin this section with an exercise. Spend a few moments thinking about the neighborhood in which you live, or one in which you lived while growing up. After you have refreshed your memory, study the six types of neighborhoods in Table 7.4. Choose the type(s) that best fit(s) the neighborhood you were thinking of in your life. Be able to explain why you chose that type.

The classification in Table 7.4 is based on ethnographic interviews in one U.S. city (Detroit) and is designed to aid organizers working to build urban neighborhood organizations (Warren & Warren, 1977). For this purpose, its authors found that demographic descriptions, such as ethnicity and income level, were not useful in describing neighborhoods. They developed a system for classifying urban neighborhoods in terms of three contextual variables. The first is the sense of neighborhood identity shared by residents, a sense of connectedness among residents and distinctiveness as a neighborhood. This seems similar to the membership and shared emotional connection elements of the D. W. McMillan–Chavis (1986) definition of sense of community. From the descriptions provided by Warren and Warren (1977), identity seems strongest in integral and parochial neighborhoods and lowest in transitory and anomic neighborhoods.

The second variable is the internal interaction among neighborhood residents (Warren & Warren, 1977). In part, this concerns informal contacts among neighbors. For instance, in a study of informal neighboring, D.G. Unger and Wandersman (1983, p. 295) asked residents of city blocks, "How many of the people on this block would you:

- recognize or know by name?"
- consider close friends?"
- feel comfortable asking to borrow some food or a tool?"
- feel comfortable talking about a personal problem?"
- feel comfortable asking to watch your house while you're away?"
- feel comfortable asking for a ride when your car is not working?"

In addition, internal interaction involves the number and strength of local community organizations, such as clubs for adults and youth, religious congregations, parent–teacher associations, and neighborhood or homeowner associations. These provide settings for forming relationships and sharing tasks among neighbors. Internal interaction in a neighborhood especially involves the elements of membership and integration in the McMillan–Chavis (1986) definition of sense of community.

One way of visualizing internal interaction involves the "strength of weak ties" in a neighborhood (Granovetter, 1973). "Weak ties" are relationships between persons who are not close friends, but acquainted sufficiently to recognize each others' mutual interests as neighbors, provide limited assistance when needed, pass on information and news, and form the basis of a sense of community or neighborhood identity. Look again at Table 7.4; one of the limits to developing a sense of community in a diffuse, transitory, or anomic neighborhood is the lack of weak ties among neighbors. In transitory and anomic neighborhoods, neighbors may not even recognize each other as neighbors. In terms of the McMillan–Chavis elements of sense of community, membership boundaries for such neighborhoods are weak.

The third Warren and Warren (1977) variable concerns the degree of external linkages with the larger community. Either individual residents or neighborhood organizations may forge such linkages. The economic and social forces that create, for instance, ghettos, shopping malls, housing projects, sports stadiums, highways, and suburban housing developments represent challenges and opportunities for neighborhoods. The strength of a neighborhood to meet those challenges depends in part on its external linkages to other neighborhoods and to sources of power or funding in the larger community (Florin et al., 1992; D.G. Unger & Wandersman, 1985). This external dimension is not addressed among the four McMillan–Chavis (1986) elements of sense of community.

The Warren and Warren (1977) typology, developed in a North American city, may not be useful for describing small towns or rural areas, neighborhoods outside North America, or for purposes of neighborhood description not linked to neighborhood organizing. Yet it is a good introduction to thinking about the neighborhood as a social unit. Furthermore, it calls attention to the character of each particular neighborhood. Even

| TABLE 7.4 | SIX TYPES OF NEIGHBORHOODS (WARREN & WARREN) |
|---|---|

### Integral

High sense of neighborhood identity, internal interaction, and external linkages.

This neighborhood is active and involved. Internally, many civic, religious, educational or other neighborhood organizations exist. Externally, these are linked with resources in other neighborhoods and the larger community. Residents share social ties and a sense of identity as a neighborhood, and like living there. There is a feeling of small-town friendliness, but also being an integral part of the city. When a problem occurs, residents mobilize and take action, with internal neighborhood or external resources, or both.

### Parochial

High sense of neighborhood identity, high internal interaction, low external linkages.

This neighborhood is insular, with a strong sense of identity and shared values, often based on ethnic or religious heritage (but *parochial* does not necessarily mean *religious* here). There is also the sense that the neighborhood is different from the larger community. The neighborhood is likely to be homogeneous in terms of ethnicity, social class, religion, or age. Internally, neighborhood organizations exist that are important in residents' lives, but these are not linked closely to the larger community, and community self-reliance is valued. Mechanisms exist for enforcement of the prevailing social norms and values. Residents like the neighborhood's closeness.

### Diffuse

High sense of neighborhood identity, low internal interaction, low external linkages.

This neighborhood is usually homogeneous in physical appearance (e.g., suburban subdivision with similar homes, or rental or public housing with similar apartments). The neighborhood also is usually homogeneous in income level; residents are often similar in outlook and like the neighborhood. Yet there are few neighborhood organizations, little recognition of how much values and concerns are shared by other residents, and little organized linkage with the larger community. Most residents' friends are outside the neighborhood; there is little interaction with neighbors.

neighborhoods with similar socioeconomic levels may differ greatly in their sense of community and degree of interdependence among residents (e.g., Brodsky, O'Campo, & Aronson, 1999; Chavis & Wandersman, 1990).

## Research on Sense of Community in Neighborhoods

Can sense of community be studied empirically? Do neighborhoods really differ in the sense of community? Is sense of community important in different societies? These are questions addressed in empirical research on the sense of community. This research, most of it influenced by the McMillan–Chavis (1986) formulation, has validated the concept of sense of community.

Many investigators have measured sense of community in neighborhoods and localities (Buckner, 1988; Chavis, Hogge, McMillan, & Wandersman, 1986; Chipuer & Pretty, 1999; W. B. Davidson & Cotter, 1986, 1989, 1993; Glynn, 1986; D. D. Perkins et al., 1990; Pretty et al., 1994; Pretty, Conroy, Dugay, Fowler, & Williams, 1996; D. Robinson & Wilkinson, 1995; Sagy, Stern, & Karakover, 1996; Skjaeveland, Garling & Maeland, 1996).

**TABLE 7.4**    *(continued)*

### Stepping Stone

Low sense of neighborhood identity, high internal interaction, high external linkages.

High turnover occurs among residents, yet neighborhood organizations are active. However, residents are active in these largely due to their career commitments or immediate interests, not for long-term commitment to the neighborhood. Residents are often professionals with external linkages to the larger community through their work. They bring these resources to the local organizations, yet soon move on and the organizations must recruit new leaders. Neighborhood organizations quickly welcome new residents and get them involved, yet residents seldom identify themselves strongly with the neighborhood.

### Transitory

Low sense of neighborhood identity, low internal interaction, high external linkages.

High turnover occurs among residents, few neighborhood organizations exist, and there is little interaction among neighbors. Cliques of residents may exist, but these are not linked to each other or to the larger community. There is little sense of belonging to a neighborhood or of shared values or concerns. New residents are not welcomed or integrated well into the neighborhood. Many residents are linked more strongly to work or the larger community than to the neighborhood, and will seek help outside the neighborhood when needed.

### Anomic

Low sense of neighborhood identity, low internal interaction, low external linkages.

Few social ties exist among neighbors, few residents know neighbors from nonresidents, and suspiciousness often results. Few neighborhood organizations exist, and there is little sense of shared values or concerns. Residents usually do not like the neighborhood or do not think of it as a neighborhood, even if they like their own house/apartment. Residents are often individualistic and private, yet the neighborhood is vulnerable to external forces, and residents have little neighborhood help in facing these challenges. This neighborhood type may occur among residents at any income level.

Note: Adapted from Warren and Warren (1977, pp. 95–112) and Heller et al. (1984, pp. 134–135).

These studies measured constructs related to the McMillan–Chavis (1986) elements of sense of community. Their findings indicated the validity of sense of community in urban, suburban, and rural town settings, in Norway, Israel, Canada, and the United States.

For example, Glynn (1986) compared the sense of community in two relatively affluent suburbs of Washington, D.C. (each with a population of nearly 20,000) and Kfar Blum, an Israeli kibbutz (population about 1,000). One of the U.S. suburbs, Greenbelt, had originally been a planned town and had a defined town center and boundaries; the other, Hyattsville, lacked a central district and readily identifiable boundaries. As a kibbutz, Kfar Blum is a smaller, collectively organized community, and its residents share a commitment to a distinctive set of values. Glynn's results showed that the sense of community and satisfaction with the community were highest in Kfar Blum, next highest in Greenbelt, and lowest in Hyattsville. In addition, in Greenbelt and Hyattsville, residents' sense of community within their neighborhood was correlated with their ratings of overall sense of community and satisfaction with the overall community.

Two studies of urban neighborhoods also documented the importance of sense of community (Chavis & Wandersman, 1990; D. D. Perkins et al., 1990). These studies concerned urban blocks, a unit smaller than the entire neighborhood. They defined a block as the area along both sides of a street, bounded by two cross streets. In New York City and Nashville, Tennessee, they surveyed residents of a large number of blocks, which varied in race, ethnicity, and socioeconomic status. In both studies, residents' sense of community (based on the McMillan–Chavis, 1986, elements) was associated with the following factors: neighboring relationships and behavior, satisfaction with the block as a place to live, and participation in citizen block associations. Moreover, longitudinal analyses of the Nashville data suggested the causal influence of sense of community. Increases in sense of community preceded increases in residents' level of neighboring, as well as in their sense of individual and group power over issues concerning the block. In chapter 10, we discuss in detail the links between sense of community and citizen participation in community associations.

Sense of community in the neighborhood or block appears to be strengthened by several factors. First, the physical environment may encourage neighboring and community. In chapter 5, we described the planned town of Seaside, Florida. Plas and Lewis (1996) conducted a qualitative study of sense of community among Seaside residents, visitors, and workers. All linked Seaside's environmental features, such as front porches and limitations on auto traffic, to a strong sense of community. Respondents often spontaneously mentioned ideas related to three McMillan–Chavis (1986) elements: membership, integration, and shared emotional connection. Also in chapter 5, we mentioned a study of how greenery in an urban housing project was associated with social ties among neighbors and with sense of safety (Kuo et al., 1998).

Involvement in community institutions or organizations represents another factor that strengthens sense of community in a locality (Brodsky et al., 1999; Chavis & Wandersman, 1990; D. D. Perkins et al., 1990). Examples include citizen block associations, religious congregations, and school-based organizations. In one study, living in a neighborhood with higher levels of voter registration was correlated with sense of community (Brodsky et al., 1999).

Both physical features and community organizations can increase the amount and quality of interaction among neighbors. However, interaction with neighbors also can decrease a sense of community. Studies in California and in Norway have found neighbor annoyance an important detractor from sense of community (Paquin & Gambrell, 1994; Skjaeveland et al., 1996). In addition, cultivating a sense of community may not be adaptive for the individual or family in some neighborhoods. Brodsky (1996) interviewed 10 African-American single mothers in a risky, high-crime neighborhood in Washington, D.C. These women were chosen for a study of successful, resilient mothers in risky neighborhoods. They shared a negative sense of community about their neighborhood. The most important boundary in their lives was not between their neighborhood and the outside world, but between their neighborhood and their home. Physical and emotional safety, a key characteristic of sense of community in the McMillan–Chavis (1986) definition, seldom existed in their neighborhood. These mothers also shared few values with the neighborhood as they perceived it. Some were involved in neighborhood or school organizations, where integration and mutual fulfillment of needs did occur. Yet, in general, success as an adult and mother in a very risky neighborhood seemed most related to resisting neighborhood contact and influence rather than cultivating it.

Despite these exceptions, neighborhoods are what many people have in mind when they use the term *sense of community*. As with mutual help groups and religious and spiritual settings, neighborhoods represent an important context for research and practice concerning sense of community.

# SENSE OF COMMUNITY: CONTRIBUTIONS AND LIMITATIONS

The burgeoning research on the psychological sense of community indicates that the concept is meaningful for community psychology. The utility of the McMillan–Chavis (1986) definition of the concept has been supported in a number of studies and settings. However, consensus is lacking on some important aspects of definition for the concept (J. L. Hill, 1996). We now turn to four issues in the definition and extension of the term *sense of community*, as a way of describing the future challenges for research and community action.

## What Is a Community? A Reprise

*Sense of community* has been used both as an overarching theme or metaphor, and as a specific hypothetical construct for measurement. As we noted early in this chapter, Sarason's (1974) use of multiple referents for the term provides an overarching theme. He variously defined psychological sense of community to refer to an interpersonal network of support, to a locality with a set of community institutions and a distinctive history, and to families, street gangs, and even national organizations (S. B. Sarason, 1974). This usage is useful as a way of unifying the field, and as an expression not only of its concepts but also of its implicit values. However, an overarching theme also yields multiple, divergent, even contradictory meanings for research and action. Even with the more specific and measurable conceptions in the D. W. McMillan–Chavis (1986) model, various studies have defined *community*, for example, as a mutual help group or organization (Rappaport, 1993), a city block (Chavis & Wandersman, 1990), a city of 300,000 (W. B. Davidson & Cotter, 1989), a high school or neighborhood (Pretty et al., 1994), and members of a politically constructed racial category within a nation (Sonn & Fisher, 1996, 1998). Distinguishing between levels of analysis, such as microsystems, organizations, and localities (and within that, blocks, neighborhoods, and cities) is one way to clarify this diversity of usage.

Several researchers have distinguished between a social network of individuals who all know each other and a larger community in which a member does not know all other members personally but nonetheless feels a sense of community or shared identity with anyone who is also a member of that community (J. L. Hill, 1996; Pretty et al., 1994). This definition asserts that the difference between a social network and a wider community is the presence of weak ties, among those who do not know each other but do recognize each other as fellow community members (Granovetter, 1973). For example, if you feel a strong sense of community within your neighborhood, or university, you probably would expect significant help with a problem from others there, even if you did not know them personally. Put another way, if you meet a person for the first time, and discover that he or she is from the same locality as you, likes the same music, shares your religious affiliation, or some other similarity, how much of a sense of community do you feel with that person? Does your locality, musical taste, or religious affiliation provide a strong sense of community for you?

This definition reserves the term *community* for larger groupings. It is useful; there are differences between small microsystems and localities, for instance. Yet it does exclude using the term *sense of community* for friendship networks, small workplaces and classrooms, and other microsystems. That is a narrower usage than Sarason's (1974) overarching theme. For community psychologists, this issue is not resolved. For the near future, at least, community psychologists need to keep inquiring, of themselves and of their participants, just what is meant by sense of community, and who the members of that community are.

## Diversity and Conflict Within Communities

Each of us is a member of many communities (Hunter & Riger, 1986; Trickett, 1996; Wiesenfeld, 1996). Sometimes, however, those multiple commitments conflict in important ways. In chapter 6, we quoted W. E. B. DuBois's (1903/1986) classic description of the conflicting loyalties (and identities) of being American, and being of African descent in an American society where one's race is frequently demeaned. Another example is that a student may experience a sense of belonging both to the college in which she is enrolled and to her hometown or neighborhood, yet neither of these communities may understand or appreciate her loyalty to the other.

Many communities are not only groupings of individuals, but also groupings of smaller subcommunities (Wiesenfeld, 1996). For example, a city includes many neighborhoods; an individual's loyalty and identity may be more tied to the neighborhood than the entire city. As another example, M.A. Bond and Keys (1993) described differences and conflicts between family members and professionals working together in an advocacy group for persons with developmental disabilities.

Moreover, subcommunities can come into conflict within a larger community (Wiesenfeld, 1996, p. 342). A community's response to that conflict can be constructive or destructive. Ignoring conflict or the importance of subcommunities eventually undermines the larger community, whereas constructive resolution or management helps strengthen sense of community (Wiesenfeld, 1996).

Understanding and respecting diversity has long been a core value of community psychology (Rappaport, 1977a). Yet diversity within communities has largely been overlooked in research on sense of community, which has focused on what community members share. Wiesenfeld called this the concept, perhaps myth, of "we" in a community.

An example of the reality as well as the myth of "we" in community is provided by Kaniasty and Norris (1995), who studied social support among residents of four southeastern U.S. cities in response to Hurricane Hugo. Overall patterns of support showed citizens who suffered greater loss and personal harm received greater amounts of support, supporting the idea that communities unite to respond to widely-experienced natural disaster. In this sense, the sense of "we" within the community was strong. However, some groups received less support, especially if they suffered greater harm. These neglected groups included African-Americans, persons with less education, and (to a lesser extent) unmarried persons. In this sense, the sense of "we" did not include the entire community. Similar patterns have occurred following disasters in other parts of the United States (Kaniasty & Norris, 1995).

To illustrate Wiesenfeld's argument, let's review the four elements of the McMillan–Chavis (1986) model, looking for concepts that explicitly recognize differences among members, existence of subgroups, and conflict as a basis of constructive change. The element of mutual influence does refer to the interactive nature of power and influence (and, implicitly, of conflict) between individuals and community, but does not discuss subgroups. The element of integration, especially in the economic analogy offered by McMillan (1996), does recognize differences among members, but refers to trading resources, not resolving conflict among competing views. The elements of membership and shared emotional connection seem defined in terms of unanimity and stability rather than diversity and change. McMillan and Chavis (1986) did address issues of values and conflict in their conclusion (p. 20), but not within the four elements of their model. Yet diversity and conflict are elements of community life.

## External Relationships

At the conclusion of their original article, McMillan and Chavis (1986) recognized the darker sides of sense of community. One is the potential that strengthening communities may increase conflict between them, if they define themselves in terms of exclusion from others. In addition, some groups with a strong sense of community will embrace values repugnant to many others: for example, neo-Nazi or vigilante groups (McMillan & Chavis, 1986, p. 20). Sarason (1974), in the last chapter of his original volume, had discussed barriers and conflicts between communities that define themselves through hostility toward other communities, as well as issues of how to balance the interests of smaller community groups and the wider community.

These issues concern relationships between a community and other communities or larger society. Defining community requires membership boundaries; these issues concern the community's relationships with those outside the boundaries (recall the concepts of ingroup and outgroup from chap. 4). However, those external relationships are omitted in the four McMillan–Chavis (1986) elements of sense of community, which focus on the internal characteristics of a community. Relationships among communities or with larger society are not explicitly addressed with the four elements. Thus, the McMillan–Chavis model can be (and has been) used in pursuit of the values emphasized by its authors, but it does not provide explicit conceptual guidance for that pursuit.

Communities do exist in relationships with each other. They are affected not only by forces within themselves, but also by forces in neighboring communities and at city-wide, regional, national, and international levels (Hunter & Riger, 1986). These forces affect the psychological sense of community. Recall that the Warren and Warren (1977) typology of neighborhoods, discussed earlier in this chapter, was based on three dimensions, two similar to the McMillan–Chavis (1986) elements of sense of community and a third referring to external linkages.

The diversity within a community to which Wiesenfeld (1996) drew attention is often linked with external conditions. For instance, one of the most constructive forces for change in the rural community in which the primary author of this chapter (James H. Dalton) grew up was school desegregation, initiated through a lawsuit by local African

American NAACP members and ultimately imposed by a Federal court. As another example, survival or growth of community associations often depends on their coalition-building with other organizations and communities (K. Heller, 1989). Moreover, a palpable difference often can be perceived between a sense of community that is based on rigid ingroup–outgroup distinctions, regarding other communities with fear, disdain, or indifference, versus a sense of community based on definable yet permeable boundaries and a concern for members of other communities (Norris, 1993).

For a practical example of these issues, imagine a community psychologist who is approached for help with community development by an all-White neighborhood organization, and soon learns that their underlying aim is to exclude African Americans and other persons of color from moving into their neighborhood. Unless those exclusionary aims are changed, strengthening sense of community within the neighborhood would have racist effects (Chavis, personal communication, October, 1987). This dilemma reflects a potential conflict between core values of community psychology: sense of community in one neighborhood versus social justice and respect for human diversity (and, ultimately, individual wellness). Community psychologists and others working in communities must resolve similar value dilemmas in many specific circumstances by weighing the claims of potentially competing values carefully. In this case, many would decline to work with the neighborhood organization unless it genuinely renounced its exclusionary aims.

McMillan and Chavis (1986) concluded their original article with a call for finding ways to build "free, open, accepting" communities "based on faith, hope, and tolerance" and to "use sense of community as a tool for fostering understanding and cooperation" (p. 20). Pursuing those aims requires considering the relationship of a community to other communities as well as its internal sense of community.

## The "Competent Community"

One framework for conceptualizing a broader conception of community is the concept of a competent community suggested by Iscoe (1974) and Cottrell (1976). This offers a perspective on communities that addresses some of the issues identified in the critique above.

On the basis of his experience in working with communities to develop plans and resources for community development, Cottrell (1976) proposed a list of characteristics of a competent community (see Table 7.5). These include explicit attention to the role of conflict in community development, the importance of recognizing and articulating differences in viewpoint between subgroups within a community, and the significance of external relations with the larger society. Some of the qualities in Cottrell's model appear similar to some of the elements in the McMillan–Chavis (1986) model. For instance, Cottrell's concept of commitment involves a shared emotional connection and is partly based on mutual influence of individual members and the overall community. The qualities of self–other awareness and participation also overlap with the McMillan–Chavis' concept of mutual influence, although Cottrell assumed the existence and importance of subgroups within a community that are emphasized by Wiesenfeld (1996). The shared meanings that are the basis of communication in Cottrell's framework seem similar to the common symbol systems that are an element of membership in the McMillan–Chavis model. However, the other qualities in Cottrell's list go beyond the McMillan-Chavis model.

| TABLE 7.5 | QUALITIES OF THE "COMPETENT" COMMUNITY |
|---|---|

1. Commitment
   Individuals are motivated to engage in the shared work of the community; community and individuals have an impact on each other.

2. Self–other awareness
   Members have a clear understanding of the interests and views of oneself or one's subgroup, as well as those of other members or subgroups.

3. Articulateness
   Members have the ability to state clearly the views of oneself or one's subgroup to others in the community.

4. Communication
   Ideas and terms with a shared meaning are used to communicate within the community. These are based on an understanding of multiple perspectives within the group, and lead to genuine collaboration among members and subgroups.

5. Conflict containment and accommodation
   A set of agreed-upon procedures exists to recognize and resolve conflicts within the community, which are assumed to be inevitable yet resolvable.

6. Participation in decision making
   Members contribute actively to community goal-setting, decision-making, and implementing of plans. A set of agreed-upon procedures insures optimal communication among members for this.

7. Management of relations with larger society
   The community identifies and uses resources available outside itself and responds to demands or threats coming from outside the community.

8. Utilization of resources
   The community makes the best use of tangible and personal resources and skills among community members and those acquired from outside.

9. Socialization for leadership
   Work is conducted so that skills for participation, leadership, power and responsibility are learned by citizens who have not had them in the past but can assume them in the future. This includes transmitting power while accommodating conflict (see no. 3 above).

10. Evaluation
    Reflective, systematic, action research on the nature of community problems and proposed responses, with allowance for failure and use of feedback for improvement.

Note: Items 1–7 are based on definitions provided in Cottrell (1976); Items 8–10 are based on Iscoe (1974).

Iscoe drew on Cottrell's earlier work (Cottrell, cited in Iscoe, 1974) and offered three additional concepts. He was primarily concerned with the collaboration of professionals (e.g., community psychologists) and grassroots community members, especially with setting up the transition of power as community members assume more control over their community organizations. He also emphasized the importance of action research. However, that research needs to be helpful to community members and promote an atmosphere of innovation and citizen participation rather than expert judgment.

The McMillan–Chavis (1986) conception of sense of community has proven to be a useful guide to many aspects of research and community action. The elements of a competent community, as formulated by Cottrell (1976) and Iscoe (1974), complement the

McMillan–Chavis elements by drawing attention to issues such as recognizing differences and resolving conflict within a community, and relations with wider communities. Both frameworks are useful for community psychology and provide ways of actualizing Sarason's (1974) overarching theme of sense of community.

## CHAPTER SUMMARY

**1.** In this chapter, we have examined the various meanings of the idea of community and its implications for community psychology. Understanding community requires specifying what is meant by the term.

**2.** Two general types of communities are relevant to community psychology: *locality*, and *relational*. Relational communities include *organizations* such as *workplaces* and *collective power structures.*

**3.** Most people belong to multiple communities that exist at different levels: *microsystems, organizations*, and *localities* (e.g., neighborhoods, cities). *Mediating structures* provide links between individuals and larger communities or society.

**4.** *Sense of community* was first proposed as an organizing concept for the field by Sarason (1974). It was defined in more specific terms by McMillan and Chavis (1986) as involving *membership* characteristics and boundaries, *mutual influence* between individual and community, *integration and fulfillment of needs* among members, and *shared emotional connection.*

**5.** Mutual help or self-help groups provide an important and growing form of community, especially the sense of community. Their distinctive features are (a) a *focal concern*, (b) *peer relationships*, (c) *reciprocity of helping*, and (d) *emphasis on experiential knowledge.* The *helper-therapy principle* is important for understanding these groups. Mutual help groups are best understood not as alternative forms of treatment for personal problems, but as normative communities that one joins.

**6.** Religious and spiritual communities represent an important form of community. We defined *spirituality* more broadly than *religion*, to include awareness of a transcendent power not necessarily associated with a religious institution or belief. Sense of community in both concerns *relationality* and a sense of *transcendence.* Religious and spiritual communities fulfill a number of functions in community and individual life.

**7.** Another important level of community is the neighborhood. We summarized research on the importance of neighborhood sense of community and described six types of neighborhoods: *integral, parochial, diffuse, stepping stone, transitory*, and *anomic.* These are based on the dimensions of *neighborhood identity, internal interaction*, and *external linkages.* Research on sense of community in neighborhoods and blocks generally shows it to be an important aspect of community and individual life.

**8.** Current conceptions of sense of community have several limitations. Should sense of community be defined as an overarching theme for community psychology, at many levels of analysis, or a specific construct at one or two levels? Is there a difference between a social network and a community? How can research and action be expanded to address diversity and conflict within a community and external relationships with other communities? Cottrell's and Iscoe's ideas of the *competent community* address some of these concerns.

## BRIEF EXERCISES

**1.** Return to the list of communities in your life that you wrote at the outset of this chapter. Answer the following questions.

- Which of those communities are localities? Relational communities? Workplaces?
- Which are organizations based in a locality but defined by relational bonds, such as a college or religious congregation?
- Which are collective power structures that seek to influence the wider community (even if they are not overtly political)?
- Which communities are microsystems? Organizations?
- Which are mediating structures that link you to larger communities?
- When have the communities on your list generated competing expectations for your time and involvement?
- To which communities on your list do you feel the strongest commitment? Why?
- In which communities would you feel a sense of connectedness with other members of the community, even if you did not know them personally?

**2.** Describe to a classmate or friend an important community in your life, and what it means to you. Review the four D. W. McMillan–Chavis (1986) elements of sense of community, and apply these to the community you chose.

- What boundaries exist for membership, and how are these communicated with a common symbol system? How do these boundaries provide you with a sense of emotional safety and belongingness?
- How are you as an individual influenced by the norms or decisions of the overall community? How do you influence that community or its decisions?
- What needs do you or others satisfy by being part of this community? What resources do members provide each other? What values are shared by community members?
- Is there a shared emotional connection or spiritual bond among members? What shared events or rituals promote this bond?

**3.** Think back to your first year in college. List the communities that were important in your life that year. What types and levels of communities were important? Which of these provided mediating structures, linking you as an individual and the larger community of the college and university? Which provided you with a sense of belonging or community? Were any of your important communities "holdovers" from your life before college? How were they important to you? Did your membership in these multiple communities create any conflicts in commitment (e.g., time, personal involvement) for you?

**4.** Find someone in your community who is affiliated with a self-help organization and willing to be interviewed (perhaps your instructor can help; often such persons function as spokespersons for their groups). Interview that person about the aims of the organization, how it operates, the nature of group meetings, and their experiences with the organization. Review the literature the organization distributes. If possible and if invited, visit a group meeting to learn more about the group. A genuine willingness to respect and learn from group members is needed to learn as much as you can through this experience. After you have learned about the group in its own terms, identify elements of membership, influence, integration, and shared emotional connection if you can.

**5.** Find someone active in a neighborhood organization, a religious or spiritual congregation or group, or some other community organization. Interview that person about the ways in which sense of community is fostered in that group and how it has affected the interviewee's life. If possible and if invited, visit a meeting or worship service to learn about the community. You can broaden your learning by visiting a neighborhood or group different from your own background. If you do, a genuine willingness to respect and learn from group members is needed to learn as much as you can through this experience. After you have learned about the group in its own terms, identify elements of membership, influence, integration, and shared emotional connection if you can.

## Recommended Readings

Sarason, S. B. (1974). *The psychological sense of community: Prospects for a community psychology.* San Francisco: Jossey-Bass.

Sarason, S. B. (1993). American psychology, and the needs for transcendence and community. *American Journal of Community Psychology, 21,* 185–202.
  Two groundbreaking works by a major theorist of sense of community.

McMillan, D. W., & Chavis, D. M. (1986). Sense of community: A definition and theory. *Journal of Community Psychology, 14,* 6–23.

Newbrough, J. R., & Chavis, D. M. (Eds.). (1986). Psychological sense of community, I: Theory and concepts [Special issue]. *Journal of Community Psychology, 14*(1).

Newbrough, J. R. & Chavis, D. M. (Eds.). (1986). Psychological sense of community, II: Research and applications [Special issue]. *Journal of Community Psychology, 14*(4).

Newbrough, J. R. (Ed.). (1996). Sense of community [Special issue]. *Journal of Community Psychology, 24*(4).

Chavis, D. M. & Pretty, G. M. H. (1999). Sense of community II [Special issue]. *Journal of Community Psychology, 27*(6).
  The original statement of the McMillan–Chavis model of sense of community, and special journal issues devoted to the topic.

Maton, K.I., & Wells, E. A. (1995). Religion as a community resource for well-being: Prevention, healing, and empowerment pathways. *Journal of Social Issues, 51,* 177–193.

Pargament, K.I., & Maton, K. I. (2000). Religion in American life: A community psychology perspective. In J. Rappaport & E. Seidman (Eds.), *Handbook of community psychology.* (pp. 495–522). New York: Plenum.

Kloos, B., Moore, T. (Eds.) (2000). Spirituality, religion, and community psychology. *Journal of Community Psychology* [Special issue], *28*(2).

Kloos, B., & Moore, T. (Eds.) (in press). Conceptualizing spirituality for community psychology: Resources, pathways, and perspectives. *Journal of Community Psychology* [Special issue].

Reviews of empirical research and action on religion/spirituality in community life.

Humphreys, K., & Rappaport, J. (1994). Researching self-help/mutual aid groups and organizations: Many roads, one journey. *Applied and Preventive Psychology, 3,* 217–231.

Editors of *Social Policy.* (1997). The future of self-help [Special issue]. *Social Policy, 27*(3).

LaVoie, F., Borkman, T., & Gidron, B. (Eds.). (1994). Self-help and mutual aid groups: International and multicultural perspectives [Special issue]. *Prevention in Human Services, 11* (1).

Borkman, T. (Ed.). (1991). Self-help groups [Special issue]. *American Journal of Community Psychology, 19*(5).

Empirical research and conceptual reviews concerning mutual aid and self-help groups.

This article appears in journals in the InfoTrac College Edition on-line library available from Wadsworth.

## INFOTRAC KEYWORDS

*community(ies), mutual aid, mutual help, neighborhood, self help (self-help), sense of community, religion, spirituality* (or any specific religious-spiritual tradition, e.g., *Buddhism*).

## RECOMMENDED WEBSITES

See chapter 8 for suggested Websites on self help and religion and spirituality. See chapter 13 for those on community development.

# Understanding Coping and Social Support

## OPENING EXERCISE

Let's begin this chapter with an exercise. Think of an important stressful experience in your life. It may have been a single event: serious illness or injury, flunking a test, or failing to attain an important goal. It may have been a life transition: beginning college or graduate school, becoming a parent, divorce, loss of a job, bereavement. It may be a long-term situation: living on a low income, a chronic illness, or having to balance several demanding roles such as mother, wife, student, and worker. It may be an experience that fits none of these categories well.

Consider the following questions about your experience.

- What was stressful about it for you?
- Was it a short-term or single event, or a long-term situation?
- How controllable was the stressful experience? Was it something you had much control over, or little, or in between?
- What resources helped you cope with this stressful experience? Some resources might include different forms of support from others, skills you already had, beliefs that sustained you, or tangible things such as money, time, or a quiet place to study.
- What things did you do to cope with this experience?
- Are you a different person now as a result of this experience? What did you learn, or how did you grow, through this experience?

Box 8.1 contains an answer to these questions by the primary author of this chapter.

## WHAT ARE THE KEY POINTS OF THIS CHAPTER?

In this chapter, we present an ecological framework of how people cope with stressful events and situations. It addresses each of the questions you answered above about your experience. As an ecological framework, it emphasizes the links between social and cultural environments and individual coping. We first describe the basic elements of the coping process: resources, stressors, appraisal, emotional states, coping responses, and outcomes. We then review in more detail three resources for coping: social support, psychosocial competencies, and religion and spirituality. Throughout, we note some of the many ways in which coping is related to social and cultural context. Our framework is illustrated in Figure 8.1.

# An Overview of the Coping Process

Understanding psychological stress and coping has been a focus of community psychology since its inception. Lindemann (1944) laid the foundations of community mental health in his pioneering study of coping with bereavement. G. Caplan (1974) extended Lindemann's work in ways that influenced both community mental health and community psychology. The ecological framework of coping in this chapter extends this tradition, framing coping in the context of community. Individuals do not cope in isolation; instead, we cope in relationships with others.

This framework was influenced principally by the models of coping proposed by Dohrenwend (1978), Hobfoll (1988, 1998), R. S. Lazarus and Folkman (1984), and Moos (1984). In addition, our thinking was influenced by the concepts of Albee (1982), Elias (1987), and Kelly (Trickett et al., 1972).

Two terminological notes are necessary. First, we generally avoid the use of the term *stress* throughout this chapter. A familiar term in everyday conversation, it has too many meanings for conceptual precision (see R. S. Lazarus & Folkman, 1984, chap. 1). *Stress* is used in at least three ways: to refer to external demands that threaten or reduce one's resources (Hobfoll, 1998), to one's perceptions of those demands (R. S. Lazarus & Folkman, 1984, p. 19), and to internal states such as anxiety resulting from external demands

## 8.1   *A Stressful Experience in My Life*

When I was 21, in the summer between my junior and senior years of college, my mother died after long being ill with cancer. My father, sister, and I knew her death was coming, even welcomed it with relief; her cancer had been very painful. But it still came hard, with an emptiness and sense of great loss. Several things about that experience still stand out for me, decades later.

Within hours, friends from our church and town began what is a bereavement tradition in many communities: delivering home-cooked food for us and the mourners who would join us. This and many other acts of kindness continued for days.

The next few days were a blur as we attended to the duties and rituals of bereavement in our culture. Some of those were not easy, but they were helpful, even inspiring. I felt I belonged, in extended family and community. I cannot count the ways that my family and I received support from others. Cultural and religious traditions helped make her life and death meaningful to me.

Sometime later that summer, while still recovering emotionally, I realized that I now had to grow up, especially to make decisions for myself. Like most mothers, mine had been a close personal guide even when I disregarded her advice. Her passing was a turning point for me. With the support of my family, friends, and my academic mentor, and with spiritual support, the next year was a time of spiraling growth, a year of making choices, the beginning of adulthood.—James H. Dalton

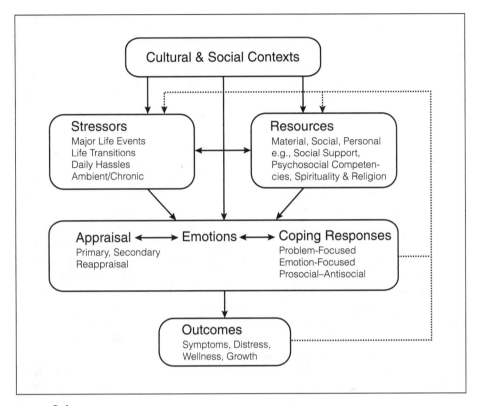

**FIGURE 8.1**

Ecological framework of coping

(what most people mean by the term). In our ecological framework of coping, we refer to external demands as *stressors* and to specific emotions rather than generalized internal *stress*.

Second, the coping process in all its aspects is *contextual*. Culture, social structure, and community norms all affect individual coping. Cultural and social forces influence everything from what resources are available to how stressors are defined and to how coping outcomes are evaluated. One's coping with a stressor, and whether that coping is effective or adaptive, also depends on the demands of that stressor. Coping with bereavement, for instance, is different from coping with work stressors. An ecological model emphasizes contextual influences on the individual, and we turn first to describing them.

## Cultural and Social Context

Everything in our ecological framework begins with cultural and social environments. Cultural factors include ethnocultural traditions, beliefs, practices, and institutions that influence coping. In a multicultural society, these include the dominant culture as well as other cultural forces. Social factors include social structure, especially socioeconomic class and other structures of power and status in a society. (Recall these concepts from chap. 6.) Neighborhood context also affects coping; we discussed neighborhood context and environmental stress in chapter 5. Settings such as family, school, and workplace also create stressors and influence coping. Because cultural groups, neighborhoods, settings, and other contexts differ, generalizations across contexts are difficult to make. Throughout the chapter, we point out examples of contextual influences on coping.

## *Resources*

Resources include material, social, and personal factors that promote health and personal well-being (Hobfoll, 1998). As you will learn in the next chapter, they are also termed *protective factors,* particularly in developmental psychology and public health, because they help to protect the person against stressors. *Material* resources relevant to coping include money, employment, housing, food, clothing, transportation, and health insurance. A quiet place to study is a material resource for students. *Social* resources include support from friends and family, social connections in the community, and social status or power. Social or community institutions such as youth groups, mutual help organizations, and religious congregations also comprise social resources. Cultural traditions, rituals, beliefs, and narratives are also social resources for coping, providing systems of meaning for interpreting stressors, examples of skillful coping, and guides to coping choices. Religious writings, widely read stories, and folk sayings are examples of these. The rituals of bereavement in any culture provide resources to the bereaved. *Personal* resources include competencies or skills, such as job, problem-solving, and interpersonal skills (Goleman, 1995). Personal resources also may include cognitions such as optimism in the face of challenges. These skills and beliefs promote adaptive coping.

Social resources often reflect the idea stated in the African proverb, "It takes a village to raise a child." Personal and family resources are certainly important, but wider levels of resources are also involved in individual development and coping. Recall from chapter 1 the finding that child abuse and neglect was more common in neighborhoods lacking a sense of community and supportive ties than in similar neighborhoods that possessed those neighborhood resources (Garbarino & Kostelny, 1992).

Social, personal, and material resources are interrelated. Material aid may come from social institutions; social norms influence how resources such as coping skills are used. In addition, resources affect other factors in the ecological framework: appraisal, emotions, coping responses, and outcomes all depend on resources. Coping also draws on or builds up resources; thus there is also a causal arrow from coping back to resources in Figure 8.1.

## *Stressors*

What are stressors? In our ecological framework, stressors are circumstances that represent a threatened or actual loss or scarcity of resources (Hobfoll, 1988; 1998; R. S. Lazarus & Folkman, 1984). As you will learn in the next chapter, they are also termed *risk factors.* Stressors are shaped by cultural and social contexts; they influence resources and in turn are shaped by the presence of those resources. Four types of stressors, listed in Table 8.1, have been defined by psychologists.

| TABLE 8.1 | TYPES OF STRESSORS |
|-----------|--------------------|

Major life events

Life transitions

Daily hassles

Ambient/chronic stressors

*Major Life Events*   Holmes and Rahe (1967) initiated the life events approach by developing the Social Readjustment Rating Scale, which is a standardized list of major stressful life events such as bereavement or loss of job. On the basis of empirical studies, they assigned each stressor a point value for its severity; a total score of stressfulness of life events could then be computed for an individual. Holmes and Rahe documented correlations of individual life-event scores with occurrence of illness. This approach spawned a number of studies with varied populations and enabled study of the effects of multiple stressors in one sample.

However, the life events approach also has a number of conceptual and methodological shortcomings. Correlations of life-events scores and outcomes have been modest (Hobfoll & Vaux, 1993). The lists often include both positive events or "entrances" that have some stressful aspects, such as marriage, and more clearly stressful events, usually losses or "exits" such as divorce or job loss. Losses are much more strongly associated with psychological distress or illness (Thoits, 1983; Vinokur & Selzer, 1975). Uncontrollable, unpredictable events appear especially stressful (Thoits, 1983). In addition, the use of a standardized list of life events is not sensitive to the cultural, economic, and individual meaning of those events (Mirowsky & Ross, 1989). For instance, divorce is given a single score, regardless of its cultural acceptability or the impact of divorce on one's material, personal, and social resources.

*Daily Hassles*   The study of daily hassles and uplifts (Kanner, Coyne, Schaefer, & Lazarus, 1981) is similar to the life-events approach, but focuses on very short-term, smaller scale stressors. Examples of daily hassles include family arguments and car problems. The larger causes of these hassles are not identified in a daily hassles measurement; it is the frequency or intensity of hassles themselves that matters. The daily hassles approach allows a more individualized understanding of the immediate, proximal antecedents of stress, although not long-term causal factors. The Kanner et al. (1981) approach also considers daily uplifts (positive events) related to resources.

*Life Transitions*   Some major life events are transitions, long-lasting changes in life circumstances. Examples include entering kindergarten, middle school, or college, or becoming married, divorced, or widowed. These are more lasting changes than a short-term life event, and they demand learning of new skills and roles. For instance, recall the skills demanded of you when you entered college or graduate school: academic, interpersonal, time management, and decision-making skills. Studying a sample of persons experiencing a single life transition (e.g., effects of divorce among children) allows a more contextual approach to understanding that transition and the particular coping skills and strategies it demands. However, life transitions can be difficult to define: Determining specifically what is stressful about the transition, and whether that stressfulness differs across individuals or groups, can be challenging.

***Ambient/Chronic Stressors***    Many stressful circumstances involve long-term resource scarcity, rather than sudden, dramatic changes. Ambient or chronic stressors are relatively stable conditions of the physical or social environment (Wandersman & Nation, 1998). Examples include long-term environmental pollution, poverty, noise, crowding, neighborhood crime, and lack of health care.

Chronic stressors also may be based on role demands such as a difficult job, caregiving for a sick relative, or parenting a challenging child, or on family conditions such as parental alcoholism (Barrera, Li, & Chassin, 1995). One's own chronic illness is also a stressor. Many daily hassles also grow out of ambient/chronic stress, as money, time, and other resources wear thin, tempers grow short, and machines break down.

***Vicious Spirals***    Loss of one resource may trigger other losses in a vicious spiral, a process emphasized in Hobfoll's conservation-of-resources theory of coping (Hobfoll, 1998). For instance, a low-income single mother whose car breaks down cannot afford to fix it, which results in the loss of the job for which she needs transportation. With the financial strain, she can no longer afford child care, which makes finding a new job even more difficult. The spiral also undermines her self-esteem and belief in her ability to cope. Vicious spirals are particularly common for those with fewer material, social, or personal resources. In the example given, any single resource such as an understanding employer, a community short-term loan fund, a relative or friend who can provide child care at least temporarily, or a friend with car repair skills might arrest the spiral long enough to allow sufficient recovery of resources. A vicious spiral is not a fifth type of stressor, but a pattern of multiple stressors.

## Stressors in Community Psychology Research

Recent study of stressors in community psychology has often sampled individuals who experienced the same life event, transition, or chronic/ambient stressor. Table 8.2 lists some specific stressors studied in recent community psychology research.

***Homelessness***    Studies of homeless persons illustrate the impact of economic and social stressors and vicious spirals. In a predominantly male sample in Spain (M. Munoz, Vazquez, Bermejo, & Vazquez, 1999), over 60% of the sample had experienced unemployment lasting more than 1 month, a major financial crisis, feeling abandoned by relatives and friends, and death of a close relative. These often had occurred in a 3-year period before and during their first episode of homelessness, suggesting vicious spirals.

Roll, Toro, and Ortola (1999) compared stressors and resources among homeless women with children, single women, and single men in Buffalo, New York. All three groups had experienced severe economic problems, but the women with children had the least lifetime income whereas the single men had the most. Women were also more likely to have been assaulted recently, often involving domestic violence. Women also experienced higher rates of depression and anxiety than the men. This suggests that the pathways into homelessness may be different for men, single women, and mothers with children.

| TABLE 8.2 | STRESSORS RECENTLY STUDIED IN TWO COMMUNITY PSYCHOLOGY JOURNALS |
|---|---|

| | |
|---|---|
| Acculturation, immigration | Parental divorce |
| Bereavement | Racism and sexism |
| Caregiving for someone with a chronic illness | Substance abuse problem |
| Crime victimization, neighborhood risk of crime | School transitions |
| Homelessness | Transition to college, college coping |
| Illness (arthritis, breast cancer, HIV/AIDS) | Unemployment |
| Motherhood | Victimization of lesbians/gays/bisexuals |
| Natural disasters (e.g., hurricane) | Workplace/job stressors, work–family conflicts |
| Parental alcoholism | |

Note: This list is illustrative, not exhaustive. Journals sampled were the *American Journal of Community Psychology* and the *Journal of Community Psychology*.

*School Transitions*    Studies of school transitions in adolescence also illustrate the study of stressors. Two research programs in large U.S. cities have documented the stressful effects for students of transition from elementary to middle and high school. This occurs especially for low-income students in large, bureaucratized school systems that diminish individual contacts between students and staff.

Seidman and associates studied multiracial samples of low-income adolescents in New York City, Baltimore, and Washington, D.C. (Seidman, 1991). Seidman, Allen, Aber, Mitchell, and Feinman (1994) found that the junior high school transition had strong effects on the students, chiefly on their academic performance and engagement with school. Grades, preparation for school, involvement in school activities, social support from school staff, and self-esteem all dropped, while daily hassles at school increased. Engagement with peers increased, but this was not necessarily constructive, because students reported that peers' values were becoming more antisocial (Seidman et al., 1994). At the transition to high school, similar but less negative effects occurred (Seidman, Aber, Allen, & French, 1996).

Reyes et al., (1994) studied the transition to high school among low-income, mainly Hispanic students in Chicago, where students moved directly from elementary school to high school. Decreases occurred in student grades, attendance, and perceptions of support from family, peers, and school staff (Gillock & Reyes, 1996).

These declines in academic engagement are especially serious given the developmental importance of the early adolescent years (Reyes et al., 1994; Seidman, 1991; Seidman et al., 1994). These studies document a loss of resources for many youth. Social support from adults, especially at school, decreases. For low-income youth, lack of economic resources in family and community pose further obstacles.

*Racism*    Research on racism provides examples of how a single ambient threat may express itself in multiple specific stressors. Harrell and associates (Harrell, 1997, 2000; Harrell, Merchant, & Young, 1997) studied racism-related stress among a multiracial sample of U.S. students and African American community members. They measured a variety of stressors. Specific racism-related life events, such as being harassed by police or being unfairly rejected for a loan, were infrequent but stressful. "Micro-aggressions" (similar to daily hassles) such as being followed in stores, being avoided by others, and subtle expressions of disrespect or fear were experienced almost daily. Also stressful were observations of racism that targeted others, seeing one's group blamed for problems, and chronic inequalities of income and material resources. Harrell (1997) found symptoms of depression, anxiety, and psychological trauma correlated with each type of stressor. Interestingly, daily micro-aggressions were the stressor most strongly associated with symptoms.

## Stressors in the Ecological Framework

In our framework, stressors are antecedents near the top of the model in Figure 8.1, prior to appraisal and coping. However, in real life stressors exist in a bidirectional relationship to coping (denoted in our framework by a causal pathway from coping strategies back to stressors). Adaptive coping can add to resources and reduce stressors. Maladaptive coping efforts create additional stressors that may lead to vicious spirals. For instance, avoidant coping such as binge drinking can create stressors at work or school and in personal relationships.

Some stressors result from purposive efforts toward goals. For instance, students take on the demands of college in order to attain ultimate goals. Hobfoll (1998; Hobfoll & Vaux, 1993) argued that this interplay of resources, stressors, goals, and choices has not received enough attention in the stress literature. However, chosen stressors may be less harmful than those imposed on the person (recall the finding mentioned earlier that "entrances" are less stressful than "exits"). Moreover, we do not wish to blame victims; many damaging stressors are in no way the responsibility or choice of their victims.

Are stressors always harmful? Stressors often can be transformed into experiences that develop resources. Many developmental transitions are sources of individual learning, growth, and joy. A natural disaster is often cited as the catalyst of a stronger (usually temporary) sense of community (Kaniasty & Norris, 1995). Yet a stressor is a stressor because it poses a threat, even if it also brings opportunities. It is the response to a stressor that creates growth. That response begins with appraisal of resources and stressors.

## Appraisal: Comparing Stressors and Resources

How does an individual decide what constitutes a stressor, a threatened or actual loss of resources? That determination involves appraisal, the ongoing process of constructing the meaning of a stressful situation.

***Primary Appraisal***    R. S. Lazarus and Folkman (1984, pp. 31–37) defined two inter-related appraisal processes. Primary appraisal refers to personal estimation of the strength or intensity of the stressor(s). For some, an upcoming public presentation or speech is a very intense stressor, for others just another task. R. S. Lazarus and Folkman distinguished between three types of stress appraisals. Harm/loss appraisals occur when some loss of resources has already happened. Threat appraisals concern potential losses in the future. Challenge appraisals may accompany threat appraisals, and focus on the potential for growth or gain in the stressful experience.

***Secondary Appraisal***   This involves personal estimation of resources and coping options for responding to the stressor. It involves at least three specific appraisals: estimating available resources, enumerating possible options or strategies for coping, and elaborating on their possible consequences and likelihood for success. If these seem likely to meet the threat estimated in primary appraisal, little or no internal stress results (R. S. Lazarus & Folkman, 1984).

Both forms of appraisal are likely to be affected by personality factors. For instance, locus of control, whether one believes that in general one controls the outcomes of one's actions (Rotter, 1966), influences individual perception of whether a stressor is controllable and how one perceives and uses resources (e.g., Liang & Bogat, 1994; Sandler & Lakey, 1982). A fuller discussion of such personality factors in coping goes beyond the scope of the ecological framework of this chapter (see Pierce, Lakey, Sarason, & Sarason, 1997).

In Figure 8.1, appraisal, emotion, and coping responses are portrayed as an interconnected system. For instance, research on neural pathways involving the limbic system and the frontal cortex indicates that some external stimuli are so threatening that coping occurs outside conscious awareness. Emotional response is nearly instantaneous, and any appraisal that occurs is rudimentary (see Goleman, 1995, for a description of this "emotional hijacking"). Even in less dramatic circumstances, emotions influence cognitive appraisal and vice versa. Appraisal is emotionally alive, not dry and rational. Also, the pathway between appraisal and coping is bidirectional. Appraisal influences later choices of coping strategy. Yet coping efforts may lead to reappraisal of stressor and resources.

***Reappraisal***   A process involving both appraisal and coping is "reframing" or reappraising the problem (R. S. Lazarus & Folkman, 1984; Watzlawick et al., 1974). (Recall reframing the nine-dot problem that opened chap. 1.) It may involve changing one's perception of the stressor's intensity, identifying unrecognized resources, or finding meaning in the situation. Reappraisal does not change the stressor, only one's perception of it. For instance, you might reappraise a stressful circumstance as an opportunity to learn new skills, or change a threat appraisal to a challenge appraisal.

An important role of social support is suggesting reappraisals. Reappraisal is influenced by cultural and social context; cultural values, for instance, influence what reappraisals are perceived as realistic or constructive.

***When Does Appraisal Matter?***   An emphasis on appraisal is limited from an ecological point of view (Hobfoll, 1998). If stress and stressors are defined solely "in the eye of the beholder," is there no inherently stressful situation? Aren't bereavement, job loss, chronic illness, or poverty stressful, regardless of how one appraises them?

Individual cognitive appraisals perhaps matter most when resources are ample and threats to them are moderate (Hobfoll, 1998). This situation allows room for individual differences in appraisal of threat. For instance, in families with ample material resources, many stressors can be viewed as temporary setbacks. However, in circumstances where the threats or losses are more serious, appraisal becomes less important because almost everyone will appraise them as highly stressful: for example, natural disasters, conditions of poverty, serious illness, and family violence. Moreover, appraisals of commonly experienced stressors are culturally and socially constructed. One's views of death, violence, and other stressors are not just matters of individual cognitions, but also of culture. In sum, where stressors are appraised similarly by many individuals, appraisals contribute less to coping than do resources.

## Emotional States

When people speak of stress, an emotional state is what they usually mean. It is helpful here to think of specific emotional states: for instance, fear and anxiety, anger, sadness, disgust, guilt, shame, regret, frustration, or jealousy. Positive emotions such as joy also can flow from stressful circumstances if the stressor can be appraised as an enjoyable challenge. The emotions of stress may be experienced as intense, passionate bursts, or as longer term states at lower intensity. A detailed discussion here goes beyond the scope of our ecological framework (see, for instance, Goleman, 1995; R. S. Lazarus, 1991; Markus & Kitayama, 1991).

Emotions are related to other factors in the ecological framework. As we have noted, emotions exist in interplay with appraisal. In addition, as we soon discuss, emotion-focused coping strategies intervene primarily with emotional states. Emotions also are reflected in many indicators of coping outcome, such as depression, anxiety, or well-being. Finally, emotional experience and expression are influenced by cultural environment (Markus & Kitayama, 1991); recall our discussion in chapter 6 of ego-focused emotions in the independent self, and others-focused emotions in the interdependent self.

## Coping Responses

Researchers have proposed a number of descriptive dimensions to classify various approaches that individuals use to cope with stressors (e.g., Carver, Scheier, & Weintraub, 1989; L. H. Cohen, Hettler, & Park, 1997; Hobfoll, 1998; Holahan & Moos, 1994; Humphreys, Finney, & Moos, 1994; R. S. Lazarus & Folkman, 1984; Shapiro, Schwartz, & Astin, 1996). Our ecological overview emphasizes two dimensions: problem-focused versus emotion-focused coping (R. S. Lazarus & Folkman, 1984) and prosocial versus antisocial action (Hobfoll, 1998). Coping is important to community psychologists because it concerns how resources like social support are used to deal with stressors (Holahan, Moos, & Bonin, 1997).

### Problem-Focused Coping    R. S. Lazarus and Folkman (1984) originally classified coping strategies into two general types: problem-focused and emotion-focused. The first addresses the stressor or problem directly, and does something active about it. It is goal-oriented, and similar to Hobfoll's (1998) concept of active coping, and the concept of active-behavioral coping (Holahan & Moos, 1994; Humphreys et al., 1994).

Problem-focused or active coping includes both cognitive and behavioral forms. Its primarily cognitive forms include analyzing information about the problem, planning, and decision making. Its behavioral forms include seeking information, increasing one's own efforts toward a goal, recruiting allies, asking for help, and assertively discussing a conflict with the person involved (Hobfoll, 1998; Holahan & Moos, 1994; Humphreys et al., 1994). *Judicious action,* such as reviewing one's resources and options, considering consequences, and seeking others' advice before acting, combines cognitive and behavioral aspects (Hobfoll, 1998).

Problem-focused strategies are especially likely to be adaptive if the stressor is relatively controllable (Hobfoll, 1998; R. S. Lazarus & Folkman, 1984). If you receive a low grade on a test, changing study tactics, increasing your study time, and seeking a tutor or help from the instructor are all problem-focused approaches. If you develop a serious illness, seeking information and treatment, asking for tangible help from others, and planning your recovery efforts are problem-focused strategies.

***Emotion-Focused Coping*** This addresses the emotions that accompany the problem, not the environmental stressor itself (R. S. Lazarus & Folkman, 1984). Meditation, quiet reflection, prayer, exercise, and seeking emotional support represent emotion-focused approaches (Shapiro et al., 1996). Venting to a friend and ruminating on painful feelings are also emotion focused, although usually less adaptive (Goleman, 1995; Hobfoll, 1998; Holahan et al., 1997).

Strategies of reappraisal and generating positive expectations, categorized as active-cognitive methods by Moos and associates (Holahan & Moos, 1994; Humphreys et al., 1994), can be categorized as emotion focused. Seeking religious or spiritual meaning in the situation (Pargament, 1997; Shapiro et al., 1996) is also emotion focused rather than problem focused. These strategies illustrate how coping and appraisal influence each other.

Use of primarily or solely emotion-focused strategies is especially likely to be adaptive if the stressor is relatively uncontrollable or must be endured, such as bereavement (Hobfoll, 1998; R. S. Lazarus & Folkman, 1984; Pargament, 1997). If you receive a low grade on a test, seeking emotional support from a friend, exercising to release your disappointment or anger, and reappraising the situation to find its hopeful or energizing aspects, are emotion-focused approaches. If you develop a serious illness, learning relaxation or meditation techniques, seeking emotional support, and finding personal or spiritual meaning are emotion-focused approaches.

*Avoidant* coping strategies (Holahan & Moos, 1994; Humphreys et al., 1994) can be said to comprise a subgroup of emotion-focused strategies (Hobfoll, 1998). These include denial, behavioral avoidance of the stressor, blaming others, and drug use to reduce tension (Humphreys et al., 1994). Although seldom adaptive with controllable stressors, some forms of denial and behavioral avoidance can be adaptive if the stressor is uncontrollable or if dealing with it is not necessary. Drug use, however, often increases risks and long-term stressors.

A person may combine problem-focused and emotion-focused strategies in response to a single stressor (for instance, exercising, then reviewing notes before an exam). With a relatively controllable stressor, emotion-focused coping can precede and facilitate problem-focused planning and action.

***Coping and Interpersonal Context*** The problem-focused versus emotion-focused distinction does not address a further question particularly important in community context: whether coping is prosocial or antisocial (Hobfoll, 1998).

*Prosocial* coping includes acts intended to care for others, seek their care, or promote interpersonal relationships. Seeking support or advice is prosocial, as are establishing relationships and considering others' feelings. Prosocial coping often involves a form of judicious action, mentioned earlier: consulting others, then acting with them in mind (Hobfoll, 1998; Hobfoll, Dunahoo, Ben-Porath, & Monnier, 1994).

*Antisocial* coping includes aggressive acts that harm others, as well as impulsive acts that disregard consequences for others. Less extreme strategies include dominating a social situation and behaving competitively, which are more likely to be adaptive, at least in individualistic cultures (Hobfoll, 1998).

Of course, some coping responses are neither prosocial nor antisocial. Studying or reading alone and solitary practice for an artistic or athletic performance are examples of constructive coping that are neither.

Hobfoll and others have studied the effects of prosocial versus antisocial coping among university and community (including both middle-class and low-income) samples in the United States and Europe (Hobfoll et al., 1994; Hobfoll, 1998). In general, judicious-prosocial coping was associated with less psychological distress than antisocial coping among both men and women (Hobfoll, 1998). Although judicious-prosocial coping thus appears often adaptive, it does involve more communication with others and consideration of their wishes, thus demanding time, patience, and sometimes self-sacrifice for the benefit of the larger group (Hobfoll, 1998).

**Coping Is Contextual**     A number of studies have found that forms of coping involving problem-focused, instrumental efforts to understand the stressor, use available resources, and attempt to alter the stressor or situation directly often are adaptive (see reviews by L. H. Cohen et al., 1997; Hobfoll, 1998; Holahan, Moos, & Bonin, 1997). However, there also are many reasons that such a generalization is too sweeping (L. H. Cohen et al., 1997; Hobfoll, 1998; Holahan & Moos, 1997; Shapiro et al., 1996). Many of the studies that provide evidence to support this conclusion are U.S. samples, often of college students or other middle-class persons, often not distinguishing between genders, racial or ethnic groups, or other diverse populations, and dealing with stressors that often are relatively controllable. For instance, being individualistic, pragmatic, and action oriented is prized in the dominant U.S. culture, particularly for men. Some actions considered appropriately assertive in European and North American cultures would be viewed as rude, at best, in East Asia (recall our discussion of individualism–collectivism in chap. 5). In addition, academic situations may be more controllable than other stressors such as bereavement, serious illness, or loss of a job. Finally, think of situations in your life when it was wiser to avoid a stressor if possible, or to manage your emotions and take no overt action, rather than pursuing problem-focused action.

From an ecological perspective, coping is contextual. There is no coping style or strategy that is always superior. Societal and cultural factors, gender and other forms of diversity, ecological levels such as neighborhood or organization or microsystem, and the nature of the stressor also must be taken into account. With this in mind, Table 8.3 summarizes some of the contextual questions to ask when reading an empirical study of coping.

## A Contextual Study of Coping with Homelessness

Coping in real-life situations has a richness that the categories described above cannot capture fully. Another approach to studying coping seeks to understand it through the thinking of the people coping with a specific stressor. For instance, Banyard (1995) studied coping methods used by homeless mothers with children in three U.S. cities. She interviewed the women with a semistructured format that allowed them to discuss their experi-

| TABLE 8.3 | CONTEXTUAL QUESTIONS TO ASK ABOUT A STUDY OF COPING |
|---|---|

What stressor(s) were studied? What personal, social or material resources were lost or threatened?

What community(ies) or population(s) were studied? Did the study report gender, race or ethnicity, cultural characteristics, age, income, or other relevant variables in the sample? Did the study test for differences along these variables in the sample?

Did the study recognize or analyze cultural or social strengths or resources for coping present in the community studied?

Were the instruments and methods used in the research examined for their cultural appropriateness or sensitivity?

Were respondents asked to voice their coping experiences in their own words, through open-ended questioning?

What coping responses were studied? Were these all the means that participants used to cope?

Were psychosocial competencies studied? Which? How?

Was social support studied? What forms and sources were studied?

What indicators of coping outcomes were studied? Do these reflect wellness and growth/thriving, or distress and symptoms?

Did the study follow changes over time in a longitudinal design?

ences in their own terms. She then constructed a classification of the coping strategies they used to cope with the financial, parental, health, interpersonal, and bureaucratic stressors they faced (an example of qualitative research methods described in chap. 4).

The women very often pursued coping with the help of others rather than alone. Coping strategies used by more than half of the sample included directly addressing the problem, finding social support, "patient endurance," thinking positively about the problem, and thinking about how to solve the problem. Other strategies included getting distance from the problem by taking time for themselves, expressing feelings, prayer, focusing on the future, and focusing on their children. These findings reflect themes of concepts we have discussed: problem-focused, emotion-focused, and prosocial coping, and reappraisal. Yet they also reflect the particular realities of the situation with ideas such as patient endurance and focusing on children.

## Coping Outcomes

Discussions of coping inevitably raises questions: What are its outcomes? By what criteria can we evaluate those outcomes?

***Symptoms and Distress***   From a clinical perspective, the most obvious goal of coping is to lessen, remove, or avoid negative outcomes: symptoms of psychological disorder or physical illness. Measurements of constructs such as depression, anxiety, substance abuse, and physical illness are often used in studies of coping.

Researchers do not focus only on symptoms of mental disorders. Sadness or anxiety, for instance, indicate psychological distress even if they are not marked enough to indicate disorder. Much research relevant to coping concerns persons in distress but not with disorders (Mirowsky & Ross, 1989).

**Wellness and Thriving**    Wellness is not simply the absence of illness symptoms, but positive outcomes associated with physical health and psychological well-being. Effective coping promotes positive functioning. Measurements of psychological constructs such as life satisfaction (e.g., Maton, 1987), job satisfaction (e.g., Hirsch, Engel-Levy, DuBois, & Hardesty, 1990), positive affect (e.g., Ying, 1995), self-esteem (e.g., Seidman, 1991), development of coping skills (Albee & Gullotta, 1997), and academic achievement and commitment (e.g., Maton et al., 1996) also represent wellness outcomes that go beyond mere absence of symptoms.

In addition, some people do not simply cope with a stressor, returning to a prior level of equilibrium. Their encounter with a stressor initiates growth that goes beyond that prior level to higher levels of functioning. For instance, after learning to cope with a demanding life transition such as motherhood or going to college, life satisfaction may increase to a new, higher level. That gain indicates growth or *thriving*, an especially positive outcome of coping (Carver, 1998; O'Leary, 1998). It may be associated with transformation of life goals, daily behaviors, and identity (Ickovics & Park, 1998) or even spiritual change (Pargament, 1997).

**Social Outcomes**    Finally, changes in interpersonal relationships or social embeddedness are not often explicitly considered outcomes of coping. Social support variables are typically viewed as means to the ends of lessening individual distress or improving individual wellness, not as ends in themselves. Yet the importance of social outcomes is illustrated in research in which outcome variables involve marital or relationship quality (e.g., Cutrona, 1996) and parent–child interaction (P. A. Andresen & Telleen, 1992; Wolchik et al., 1993). Social outcomes deserve more attention; community psychology seeks to understand and strengthen connections among individuals, not individual wellness in isolation.

**A Cyclical Process**    Coping and its outcomes, positive or negative, lead to new processes of coping. The presence of psychological distress or disorder or of physical illness or injury represents a loss or threat to resources, thus becoming a stressor for a new round of coping. Even a positive outcome leads to future challenges, as well as to changes in resources. As is illustrated in Figure 8.1, coping is an ongoing, cyclical process.

# SOCIAL SUPPORT: RESOURCES FOR COPING

Now that you have an overview of the coping process, we return to resources, to cover three of them in depth: social support, psychosocial competence, and religion and spirituality. These are not the only important resources for coping, but they do illustrate ecological relationships in the coping process.

## Social Support: Overview

Community, social, clinical, health, and developmental psychologists, as well as sociologists, anthropologists, psychiatrists, social workers, and public health professionals, have studied social support intensively (see G. Caplan, 1974). Interest in social support increased after studies of coping showed that some individuals coped well even with high levels of stressors. Perhaps support from others provided a buffer that moderated the effects of stressors.

Table 8.4 illustrates some of the coping outcomes associated with the presence or strength of social support in recent studies and reviews. A caution: These associations, especially when based on cross-sectional designs, may not indicate a causal buffering role for support. For instance, occurrence of symptoms may lead to loss of support, or happier

| TABLE 8.4 | COPING OUTCOMES CORRELATED WITH SOCIAL SUPPORT: OUTCOMES, POPULATIONS, AND RELATED RESEARCH |
|---|---|

**Part 1: Greater Social Support Correlated with Lesser Symptomatology**

| Symptoms | Population | Related Research |
|---|---|---|
| Anxiety | Elementary school students | Hill & Madhere (1996) |
| | High school students | Barone et al. (1991) |
| | Crime victims | Cutrona & Russell (1990)*, Kaniasty & Norris (1992) |
| Depression | Adolescents, young adults | Barrera & Li (1996)*, Gore & Aseltine (1995), Maton et al. 1996 |
| | Adults with mental illness | Wood, Hurlburt, Hough, & Hofstetter (1998) |
| | African American men | Peterson, Folkman, & Bakerman (1996) |
| | HIV-positive adults | Carels, Baucom, Leone, & Rigney (1998), Siegel et al. (1997) |
| | Mothers | Cutrona & Russell (1990)*, Henly (1997), Maton et al. (1996), Rhodes et al. (1992, 1994), Rhodes & Woods (1995) |
| | Unemployed adults | Cutrona & Russell (1990)* |
| Behavior problems | Adolescents | Barrera & Li (1996)*, Wills, Vaccaro, & McNamara (1992) |
| Generalized, psychological distress | Bereaved children, adults | Cutrona & Russell (1990)*, Sandler et al (1992) |
| | Caregiver for ill persons | Cutrona & Russell (1990)*, Tausig (1992) |
| | Children of divorced parents | Lustig, Wolchik, & Braver (1992) |
| | College students | Liang & Bogat (1994) |
| | HIV-positive adults | Carels et al. (1998) |
| | "Latchkey" children | Shulman, Kedem, Kaplan, Server, & Braja (1998) |
| | Teachers, nurses | Cutrona & Russell (1990)* |
| | Young adolescents | DuBois, Felner, Sherman, & Bull (1994), Hirsch & DuBois (1992) |
| Health problems | Adults | Bates & Toro (1999), Burman & Margolin (1992)*, Cutrona & Russell (1990)*, Dunkel-Schetter, Sagrestano, Feldman, & Killingsworth (1996)*, Uchino et al. (1996)* |

*(continued)*

| TABLE 8.4 | *continued* |
|---|---|

**Part 2: Greater Social Support Correlated with Positive Outcomes**

| Outcomes | Population | Related Research |
|---|---|---|
| Academic performance & commitment | High school students | Gonzales et al. (1996) |
| | College students | Maton et al. (1996), Zea, Jarama, & Bianchi (1995) |
| Cardiovascular, endocrine, & immune functioning | Adults | Uchino et al. (1996)* |
| Job, life satisfaction | Adults | Hirsch et al. (1990),* Hobfoll & Vaux (1993)*, Maton (1987, 1988, 1989) |
| Parenting skills | Mothers | Andresen & Telleen (1992)*, Silver et al. (1997) |

Note: This list is illustrative, not exhaustive. Literature reviews are indicated by asterisks. See discussion in text.

persons may assemble stronger support networks, or a third variable such as social skills may determine both support levels and well-being. Clearly, however, being embedded in a network of supportive relationships is associated in general with health and psychological well-being (see reviews by S. Cohen & Wills, 1985; Hobfoll & Vaux, 1993; Kessler, Price, & Wortman, 1985; M. Levine & Perkins, 1997; Uchino, Cacioppo, & Kiecolt-Glaser, 1996).

Social support is not a simple, unitary concept (Hobfoll & Vaux, 1993; B. R. Sarason, Sarason, & Pierce, 1990a). Rather, it represents a collection of social, emotional, cognitive, and behavioral processes occurring in personal relationships that provide aid that promotes adaptive coping. This complexity makes it important to understand varying definitions and measurements of social support.

## Forms of Social Support: Generalized and Specific

Social support can be understood as occurring in two forms: generalized and specific (B. R. Sarason et al., 1990a). These differ in the functions they play for the recipient of the support. Generalized support occurs in ongoing interpersonal relationships; specific support is provided to help a person cope with a particular stressor.

***Generalized Support***    This refers to ongoing support, whether or not the person currently faces demanding stressors. It involves a general sense of belongingness, acceptance and being cared for (B. R. Sarason et al., 1990a). In turn, it can be understood as occurring in two types: social integration and emotional support (Cutrona & Russell, 1990).

*Social integration* refers to a sense of belongingness in a social network or community. Friendships, workplace relationships, and membership in a religious congregation or neighborhood association are examples of settings in which social integration occurs. In a study of senior citizens, for instance, Felton and Berry (1992) found that interviewees cited extended family, religious congregations, and other groups as sources of support, not just individuals. Social integration in this sense may resemble the psychological sense of community described in chapter 7.

However, not every instance of objective membership in a community or relationship is necessarily supportive. Not every marriage, workplace, or religious congregation provides support. If membership is bolstered by a sense of mutual commitment and belongingness, supportive social integration is occurring (Cutrona & Russell, 1990).

*Emotional support* refers to comfort and caring provided within personal relationships (Cutrona & Russell, 1990). It is often the most intimate and intense form of support and is present in a strong marriage, parent–child relationship, or friendship. It is often unconditional, and may be related to attachment in close relationships (Bartholomew, Cobb, & Poole, 1997). Although social integration refers more to the breadth of one's network of supportive relationships, emotional support refers to depth of relationships, usually with close friends or family.

Strong generalized support provides a resource that is stable over time and across many situations in one's life. It provides the person with a secure base for living and coping. It is not specific to one kind of stressor and does not necessarily involve obvious helping with a specific challenge. It is most clearly measured in terms of perceived support, in which the research participants are asked about the general quality of support that is available in their lives, not about specific instances in which they have recently received support (Barrera, 1986; B. R. Sarason et al., 1990a). Because it becomes stable over time and across situations, generalized support can become internalized within the person, influencing the individual's worldview and appraisal of stressors and resources. It thus becomes as much a personal resource as a social resource, an integration of personality and environmental support (Pierce, Lakey, Sarason, Sarason, & Joseph, 1997).

**Specific Support**    This form of support more directly concerns problem-focused coping with a specific stressor, often in a particular setting such as neighborhood, work, or school (Hobfoll & Vaux, 1993). Three types of support can be considered specific: encouragement, informational, and tangible (Cutrona & Russell, 1990).

*Encouragement* (termed "esteem support" by Cutrona and Russell, 1990) concerns bolstering of a person's sense of competence for dealing with a specific challenge. It is task-focused reassurance, not deeper emotional support. It may come from family or close friends, but is may also come from less-intimate sources such as coworkers. *Informational support* involves providing advice or guidance. It is primarily cognitive rather than emotional and is usually tailored to a specific situation. *Tangible support* is concrete assistance, usually referring to material resources such as money or tasks such as car repair.

Regarding tangible support, Stack (1974) analyzed the exchange of assistance among low-income families in a housing project, including providing money, child care, and clothes, as well as sharing meals and other costs. These gifts were provided in an atmosphere of reciprocity, with the expectation of receiving help from others when it was needed. Maton (1987) studied the giving of money, goods, and services among members of a religious congregation, also finding reciprocity important. Berkowitz (1987) profiled the founder of the Useful Services Exchange, a community service listing residents of a town and the skills or services they would provide for free to other community members.

Specific support is provided as needed, to help with a particular stressor. It is perhaps best measured in terms of received support, in which research participants are asked to record or remember specific instances in which they receive support (Barrera, 1986; B. R. Sarason et al., 1990a). It may be provided by close friends or mere acquaintances. It usually requires some form of asking for help from others. Its effect on personal adjustment is likely to appear only when the person encounters stressful circumstances requiring a specific form of helping (L. H. Cohen et al., 1997; S. Cohen & Wills, 1985). Thus, it has a buffering effect, moderating the effects of stressors only when they occur (Maton, 1989).

The effects of specific support also depend in part on culture. Comparing U.S. and mainland Chinese students, Liang and Bogat (1994) found that specific, received support meant different things in these two samples. Among Chinese students, such support, when openly provided, often was not helpful. In a collectivistic culture, receiving support in a noticeable way may have reflected poorly on one's family or other ingroup, embarrassing them. Culture thus affected the perception and use of specific support.

***Optimal Matching Research***    Differing types of social support appear most effective when matched with particular stressors, an idea known as the *optimal-matching hypothesis* (Cutrona & Russell, 1990). In the nearly 40 studies Cutrona and Russell reviewed, emotional support was more effective than other forms for many uncontrollable stressors, such as having a severe physical illness or caring for a relative who did. Social integration and encouragement were more helpful in dealing with job loss, which requires both problem-focused and emotion-focused coping. Encouragement alone was most effective in dealing with chronic work stress among nurses and teachers. Tangible support best predicted positive coping with chronic financial strain among low-income persons. These findings support the optimal-matching hypothesis.

Cutrona and Russell's (1990) review revealed that some stressors, such as bereavement and loss of job, require multiple forms of aid. Depending on the nature of the stressor, one type or multiple types of support may be needed.

## The Relationship Context of Social Support

Social support occurs not in a vacuum, but within relationships with friends, family, coworkers, and others. It is shaped by the dynamics in those relationships. In a number of studies, having close, confiding, reciprocal relationships has been linked to higher levels of social support, and to less loneliness and greater life satisfaction (Hobfoll & Vaux, 1993). Such relationships provide a strong base of generalized support as well as specific forms of support when needed.

***Sources of Support***    Support relationships may be categorized by source, such as whether they are with family members, peers or friends, teachers or fellow workers, or persons with the same problem.

Family members, particularly parents and spouses, are important sources of support (especially generalized support) in many contexts, including school, college and young adulthood, adolescent motherhood, and for women with breast cancer (Barone, Aguirre-Deandreis, & Trickett, 1991; Cauce, Hannan, & Sargeant, 1992; Chen, Telleen, & Chen, 1995; Maton et al., 1996; Pistrang & Barker, 1998). Family relationships, compared to other social ties, often involve greater commitment and personal knowledge of the individual and support that is generalized as well as specific. However, they also mean greater obligation for reciprocity and greater potential for conflict (Hobfoll & Vaux, 1993; Pistrang & Barker, 1998), and they may not be useful for every stressor (Gore & Aseltine, 1995).

Studies of middle school and high school students have found support from school staff associated with student satisfaction with school, student perceptions of competence at school, and with grades (Barone et al., 1991; Cauce et al., 1992; Gillock & Reyes, 1996).

Friends are an important source of support across the life span, although their influence does not always promote adaptive coping (e.g., Seidman et al., 1994). Differences in the effects of support from friends is likely to be very contextual. For instance, in one study of urban African Americans aged 12–14, peer support was associated with higher grades in school in safer neighborhoods, but with lower grades in neighborhoods with more gang activity and crime (Gonzales et al., 1996). A study of mostly middle-class and White adolescents found that girls, compared to boys, develop closer friendships and use social support from friends more often, but they are also more vulnerable when those relationships are disrupted (Gore & Aseltine, 1995).

Stack's (1974) classic study in an African American community identified another source of support, namely "fictive kin," or friends with whom relationships were similar to extended family membership. Similar to the idea of fictive kin is the *natural mentor,* a key support source in studies of African American and Latina young mothers (Rhodes, 1994; Rhodes, Contreras, & Mangelsdorf, 1994; Rhodes, Ebert, & Fischer, 1992). Rhodes and her associates defined a mentor as a person at least 8 years older than the mother, not a relative, who provided emotional, encouragement, informational, and other forms of support (Rhodes et al., 1992, p. 449). In their samples, 35%–45% of mothers identified such mentors. Many of these relationships had begun in childhood, and most mothers with a mentor saw that mentor at least once weekly (Rhodes et al., 1994). In both studies, mothers with mentors were less likely to become depressed than those without mentors, despite similar levels of stressors and overall support in the two groups.

Similar to natural mentors are *natural helpers,* individuals whose informal role in a community includes providing informational or emotional support. Some become natural helpers because their jobs lead to conversations with personal–emotional meaning, such as beauticians and bartenders (Cowen, McKim, & Weissberg, 1981). Others become natural helpers by means of taking an active role in providing support, for instance in helping youth with personal problems.

*Comparing Sources of Support*    Does support differ by source? We have discussed some ways in which parent, school staff, and peer support differ in their effects on adolescents. Do spouses and fellow patients also differ in the helping they provide to women with breast cancer? To study this question, Pistrang and Barker (1998) audiotaped 10-minute conversations in which English women with breast cancer (disclosers) talked about their condition with either their husband or a fellow patient with breast cancer previously unknown to the discloser. The disclosers rated both conversations positively, but trained observers of the tapes rated the fellow patients more supportive, empathic, self-disclosing of own feelings, and less critical than husbands. Marital satisfaction did not explain these differences, although husband fatigue with the ongoing demands of caretaking may have had an effect (Pistrang & Barker, 1998). In addition, the first-hand experiential knowledge

| TABLE 8.5 | SOURCES OF SOCIAL SUPPORT STUDIED IN COMMUNITY PSYCHOLOGY |
|---|---|

Family

Friends

School staff

Natural mentors, natural helpers

Self-help groups and other peer helpers

Sources available through telephone and computer-mediated support

of the fellow patients may have been especially helpful. These findings support the value of *peer helpers* (persons who have experienced the same problem) in self-help groups (see chap. 7).

The importance of sources of support also differs in terms of the setting. A study of student coping with the first year of college in a suburban, mainly European American university found differences in what constituted the most important source of support for African American and European American students (Maton et al., 1996). For European Americans, peer support was the most important factor in commitment to college during the first year. Peer support for them was easily available on campus. In contrast, for African Americans, for whom fewer peers were available there, family support was a stronger predictor of commitment to college. Among high-achieving African American male students, family support was especially important (Maton et al., 1998).

**Support Through Communications Media**    New technologies can make sources of support more accessible. An example is the Grandma Please program in Chicago (Szendre & Jose, 1996). During after-school hours, children can call a central number and be connected to an elder volunteer for conversation and support. The program benefits both children and elders.

A newer medium of support is electronic communication in computer-mediated on-line mutual help groups (Madara, 1997; Salem et al., 1997). These provide a resource to those with privacy concerns or who cannot attend face-to-face groups. Similarly, Dunham et al. (1998) developed a local computer mutual-help network for single, low-income mothers. Each mother who volunteered to join received a computer donated by local organizations and access to the network. A core group of mothers, almost one third of the sample, used the service intensively and experienced declines in parenting stress over 6 months.

Table 8.5 lists the sources of support we have described.

**Relationships as Stressors**    Of course, relationships create stressors as well as support. A recent study of HIV-positive men revealed that depressive symptoms were associated with the occurrence of negative interactions with others (Siegel, Raveis, & Karus, 1997). A study of adolescent mothers found that depression was predicted by both the amount of received social support from members of their support network and the amount of social strain (criticism, conflict, and disappointment) in those same relationships (Rhodes & Woods, 1995). A study of Israeli women during the Israel–Lebanon war revealed "pressure cooker" effects (Hobfoll & London, 1986). These occurred because the women all experienced a simultaneous stressor, many individuals sought support, and the shared resources of the group were strained. In other contexts, if support is required over an extended time, for an illness or other chronic problem, conflict often occurs as supporters tire (Coyne, Ellard, & Smith, 1990). Receiving support from others may lead to feeling patronized or helpless. Providing support to others takes energy and time, as you know if you have ever provided help to a friend in an emotional crisis. Studying support in the context of relationships helps clarify its positive and negative effects.

## Social Networks

Social support occurs not only within single relationships, but also within networks of relationships. A social network consists of a focal person and that person's relationships with others. Depending on the purposes of study, a network may be defined to include relationships with acquaintances, friends, or providers of support (generalized or specific types). Researchers analyze social networks in terms of many variables related to social support. We will focus on three: multidimensionality, density, and reciprocity.

***Multidimensionality***    Multidimensional relationships are those in which the two persons involved do a number of things together and share a number of role relationships. Multidimensional relationships exist when a coworker is also a friend we see socially or when we share multiple interests and activities with neighbors. *Unidimensional relationships* are confined to one role. One sees a coworker only at work; neighbors are not friends or fellow members of organizations. As a student, you have a multidimensional relationship with a classmate who is also a neighbor or who is involved in the same organization. With a person you know only in class, you share a unidimensional relationship.

Because a multidimensional relationship means we see the other person more often, forming and deepening friendships is often easier. Multidimensional relationships also mean that ties are more resilient. For instance, loss of a job effectively means the end of unidimensional relationships with coworkers, whereas multidimensional relationships would survive and help the individual to cope with that stressor.

Hirsch (1980) studied multidimensionality in the social networks of two groups: recently widowed young women and adult women students returning to college. In both groups, self-esteem, satisfaction with socializing, and tangible support were associated with multidimensional relationships rather than unidimensional ones.

***Density***    A social network also consists of relationships between the persons in that network other than the focal person. Network density refers to the extent of these relationships. A high-density network exists when many ties exist between network members; for instance, when most network members are friends of each other. Residents of small towns and even some urban neighborhoods often live in high-density networks. A low-density network exists when few of the members are closely connected (of course, all are closely connected to the focal person). A person with many friends in different settings, yet whose friends do not know each other, has a low-density network.

High-density networks usually offer greater consensus on norms and advice (Hirsch et al., 1990) and often quicker help in a crisis, because the network members are more interconnected. However, low-density networks often hold a greater variety of persons with a greater variety of life experiences. Thus, they can provide a diversity of resources needed during life transitions such as divorce, bereavement, or entering college (Hirsch, 1980; Hobfoll & Vaux, 1993; Wilcox, 1981). In such transitions, too much density of inter-connections within one's network may inhibit the development of new roles and personal identities or adaption to changed circumstances.

Hirsch (1980) analyzed network density in his study (mentioned above) of recently widowed young women and adult women college students. In those samples, low-density social networks were more adaptive than high-density ones. As these women moved into new roles as single person or college student, they needed a variety of friendships and support resources. In a study of women experiencing divorce, Wilcox (1981) reported similar findings.

***Reciprocity of Support***    Social networks also vary in the extent of reciprocity of support, the extent to which the individual both receives support from others and provides it to others. Reciprocity may be the most important aspect of friendship across the life span (Hartup & Stevens, 1997).

In studies of self-help groups and of a religious congregation, Maton (1987, 1988) found that reciprocity of support was associated with greater psychological well-being. When individuals provided support as well as received support (a state of reciprocity), well-being was higher. Among those who mostly provided or mostly received support and those who did little of either, well-being was lower. These findings support the helper-therapy principle (Riessman, 1990): Providing help for others benefits the provider (recall this idea from chap. 7). Receiving help may be stigmatizing or may lead to a sense of indebtedness. Providing help, as long as the person does not exhaust personal resources, can generate feelings of self-worth and competence.

Maton's (1987, 1988) findings refer to overall reciprocity of providing and receiving support in the person's social network, not to reciprocity within each dyadic relationship. An individual may primarily provide support to one other person while primarily receiving support from another, yet have an overall balance of providing and receiving (Maton, 1987, p. 201).

Maton's (1987/1988) correlational findings cannot indicate the direction of cause and effect. A balance of providing and receiving may increase well-being, or it may be that happier individuals create such a balance in their lives, or that each factor strengthens the other. However, the correlational findings indicate the general importance of balancing providing and receiving support. Moreover, the findings are noteworthy because professional forms of helping often place clients in a position in which they receive but cannot provide help. In contrast, self-help groups provide opportunities for both giving and receiving aid.

## Social Support: Contributions and Limitations

Researchers interested in stress and coping originally became interested in social support as a way of explaining why some individuals with high levels of exposure to stressors did not suffer negative outcomes (B. R. Sarason et al., 1990a; Hobfoll & Vaux, 1993). Social support was presumed to offset or moderate the effects of stressors. However, later research indicated that its effects are complicated by many interacting factors, and the negative effects of supportive relationships also became clearer (Coyne et al., 1990; Hobfoll & Vaux, 1993). Researchers now agree that social support is not a panacea and that it must be examined in terms of its interaction with many factors (L. H. Cohen et al., 1997). Its effects depend on the context, which involves the following factors, at least:

- cultural forces that influence the perception of resources, stressors, and forms of support
- characteristics of social units such as neighborhood, setting and social network (e.g., multidimensionality)
- relationship issues and how they influence (positively and negatively) the exchange of support
- opportunities for reciprocity and the benefits of providing support
- the nature of the stressor, especially its controllability
- the forms of support available and used in coping
- the presence of other personal, social and material resources.

In other words, social support must be understood in ecological terms.

# PSYCHOSOCIAL COMPETENCIES: RESOURCES FOR COPING

Competencies for coping are a resource needed to carry out coping strategies. Without them, we may not recognize or use resources available from others. Competencies also are the focus of many preventive interventions and are a key element of individual wellness.

Table 8.6 lists key personal and social competencies identified in psychological research, including but not limited to community research. We do not discuss that research in depth; much of it goes beyond this chapter's purposes. We have used Goleman's (1995, 1998) empirically based description of emotional intelligence for much of Table 8.6, while attempting to put that framework in a wider community context. Chapters 9–11 examine interventions to prevent disorders and promote such competencies.

TABLE 8.6    **PSYCHOSOCIAL COMPETENCIES FOR COPING**

| Personal Competencies | Social Competencies |
| --- | --- |
| Self and emotional awareness | Empathy |
| Self and emotional regulation | Social analysis |
| Problem-solving | Collaboration |
| | Personal connection |
| | Conflict management |
| | Interpersonal influence |

Note: This list is illustrative, not exhaustive, and is based primarily on Goleman (1995, 1998).

## Personal Competencies

These include skills related to managing emotions, motivation, cognition, and other intrapersonal processes in coping (Goleman, 1995, 1998, pp. 26–27). *Self and emotional awareness* involves sensitivity to one's own emotions and intuitions, as well as insight into one's strengths and limitations. *Self and emotional regulation* involves management of emotions in adaptive ways, including resisting impulses. It also includes flexibility in the face of changing circumstances and conscientious attention to task detail and responsibilities. Both of these are important for careful appraisal of stressors and resources and for judicious, adaptive coping.

*Interpersonal cognitive problem solving* (ICPS; Shure, 1997; Shure & Spivack, 1988) is a set of personal competencies studied by community psychologists. Personal competencies associated with the process of problem solving include identifying and framing problems, setting goals, generating alternative strategies, elaborating on and considering consequences and obstacles, and decision making. Shure and associates have developed intervention programs in schools and other settings that effectively promote ICPS and related skills among children, adolescents, and adults (e.g., Bruene-Butler, Hampson, Elias, Clabby, & Schuyler, 1997; R. Caplan, Vinokur, & Price, 1997; Cowen et al., 1996; Shure, 1997; Shure & Spivack, 1988; Weissberg, Barton, & Shriver, 1997). We cover such programs in detail in chapter 10.

## Social Competencies

The most basic social skill is *empathy,* the accurate understanding of another's emotions and attunement to that person (Goleman, 1995). Empathy was correlated, for instance, with resilience and adjustment in a study of highly stressed, low-income urban U.S. children (Hoyt-Meyers et al., 1995). ICPS training includes development of increased empathy (Shure, 1997). More broadly, *social analysis* (Goleman, 1995) involves understanding groups (for instance, identifying the resources and talents of others) and insight into the emotional and power dynamics of groups (from school-playground groupings to complex organizations). Social network orientation (i.e., the awareness of one's social support network and how to mobilize it for help) is a social analysis skill (Barone, Iscoe, Trickett, & Schmid, 1998).

*Collaboration* and teamwork require several other competencies. The skill of making *personal connections*, building and maintaining personal relationships, from small talk to deeper support, is crucial among adults and children (Goleman, 1995). Some specific aspects include making conversation, asking open-ended questions, discussing feelings, and accepting criticism (Botvin & Tortu, 1988; Rotheram-Borus, 1988). *Managing conflicts* to promote teamwork and resolve disputes comprises another essential family of skills (Goleman, 1995, 1998).

Finally, *interpersonal influence* involves a family of competencies in moving others to action or resisting unwanted influence (Goleman, 1995, 1998). Training in assertion and related skills has been empirically related to adolescents' ability to resist drug use (Botvin & Tortu, 1988) and a number of positive outcomes for children (Rotheram-Borus, 1988). The JOBS Project included training in interviewing and other job-search skills, helping unemployed workers rejoin the workforce (R. Caplan et al., 1997). Many leadership skills are important in work and community settings (Goleman, 1998; Maton & Salem, 1995).

## Contributions and Limitations

These competencies are generally adaptive and are often the focus of prevention and competence promotion programs. However, their utility is contextual. They do not represent skills specific to particular transitions or stressors such as parenting, bereavement, or entering college. For instance, the same skill (e.g., assertive persuasion) may be adaptive in some situations and cultures, yet ineffective or counterproductive in others.

## SPIRITUALITY AND RELIGION: RESOURCES FOR COPING

On April 19, 1995, an explosion ripped through the Murrah Federal Building in Oklahoma City, Oklahoma. Over 100 people died, including both adults at work and children in a day care center. The bereaved were left with difficult grieving. Many turned to their spiritual and religious practices and congregations for support and to make sense of their experience (Pargament, 1997, p. 170). A spiritual perspective can help make sense of the "incomprehensible, unfathomable, uncontrollable" (Pargament, 1997, p. 8). It is perhaps most useful at the limits of an individuals' resources and ability to cope, which is when the Western cultural and psychological emphasis on controlling outcomes are most likely to fall short (Pargament, 1997).

We discussed the distinction between religion and spirituality in the previous chapter. Both offer personal and social resources. Personal resources include a spiritual relationship with God or other transcendent force, a set of beliefs that provides meaning in life and may promote coping, and specific coping methods such as prayer and meditation. Social resources include membership and support within a religious congregation and cultural spiritual practices (e.g., Hazel & Mohatt, in press). As we noted in the previous chapter, these include a diversity of religious and spiritual traditions.

Spiritual and religious resources influence coping and well-being, empowerment, and prevention of problems in living (Paloutzian & Kirkpatrick, 1995; Pargament et al., 1992; Pargament, 1997). For instance, 90% of U.S. residents report a belief in God, and 80% report being conscious of God's presence in their lives. U.S. survey respondents would seek help for a personal problem more often from a clergy member than any other professional (Pargament, 1997, pp. 2 and 210). Many community resources for help are religious in nature, and many self-help groups are based on spiritual beliefs and practices (Maton & Wells, 1995). In addition, a survey of U.S. adults found that 40% of respondents were involved in some form of "small group that meets regularly and provides caring and support for its members" (Wuthnow, 1994, p. 45). This definition included fellowship and prayer groups as well as self-help groups (Wuthnow, 1994, p. 65).

However, the personal and social impact of religion and spirituality can also be negative. For instance, a survey of U.S. battered women found that over one quarter said religion had hurt them, not helped them, and another one quarter reported both harmful and helpful influences of religion (Horton, 1988, cited in Pargament, 1997). Spirituality and religion can create or worsen stressors, such as when the person interprets a stressor in a spiritual way that prevents helpful coping, or when a congregation shuns an errant member (Pargament, 1997).

## Purposes of Spirituality

Neither religious beliefs and institutions nor personal and cultural forms of spirituality exist simply as resources for coping. Both have much larger purposes. Their usefulness for coping must be understood within those larger aims.

Spirituality and religion involve a sense of transcendence, of going beyond oneself and daily life (S. B. Sarason, 1993). They cannot be reduced to other psychological and social resources for coping. They represent more than personal resilience and social support in pious form. Spiritual–religious persons often view their relationship with God or a spiritual world as distinct from other relationships (Pargament, 1997). Empirical study of spiritual and religious coping concerns psychological and health outcomes, but not other spiritual aspirations or ends. Thus, it concerns only part of the meaning of religion and spirituality.

## Empirical Research on Spirituality, Religion, and Coping

Empirically, how do spiritual–religious factors affect coping outcomes? Pargament (1997) reviewed empirical studies of spirituality, religion, and coping. These studies are correlational, so direct conclusions about the causal impact of spiritual–religious coping on coping outcomes cannot be drawn. However, researchers can study the strength of spiritual variables as predictors of coping outcomes, particularly in longitudinal designs. Participants in the studies Pargament reviewed were mostly North American adults, including persons with chronic and terminal illnesses, bereaved widows and children, victims of automobile accidents and of floods, Whites and African Americans, heterosexuals and gay men, and senior citizens as well as other adults. Not all persons studied were religious in belief or practice; most who indicated religious involvement were Christian. Researchers measured a variety of coping outcomes, including psychological distress and well-being, general health, and mortality in some studies of illness.

## Specific Coping Methods and Outcomes

Spiritual–religious coping practices include prayer, a sense of a personal relationship with God, framing stressors in spiritual terms, engaging in spiritual practices and rituals, and seeking support from congregation members. Both very religious and nonreligious persons may use them in particular circumstances. How are spiritual–religious coping practices related to psychological coping outcomes?

Pargament's (1997, chap. 10) review revealed four general findings regarding this question. First, spiritual–religious coping was particularly important with highly stressful, largely uncontrollable situations. Second, spiritual–religious coping methods were often significant predictors of coping outcomes even after nonspiritual coping methods were statistically controlled. Spiritual–religious coping thus seems to play a distinctive role in coping, especially with uncontrollable stressors.

Third, coping methods with positive impact included (a) perceiving a spiritual relationship with a trustworthy and loving God, (b) activities such as prayer, (c) religious reappraisal promoting the sense that growth can come from stressful events, and (d) receiving support from fellow members of a religious congregation (Pargament, 1997). However, many studies found nonsignificant associations between spiritual–religious coping and outcomes, and some found negative associations (Pargament, 1997, p. 285). Negative effects included self-blame for stressful events and lack of support from one's religious congregation. These findings suggest that spiritual–religious coping is influenced by many other factors and is not always positive in effect.

## Contexts of Coping

For whom are spiritual–religious methods most helpful in coping? National surveys of U.S. residents reveal that women, those with low incomes, the elderly, African Americans, and the widowed find religion and spirituality more useful for coping than do other groups. What these groups seem to have in common is less access to secular sources of power and resources (Pargament, 1997, p. 301). Religion and spirituality thus represents an especially important, accessible coping resource. For instance, Moore (1992) reviewed the history of the African American church as a community institution, arising even under slavery, that has supported individual coping as well as personal and community empowerment (but see also Brodsky, 2000).

## Contributions and Limitations

Pargament's (1997) review indicates religious and spiritual coping methods are important for understanding coping. Their impact may be positive or negative. Their most distinctive contributions may occur when other resources are lacking or when stressors are uncontrollable. Yet this research is in its early stages, with much to be learned (Pargament, 1997). Especially needed are longitudinal studies of coping and resources. In addition, more studies are needed to delineate the differing significance of religion and spirituality in differing social and cultural contexts (Maton & Wells, 1995; Pargament, 1997; Pargament & Maton, 2000). In particular, more studies of diverse faiths and forms of spirituality are needed. Also needed are studies of how religion and spirituality relate to other forms of diversity, such as gender, race, culture, nationality or socioeconomic class. For instance, in one study, Protestant Christians in the United States and Korea differed in beliefs about locus of control (Bjorck, Lee, & Cohen, 1997).

# PUTTING IT ALL TOGETHER: PROCESSES OF COPING

The ecological framework of this chapter emphasizes (a) the role of resources in defining stressors and in coping; (b) coping as a process of appraisal, coping responses, and outcomes; and (c) the importance of social, cultural, and situational contexts in coping. To integrate your learning of this framework, let's consider two examples of coping. How does the ecological framework apply to an individual coping with bereavement? To adults returning to college, coping with the demands of that new commitment?

## Bereavement

This stressor accounted for the highest stressfulness score and two of the five highest scores on the original Social Readjustment Rating Scale (Holmes & Rahe, 1967). If the bereaved was especially close to the deceased, bereavement usually represents the beginning of a life transition. It may require relatively permanent changes in social roles, identity, and even living arrangements. Bereavement may also pose daily hassles, as when a spouse discovers that he or she must now perform unfamiliar tasks. Bereavement represents an actual and potential loss of many resources: a life companion, specific forms of guidance and support from the deceased, old personal identities, and material resources.

Bereavement is a universal human experience, and every culture has beliefs and rituals to guide its members through it. Spiritual traditions, writings, and rituals are often central to bereavement. They provide meaning or ways of understanding the experience (appraisal) and forms of support for the bereaved. The experience of bereavement poses the kind of difficult questions and uncontrollable circumstances for which spiritual perspectives are often crucial resources.

As an uncontrollable and emotional event, bereavement requires emotion-focused coping. Social support may be provided by social integration, emotional support from one's closest friends and family, and spiritual sources. These are often provided by others without explicit requests for help. Life after bereavement may also require problem-focused coping. Encouragement, informational, and tangible support are often needed to cope with new demands. Obtaining specific help may require asking for assistance, a psychosocial skill. Becoming involved in providing helping to others, not simply receiving it, may be helpful. If the bereaved has a high-density social network, looking beyond it to form new friendships also may be helpful.

The outcomes of bereavement are often painful emotions in the first weeks, and even months. Yet, as with life transitions generally, the person eventually may experience growth in personal strengths, skills, and resources.

## Adult Students

Let's consider another example: adult students entering college (e.g., Hirsch, 1980). In this case, the stressor is an "entrance" rather than an "exit," but still it represents a life transition demanding changes in social networks and roles, academic competencies, and a new social identity. It also represents a loss of time for other, competing commitments such as family or job or personal time, and a demand for new material, social, and personal resources.

Adult students use problem-focused coping, such as studying, seeking academic advice, finding classmates or others with whom to study, and creating a place and time to study at home. These are often more challenging for the adult (and for other commuter students) than for students living on campus. Emotion-focused coping is often needed, too. Existing, generalized emotional support, the sense of being cared for, provides an important base for the exploration of college studies. New adult students also need specific forms of support: encouragement in academic work, informational guidance, and tangible assistance with accomplishing many competing tasks in their lives. Help with housework is one example of the latter.

Hirsch (1980) found that for adult women students, two social network factors were important: having rewarding multidimensional relationships and having supportive networks both with family and outside the family. In his sample, these promoted adaptation to college. Developing relationships with other adult students not only provides social integration but also affords encouragement, informational, and tangible support. Moreover, the experience of college is not simply a stressor, but can lead to growth and thriving.

These examples illustrate how coping is a process. Although we can divide it into pieces to describe its workings, it occurs in everyday life as a seamless process. In addition, it is a cyclical process in which later pieces of the puzzle may lead to changes in the placement of earlier pieces, as when a coping response that fails may lead to reappraisal of the problem and to new responses. Resources, appraisal, and coping each affect the other. Outcomes, positive or negative, create new puzzles to solve. Living is coping. Our ecological perspective is designed to help you grasp how people conduct that process of living in social contexts, not alone.

To communicate the importance of context in coping, this chapter built on the previous chapters on ecological concepts, human diversity, and conceptions of community. In the next three chapters, we examine interventions designed to promote some of the personal and social resources we have discussed, as a means of preventing or lessening psychological problems before they occur.

# CHAPTER SUMMARY

**1.** This chapter presents an *ecological framework* for understanding the coping process. That framework emphasizes (a) the role of resources in coping; (b) the importance of social, cultural, and situational contexts in coping; and (c) coping as a process of appraisal, coping, and outcomes.

**2.** *Resources* for coping include *material, social,* and *personal* resources. Examples of resources include social support, religion and spirituality, and psychosocial competencies.

**3.** *Stressors* are external circumstances that represent a threatened or actual loss or scarcity of resources. They include *major life events, life transitions, daily hassles,* and *ambient/chronic* stressors.

**4.** *Primary appraisal* is the individual estimation of the strength of a stressor. *Secondary appraisal* is the estimation of the strength of resources for coping and of coping options. Appraisals begin the process of coping. They interact with emotional states such as anxiety and anger. *Reappraisal,* when appraisals are changed to promote coping, is a bridge between appraisal and coping.

**5.** *Coping responses* include both *problem-focused* and *emotion-focused* strategies, and may be *prosocial* or *antisocial. Judicious action* is one important problem-focused strategy, and *avoidance* is included under emotion-focused strategies. Problem-focused approaches are likely to be more effective when stressors are *controllable*, emotion-focused approaches when stressors are *uncontrollable*.

**6.** *Coping outcomes* refer to the psychological or health effects of coping and to how coping strategies may be evaluated. These include *symptoms* of psychological disorder, psychological *distress, wellness,* and *growth* or *thriving.*

**7.** *Social support,* the provision of helping by others, is a key resource for coping. It may be *generalized (emotional, social integration)* or *specific (encouragement, informational, tangible).*

**8.** Social support occurs in relationships, which affect its nature and effect. *Sources* of support include family, friends, school staff, *natural mentors* or *natural helpers, peer helpers* and self-help groups, and sources available through communications media such as telephone services and the Internet. *Social networks* can be analyzed in terms of *multidimensionality, density,* and *reciprocity.* Multidimensionality and reciprocity of support are important for coping outcomes.

**9.** *Psychosocial competencies* are important resources for coping. These include *personal competencies,* such as problem-solving, and *social competencies,* such as empathy and personal connection.

**10.** Religion and spirituality provide personal and social resources for many individuals. General measures of spiritual–religious orientation do not predict coping outcomes as well as specific *spiritual–religious coping methods,* such as prayer. These can have positive or negative effects.

## BRIEF EXERCISES

**1.** Brainstorm a list of stressors with which you, or someone you know well, has had personal experience. Include any external stressor that required effort in coping, including daily hassles that were frequent or especially bothersome.

　　When you have a good-sized list, categorize them in terms of the four types of stressors in Table 8.1. Try to think of stressors in all four categories. If you have trouble thinking of stressors, review our description of them early in the chapter (and count your blessings).

　　Choose two stressors from your list. Identify the resources (personal, social, material) that were harmed or threatened by each stressor.

**2.** Choose a significant stressor from your list in Exercise 1 above. What forms of problem-focused and/or emotion-focused coping did you employ to cope with that stressor?

　　What aspects of the stressor or situation could you personally control? What aspects were beyond your control?

　　Did the stressor lead to psychological distress? Of what sort, for how long?

　　Did you grow through the experience? How? Did you develop greater competencies, or social or personal resources?

　　Discuss your experiences with a friend or classmate.

**3.** Think back to your first year of college. What psychosocial competencies were required for you to succeed?

　　Write a list of these competencies. Be as specific as possible. For instance, many different social skills may have been required, including making conversation, resolving roommate conflicts, asking for help, disagreeing constructively with a roommate, and so on. (It may also include doing your own wash, waking up on time, and writing papers before the last minute.) If you have trouble writing a list, review Table 8.6 and the related section in the chapter. Discuss your list with a friend or classmate.

# RECOMMENDED READINGS

## Books

Goleman, D. (1995). *Emotional intelligence.* New York: Bantam.

Goleman, D. (1998). *Working with emotional intelligence.* New York: Bantam.

Hobfoll, S. (1998). *Stress, culture, and the community: The psychology and philosophy of stress.* New York: Plenum.

Lazarus, R., & Folkman, S. (1984). *Stress, appraisal, and coping.* New York: Springer.

Pargament, K. I. (1997). *The psychology of religion and coping.* New York: Guilford.

Pargament, K. I., Maton, K. I., & Hess, R. (Eds.). (1991). Religion and prevention in mental health. *Prevention in Human Services, 9*(2). Also published as a book in 1992: *Religion and prevention in mental health.* New York: Haworth.

Pierce, G. R., Lakey, B., Sarason, I. G., & Sarason, B. R. (Eds.). (1997). *Sourcebook of social support and personality.* New York: Plenum.

Pierce, G. R., Sarason, B. R., & Sarason, I. G. (Eds.). (1996). *Handbook of social support and the family.* New York: Plenum.

Sarason, B. R., Sarason, I. G., & Pierce, G. R. (Eds.). (1990). *Social support: An interactional view.* New York: Wiley.

## Articles and Chapters

Hobfoll, S., & Vaux, A. (1993). Social support: Social resources and social context. In L. Goldberger & S. Breznitz (Eds.), *Handbook of stress: Theoretical and clinical aspects* (2nd ed., pp. 685–705). New York: Free Press.

Liang, B., & Bogat, G. A. (1994). Culture, control, and coping: New perspectives on social support. *American Journal of Community Psychology, 22,* 123–147.

Maton, K. I. (1988). Social support, organizational characteristics, psychological well-being, and group appraisal in three self-help group populations. *American Journal of Community Psychology, 16,* 53–77.

Maton, K. I., Teti, D. M., Corns, K. M., Vieira-Baker, C. C., Lavine, J. R., Gouze, K. R., & Keating, D. P. (1996). Cultural specificity of support sources, correlates, and contexts: Three studies of African-American and Caucasian youth. *American Journal of Community Psychology, 24,* 551–587.

Humphreys, K., Finney, J. W., & Moos, R. H. (1994). Applying a stress and coping framework to research on mutual help organizations. *Journal of Community Psychology, 22,* 312–327.

Rhodes, J. E., Ebert, L., & Fischer, K. (1992). Natural mentors: An overlooked resource in the social networks of young, African American mothers. *American Journal of Community Psychology, 20,* 445–462.

# InfoTrac Keywords

*coping, competence(ies), religion, spirituality, stress(or), support, social support.*

# Recommended Websites

## Mutual Aid and Self Help

Information on mutual aid and self help has grown explosively on the Internet. Rather than provide listings of all available types of resources, we list several international self-help clearinghouses. If you have a specific topic or problem of interest, check the clearing-house listings for that topic.

http://mentalhelp.net/selfhelp

>This is the American Self Help Clearinghouse site, with links to international sites, which is part of the larger Mental Health Network site. Resources include listings of on-line resources and of local self-help resources for health and mental health concerns, including illnesses and disorders as well as other topics such as parenting, aging, and gay/lesbian issues. A reading room has excellent resources. This site also provides assistance in starting and working with self-help groups, and forums and chat rooms.

http://wsupsy.psy.twsu.edu/shnok

>This, too, is a good introduction to concepts and resources regarding self help, including reviews of its effectiveness and links to websites regarding psychological and medical problems. It is associated with the Self-Help Network of Kansas but has international scope.

http://psychwww.com/resource/selfhelp.htm

>Psychology Self-Help Resources on the Internet provides lists and links to on-line resources concerning psychological and related disorders, mental health information, and mutual aid and self-help clearinghouses. Part of the larger PsychWeb site on the discipline of psychology.

http://mhselfhelp.org

>This site provides technical assistance for those interested in starting or working with consumer groups in mental health.

## Advocacy for Persons with Mental Illness

http://nmha.org

>This is the National Mental Health Association site, with information on policy advocacy, general mental health topics, and local affiliates.

http://www.nami.org

>This is the National Association for the Mentally Ill site. It provides mental health information and opportunities for mental health consumer and family involvement and advocacy through local affiliates.

## Coping Information: Health and Mental Health

http://psychcentral.com

>This site provides chat rooms, newsgroups, frequently asked questions, information and book reviews, and links to other Websites. It is a good introduction to many mental health sites.

http://mentalhealth.org
> This is the Website of the U.S. government's Center for Mental Health Services, providing general and consumer-oriented information on mental health.

http://www.apa.org/psycnet
> This is part of the American Psychological Association Website. In addition to information on disorders and treatments, it provides a search engine for on-line psychological (including journal) resources.

http://www.goaskalice.columbia.edu
> This site has a question-and-answer format with information on health, wellness, nutrition/fitness, sexuality, stress management, and other health topics.

http://www.cdc.gov
> This is the Website for the U.S. Government Centers for Disease Control and Prevention. Includes information on a variety of diseases and conditions, including treatment and prevention; information on health issues in the news; public health statistical summaries; and links to other health sites.

## *Spirituality, Religion, and Psychology*

http://psychwww.com/psyrelig
> This is part of the larger PsychWeb site (see above), with general information on psychology and religion. It includes email discussion groups, lists of books and journals, and information on graduate study.

http://www.spiritualityhealth.com
> This site concerns spirituality and religion, health, and psychology. Contributors include scholars and writers from many fields, including psychology.

# Mapping Your Social Support Network[1]

Social support, as you learned in chapter 8, is a key resource for coping. The personal meaning of social support is best conveyed by constructing a map of one of your support networks.

In this exercise you will list your sources of emotional support, map them in terms of settings and interrelationships, analyze some characteristics of this network, and integrate your learning with social support concepts.

## Network List

First, write a list of the people to whom you would go to seek help with a personal or emotional problem of your own. List only those who you would seek out for this kind of help, not your entire network of friends. You may include persons you would contact by telephone, not just face to face. Write this list down the left margin of your paper, each name on a separate line.

Second, on the line for each person write the relationship(s) you share with that person. You choose the term(s) for these; examples include *sister, friend, roommate, fellow worker, neighbor.* This is an indicator of the sources of your support and of unidimensional and multidimensional relationships.

Third, on the same line list the setting (just one) where you most frequently encounter that person. Examples include *work, apartment* or *home, classes,* and *student union.*

Fourth, put a check mark on the line of each of the persons who you believe would probably seek you out for help with *their* personal-emotional problems.

## Network Map

You need a clean sheet of paper for this part. First, in the center of the page, put a small circle or dot, which represents you. Second, use dotted lines to divide the space into segments radiating out from the center like pieces of a pie. Each segment represents a setting in which you encounter at least one person in your emotional support network (from the third step above). Make a segment bigger if it includes many persons, smaller if it does not.

Third, put small circles or dots in the segments to represent the people on your network list. Label them with initials. You may put your closest confidants closer to you on

---

[1]David Todd (1979) was our original source of an earlier version of this exercise.

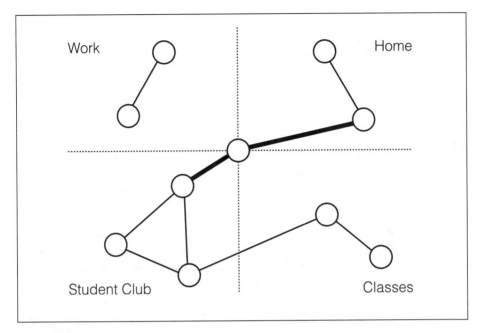

**FIGURE 8.2**

Social support network map

the map, and others farther away. *However, spread all of them out, and use the entire page.* That makes the next steps easier. (Remember, everyone on this list is close to you in some way.)

Fourth, draw a heavy line between your circle and the circles of those persons with whom you share a multidimensional relationship. The heavier the line, the more dimensions of relationship you share with that person.

Fifth, draw a light line between any two persons on the map, other than yourself, who you believe to be friends or confidants of each other. (Don't worry about whether these are multidimensional or not.) Lines may cross setting boundaries (dotted lines drawn between segments). This is your indicator of network density.

Figure 8.2 illustrates a network map.

## Analyzing Your Network List and Map

Your list and map represent your perceived network for emotional support (see chap. 8).

**Network Size**    This is simply the number of persons on your list. Network size is not an important predictor of coping outcomes unless it is very low (B. R. Sarason, Sarason & Pierce, 1990). A person with few or no confidants is socially isolated (at least emotionally) and lacks a key resource. In addition, conflict, loss, or other stressors in a relationship have a proportionally larger effect when there are only a few supportive ties. On the other hand, there is an upper limit to how many close, emotionally supportive relationships a person can realistically engage in. More is not always better.

Is there anything you would consider changing about your emotional support network's size?

**Sources and Quality of Support**    On your network list, you labeled relationships.

How many family members are on your list, and what is your perception of the quality of their support for you? What sort of support do you perceive to be available from your family? With what stressors are family members able to help you?

How about the number and quality of supportive relationships with friends? What sorts of support are available from them, to cope with what stressors?

Do you have a mentor, an older person who is not a relative and who provides emotional and/or other forms of support? Rhodes and associates (Rhodes, et al., 1992; 1994) studied natural mentors among African American and Latina mothers, but mentor relationships occur in many contexts. A mentor may provide advice and support in one setting, such as work, or be a source of more generalized support.

This is also a way to consider the diversity of resources in your network. Does your network contain persons of both genders, and of varying ages? Of differing life experiences and backgrounds? Does it contain anyone who has experienced stressors such as bereavement, unemployment, divorce, or serious illness/injury, and who could provide support if one of these stressors happened to you?

Is there anything you would consider changing about your sources of emotional support?

**Reciprocity**    In constructing your network list, you checked persons who you expected would seek emotional support from you for their problems. That is a rough measure of reciprocity within each relationship.

Which relationships in your network are reciprocal? How are they different from those that aren't? Is there an overall balance of providing and receiving emotional support in your life, when all your relationships are considered? What are the psychological benefits for you of providing support to others?

Is there anything you would consider doing to strengthen reciprocity in your emotional support network?

**Multidimensionality**    Heavy lines between you and others in your network map represent multidimensional relationships. (Unidimensional relationships you share with others are not drawn on the map.) Multidimensional relationships often offer high-quality support (e.g., Hirsch, 1980). Do you have any of these? Do they offer more quality of support, or more rewarding contact, than unidimensional ones?

Is there anything you would consider doing to increase multidimensionality in your network?

**Network Segments**    These are separated by dotted lines on your map. Many students have segmented networks, with supportive relationships in each segment, but few connections across segments. Hirsch (1980) found that for samples of young widows and adult women college students, having supportive relationships in different settings or segments of their lives was more adaptive than one densely connected network. Is that true for your network?

Is there anything you would consider doing to build supportive relationships in each setting in which you spend a lot of time?

***Network Density***    Density refers to the extent of ties among network members *other than yourself.* A high-density network has many such connections, a low-density network does not. A low-density network has been shown helpful for persons experiencing life transitions that involve forming new relationships, such as divorce, widowhood, and adults re-entering college (Hirsch, 1980; Wilcox, 1981). A high-density network may respond more quickly in a crisis, since its members are more interconnected.

Is there anything you would consider doing to change the density in your network?

***Summary***    The effects of social network variables on your coping is contextual, and some of the ideas and findings we have mentioned may not fit your personal experience. In addition, your emotional support network represents just one form of social support. Your lists and maps for other forms of support (social integration, or encouragement, informational, or tangible support for a specific purpose) would probably look different. Try mapping and analyzing those as well.

# four

# Preventing Problem Behavior and Promoting Social Competence

# PREVENTION AND PROMOTION: KEY CONCEPTS

# OPENING EXERCISE: A PREVENTION PARABLE

A story is told about a man at the side of a river, reaching in and hauling to shore person after person, all of whom were struggling, often drowning, as they were pulled downstream by the strong current. A woman came by and saw what he was doing, and pitched in to help. But despite their hard and constant work, for every body they pulled out, ten more went past them. The condition of those who remained in the river became more and more desperate.

As they worked, the woman asked the man, "How are these people getting into the river?" The man did not know. "Why don't you go upstream and see what the problem is?" she asked. "I am too busy," the man replied. "There is much to do here. Besides, if I stop, even more people will be lost." She thought about what he said and agreed and went back to work. But after more and more days, with the flow of people growing and their own strength diminishing, she decided to go upstream and find out what was going on. "It's true that some extra people may be lost while I am gone, but if I can stop, or even cut down the flow, we all will be better off." And so she went.

Upstream, she saw that one part of a path was leading people to go directly into the river. As she moved toward it, she realized that this was where she would stay; her work would no longer be to fish drowning people out of the river, but rather, to keep as many as possible from going in at all. She would work to redirect people from the path, and try to change the path. Soon, others followed her example, positioning themselves just downstream from the entry point so they could get people out before the current got full hold of the people in the river, making them harder to save. Finally, some decided that people needed to live so that they were not drawn to the river at all, in a way that kept them away from taking the harmful path in the first place (after all, it did not seem as if *everyone* was equally likely to be going down the river). Even for those people reached early, however, it would be important to prepare them so that if they did take the harmful path, they would have the support and strength to resist its pull. The woman and her colleagues began to work toward those goals.

As you read this parable, ask yourself, "What does it mean to prevent something?" No doubt, the reader has had some experience as the recipient of a prevention program. Perhaps your health classes in high school, middle school, or even elementary school involved programs to prevent drug and alcohol abuse, smoking, teenage pregnancy, violence, and HIV/AIDS. Your college or university no doubt has programs to prevent bias, drunk driving, and academic failure. What do you remember about these programs? How did they go about trying to help you prevent one problem or another? What is your opinion about the effectiveness of these efforts? What accounts for their strengths or shortcomings? For example, were they based in any sound theory of prevention or promotion, specifying when and how it should take place? In this chapter, we give you some tools to start answering questions like these systematically, as well as share ways in which community psychology concepts are leading to new thinking about prevention.

Before we go further, we want to emphasize that a focus on prevention and a focus on treatment can be complementary. Our parable, a version of a story often told by prevention advocates, is intended to highlight the need for a diversity of approaches to mental disorders and other psychological problems in living. Treatment of those already experiencing a mental disorder is a humane goal and often means taking into account biological and individual factors as well as social ones. Prevention, in contrast, focuses on factors that can be changed before disorder develops, whether environmental or personal. Although budget constraints often mean that prevention and treatment advocates compete to some extent for scarce resources, their activities and choices of emphasis are complementary and worthy of mutual respect.

## WHAT ARE THE KEY POINTS OF THIS CHAPTER?

In this chapter, we review the historical and conceptual building blocks of the concept of prevention and introduce concepts concerning promoting competence and/or preventing disorder. We explain the background of the two points of view concerning prevention represented in the parable, why they have come to exist, and what the implications are for carrying out prevention programs. Central to our thinking is that prevention cannot be thought of as an inoculation. Successful efforts require an ecological and developmental approach, addressing not only people but also the contexts in which they live and interact. We also demonstrate that prevention, or the absence of illness, actually is no longer the goal of community psychology intervention. Promotion of health and social competence, of strengths in people and in the places they live, work, and play, has become the goal. We also note emerging interest in concepts that emphasize resilience, strengths, and thriving despite adverse life circumstances. We next discuss the prevention equations, a practical way of integrating many of the concepts of community psychology and applying them in research and action related to prevention and promotion. We end the chapter with some pizza.

## INTRODUCTION: BACKGROUND
## TO PREVENTION AS A FIELD OF STUDY

What do you think needs preventing now? What two or three areas would you prioritize? Why? You will find that in different eras, different problems seem to be emphasized. In the 1960s, there was a focus on poverty and the way its consequences created disadvantage for children in schools and for all of its victims in terms of health and well-being; in the 1970s, the end of the war in Southeast Asia and the intensification of the Cold War between capitalism and communism highlighted many issues of social and economic justice. In the 1980s, there was a "war" on alcohol, tobacco, and other drugs. Many feel that this war was most successful in the area of smoking prevention. In the early and middle 1990s, the emphasis shifted to the prevention of violence. At the time of this writing, many social issues were being debated, such as abortion; so-called entitlement programs, such as welfare and Medicare; immigration; and racial and ethnic tolerance. These shifts were, in turn, reflected in legislative changes. Among the most noteworthy is the switch of the Drug Free Schools and Communities Act, which funded local, school, and community-initiated substance abuse programs, to the Drug Free, Safe Schools and Communities Act,

## 9.1 From "What's Happening"
(Camden County Youth Center, New Jersey, October 1992)

"Dreams Going Up In Smoke"

I used to watch my dad do drugs.

Smokin his pipe. Rock of cocaine on the screen. Light up with a match or lighter.

I wished he wouldn't.

But what could I do? Thirteen year old.

Talk to him. Hug him. He said he couldn't stop.

They wouldn't tell me how he died.

—T.T., age 15

"If I Gonna Die . . ."

If I gonna die . . . I want people to have good things to say about me—not die from some gunshots or some drug war. I wanta be something—job, church, family—not be the one my aunts hear about shot dead—read about in the papers.

I've got jumped. I've got shot. Next time around I might be dead.

—T., age 17

---

which added violence to the portfolio, but actually reduced the total pool of available funding. Drugs, guns, other forms of violence, and dysfunctional families continue to act as sources of harmful influence and provide potential current foci for prevention efforts.

Prevention is a common sense concept that derives from Latin words meaning "to anticipate" or "before something to come." The language of prevention is found in all aspects of public endeavor. Parents try to prevent children from hurting themselves; police try to prevent crimes; the legal system is designed to prevent violation of certain rights; road signs are created and posted to prevent people from getting lost.

In the field of community psychology and community research and action, ideas about prevention have been evolving. Because the field of community psychology is linked to societal events and forces, this is an evolution that will continue. It is this dynamic that makes the field so important and exciting, but also hard to capture in a text book.

As you learned in chapter 2, the concept and practice of prevention links the fields of public health and psychology. Psychiatrists Erich Lindemann and Gerald Caplan were particularly important in forging that link. An analysis of available "personpower" in the mental health field by George Albee (1959) supported the growing interest in prevention. Albee showed that there were not and could not be a sufficient number of clinicians trained to provide all of the needed mental health services for the population. Consider the implications of this extraordinary finding. Therapeutic resources are scarce and will realistically remain scarce. As in the parable that opened this chapter, need will always outstrip the supply of services. Prevention of psychological problems (reduction of need) becomes a justifiable use of scarce resources.

Another issue raised by Albee's (1959) findings concerns how scarce treatment resources are distributed. A series of epidemiological studies (Hollingshead & Redlich, 1958; J. K. Myers & Bean, 1972) provided some insights. There was a strong relationship between socioeconomic status, ethnicity, and services received. The poor and minority groups were more likely to receive severe diagnoses, to receive medication rather than psychotherapy, and to be seen in groups rather than individually. The preferred clients were those most like the therapists—male, Caucasian, verbal, and successful. Both preventive concepts and innovative services were central in the Community Mental Health Centers Act in 1963, advocated by President Kennedy. In terms of the parable at the outset of this chapter, there were a growing number of reasons to go upstream and keep people from getting into the river.

Although community psychology has embraced the concept of prevention, there is another aspect of the concept that merits consideration. It can be derived by taking another look at the examples mentioned earlier. Parents try to help children learn how to care for themselves safely; educators encourage learning in different forms; employers train and supervise employees to work effectively; road signs are posted to help people get to where they want to go. These examples focus on developing desired competencies, skills, and abilities. Overall health and quality of life becomes the goal, more than simply preventing psychiatric disorders or types of problem behaviors. Cowen (1991) championed the term *wellness* as a more fitting goal of preventive efforts. He went on to say that whereas wellness refers to life satisfaction or gratification in living, it is a transactional concept linked to the social ecology within which people live. Again, in Cowen's (1991) colorful words: "The pot-of-gold behind the pursuit of a wellness rainbow might be a genuine betterment of the human condition" (p. 408). Cowen's views have become central to how community psychologists think about prevention of disorder and promotion of competence and wellness.

# A FOCUS ON COMPETENCE: BOWER'S MODEL

A focus on the promotion of social competence, wellness, and health and the prevention of problem behavior is common to many professional disciplines. It also is a shared concern among policy makers, elected officials, educators, sports and recreation leaders, and parents. Bower (1972) proposed a useful way of conceptualizing how society is organized to accomplish these goals. He described three types of settings through which all societies prepare their young citizens for adult life, using the catchy acronyms, *KISS, AID*, and *ICE*.

## Key Integrated Social Systems (KISS)

*Key integrative social systems* (KISS) are formal and informal settings within which individuals interact from conception through childhood. The first of these is the health care system, which includes prenatal care, the management of the birthing process, and postnatal care. The second KISS system is the family, which begins to shape a child's values and outlook on life and provides opportunities to build important cognitive, affective, motor, interpersonal, and academic skills.

School is the third system, and its impact is felt at an increasingly early time as more and more children enter child care and preschools before kindergarten. Head Start, for example, is designed primarily for preschool children from impoverished families and provides not only pre-academic skills, but also medical and dental services, housing, parenting support, job training and placement, linkage with social services, and transportation. It is paradoxical that as children move into the public school system, their access to these services tends to become far less organized and systematic. Nevertheless, the school years from kindergarten through 12th grade exercise substantial influence on a diverse array of skills, of which academic abilities are only a part.

An informal KISS system that has a pervasive influence is peers. Aristotle was among the first to state that humans are "polis" animals, meaning that we are inherently social and that we organize ourselves around this central shared feature. From toddlerhood on, peers serve as models and mirrors, sources of new behaviors, advice, feedback, questions, and support or discouragement. Developmental psychologists have studied how, at different time periods in one's life, peer influences vary in strength and nature. Pre-adolescence is a time when peer influences begin to compete with those of parents and teachers, increasing in strength into the adolescent years. Shared experiences with peers can strongly influence career, higher education, lifestyle, and religious choices.

Indeed, religion is the final KISS system discussed by Bower (1972). At the time of his writing, religious institutions were in a decline. The late 1960s and early 1970s in the United States were times of disillusionment and confusion for many, and the role of religion and the operation of religious institutions were questioned or ignored. Yet through the late 1980s and the mid 1990s, there has been a resurgence in the role of religion and religious organizations as sources of influence and support. This trend can be seen perhaps most dramatically in Eastern Europe, in the countries of the former Soviet Union. Poland and Russia have seen previously outlawed religious observance flourish, with religious leaders taking strong stands on social issues and the provision of human rights.

The term *secondary KISS contexts* can be used to refer to other key aspects of socialization not mentioned as part of Bower's (1972) initial theory and include the following:

- *Workplaces* affect individuals through scheduling, roles and work strain, interactional patterns, opportunities for growth or frustration.
- *Leisure/recreational systems* can be formal or informal: country clubs or midnight basketball games, senior citizen centers or a card game with friends, concerts or reading in a coffee house.
- *Community organizations* include parents' groups affiliated with schools; civic groups such as Kiwanis, Scouting, B'nai B'rith, and Mothers Against Drunk Driving; local business associations; and advocates for local beautification/preservation. These may influence individual development of their members or exist to help others develop (e.g., parenting groups).
- *Media/Internet/cyberspace* communication is eclipsing more traditional forms of communication and interaction, and "bits" of information flow more quickly. This information influences individual development in many direct and indirect ways.

Obviously, the influence of KISS can be the kind that promotes competence or thwarts it. If the KISS settings work as they were designed to, by providing the intended health care, schooling, parenting, friendships, and spiritual supports, individuals passing through them would develop considerable strengths. In such circumstances, KISS would be exercising a substantial preventive effect. But the reality is that KISS settings do not function flawlessly. Inequitable distribution of resources leads some schools, families, and hospitals to work less than optimally. Further, the degree of integration of these social systems with each other varies quite dramatically from country to country, state to state, and municipality to municipality. KISS systems thus may interfere with each other rather than complement each other. For many children, passage through KISS can be quite perilous.

## Ailing-in-Difficulty (AID) Institutions

When difficulty is encountered in the KISS settings, society provides AID: ailing-in-difficulty institutions. Those who are not able to function as well as desired in one context of KISS can go to such places for short-term assistance. Following this help, the person is expected to be able to function well. If one thinks of KISS as the main turnpike of socialization, AID can be thought of as rest stops or service areas. Examples of AID include guidance counseling and special services in the schools, outpatient mental health facilities, local police, a short-term detention or crisis center, hospital emergency rooms, and work-site personnel counseling.

## Illness Correctional Endeavors (ICE)

The final part of Bower's (1972) model is ICE: illness correctional endeavors. ICE is provided by psychiatric hospitals, prisons, and long-term health care facilities. These may appear to be places where those in need of high degrees of assistance can go so they can return to AID or KISS, but the reality is that it often can be easier to enter ICE institutions than to emerge from them back into KISS systems. Bower (1972) viewed these institutions more as agents of social control than as venues for rehabilitation.

Present societal forces (such as greater public scrutiny of care facilities and the rise of cost-oriented managed care and short-term services) make ICE settings less effective as repositories for those felt to be social outcasts and misfits than was the case when Bower (1972) was writing. However, in certain countries, especially those run by dictatorships and other de facto totalitarian regimes, ICE institutions continue to be used overtly as holding tanks for those who do not "fit smoothly" into KISS systems. Bower's (1972) point, however, still holds: In ways subtle and not so subtle, people who are deemed "different," "defective," "inferior," "evil," or "bad" are kept away from the social mainstream that constitutes the KISS and even AID systems.

## Summary

Taken as a whole, Bower's (1972) model can be expressed as follows: With a good, loving KISS early in life, people will need less AID and fewer will have to be treated with ICE. From this simple conceptualization, many implications follow about the process of socialization in a nation, community, agency or social organization, or family. If socialization occurs properly throughout life, the large apparatus of repair and diversion can be reduced. Problems of all kinds can be prevented or reduced in severity.

## Linkage to Social Ecology and Developmental Psychology

It's helpful to think of KISS in terms of the social–ecological levels of analysis you learned in chapter 1. Parents and other caregivers, as well as educators, medical personnel, and others whose responsibilities include navigating children through the KISS settings, are themselves embedded within *microsystems, organizations, localities,* and *macrosystems* that influence how well they function in their task of socializing children. The macrosystem consists of beliefs about children and child rearing and such social policies as flexible work scheduling and paternity leave that are of general influence on parents and parenting, but the nature of that influence depends most on the microsystems, organizations, and communities within which parents interact most directly (Belsky, 1984). Among the relevant organizations or communities are religious congregations, tenant associations, neighborhood or town libraries, colleges, chamber of commerce chapters, farmer's cooperatives, neighborhood crimewatch organizations, or political clubs. Some examples of microsystems include families, a small civic group, an informal network of friends, a bowling team, a sewing or quilting group, or a small family-run business.

The social–ecological point of view provides a way of putting Bower's (1972) concepts into motion and applying them dynamically. For example, macroeconomic trends create financial pressures on corporations, which cut costs by downsizing, laying off workers, and increasing overtime for those who remain. This, in turn, reduces the time and energy of parents for their families and for volunteer organizations related to school, civic, recreational, and religious life. When the KISS systems are deprived of resources and do not work optimally, more individuals require the services of AID stations and ICE institutions.

The practical value of Bower's (1972) focus on KISS systems is linked to advances in knowledge that improve socialization efforts. In the social–ecological model, the individual is viewed as developing and adapting at the center of numerous surrounding interactive environments (e.g., Belsky, 1980; Bronfenbrenner, 1979; Holahan & Spearly, 1980). Our biological attributes, knowledge and attitudes in all domains, personal identity, personal history, socioemotional skills, and physical characteristics all are involved at all times. Seeing this, Masterpasqua (1981) commented on what he saw as the essential synergy between developmental and community psychology. He put forth the notion of developmental rights as a key integrative concept, something restated often since then as community psychologists and those interested in the intersection of law and children's rights have been addressing these issues more prominently (Melton, 1991; Wilcox, 1993).

Developmental rights means that children born into a society have the right to conditions that will allow them to grow in a healthy manner, if not also to thrive. These conditions serve as a powerful force for prevention of problem behavior and promotion of competence. Some of these follow from Bower's (1972) model, such as adequate health care in the prenatal period and sound parenting skills. However, research is necessary to constantly fill in the details, help find critical periods of growth and influence, and guide the specific timing and content of interventions and services. Research also is necessary to refine our understanding of variations due to cultural and racial factors, gender, socio-economic and education status, and developmental level.

Hence, it was with great wisdom that early community psychologists advised that participant conceptualization should and must precede the onset of interventions and occur throughout them. This acknowledges the richness, complexity, and history of social systems, the individuals within them, and their response to change. And participant conceptualization, as the name implies, is rooted in key concepts for understanding prevention and promotion.

# CONCEPTS FOR UNDERSTANDING PREVENTION AND PROMOTION

In this section, we describe the historical progression of concepts from prevention of disorder, to promotion of competence, to ideas of strengths and thriving. In so doing, we define and illustrate key concepts in the contexts in which they are used.

## Historical Perspective: G. Caplan's (1964) Concepts

There is a rich history to the concept of prevention, rooted in the field of public health and the mental hygiene movement of the early 20th century (K. Heller et al. 1984; Spaulding & Balch, 1983). However, Gerald Caplan is recognized as the individual whose use of the term, *prevention,* led to its becoming a part of the mental health lexicon. G. Caplan (1964) made a distinction between the following three types of prevention.

***Primary Prevention***    This is intervention given to entire populations when they are not in a condition of known need or distress. The goal is to lower the rate of new cases (from a public health perspective, to reduce incidence) of disorders. Primary prevention intervenes to reduce potentially harmful circumstances before they have a chance to create difficulty. Examples of this are such things as vaccinations, fluoridating water, and providing decision making and problem solving skill-building programs to children in preschool. Similarly, primary prevention also can be thought of as being applied to all persons in a given setting, regardless of potential need (e.g., all fifth graders in preparation for transition to middle school, or all first-year college students).

***Secondary Prevention***    This is intervention given to populations showing early signs of a disorder or difficulty. Another term for this is *early intervention.* This concept is a precursor of current notions of being "at risk," which are discussed shortly. Examples of secondary prevention are programs targeted to children who are shy or withdrawn, those who are beginning to have academic difficulty, or adults who are getting into conflicts with coworkers on the job.

Secondary prevention presupposes some method of determining which individuals are at risk or demonstrating early signs of disorder. Identifying such individuals creates a potential for stigmatization, both because they do not currently have a disorder and because they might never develop one. Improving methods of risk identification represents an important area of work in community psychology.

***Tertiary Prevention*** This is intervention given to populations who have a disorder, with the intention of limiting the disability caused by the disorder, reducing its intensity and duration, and thereby preventing future re-occurrence or additional complications.

If it strikes you that it is difficult to differentiate tertiary prevention from treatment, you are not alone. But Gerald Caplan had a purpose that often is forgotten by his critics today. A child psychiatrist by training, Caplan was trying to introduce a preventive way of thinking to the treatment-oriented medical, psychiatric, mental health, and social service fields. By emphasizing the similarities of prevention and treatment, he was able to link these concerns. Ultimately, he was successful in that the idea of prevention took hold, becoming a central tenet of fields such as community psychology and school psychology, and, increasingly, clinical and health psychology.

However, G. Caplan's (1964) framework appealed to those seeking resources for treatment. Some early prevention grants were given to programs designed for such things as the tertiary prevention of schizophrenia: a worthy goal, but not exactly what Caplan had in mind. Yet, as many have noted, prevention is a difficult concept to grasp. One is trying to keep away what is not (yet) there. Would it ever arrive if the prevention effort was not in place? Others have stated that if prevention is to be worthwhile, then one must specify what one is preventing. Recent emphasis on defining the prevention of specific conditions such as suicide, depression, and conduct disorder as part of the nation's mental health agenda reflect this point of view.

Klein and Goldston (1977) were among a number of community psychologists who attempted to clarify the issues raised by G. Caplan's (1964) definitions and others' interpretations. Although agreeing with the definition of primary prevention, they felt it important to relabel secondary prevention as treatment given because of early identification, and tertiary prevention as rehabilitation services. This helps to provide a clearer distinction between prevention and treatment for specific or severe problems. Debate still ensues over whether interventions given to shy children, for example, are best thought of as prevention or treatment. But other models now have risen to prominence, and thus it pays little to dwell on past inconsistencies when current inconsistencies are available for examination.

## The Institute of Medicine (IOM) Report

The IOM Report (Mrazek & Haggerty, 1994) will likely greatly influence thinking about prevention well into the 21st century. Its main conceptual contribution is the idea of universal, selective, or indicated measures or methods for prevention.

***Universal Preventive Measures*** These interventions are good for everyone in a given population group, and they typically are administered to populations that are not in distress. This is similar to primary prevention.

***Selective Preventive Measures*** These are desirable for people at above-average risk for developing mental disorders. That risk may be based on their environment (e.g., low income or family conflict) or personal factors (e.g., low self-esteem, difficulties in school). These risk characteristics are associated with the development of particular disorders, but are not symptoms of the disorder itself.

***Indicated Preventive Measures***     These are applied to individual people who are at high risk for developing disorder in the future especially if they show early symptoms of the disorder. However, they do not meet criteria for full-fledged diagnosis of a Mental Disorder.

Interestingly, the IOM Report places mental health promotion (including concepts related to competence and wellness) into a separate area, distinct from prevention. The editors viewed self-esteem and mastery as the main focus of mental health promotion, with *competence, self-efficacy,* and *individual empowerment* all terms commonly used in describing such efforts. The IOM Report defined its focus in terms of whether or not an approach prevents a specific disorder, not in terms of competence enhancement.

Weissberg and Greenberg (1997) raised some thoughtful questions about the IOM framework. For instance, should a violence prevention program be considered a universal intervention in a school with few incidents of violence, yet selective in a school where violence is more common? Because depression is diagnosed more often among girls than boys, should a program for prevention of depression be considered universal if given to a troop of Boy Scouts but selective if given to a Girl Scout troop? For disorders such as conduct disorder, what is the boundary between predictors of a disorder (for selective prevention) and early symptoms (for indicated prevention)? Consider a program delivered to a class in which there is a diversity of students: (a) a student with conduct disorder, and another with attention-deficit hyperactivity disorder; (b) several disaffected, underachieving, unmotivated students; and (c) others with no behavioral or emotional difficulty, some even with great strengths. Is the same program considered universal for the latter group, selective for the disaffected students, and indicated for the children with diagnosed disorders? Beneath these definitional questions is a fundamental concern for the direction in which preventive efforts should be headed, both in terms of research and action.

## Two Points of View: Prevention of Disorder and Promotion of Wellness and Competence

As can be seen in the historical overview, there is a continuing debate about where the emphasis of time and resources for prevention efforts is best placed. Articulate spokespersons of each point of view arise periodically, and readers are urged to engage in this debate on the basis of the current state of knowledge. In general, the debate can be framed between proponents of prevention of disorder and promotion of wellness and social competence.

Advocates of the prevention of disorder view argue that we are learning a great deal about how to prevent specific disorders such as depression, suicide, conduct disorders, and schizophrenia. Research should be directed toward isolating and reducing the operation of risk factors most closely targeted with specific disorders. This view is most likely to be associated with selected and indicated interventions, based on the IOM Report.

Advocates of the promotion of wellness and social competence view note that many people are not in a state of sound psychological well-being despite not having specific disorders. As we look at the future in the United States and in every country in this increasingly interconnected and technological world, it is necessary to help people be more than "not ill." Promoting and strengthening overall health is important; even planners are not able to specify a disorder that is being prevented. We know a great deal about how to promote sound health and social competence, drawing in part from interventions in public health in such areas as prevention of cardiovascular disease, from school settings in areas such as social and emotional skill building, and from workplace efforts to increase organizational effectiveness. Research should be directed toward identifying and understanding the factors that promote health, wellness, and competence in daily living. These will differ in different living environments, cross-culturally and internationally.

As you learned in chapter 2, issues of prevention and mental health have never been isolated from political and ideological considerations. Historically, in U.S. society, the social zeitgeist during conservative times favors individual, illness-oriented conceptions of mental health and other social problems. Prevention in those times tends to be understood in terms of preventing specific disorders. In more progressive times, an environmental focus supports a definition of prevention closer to promotion of overall health and wellness and competence.

As we noted in chapter 2, the United States is now in a conservative period that in the 1990s moderated in intensity. Research in recent years has focused on biological factors in mental health, and the mental health field is seeking to prove itself to be rigorous (at least as rigorous as medicine is perceived to be) and cost conscious. Insurance companies and Federal granting agencies prefer to pay for clear prevention outcomes, rather than support efforts to improve health. However, organizations such as the World Federation of Mental Health and the World Health Organization tend not to share the view of the United States. Theirs is a more holistic view of health, in which mental health and physical well-being—which extends to basic issues of shelter, food, and freedom from war, societal anarchy, and enslavement—are essential parts of the overall picture. Many community psychologists embrace this broader view of health.

The goals of preventing specific disorders and promoting wellness and competence are not mutually exclusive, and the techniques to pursue them may be the same in particular circumstances. There are strong parallels with physical health, where health-promoting activities such as a sound diet are valuable and may also serve to prevent such problems as cardiovascular disease—but also may not have specific preventive effects on specific conditions or illnesses. Community psychologists try keep a perspective on prevention that is best understood as an umbrella providing a common cover for both points of view, or as a bridge linking them. Community psychology knowledge is used sometimes to provide preventive interventions to specific populations to prevent specific disorders, and at other times to general populations in KISS settings to promote overall wellness. The outcomes of these interventions are measured in terms of lowered incidence of a specific disorder and/or in terms of increased competence for coping, as appropriate.

We turn next to community psychologists' conceptual frameworks of risk and protective processes, for it is these frameworks that energize the work of prevention and competence promotion and provide the stimulus for the kinds of creative approaches needed to address diverse settings and circumstances.

## Five Concepts for Prevention and Promotion, Today and Tomorrow

Critical to the perspective of the IOM report are concepts of risk, protection, and resilience. As of this writing, momentum toward the concepts of strengths and thriving appear to be building and some preliminary discussion of these ideas also is in order. In most writings to date, risk and protection have been described in terms of factors: risk factors and protective factors. However, this has created a misperception of risk and protection as static and unchanging. Instead, risk and protection are best viewed as processes, and dynamic ones, at that. Referring to these as processes, or at least redefining factors as dynamic, changing processes, helps convey their interrelated and ongoing nature.

**Risk**    Risk processes can be defined as those features of individuals and environments that reduce the biological, psychological, and/or social capacities of individuals to maintain their well-being and function adaptively in society. This often involves a reduction of the individual's ability to cope with stressors or to sustain desired or expected social roles. A simple example is a family in which one or both parents have chronic physical or mental illness. This interferes with a number of parental roles. For the children involved, it comprises a set of risk processes that includes biological predispositions. When a family is organized around a mother's chronic illness, for example, it may be more difficult, if not impossible, for children to be driven to friends' houses, or back to school for special programs, or to music lessons or enrichment programs. Even when these things are accomplished, it is at a cost to the family, in terms of time, money, energy, or something else that they were unable to do as a result. Because of his burden of responsibilities, the children's father may be less available to sit and read to them, to go to the library with them to work on homework projects, or even to engage in weekend recreation. Characteristics of the children interact with these situations to ameliorate or exacerbate their impact.

The research literature discusses how risk processes accumulate to increase the likelihood that disorder will result (Haggerty, Sherrod, Garmezy, & Rutter, 1994). There has been discussion over whether this increase is additive or multiplicative, but this point is less critical than our understanding of the life meaning of such occurrences. Continuing with the above example, think about what additional burdens would be placed on the family and children if they lived in poverty. Their access to resources and services, their options for getting assistance from others, their nutrition, all of this and much more would be added to the burdens of the family and interfere with developmental opportunities for the children. What if one of the children had a learning disability? What if this was a single-parent family? What if they were recently arrived immigrants or not fluent in English? Imagine this scenario transferred to one of a war-torn region in Africa or Eastern Europe or the Middle East, or a violent U.S. neighborhood. We can debate the mathematical relationship of these risk processes to the likelihood of disorder, but it is essential to keep in clear view the continuous human toll as these ongoing risk processes operate.

**Protection**    Protective processes provide a significant counterpoise to the operation of risk processes. The definition can be seen as the opposite of risk: those features of individuals and environments that operate in ongoing ways to increase or enhance the biological, psychological, social, and emotional capacities of individuals to maintain well-being and function adaptively in society. Hancock (1996) studied the relationship of risk and protective processes and their relative potency in prediction of substance abuse. Her findings, although not broadly generalizable, did suggest that protective processes are especially potent, and that to a surprising degree, a little protection can offset a lot of risk. It is likely that we have yet to fully understand the way in which protective processes work at the individual and interactional levels.

Using our running example, let's introduce some protective processes and see their impact. Bronfenbrenner (1979) was among the first to say that the presence of an irrationally caring adult is the most essential protective influence, especially for children. By this, he did not mean that association with individuals with acute psychoses is great for your health. Rather, he meant that people appear to derive benefits when they know that someone cares about them beyond what might be rational—akin to what Carl Rogers referred to as "unconditional positive regard." No matter what happens, there is a person in one's corner. The processes involved no doubt include words of reassurance, confidence, optimism, and suggestions for solving problems. In some cases, there will be physical comfort, hugs, or a blanket before bedtime.

Work by Salovey and Mayer (1990), LeDoux (1995), Goleman (1995), and Salovey and Sluyter (1997) has shown that our emotional experiences have deeply important impact on our psychological health and interpersonal functioning. Human beings seem primed to latch on to the positive exception, rather than the negative rule. In a sea of calamity, our biological mechanisms are set up to store and activate even the most isolated positive memories. Often, it is the task of psychotherapy to recall and reactivate the positive memories that have become crowded out of our consciousness and therefore rendered less potent as protective processes in our lives. When children are abused and neglected early in life, they have not had the opportunity to forge these positive memories; thus, their prognosis is accordingly less hopeful. Protective processes to make maltreatment less likely thus are needed for young children, as well as protective processes involving positive emotional experiences and positive connections with caring adults.

In the context of our running example, let's place into the scenario several relatives who think the kids in this family are the best in the world and never tire of telling them so. They do this even after a child has gotten into trouble at school, perhaps acting out frustration from not getting attention at home recently, from not being able to complete a homework assignment, from lack of sleep or good nutrition, or from all of these difficulties. Reassurance and social support in the face of these obstacles can be powerful. Add to that some stories about the future and confidence that all will work out. Add to that a caring school environment, with programs that provide emotional support to kids whose families are in crisis. Add also a teacher who recognizes that the children in this family need some special help or after school enrichment and figures out a way to make it available. And instead of poverty, what if this scenario were to be played out in a context of wealth, where resources to handle some of the household and illness-management tasks could take some of the burden off Dad and the kids. Would it be unreasonable to contemplate a health care system in which children of chronically ill parents, regardless of income or other factors, were routinely placed in groups to offer explanation, support, and practical help with being kids in this situation? Such programs have been provided in the schools for children whose families are undergoing separation and divorce; the benefits have included reduction of depression, acting out behavior, low self-esteem, and self-blame on the part of children (Pedro-Carroll, 1997; Wolchik et al., 1993). Yet ongoing programs of this kind are all too rare.

***Resilience***    Resilience also has a place in this scenario. It can be thought of as a special case of protective processes, that is, those that allow someone to adapt to adverse, challenging, or threatening contexts. In reading about this concept, one is likely to come away with the idea that resilience, or resiliency, is a trait, an attribute of individuals that renders them less subject to the negative effects of stress. Garmezy's (1971) early work referred to "invulnerable children" as those who appeared to come through the most dire circumstances—wars, floods, severe parental disability—with psychological and physical health intact. Indeed, it was even considered that such experiences were somehow strengthening to these resilient individuals. Although it would be foolish to doubt categorically that such people exist, it is not helpful in general to think of resilience as a trait (Werner & Smith, 1992). Rather, we find it most useful to think of resilience as involving the environment and the individual in combination. That is, if we were to look carefully at instances of resilience, we would find that in most cases, environmental protective processes were operating. There were key people who showed help and caring; there were tangible support resources at key moments; loving adults provided early emotional experiences that left the ability to feel love, hope, and optimism.

A trait-based concept of resilience is likely to place disproportionate emphasis on searches for genetic factors or other early biologically linked attributes that serve as markers of this valued capacity. A concept of resilience that includes the strong role of the environment is likely to fuel efforts to provide protective guideposts, guardrails, way-stations, and other supports in the environment. Indeed, encounters with such supports are likely to be strengthening to virtually all individuals. Either a genetic or environmental view alone is incomplete, of course. But focusing on the environmental perspective, consistent with a community psychology perspective, suggests pathways for action and serves as a useful balance for other areas of psychology that tend to emphasize a biological and genetic point of view.

**Strengths**    The concepts of strengths and thriving are not new, but they are unfamiliar in mainstream psychology (S. B. Sarason, 1978). A focus on strengths asks the question, what are a person's assets and how are these brought to the center of his or her life, especially in times of difficulty? Paradoxically, the notion draws support from neurobiology, where the concept of compensatory functioning has long been understood as the brain's way of circumventing deficits in its seemingly constant attempt to maximize our functional and adaptive capacities (Sylwester, 1995). Indeed, much of rehabilitation psychology is about finding ways to restore functioning when the primary mechanisms for that functioning are damaged. Health psychology is recognizing the powerful role of humor and optimism in fighting and preventing disease (Goleman, 1995). Those involved in youth work recognize that at risk adolescents can be "reclaimed" as their strengths are identified, enhanced, given recognition and value, and then linked to areas of difficulty (Brendtro, Brokenleg, & Van Bockern, 1990; Elias & Cohen, 1999). Community psychology research from a "strengths-based" perspective is likely to become more prominent in the near future.

**Thriving**    That focus on strengths likely will be joined by research driven by the concept of thriving. This stems directly from applying an ecologically based concept of resilience to populations at high risk. It is exemplified by studies such as that of Abraido-Lanza, Guier, and Colon (1998), who examined the process of thriving among Latinas with chronic illness living in impoverished neighborhoods. An individual is deemed as thriving to the extent to which she appears to experience positive growth despite her adverse life circumstances and, additionally, finds strength, insight, or meaning in life as a result of what she goes through. Although the authors acknowledge many methodological complexities in their research, the main finding seems clear: Thriving is related to positive affect and self-esteem and represents something beyond coping, or even resilience.

Two other studies shed some light on ecological factors that might account for individual differences in thriving. O'Leary (1998) reviewed the literature on developing strength in the face of adversity. She identified three stages of response to severe stressors: survival, recovery, and thriving. Thriving is defined as a transformation of one's personal priorities, sense of self, and life roles. Interestingly, this phenomenon was observed by Erich Lindemann and served as the impetus for his work in crisis intervention.

O'Leary (1998) also identified microsystem and organizational level resources that foster thriving. Social relationships appear to be especially potent for women, to the extent to which having and perceiving strong support is linked with improved immune system functioning. Certain conditions within organizations such as workplaces and schools provide opportunities for thriving to take place. These factors include caring, openness of communication, encouragement of individual contributions and growth, and organizational risk taking. Under such conditions, individuals appear to be free to contemplate new roles, to make changes in their jobs and roles and still feel accepted within an organization, and to feel involved in organizational decision making.

Thriving also appears to be fostered by nations that respond to challenges in certain ways. O'Leary (1998) reviewed the emergence of the African National Congress and democracy in South Africa, concluding that collectivist traditions and a strong set of positive, supportive, reaffirming rituals in the face of setbacks led to results that have gone beyond recovery to transform a nation. Another example can be found in Armenia (Karakashian, 1998). Over a period of 4 millennia, Armenia has endured calamities that have led neighboring countries and civilizations to crumble. What accounts for this? Karakashian (1998) identified three main factors that she pointedly labels not as prevention (which implies absence of illness) and not as resilience (which implies a return to former health, a "bouncing back" to prior equilibrium) but thriving (which implies continued strengthening and growth beyond that equilibrium). These factors include (a) development of identity-affirming family traditions and community life; (b) an identity as "dogal," associated with survival of adversities such as forced deportations and migrations; (c) strong family education in Armenian history, culture, and values; and (d) parenting approaches that appear to equip Armenian children with as much feeling of support and being loved as children from other countries, as well as skills of alternative thinking, overcoming obstacles, and communicating their feelings. The latter are among the skills identified as essential aspects of emotional intelligence (Goleman, 1995). By focusing on cultural traditions and practices, Karakashian (1998) identified processes that go beyond individual resilience.

For community psychologists interested in prevention, strengths and thriving are concepts that hold great promise. They enable us to move beyond an individual perspective and see how prevention, social competence, wellness, and related outcomes result from a convergence of influences at multiple ecological levels. Next, we use the vehicle of the prevention equations to provide a feasible way of conceptualizing and enhancing ecological influences that are associated with the generic term, *prevention,* but also are linked to a broader set of wellness-related goals.

# The Prevention Equations: Integrative Guides for Research and Action

> If children are to experience healthy relationships and occupy meaningful and productive roles in society as adults, they must be competent at communicating and working cooperatively with others. They need to be able to express their own opinions and beliefs, to understand and appreciate the perspective of others who differ from them in background, needs, or experiences, and to become skilled at reasoned disagreement, negotiation, and compromise as methods of solving problems when their own needs or interests conflict with those of others. Indeed, in the face of decreasing resources and increasing global interdependence, it can be argued that such qualities are essential to our survival. The question, then, is not *whether* we must enhance children's social competencies, but rather *how* to accomplish this goal. (Battistich, Elias, & Branden-Muller, 1992, p. 231)

The complexity of ecological, developmental, and transactional models and their application to notions of risk, protection, resilience, strengths, and thriving can seem daunting. Some simplification strategies are necessary to help make directions for research and action more clear. Prevention equations serve this role.

## Two Prevention Equations

The literature concerning social competence promotion over the past decade can be summarized in terms of the prevention equations of Albee (1982) and Elias (1987; see Table 9.1). Albee's (1982) formula is framed at the individual, person-centered, level; its focus is on reducing the likelihood of disorder (or improving the likelihood of wellness) in a single person. Individual risk is heightened to the extent that the individual experiences stress and/or physical vulnerabilities, and is lowered to the extent that the individual possesses coping skills, perceives him or herself as well supported, and has positive self-esteem. For each term in the equation, there is a corresponding approach to intervention that one might take. These are numbered 1–5 in Table 9.1.

Elias (1987) extended these ideas to the level of environments to complement Albee's (1982) equation. In social learning theory, predicting individual risk actually would involve a set of equations for the multiple settings one inhabits. Further, these equations would have to be modified to reflect developmental changes in the individual. Additionally, community psychology calls for ways of examining the risk (and protective) processes for populations and communities, not just for individuals.

The environmental level formula in Table 9.1 indicates that risk is increased as a function of stressors and risk factors in the environment, and decreased to the extent to which protective processes are enhanced: positive socialization practices in key socialization environments, access to social support and socioeconomic resources, and opportunities for positive relatedness and connectedness of the kind that allows for prosocial bonding and the development of a sense of being valued. Note that these terms are attempts to denote properties of settings, not attributes of individuals. The derivative interventions shown in Table 9.1, numbers 6–10, are correspondingly focused on ecological levels that surround individuals.

| TABLE 9.1 | INDIVIDUAL AND ENVIRONMENTAL LEVEL PREVENTION EQUATIONS |
|---|---|

### INDIVIDUAL LEVEL (Albee, 1982)

Incidence of behavioral and emotional disorder in individuals =

$$\frac{\text{stress (1)} + \text{physical vulnerability (2)}}{\text{coping skills (3)} + \text{social support (4)} + \text{self esteem (5)}}$$

*Interventions derived from individual equation:*

1. Reduce/better manage perceived stress
2. Reduce the negative impact of a physically/biologically-based vulnerability
3. Increase coping skills, problem solving/decision making, social skills
4. Increase perceived social support
5. Increase self-esteem/self-efficacy

### ENVIRONMENTAL LEVEL (Elias, 1987)

Likelihood of behavioral and emotional disorder in settings =

$$\frac{\text{stressors (6)} + \text{risk factors in the environment (7)}}{\text{positive socialization practices (8)} + \text{social support resources (9)} + \text{opportunities for positive relatedness and connectedness (10)}}$$

*Interventions derived from environmental equation:*

6. Reduce/eliminate stressors in key socialization settings, other aspects of environment
7. Reduce operation/presence of physical risk factors in the environment that result in increased physical/biological vulnerability
8. Improve socialization practices, ways in which key socialization settings carry out their tasks
9. Increase accessible social support resources
10. Increase opportunities for positive relatedness to others and connectedness to positive social institutions, positive social groups, agencies, and other formal and informal settings

It might occur to you that the numerators of each equation summarize the literature on risk processes and the denominators do the same for protective processes. Good! It occurred to us, as well! In what follows, we use introductory examples to show how the equations can be used to guide both research and action, as well as to illustrate the complementary nature of terms used at the person and environmental levels.

## Defining the Terms in the Prevention Equations

*Stress* (in the individual-level equation) has been linked clearly to individual distress and various types of psychopathology. Although it is recognized that the absence of stress can be as debilitating as an excess of stress (Goleman, 1995), it is generally noted that stress past an optimal level of arousal inhibits optimal performance of specific tasks or life roles.

Techniques that teach individuals how to better manage their stress, such as meditation (Kabat-Zinn, 1993) or relaxation training (Cartledge & Milburn, 1989) reduce the likelihood of disturbance, although of course many factors impinge on this.

In a similar way, it is recognized that *stressors* (in the environmental-level equation), aspects of environments or contexts that engender stress in their inhabitants, are associated with dysfunction. School transitions, especially to kindergarten, to middle school or high school, as a transfer student, and out of high school, are accompanied by increased rates of referrals for mental health and related services, as well as decreased academic performance that can set off a trajectory or negative accomplishment and school failure (Carnegie Corporation of New York, 1994; Chung & Elias, 1996; Reyes et al., 1994). Although each student is not automatically affected by these conditions, overall rates of dysfunction increase at times of transition. Programs directed at reducing the factors that engender stress during those transitions, such as the STEP program discussed in chapter 5, often change structural features of the setting in which transition occurs. As with STEP, that often results in lower rates of problems for students (Elias et al., 1986; Felner & Adan, 1988).

*Physical or biologically-based vulnerabilities* in individuals have many causes but one common effect: They make it more difficult for a person to participate in mainstream KISS contexts. This says far less about the capabilities of such individuals than it does about the willingness and flexibility of social settings to accommodate to their special needs. (Recall from chap. 2 the insistence of Lightner Witmer, founder of the first U.S. psychological clinic, that every child can learn, given a supportive environment.) Person-centered interventions at the person level reduce the impact of such vulnerabilities by providing tools that can allow better mainstream access as well as strengthening an individual in areas where help is needed. One positive effect of Head Start for many children is that it gets them earlier access to services for visual, hearing, dental, and health impairments. If children attend school with these vulnerabilities undetected, they encounter academic and social difficulties, loss of motivation, frustration, or self-doubt.

*Risk factors in the environment* refer to such conditions as lead in paint and water, malnutrition, and poor prenatal care, all of which create physical and psychological vulnerabilities that, in turn, hamper coping and development. Examples include exposure to hazardous wastes that lead to increased incidence of cancer in children. (In chap. 5, we discussed research on such factors in neighborhoods.) Epidemiological research that uncovers such situations is important in community psychology, as are interventions to correct such factors or ameliorate their effects. For instance, A. Levine (1982) studied community responses to discovery of the effects of a toxic waste dump at the Love Canal in New York State. When child advocacy groups such as the Association for Children of New Jersey, the National Association of Child Advocacy Organizations, and the Children's Defense Fund advocate state or federal legislation regarding lead or housing policies that allow children to live in dangerous environments, they are operating within the spirit of intervention term number 7 in the environmental level prevention equation.

*Coping skills* in individuals are perhaps the most widely studied aspect of prevention. All manner of programs to build individuals' social, emotional, and cognitive skills fall under this term. These represent interfaces with clinical, school, and other branches of applied psychology and allied fields. Many of these focus on teaching skills such as problem solving, communication, self-regulation, and social approach behaviors. Social skills training occurs in schools, mental health programs, and workplaces; and with individuals being strengthened for the future as well as those who are experiencing problems and disabilities.

*Positive socialization practices* denotes the way in which KISS systems fulfill their socializing functions. Caregivers are prepared for their roles, equipped to help individuals learn and use coping and social skills. As Bower (1972) observed, are those in a position to give a good KISS able and willing to do so? Are parents prepared for what they are called upon to do by society? Are teachers? We know, for example, that nearly 50% of beginning teachers leave the profession within 5 years because they are not equipped to handle the behavior of their students and to turn their classes into constructive learning environments. This reflects not poor capacity on the part of new teachers as a group (although, as in any field, some people are not destined to be teachers and will not find out until they attempt it). The cause is just as much failure of the socializing agents that are supposed to prepare them for teaching, and the conditions under which they work.

For any job, how do its socializing contexts (schools, families, neighborhoods, employers, and others) prepare their members for effective role performance? The likelihood of psychological difficulties in a factory, for instance, decreases when supervisors as a group are skilled in training and developing those who work under them. Communities are healthier when, for instance, their teachers know how to deal with children's hearts as well as their minds, and the school administrators know to do the same with their teachers.

In chapter 8, we discussed the concept of *social support* as a coping resource, primarily at the individual and microsystem (social network) level. Albee's (1982) individual-level equation recognized this resource. Yet social support resources are accessible and easily used in some settings, but missing or inaccessible in others. Their strength and availability is an important setting characteristic.

The area of *self-esteem* and self-efficacy is one that has had a long-standing link to positive mental health outcomes. Rotter (1982) and Bandura (1982) have shown that individuals with negative expectancies for their ability to impact on their environments and a poor recognition and appreciation of their strengths are more likely to develop a variety of psychological disorders. Similarly, settings vary in the extent to which they provide *opportunities for relatedness and connectedness* and positive contributions by the people within them (Barker, 1968; Cottrell, 1976; S. B. Sarason, 1974; Wicker, 1979). Those settings that do provide such opportunities are likely to have more individuals who feel a positive sense of efficacy, and in turn, rates of disorder will be lower in them than in comparable types of settings that do not provide such opportunities.

Recall from chapter 5 that behavior settings that are "optimally manned" or "populated" (Barker & Gump, 1964; Schoggen, 1989) are less likely than somewhat "underpopulated" settings to promote individual development and sense of connectedness. Individuals in environments with mostly optimally populated behavior settings are likely to be less loyal, more disgruntled, feel left out, and leave sooner. You no doubt can think of some settings in which you have had similar feelings. Organizations with many underpopulated behavior settings, however, generate greater perceptions of involvement, connectedness, and individual satisfaction. Many things need doing in an underpopulated setting, and those who do them often recognize they are providing something worthwhile for the setting. Hopefully, you have had this kind of experience, as well.

## *Integrating Person and Environment*

Perry and Jessor (1985) have taken a leadership role in linking health and mental health outcomes to risk and protective processes at the person and environmental levels. They identified four domains of health and competence: *physical,* referring to physiological functioning; *psychological,* referring to subjective sense of well-being; *social,* referring to effectiveness in fulfilling social roles; and *personal,* referring to realization of individual potential. Within each domain, knowledge, attitudes, and behaviors comprise health-compromising (risk) or health-enhancing (protective) processes.

In Perry and Jessor's (1995) model, three facets of intervention must converge to maximize likelihood of success: environmental contexts, personality, and behavioral (coping) skills. Personality serves an important integrative role, mediating between individual behavioral skills and environmental contexts that influence how the person applies those skills. The focus of personality as Perry and Jessor defined it is the meaning that an individual attaches to events, relationships, and oneself. It influences, for instance, one's identity as a problem solver, as a valued person, as one who is entitled to and wants good health, and as a person who can positively influence the course of his or her life. Future work in community psychology is likely to build on integrative models such as Perry and Jessor's, leading to improvements in the prevention equations as guides for research and action.

## CONCLUSION: APPLYING THE CONCEPTS

Our use of prevention equations may suggest a certain precision to prevention and promotion concepts and interventions. However, that is not our intent. As participant conceptualizers, community psychologists are very aware of the complexity of individuals and settings. The prevention equations are merely guides to exploration in a messy, challenging, exciting world.

Moreover, prevention/promotion interventions that work in their original settings may fail miserably in other contexts. Even highly effective interventions will not automatically generalize to new circumstances. As the sage Hillel commented many centuries ago, one can never stand in the shoes of another because time does not stand still. No two situations are identical. Yet we know there are continuities within the diversity of ecological contexts. Respect for uniqueness is balanced with aspects of shared humanity, diversity with commonality, present circumstances with transcendent realities.

How better to think of these high concepts than in terms of a pizza? When one takes a bite of a pizza with "everything," it has a certain taste that is hard to attribute to any particular ingredient. What really makes the pizza great? The sauce? The cheese? The spices? The crust? The way it was cooked? The water used to make the dough? Whether we tossed the dough wearing gloves or not? The kinds of toppings used, how much, and when and where they were placed? There are many factors that come together to influence an overall outcome. Yet there is still something most can agree is pizza and although one cannot define it precisely, it is possible to agree on what great pizza tastes like.

Community psychologists are not content with having great pizza. We want to know what made it great, who might not have thought it was so great and why not, and how can we make sure that more great pizza reaches more people more consistently. Take as an example Seidman's (1991) Adolescent Pathways Project. His interest is in understanding ways in which five sets of outcomes occur: psychological symptoms, antisocial behaviors, academic achievement, extracurricular achievement, and sound health. Clearly, a complicated set of outcomes and pathways are possible if we are to understand how these outcomes arise as a function of risk and protective processes as arrayed in the prevention equation, and mediating influences unique to the contexts under study. For a community psychologist, drawing patterns often occurs from examining a series of cases. Seidman (1991) reviewed studies of 32 elementary and middle/junior high schools in low-income urban areas. Among the findings was the importance of ethnic diversity in understanding pathways. For example, low involvement/participation is significantly related to a negative developmental outcome, antisocial behavior, when one examines the data for the entire sample. Yet when one looks at subgroups, one finds the relationship is not significant for Black and White females, but is so for Latina females.

This is one of many examples of the importance of considering how ethnicity and other mediators can refine our views of what predicts developmental outcomes and, therefore, of what kinds of preventive efforts are likely to be most effective for what kinds of contexts. Clearly, no single pizza recipe will work across all nations and their ecologies and inhabitants.

From the basic recipes of prevention and competence promotion theory, different ingredients must be added to address the diversity of situations. Often, and appropriately, those additions will reflect the chef, the chef's mentors, the circumstances, the ingredients available, and the nature of the order. The great chefs know the basic recipes, but their greatness comes in knowing how to modify and improvise without compromising the essence of what is being prepared.

In the next two chapters, we look at some great recipes and ingredients in the form of effective prevention and promotion programs, and at the challenges of improvisation that arise in particular settings. In chapter 10, we visit exemplary and promising approaches to promoting competence and preventing problem behaviors, both in the United States and internationally. In chapter 11, we take a more detailed look at implementation of these approaches, and identify key components and processes that are characteristic of viable approaches to prevention and promotion.

## CHAPTER SUMMARY

**1.** Prevention is an evolving field of study in community psychology and related disciplines. We began with a parable that illustrates in common sense terms the logic of taking a preventive approach to dealing with mental health problems.

**2.** Bower's (1972) model illustrates how individual development through the socialization process is related to prevention. These include *Key integrated social systems (KISS)*, *ailing-in-difficulty (AID)* settings, and *illness correctional endeavors (ICE)* institutions. KISS settings are the focus of preventive efforts. These include prenatal care, schools, parents, peers, religious organizations, and the Internet.

**3.** The social–ecological approach stresses the importance of environment, a person's individual attributes, and how these elements interrelate and also impact on the effectiveness of preventive efforts. Prevention occurs not through inoculation but as people pass through social institutions that are strengthening and supportive.

**4.** G. Caplan's (1964) view of prevention as involving *primary, secondary,* and *tertiary* components was an early and highly influential conceptualization of prevention. More recently, the Report of the Institute of Medicine defined prevention in terms of *universal, selected,* and *indicated* approaches. In general, *prevention* really is a term that denotes two complementary foci: *prevention of disorder and problem behavior* and *promotion of wellness and social competence.*

**5.** Key concepts in prevention and promotion were defined and discussed: *risk, protection, resilience, strengths,* and *thriving.* All are best thought of as social–ecological and developmental processes, not static factors or attributes of individuals.

**6.** Albee (1982) and Elias (1987) created two *prevention equations* useful for integrating the concepts presented. From these equations, one may derive 10 specific types of intervention at either the individual or environmental levels. These are listed in Table 9.1.

**7.** Community psychology does not shy away from real-world complexity and tries to avoid overgeneralizing from one context to another. Nevertheless, there are continuities across contexts in prevention and promotion. Understanding prevention, with all its facets, is like understanding all that goes into making a great pizza.

# Brief Exercises

**1.** For your community, identify the KISS, AID, and ICE settings. Explain why you categorized each setting in each category. A phone book, services directory, or even a walk around the community can help identify settings, as does doing this with a partner. Try to find settings in the health, mental health, educational, justice, and other human service systems. Some of these, especially ICE settings, may serve your community yet be located elsewhere.

**2.** One aspect of KISS that has mushroomed since Bower (1972) is media/cyberspace/Internet. It raises three critical questions for the future:

- How can our system of education, both for children and adults, be transformed to take into account the changes in information availability?
- How we can do this in a way that is equitable with regard to communities and individuals of various income levels and conditions of physical or learning abilities?
- How can KISS systems respond to the penetration of information in various forms into our homes, cars, and brains? Is the media/cyberspace/Internet system reducing our involvement in our families, social networks, and communities, or increasing it (or both)?

Consider these future areas and your views of them. What questions do they raise for you? After you have thought about it on your own or with classmates, consider some of our questions. For instance, regarding the third issue, how much time is taken from interpersonal interaction? From participation in community groups and the kinds of meetings that, to this point, have been the backbone of a sense of community? Are there differences between a sense of community based on direct personal contact and that derived from cyberspace encounters? Will video technology, such as face-to-face email chats across huge distances, change such perceptions? How do families deal with the massive influx of information into the home? To what should children be exposed? At what ages? For that matter, to what should adults be exposed?

**3.** Generate some examples of prevention/promotion interventions. Discuss each step below with a classmate if possible.

A. First, choose a *problem in living* that is at least partly psychological in nature. The problem may be defined by symptoms or behaviors (e.g., depression, anxiety, health problem, poor school performance, criminal arrests) or by a stressful situation (e.g., bereavement, divorce, loss of job, poverty). Also choose an *age group* in which you are interested that experiences this problem; and a *community* with which you are familiar, where this problem occurs.

B. Second, for this problem, age group, and community, *list the risk and protective processes* that you can identify. Write a sentence to define each process; tell why each protective process is protective. Use Table 9.1, the prevention equations, to help identify risk processes (numerators in the equations) and protective processes (denominators).

C. Third, for this problem, age group, and community, identify examples of *primary prevention* activities, and of *secondary prevention or early treatment* activities. List activities that exist and those that you can suggest. Write a sentence or two to describe each existing or suggested intervention. Include what setting that intervention would be based in (e.g., school, neighborhood, workplace). Tell why it represents primary or secondary prevention.

**4.** *Reading with emotional intelligence.* Try reading one of the recommended readings or other relevant prevention/promotion readings, using our 6R/3E/4Q Method below. Your reading should lead you to record, when you are finished:

- 6 *Revelations*, facts you did not know, things you find especially interesting and meaningful to you,
- 3 *Emotional reactions*, things to which you found your self reacting with upset, joy, pride, puzzlement, shock,
- 4 *Questions* that are raised by what you read that you would genuinely like to know the answers to.

Looking at the prevention/promotion aspect of community psychology in this way is likely to lead you to put your reading to much more active use than will the usual under-lining/ highlighting methods.

# RECOMMENDED READINGS

Albee, G. (1982). Preventing psychopathology and promoting human potential. *American Psychologist, 37,* 1043–1050.

Elias, M. (1987). Establishing enduring prevention programs: Advancing the legacy of Swampscott. *American Journal of Community Psychology, 15,* 539–553.

Sources of the prevention equations.

Bloom, M. (1996). *Primary prevention practices: Issues in children's and families lives* (Vol. 5). Thousand Oaks, CA: Sage.

An excellent, recent complement to the prevention equations.

The Carnegie Corporation of New York. (1994). *Starting points: Meeting the needs of our youngest children.* New York: Author.

One example of a large and growing source of prevention and health promotion information: private foundations and research organizations. (The William T. Grant Foundation, Annie Casey Foundation, Pew Charitable Trusts, Packard Center for the Future of Children, Carter Center at Emory University in Atlanta, Institute of Medicine, and National Research Council represent others.) This report outlines problems and theories of early child development and child care and provides examples of programs in key areas: promoting responsible parenthood, guaranteeing quality child care choices, ensuring the health and safety of youth, and mobilizing communities to support young children and their families.

Kelly, J. G., Dassoff, N., Levin, I., Schreckengost, J., Stelzner, S., & Altman, B. (1988). *A guide to conducting prevention research in the community: First Steps.* New York: Haworth.

Applies social–ecological models to prevention research. Rich examples of how to use a prevention/promotion theory to guide action.

## InfoTrac Keywords

*competence(ies), health, intervention, prevention(ive)(ing), primary prevention, promotion(ing), protection(ive), risk.*

## Recommended Websites

http://www.prevention.org

This is the Website of Prevention First, an Illinois-based organization that serves as a clearinghouse for local and national prevention programs, resources and materials, other prevention Websites, and its journal, *Prevention Forum.*

http://www.cmmtypsych.net/

This is a good site on community psychology, with resources on prevention and promotion. For details, see Recommended Websites for chapter 1.

http://www.samhsa.gov/csap/index.htm

http://www.samhsa.gov/cmhs/cmhs.htm

Within the Substance Abuse and Mental Health Administration of the U.S. government are Centers for Substance Abuse Prevention (CSAP) and Mental Health Services (CMHS). These sites provide information on U.S. government resources in prevention in these areas.

http://www.journals.apa.org/prevention

The latest edition of the American Psychological Association's electronic journal, *Prevention and Treatment,* can be accessed directly via this site.

## Sites for Information on Social Issues Related to Prevention

http://www.unicef.org
>This is the multilingual Website of the United Nation's Children's Fund, with worldwide information on children's rights and issues such as child labor, safe motherhood, and response to disasters affecting children.

http://cpmcnet.columbia.edu/news/childpov/
>This is the site of the National Center for Children in Poverty, and a source for policy and legislative information.

http://childstats.gov/index.htm
>This is the site for the U.S. Federal Interagency Forum on children, for viewing reports such as the yearly "America's Children: Key National Indicators of Well-Being," a summary of statistical indicators of child and family health, economic status, education, social environment, and related measures. This site provides valuable information for a national overview of child well-being.

http://www.aecf.org/kidscount/index.htm
>*Kidscount* is a useful yearly summary of U.S. health, economic, and demographic social indicators regarding children. Contained within the site of the Annie E. Casey Foundation, this site provides information about private nonprofit philanthropy focused on children and families.

http://www.frca.org
>Family Resource Coalition of America provides news affecting families and communities, family support legislation and policy alerts, bulletin boards and other ways to network, and access to books and resources.

http://www.elderweb.com
>ElderWeb is an on-line sourcebook with links to information about health and other issues related to maximizing the competence and preserving the dignity of frail elderly individuals.

## Selected Sites on Child Abuse and Neglect

http://www.childabuse.org/
>This is the site of the National Committee for the Prevention of Child Abuse.

http://www.acf.dhhs.gov/programs/cb
>This is the site of the Office on Child Abuse and Neglect in the Children's Services Bureau in the U.S. Department of Health and Human Services.

http://www.childwelfare.ca/index.shtml
>This is the site of the Child Welfare Resource Centre in Canada.

http://child.cornell.edu/capn.html
>The Child.Cornell site is supported by the Family Life Development Center there and by the Child Abuse Prevention Network. It has an extensive array of resources and links to other sites for professionals, researchers, and students.

# Prevention and Promotion: Current and Future Applications

# PREVENTION AND PROMOTION ARE ALL AROUND YOU

In *Always Wear Clean Underwear,* Gellman (1997) gives children humor-laced insights into why advice kids get from parents is filled with potential to promote our well-being and to prevent difficulties. We learn, for example, that "share your toys" is a way of saying that people should be more important to you than things. "Always say please and thank you" is important, Gellman believes, because people who steal cars start out by stealing candy bars and people who cheat in business start out by cheating in school. By saying please, we learn that we are not entitled to anything and everything we want when we want it. Thank yous teach us that we should be grateful for good things that happen and we should tell people who do good things for us that we appreciate them. Then, they will care for us more and do even more for us. What about the title, you are wondering? No, it's not about germs, and it's not about avoiding embarrassment if you get into an accident. The message is that what people don't see about you should still be as good as what they do see about you.

No doubt you are questioning what this has to do with community psychology. Our point is this: Parents and many others conduct prevention/promotion programs, mostly without the assistance of community psychologists, every day. Prevention and promotion efforts are ubiquitous. Try this exercise: Think of examples in your own life of efforts (formal programs or informal actions) to promote social competence and prevent problem behaviors. On the basis of what you learned in chapter 9, ask yourself the following: What risk processes might be weakened, or protective processes strengthened, by these efforts? Do these efforts promote strengths and thriving? Which efforts had a lasting effect? Why?

In addition, ask yourself this: Can you tell if a formal prevention/promotion program is the work of community psychologists? Does it matter? Snowden (1987) wrote about the "peculiar success" of community psychology: Its approaches are widely adopted, but as a field it is not well-known. Since its founding, the field has been actively interdisciplinary, so much so that its members and their work in prevention and promotion appear in many places: for instance, law, education, government, public health, social work, the corporate world, and several fields of psychology (especially developmental, organizational, educational, and clinical). At the same time, members of other disciplines often collaborate on research and interventions that appear in community psychology. In this chapter, we help you recognize some of the work community psychologists are doing in prevention and promotion along with practitioners from other fields.

# WHAT ARE THE KEY POINTS OF THIS CHAPTER?

The literature on prevention and social competence promotion is expanding at a remarkable rate. Significant new compilations of programs and research emerge monthly, nationally and internationally. In this chapter, our goal is to provide you with a look at a variety of ways in which concepts of prevention and social competence promotion are applied in action research and experimental social innovation (recall these from chaps. 3 and 4). These programs represent both prevention/promotion interventions designed to improve individual, organizational, or community life and research projects designed to study whether the intervention had the planned effect and how to improve it for the future.

First we conduct a tour of the prevention/promotion field. We begin with person-centered programs in developmental sequence, reviewing some programs for early and middle childhood, adolescence, and adulthood. Next we consider organizational, locality, and macrosystem levels, looking at programs in schools, workplaces, and localities, and at policies affecting populations. We include examples from community psychology and other sources to illustrate the diversity of the field.

In the rest of the chapter, we examine several issues that cut across all prevention/promotion efforts. We provide a brief overview of the importance of cultural and community context for prevention/promotion. We review evidence of the effectiveness of prevention/promotion programs in general and two approaches to addressing issues of studying effectiveness. Even at a very general level, prevention/promotion initiatives show surprisingly strong effects. Finally, we suggest a few issues likely to be the focus of increased prevention/promotion efforts in the near future.

# PERSON-CENTERED PREVENTION/PROMOTION: A DEVELOPMENTAL TOUR

In this section, we review selected prevention/promotion programs for four age groups: early childhood, middle childhood, adolescence, and adulthood. These represent approaches that focus on preventive changes within individuals or microsystems such as families; thus, they are termed *person-centered*. Under some conditions these may lead to changes in a setting (e.g., a classroom or school), but the focus here is on individuals and microsystems. We have selected interventions that have been found effective in longitudinal empirical research and that provide an illustration of prevention/promotion practices and emphases for each age group. However, you should understand that for reasons of space we have had to omit a number of exemplary, effective programs, as well as a number of promising innovations. Prevention/promotion is a growing field with many promising pathways to the future.

Where possible, we indicate the risk and protective processes (from the prevention equations in chap. 9) that represent the foci of a particular program. We present these in parentheses in the text as (EQ # . . . ), listing the numbers of the processes in the equations. Table 10.1 lists these processes (see also Table 9.1 in the prior chapter).

| TABLE 10.1 | INTERVENTIONS DERIVED FROM PREVENTION EQUATIONS |
|---|---|

Interventions derived from individual equation

1. Reduce/better manage perceived stress
2. Reduce the negative impact of a physically/biologically based vulnerability
3. Increase coping skills, problem solving/decision making, social skills
4. Increase perceived social support
5. Increase self-esteem/self-efficacy

Interventions derived from environmental equation

6. Reduce/eliminate stressors in key socialization settings, other aspects of environment
7. Reduce operation/presence of physical risk factors in the environment that result in increased physical/biological vulnerability
8. Improve socialization practices, ways in which key socialization settings carry out their tasks
9. Increase accessible social support resources
10. Increase opportunities for positive relatedness to others and connectedness to positive social institutions, positive social groups, agencies, and other formal and informal settings

Note: See also Table 9.1, page 275.

## Programs for Early Childhood: Parents and Problem Solving

***Prenatal/Early Infancy Project***    Olds (1997) developed an exemplary program that provided social support and training in parenting and coping skills training to mothers of at-risk infants, leading to reductions in abuse and neglect and improved child health outcomes (EQ #1,4,5,8,9,10).

The purpose of the intervention was to assist first-time mothers whose children were at risk for birth and early childhood difficulties because the mothers were low-income, teenaged, and/or unmarried. The program involved home visits by a trained nurse and health care screenings. Home visits began in the 30th week of pregnancy and continued through the second year of a child's life. The psychological aspects of home-visit discussions were based on developmental concepts of family and community relationships (Bronfenbrenner, 1979), self-efficacy (Bandura, 1982), and mother–child attachment (Bowlby, 1969). The program was first implemented in Elmira, New York, primarily with European American mothers, and later in Memphis primarily with African American mothers, and in Denver with a multiracial sample.

A randomized field experiment with the Elmira sample compared mothers and children who received home visits with a comparison group who received only health screenings at a clinic. The comparison group had significantly higher rates of child maltreatment, use of emergency medical services, safety hazards at home, and smoking during pregnancy (a health risk for infants). On average, the comparison group provided a less stimulating environment for intellectual and emotional development. Clearly the home visits made a difference in the lives of young mothers.

Olds's (1997) program has not been implemented widely because funding cutbacks in human services have not allowed necessary staff to be employed. When client caseloads were increased for the nurses, the effectiveness of the program was reduced (Schorr, 1988). Yet when long-term effects of the original program were studied, services to low-income families who received the home visits cost over $3,000 less per family than those in the comparison group by the child's fourth birthday. Preventive services thus were significantly less costly than health care and other costs after problems developed (Olds, 1997).

**High/Scope Perry Preschool Project**    The Perry Preschool Project (PPP), using the High/Scope curriculum, is a widely adopted and very important social and educational innovation. The premise of the PPP is that comprehensive early childhood education, especially for children at risk for poor public school performance due to growing up in poor economic circumstances, could avert early school failure, subsequent school dropout, adult poverty, and an array of associated problems. There are many elements to the High/Scope curriculum; all must be implemented for positive effects to be obtained. These include a classroom and daily routine in which children have time for planning activities, performing them, clean-up, and recall and discussion of the activity, in small and large group formats. Based on Piagetian and early childhood development theory, PPP methods involve children as active learners and adults as coordinators of child-centered, developmentally appropriate activities (EQ #3,4,5,6,8,9; Weikart & Schweinhart, 1997). The Head Start program has often used a High/Scope curriculum with health and social welfare services for parents (EQ #1,2,10).

The PPP transforms key microsystem events for young children at a critical developmental period, setting up a positive trajectory that is expected to endure through later development. Follow-up data suggest that this indeed can occur; studies of PPP children 20 years later show positive impact compared with control children on such indices as arrests, educational attainment, income, and duration of marriages (Berreuta-Clement, Schweinhart, Barnett, Epstein, & Weikart 1984; Weikart & Schweinhart, 1997).

Although there have been some controversies over methodology and specific findings, the consensus is that when PPP or Head Start are implemented according to their performance standards, they are powerful interventions for prevention and promotion. Cost–benefit analyses comparing treatment and comparison groups from PPP studies suggest that the program saves $7.16 in future costs (of social, health, and educational services) for each $1 invested (Weikart & Schweinhart, 1997). However such benefits are computed, there is general agreement that the monetary and human benefits of the program are substantial. Nevertheless, PPP and Head Start methods are not always implemented rigorously, and findings show that without such rigor, benefits are diluted. (We discuss the importance of implementation in chap. 11).

Social concern has surfaced recently about U.S. national policy on early childhood development, fueled by research on critical growth periods, developmental risks associated with poverty, and the benefits of early intervention (Brooks & Buckner, 1996; Carnegie Corporation of New York, 1994; Rickel & Becker, 1997). Comprehensive intervention is advocated at the person and environmental levels, similar to the Prenatal/Early Infancy Project and High/Scope Perry Preschool programs, including Head Start services for the "under threes" (Carnegie Corporation of New York, 1994).

*Interpersonal Cognitive Problem Solving* Shure and Spivack (1988; Shure, 1997) developed a preschool curriculum to increase children's interpersonal cognitive problem solving (ICPS, now known as "I Can Problem Solve") skills. These are critical thinking skills; the focus at the preschool level is on children's feelings vocabulary (words such as *sad, glad, mad, proud, bored*) and prerequisite cognitive concepts, such as "or," "else," "before and after," and "not." The key to this approach is that a set of caregivers (e.g., preschool teachers) is being helped to deliver not only certain content to children but to give children opportunities to practice the skills being taught, applying their learning throughout the school day (EQ #3,8).

The centerpiece of ICPS is teaching caregivers to "dialogue" with children. In essence, "dialoguing" involves asking open ended questions first, to promote children's own thinking and problem solving, reverting to more of a "telling" mode only as needed. For example, here are two sets of examples of how teachers in a kindergarten classroom context might handle a situation:

Example 1: Who will help Golnar with the blocks?

1. "Golnar, how can you find someone else to work with you in the blocks area, to help you build that fort?"

2. "Could you ask Pedro or Liang or Rivka to work with you, or maybe Pat?"

3. "Go ask Sara. If she says no, call me and I will tell her to work with you, or else I will tell George to do it."

Example 2: How will Samara and her friends find something to do at recess?

1. "Girls, what are all the things you can think of to do when you get outside?"

2. "Are you going to want to play on the swings, use the jump ropes, or play tag?"

3. "When you get outside, I want Samara to go to the climbing area, Julie to go to the bikes and cars, and Carol to go to the blacktop. We will switch in 15 minutes so everybody has a chance to do at least two different things."

In each set of examples, there are illustrations of three levels of caregiver methods to facilitate children's own thinking processes. The first option is an open-ended question, which is likely to result in an interchange between adult and child that requires children to think about their preferences, to envision possibilities, and to make a choice. The second keeps the choice in the hands of the child and stimulates possibilities, albeit with more structuring than the first way. The final approach is to tell this child what to do, with or without explanation. ICPS approaches emphasize the first two methods in the examples above, teaching through dialoguing.

The learning outcomes of frequent "telling" will be no surprise to students who have sat through many lectures (a fancy form of telling). Learning is promoted by actively working with materials and situations, and with creating our own meanings. That is what ICPS, and an entire genre of similar problem solving and decision-making approaches, aspires to do for children of preschool through high school age (Elias & Clabby, 1992; Elias et al., 1997).

The ICPS approach can be used in many preschool settings, and especially in Head Start. However, funding is not available within Head Start to allow for widespread staff training and follow-up. Without proper initial training and follow-up, ICPS-related programs do not sustain their effectiveness (Elias et al., 1997).

## Programs for Middle Childhood: Social Problem Solving

**Social Development Model**    The Social Development Model is a universal preventive intervention focused on elementary schools (Hawkins, Catalano, Morrison, et al., 1992; Hawkins & Lam, 1987). It addresses the need to teach skills to children but also to change the norms of home and classroom settings and to create opportunities to practice new skills. Teachers were trained in classroom management, cooperative learning, and the use of the ICPS curriculum; parents were trained to create norms in the home for child self-control and for performing academic work (EQ #3,5,8). When researchers followed children from first into fifth grade, children in the intervention group were less likely than controls to initiate alcohol use, more psychologically attached to school, their families were stronger in communication and involvement, and school rewards and norms were more positive than among controls (Hawkins, Catalano, Morrison, et al., 1992).

**Social Decision Making and Social Problem Solving**    Elias, Gara, Schuyler, Branden-Muller, and Sayette (1991) examined the impact of an elementary school version of ICPS, the Social Decision Making and Social Problem Solving Program (SDM/SPS; Elias & Tobias, 1996), on problem behaviors. SDM/SPS differs from the ICPS program in two major ways. SDM/SPS emphasizes readiness skills designed to build student self-control and group participation and to foster classroom norms to support these skills. SDM/SPS also contains an application phase in which the skills of the program are systematically infused into all aspects of the school routine, including the discipline system, academic areas such as language arts and social studies, and community service (EQ #1,3,5,8,9,10). Elias et al. (1991) found that students followed up 6 years after receiving a 2-year intervention in elementary school showed significantly less likelihood than controls to use alcohol and tobacco.

## Programs for Adolescents: Competencies and Community Service

**Life Skills Training (LST)**    This program provides junior high school aged children with knowledge, motivation, and skills to resist influences to use tobacco, alcohol, and other drugs (EQ #1,5; Botvin & Tortu, 1988). The LST curriculum focuses on awareness of negative consequences of substance use, accurate norms regarding peer use, building self-esteem, coping with social anxiety, and social-communication skills (including resistance to peer pressure). The curriculum structure includes 15 lessons in Grade 7 and "booster" sessions in Grades 8 and 9. Teachers are extensively trained and provided with a detailed manual; another version of LST uses 11th and 12th graders as peer leaders. Assessments of the research findings on LST program effectiveness have concluded that the program reduces smoking and is promising in its impact on future alcohol and drug use (Botvin & Tortu, 1988; Rogers, Howard-Pitney, & Bruce, 1989). Elements of LST have been adopted in many drug abuse prevention programs in schools.

Successful programs directed specifically toward preventing adolescent drug use have combined an informational component, training in social influence and skills (often resistance to peer pressure and media advertising), and interventions to alter student norms about the prevalence and acceptability of peer drug use. Reduced alcohol use immediately following programs such as Adolescent Prevention Trial (Hansen & Graham, 1991) and ALERT Drug Prevention (Ellickson & Bell, 1990) have been documented, but enduring effects have been rare.

***Lions-Quest Skills for Action***   Skills for Action (SFA) is a program of Lions-Quest International with three components: (a) a classroom-based curriculum to develop social–emotional and decision making skills and to address problem behaviors such as substance use, (b) a highly structured community service component, and (c) a skills bank containing a series of enrichment activities. Thus, SFA can be understood not only as preventing problem behaviors, but as promoting social–emotional competence and community citizenship. An evaluation study involving students in Grades 9–12 in 29 high schools in urban, suburban, and rural settings found preliminary support for the effectiveness of the program. In two alternative high schools, where the program was a selected intervention (see chap. 9), students in SFA were suspended less often and had higher grades than controls. No impact was found on substance abuse. In the other 27 high schools, the strongest overall effect was on prevention of dropping out; ninth graders made the most gains, including lower drug and cigarette use (Laird, Bradley, & Black, 1998).

SFA evaluators also found that if students gave fewer than 15 hours of community service, no program effects were obtained. Their attention to monitoring allowed them to note a high degree of satisfaction with the program but highly variable conditions of implementation. In addition, schools with the SFA program varied considerably in what elements of the program were actually implemented, whereas control schools often had some similar programs in place. These factors make it difficult to form firm conclusions about program impact. However, with 3,500 students performing 29,000 hours of service touching the lives of 12,000 people in the pilot studies alone, SFA clearly has an ecological presence in schools and communities.

## Programs for Adults: Social Support and Coping Skills

***Widow-to-Widow Program***   This program (Silverman, 1988) was an early example of a program for mutual aid and social support. Silverman recognized that bereavement was a significant stressor that was destabilizing and also isolating for many women. Bringing together those who were experiencing similar trauma would promote sharing of emotional, social integration, informational, and tangible support (EQ #1,4,5,9,10). Data from outcome studies showed that the program assisted participants to find greater joy and excitement in their lives, supported them in meeting problems of daily living, and lowered the need for psychiatric care. The mechanism most often viewed as accounting for these findings was the acceptance the widows felt as members of a supportive network (Silverman, 1988). Similar programs have been adopted by the American Association of Retired Persons and other groups. Widow-to-Widow was developed by professionals, but it shares many elements in common with self-help groups discussed in chapters 7 and 8.

***San Francisco Depression Prevention Research Project (DPRP)***   Directed toward adults, the DPRP is a selected preventive intervention (see chap. 9) focused on patients in public primary health care clinics serving low-income populations, a group at statistically higher risk for depression (Munoz, 1997). The DPRP recruited patients seen at these clinics for general health problems and who were not already clinically depressed. Those who chose to enroll in the intervention participated in eight group sessions, once per week. These sessions focus on learning cognitive–behavioral coping skills, including monitoring thoughts, moods, and actions, increasing pleasant activities, and building interpersonal skills (EQ #3). In a randomized field experiment, the DPRP intervention lowered incidence of depressive symptoms and onset of depression (Munoz, 1997).

*JOBS Project*    Adult workers who lose their jobs are clearly at risk for a variety of psychological problems. The JOBS Project intervenes at the point at which these workers begin looking for new jobs, and represents a selected intervention. Laid-off workers are offered the opportunity to attend 20 hours of group training focused on problem solving, overcoming setbacks, job search skills, and exchange of social support (EQ #1,3,4,8). A series of evaluation studies using experimental designs has yielded evidence that the program reduced incidence of serious depression and led to obtaining better jobs. Cost–benefit analysis also revealed that the money expended on the program, approximately $300 per person, was made up in less than a year in the form of tax revenues contributed by workers once they were back in the work force (R. Caplan et al., 1997).

*Worksite Coping Skills Intervention*    Kline and Snow (1994) developed an intervention directed at mothers employed in secretarial positions. Their preliminary research uncovered risk for work and family stressors in this population, and their intervention focused on stress management, problem, and emotional focused coping skills, and cognitive restructuring techniques (EQ #1,4,5). It was carried out in four different corporate work sites. When compared with a matched comparison group, participants reported lower role stress, less tobacco and alcohol use, and higher perceived support from others at work. These effects were maintained at 6 month follow-up, with an additional impact on lower psychological symptomatology.

# BEYOND INDIVIDUALS:
# ORGANIZATIONS, COMMUNITIES, MACROSYSTEMS

Prevention/promotion goals can be pursued by changing the interpersonal environment or formal policies of an organization (e.g., school, workplace), locality, or even nation. Like the programs we have discussed, these efforts aim to increase individual quality of life, but seek to do that by altering an entire setting, community, or larger unit.

## Whole Setting Approaches: Schools and Workplaces

Many of the interventions we have reviewed represent person-level preventive approaches in which the characteristics of the setting are left unchanged. However, clearly many settings create stressors for individuals, and reducing these or increasing protective processes within the setting would have preventive effects. Next, we review programs that reduce risks and enhance protective processes in whole settings.

*Child Development Project*    Based in Oakland, California, the Child Development Project (CDP) seeks to produce a caring community in the classroom and elementary school by creating environments that foster self-determination, social competence, social connectedness, and moral guidance (EQ #3,4,5,8,9,10) (Solomon, Watson, Battistich, Schaps, & Delucchi, 1996). Walk into a CDP classroom and you will find students working in cooperative groups and discussing issues of social responsibility and prosocial values in their academic subjects and in class meetings and projects. Schoolwide activities reflect similar values, as do the operation of parent–teacher teams and the concept of "family homework." Data from a variety of studies indicate that changes have been produced in social skills, social adjustment, classroom behavior, and a balance of gains in self-assertion and in concern for others (Battistich et al., 1992).

*Schools Without Bullying*    Olweus's (1991) work in Norway involves preventing conduct disorder by focusing on the school rules for acceptable interaction in all aspects of the environment, including the playground. His approach includes parents, whose approach to discipline often contributes to a bully's problems. Intervention components include an educational booklet on bullying used with all students, a parent education booklet, a video depicting the lives of victims of bullying, and a strong school discipline code that labels even nasty verbal comments as bullying and calls for swift consequences, such as removal from the playground or classroom (EQ #7,8). Repeated offenses bring calls for parents to come into the school. Evaluation data have been supportive, indicating significant improvements in satisfaction with school life, feelings of comfort and safety, and, most importantly, less bullying of others; replications in the United States also have been effective. In essence, Olweus's approach, and those modeled after it, create a school with a different environmental "feel" and set of interactions than was the case prior to its implementation.

*School Development Program (SDP)*    SDP and related approaches focus on the entire atmosphere and structure of the schools that adopt them. The "Comer process" (Comer, 1988; Comer, Haynes, Joyner, & Ben-Avie, 1996) is in essence a school-based management approach that transforms the relationships among educators and parents so that there is a shared decision-making and responsibility base for an individual school. The key components include a School Management Team, a school-based Mental Health Team, programs to encourage parent support and involvement, and a social and emotional skills development curriculum (EQ #3,4,5,6,7,8,9,10). This model generates powerful radiating effects, which Comer has described as a sense of empowerment that flows into the classrooms and touches the students while also flowing out in the community and touching residents and service providers who interface with the school. Initial evaluation results have found an impact on school-wide levels of academic achievement and an invigoration of many parents and educators to participate in the educational system. But as of this writing, preliminary reports of replication studies tell the familiar story that positive effects are not obtained without rigorous implementation.

*School Transitional Environmental Project (STEP)*    As we discussed in chapter 5, Felner and Adan (1988) developed an approach that changed the usual configuration of high school environments, so that new high school students were in a more contained environment with greater social supports (EQ #6,8,9,10). Ninth graders, entering high school, remained with the same classmates for most of their classes and had a smaller number of teachers, who thus knew each student better. This promoted social support from peers and adults. Homeroom teachers also were taught to handle more of the students' guidance needs. At year's end, students in the STEP program had better grades, less absenteeism, and a more positive view of school than those in a comparison group. The IOM report suggested that these gains reduce the risk of conduct disorder (Mrazek & Haggerty, 1994).

**Worksite Interventions**    In recent years, companies have recognized that the well-being of their employees can have many economic benefits. American Express, Kimberly-Clark, and Ford Motor Company are among the organizations that have devoted substantial resources to changing their microsystems and organizations and building the emotional competence of key managers and work groups. An example that reflects a community psychology perspective comes from Ford. In their attempt to redesign the Lincoln Continental, executives gave the design team extensive contact with owners and potential owners. The improvements in empathy and perspective taking improved their ability to create a successful design. But beyond that, the employees felt strongly empowered and supported by their larger organization (EQ #1,3,4,5,8,9,10; Goleman, 1998). Some organizations, such as Disney, work extensively to ensure that employees have a high degree of social and emotional skills and that Disney theme parks and stores create a minimum of stress and a maximum of support for consumers.

## Community-Wide and Policy-Level Interventions

Prevention/promotion efforts can be pursued at the level of neighborhoods, localities, and macrosystems. These initiatives may involve new programs, as do most of the examples we have discussed above, or changes in the policies and/or practices of localities or larger units, including nations.

**Better Beginnings, Better Futures Project**    Canada has long been committed to pursuing the benefits of prevention for its children. In the 1980s, the province of Ontario created Better Beginnings, Better Futures as a primary prevention project. Government representatives work actively with local boards comprised of residents and local service providers to create projects to prevent behavioral, emotional, learning, and health problems among children, particularly in economically disadvantaged populations. Although the 25-year project is not yet completed, promising community actions have been taken. Research findings indicated that the participation of community residents in developing prevention/programs had many beneficial effects, such as creating a sense of empowerment, fostering new individual and community competencies, and forging informal social support. However, it is difficult for a community to keep resources and energies focused on prevention in children over such a long period of time (Sylvestre, Pancer, Brophy, & Cameron, 1994). Better Beginnings, Better Futures illustrates a community-wide initiative of the type we discuss in more detail in chapter 13.

**Interventions Using Mass Media**    Jason (1998a) carried out a series of interventions designed to change the localities and macrosystems within which people live, leading to change in microsystems and individuals. Among the most effective was a collaboration with the Chicago Lung Association and the Chicago Board of Education to work toward smoking prevention among African American youth. A school-based anti-smoking curriculum developed by the American Lung Association was combined with a three-pronged media intervention: (a) a smoking prevention curriculum run each week on the children's page of *The Chicago Defender,* a local newspaper with a strong African-American readership; (b) a series of eight public service spots on WGCI, a radio station with a listening audience of 1 million, mostly African-American, along with a call-in talk show for parents; and (c) an anti-smoking billboard contest, which also posted the five best entries (EQ #4,5,6,7,8,9). Findings indicated lower cigarette use among adolescents, and lower rates of cigarettes, alcohol, and marijuana use in families. Jason's work suggests that media-based interventions must reach directly into microsystems in order to be effective and that careful targeting, including attention to cultural and ethnic issues, is important (Jason & Hanaway, 1997).

***Revitalizing High-Risk Neighborhoods***    In the United States, Federal Center for Substance Abuse Prevention grants have been used to develop comprehensive strategies to revitalize communities beset by crime and drugs. In Vallejo, California, community groups including the chamber of commerce, private employers, police, employment and housing departments, and grassroots neighborhood groups worked together to clean up the physical environment, reduce crime, provide social services for all, and reduce alcohol abuse (EQ #1,3,4,6,7,8,9,10). They identified neighborhood "hot spots," working street by street, and intervened in these localities first. In the first year of the project, two neighborhoods were cleaned up and initiatives into two others were being made. The Vallejo project is among many similar initiatives that are meeting their initial goals, but ultimate results will take years to measure (Sparks, 1998).

***Reducing Substance-Abuse-Related Outcomes***    Another level of intervention involves macrosystem policy, chiefly laws but also including decisions by other government bodies, including the courts. In the United States, increasing the legal age for drinking alcohol and/or increasing taxes on alcohol purchases have had preventive effects (EQ #7; P. Cook & Tauchen, 1982; O'Malley & Wagenaar, 1991). These macrosystem policy changes have had significant impact on alcohol use, alcohol-related illness, and alcohol-related fatal auto accidents. However, if local communities do not enforce tighter laws, the effects are neutralized. Perry and Associates (1989), working with the World Health Organization, have shown that in countries where the norms for alcohol use are liberal (Australia, for example), interventions that work in other countries are far less effective.

A more specific community-wide effort is Project TRAC (Targeted Reduction of Alcohol/Drug-Related Crashes) in San Diego County, California. In that county alone, the annual death rate from these accidents was 3.9 people per 100,000, and the injury rate 111.2 people per 100,000. The cost per year was estimated in excess of $100 million, the human cost inestimable. All of these accidents were viewed as preventable because of the substance use involvement. A public awareness campaign led by victims and offenders involved in accidents focused on populations determined to be most at risk, including college students and military personnel. Results were evaluated through data from hospitals and emergency services; preliminary findings were favorable, but longer term impact remains uncertain (McQuancy, 1999).

*International Perspectives*    Community-level and policy interventions differ by nation. We have mentioned initiatives originating in Norway and Canada, for instance. The Netherlands (Verburg, Janssen, Rikken, Heofnagels, & van Willenswaard, 1992) have a well organized system of prevention through Regional Institutes for Outpatient Mental Health Care, known as RIAGGs. RIAGGs conduct prevention projects involving schools, parent education, sexual violence, work and unemployment, ethnic groups, women, elderly, suicide, and social functioning. It is noteworthy that the RIAGG structure, which has been regional, is gradually becoming more centralized, to reduce variance in the quality and nature of programs across regions. This approach allows for an integration of various levels of prevention and for sharing of solutions participants have identified. It represents a shift from a local–regional focus to a national one.

Community-level preventive initiatives also have occurred in South Africa with the creation of community settings to address community violence and with health-promoting schools (Lazarus & Prinsloo, 1995). In Venezuela, preventive initiatives include creation of L'Esperanza (Hope), a legal association for homeless victims of landslides, and the Center for Popular Action Service, a nongovernmental agency that works with groups of women, workers, youths, farmers, and slum communities to empower them in terms of health, legal rights, and community decision making (Montero, 1995). These efforts resemble initiatives for citizen participation and empowerment that we describe in detail in chapters 12 and 13.

Prevention/promotion takes a different, health-oriented focus in Ghana (Sefa-Dedeh, 1992). In this West African country, children make up nearly 50% of the registry of deaths. Eight major preventable diseases are prevalent, including polio, diarrhea, and measles. Malnutrition and poverty are widespread, as is a lack of maternal and child health care. These problems are exacerbated by widespread cultural practices, such as men eating first and having the most nutritious foods available, followed by women and children. These examples serve as essential reminders that any innovation must take into account local cultural practices and issues (see chap. 6).

National-level preventive efforts in Ghana have begun, but their impact has been limited by lack of resources. Family planning programs are appearing, but only in some of the more urban areas; a primary health program has started to get information on nutrition and health to women but has done little with regard to mental health needs. Ghana also ratified the U.N. Convention on the Rights of the Child, which led to significant progress in areas of child health. However, conditions of poverty and the lack of well-functioning schools limit current efforts and clearly remain as an important agenda for prevention.

To help remember the prevention/promotion programs we have discussed, review the outline at the beginning of the chapter, which lists programs by category.

## THE IMPORTANCE OF CONTEXT: CULTURAL AND LOCAL

The concept of context has long been seen as sensible for community psychology. It grounds us in the real world which we are attempting to understand and improve. It rings true. But it has been slippery to grasp. . . . Community psychology can make a distinctive contribution by clarifying the many meanings of the diversity concept through attention to the contexts in which diversity develops, and the social milieu in which it is expressed. Such a clarification can support intervention that is both empowering and respectful of the contexts of those with whom we intervene. (Trickett, 1996, p. 226. Reprinted by permission of Kluwer Academic/Plenum Publishers.

Most of the prevention/promotion initiatives we have discussed have originated in North America or Europe. Is there a way of estimating how well programs developed there might transfer to countries in Asia, Africa, or Latin America?

Sundberg, Hadiyono, Latkin, and Padilla (1995) studied this question in selected Asian and Latin American countries. They chose five programs from among those designated as model prevention programs by the American Psychological Association in *14 Ounces of Prevention* (Price et al., 1988). Empirical research has shown each of these programs effective in the United States. We have already discussed four of these interventions: the Prenatal and Early Infancy program (Olds, 1988), High/Scope Perry Preschool program (PPP; Schweinhart & Weikart, 1988), Interpersonal Cognitive Problem Solving (ICPS; Shure & Spivack, 1988), and Life Skills Training (LST; Botvin & Tortu, 1988). A fifth program was the Stanford Heart Disease Prevention Program, a community-wide intervention to promote health through nutrition, exercise, smoking cessation, and other methods, using media and training groups (Maccoby & Altman, 1988).

Sundberg et al. (1995) used a key informant methodology, asking experts in 12 countries to examine these five programs and consider the need and the economic, political, cultural, and general feasibility of applying them in their nations. With regard to need, only the LST program was ranked highly in Latin American countries. Asian countries showed little consensus on estimations of need, with least enthusiasm for the PPP, ICPS, and LST programs. Only the LST program was seen as quite feasible in most countries.

Cultural differences reduced the desirability of many of the programs outside the United States. Some of these match the concepts of individualistic and collectivistic cultures we discussed in chapter 6. In India, the Prenatal/Early Infancy project would likely only be applied to married women, because of the unacceptability of unwed mothers in that society. Training children to be independent problem solvers was not valued in most countries, in which respect for elders is paramount. Cigarette smoking was not seen as a large problem in many countries outside the United States, and there was little concern about its role as a "gateway" to more serious substance use. Peer-resistance or refusal skills, part of LST and many other drug-use prevention programs, might conflict with the value of machismo in Latin America. Finally, the implicit future orientation of prevention concepts conflicts with the focus on the present in many cultures: the Thai concept of *mai pen rai*, translatable as "don't worry," is an example. Beyond these cultural differences, resource issues such as poverty and population were mentioned by key informants as limiting feasibility of these programs.

However, Sundberg et al. (1995) also found that the elements of the prevention equations (chap. 9) were highly valued across different countries. What is necessary is to ensure that specific preventive efforts directed toward the goals indicated in those equations are consistent with the cultural norms, resources, and social and political structure of a nation.

One approach to transferring and developing effective prevention/promotion initiatives is through communication about programs and findings. The World Health Organization's Division of Mental Health has had a special concern with prevention and life skills since the early 1990s. Their newsletter, "Skills for Life," highlights prevention theory, research, and practice around the world. The World Health Organization Mental Health

Promotion Unit also reports on Life Skills Education in the Schools (Orley, 1996). For example, programs directed at violence prevention among Greek and Lebanese primary school children found that their greatest impact was on girls and rejected children (Chimienti & Trivilas, 1994), a finding similar to those of Shure's (1997) ICPS curriculum.

Clearly, prevention at an international level requires a detailed familiarity with the contexts and histories of the areas involved. Even within countries with seemingly high degrees of geographic and cultural homogeneity, one must avoid assuming that what is effective in one area will automatically work in another. For instance, Bierman (1997) found it challenging to apply a conduct disorder prevention program that had been developed in urban areas to rural Pennsylvania. Limited human services and recreation, predominance of politically conservative climates, and homogeneous populations were among the factors that, for example, required changes in recruitment of families for that part of the intervention design. In addition, Gager and Elias (1997) found that implementing school-based substance abuse and competence enhancement programs in high-risk versus low-risk neighborhood schools led to differential effectiveness. Such factors as having an ongoing program coordinator or committee, ongoing training, and explicit linkage of programs to the goals and mission of schools were markers of "resilient" programs (those that were effective under the most difficult circumstances).

## EVIDENCE FOR THE EFFECTIVENESS OF PREVENTION AND PROMOTION PROGRAMS

In this section, we present two approaches to generalizing across a broad range of action research studies. The first, meta-analysis, represents a quantitative approach. The second, the best practices approach, is more qualitative (recall this distinction from chap. 4).

### Meta-Analyses of Prevention Programs

*Meta-analysis* compares statistical findings of all quantitative studies done on a given topic that meet certain methodological criteria (e.g., comparison of program and control groups in randomized field experiments, all of which used similar dependent variables). A statistical formula is applied to the measured differences between groups in each study, resulting in a statistical estimate of the size of the effect of that intervention on the chosen outcomes (dependent variables). Comparison of effect sizes for all similar studies yields an estimate of the effect of similar interventions (e.g., primary prevention programs) on outcomes. Although not without controversy (e.g., Trickett, 1997; Weissberg & Bell, 1997), meta-analysis is one useful tool for broad comparisons.

Durlak and Wells (1997) used meta-analysis to examine 177 primary prevention programs directed at children and adolescents. The programs dated from 1953 to 1991, with many in the 1970s. This is a very broad focus, yet provides a useful overview. The authors looked at both person and environment (e.g., school) level interventions, and both high-risk selected ("high-risk") and universal target populations (Mrazek & Haggerty, 1994). Their conclusions, which have many qualifiers that are best read in the original study, are that from 59% to 82% of participants in a primary prevention program surpassed the average performance of those in control groups. This indicates clear superiority of prevention groups to controls. In terms of outcomes, many programs both reduced problem behaviors and increased competencies.

Meta-analyses also have the value of revealing gaps and strengths in the literature. As an example of the former, there were virtually no health promotion programs directed toward high school students. Regarding strengths, consistently positive effects were found to result from programs that helped people cope with significant life transitions, such as first-time motherhood, children of divorce, school entry or transition, children dealing with stressful medical and dental procedures, and creating supports for parenting (Johnson & Breckinridge, 1982).

Durlak and Wells (1998) also applied the meta-analysis model to secondary prevention programs delivered in situations where children showed early signs of difficulty. Such signs include persistent shyness or withdrawal, early academic problems (especially in reading), and antisocial behavior. The evidence showed clearly that the average participant in these programs was better off than 70% of comparable peers who did not receive similar intervention.

Cognitive–behavioral approaches, often involving social problem-solving strategies, appeared most effective, especially in terms of long-term effects. Nonbehavioral programs had little preventive effect. Positive effects occurred most easily with children in Piaget's preoperational stage (approximately ages 3–7) and then with children in formal operations (beginning at age 12); lesser benefits accrued to children in concrete operations (ages 8–11).

Children with externalizing problems responded relatively well to early intervention efforts. This is important because such children, once they progress to diagnosed conduct or oppositional disorder, are notoriously difficult to treat. This finding indicates the utility of primary and secondary prevention in such areas as bullying and fighting and promoting positive group participation and friendship skills.

## Best Practices in Promoting Social–Emotional Learning

The second approach to comparing prevention/promotion programs is termed the *best practices* approach. It involves studying a specific type of program that has been empirically shown to be effective across multiple settings and gleaning from further studies of those settings the procedures that effective programs of that type have in common. Doing this effectively requires site visits and qualitative studies (see chap. 4) that are much more detailed than brief journal articles. Here, we present a specific example of this kind of study based on school-based prevention and promotion programs.

Action researchers and others in the field of prevention of problems behaviors and promotion of social–emotional competence joined in 1995 to establish the Collaborative to Advance Social and Emotional Learning (CASEL). Its mission is to increase awareness of educators, trainers of school-based personnel, the scientific community, policy makers, and the public about the need for, and the effects of, systematic efforts to promote the social and emotional competencies of children and adolescents. These competencies are also termed *emotional intelligence* (Goleman, 1995). CASEL also facilitates effective implementation, ongoing evaluation, and refinement of comprehensive programs in social and emotional learning throughout all school grade levels. Nine action-researchers with many years of experience in the field created a document reflecting their consensus on how best to conduct these programs in schools: "Promoting Social and Emotional Learning: Guidelines for Educators" (Elias et al., 1997). It exemplifies the best practices approach.

These authors put best practices for school-based promotion of social–emotional learning in the form of guidelines for program development, implementation, and evaluation. These guidelines grew out of a consensus of authors who reviewed programs that met at least two of these criteria at the time of writing: (a) is supported by the best available research evidence; (b) having existed in practice in the schools for multiple years as part of the normal service system of school, not as a grant-funded or demonstration project; and (c) having received recognition by many practitioners as a theoretically sound and practically effective approach.

***Guidelines for Program Development***   The Guidelines cover a variety of ecological contexts: classrooms, school buildings, and school districts. Programs featured in the book include some by community psychologists (e.g., ICPS; SDM/SPS; Primary Mental Health Project) and others that community psychologists would be proud to claim (School Development Program; Responsive Classroom; Second Step; Raising Healthy Children; Success for Life; Elias et al., 1997). Noteworthy is that these programs cross all ecological levels and grade levels.

Here are 4 of the 39 Guidelines, selected because they are points that are addressing aspects of schools that are clearly recognizable, make a great deal of common sense, and yet tend not to be followed rigorously in everyday practice:

Guideline #1:

Educators at all levels (elementary, middle, and high school) need explicit plans to help students become knowledgeable, responsible, and caring. Efforts are needed to build and reinforce skills in four major domains of social and emotional learning:

    a. Life Skills and Social Competencies

    b. Health Promotion and Problem Behavior Prevention Skills

    c. Coping Skills, Conflict Resolution, and Social Support

    d. Positive, Contributory Service

Guideline #17:

A caring, supportive, and challenging classroom and school climate is most conducive to effective social and emotional teaching and learning.

Guideline #31:

Long-lasting social and emotional learning programs are highly visible and recognized. These programs act "proud" and are not "snuck in" or carried out on unofficially borrowed time. They do not act in opposition to school or district goals, but rather are integral to these goals.

Guideline #36:

Effective social and emotional learning programs are monitored and evaluated regularly using systematic procedures and multiple indicators.

Think about the schools you have been a part of. Have they been places in which you have felt that social and emotional learning—the skills you need to better handle everyday life issues and to grow as a person—were given clear attention? Did you experience all aspects of Guideline #1? At which grade level(s)? Did you feel that year in and year out, your schools met Guideline #17? Were prevention programs publicized in your school from year to year or was there a big push for a single year program? Did you participate in any kind of evaluation of prevention programs in your school, as indicated by #36?

Something uncovered in site visits to the Success for Life Program illustrates aspects of best practice that go beyond formal listings in curricula and explicit, standardized guidelines. Members of all high school athletic teams at LaSalle High School in Providence, Rhode Island must create and agree to a set of personal goals, team goals, and school goals. These are monitored by athletic staff and counselors. Site visitors learned that two high school star football players blew off their community service project, which led to their suspension from the subsequent game for violating their school goals. There was a community outcry, reflecting the role of high school sports in many American neighborhoods. However, the school administration stuck to their rules, and the players sat. What followed was an even louder outpouring of acclaim for the school, from community residents, business owners, and many parents. The school was praised for articulating and maintaining a set of values.

Remarkably, what might appear to most as common sense is, in reality, an act of courage on the part of school administrators, given the normative context that has been set up in most communities. School sports often is given high priority and sometimes is a considerable source of community pride, identity, and rivalry. When the values of school sports and school rules clash, it becomes a defining moment for the school and the community. Interestingly, LaSalle's educators were clear on their priorities. What they did not count on was the extent to which others in the community shared their views.

## EMERGING AREAS FOR PREVENTION/PROMOTION

The areas of prevention/promotion focus that we have discussed show no signs of diminished interest or application for the future. However, four areas seem to be emerging as new foci for community psychology's preventive efforts in upcoming years, possibly decades.

### Aging Citizens

Community psychologists have been relatively inattentive to the needs of the elderly and to preventing problems associated with aging. Nevertheless, there is some consensus that prevention efforts for this population must (a) be a source of empowerment, (b) foster active participation by aging citizens, and (c) address living arrangements and communities. Austin Groups for the Elderly (Smith, 1992) found that by locating an array of services for the elderly in one place, not only were costs savings made but greater coordination of care took place and many problems were prevented that otherwise would have persisted. Further, the types of services included child care, eldercare, exercise groups, legal services, transportation, and advocacy, all of which helped bring the elderly into contact with others and foster a continuing sense for relatedness and connectedness. L. A. Bond, Cutler, and Grams (1995) provided additional information on working with this population.

## Preventing Youth and School Violence

During the final writing of this book, violent incidents came to the forefront in the schools. A tragic mass shooting of students at Columbine High School in Colorado attracted intense media attention while continuing a trend of shootings in schools in many different communities. There is rising concern about safety, violence, and how youth are being prepared for adult roles.

Responses to these problems by public officials and educators initially focused on security measures and individual personality predictors of violence. However, the latter have been difficult to identify and apply, especially as a preventive method. Moreover, CASEL (see above) and other groups have maintained that violence needs to be addressed organizationally and is an outcome of failing to build promotion of social and emotional (or emotional intelligence) competencies into the ecology of schools (Elias, 1997) and homes (Elias, Tobias, & Friedlander, 1994). Accordingly, community psychologists are among those urging an examination of how certain schools are organized so that their levels of violence and vandalism are lower than those of other schools. The following conditions have been identified as conducive to low rates of school violence (Felner & Adan, 1988; Hawkins & Lam, 1987; I. S. Levine & Zimmerman, 1996; Pepler & Slaby, 1994; Wager, 1993):

1. School courses are perceived as having a high degree of relevance.
2. School rules and structures allow students some control over what happens to them at school.
3. School discipline policies are viewed as firm, fair, clear, and consistently enforced.
4. There is a rational reward structure in the school that recognizes students for their achievement.
5. There is a strong and effective school governance, with a consistent structure of order and strong principal leadership.
6. Ways are found to decrease the impersonality of the school and increase the amount of continuing positive contact between students and teachers.
7. The curriculum includes education in social and emotional competencies. These include self-control, group participation and social awareness skills, and cognitive strategies for thinking through everyday problems and decisions, as well as for managing difficult choices when under stress.

These individual skills and setting characteristics are the foci of many prevention/promotion programs we have described in this chapter. When fortified by programs that address these skills comprehensively and developmentally, children are able to be effective learners and, most importantly, participating citizens in the many communities of which they are a part. School violence can be reduced as children find they have the social and life skills to participate in prosocial, competent communities. However, it is essential that all students are given the opportunity for such participation and are not marginalized or threatened physically or psychologically (Cottrell, 1976; Coudroglou, 1996; Elias et al., 1997).

## Prevention Policy and Advocacy

Addressing youth and school violence at community and national levels leads to a third emerging area for prevention/promotion: policy and advocacy. These concern efforts to create resources for prevention programs, or changes in laws or other policies that can have preventive effects. The following represent examples of prevention policy and advocacy:

- serving as a Congressional staff member for social and health issues, or working with legislative or executive branches of government on creation of policy positions, laws, and regulations relating to prevention issues (e.g., Rickel & Becker, 1997)
- research, writing, and giving testimony regarding effective prevention/promotion interventions (e.g., Jason, 1998; see also chap. 13 of this text)
- staff positions or consulting with state-level human services, mental health, children and youth, and prevention services departments
- public policy staff and legislative liaison positions with the American Psychological Association or other professional organizations
- staff or board positions in advocacy organizations such as the National Mental Health Association, World Mental Health Association, World Health Organization, Children's Defense Fund, or National Association of Child Advocacy Organizations

In addition, community psychologists continue to be authors of important works related to public policy in such issues as media and violence (Jason & Hanaway, 1997) and children's rights (Melton, 1991; Rickel & Becker, 1997).

Advocacy is also involved when a community psychologist sits on the board of a local school district or agency and makes his or her perspective known in the context of ongoing meetings. When this occurs, community psychology might remain invisible to the groups involved, although its principles will be influential. For example, the primary author of this chapter, in his capacity as member of the Board of Trustees for the Association for Children of New Jersey, was able to raise issues related to the need for preventive considerations and strengths-oriented programs as part of welfare reform decisions. The latter point was especially important: Policy makers had not realized that their reforms would do little to change the cycling of people into services systems, especially those who were finding their way there through poor academic skills, inadequate workplace skills, difficulties in self-control and self-regulation, and substance abuse.

In another context, the same author was able to invoke a community psychology approach to religious school education, which had been predominantly viewed in person-centered terms. The well-known phrase, "It takes a village to raise a child," was invoked with an appropriate cultural modification, "It takes a Kehilla to raise a mensch" and then supplemented with some ecological–developmental considerations: "and it requires everyone to do so with integrity and collaboration over a period of many years." This perspective helped shift how religious school education was conceptualized and carried out at the local level and beyond (Kress & Elias, 2000).

In chapter 13, we discuss in detail the dynamics of community and social change, including policy research and advocacy.

## *Implementation of Prevention/Promotion Programs*

A final emerging area for research and action concerns the actual implementation of prevention/promotion initiatives in local contexts. As we have noted throughout this chapter, ideas and approaches may work very well in one organization, locality, culture or other context, yet not be applicable in another. Interventions identified as effective by empirical research in multiple settings, even when backed by meta-analytic findings or best practices, must be adapted to the "local and particular" dynamics and resources of each setting. As they develop more opportunities and applications for prevention, community psychologists and other prevention advocates are increasingly learning about the importance of carefully considering implementation plans in context. That is the focus of chapter 11.

## CHAPTER SUMMARY

**1.** The literature on prevention and promotion is constantly growing. The most reliable conclusions can be gleaned from programs that have been in operation for a number of years and whose effectiveness has been studied empirically.

**2.** Person-centered prevention and promotion programs focus on change in individuals and microsystems, chiefly families. We described a selection of programs for early childhood, middle childhood, adolescence, and adulthood. These often focus on teaching social–emotional competence or skills for coping, sometimes on social support.

**3.** Other prevention/promotion approaches focus on changing organizations, localities, and macrosystems. Some focus on organizational settings such as schools and workplaces, seeking to change the "climate" and social norms of these settings. Others focus on citizens and organizations in localities working together to address prevention/promotion and on policies (such as laws) and programs that have preventive effects in macrosystems.

**4.** Context, the ecology of a particular culture, population, community, or setting is crucial for the effectiveness of prevention/promotion efforts. Some programs that we had described in this chapter are effective in some cultures or nations but are not considered needed or feasible in others. Even within a nation, differences in programs are necessary in different settings or communities.

**5.** The question of the effectiveness of prevention and promotion efforts was addressed through quantitative and qualitative approaches. Meta-analysis is a quantitative way of summarizing vast amounts of literature systematically. It also provides a way to assess interventions across investigators and contexts and shows where gaps in literature exist. Examples of meta-analyses for primary and secondary prevention were presented.

**6.** Best practices represents a qualitative approach to understanding the effectiveness of prevention and promotion interventions. We illustrated it through the work of the Collaborative to Advance Social and Emotional Learning (CASEL). Some of CASEL's guidelines for carrying out school-based programs were highlighted.

**7.** Areas in which the potential for future prevention/promotion research and action are particularly exciting include aging, youth and school violence in the schools, prevention policy and advocacy, and implementation of prevention/promotion programs.

# BRIEF EXERCISES

**1.** Which prevention/promotion program described in this chapter was most interesting or appealing to you? Why?

In what settings or communities or cultures might it work best? Why? In which might it not be effective? Why?

**2.** Design a prevention or promotion program.

- Choose a target population (e.g., by age, or those who share the same recent stressor or are in the same setting, or some other similarity).
- Choose a goal: a problem to prevent and/or competence to promote.
- Decide whether your program is better termed primary or secondary prevention.
- You may wish to focus on a setting for your program with which you are familiar, such as middle schools, a workplace, or your university. (Your aims may not involve a single setting, e.g., a program for children of recently divorced parents).
- Describe the specific methods your program would use to accomplish your goal and how these are related to the problem being prevented or competence being promoted.
- Describe the connection between your program and the concepts of community psychology, in this or previous chapters. Especially show similarities with the prevention/promotion programs described in this chapter.
- Suggest a way to measure or otherwise evaluate the effectiveness of your program.

**3.** Imagine yourself as a board member for a local school. Which program(s) described in this chapter would you recommend be incorporated into the school curriculum and/or services (if necessary spending money from the budget to do so)? Why?

**4.** Imagine yourself as a local government official in your community. Which program(s) described in this chapter would you recommend be developed in your community (if necessary spending tax money to do so)? Why?

**5.** In this chapter, we distinguished between quantitative (e.g., meta-analysis) and qualitative (e.g., best practices) methods of determining the effects of prevention/promotion programs. In chapter 9 we discussed the Institute of Medicine (IOM) report on mental health prevention. That report identified effective programs, which were chosen on the following basis: (a) top priority to those shown effective in multiple randomized controlled experimental trials (termed *field experiments* in chap. 4), (b) second priority to those with at least one randomized controlled trial, (c) lesser priority to those studied with other designs, and (d) least priority to those suggested by respected authorities, based on clinical experience, descriptive studies, prior service delivery programs, or reports by expert committees (i.e., evidence that often appears in best practices studies; Mrazek & Haggerty, 1994, p. 418).

The impact of this kind of prioritization is well worth thinking through. Consider these questions:

- What kinds of programs are likely to be considered most valid by the IOM criteria? Who would have the resources to develop them?

- Is there a way in which seeking to have the scientific precision of a randomized controlled trial or field experiment might shape the nature of the prevention program that one is planning?
- Do you agree that one properly controlled randomized trial is more valid than a series of descriptive or qualitative studies of service delivery programs in actual practice over a series of years?
- What is your view of what should be viewed as adequate "evidence" that a prevention program is successful?

You learned from chapters 3 and 4 (and will see again in chap. 14) that community psychologists have learned that there are many ways of construing "research evidence," and that evidence depends in part on the context and purpose of study.

**6.** In their meta-analysis of secondary prevention programs, Durlak and Wells (1998) found greater effectiveness of programs with preoperational-aged children (generally children roughly aged 3–7 years), and then with children in formal operations (beginning typically around age 12); least benefits appear to accrue to children in concrete operations (roughly ages 8–11). What about children's cognitive development, school structure or social regularities, or family and neighborhood factors might account for this? (Remember that these are secondary prevention programs, for children who are already experiencing some problems, although not a diagnosable mental disorder.) What changes might you recommend in programs for children aged 8–11 to make them more effective?

# RECOMMENDED READINGS

Albee, G., & Gullotta, T. (Eds.). (1997). *Primary prevention works.* Thousand Oaks, CA: Sage.
  A recent review of exemplary prevention/promotion programs across the lifespan. Features the latest findings from programs honored with the Lela Rowland Award by the National Mental Health Association. Contains descriptions of program goals, processes and practices as well as evidence of effectiveness.

Mrazek, P., & Haggerty, R. (1994). *Reducing risks for mental disorders: Frontiers for preventive intervention research.* Washington, DC: National Academy Press. ["The IOM Report."]
  Contains extensive reviews of prevention research and programs and proposes the distinction among universal, selected, and indicated prevention approaches and between prevention and mental health promotion. Emphasizes prevention of specific disorders such as conduct disorder and substance abuse.

Price, R., Cowen, E., Lorion, R., & Ramos-McKay, J. (Eds.). (1988). *Fourteen ounces of prevention.* Washington, DC: American Psychological Association.
  Descriptions of exemplary programs chosen in 1988 as the best, empirically verified, enduring examples of prevention across the life span. Not as recent as *Primary Prevention Works,* but contains chapters on exemplary programs not covered in the later volume.

Prilleltensky, I., & Laurendeau, M. (Eds.). (1994). Prevention: Focus on children and youth [Special Issue]. *Canadian Journal of Community Mental Health, 13*(2).
  Presents prevention/promotion innovations and issues in Canada. The editors' macrolevel perspective highlights the role of government, social policy, societal norms, and citizen participation in perpetuating and preventing social problems.

Weissberg, R., Gullotta, T., Hampton, R., Ryan, B., & Adams, G. (Eds.). (1997a). *Enhancing children's wellness.* Thousand Oaks, CA: Sage.

Weissberg, R., Gullotta, T., Hampton, R., Ryan, B., & Adams, G. (Eds.). (1997b). *Establishing preventive services.* Thousand Oaks, CA: Sage.

> This two-part series represents the "Healthy Children 2010" report. *Enhancing Children's Wellness* provides perspectives from leaders in the prevention/promotion field. *Establishing Preventive Services* focuses on policy and practices to improve the health of U.S. children by 2010.

### Guide for Action

Barton, H., Hopkins, K., McElhaney, S., Heigel, J., & Salassi, A. (1995). *Getting started: The NMHA directory of model programs to prevent mental disorders and promote mental health.* Alexandria, VA: National Mental Health Association.

> A practical resource for program development. Describes implementation, evaluation, and dissemination for 39 exemplary programs. Covers more programs, with briefer entries more focused on "how to" ideas than *Fourteen Ounces* and *Primary Prevention Works.* "How to" guides for planning and implementing community change initiatives, including prevention/promotion, are also listed after chapters 11 and 13.

### International Perspectives

Albee, G. W., Bond, L. A., & Monsey, T. (1992). *Improving children's lives: Global perspectives on prevention* (Volume XIV of the *Primary prevention of psychopathology* series). Thousand Oaks, CA: Sage.

> Researchers, practitioners, policy makers, and educators from around the world discuss their priorities in the area of prevention and the approaches, obstacles, and solutions they have identified.

World Health Organization, Division of Mental Health. *Skills for Life* [Newsletter.] Geneva, Switzerland: Author.

> The World Health Organization (WHO) publishes an outstanding newsletter, highlighting prevention theory, research, and practice. Information can be obtained at the WHO Division of Mental Health, CH-1211 Geneva 27, Switzerland. Fax number: 022-791-4160.

## INFOTRAC KEYWORDS

> *community-based, competence(ies), health, intervention, prevention(ive)(ing), primary prevention, problem solving, promotion(ing), school-based, parent, social-emotional learning, violence.*

## RECOMMENDED WEBSITES

http://nmha.org/children/prevent/index.cfm

> This section of the National Mental Health Association Website is devoted to prevention/promotion. It includes programs for children, youth, and adults. Examples cover the lifespan and include both universal and selected approaches. Includes programs that

are winners of the NMHA Lela Rowland Prevention Award, many created by community psychologists.

http://www.CASEL.org

The Collaborative to Advance Social and Emotional Learning (CASEL) brings together community psychologists and other scientists, educators, policy makers, foundations, and citizens to promote social and emotional learning in children. The CASEL Website is an excellent introduction and linking site to resources for prevention/promotion initiatives in schools, including materials on empirically based, "best practice," SEL programs, SEL and academics, SEL and health, and educator preparation for implementing SEL in schools.

http://www.tc.columbia.edu/academic/psel

The Project for Social and Emotional Learning focuses on teacher, administrator, and special educator preparation to build social and emotional skills.

http://smhp.psych.ucla.edu

The School Mental Health Project at UCLA seeks to enhance the mental health of children through school-based initiatives and fostering school-community collaboration. Their Website is an excellent source of information, publications, and links to various sites related to school policy, programs, and practices.

http://www.eiconsortium.org

This is the Website of the Consortium on Research on Emotional Intelligence in Organizations, a research group that works with organizations to assess and improve emotional intelligence in all kinds of workplaces and sponsors an annual volume reviewing research and application in emotional intelligence.

http://www.esrinternational.org

Educators for Social Responsibility is a source of information on programs related to peacemaking and conflict resolution in all parts of the world.

http://www.communitiesofhope.org

The HOPE Foundation is dedicated to developing programs for communities, schools, and community agencies, and youth organizations related to violence prevention and building youth as resources.

http://www.pavnet.org

The Partnerships Against Violence Network maintains a national online data base of violence prevention strategies for communities, families, and youth.

http://www.NASPWEB.org

This Website of the National Association of School Psychologists includes updated information on school violence.

http://www.un.org/esa/socdev/iyop

This is the United Nations Website on prevention and promotion for people over age 60.

# PREVENTION AND PROMOTION: IMPLEMENTING PROGRAMS

# OPENING EXERCISE: LESSONS LEARNED FROM FAILURE

In *The Path of Most Resistance: Reflections on Lessons Learned from New Futures,* staff of the Annie E. Casey Foundation (1995) described the failure of a program, which cost in excess of $100 million over 5 years, to help 10 mid-sized cities develop and implement plans to prevent problem behaviors in at-risk youth. The cities receiving the grant awards ensured that their plans reflected the best-known work in the literature to date. All plans received extensive review and comment. The level of funding was far more than typically is available for implementing prevention/promotion initiatives. Here is an excerpt from their report:

> At the heart of New Futures was the belief that at-risk youth are beset by multiple challenges and served ineffectively by multiple systems of service delivery. Real changes in aggregate youth outcomes would require fundamental and deep changes in existing institutions and systems. Such an approach would not only serve vulnerable children and families more effectively, but it was also the only way to proceed, given the scarce public resources available for significant additions to existing youth-serving systems.
>
> By challenging communities to design comprehensive systems reforms rather than to add programs, New Futures had embarked on the path of most resistance. . . . Vested interests in current practice, fiscal constraints, and political risks created a constant force capable of minimizing system change. Some parts of the reform agenda threatened the stability of the current system, and others seemed to discount the importance of the good aspects of the system that already existed. . . . True integration at the service-delivery level, we learned, requires unprecedented commitments by school boards, child welfare agencies, and other youth-serving institutions to subordinate their traditional authority over critical functions—including budgeting, staffing, and resource allocation—in favor of collective decision making (Annie E. Casey Foundation, 1995, pp. 1–2).

What lessons can—MUST—we learn from this? What accounts for what happened? Is there any hope in continuing such efforts? Some things that may have occurred to you are these: Money alone will not bring about effective competence promotion and problem prevention efforts, incorporating best practices into one's plans does not ensure success, and, despite the failure of New Futures, many other, often smaller and less-well-funded, prevention efforts succeed.

In fact, community and preventive psychologists have learned a great deal about the art and science of implementing preventive efforts. Bringing good ideas and sound procedures of the kind you read about in Chapters 9 and 10 into high-quality, enduring practice is not impossible. The challenge can be likened to the difference between reviewing for a test in the library and actually taking the test, or the difference between pitching in the bullpen and facing live batters in a stadium with a huge crowd roaring on every pitch. Performance in the "practice" situation does not always match what can be demonstrated under "real world" conditions. See what other examples you can think of in which you have noticed a difference in performance under "real world" and more "protected" conditions. How could those differences be bridged or overcome? Now, you can better see why this chapter is an important part of community psychology's understanding of prevention and promotion.

Community psychology has been at the forefront of looking at the fascinating and important question of what happens when community brings a community action program into a new setting—whether the goals are promoting competence, preventing problems, treating existing difficulties, or a combination of these. This is a topic that allows one to integrate personality theory, learning theory, social psychology, environmental psychology, community mental health, public health, health psychology, and, of course, community psychology. For those whose interests are in action research, the cycle of action and studying to address social issues, the topic of *implementation* represents a crucial frontier between action and research.

## WHAT ARE THE KEY POINTS OF THIS CHAPTER?

In this chapter, we discuss how prevention and promotion initiatives really are complex "operator-dependent innovations." That is a fancy way of saying that implementing them consistently and with high quality is difficult because they are greatly influenced by critical decisions made by the people who carry them out. First, we outline why implementation of prevention/promotion interventions is important. Second, drawing on available research, we ask whether available effective prevention/promotion interventions are widely implemented effectively, and find the answer is often "no." Third, we describe some reasons why this is so, mainly concerning organizational and setting ecological context. Fourth, we present an "implementation equation" that summarizes the elements of effectively implemented programs and their relationship to setting constraints and resources. Fifth, we outline how this equation and related concepts of action research can be applied to prevention/promotion programs. Sixth, proposing an analogy to a conductor and orchestra, we present a conductor's guide to implementation, and illustrate it with a description of the 17-year process of implementation of one prevention/promotion program. We conclude with thoughts about the current and future importance of attending to implementation issues in prevention/promotion.

## WHAT REALLY HAPPENS WHEN PREVENTION/PROMOTION IS CARRIED OUT IN COMMUNITIES?

> "What is seen often is not real;
> what is real often is not seen."

How does this saying apply to prevention and promotion initiatives? Articles in research journals devoted to these topics describe well-funded demonstration projects, involving committed and well-trained staff, occurring in settings that value innovation, supported with a variety of resources, and studied in detail by program evaluation researchers. The unseen is what happens in community contexts: classrooms, Head Start centers, after school youth groups, workplaces, senior citizen programs, community-based drug abuse prevention coalitions, and other settings where there is rarely an experimental design in place and no one is available to chronicle what actually is happening towards reaching prevention/promotion goals.

What else does the saying imply? What does it say to those who want to bring programs into their home settings? From a community psychology perspective, it is important that there be an ecological match, or fit, between the context in which a program has been demonstrated and the context of its future application. Programs developed and studied under conditions of heavy funding, motivation, and resources rarely find their future environments to be similarly endowed. As a result, there are many failures to replicate "successful" efforts reported in the literature.

Yet, there are local settings that contain programs that might be quite valuable in other places. However, documentation of how these programs operate may be lacking, inadequate, or not widely distributed. In the previous chapters, we reviewed various types of prevention/promotion programs with sound empirical evidence for their effectiveness. In this chapter, we describe ways to close the gap between rhetoric and reality, to move from images of what is possible held out in journal articles, demonstration projects, and well-funded program initiatives toward what will endure in the day-to-day grind of everyday settings such as those in your neighborhood, settings that too often have limited resources.

These issues are not mere technicalities; they are a significant matter of public health and quality of community life. They are as essential for treatment as for prevention/promotion. Relevant data are available from a mid-decade review of progress toward achieving national health objectives for youth by the year 2000 (Fleming, 1995) and Kids Count (1996), which monitors indices of well-being among youth in each of the 50 states. Widespread progress has not been made across key areas such as tobacco/alcohol/other drug use, mental health and mental disorders, violent and abusive behavior, sexually transmitted diseases, and child protective services. Trends suggest that ever more youth are being caught in the grips of poverty and dangerous environments in their schools and communities. What can community psychology do to make sure that what we know about prevention/promotion is actually used in communities?

# HAVE PREVENTION/PROMOTION INNOVATIONS BEEN WIDELY ADOPTED?

The challenges for implementing prevention and promotion approaches are illustrated by a recent study of the operation of such approaches in schools. As you learned in chapter 10, the evidence is clear that school-based prevention/promotion innovations can provide children with skills, supportive environments, and positive life opportunities that lessen their risk for a variety of health-compromising actions. Have these programs been implemented widely or effectively in schools?

## The School Intervention Implementation Study (SIIS)

The School Intervention Implementation Study (SIIS) emerged from the realization that there has been little examination of the nature and impact of the dissemination of prevention/promotion programs. The SIIS sought to learn what happens when programs developed under carefully controlled conditions are placed into the schools, typically with fewer resources and without systematic evaluation.

Surveys were sent to the approximately 550 operating school districts in New Jersey, a state that can provide an indication of trends in other parts of the country (Elias, Gager, & Hancock, 1993). New Jersey has metropolitan areas, various types of suburbs, significant rural areas, and shoreline districts. Further, few states in the United States have so many school districts. There exists a variety of district organizational arrangements and styles that covers the range of what can be found nationally. Finally, New Jersey is a national leader in mandated prevention programs, particularly on substance abuse prevention and AIDS prevention. Thus, the findings from the SIIS were likely to portray the state of the art as contained in the more progressive states, and provide valuable lessons for states that are following down the path of increasing mandated preventive and competence promotion programs. The SIIS overall response rate was 65%, highly satisfactory for a study of this kind and scope.

Although the SIIS survey revealed many programs in operation across New Jersey, there was little consistency in their implementation. The vast majority of districts are doing "something" related to the prevention of substance abuse and the promotion of social competence. However, what is taking place is not systematic. In spite of mandates and encouragement for programming from kindergarten to 12th grade, only 10% of the districts have a program running throughout the elementary years, 6% have a program throughout middle school, and 12% throughout high school. One third of the districts had at least four grade levels that received no prevention programming. Children receive little continuity in prevention programming within or across communities, and there appears to be an inexplicable neglect of programs for children classified as needing special-education services. Further, the programs that are used are not necessarily those supported by a track record of empirical evidence for success, or even a documented history of effective use and positive impact in districts similar to those in which they are being carried out locally. One surprise: Even in districts where well-supported programs were implemented under favorable conditions, instances of implementation success were matched by instances of failure. Finally, even the most promising programs showed an uneven record of being adopted.

Goleman (1998) found similar trends in many workplaces. In his study of hotels, police departments, manufacturing plants, teaching hospitals, and other work settings, programs to strengthen employees' social and emotional well-being were often successful in one setting but not in another. Best practices for implementing programs often were not recognized or followed. Therefore, understanding implementation of innovations, and how to bring "best practices" into common practice, is becoming central to a prevention/ promotion perspective.

## An Action-Research Perspective on Program Development

There is much consensus that the guiding approach for the operation of social competence promotion and problem behavior prevention programs in school and community settings should be Lewin's concept of *action research* (see chap. 3 and the concept of experimental social innovation in chap. 4). Action research involves the idea of testing theories and methods by putting them into practice, evaluating their impact, and using the results to refine future theory, method, and practice. Action research is seen as involving ongoing cycles of problem analysis, innovation (intervention) design, field trials, and innovation diffusion (dissemination), leading to ever more precise variations and targeting of programs to recipient populations and settings (Price & Smith, 1985). The entire model is cyclical because ongoing monitoring of problem areas will yield information as to whether or not the program is having a significant impact, with which populations, and in which settings. Such information then leads to the development of refined or new problem statements, which in turn inspire further cycles of prevention research, development, and evaluation directed toward further problem reduction and health and competence promotion (Mrazek & Haggerty, 1994; see also chap. 14).

Rossi (1978) addressed the issue of how a program evolves from its beginnings to having real public health impact. He believed the central question to understand is how the program operates when carried out by agents other than the developers. That issue represents the core of this chapter. Combining his work with a community psychology perspective, four stages of program development and implementation can be identified on the path toward having a policy impact. This process of going from original development of an innovation to its widespread implementation is sometimes referred to as *scaling up* (Schorr, 1997).

1. *Experimental:* A program demonstrates its effectiveness under small-scale, optimal, highly controlled conditions, compared to a control group.

2. *Technological:* A program demonstrates effectiveness under real-world conditions, similar to the conditions for which it is eventually intended, but still under the guidance of its developers.

3. *Diffusional:* A program is adopted by other organizations or communities and demonstrates effectiveness under real-world conditions when not under the direct scrutiny and guidance of its developers.

4. *Widespread implementation:* From a community psychology perspective, progress through the diffusional stage brings the program to one or a few communities only. Implementation becomes widespread when a program continues to show its effectiveness in a wide variety of settings and is transferred from its developers to new implementers, who in turn conduct further program diffusion. The program has widespread impact on communities and society only when this final stage occurs.

The challenge of dissemination can be concretized by efforts to reform schools in the United States. A developer of innovative science education programs at the American Association for the Advancement of Science noted that he gets calls, requests, letters, and the like from all over the country from people who are excited about the work of his innovative project and want his help to implement it in their communities. He tells them he can't. Why? Because "There are more of you than there are of us." (Rutherford in Olson, 1994, p.43).

Even those who have created successful demonstration models of school reform and community development, such as Sizer (Coalition of Essential Schools); Slavin (Success for All); Pinnell (Reading Recovery); Levin (Accelerated Schools Project); Dryfoos (Full Service Schools); Comer (School Development Program); Wandersman, Chavis, and Florin (Block Booster and Center for Substance Abuse Prevention Coalition-Building Programs); and Wolff (Community Partners), have achieved some measure of success in a limited number of settings but have not solved the problem of how to bring their work to the public more broadly. Similar tales of woe have been told by those working in the mental health field (Schorr, 1988).

From a community psychology perspective, then, one good way to implement and disseminate prevention/promotion activities is to focus on working with existing settings to help them become more innovative. When this happens, settings become dedicated to the continuous improvement of their impact on individual well-being. That leads to adopting innovative practices in ways that are effective in that setting. This is especially true with the KISS settings you learned about in chapter 9. It has been argued that creating such organizational cultures, particularly in the schools, is among the most powerful ways to build and maintain competence in children and adolescents and serve the goal of prevention (Elias & Clabby, 1992).

## WHY HAVE PREVENTION/PROMOTION INNOVATIONS NOT BEEN WIDELY ADOPTED?

The SIIS and Goleman (1998) studies cited earlier indicate that the effectiveness of prevention/promotion programs and even their very nature have been very inconsistent. Why? The answers have to do with *context,* the ecological characteristics of each setting. The qualities of settings that we described in chapter 5, the aspects of diversity in chapter 6, the nature of a community in chapter 7, and other factors yet to be understood greatly influence the nature and impact of prevention/promotion initiatives.

Let's think of settings in terms of Kelly's (1970) ecological concepts, for instance (recall these from chap. 5). Every setting has a unique set of relationships of *interdependence* among its members. In one workplace, for instance, the supervisors may be more approachable and informal with employees, which may help generate employee participation in a workplace exercise program or in group meetings designed to foster teamwork. In a different setting, the same programs may fall flat because the supervisors and line staff are more formal and distant.

Further, every setting has a set of tangible and intangible *resources* that are cycled among its members. A high school may have an English teacher whose interpersonal skills and trustworthiness lead many students to seek her advice. She may be the ideal choice for leading a suicide or drug abuse prevention program, whereas in another setting it may be the soccer coach or even someone from outside the school. These persons may put their stamp on the program, making it different from a program elsewhere that looks the same on paper. Resources may also include money, level of support from parents or administrators, and even whether the room where the program occurs is appropriate for the activity.

Prevention/promotion innovations inevitably are influenced by the ways in which individuals naturally *adapt* to their settings. The culture and customs of an urban school mainly attended by students of Caribbean ancestry, for instance, will differ from those in a European American suburb. Thus, the interpersonal skills and adaptive behaviors will also be different, and any prevention/promotion innovation must recognize and address these.

Finally, Kelly's (1970) principle of *succession* means that a setting has a history, representing both continuity and change over time. An effective prevention/promotion innovation must address that history, respecting the culture of the setting while offering new directions for its development. Taken as a whole, Kelly's concepts suggest many issues for prevention/promotion practitioners to consider when transferring an effective, innovative program to a new setting. In the next section, we elaborate these issues.

# SEVEN CHARACTERISTICS OF PREVENTION/PROMOTION INNOVATIONS IN HOST SETTINGS

In Table 11.1, we have listed seven characteristics of prevention/promotion program innovations in terms of their ecological relationship to a host setting that adopts the innovation. These characteristics can be obstacles to dissemination or transfer of an effective program from one setting to another. When planners of an innovation address these issues, their efforts are much more likely to be effective.

***Operator Dependent***    Rossi (1978) coined this term to refer to the fact that innovation and social change rely on human beings as the means of change. Clinical trials of a new medication use the same substance, in standardized dosage and treatment procedure, in every setting tested. The nature of a prevention/promotion program, in contrast, is very dependent on the persons involved in it. For instance, consider a school curriculum intended to lessen student drug use. Teacher/staff attitudes and commitment to the program and their enthusiasm or lack of it play an important role. Student peer leaders or outside speakers may enhance the program impact, depending on how they are selected, trained, and used. Program leaders may use curriculum activities carefully or they may devise their own approach. Support from administration and from parents is also crucial for success. Similar factors affect how corporate or community programs are conducted.

In any psychologically relevant prevention/promotion initiative, the decisions made by program staff and participants are perhaps the single greatest influence on its impact. Those decisions are strongly affected by the relationship between the developer of an innovation and the staff who will implement it (Stolz, 1984).

One aspect of operator dependence is that to be taken seriously, an innovation must mesh with the developmental stage and self-conceptions of the staff who will implement it. Skilled staff in any setting take pride in their craft and view their work with a sense of ownership. To gain their approval, an innovation must fit their values and identity: for instance, a police officer's sense of what police work involves. At the same time, an innovation must also offer something new that increases the staff's effectiveness as they define it. Staff members of different ages, ranks in the organization, or levels of seniority may support or resist an innovation, depending on how they understand their work and roles.

***Context Dependent***    Staff members or operators are not the only humans involved in a prevention/promotion innovation. The participants or recipients of the initiative also influence its impact, as does the social ecology of the setting. In the example of a school-based drug use prevention program mentioned above, student culture and expectations affect the classroom climate and may even undermine any impact of the program. For instance, research indicates that such a program is more likely to be effective with younger adolescents, before drug experimentation or mistrust of adults become more common (Linney, 1990). Thus, developmental stage and self-conception are as important for program participants as for program operators.

Each school, workplace, or community has a mix of ages, genders, races and ethnicities, income levels, and other forms of diversity and personal identity that an innovation must address. These affect the social norms of the setting and the skills and resources its

| TABLE 11.1 | SEVEN CHARACTERISTICS OF PREVENTION/PROMOTION INNOVATIONS IN HOST SETTINGS |
|---|---|

Operator dependent

Context dependent

Fragile, difficult to specify

Core versus adaptive components

Organizationally unbounded

Challenging

Longitudinal

members need to adapt, and therefore the goals of a prevention/promotion innovation. Furthermore, an innovation may draw a different response in a setting with a strong sense of community among its members compared to one without it.

Finally, the program circuits of the setting (Barker, 1968; recall this from chap. 5) constrain any prevention/promotion innovation. Middle and high schools restrict most activities to strictly timed periods, for instance. Neighborhood programs must provide child care and other practical support to meet the needs of their participants.

***Fragile, Difficult to Specify***   As with any means of teaching or social influence, the key elements of a prevention/promotion program may be difficult to specify (Tornatzky & Fleischer, 1986). At first, it is easy to assume that the new curriculum in a school-based initiative or the new policy in a corporation or community is the critical element. But a moment's reflection on our first point above undoes that assumption: Psychological innovations are operator-dependent, not standardized. Yet what aspect of that operator dependence is the key? Is it participant expectations, staff skill or commitment, extent of staff training or supervision, how much time or money is committed by the organization to the program, whether the top leadership makes clear its support, or other factors? Is a committed, energetic staff the key, regardless of what curriculum they use? Is it the use of small-group exercises and discussion, rather than lecture? In one setting, one of these factors may be the key, while another variable is crucial elsewhere. There are often multiple keys to success. This uncertainty makes the program fragile, in the sense that it will assume different forms in different settings, with different effects. It may never be implemented the same way in different settings.

Transferring an effective innovation to a new host setting is, in a sense, impossible (London & MacDuffie, 1985). Operators in the new setting inevitably will make changes in the program to fit their needs, values, and local culture. Indeed, some of these changes are necessary to respect the history and culture of that setting.

In the long run, this can be a strength, because a setting committed to innovation can develop prevention/promotion initiatives that fit its context. However, an innovation that is difficult to specify may leave its operators unsure of their roles and responsibilities at first. That uncertainty may be welcomed by bold personalities and by those who are confident of support from their superiors, but resisted by others who like more structure or who feel unsupported by supervisors.

***Core Versus Adaptive Components*** Developers of prevention/promotion innovations should try to specify the key components of their programs. This is especially important when they attempt to transfer their initiatives to new host settings. Two types of components have been identified. *Core components* are crucial to the identity and effectiveness of the program. *Adaptive components* are not and may be altered to fit the social ecology or practical constraints of the new host setting (Price & Lorion, 1989).

For one school-based innovation, the core aspect may the written curriculum and skills to be taught. For another, it may be that a characteristic method of small-group exercises and discussion is the key and that the written curriculum is an adaptive feature. For some innovations, building social support among program participants is the core feature regardless of how that is done. For other innovations, particularly educational ones, learning skills is the core feature, whereas methods of promoting that learning may be adapted to the setting.

Developers and advocates need to pay considerable attention to how core features are being used by the operators in a new host setting. They also need to help those operators develop their own ways of implementing the adaptive features, to fit the circumstances of the setting. Of course, the more difficult it is to specify the core components (see the section just above), the more difficult this task becomes.

***Organizationally Unbounded*** For many prevention/promotion initiatives, effectiveness means changes in many areas of the host setting or organization (Tornatzky & Fleischer, 1986). The program is not isolated, but connected to many persons and activities of the setting. This is similar to Kelly's (1970) principle of interdependence. For instance, Comer's (1988) approach to improving school climate involves strengthening relationships between teachers, all other staff, students, and parents. Comer (1992) noted that in a middle school using this approach, a new student, whose foot was stepped on by another student, immediately squared off to fight, a behavior expected in his former school. "Hey, man, we don't do that here," he was told by several other students, who succeeded in defusing the tension. That is an organizationally unbounded innovation: It began with strengthening adult–adult and adult–student relationships, yet spread to student–student relationships. Those outcomes may be affected as much by a janitor, secretary, or parent volunteer as by the teachers or administrators. They may include changes in behavior out of class, not just in it.

An effective, organizationally unbounded innovation is a fine thing to have, but difficult to introduce. To members of the host setting, it may seem to lack focus, or to require abrupt changes from everyone all at once. Those who believe that a problem is limited to one area of the organization will resist involvement. For instance, a school may implement a number of innovations to prevent violence in school. Those who believe that violence prevention is solely a disciplinary matter will resist changes in curriculum to teach students skills in conflict resolution, or training of student peer mediators for informal resolution of conflicts. They may say things like "That's the vice-principal's job, not mine," or "Dealing with misbehavior is an adult's job."

***Challenging*** Any innovation is a challenge to a setting. By its nature, it suggests that change is needed. At the same time, that challenge may be understood by staff or program participants as an opportunity for growth, or as an answer to a problem. These perceptions may depend on whether the organization is responding to a crisis and whether the innovation is believed to require change that is difficult or feasible, or abrupt or gradual. Even the language that innovators use may contribute to those perceptions.

If you have studied developmental psychology, you have no doubt encountered Piaget's distinction between *assimilation* and *accommodation* (Flavell, 1963, p. 47). Like individuals in Piaget's theory, organizations also tend to assimilate their experiences to fit their existing ways of thinking if possible. Only if necessary do they accommodate those ways of thinking to incorporate new ideas or practices. Interventions that fail to respect and use the existing culture of a setting—its history, rituals, symbols, and practices—will be rejected or assimilated only partially or in distorted form. A program that is adopted because of pressure from above or outside an organization also is likely to be abandoned as soon as that pressure abates. Innovations that respect organizational culture and that are based on collaboration with stakeholders, can lead to accommodation in organizational thinking and practices, and thus to lasting changes.

Weick (1984) mustered evidence from social and cognitive psychology for the conclusion that when extensive changes are required of humans in organizations, their sense of being threatened rises, as does their resistance to change. When the proposed change seems smaller, the perceived threat is smaller, risks seem tolerable, and opponents are less mobilized. "Small wins" is Weick's (1984) term for limited yet tangible innovations or changes that can establish a record of success and sense of momentum. In such a context, advocates of prevention/promotion must consider their language. If they portray their innovation as a logical outgrowth of the setting's history to date, and as a sensible response to current challenges, resistance is lessened.

When an organization or community believes itself to be in crisis or facing problems that require sweeping change, more challenging innovations may be accepted. Indeed, under those conditions, small wins may be seen as inadequate. However, most innovations take place in a climate less charged by a sense of crisis.

***Longitudinal***    This idea is similar to Kelly's principle of succession. An innovation takes place in a setting with a history and culture. To be effective, it must change that setting in some way (Tornatzky & Fleischer, 1986). To be lasting, it must become part of that history and culture, not dependent on an influential leader or a few staff members, all of whom will eventually leave the setting. It must be *institutionalized*, made a part of the setting's routine functioning. Consider a youth group, a support group for senior citizens, or an formal or informal organization at your college or university. How would it be different if it is run by a new, untrained leader every year versus having a longer term leader who, when she does leave, trains her successor well?

Moreover, any effective prevention/promotion innovation must be repeated or elaborated periodically for effect. One-shot presentations or activities seldom have lasting impact. Teaching a child to read is a multiyear effort, from identifying letters to reading novels (Shriver, 1992). Should it be any surprise that learning social–emotional skills or developing attitudes that limit risky behavior cannot be done quickly?

***Summary***    Prevention/promotion innovations, by their nature, face obstacles to being adopted within organizations and communities. They are dependent on operators, usually staff who must implement the innovation. They also are dependent on the social context and even physical environment in which the innovation takes place. Their key elements may be difficult to specify or explain and fragile or difficult to transfer to new settings.

They challenge organizational thinking and tradition and may generate resistance. They must be sustained over time to be effective.

These qualities represent obstacles for the advocate of a prevention/promotion innovation. Yet they can also be understood as suggesting the presence of resources. The operators and participants on whom a program is dependent represent potential resources for enriching that innovation, if they are approached as partners and their life experiences and culture respected. Resistance to a proposed change may be rooted in loyalty and commitment to the setting or community, a resource that can also be channeled for change. Advocates of prevention/promotion need to understand these challenges, respect their sources, and work with members of a setting or community to overcome them.

# IMPLEMENTING PREVENTION/PROMOTION INITIATIVES WIDELY AND EFFECTIVELY

For an article discussing the challenges of doing effective preventive work in community settings, Kelly (1979b) took his title from a hit song of the 1940s, "Tain't what you do, it's the way you do it." In working to improve community life, means, or how we do things, matter as much as ends or goals. How the implementer of a prevention/promotion effort forms relationships with collaborators and citizens is critical to the success and integrity of those efforts. Our discussion above of prevention/promotion as complex, operator-dependent initiatives suggests some reasons why this is so. Human beings (teachers, nurses, parents, program staff) implement programs. The work of the implementer involves forming relationships with these persons. Implementers must communicate clearly the core program elements that must be faithfully replicated, while also collaborating with those in the host setting to modify adaptive features so that they will "fit" the local and particular qualities of that setting. Moreover, both the intended and unintended effects of the program must be studied, because these are not necessarily going to conform to patterns shown in the original setting in which the program was developed. To paraphrase Kelly (1979b), it's both "what you do" *and* "the way you do it" that matter.

## The Prevention/Promotion Implementation Equation

Thus, the implementer of a prevention/promotion initiative must consider many factors. These can be summarized in the form of an equation, following in the tradition of Albee (1982) and Elias (1987; see chap. 9). The implementation equation (Elias, 1994) summarizes the main parameters that implementers need to consider. It draws on reviews of community psychology practices (e.g., Chavis, 1993; Price, Cowen, Lorion, & Ramos-McKay, 1988; Vincent & Trickett, 1983; Wolff, 1987, 1994). (See Table 11.2).

The equation articulates the notion that the greater the strength of the prevention/promotion program (the sum of the terms in the numerator on the right side of the equation), relative to the constraints of that setting and its resources for implementing the program (in the denominator), the more effective implementation or *praxis* will be. Praxis denotes a certain type of program implementation, linked with community psychology's commitment to participant-conceptualization. It refers to implementation that integrates action, research, and reflection concerning program objectives and actual ongoing pro-

| TABLE 11.2 | PREVENTION/PROMOTION IMPLEMENTATION EQUATION |

$$\text{Praxis}_{D, H, S} = \frac{\text{Grounding} + \text{Theory} + \text{Learning} + \text{Instruction} + \text{Tactics} + \text{Materials} + \text{Contexts}}{\text{Constraints} / \text{Resources}},$$

where

| | | |
|---|---|---|
| Praxis | = | implementation with integration of action, research, and reflection on program objectives and actual ongoing program effects |
| D, H, S | = | the specific *Developmental, Historical,* and *Situational* context of the prevention/promotion program |
| Grounding | = | grounding in the problem and the literature |
| Theory | = | clarity about theoretical perspectives |
| Learning | = | principles of effective learning |
| Instruction | = | appropriate tailored instructional strategies |
| Tactics | = | relevant applicable tactics |
| Materials | = | available user-friendly materials |
| Contexts | = | hospitable organizational contexts |
| Constraints | = | limitations/obstacles to program implementation |
| Resources | = | available resources to support implementation |

gram effects. In the equation, praxis is conceptualized in terms of the *Developmental* levels and concerns of its staff (e.g., both their age-related concerns and their seniority in the setting), *Historical* issues in that setting (e.g., prior experiences with similar innovations), and *Situational* factors salient there. Thus praxis refers to implementation that is at least somewhat different in every setting, responding to the mix of contextual forces there.

The first two terms in the numerator on the right side of the equation are Grounding in the Problem and Literature (*Grounding*) and Clarity About Theoretical Perspectives (*Theory*). These reflect the need for implementers to be grounded not only in past work but also in the conceptual underpinnings of what one is attempting. Whose previous work is a useful guide? What theory or concepts are being drawn upon? What are the implicit values? How closely do these match those of the prospective or current host setting? How similar are previous implementation contexts to the one being considered now?

Have you ever attended a class or workshop on an interesting, timely topic, yet found that it was primarily a lecture, with unclear objectives, poor handouts, delivered without evident caring, and with inadequate time for questions? That experience illustrates the importance of the next four terms in the equation: use of Principles of Effective Learning (*Learning*), Appropriate Tailored Instructional Strategies (*Instruction*), Relevant Applicable Tactics (*Tactics*), and Available User-Friendly Materials (*Materials*). These terms relate specifically to the mechanics of creating change.

Change often involves some kind of education, or reeducation. Much has been learned about techniques for accomplishing this kind of education, although remarkably little of it finds its way into the psychological literature, in part because of traditional research design and publication-related constraints. For even the most sound intervention or "practice" ideas to have a chance of coming to fruition as intended, they must use effective learning principles, such as attending to the amount of information presented and the pace of presentation; strategies that are geared to the audiences, whether adults or children, professionals or novices, or members of particular cultural groups; consonant behavioral tactics, which typically involve active learning and examples and a style that communicates caring; and supportive materials that enhance the learning and give people something to "take home" with them.

The seventh term in the numerator, Hospitable Organizational Contexts (*Contexts*), refers to the readiness of the host setting for an innovation. Price and Lorion (1989) and Van de Ven (1986) emphasized that members of an organization must be ready to accept an innovation, preventive or otherwise. There must be a perception that there is environmental pressure, or at least support, for the innovation, an awareness and acceptance of a problem by the host organization, and a set of attitudes, beliefs, and practices on the part of staff that is compatible with the prevention/promotion effort being proposed. The innovation must be able to find a place within the structures and services already in the host organization, and staff need to be able to imagine how they can relate to it.

The denominator consists of the balance of *Constraints* and *Resources.* The higher the proportion of constraints to resources, the more that strengths in the numerator in the equation are offset. Certain types of resources—funds, facilities, and expertise—must be accessible, and potential implementers will require reassurance that all these supports are in place. Constraints, which include shortages of resources but also such factors as a negative history with prior innovations, poor morale, distrust among different levels within the host setting, unstable hiring or retention practices, and other types of organizational instability, all work against effective implementation. If resources are not in place and/or constraints are considerable, more "groundwork" needs to be done before the innovation is introduced, a process aptly referred to by Sarason (1982) as what happens "before the beginning." Even a cursory look at the implementation equation makes clear the challenge of innovations occurring in contexts of poverty, violence, distrust, and apathy, and the need for much groundwork to be done before embarking upon them with a hope of lasting success.

In summary, change agents interested in prevention must be prepared to immerse themselves into local settings and contexts, to be patient, and to build and extend their ranks through participation, collaboration, and explication (O'Donnell, Tharp, & Wilson, 1993). It is a tenet of the field that the energy and direction for solutions for social problems comes from the local level (Cowen, 1977; Price & Cherniss, 1977; Tolan et al., 1990). As we learned earlier, another tenet is that small wins are very powerful. There is much that can be accomplished in the area of prevention and promotion if innovators are prepared to implement efforts with creativity, tenacity, and integrity.

# ADAPTING PREVENTION/PROMOTION INITIATIVES IN A NEW HOST SETTING

Imagine that you are in charge of adapting a prevention/promotion program for a middle school to reduce the risk of violence among students in school. You use the implementation equation as a guide to planning your approach.

First, you will gather information about the developmental, historical, and situational context of the school and community. What violent acts are of concern here? What violence has occurred here, and what sort of violence occurs regularly (e.g., fights)? Are these linked to other problems, such as hazing or harassment, cliques among students, gang activity, sexual harassment, or drug use? Is violence condoned as a means of resolving conflicts by adults in the school? What are community attitudes about violence? Who else in the community is conducting similar efforts? What have they learned, and how might they be resources? How has the school addressed this issue before, and what were the results?

Second, you look closely at the research and practice literature about the problem and how it has been addressed (Grounding). You identify a program that has been shown to be effective in a demonstration project at a school located near the university where this program was developed. However, the school is different from yours in many ways, including the socioeconomic and racial profile of your students, the makeup of the teaching staff, and the extent of monitoring of program implementation by the developers of the innovation. Following the terms *Theory, Learning, Instruction,* and *Tactics,* you look at the way in which the program is structured. You note positively the presence of a skills-oriented approach, with many interactive exercises, multimedia, and modules to address different cultural subgroups. A trip to an educational materials library shows you that the materials are moderately user-friendly. As you turn your attention to the middle school in which you will work, you note there is a new principal but an experienced staff and an involved, supportive parents' group. Both teachers and parents believe that something should be done to address the issue of violence, although they have a diversity of ideas about how to do that. Overall, resources appear to outweigh constraints, as long as the experienced staff members support an innovation (Hospitable Context). Your question now is, how can you bring the core elements of the program into your school, retaining its effectiveness while adapting it to the local and particular qualities of your setting?

## Stages in the Process of Adapting Innovations to Settings

Historically, concepts of how best to transfer effective educational programs and adapt them to new host settings have evolved through four stages (RMC Research Corporation, 1995), which we summarize below.

*Cookbook:* In the 1970s it was believed that programs had to be thoroughly documented, ideally in "kits" that could be followed precisely, step by step.

*Replication:* Later, model programs were replicated by having staff trained in the methods used by program developers and then bringing these methods back to one's own settings to be carried out as similarly as possible, but with some room for adaptation to the setting.

*Adaptation:* By the late 1980s, models were understood to require adaptation to the unique context of the host site, ideally by having the developer serve as a consultant in making the necessary changes.

*Invention/Innovation:* Recently, models have been seen as sources of ideas and inspiration rather than procedures to replicate or adapt. There is emphasis on creating one's own program, tailored to the unique circumstances at a given time, yet using ideas gleaned from best practices literature. The implementation equation presented above embodies an invention/innovation approach.

Interestingly, these stages parallel some aspects of individual development illuminated by Jean Piaget and Erik Erikson. Like Piaget's stages of cognitive development (sensorimotor, preoperational, concrete, and formal operations), they progress from concrete experience and thinking to use of abstract principles applied to specific problems (e.g., invention/innovation).

In addition, many adult learners who play major roles in implementing prevention/promotion programs (e.g., teachers, parents, health professionals, community leaders) will be in Erikson's stage of generativity in middle adulthood (Erikson, 1950, 1982). At this stage, people have accumulated a certain amount of wisdom. They have "been there, done that." Yet they are open to change if it promises to lead to some positive impact on the next generation, especially something that transcends themselves (S. B. Sarason, 1993). They often will value creating more than following. Thus, development and ownership of an innovation are key elements. There is a special sense of fulfillment in being generative, as opposed to replicating precisely that which others generated. This directly supports RMC's findings, as well as those of the SIIS, and helps explain why so many schools create their own programs out of existing ones rather than adopt programs developed by others. SIIS and other data indicate that the tendency to invent is greater than the tendency to adapt or adopt.

Thus, successfully disseminating a model program involves implementing and institutionalizing it in a new site while capturing the excellence of practice by linking practice to theory. What is transferred to others includes not only procedures but also an understanding of the principles that undergird and comprise that specific example of practice. From this perspective, it is not only necessary to "talk the talk and walk the walk;" it is necessary to "talk the walk," to explicate practice activities in an articulate and heuristic, generative, instructive, and inspiring manner (Elias, 1994; Fullan, 1994), as the implementation equation attempts to delineate. This provides guidance for a journey of development for the prevention/promotion innovation in the new host setting. The destination and general route are indicated, but specific pathways, timing, obstacles and detours, and resting points are to be chosen by members of the setting.

This especially involves the *D, H,* and *S* variables in the implementation equation: *developmental, historical,* and *situational* contexts. Community psychology, with its rich use of ecological and historical concepts, has much to offer to the study and practice of improving the way in which preventive and health-promoting innovations are organized to influence local settings and beyond.

To return to our example above regarding implementing a program to prevent school violence, you might decide to study the context of the school deeply, and to gather the ideas, support and willing involvement of teachers, administrators and school board, parents, and students before implementing a program. You also might want to allow staff and others involved to exercise creative judgment and control over adaptive features of the program, rather than expect them to implement someone else's program in a concrete way. Yet you would also want to identify the core principles of that program, implementing them in ways faithful to its basic premises and that are necessary for it to be effective. How can you balance these expectations? A musical analogy may help.

# A CONDUCTOR'S GUIDE TO ENDURING IMPLEMENTATION

Our favorite analogy for implementing prevention/promotion innovations is that of a musical conductor, especially one who also arranges the orchestration of the music. As a conductor begins to practice the piece with a particular orchestra's musicians, in a particular concert hall, the phrasing, tempo, and dynamics of sound may require adaptation from the music as written. In addition, there are times when, indeed, the music itself has a few gaps in detail. Moreover, performing a piece is more than reading and literally reproducing the written score; performers and conductors must find ways to express the spirit of a composition. Conductors have certain principles that they follow to provide some guidance even as they must make unique and creative decisions. Similarly, there are principles that can guide those who embark on the complex, operator-dependent task of implementing a prevention/promotion initiative (Elias et al., 1997; Kelly et al., 1988; see Table 11.3).

1. *Carry out environmental reconnaissance* (Trickett, 1984). Do not promise or deliver a totally "finished" product. Instead, build the basis for action research by discussing the need for modifying any program adapted from elsewhere, through careful study of its effects in this setting. The guiding principle is to start a pilot using the most basic model that has been used in a setting closest to one's own and subsequently modify it. This can be done through the process of monitoring program implementation procedures, evaluating outcomes, providing feedback to the setting, and making appropriate modifications in the program, a process we discuss further in chapter 14 (see also Elias & Clabby, 1992).

2. *Ensure strong agreement on program goals among all stakeholders.* Teachers, administrators, parents, students, and other important groups are *stakeholders* in a school setting. In a locality, stakeholders include elected or other government officials, representatives of community and private organizations, and interested citizens. Stakeholders need to be included in wide-ranging discussion of the problem to be addressed by a

---

**TABLE 11.3**    CONDUCTOR'S GUIDE TO ORCHESTRATING PREVENTION/PROMOTION INNOVATIONS

---

1. Carry out environmental reconnaissance.

2. Ensure strong agreement on program goals among all stakeholders.

3. Ensure connection of program goals to the core mission of the host setting.

4. Consider a coalition with related local settings.

5. Develop strong, clear leadership.

6. Describe the innovation in simple terms, especially in the beginning.

7. When the program begins, ensure implementation of its core principles and elements.

8. Measure program implementation and attainment of program objectives throughout the operation of the program.

9. Search for unintended effects of the program.

10. Plan for institutionalization of the program in the host setting.

11. Establish external linkages with similar programs in other settings.

---

prevention/promotion initiative. For instance, they need to discuss the nature of violence in your school district and community. They also need to set the goals of an intervention or program. Once goals are agreed upon, participants will have a guide for decisions about choice of model programs, implementation details, measuring program effects, and responding to critics.

3. *Ensure connection of program goals to the core mission of the host setting.* A host setting (e.g., school, worksite) is unlikely to adopt a prevention/promotion initiative unless its members can grasp a clear relationship between its purpose and the mission of their setting. For instance, in a school, prevention/promotion relates to students' needs in the areas of behavior and health, but it also relates to their academic education. A prevention/promotion program such as Interpersonal Cognitive Problem Solving (Shure & Spivack, 1988) that teaches skills for everyday decision making and problem solving also can and should have implications for reasoning skills needed in academic subject areas (Elias et al., 1997).

4. *Consider a coalition with related local settings.* Many prevention/promotion initiatives concern a community problem not limited to a single school or setting. If your aims involve a community-level problem, involve related community settings in the process of goal formation and program development. For a school-based violence prevention program, this might include police, domestic violence agencies, mental health or family guidance agencies, substance abuse treatment facilities, youth centers or recreation programs, local businesses, and religious congregations. Sometimes the stakeholders are more numerous than first appears obvious.

5. *Develop strong, clear leadership.* Hard choices will have to be made and midcourse corrections will be frequent. The effectiveness of a prevention/promotion initiative may require collaboration and sharing of resources among multiple, often competing groups. Strong leadership helps to build collaboration, especially by listening carefully, working slowly for small wins, and keeping participants focused on shared goals.

6. *Describe the innovation in simple terms, especially in the beginning.* Price and Lorion (1989) emphasized the value of focusing on a few, simple objectives and characteristics of the innovative program, even if its implementation ultimately will be more complex and have many components. Articulate to others, "We are here to . . ." and "The way we do this is through 1 . . . 2 . . . 3 . . .". This allows for mobilization of internal resources and overall improved project management. While the reality is more complex, focusing allows communication and key elements to be prioritized planfully (Van de Ven, 1986).

7. *When the program begins, ensure implementation of its core principles and elements.* Identify the core elements of the program innovation and replicate these as faithfully as possible in your setting. This typically requires intensive staff training and ongoing coaching and supervision. Also valuable is consultation by the original program developers or others who have implemented the program in settings similar to yours.

8. *Measure program implementation and attainment of program objectives throughout the operation of the program.* This measurement may range from practical to scientifically precise (see chap. 14). However, some form of assessment is essential. Foremost, it is a statement of values, of ongoing commitment to goal achievement, and accountability to those who are carrying out and receiving the initiative. Secondarily, continuous assessment of process and outcome allows adaptations of a program to be made as its context changes. Finally, measurement provides evidence of program performance that funders and stakeholders require.

9. *Search for unintended effects of the program.* Any innovation in a host setting will have unintended effects, both positive and negative. Being alert to these possibilities during the assessment process can lead to revision or refinement of the program. For example, in early prevention programs, outside experts would come in and carry out interventions in schools. Teachers were thrilled; they would leave the class and use the time for extra preparation or grading papers. However, when the experts left, there was little of the program left behind and little chance for teachers to reinforce the principles of the program throughout the rest of the school day. Documentation of such unintended effects has led to rethinking about the role of setting members in the implementation of prevention/promotion innovations, toward the necessity of their having direct and ongoing involvement.

10. *Plan for institutionalization of the program in the host setting.* Assume that the program will need to outlast the staff who initiate it. Plan for how to institutionalize it, incorporating it into the host setting's routine functioning, so that it survives after its founders have moved on. In addition, develop a process of program renewal, so that it can be adapted to changing needs and circumstances in the host setting. Failure to consider this aspect of the implementation process is probably the main reason why good programs do not persist.

11. *Establish external linkages with similar programs in other settings.* Networking is the lifeblood of enduring innovations. Relationships with other implementers—via meetings, distance learning technology, Internet, shared newsletters, conference calls—provide ideas and technical assistance, opportunities to share triumphs and frustrations, and social support from individuals who are going through the same things. In addition, networking provides a base for actions on broader issues, such as advocacy or funding.

In case you are wondering if you have to do all of these things in order to be successful, the answer is a definitive "yes and no." The first time one looks at a piece of music, before one has mastered the notation, it makes very little sense and one wonders if it can ever be mastered. With practice and attention to feedback and learning, and often through working with others, one learns to play compositions that seemed imposing at first.

Prevention/promotion work is similar. It uses a process of action research, so that there is continual feedback and adjusting to the specifics of the context. This feedback often involves both qualitative and quantitative research (chap. 4). The accumulation of feedback through the action-research process lead to modification that continuously balances and strengthens both core and adaptive features of the program. Prevention/promotion work occurs in teams, to an even greater extent than music. Creative leadership, flexible adaptation to context, and appreciation of the interdependencies among stakeholders and the resources each brings to the shared work all converge to create ongoing innovation and high-quality programs.

# IMPLEMENTING A PREVENTION/PROMOTION INNOVATION: A CASE EXAMPLE

In this section, we describe a case example of implementing a school-based prevention/promotion program in multiple school settings. Its path of implementation took many twists and turns, influenced by action research, a commitment to continuous program improvement, and the practicalities of school and community life. Our example is the Social Decision Making and Social Problem Solving (SDM/SPS) Project (Elias, 1994; Elias & Clabby, 1992), a school-based prevention initiative.

The SDM/SPS Project has been guided by many points in the Conductor's Guide above, over a period of 17 years. It has spread from a demonstration project in two experimental and three control classrooms to hundreds of classrooms in schools in two dozen states and several countries. The core of the project involves building the social and emotional skills of students, with a focus on self-control, group participation and social awareness, and a decision-making strategy to use when faced with difficult choices under stress or when planning. Its ultimate goals include promoting successful social and academic performance and preventing problem behaviors (Elias & Clabby, 1992; Elias & Tobias, 1996).

The task of orchestrating the development and spread of this innovation, with which the primary chapter author (Maurice Elias) was involved from the onset, will appear much more organized in its description than in its reality. Think of orchestrating in the context of an orchestra where all members are standing, wearing roller blades, on a boat in stormy seas. The wind is blowing, pages of the musical score are regularly getting washed overboard, even a few members of the orchestra are slipping into the water every now and then, and at times there are several people who feel they are the conductors. If you read the following with this scene in mind, you will be closer to the reality than what the printed page typically allows. Keep in mind, however, that after 17 years, the boat is still afloat, many more people have joined the orchestra, and we have learned a lot not only about orchestration but about sailing in heavy seas.

We drew initial guidance from the principles in the implementation equation presented earlier, although we were only dimly aware of all of its terms when we started. It is important to note that from the inception of the project, we tried to make the initial implementation conditions match those likely in the school environments where the program would eventually be implemented. Thus little of the available funding went into creating ideal training conditions, providing resources and materials to implementing teachers, paying for any training or implementation work, having experts work directly in classrooms, or finding locations with strong receptivity to prior innovations. Instead, we sought to work in conditions as close to the real world as possible. Furthermore, we were acutely aware of developmental factors and of the need to modify what we were doing for diverse populations, particularly children with special-education classifications.

## *Evolution of the Elementary School Level Program*

The history of much of this effort, as well as the way in which planned and unplanned variations in conditions were addressed, is detailed in Elias and Clabby (1992). Key points in the voyage, however, can be described here. At the elementary school level, we created a scripted curriculum with extensive accompanying materials, all developed through nine years of continuous improvement in an action research cycle. Other action research cycles were created to support modifications of the approach for special education and middle and high school populations. In particular, the creation of an acronym for the eight steps of social decision making—FIG TESPN—led to dramatic differences in delivering the program to special education students (Elias & Tobias, 1996). Another important finding was the need to integrate the learning of problem-solving skills with the application of those skills in practice to academic and interpersonal situations, as soon as possible after learning them in class.

We also discovered the value of sharing learning across implementation sites in a systematic way. The *Problem Solving Connection Newsletter* was created as a resource exchange network for those using social problem solving or related interventions; it became a place to ask questions and to share innovations, to incorporate diversity and change into the implementation context. It is where such creative adaptations as the "Keep Calm Rap" was developed and redeveloped, as well as "Be Your Best," which one class began to sing to the tune of Disney's "Be Our Guest," from *Beauty and the Beast*. Most recently, branches of the project have been focusing on distance learning coalitions and Internet exchanges as vehicles for implementation sharing and support.

## Adaptation to the Middle School

Although there is far less uniformity among elementary schools than unsuspecting outsiders might think, there is even greater diversity among middle schools. This means that intervention technologies are not easily transferred from elementary to middle school. It also means that successful interventions in one middle school context must be transferred to others with much care. In attempting to provide follow-up for the elementary school level social decision-making and problem-solving program into middle school, we found that numerous adaptations had to be made. This was discovered as an outcome of action research and by being clear about the core features and goals of the program. Even after creating successful demonstration projects, however, those involved were not filled with a sense that the work was completed. There was the matter of providing a well-annotated musical score for others to use. This gave rise to the book, *Social Decision Making and Life Skills Development* (Elias, 1993).

We were wary of providing a set "score"; therefore, we chose to provide key principles and specific examples as inspiration, rather than fully scripted materials. Those who had brought social problem solving successfully into their local settings (in our orchestral analogy, local conductors, the first players of different orchestral sections, and some individual musicians) explained clearly their own use of problem-solving principles in the classroom. This helped readers imagine themselves using program materials; at first, this would take place in a way similar to the examples provided, but soon thereafter their applications would have to be integrated with their own skills and context.

To introduce each innovation to prospective implementers, we first presented a sales pitch that made the program sound attractive and viable to those who might implement it. Then came a discussion of program materials and how they could be used. Next, we discussed evidence of its effectiveness, accompanied by listings of follow-up and support resources. Finally, we presented sample activities, to allow readers to try out specific modules and get a feel not only for the particular details but also get a sense of the flow of the activities with the individuals and groups involved (Elias, 1993). Some examples of modules follow.

1. A video program that shows children how to watch television and then use social decision making and problem solving to create their own programs, series, documentaries, and public service advertisements.

2. A program to allow students to create school and community service projects.
3. A procedure for creating parent newsletters and other school-home communications; the detail includes such things as what to tell the printer when it comes to reproducing photographs.
4. FIG TESPN, an approach to social decision making and problem solving that takes into account the special learning needs of many children. The acronym includes the following:

> *F*eelings are my cue to problem solve
> *I* have a problem
> *G*oals guide my actions
> *T*hink of many possible things to do
> *E*nvision the outcomes of each solution
> *S*elect your best solution, based on your goal
> *P*lan, practice, anticipate pitfalls, and pursue it
> *N*ext time, what will you do the same or differently.

5. Troubleshooting sections, where the practitioners in the field talk about the tough issues and how they have dealt with them. Examples include issues of getting started, not having enough time, and working with children who seem to place a positive value on aggressive behavior.

## Setting Up an Infrastructure to Support Widespread Implementation

To support the process of widespread implementation with fidelity and effectiveness in diverse contexts, it was necessary to pay great attention to implementation infrastructure. Using the analogy of music, one can imagine the difficulty in playing a piece of orchestral music one has not heard in its entirety. For this to happen, it is helpful to have ongoing concerts that others can attend, to be able to train master conductors and musicians who will have had experience with the musical work and then can go back and teach it to others, and to have the capacity to send out conductors and musicians to local settings to assist them in learning to play, as well as to help them make modifications in light of their own orchestral strengths and weaknesses and to avoid making modifications that will change the nature of the composition.

A Social Problem Solving Unit was created within Rutgers University and its affiliated mental health center. The Unit's mission is to foster effective implementation of SDM/SPS programs in school districts nationally and internationally, with an action research orientation. Many of the principles of effective implementation in multiple settings that we have discussed in this chapter grew out of the experiences of this Unit. The SDM/SPS program and implementation unit gained approval from the National Mental Health Association, the National Diffusion Network of the U.S. Department of Education, and the National Education Goals Panel, critical steps in building credibility and opening up contacts with networks of potential and actual implementers from which further refinements in practice and sources of implementation support could be derived.

Data concerning the evaluation of the dissemination of the approaches of the SDM/SPS Project are available from three major studies. Commins and Elias (1991) undertook an examination of the first four sites to implement the SDM/SPS program. The methodology involved empirically identifying key conditions most likely to facilitate long-term program implementation. Ten such conditions were identified. The two districts showing all 10 conditions were found to have made substantial progress toward institutionalizing the program. A district showing 9 of 10 conditions had made substantial progress. The remaining site met only 4 of 10 conditions, and showed almost no progress. This study was the first to show that the program could be disseminated effectively. Anecdotally, it is worth noting that 11 years after the Commins and Elias (1991) study, the SDM/SPS program has a clear, visible presence in the both districts that earlier had met all conditions, has been integrated into the elementary guidance program in the district that met 9 of 10 conditions, and continues to be implemented only on a sporadic basis in the remaining district.

M. Heller and Firestone (1995) conducted a study of the sources of leadership in schools that had implemented long-term social and emotional learning programs. As part of this study, nine elementary schools that had implemented SDM/SPS Solving for at least 3 years were identified. An interview procedure was set up to determine the degree of institutionalization of the program. They found that five of nine schools had institutionalized the program to a significant degree. Four were deemed *fully institutionalized*, meaning that all teachers were using the program with high fidelity. One was designated as *mixed*, in that there was a core group of teachers that were high fidelity users of the program, with others using the program less rigorously, and four had a *partial* status, meaning that they maintained affiliation with the SDM/SPS programs and teachers were using the program, although in generally limited, low-fidelity ways.

Detailed analysis of mediating factors indicated that full institutionalization was related primarily to leadership roles being filled consistently and by multiple individuals, usually from varied roles, and to having school-based SDM/SPS coordinating committees. The teachers played the most critical role in institutionalizing SDM/SPS programs. In every school, long-term, high fidelity institutionalization was more likely when there was an active group of teachers who implemented the program and knew its impact. Essential among the activities of such groups were providing a sustained vision of the program, offering encouragement, and setting up in-house procedures to monitor its progress and improve its effectiveness (M. Heller & Firestone, 1995).

As the SDM/SPS program expanded through involvement with the National Diffusion Network, trainers were bringing the program to sites inside and outside of its New Jersey base. Beyond a focus on implementation, we felt it was important to examine the extent to which teachers and student recipients of the program were developing their skills to the same degrees as they did in the initial validation sample. In the initial samples, of course, the program was smaller, there were fewer implementation sites, and program management was closer and more intensive. For the more recent study, three new sites in New Jersey plus sites in Arkansas and Oregon were studied.

Results are summarized in Bruene-Butler, Hampson, Elias, Clabby, and Schuyler (1997). Briefly, extent of teacher acquisition of skills in "dialoguing" and "facilitative questioning" met or exceeded those of the original sample in all of the new sites. Comparing the Oregon and the original New Jersey site, use of inhibitory questioning strategies declined from pretest to posttest; use of facilitative (discussion-oriented) questioning increased greatly. With regard to acquisition of interpersonal sensitivity, problem analysis, and planning skills, students in all of the recent dissemination sites showed significant gains during the program, and the effect sizes in all cases were equal to or as much as twice as large as those in the original validation sample. The Bruene-Butler et al. (1997) data suggest that the implementation of the SDM/SPS program in sites assessed in 1994 and 1995 can occur in ways that allow its impact on teachers and students to be as strong as it was in the initial implementation site, where it was begun in 1980.

## Technology-Based Applications

The most recent set of innovations relates to the use of technology to deliver SDM/SPS approaches. The Hallmark Child Philanthropic Foundation initiated a project to bring together many who felt that disaffected elementary-school-aged children often were not receptive to school-based programs, largely because they were in school environments that did not value the building of their social competence or the transfer of health and life skills outside the classroom. This exciting project involved the development of a video-based program for 9- to 11-year-olds, to be disseminated by existing networks for training within Boys and Girls Clubs, Girl Scouts, and 4-H Clubs around the nation, a strategy designed to help reach at-risk and disaffected youth who are not responsive to school-based programs. SDM/SPS was used as a conceptual base for the program.

This is an action research project of remarkable scope, centered around the character of TJ, a wheelchair-bound African-American girl who is the problem-solving DJ for a radio call-in show for kids, along with support characters Jeff, her sort of spaced-out engineer and sound-effects man, and station manager Ray Dio, a former DJ who had his heyday in the 1960s and 1970s and brings maturity, perspective, and a lot of Latin music and rhythms to the station. The themes for the program are teamwork and cooperation, and peaceful conflict resolution and dealing with anger. Initial data from pilot testing of portions of the program showed meaningful and higher-than-expected impacts on children's self-reported skill knowledge and attitudes and observed behaviors in the clubs (Johnston, Bauman, Milne, & Urdan, 1993). Extensive formative evaluation has taken place to ensure that key aspects of implementation-receptivity and responsiveness of diverse audiences of children, retention of program content and themes, enthusiasm for carrying out activities and follow-up projects based on the videos, and clarity of implementation directions for local group leaders would be built into the program from the inception. At this point, TJ materials have reached over two million children, making it perhaps the largest systematic program of its kind since Head Start (cf. Elias & Bartz, 1995; Elias & Tobias, 1996; Hallmark Charitable Foundation, 1994, for details).

To take further advantage of the ways in which video and computers enhance receptivity and effectiveness of social competence-building efforts among populations that are diverse with regard to culture and learning skills, an organization called Psychological Enterprises Incorporated was developed. Its first activities involved generating a computer software program that provides a tutorial on the steps of social decision making, as well as a vehicle for individual students to work through discipline problems, clinical issues, or even to problem solve preventively (Psychological Enterprises Incorporated, 1993). Action research on this technology and its applications in clinical (Elias, Tobias, & Friedlander, 1994) and school (Elias, Hoover, & Poedubicky, 1997; Nigro, 1995) contexts has begun (Elias & Tobias, 1996).

## *Concluding Perspectives*

What is the essence of this case example? It chronicles the use of a social decision-making approach, informed by community psychology principles and implementation considerations, including the prevention and implementation equations, the four stages of development of innovations, and the Conductor's Guide to Orchestrating Prevention/Promotion Innovations (see Table 11.3). The SDM/SPS process has been context-sensitive and operator-dependent, yet faithful to basic program principles. The emphasis is on implementing core features while adapting its methods to diverse host settings. In the spirit of continuous improvement, SDM/SPS developers and adopters conduct ongoing action research to maximize its effectiveness and serve a broad range of populations and settings. This process is, in fact, at the core of what community psychology has to contribute as a discipline. There are no short cuts; on the other hand, every accomplishment, every small win (Weick, 1984) and "baby step" (Cowen, 1977) is celebrated as a positive action, an instructive example, and part of moving problem prevention and competence and health promotion from rhetoric to reality.

# CONCLUSION: FINAL THOUGHTS, FUTURE THOUGHTS

Issues like violence, alcohol and other drugs, AIDS, academic failure and school disaffection and dropping out, and child abuse and neglect require bold, definitive, effective, widespread, sustained efforts. What is at stake is the future health of our youth and what they will become when they are adults and in a position to take over the responsibilities of citizenship in a democracy.

Community psychologists have particular concerns about situations in which the spread of prevention/promotion innovations is approached naively, unrealistically, or misleadingly. All too often, the result is failure and fatalism about resolving future community problems. There are no shortcuts, inoculations, or preventive approaches that can succeed in the absence of careful oversight and continuous monitoring and feedback. Policy advocacy also is required if implementation of prevention is to reach the point of having a widespread impact on public health (Montero, 1996).

The SDM/SPS Project was presented as an example of how conditions can be created so that health promotion and risk reduction programs can be brought into schools and implemented with integrity, skills acquisition, and generativity in multiple contexts. Space did not allow us to describe initiatives in other community settings, but review the programs in chapter 10 to understand and imagine the impact of widespread implementation on families, neighborhoods, workplaces, and other settings.

Ultimately, there is no substitute for creating an infrastructure within which implementation of prevention/promotion innovations can occur with care. If we do not implement with care, we are likely to see public interest in prevention and promotion diminish. Documentation of process and outcomes in ways that policy makers, the public, professionals in caregiving fields, and scientists can all use with confidence also will become a high priority in the field of prevention/promotion. Finally, the current emphasis on invention that predominates in university settings must be complemented with realization of the intellectual value of understanding how operator-dependent innovations can be implemented in nondemonstration contexts. The challenges are both intellectual and practical and must be met if we are to have health-enhancing communities for our youth and for all citizens.

## CHAPTER SUMMARY

**1.** Successful prevention/promotion programs cited in research journals are not necessarily successfully replicated in multiple settings. We used Kelly's (1970) ecological concepts of interdependence, resource cycling, adaptation, and succession to analyze some of the reasons for this.

**2.** *Action research* is a cyclical approach to developing prevention/promotion programs and transferring them to multiple settings. It consists of four stages: experimental, technological, diffusional, and widespread implementation. This process is sometimes termed *scaling up*.

**3.** Seven characteristics describe prevention/promotion innovations and the settings where they usually take place. These are listed in Table 11.1. Innovations are *operator-dependent, context-dependent, organizationally unbounded,* and *fragile and difficult to specify.* Effective innovations thus require identifying *core and adaptive components, challenging* the setting in growth-producing ways, and *longitudinal* attention to program quality. Because of these factors, operators of such systems must have or acquire specific skills in order to put in place successful and enduring prevention/promotion innovations.

**4.** There are numerous challenges in implementing prevention programs effectively. Such challenges are summarized in the prevention/promotion implementation equation in Table 11.2.

**5.** Approaches to exemplary education programs have evolved from *cookbook, replication,* and *adaptation* approaches to an emphasis on *invention/innovation.* Implementing an invention/innovation approach requires taking the developmental levels of implementers into account; for instance, a desire for generativity in one's work.

**6.** On the basis of an invention/innovation approach, we presented a Conductor's Guide to Implementing Effective Prevention/Promotion Innovations in Multiple Settings. These are listed in Table 11.3.

**7.** The Social Decision Making and Social Problem Solving Project is an example of a long-term prevention/promotion effort that has encountered many of the challenges of implementation and has attempted to address them using the principles outlined in this chapter.

**8.** There is no magic formula for successful widespread implementation of a model program; however, a process of continuous monitoring, feedback, and modification, respecting local ecology and needs of implementers, encouraging diverse inputs, and building a sense of community allows innovations to have the best chance to adapt to their environments for extended periods of time.

# Brief Exercises

**1.** Recall a prevention/promotion educational program you have experienced as participant or implementer/leader. This may, for instance, involve drug abuse prevention, parenting skills classes, conflict resolution training, a program teaching social or communication skills, or other intervention. Using the concepts in this chapter, analyze the quality of its implementation.

First, use some of the seven characteristics in Table 11.1 to describe the situation in which this program occurred.

- Was it operator-dependent and context-dependent? How?
- Were its effects organizationally unbounded? How?
- What were its core and adaptive features, as you perceive them?
- Do you believe the program was implemented effectively? What factors influenced whether it was effective or not?
- Was the program evaluated and improved longitudinally?

Second, if possible describe the educational effectiveness of the program using terms from Table 11.2.

- Did it use appropriate instructional strategies? For instance, did it use group discussion, exercises to apply learning, and other ways to strengthen learning?
- Were its materials (e.g., written, visual, computerized) user-friendly and helpful?
- Was the organization or setting genuinely committed to the program (hospitable context)?
- What were the constraints, limitations, or obstacles to program implementation? How could these be overcome?
- What persons represented resources of talent, commitment, or other qualities that increased the effectiveness of the program?

**2.** This chapter focused on educational settings. List some other KISS and AID systems, or other systems in society, that are operator-dependent, context-dependent systems, whose effects are organizationally unbounded and difficult to specify.

In what respects might health care, retail sales and services, finance, computer technology, religion, politics, and diplomacy represent such systems? Justify your opinion with recent news stories or with your own experiences.

# Recommended Readings

McElhaney, S. (1995). *Getting started: NMHA guide to establishing community-based prevention programs.* Alexandria, VA: National Mental Health Association.

> Tells how to create the partnerships and resources required to engage in a serious prevention effort in an organization or community. Part of a set that includes the NMHA directory of prevention/promotion programs described after chapter 10.

See also Recommended Readings for chapters 13 and 14 for resources on implementing change in communities. The Community Tool Box Website, listed as a Recommended Website for chapter 13, also includes many resources for developing and implementing prevention/promotion innovations in communities.

# InfoTrac Keywords

*action research, dissemination, implementing(ation), intervention, prevention(ive)(ing), primary prevention, program, promotion(ing).*

# Recommended Websites

http://www.landmark-project.com/ncsh

This site contains a special project that asks educators to visit a 1960s-style school building gutted of all relics of industrial age learning. The goal is to establish a resource of innovative ideas of what school should be like and what students and staff should be doing to better prepare to build children's competencies for the future.

http://www.cecp.air.org

The Center for Effective Collaboration and Practice works to improve services to children and youth at risk for or experiencing emotional or behavioral problems. Their Website contains information on both established and effective programs and those at an earlier stage of development that appear promising. It also has resource lists, online discussions, and links to many related sites.

# TOURING THE PREVENTION/ PROMOTION LITERATURE

The literature in prevention and promotion is expanding far more rapidly than any text-book will ever be able to capture. Relevant literature comes from many fields, including the mass media and the Internet. Particularly for the latter outlets, it becomes important to know how to recognize high-quality work that is useful for prevention/promotion purposes.

The purpose of this exercise is to provide you with ways to do your own investigations of the literature so you can keep up to date and determine what it is that is worth studying in more detail. We invite you to look at a wide array of outlets for examples that reflect prevention and promotion. Articles in the journals listed after chapter 1 will show you the diversity of topics and disciplines represented in prevention/promotion efforts. Articles in major newspapers and newsmagazines regularly address the social issues that are the central concern of community psychology, although rarely will you see community psychology mentioned. One particular reason for this reading concerns our responsibilities as citizens to inform ourselves about those issues. Prevention and promotion are linked to areas that come up for public consideration in the media and in our legislative bodies. The prevention/promotion literature also can inform many college and university policies that impact considerably on students.

The analytic method we recommend is summarized below. It reflects our view that reviews of the literature, as well as students' reviewing of the literature, are best done in a particular context and for particular purposes. We find it is more valuable to read purposefully than generically.

The framework below also draws from Bower's (1972) KISS-AID-ICE distinction, social ecological concepts, and the literatures on risk and protective processes and implementation. It provides readers with a way of capturing essential information about articles in a way that we and our students have found useful.

You may find that there are additional considerations you want to add, perhaps from the implementation equation. You might want to keep track of certain problem areas, make a separate file for work done in different parts of the United States and the world, or have a special focus on mass media and Internet sources or doings in your current community or home town. You may find that initial sources you examine will not have the information you need to answer a number of the questions we suggest, and that you need to read further. Part of the participant–conceptualizer role of community psychologists is to shed light on knowledge needed for responsible citizenship. You now have a format to gather that information for key social issues.

## *Guidelines for Reviewing*
## *Prevention/Promotion Articles/Materials*

1. Record full reference information, to be sure you know the source and context of this work.
2. What is the purpose of the work? Does it discuss a community or social issue that could be addressed by prevention/promotion initiatives? Or does it report on a specific prevention/promotion intervention?
3. If a prevention/promotion intervention is described, what protective processes is the program trying to strengthen? What risk processes is the program trying to weaken?
4. What population is being focused on? How were particular participants chosen? Some criteria may include age, gender, race or ethnicity, socioeconomic status or class, urban/suburban/rural location or geographic area, nation, or historical /political/cultural context.
5. What Key Integrative Social System(s) is involved? Health care (includes prenatal/ birth/postnatal care), parents/families, peers, schools, religious settings, workplaces, leisure/recreational, community organizations, media/Internet/cyberspace, other?
6. What ecological level or levels of analysis does the article address? Individual, microsystems, organizations, localities, and/or macrosystems? What specific persons or groups does it address at that level? Is it targeted at the right level(s)?
7. If a prevention/promotion intervention is described, does it respond to a planned or predictable life situation (such as an education-related transition) or to an unpredictable life event (a reaction to a stressful or crisis event, such as divorce, bereavement, unemployment)?
8. Does the article focus on a wider community or social issue, such as poverty, social injustice, prejudice, or drugs? How might "small wins" thinking be applicable in prevention/promotion efforts on that issue?
9. If a prevention/promotion intervention was conducted, who planned it? How much were various constituencies and stakeholders involved? At what points? Were the persons most affected by decisions made in this program involved in making those decisions? Was there sufficient sensitivity to cultural and contextual factors?
10. How was the intervention implemented? Where? By whom? Under what conditions? When was it carried out? How often? Over what period of time? Did the program developers check to see if the program was actually implemented as planned?
11. What is the evidence for the effectiveness of the intervention? What are the sources of that evidence?
12. Which of the objectives were clearly met? Not met? Met partially? Did it have an impact on the wider community? How?
13. Was the intervention implemented in multiple settings or contexts? Was it effective in all settings?
14. Are you convinced that the authors' interpretations or claims of effectiveness are true? Why or why not?
15. What are the most important things you think can be learned from what you read? What important questions does it raise?

# five

# COMMUNITY AND
# SOCIAL CHANGE

# CITIZEN PARTICIPATION AND EMPOWERMENT

Nobody is wise enough, nobody is good enough, and nobody cares enough about you, for you to turn over to them your future or your destiny.

(Benjamin Mays, cited in Wandersman & Florin, 2000)

First I would like to tell you the story of how I came to volunteer my time to the community instead of going off and having a good time by myself. It started in 1979, after I had a contractor build a shower in my basement and a year later, the shower collapsed. I called up the contractor and he said he would come around in a week. Three months later, he still had not shown up, so I called the Better Business Bureau. The first questions they asked me were 'What block association do you belong to? What community board are you in?' I did not even know at the time that a community board existed. So I called the community board, who filed complaints against the contractor and ultimately restitution was made. Until this point in my life, I literally did not know about citizen participation.

In 1980 the East 48th Street Block Association #135 was formed to improve the quality of life on our block. Almost immediately changes were visible such as property improvement, communication, and a cleaner block as a whole. Since then we have formed a Block watcher group; we have continuous patrols on the block; we have installed outdoor lights in front of almost every home. . . . Believe it or not, it is a deterrent to crime. We have a youth softball team. . . . During the summer, we have bus rides to parks for youths and families. Last year on July 4th we had a block party. We have a block party about every year. We get free tickets to see the Yankee baseball games. All of this is achieved through my affiliation with different community groups.

Even though volunteer service is a lot of hard work, it enhances the quality of life and is quite rewarding.

Louis Burgess (1990, pp. 159–161)
Reprinted by permission of Kluwer Academic/Plenum Publishers

The remarks above, by a community leader from Brooklyn, New York, embody the three themes of this chapter: *sense of community, citizen participation* and *empowerment*. Louis Burgess's willingness to become involved in a block association led to tangible changes in his own life and, together with other citizens, in the life of their community. These changes are not unique to Mr. Burgess or to New York City, but occur widely in many societies. They represent social change not at the level of national government, or the global economy, or through large-scale social movements, but in local neighborhoods, schools, religious congregations, workplaces, and behavior settings (Barker, 1968) in which citizens live. They embody the process of participation by citizens in their community's life and the process of empowerment that occurs as they, individually and collectively, learn to influence the environment of their communities. Citizen participation and empowerment link ecological contexts (chap. 5) and sense of community (chap. 7) with community and social change.

Although citizen participation and empowerment may not seem "psychological" at first glance, they are actually intensely so. They involve cognitions, emotions, and motivation regarding community life and citizens' collective ability to change it. Working together with others to improve the quality of community life requires psychologically important skills and behaviors. Some settings promote learning these skills more than others, for psychologically meaningful reasons. Cooperation and prosocial behavior, group dynamics, leadership, interpersonal and intergroup conflict, and other concepts related to citizen participation and empowerment have long histories in the field of psychology.

The study of citizen participation and empowerment does require a reorientation from an exclusive focus on individual well-being to a broader concern with individuals in communities. It also requires debunking myths that often surround discussion of community life and community change. Table 12.1 lists several of these myths and insights that about individual life and public life. (Lappe & DuBois, 1994)

## What Are the Key Points of This Chapter?

In this chapter, we first define citizen participation and empowerment. Second, we describe a study of citizen activists, which illustrates the development of both participation and empowerment at the individual level. Third, we propose a model that emphasizes how sense of community (covered in chap. 7), citizen participation, and personal empowerment are intertwined, strengthening each other. Finally, we review research and conceptual issues on these three topics, discussing findings in terms of the model.

## Defining Citizen Participation and Personal Empowerment

### Citizen Participation

A useful definition of *citizen participation* is as follows:

> a process in which individuals take part in decision making in the institutions, programs, and environments that affect them. (K. Heller et al., 1984, p. 339)

Let's unpack this definition. "Institutions, programs and environments" includes workplaces, health settings such as hospitals or mental health centers, neighborhoods, schools, religious congregations, and society at large. They also include grassroots organizations formed for the purpose of influencing larger environments; such groups may include a block association, a political action group, or a labor union. In addition, citizen participation involves decision making. It does not necessarily mean holding the power to control all decisions, but involves making one's voice heard and influencing decisions in democratic ways.

Citizen participation is not simply volunteering time or resources, but occurs when citizens take part in making decisions for the community. Assisting with a kindergarten class field trip or with recreational activities in a nursing home constitutes community service, but not citizen participation. Citizen participation also is not simply social support or mutual help among members of a group. Participation involves citizen or member input for group decisions, not just mutual support for individual adjustment. Finally, citizen participation includes but is not limited to electoral participation, such as voting. Community psychologists typically are interested in forms of participation that go beyond merely voting.

Participation is a process; it is not a static characteristic of persons or of organizations. It occurs in a diversity of forms. Serving on a community coalition to address prevention of

| TABLE 12.1 | MYTHS AND INSIGHTS ABOUT PRIVATE LIFE AND PUBLIC LIFE |
|---|---|

*Myth:* Public life is for celebrities, politicians, and activists, people who like to be in the limelight or who want to make waves.

*Insight:* Every day, at school, where we work, where we worship, within civic or social groups, our behavior shapes the public world and is shaped by it. We are all in public life.

*Myth:* It's too depressing to get involved in public life, too easy to burn out.

*Insight:* Public life serves deep human needs: for instance, to work with others or to make a difference. It is as essential as private life.

*Myth:* Public life is always nasty, cutthroat, all about conflict.

*Insight:* Public life involves encountering differences, but conflict doesn't have to be nasty. When understood and managed well, it can be healthy and informative, a source of growth.

*Myth:* Public life is about pursuing one's own selfish interests.

*Insight:* Selfishness and enlightened self-interest aren't the same thing. Understanding how our true interests overlap with those of others comes only through involvement in public life.

*Myth:* Public life interferes with a private life.

*Insight:* Public life often enhances private life, making it more meaningful and enjoyable.

Note: Adapted from Lappe and DuBois (1994, pp. 21, 24, 29, 33, 39).

drug abuse, writing a letter to the editor, debating the budget at a school board meeting, and testifying at a public hearing about a proposed zoning ordinance are different forms of citizen participation (Wandersman, 1984). Table 12.2 presents a few of these.

***Participation: Means or End?*** We must also distinguish between citizen participation as a *means* or an *end*. As a means, participation is often encouraged as a technique: For instance, a decision or plan is improved because citizens affected by it participate in shaping it, or citizens' commitment to a decision is greater if they had input in making it. As an end, citizen participation is a *value* to be enacted, often seen as one of the essential qualities of a democratic society, regardless of whether it generates practical benefits as a technique.

This means–end distinction is not merely academic. First, participation is not always a means to better decisions, particularly if conflicts erupt and are not resolved, or if valid expertise is ignored. Second, participation and efficiency may be contradictory ends for community organizations. Riger's (1993) research on feminist movement organizations (e.g., women's centers, shelters for battered women, and rape crisis centers) showed that maximizing participation by organization members in decision making can require long meetings and interfere with the most efficient use of organizational resources (money, staff time, expertise). Finally, many societies, including Western democracies, endorse competing ideals. Citizen participation competes with economic efficiency, budget constraints, shifts in public attention to social/community problems, and the influence of experts and of lobbyists in influencing public decisions. (Recall the competition in U.S. society of the traditions of utilitarian and expressive individualism vs. citizen participation, described

**TABLE 12.2**  **EXAMPLES OF CITIZEN PARTICIPATION**

**Healthy communities.** Citizens in a community join in coalitions to plan for improving health services. Their plans may concern issues linked to health status and important to citizens, yet often excluded from health planning: prevention and health promotion, drug abuse, unemployment, or violence.

> Partners for a Healthy Community is governed by a board of 22 community leaders representing business, industry, education, health care, government, and human services. Current projects include a parish nursing program in church congregations, a study committee on depression (identified as a key health concern), a neighborhood program to train citizens in basic health interventions, and study circles that bring together individuals of varied racial, economic, and social backgrounds to discuss issues that create conflict. (Partners for a Healthy Community, Anderson, South Carolina, in Wolff & Lee, 1997)

**Block and neighborhood associations.** Citizens in a neighborhood or smaller area work together to prevent crime or drug abuse, promote recreation and a sense of community, improve housing, support education, or other purpose. (The quotation from Louis Burgess at the outset of this chapter illustrates such a group.)

**Alternative settings.** Citizens dissatisfied with existing community services join to create a new setting to provide such services; for instance, a shelter for battered women, a rape crisis center, a child care center, an alternative school, or a self-help group.

> In 1977, Mimi Kaplan learned she had breast cancer. The doctors couldn't answer her questions. They couldn't address her fears, particularly her main concern, 'How can I cope with chemotherapy while holding down a job?' So Mimi reached out to women facing similar problems. Their first support meeting led to a national organization, Y-ME. . . . Today Y-ME supports women cancer patients throughout the world and even guides physicians in improving their patients' care. (Lappe & DuBois, 1994, p. 5)

**Work settings.** A community psychologist interviewed workers in a statewide organization providing human services to persons with disabilities. This organization had implemented efforts to empower its staff through granting them more control over decisions about their work. Some interview excerpts regarding participation in decision making are as follows:

> "[I have] the ability to figure out what needs to be done . . . to prioritize my own work and to set my own agenda."
>
> "I am a [secretary] but I am not treated like I am below them or that I don't have any good ideas."
>
> "I am able to problem solve . . . . I'm able to create a solution for a need."
>
> "Results. When I make a decision . . . and it works . . . . I feel good when I get results."
>
> "If I have a suggestion . . . I will go to someone . . . . They listen to my ideas." (Foster-Fishman et al., 1998). Reprinted by permission of Kluwer Academic/Plenum Publishers

**Public input on environmental issues.** Governments mandate public hearings or review boards regarding the environmental impact of proposed developments by business or government. Environmental groups, national or local, advocate changes in legislation.

**Education.** Citizens join in community councils to review and advise public schools and their elected boards. Students assume greater roles in teaching each other through cooperative learning and in school governance in innovative schools.

Note: Sources were Foster-Fishman et al. (1998), K. Heller et al. (1984), Lappe and DuBois (1994), Wolff and Lee (1997), Wandersman and Florin (1990), Zimmerman and Perkins (1995).

in chap. 2.) In short, citizen participation is often, but not necessarily, a practical means to better decisions. If pursued as an end in itself, it incurs costs that must be weighed against pursuit of other aims.

Having said this, however, advocates of citizen participation can cite many examples of its advantages. Reviews of field research in organizations show that participation by employees or organization members usually (but not always) increases the quality of decisions and overall organizational effectiveness. This generalization is true especially if cooperation among members is stressed, and if disagreement and conflict are seen as a source of information rather than a threat (Bartunek & Keys, 1979; Fawcett et al., 1995). Members of an organization will be more committed to implementing a decision if they contributed to it (Bartunek & Keys, 1979), a finding especially important for voluntary organizations. Studies of voluntary organizations also indicate that emphasizing participation promotes effective leadership and a concern with accomplishing tasks (Fawcett et al., 1995; Maton & Salem, 1995). Finally, a setting that encourages participation and hearing different points of view may recognize and grapple with dilemmas before they are recognized elsewhere.

## Defining Empowerment

The conceptual and value issues involved in defining citizen participation become even thornier when we turn to *empowerment*, a more value-laden term. *Empowerment* has passed into common language with a number of meanings and connotations. It has been appropriated as a buzzword for diverse and inconsistent usages by competing groups: for instance, as, a rhetorical tool for both progressive and conservative forces in U.S. politics (D. D. Perkins, 1995). Corporations speak of empowering their employees, sometimes with no clear intent to share power. It is common to hear physical exercise, meditation, or psychotherapy described as empowering; this is a very different meaning from empowerment associated with citizen participation. Riger (1993) has discussed varying, inconsistent usages of the term even within community psychology. A word that means everything also means nothing distinctive, and sometimes it seems that empowerment has suffered that fate.

Rather than abandon the term prematurely, let's look at it more closely. In community psychology, Rappaport (1987) defined empowerment generally as "a process, a mechanism by which people, organizations, and communities gain mastery over their affairs" (p. 122). A specific definition was proposed by the Cornell Empowerment Group:

> an intentional, ongoing process centered in the local community, involving mutual respect, critical reflection, caring, and group participation, through which people lacking an equal share of resources gain greater access to and control over those resources. (cited in D. D. Perkins & Zimmerman, 1995, p. 570, and by Rappaport, 1999).

Certainly this definition contains elements similar to the definition of citizen participation. The principal distinction between the two is that participation is a behavior, involving actively engaging in decision making within a group, organization, or environment. Empowerment is a broader process that includes variables that may lead to citizen participation, accompany it, or result from it. For individuals, empowerment involves cognition ("critical reflection," for instance, in the Cornell definition above), emotion ("caring"), motivation, and perhaps other factors, not just the behavior of participation (see also Zimmerman, 2000). At the organizational level of analysis, empowerment strategies such as recruiting new members, mobilizing resources, or building alliances with similar groups may precede behavioral participation in a community-wide decision.

Clearly this definition of empowerment does not refer to the transforming effects of exercise, meditation, psychotherapy, or similar activities devoted to individual change. Those are better understood by language that refers to personal development or growth, not power. In this chapter, we exclude such purely internal, individual uses of the term. Instead, we define empowerment as a collective, social process, accomplished with others, not alone. We also focus on how it involves individual *and* community change, through citizen participation, occurring through empowering community settings.

Use of the term *empowerment* remains diverse, even within community psychology. However, that diversity can be a strength, as long as students of empowerment define clearly what they mean, and remain open to alternative views and to the role of debate in deepening understanding of the concept (Rappaport, 1995). Rappaport has intentionally sought to keep the definition of *empowerment* open, arguing that a simple definition is likely to limit understanding of empowerment's different forms in different contexts (see also Foster-Fishman, Salem, Chibnall, Legler, & Yapchai, 1998). The tension between efforts to define empowerment clearly and precisely and efforts to avoid prematurely narrowing its meaning parallels the tension seen with sense of community in chapter 7. At this point, empowerment may be understood as an overarching theme with a variety of meanings and applications.

## Qualities of Empowerment

Despite the variety of ideas about empowerment, consensus appears to be growing among community psychologists on some of its key qualities. These include the ideas that empowerment is a multilevel construct, involving bottom-up change, which differs in differing contexts, occurs in a collective context, and is a process rather than a steady state. The discussion below relies heavily on the theoretical work of Rappaport (1981, 1987) and Zimmerman (1995, 2000).

**Multilevel Construct**    Empowerment occurs in individuals, organizations, or communities (Zimmerman, 2000). Through becoming a leader in a local group, an individual person may develop greater control over resources or decisions in one's life. A work organization may empower its employees, and perhaps improve productivity, by forming work teams that assume responsibility for day-to-day decisions about their work. Through networking with other groups, an organization may obtain greater resources for pursuing its mission. Through advocacy at higher levels of government, a community may gain a greater role in determining policy or control over its affairs.

Empowerment at one level does not necessarily lead to empowerment at other levels (Riger, 1993). Empowerment of individuals does not necessarily empower their organizations or communities. Moreover, feeling empowered does not always lead to actual control of resources or decisions. In addition, empowering an organization, no matter how public-spirited its mission, does not necessarily empower a whole community. Indeed, empowering organizations with competing agendas may unleash competition for resources that divides and weakens a community (Riger, 1993). Further, empowering an organization in which leadership is tightly controlled does not necessarily empower its members. Thus, it is necessary to understand empowerment at differing levels and to study how these levels are related (Zimmerman, 2000).

In this chapter, we are most concerned with empowerment at individual, microsystem, and organizational levels, while showing how these are related to issues in localities and macrosystems. One focus will be *psychological empowerment*. This is the process of empowerment for individuals, involving changes in their behavior, cognitions, and other processes, which is related to the collective process of empowerment defined above. A person who becomes more skeptical of traditional authority, more willing to oppose injustice, and more involved in citizen participation is becoming psychologically empowered. At a different level, an organization that promotes participation by its members in its decisions and work is an empowering organization. In chapter 13, we discuss how groups and organizations become empowered to change their communities.

***Bottom-Up Perspective***     Another reflection of the multilevel nature of the empowerment perspective is its concern with bottom-up rather than top-down approaches to social and community change. *Bottom-up approaches* originate at the "grassroots," among citizens of a community rather than among its leaders or most powerful members. They reflect attempts by ordinary people to assert control over their everyday lives. Perhaps the defining quality of bottom-up approaches is that they reflect the ideas and everyday experiences of the people most affected by a community problem or proposed change (Fawcett et al., 1995). *Top-down approaches*, even when well-intentioned and containing useful ideas, reflect the perspectives and experiences of the powerful, and usually preserve the existing power structure (see Gruber & Trickett, 1987). Professional mental health care represents a top-down approach, self-help groups a bottom-up approach. Centralizing the functions of city government in "city hall" agencies is a top-down approach; strengthening citizen participation in neighborhood and block associations is a bottom-up approach. Relying only on technical experts to make decisions on environmental issues is a top-down approach; involving citizens in the process of decision-making about those issues in their community is a bottom-up approach.

Neither the top-down nor the bottom-up approach is always wiser. Moreover, these seemingly opposing approaches can complement each other in specific cases, as when medical professionals and mutual help groups collaborate. The empowerment perspective is usually concerned, however, with understanding the nature of bottom-up change and with understanding the perspectives of those it directly affects. Moreover, the empowerment perspective presumes that the best way to address a community problem or issue is to listen to the views and experiences of those most affected and to incorporate those views and experiences into plans for action (Fawcett et al., 1995).

***Contextual Differences***     Empowerment differs across organizations, localities, communities, and cultures because of the differing histories, experiences, and environments of each (Zimmerman, 2000). For instance, a person may develop skills for influencing decisions in a voluntary civic group that values teamwork, discussion, and maintenance of friendly relationships, but that person may find these skills ineffective for wielding influence in a workplace that rewards directive, task-oriented decision making. The person thus is empowered in the first context, but not the second. Even the nature of empowerment may be different at the workplace and in the civic group.

**Process of Empowerment**   Empowerment is a dynamic process that develops over time (Zimmerman, 2000). It is the process of acquiring resources, power, influence, or a voice in decision-making. It is reversible and can deteriorate as well as grow, but it is not reversed by small setbacks. Moreover, empowerment is not a personality trait; to be empowered in one domain (e.g., work) is not necessarily to be empowered in other domains such as family or neighborhood (Zimmerman, 2000). Because it is a process, empowerment is best understood by longitudinal research.

**Collective Context**   Empowerment, as conceptualized by community psychologists, occurs through linkages with other individuals. It is not a solitary process, but proceeds through participation in a group or organization. Psychological empowerment, defined above, most often occurs through cooperating with others. As studied by community psychologists, this almost always involves grassroots groups and organizations that are limited in size, possess a strong sense of community, offer opportunities for participation in decision making, and emphasize shared leadership and mutual influence among members. These groups may be independent of traditional social institutions (e.g., a local environmental group or a mutual help group) or related to them (e.g., a work team in a factory or a small group within a church). In addition, empowerment may involve not only linkages between individuals, but also between *organizations* that form coalitions to pursue shared aims more effectively (Zimmerman, 2000). Table 12.3 lists these five qualities of empowerment.

**Contributions and Limitations**   Empowerment involves a process through which individuals collectively acquire control of resources. These resources may be material, or may involve social resources, knowledge, peer helping, or other less tangible resources. Its end is a more equitable distribution of these resources. The process of empowerment may promote ends such as justice, equality, respect for diversity, or sense of community.

However, in other contexts, empowerment may conflict with some of these principles. For instance, in individualistic, Western societies, empowerment may be defined and understood in individualistic terms, and used to promote personal self-advancement without regard for one's community or for others. Or it may be understood to mean strengthening the position and resources of one's in group, at the expense of competing out groups (Riger, 1993). Examples such as an anti-immigration group or a White supremacy group come to mind. In addition, concepts of empowerment originated in Western societies, and

---

**TABLE  12.3    QUALITIES OF EMPOWERMENT**

Multilevel construct

Bottom-up perspective

Contextual differences

Process of empowerment

Collective context

---

must be understood in cultural context. Empowerment in a collectivistic culture may mean something different than in a more individualistic one (see, for instance, Silka & Tip, 1994).

Such issues underscore the need to specify the relationships and potential conflicts between empowerment and values such as sense of community (Riger, 1993). These issues can be clarified in particular situations by asking questions such as "Who is to be empowered?" "For what purpose or end?" "What community is involved?" "What are its cultural traditions?" (Berkowitz, 1990; Riger, 1993). Wherever possible, we clarify such issues in discussing examples of empowerment throughout chapters 12 and 13.

# SENSE OF COMMUNITY, CITIZEN PARTICIPATION AND PSYCHOLOGICAL EMPOWERMENT: INTERTWINING PROCESSES

In this section, we describe how sense of community, citizen participation, and empowerment intertwine, strengthening each other. To communicate the richness of how these interrelate, we begin with an empirical study of citizen activists.

## A Qualitative Study

Kieffer (1984) studied the process by which individuals become psychologically empowered. He interviewed 15 community activists from a variety of locales in the U.S. These participants described how they developed from individuals uninvolved in community affairs into citizen leaders in grassroots community groups, often confronting powerful corporations or governments over local community issues. As we discussed in chapter 4, Kieffer's method aimed to discern common elements in that development across individuals, through qualitative analysis of their interview responses and with the aid of the interviewees themselves in interpreting those responses. Kieffer's study mainly concerned how citizen participation and psychological empowerment occur for individuals (the focus in this chapter). It was less concerned with how citizens can effectively influence their communities (the focus of chap. 13).

Ten of Kieffer's (1984) 15 participants were women, a common gender ratio in grassroots groups. Their ages ranged from 30 to 65. All had a high school education; 3 had completed college. Participants resided in New York City, rural central Appalachia, and other places throughout the Northeastern, Southern, and Midwestern regions of the United States. They included a

> working-class mother who had become the prime force in constructing a community health clinic, a migrant laborer who had become an organizer and boycott coordinator, a former junkie and gang leader who had become a leader in an urban homesteading program, and a retired laborer leading efforts against brown lung disease. (Kieffer, 1984, pp. 13–14)

Across these differences of age, gender, race, education, locale, and community issues, Kieffer found that all of these activists had progressed through a common set of four developmental stages of psychological empowerment. These stages are listed in Table 12.4.

| TABLE 12.4 | STAGES, OUTCOME, AND THEMES OF PSYCHOLOGICAL EMPOWERMENT IN KIEFFER'S (1984) STUDY |
|---|---|

**Stages**
    Era of entry
    Era of advancement
    Era of incorporation
    Era of commitment

**Outcome**
    Participatory competence

**Themes**
    Intertwining of growth and conflict
    Intertwining of action and reflection
    Intertwining of individual and community

The first stage, the *era of entry*, began with individuals having a strong sense of community in their localities, but not by being activists or community leaders in any sense. Their sense of community was threatened by a tangible, identifiable, direct *provocation* to the self-interest of the person and to the interests of the wider community. For one individual, this was an electric power facility that would flood the entire valley in which her community lay. For another, it was a betrayal of trust by a farmer-employer; for a third, a woman, it was being assaulted in her own yard. The provocation involved an injustice that not only generated anger, but undermined the trust previously held by Kieffer's (1984) interviewees in the authority of elites, corporate and governmental. They began, often reluctantly, to speak out and to confront those they held responsible.

In the *era of advancement*, three things occurred. All interviewees described having a *mentor* from outside the community. Often a community organizer, the mentor acted as role model, instructor, sounding board, and provider of concrete aid and emotional support. Second, all informants reported supportive peer relationships from others in their home community, through a *grassroots organization* formed to meet the threat. Third, all deepened their *critical awareness* or understanding of the social, economic, and political status quo, and of how this was influenced by their powerful opponents. Following a provocation involving injustice, they questioned authority and the status quo. Participation in the grassroots group and in the processes of confronting powerful others fostered this change of viewpoint. Critical reflection about their experiences also deepened their learning. In this stage, the developing activists advanced within their grassroots organizations and in terms of their own critical awareness.

The *era of incorporation* involved integrating their learning and experiences into a changing sense of personal identity. They began to think of themselves as leaders, as able to speak out and energized to do so. This growth also brought conflicts that occur with other commitments. Particularly for women, this often involved the competition of family and community needs. "How am I going to be able to do all these things?" was a question posed by many to themselves. Those who persisted in community activism and leadership found ways to resolve those conflicts, and their identity as community leader and their commitment to community work intensified.

The *era of commitment* was marked by fully integrating new experiences and ideas into many areas of one's life and personal identity. They searched for ways to express their altered values or newly developed skills through leadership roles or (in some cases) new careers. The activists interviewed by Kieffer (1984) reached the era of commitment in about 4 years on average, although this was variable.

Kieffer (1984, p. 31) described the outcome of these developmental stages as *participatory competence*. That involved three factors:

- self-perception of having skills for citizen participation,
- "critical understanding of the sociopolitical environment,"
- "cultivation of individual and collective resources" for community action.

Several themes occurred throughout these stages (Kieffer, 1984). First, conflict and growth seemed intertwined; conflict occurred within the person, e.g., between competing commitments, as well as between competing groups in the community. Psychological empowerment was initiated by a provocation and grew through the processes of conflict. Second, experience in community work and critical reflection on that work intertwined, leading to insights not possible through passive observation. Psychological empowerment required active involvement in community life, as well as reflective thinking about the meaning of that involvement. Finally, the development of psychological empowerment among Kieffer's participants was not simply an individual achievement. Implicit throughout Kieffer's analysis is the connection of individual to community. This included the original rootedness of individuals in their communities, their continuing commitment to the interests and work of the grassroots group and its wider community, and the support exchanged within the grassroots group. This illustrates the connections between sense of community, citizen participation, and empowerment.

Kieffer (1984) proposed that psychological empowerment and participatory competence developed whether or not the individuals and their communities won the sociopolitical struggles that they set out to fight. They did not necessarily gain the power to overcome powerful forces, but they did see themselves as having become more empowered, as gaining new skills and understanding, and as "feeling more powerful" (Kieffer, 1984, p. 32). This represents a limited definition of empowerment, because it does not necessarily involve increased influence in community decision making. Yet the experience described by Kieffer's respondents, a pervasive sense of having been empowered, even by setbacks and defeats, appears meaningful. They "unearthed seeds of fire" (Adams with Horton, 1975) that transformed them as persons, and that often fosters successful community change in the long run.

## A Conceptual Model

Figure 12.1 presents a model of the processes described in Kieffer's (1984) study and supported by studies of empowerment and participation to be discussed below. The model is based primarily on conceptual discussions by Wandersman (1984), Zimmerman (1995,

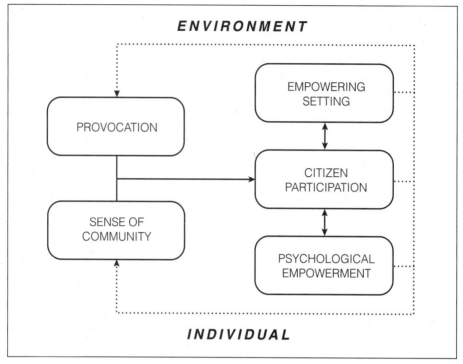

**FIGURE 12.1**

Processes of citizen participation and empowerment.

2000) and B. McMillan et al. (1995). It includes qualities of the individual (e.g., psychological empowerment), the environment (e.g., provocation, grassroots organization), and the interaction of these (sense of community, citizen participation).

The model begins with the individual living within a locality or relational community that shares a sense of community as defined in chapter 7. This experience of community rootedness was reported by all of Kieffer's (1984) interviewees and is widely reported in similar developmental accounts of empowerment (e.g., Berkowitz, 1987; Colby & Damon, 1992). Sense of community includes the qualities defined by D. W. McMillan and Chavis's (1986) definition of sense of community, such as membership, shared emotional connection, integration and fulfillment of needs among members, and mutual influence among community members. It also includes civic duty, or a personal sense of responsibility to the wider community, which was related to empowerment in empirical studies (Florin & Wandersman, 1984; Zimmerman & Rappaport, 1988). Sense of community is a link between the individual and the community environment.

The sense of community is threatened by a *provocation.* That provocation may be a recent, specific event, such as a corporation's plan to demolish a village to build a dam, a personal violent assault, or a contractor who does not honor his commitments (Burgess, 1990; Kieffer, 1984). Existence of a long-term problem also could constitute a provocation to which citizens respond, such as the unwillingness of city government and schools to collaborate on youth recreation services after school hours (Speer & Hughey, 1995). In a work setting, the provocation may be loss of profitability that prompts an organization to institute new management techniques empowering employees to make more decisions. However, an event is a provocation in this model only if it is experienced as a salient threat to the sense of community experienced by employees or community members.

A salient provocation to the community leads to the next three elements of the model: *citizen participation* by the individual, engagement in an *empowering setting*, and *psychological empowerment* of the individual. Empowering settings may include neighborhood or block associations, citizen advocacy groups, or other groups. They are empowering if they foster participation and psychological empowerment of members; we describe their characteristics later in this chapter. The three processes of citizen participation, engagement in an empowering setting, and psychological empowerment interact and affect each other (although the act of initiating participation comes first, as a response to provocation). This interplay is represented in Figure 12.1 by bidirectional arrows among them, with participation mediating the mutual effects of organization and individual. An empowering setting, citizen participation, and psychological empowerment thus intertwine and strengthen each other.

The interplay of these three elements also leads to two other outcomes: responses to the provocation and changes in the sense of community. The actions of individual or group may or may not eliminate the provocation (recall that Kieffer's, 1984, respondents did not always win their battles), but they do address it directly. Sense of community is often strengthened by collective action against a provocation, but this is not always so, especially if the issues are divisive. Of course, if the organization is not empowering for its members, if a person's life commitments preclude extensive citizen participation, or if the forces behind the provocation are overwhelming, neither these outcomes nor psychological empowerment are likely to occur.

In the next three sections, we turn to research on three central elements of this model: citizen participation, psychological, empowerment, and empowering settings.

## Sense of Community and Citizen Participation

The first of these elements, citizen participation, has long been a concern of social scientists. Much of that research has concerned the impact of demographic variables such as race, socioeconomic status, home ownership and length of residence. In the United States, for instance, it has often been found that middle-class citizens are more likely to participate in civic organizations than the poor and that if socioeconomic status is controlled, Blacks are more likely than Whites to participate. Length of local residence and home ownership (measures of "rootedness") also are generally associated with greater participation in locality-based organizations. However, the power of these variables to predict citizen participation in specific localities or to illuminate the processes of empowerment, is limited (D. D. Perkins et al., 1996; Wandersman & Florin, 2000).

In community psychology, the research literature on citizen participation burgeoned in the 1980s and 1990s. Much of it has concerned participation in voluntary neighborhood or block associations in the United States. These grassroots organizations address a variety of neighborhood issues such as zoning, housing, neighborhood appearance, crime, traffic, and recreation. They form mediating structures (recall this from chap. 7) between individual residents and city or county governments.

**Neighborhood Participation Project**    This program in Nashville, Tennessee, was the setting for several important early studies of citizen participation. Researchers studied residents of a sample of city blocks, defined as the two facing sides of a street bounded by two cross streets; residents of such a unit are more likely to interact with each other than in a larger neighborhood or in blocks otherwise defined. Louis Burgess, quoted at the beginning of this chapter, was active in a block association. These community groups give citizens a means of acting together to respond with larger forces that affect them, such as city government, absentee landlords, or crime. In the Nashville studies, participation in block associations usually was measured on a scale ranging from membership and attendance of meetings, through increasing involvement in the tasks of the association, to leadership of the association or a committee within it (Chavis & Wandersman, 1990). Samples were about equally composed of African American and European American citizens.

In these studies, participation was associated with sense of community, informal neighboring behaviors, and dissatisfaction with community problems (Chavis & Wandersman, 1990; Florin & Wandersman, 1984; D. G. Unger & Wandersman, 1983). Recall from chapter 7 that informal neighboring includes actions such as talking with neighbors, borrowing tools or other items, or watching someone's house while they are away. Dissatisfaction with block problems resembles the concept of provocation in Figure 12.1 and in Kieffer (1984). Longitudinal analyses indicated that participation in block associations led to increased sense of influence over block issues, an aspect of psychological empowerment.

**Block Booster Project**    The Nashville findings were extended by studies in New York City neighborhoods associated with the Block Booster Project (D. D. Perkins et al., 1990). Twenty-eight blocks were sampled from three neighborhoods reflecting diverse racial and ethnic composition and lower to middle income levels.

D. D. Perkins et al. (1990) analyzed differences between blocks, not individual residents, to predict levels of participation in block associations. Similar to the Nashville findings, blocks with greater levels of participation had more informal neighboring and greater satisfaction with the block among residents. Block associations perceived by residents as more effective also had higher levels of participation. In addition, blocks with higher incidence of poorly maintained properties had higher levels of participation, suggesting the importance of provocation. However, differences between blocks in occurrence of crime was not correlated with participation; this may suggest that a provocation must be visible to all residents.

**Comparative Analysis of U.S. Cities**    D. D. Perkins et al. (1996) conducted the broadest analyses in this series of studies, measuring factors related to participation in block and neighborhood organizations in New York City (Block Booster), Baltimore, and Salt Lake City. All three samples were multiracial. In New York City, associations were formed at the block level; in Baltimore and Salt Lake City associations were organized in terms of larger neighborhoods. The most consistent and powerful predictors of participation in these organizations concerned sense of community. These included beliefs about civic responsibility, sense of attachment to the community, perceptions of the efficacy of the neighborhood association, frequency of informal neighboring, and extent of volunteering for other community organizations (usually religious). Characteristics of the neighborhood physical environment, and demographic factors were less consistently related to participation.

***Sense of Community and Voting***    W. B. Davidson and Cotter (1989, 1993) studied the relationship between sense of community and voting behaviors in southern U.S. communities. Davidson and Cotter used the term *community* to refer to the entire city, not to one's residential block or neighborhood. W. B. Davidson and Cotter (1989) surveyed residents of Birmingham, Alabama, and found sense of community was significantly correlated with self-reported voting, contacting public officials, and working on public problems, but not with political campaigning or discussing politics.

***Participation in Cooperative Housing***    Saegert and Winkel (1996) studied participation in a different urban context, housing cooperatives among low-income residents of New York City. These organizations were created, with the resources of city government, to enable these residents collectively to purchase the apartment buildings in which they lived when these were sold. Studies of these cooperatives indicate they are superior to city or landlord ownership in terms of upkeep, safety, and resident satisfaction (Saegert & Winkel, 1996). Thus, housing cooperatives can be considered empowering for low-income families.

Saegert and Winkel (1996) surveyed residents in 16 cooperative housing buildings, comparing the 16 buildings on overall measures of quality of life (physical and social environment) in the building. The best predictors of building quality of life involved building-level citizen participation: the extent of residents' own participation in building activities, their perceptions of the extent of such participation by other residents, and having more frequent building meetings and less conflict among residents. Saegert and Winkel also measured (self-reported) voting in city, state, and national elections. The best predictors of voting were individual participation in building activities and perceptions of quality of life in the building. Thus, the Saegert and Winkel findings suggest that citizen participation in the building association and in voting in wider elections are interrelated and also are related to the building quality of life.

***Citizen Participation: Conclusions***    A theme emerges from these and other studies of citizen participation in locality-based grassroots organizations: The sense of community shared by residents of a building, block, neighborhood, or city is a strong and consistent predictor of citizen participation (see also Hughey, Speer, & Peterson, 1999). Specific forms of this relationship include informal neighboring behavior, involvement in citizen associations, and satisfaction with the neighborhood or building. This also implies that neighborhoods lacking in the demographic resources for participation identified by social science (long-term residents, home ownership, middle-class income) can nonetheless develop empowering citizen groups through strengthening the ties among residents and building an effective organization. Table 12.5 summarizes the predictors of citizen participation in these studies.

| TABLE 12.5 | PSYCHOLOGICAL PREDICTORS OF CITIZEN PARTICIPATION IN NEIGHBORHOOD ORGANIZATIONS |
|---|---|

Informal neighboring behavior

Sense of community, sense of civic responsibility

Satisfaction with quality of life in neighborhood, block, or building

Dissatisfaction with neighborhood problems

Involvement in apartment building activities

Volunteering for other community organizations

Perceived effectiveness of neighborhood association

## Elements of Psychological Empowerment

A second component of the model in Figure 12.1 concerns psychological empowerment, the personal aspect of citizen participation and empowerment. Psychological empowerment involves cognition, behavioral skills or competence, motivation, commitment to values, and other aspects of the person experiencing empowerment (Zimmerman, 1995, 2000). It develops through the interaction of personality factors and social experiences, particularly in situations involving citizen participation. "Empowerment appears not to be a spectator sport" (B. McMillan et al., 1995, p. 721), but is created by becoming involved actively in community work.

In this section, we focus on two components of psychological empowerment: critical awareness and participatory competence. As we do so, keep in mind that empowerment is contextual. It develops in a specific setting, community, and culture, and is strongly influenced by the qualities of those contexts (Zimmerman, 1995). A person may be psychologically empowered in one situation (at work) but not in another (in the neighborhood). Nonetheless, some generalizations can be made about psychological empowerment.

***Critical Awareness***     Empowerment involves development of a "critical awareness" about society and one's community (Friere, 1970/1993; Kieffer, 1984; Zimmerman, 1995). Serrano-Garcia (1984) listed three elements: "critical judgment about situations, the search for underlying causes of problems and their consequences, and an active role in transformation of society" (p. 178). Critical awareness includes questioning authority and the status quo and recognizing how power in relationships affects the quality of everyday life for individuals and families. The feminist motto "The personal is political" (Mulvey, 1988) is an expression of this idea.

Critical awareness also involves understanding of the causal agents or sources of power in an organization or community. Who defines community problems? How are decisions made? Whose views are respected and whose are discounted? How is leadership exerted? These patterns of behavior are influenced by formal policies and informal norms, at microsystem, organizational, community, and cultural levels. Those policies or norms can exclude citizens from participation in community decisions that directly influence their lives. Learning to see injustices as social regularities (Seidman, 1988), not as the natural order of the world, is a first step toward critical awareness and empowerment. Recall the nine-dot problem with which we began chapter 1: Critical awareness means being able to question the assumptions about social relationships that seem natural because they have been so thoroughly taught.

Critical awareness is of little use unless the person also perceives that change is possible, that citizens can change community conditions in constructive ways. *Perceptions of influence* over community problems, through joint action with others, are an important component of psychological empowerment (Saegert & Winkel, 1996; Zimmerman, Israel, Schulz, & Checkoway, 1992; Zimmerman & Rappaport, 1988). This sense of control is contextual; it refers to influence in particular circumstances. This contextual viewpoint is the chief difference between psychological empowerment and related, better known personality variables such as locus of control (Rotter, 1966) and self-efficacy (Bandura, 1986). The latter are broader constructs, concerning consistencies in behavior across many situations in a person's life.

Critical awareness emerges from life experiences and from reflection on them; neither book learning nor experience alone is sufficient. It is further developed through dialogue with others. The community activists interviewed by Kieffer (1984) had developed critical awareness through their experiences, through a relationship with an experienced mentor, and through discussion of their experiences with other community members. Through these experiences, they developed both a theory of community problems and how to address them and a commitment to action.

***Participatory Competence***   To be effective in action, the person needs to combine critical awareness with behavioral skills for participating effectively in community decisions. Participatory competence was the major outcome of Kieffer's (1984) stages of empowerment. It includes a variety of skills suggested by empirical studies (e.g., Balcazar, Seekins, Fawcett, & Hopkins, 1990) and other accounts (Berkowitz, 1987, 1996; Lappe & DuBois, 1994):

- articulating community problems
- imagining and articulating visions of a better community
- assertively and constructively advocating one's views
- actively listening to others, including opponents
- identifying and mobilizing personal and community resources
- building collaborative relationships and encouraging teamwork
- managing and resolving conflicts
- planning strategies for community change
- incorporating lessons learned through experience
- finding social support for oneself
- pacing one's efforts, to avoid burnout
- mentoring others in participation.

However, participatory competence is contextual; the nature and usefulness of these skills depends greatly on the setting. Some are more important in one setting than another.

A particularly important skill for participatory competence is *mobilizing resources* (Zimmerman, in press). Empowerment involves identifying, gaining access to, and using resources. Resources include tangible factors such as time, money, skills, knowledge, and influential allies. They also include less tangible qualities such as legitimacy or status in the community, the talents and ideas of community members, their personal commitment to community change, and social support. Further resources include shared values, and the shared rituals, narratives, or stories that embody them (Rappaport, 1995). Focusing on the resources and strengths in a community promotes participation and empowerment. Moreover, many of the resources involved in empowerment (e.g., social support, commitment, knowledge) are not scarce, but are renewable and multiplied through working together (Rappaport, 1987).

### Sustaining Participation and Empowerment

Involvement in time-consuming citizen participation requires commitment. What sustains that commitment?

Citizen participation is often initiated by questions such as "How does this problem or decision directly affect me, my family, or my community?" Recall from the outset of this chapter that Louis Burgess's (1990) original motive for involvement in his neighborhood association was to gain restitution for a poorly built shower. However, as a result of this participation, his motivation developed into a broader concern with the quality of life in his neighborhood. Lappe and DuBois (1994, p. 30) informally interviewed U.S. citizens involved in community decision making, asking them what rewards they obtained from that participation. Answers included the following:

- taking pride in accomplishment
- feeling my actions are in tune with my values
- having more energy
- a feeling of calm, serenity, well-being
- discovering how much I have to contribute
- working with those who share my concerns and hopes
- learning new skills, such as how to negotiate
- knowing my efforts will help create a better world for those I love
- enjoying better schools, jobs, housing, medical care, etc.

Two additional factors appear important in sustaining citizen participation and psychological empowerment. *Optimism* involves an enjoyment of challenges, a can-do spirit, an excitement about one's work. Citizen activists interviewed by Colby and Damon (1992) tended to attribute setbacks to temporary or situational causes and to seek to learn from them, rather than see them as evidence of personal failures or flaws. Berkowitz (1987) found similar themes, as well as an ability to react to adversity with humor, to remain optimistic, and to celebrate successes.

Both of these qualitative studies also found that *spiritual or moral commitment* often sustained citizen participation and empowerment, at least among their interviewees. For some, this involved spiritual faith and practices; for others, it centered on a secular commitment to moral principles such as justice. Spiritual support for community involvement included a sense of "that of God" or of innate value within everyone; a "calling" to their work and certainty of its spiritual necessity; the certainty that "God will provide," which enabled taking risks; a "willing suspension of fear and doubt" as they began new challenges; a "capacity for forgiveness;" and a sense of being blessed to be able to serve (Colby & Damon, 1992, pp. 78–80, 189–194, and 296). These beliefs supported the optimism of many interviewees. Berkowitz (1987, p. 323) often found what he called "traditional virtue" among his spiritual and secular respondents: a concern with caring for others, integrity, persistence, and commitment. Colby and Damon (1992, p. 78) found similar commitments to justice, harmony, honesty, and charity. Schorr's (1997) review of effective community organizations found that many promote personal relationships and a shared group climate

| | ELEMENTS OF **PSYCHOLOGICAL EMPOWERMENT** |
|---|---|
| TABLE **12.6** | IN **INDIVIDUALS** |

Critical awareness
  Perceived influence

Participatory competence
  Mobilizing resources

Factors sustaining participation and empowerment
  Rewards of participation
  Optimism
  Spiritual/moral commitment

---

based on spiritual ideals or on secular ideals that provide shared meaning and purpose. Pursuit of these values, whether within a spiritual or secular perspective, provides meaning for community involvement. Table 12.6 lists components of psychological empowerment.

# EMPOWERING COMMUNITY SETTINGS

The third area of research we will cover concerns the qualities of settings (groups or organizations) that foster participation in decision making and empowerment among their members. For instance, the empowered community activists studied by Kieffer (1984) did not become empowered alone; their growth occurred within empowering settings.

First we describe four qualities of settings that empower personal development among their members. Second, we show how those four qualities also empower citizens to work for social change in their communities. Third, we discuss the issue of conflict in community groups, and how one community organization resolved it constructively. Fourth, we describe the importance of managing benefits and costs of citizen participation for group members. Finally, we discuss how sense of community within the setting represents an overarching theme of empowering settings.

Many studies in this section were based on collaborative relationships between researchers and community organization members, often over periods of years. Thus, the research methods, as well as topics of inquiry, were guided by concepts of citizen participation and empowerment.

## *Empowering Settings and Personal Development*

Maton and Salem (1995) summarized studies of three empowering community settings that reveal much about the workings of both a sense of community and empowerment. The three settings are New Covenant Fellowship, a local Christian religious fellowship; GROW, an international self-help organization for persons with serious mental illness; and Meyerhoff Scholars, one university's program to promote science achievement among African American students. Although these settings foster individual development, not citizen participation in community decision making, the concepts identified by Maton and

Salem are important for understanding empowering settings. As we discuss below, these concepts also apply to settings concerned with citizen participation and community change.

Maton and Salem (1995) found four general characteristics that fostered personal empowerment in all three organizations: a group-based and strengths-based belief system, an opportunity role structure, peer social support systems, and shared, inspiring leadership.

***Group-Based, Strengths-Based Belief System***   Each group had a clear set of principles that defined member and organizational goals, and inspired member growth toward them. These included a religious lifestyle (New Covenant), personal growth and coping (GROW), and academic success (Meyerhoff). The belief systems were strengths-based, emphasizing the capabilities and resources of group members for pursuing these goals. GROW, for example, stresses the capability for effective coping within each member and the resources offered by the group. Meyerhoff encourages students to think of themselves as talented and as resources for each other. In addition, the principles and practices in each organization encourage members to think and act beyond themselves, to give back to the group and the wider community. In each group, pursuit of the basic goals of the group involves service and involvement with others.

A group-based belief system provides a link to several of the qualities of psychological empowerment described earlier in this chapter. It can foster critical awareness of society, and one's perception of influence in the community. It may provide a spiritual meaning for community involvement or rationale for optimism in the face of setbacks. It can provide inspiration that increases motivation for influencing the community.

Rappaport (1995) described the importance of shared community events, rituals and narratives or storytelling that embody memorable examples of empowerment. These often embody the belief system of the group, and represent resources for strengthening the sense of community among members. Berkowitz (1996) described the community-building power of celebrating a community's solidarity or accomplishments. Bettencourt, Dillmann, and Wollman (1996) found that such identification of members with the group's history and aims fostered the longevity and effectiveness of a peace group. An organization "that can articulate its core values develops the capacity to act on what it believes" (Butterfoss, Goodman, & Wandersman, in press).

We should note that group identification and its emotional basis can be a double-edged sword (Pratkanis & Turner, 1996). Belief systems and associated rituals can create stereotyped images of those outside the group, generate conflict, and foster manipulation by emotional appeals. This has been the history of many forms of ethnic, religious, and other conflicts between communities. Fostering external linkages outside the group and awareness of values transcending the group may help to reduce these risks.

***Opportunity Role Structures***   Maton and Salem (1995) found that all three organizations had developed a system of roles and tasks that involves each member actively in the life of the group. These systems are pervasive and accessible in the activities of the group, offering many chances for a new or uninvolved member to take part, and volunteering for roles is frequently encouraged by group members and leaders. GROW, for instance, creates new chapters with few members and multiple roles as a way of fostering member participation in the group (Zimmerman et al., 1991). As we have discussed before, these resemble underpopulated settings in Barker's ecological psychology (Barker,

1968; Schoggen, 1989; also see chap. 5). An opportunity role structure affords member participation and development of participatory competence.

***Peer Social Support Systems***   Each of the three empowering organizations explicitly promotes social support among its members. That support encompasses multiple forms (e.g., socializing, emotional support, informational support). New Covenant promotes the exchange of emotional, spiritual, and even financial support among members. Meyerhoff provides faculty and staff involvement with students, but especially relies on structured study groups among peers. Behavioral observations of GROW meetings (L. Roberts et al., 1991, 1999) have revealed a very high percentage of positive helping statements being exchanged.

Peer support promotes *mentoring*, the learning of new skills through partnership with a more experienced person. Recall that mentoring was one of the key factors in psychological empowerment in the Kieffer (1984) study of community activists. GROW members also are strongly encouraged to become a helping partner with another member, helping each other outside group meetings (Maton & Salem, 1995). Kroeker (1995) described a similar role of "accompaniment" in her study of empowerment among members of a Nicaraguan agricultural cooperative.

In all three groups, a strong sense of community is also reported by members. All three encourage members to develop multidimensional friendships among themselves (recall this concept from chap. 8). Reports of the sense of community in each group appear to include the elements of a sense of membership, mutual influence of member and group, integration and fulfillment of needs among members, and shared emotional connection, the four elements of a sense of community proposed by D. W. McMillan and Chavis (1986) and discussed in chapter 7.

***Shared, Inspiring Leadership***   Finally, in all three settings, committed leaders articulated a vision of the organization, acted as role models, used interpersonal and organizational skills, and socialized new leaders. Opportunity role structures and social support systems facilitated this process of leadership development.

Despite the differences in these organizations' missions, Maton and Salem (1995) termed all three "empowering" settings because their methods promoted psychological growth among members. However, these settings do not seek community or social change directly. They may be indirectly involved in social change; GROW and Meyerhoff, for instance, are concerned with promoting the strengths and capabilities of disempowered populations. However, they embody a vision of empowerment largely limited to individual and organizational development. Can a grassroots organization that seeks wider community–social change empower its members in the same four ways identified by Maton and Salem (1995)?

## Empowering Settings and Community Change

Speer, Hughey, and associates (Speer & Hughey, 1995; Speer et al., 1995) studied grassroots community organizations concerned with "community organizing for power," directly seeking social change in their localities. These researchers analyzed the organizing strategies of the Pacific Institute for Community Organizing (PICO) in the United States. The PICO approach embodies the idea that empowering members within an organization helps to create an empowered organization that influences the wider community (see Zimmerman, 2000, for a discussion of the empowering-empowered distinction). Interestingly, PICO groups empower their members in ways similar to those identified by Maton and Salem (1995).

PICO groups are based in religious congregations in low-income communities and use a "relationship-based" approach to community organizing (Speer & Hughey, 1995, p. 730). This method begins with citizens meeting in pairs to discuss issues of community concern and to build interpersonal ties. The rationale is that an organization based on strong interpersonal relationships will endure when the hot issue of the moment has passed, whereas a group solely based on one issue will falter. This interpersonal connectedness forms a peer social support system (Maton & Salem, 1995). The religious–institutional basis of the organization and its structured approach to planning community change provide a group-based belief system that provides clear, inspiring goals and is focused beyond the self, another of the Maton and Salem (1995) elements. Moreover, PICO groups follow each stage of active community organizing with a period of group reflection and evaluation of their work, including more meetings in pairs of members. This builds critical awareness, a key element of psychological empowerment, as described earlier.

PICO groups also create *participatory niches* (Speer & Hughey, 1995) by rotating responsibilities among members, thus providing roles for as many members as possible. These resemble opportunity role structures (Maton & Salem, 1995) and underpopulated settings (Schoggen, 1989). In addition, PICO methods stress participatory decision making by group members at each stage of their efforts. These methods also involve members in fact-finding about community problems, identifying powerful officials or organizations whom the group seeks to influence, and meeting with these targets to press for specific decisions. These activities structure new roles and skills for members, increasing their participatory competence.

Leadership in PICO organizing builds on the existing congregational structure and an organizing committee, which creates strong yet shared leadership based on the inspirational qualities of the religious setting. These are similar to the leadership in empowering settings studied by Maton and Salem (1995).

In a study comparing PICO groups to neighborhood groups employing more traditional issue-oriented organizing strategies in the same city, members of PICO groups perceived their groups as less controlling, more intimate, and more psychologically empowering, and reported more interpersonal contact with group members (Speer et al., 1995). These findings indicate that these groups are empowering settings, and they support the applicability of the Maton and Salem (1995) categories to settings focused on community and social change.

## Conflict and "Coempowerment" Within an Organization

> To live is to have conflict. If you don't have conflict, you aren't doing anything. Friction means fire, and fire is power. (a community organization leader interviewed by Lappe & DuBois, 1994, p. 247).

Conflict is a fact of life in community work. It may concern polite but firm disagreement over ideas or actions, or involve passionate confrontation and anger, or take a variety of other forms. Community organizers and researchers agree that a community organization that appreciates and manages conflict, rather than denies or resists it, empowers its members in the long run (e.g., Bartunek & Keys, 1979; Kaye & Wolff, 1997; Lappe & DuBois, 1994, pp. 247–256; Wiesenfeld, 1996). Conflict is a source of new or previously overlooked ideas and of challenges to unexamined assumptions. It provides an opportunity for greater inclusion of all members. It usually accompanies diversity of backgrounds, experiences, and viewpoints, and thus is a positive sign of a truly inclusive, diverse group. Creatively and wisely resolved, it often leads to better planning and to greater self-confidence within a group (Lappe & DuBois, 1994, p. 246).

The four Maton and Salem (1995) qualities of empowering settings do not explicitly address the issue of conflict within an empowering setting. Yet such conflict certainly does occur within communities and organizations, and can facilitate or impede member participation and empowerment. Kieffer (1984) found conflict and growth intertwined in his study of psychological empowerment. A case study of an organization for persons with developmental disabilities (M. A. Bond & Keys, 1993) analyzed the emergence of conflicts within the organization and how resolution of these conflicts empowered the members as well as the group.

Midwest ARC was founded in a Midwestern U.S. city by families of persons with developmental disabilities and grew to provide community services such as a day program, vocational services, residences, and an early intervention program (M. A. Bond & Keys, 1993). All of these were initially controlled by families rather than professionals; the organization had been founded in part because professional services had been patronizing and ineffective. As the organization expanded in scope, it began to seek to identify resources more widely.

However, over time Midwest ARC broadened its scope and began to bring into its governing board community members (often professionals) who had access to community leaders and resources (including funding). Thus emerged two subgroups within the organization, which held divergent and ultimately conflicting visions for the organization: a parents' group and a community members' group. Parents tended to be from the working class, valued practical knowledge, and usually had long experience with Midwest ARC. Since their views had often been discounted by professionals, some had cultivated confrontational communication styles in order to be heard (M. A. Bond, 1999). Community members tended to be educated, verbal professionals confident of their expertise, impatient with practical details, and having little experience with developmental disabilities or with the day-to-day running of the organization. A number of conflicts emerged, leading to turnover in staff and in board membership. To understand these conflicts, you must go beyond thinking of the relationship of an organization to its individual members (the focus of the Maton and Salem concepts), and also think of an organization as a collection of *subgroups* with relationships to each other (Wiesenfeld, 1996).

How did Midwest ARC resolve its problems? Bond and Keys (1993) described changes that they termed *coempowerment.* The prefix *co* refers to the fact that the subgroups within the organization were empowered together, as a unity, not in subgroups or as individuals. Coempowerment involved four processes. *Activating resources* occurred as new staff and board members built an organizational atmosphere that recognized and used resources (skills, information, interpersonal connections) offered by both parents and community members. *Appreciating interdependencies* involved recognition of superordinate goals shared by all Midwest ARC board members, such as a commitment to provide expanded services. These were endorsed by both parents and community members. To attain those goals, each group needed the help of the other, making the groups interdependent.

Activation of resources and appreciation of interdependence progressed as organization leaders adopted more *inclusive decision making*. More decisions were made by the board or through committees representative of organizational membership; fewer decisions were made by a few officers or "insiders." Research in a number of community organizations has shown that inclusive decision making promotes citizen participation and organizational effectiveness (Fawcett et al., 1995; Maton & Salem, 1995; B. McMillan et al., 1995; Prestby & Wandersman, 1985).

*Boundary spanning* (Katz & Kahn, 1978) involved individuals in the organization whose networks of personal or work relationships included members of both parent and community members. One example of this was a community member who often worked in the crafts store run mostly by parents. Another was a founding parent member who reached out to community members in several ways. Ongoing changes in board membership led to more professionals who were also parents of persons with developmental disabilities, and community members from a broader socioeconomic base. These changes promoted spanning of the boundaries between parents and community members (M. A. Bond & Keys, 1993, pp. 51–53).

It is important to note that appreciating interdependencies and boundary spanning both promote a sense of community. Inclusive decision making and appreciation of interdependencies fostered mutual influence, one of the four elements of sense of community (D. W. McMillan & Chavis, 1986). Also, these efforts helped realign membership boundaries to focus on the whole organization, not subgroups.

By empowering its members to collaborate, Midwest ARC went on to attain a number of organizational goals, including a successful capital fundraising campaign and increased funding for expanded services (M. A. Bond & Keys, 1993, p. 44).

## Benefits and Costs of Participation

Community groups rely on volunteers. If those volunteers don't find their involvement rewarding, or if its personal costs are too high, they will leave. If they find involvement rewarding, they will often become more involved. At the outset of this chapter, Louis Burgess stated that involvement in neighborhood affairs was a lot of work, but also rewarding in ways he had not originally anticipated. Empowering community settings provide benefits for citizen participation that outweigh its personal costs (B. McMillan et al., 1995; Prestby, Wandersman, Florin, Rich, & Chavis, 1990).

Benefits of participation may include learning new skills, being involved in exciting issues, making interpersonal contacts, personal recognition, and a sense of improving the community (we presented a list of these earlier while discussing psychological empowerment). Costs of participation include use of time, finding child care, and experiencing unpleasant meetings (for instance, unproductive conflict).

In the Block Booster Project, associations that intentionally sought to increase incentives and lower costs for individual involvement had greater overall levels of member participation (Prestby et al., 1990). Incentives for participation included recognizing individual accomplishments, welcoming attendees at meetings, asking for opinions, and providing discount coupons from local businesses. Efforts to lower costs of participation included arranging times and length of meetings to meet citizen schedules and offering child care.

## An Overarching Theme: Sense of Community Within the Setting

Many research findings on empowering community settings resemble ideas concerning sense of community (see Hughey et al., 1999). Here, *sense of community* refers to the relationship of the individual to the setting or organization, not to the wider locality (which appears elsewhere in the model in Figure 12.1). When members of a community organization share a sense of community among themselves, and when members participate in decision making, that setting is likely to empower its members.

All four of the Maton and Salem (1995) qualities of empowering settings involve strengthening group sense of community. The four elements of coempowerment also concern strengthening that sense of community, especially when subgroups are in conflict. Even attention to the benefits and costs of participation are relevant, especially to fulfillment of member needs and sense of membership (D. W. McMillan & Chavis, 1986). For a community organization, building a group sense of community, maximizing member participation in decision making, and empowering members are intertwined processes (Hughey et al., 1999). Table 12.7 lists the qualities of empowering settings.

## Dilemmas in Creating Empowering Settings

Creating a setting that empowers its members is not as easy as it may sound. Studies by community psychologists illustrate dilemmas that arise in seeking to empower members and foster participation. All of them raise two key questions: Who is to be empowered? How?

---

**TABLE 12.7** **QUALITIES OF EMPOWERING COMMUNITY SETTINGS**

---

Group-based, strengths-based belief system

Opportunity role structures, participatory niches

Peer social support systems

Shared, inspiring leadership

Coempowerment

   Activating resources

   Appreciating interdependencies

   Inclusive decision making (through citizen participation)

   Boundary spanning

Maximizing benefits, minimizing costs of participation

Overarching theme: Sense of community within setting

---

*The "Challenges of Success"*    Riger's (1984, 1993) studies of feminist movement organizations, such as women's shelters and rape crisis centers, illustrate how the goal of efficient services for clients (in this case, empowering women) may conflict with the goal of empowering staff members. Many feminist organizations began as small collectives in which decision-making was shared widely among volunteers. Yet as demand for their services grew, the time-consuming process of bottom-up participation in decision making became very inefficient. Moreover, many feminist organizations began to seek funding and employ staff. As they did so, the need for financial accountability to funders also led to more top-down decision making.

These changes created settings that were less participatory for members/employees. Yet they empowered the organization to provide more services. The less that staff members were involved in participatory decision making, the more women in need could be empowered. Riger (1993) labeled these tradeoffs the "challenges of success." Such challenges involve the question raised above: Who is to be empowered?

*Inequalities of Resources*    Gruber and Trickett (1987) studied the creation of the High School in the Community, an alternative high school founded by a group of parents, teachers, and students. This school was created with a governing board comprised of equal proportions of faculty, parents, and students. This board was to be the policy making body for the school, designed to foster participation by all three of its subgroups. In practice, however, the board quickly developed conflicts with teachers over issues such as faculty hiring and admissions policy. Within three years, the faculty undermined the power of the board by assuming responsibility for important decisions and bringing fewer issues to the board for discussion. Eventually, the board dwindled in significance.

One of the main reasons for this outcome was that faculty possessed more knowledge and resources. They had more expertise in educational decisions, and more information about day-to-day problems facing the school, and could more easily perform school-related tasks. When other schools and funding agencies communicated with the school, it was with faculty. Teachers also had the last word in most disputes. They granted grades and credits, and could delay or alter implementation of board policies they disliked.

Many social regularities of traditional schools thus were replicated in the workings of the new school. All of these regularities tended to empower only the faculty (Gruber & Trickett, 1987). Yet, when surveyed, parents and students felt empowered, although their actual input into school decisions was limited (Gruber & Trickett, 1987, pp. 368–369). Moreover, the High School in the Community attained many of its educational objectives. These findings raise several questions: Who is to be empowered? Who holds what resources? What does it mean to feel empowered?

*Top-Down Empowerment*    Employee empowerment and related initiatives such as quality circles have become popular in many large work organizations, often instituted by management. Foster-Fishman and associates (Foster-Fishman & Keys, 1997; Foster-Fishman et al., 1998) studied an initiative designed to empower the employees of SERVE, a large, public human service organization serving persons with disabilities. The empowerment initiative was instituted by statewide management from the top down, rather than at employee insistence. It was designed to encourage staff participation in organizational decision making and promote employee-originated innovations in services.

The studies found external and internal constraints on employee empowerment at SERVE. Externally, as a public agency, SERVE was vulnerable to political pressures, media criticism, and budget cuts. These made any innovation risky unless it was very likely to succeed, and rewarded close, tightly controlling, disempowering supervision of staff. Internally, many supervisors resisted the empowerment initiative and limited its actual adoption in practice. However, the researchers found that some SERVE managers and worksites genuinely adopted empowerment principles, resulting in contextual (e.g., work-site) differences. Foster-Fishman et al. (1998), using qualitative research methods, found evidence of genuine employee participation and innovation.

**Summary of Dilemmas**    These studies pose several dilemmas for the creation of empowering community settings.

First, who is to be empowered, by whom? The competing aims of empowering staff versus serving women in need were identified in Riger's (1993) "challenges of success." The High School in the Community experienced a similar conflict: empowering faculty interfered to some extent with empowering parents and students (Gruber & Trickett, 1987).

However, the studies we have reviewed all took place in work settings. In a volunteer organization, members can easily "vote with their feet," reducing their commitment or leaving the organization. Leaders of voluntary organizations must attract member commit-ment without pay, which can foster genuine grassroots participation and empowerment.

Second, is empowerment enacted in practice? Verbal commitment to the principle of empowerment (by faculty at High School in the Community, by some managers in SERVE) does not guarantee behavioral or organizational commitment to empowering practices. (It's easy to "talk the talk," harder to "walk the walk.")

Third, how is empowerment defined: feeling empowered or actual decision-making power? Despite clear limits on their actual influence, many parents in the High School in the Community felt empowered and satisfied with the school (Gruber & Trickett, pp. 368–369), and many employees of SERVE felt empowered (Foster-Fishman & Keys, 1997; Foster-Fishman et al., 1998). Recall from chapter 9 that Kieffer's (1984) employees felt empowered even when they did not win the community battles they set out to fight. However, in many other contexts, feeling empowered without real decision-making power may represent an illusion (Riger, 1993).

Fourth, what is the level of analysis? Recall from chapter 9 that empowerment is con-textual, differing in form across settings; even settings within the same organization, as Foster-Fishman and associates found. Empowerment may have an agreed-upon meaning in a local setting (grassroots group, single workplace, neighborhood). However, in larger social units (large organizations, cities, societies), empowerment has multiple, competing meanings, often becoming a buzzword that means nothing distinctive at all (D. D. Perkins, 1995). Thus, empowerment may be especially local and contextual in form.

Another implication of levels of analysis and the contextual nature of empowerment concerns human diversity. Most studies of empowering settings have not focused on cul-tural, racial, gender, or other population differences in what constitutes an empowering setting, although these are likely to exist in some way.

This chapter concerned the relationships between individual citizens and their com-munities, chiefly through processes of citizen participation, empowerment, and sense of community. We concluded by describing empowering settings that foster these processes among their members. In the next chapter, we take up empowered organizations that influence their wider communities, fostering social change and enhancing the quality of community life.

## Chapter Summary

**1.** Citizen participation, empowerment, and sense of community are intertwining processes through which citizens take part in community life.

**2.** *Citizen participation* occurs when individuals take part in decision making in a community: group, organization, locality, or larger unit. It is not the same as community service. It is a behavior, and may be a means of making decisions or an end or value about how decisions should be made.

**3.** *Empowerment* occurs when people lacking an equal share of resources gain greater access to and control over those resources. It may refer to behavior or to other psychological processes, and is a more value-laden term than citizen participation.

**4.** Empowerment occurs at *multiple levels* of analysis, but usually from a *bottom-up perspective.* It is a *process*, not personality trait, and differs in *different contexts.* Community psychologists are concerned with empowerment in group or *community context.*

**5.** Kieffer (1984) studied psychological empowerment among community activists. They progressed through four stages, the eras of *entry, advancement, incorporation,* and *commitment.* The outcome of these stages was *participatory competence* in citizen participation.

**6.** Citizen participation and psychological empowerment result when citizens who share a sense of community are threatened with a *provocation* to their community. They respond by forming or joining a community organization. If that organization (or setting) empowers them, increased participation and empowerment occur, responding to the provocation and strengthening the sense of community. These processes are illustrated in Figure 12.1.

**7.** Citizen participation has been studied in locality organizations such as block associations. Factors that predict citizen participation in these organizations often concern sense of community and are listed in Table 12.5.

**8.** Psychological empowerment refers to empowerment as it occurs in individuals. Two of its principal components are *critical awareness* and *participatory competence.* *Rewards* gained from participation, *optimism,* and *spiritual/moral commitment* help to sustain participation and empowerment.

**9.** Empowering community settings share a number of characteristics. These are listed in Table 12.7. Their overarching theme is strengthening the internal sense of community within the setting.

**10.** Creating empowering settings raises several dilemmas. These include who is to be empowered, whether empowerment is actually enacted, how it is to be defined, and what is the level of analysis.

# BRIEF EXERCISES

**1.** Interview a community leader or activist. (Your instructor may be able to help you find one locally.) This person may be well-known or known only in the neighborhood or organization with which she or he works most closely.

Here are some questions to ask: What is the community work that you do? How did you become involved in it? Does it involve challenging the community's status quo somehow? Who has influenced this work most greatly? Did you have mentors or role models for doing this work? Do you have partners now in this work? Has a sense of community (or a sense of belongingness and commitment to your community) been a part of your work? What lessons have you learned from it? What are the rewards of your work? How have you grown through this work? What sustains you during difficult times in this work?

If possible, apply the concepts listed in Tables 12.4–12.7 to this person's community experiences.

**2.** Read one or more profiles of community activists in *Local Heroes* (Berkowitz, 1987). Present a report to the class on what you learned. Consider the questions in Exercise 1 while you read.

**3.** Attend a meeting of a neighborhood or block association or a community group that is devoted to community change or challenging the community status quo. Interview group members if you can as well. Learn as much as you can about the purposes and history of the group, how it makes decisions, how it encourages participation by its members and the wider community, and what its impact on the wider community has been. Ask questions from Exercise 1 above in interviews if appropriate.

**4.** Explain the model in Figure 12.1, including all the terms, to a friend or classmate. Use your own words and examples.

# RECOMMENDED READINGS

## *Articles and Chapters*

Bond, M., & Keys, C. (1993). Empowerment, diversity and collaboration: Promoting synergy on community boards. *American Journal of Community Psychology, 21,* 37–57.

 Foster-Fishman, P. G., Salem, D., Chibnall, S., Legler, R., & Yapchai, C. (1998). Empirical support for the critical assumptions of empowerment theory. *American Journal of Community Psychology, 26,* 507–536.

Kieffer, C. (1984). Citizen empowerment: A developmental perspective. *Prevention in Human Services, 3,* 9–36. Also published in J. Rappaport, C. Swift, & R. Hess (Eds.), (1984). *Studies in empowerment: Steps toward understanding and action.* New York: Haworth Press.

Maton, K., & Salem, D. (1995). Organizational characteristics of empowering community settings: A multiple case study approach. *American Journal of Community Psychology, 23,* 631–656.

 This article appears in journals in the InfoTrac College Edition on-line library available from Wadsworth.

Rappaport, J. (1987). Terms of empowerment/exemplars of prevention: Toward a theory for community psychology. *American Journal of Community Psychology, 15,* 121–144.

Riger, S. (1993). What's wrong with empowerment. *American Journal of Community Psychology, 21,* 279–291.

Zimmerman, M. (2000). Empowerment theory: Psychological, organizational and community levels of analysis. In J. Rappaport & E. Seidman (Eds.), *Handbook of community psychology* (p. 43–63). New York: Plenum.

### Special Journal Issues

Wandersman, A. & Florin, P. (1990). Citizen participation, voluntary organizations and community development: Insights for empowerment and research [Special section]. *American Journal of Community Psychology, 18*(1).

Zimmerman, M., & Perkins, D. (Eds.). (1995). Empowerment theory, research and application [Special issue]. *American Journal of Community Psychology, 23*(5).

Wittig, M., & Bettencourt, B. A. (Eds.) (1996). Social psychological perspectives on grassroots organizing [Special issue]. *Journal of Social Issues, 52*(1).

### Books

Berkowitz, B. (1987). *Local heroes.* Lexington, MA: D.C. Heath.

Colby, A., & Damon, W. (1992). *Some do care: Contemporary lives of moral commitment.* New York: Free Press.

# InfoTrac Keywords

*citizen, citizen participation, community, empowering(ed)(ment), participation(tory), sense of community.*

# ORGANIZING FOR COMMUNITY AND SOCIAL CHANGE

CHAPTER

*13*

> Never doubt that a small group of thoughtful, committed citizens can change the
> world; indeed, it's the only thing that ever does.
>
> Margaret Mead

In chapter 12, we examined the intertwining processes of sense of community, citizen participation, and psychological empowerment. In this chapter, we continue the discussion by focusing on these questions:

- How do citizens, acting collectively, acquire and use power to promote positive changes in their communities?
- How can communities become empowered to address the problems and challenges they face?

Recall from chapter 12 that empowerment is a multilevel construct. Organizations and communities may become empowered, not just individuals. We devote this chapter primarily to change at the community level. Yet we also seek to promote your understanding of how community change is closely connected to quality of life for individuals, and to organizational and macrosystem forces. By chapter's end, we hope that you will have a better understanding of the ways in which Margaret Mead's oft-quoted adage comes true, and of how that involves psychological questions and concepts.

## What Are the Key Points of This Chapter?

We begin with an exercise designed to help you imagine how community and individual well-being are intertwined. Second, we discuss the distinction between *empowering* organizations and communities, covered in chapter 12, and *empowered* organizations and communities to be covered here. Third, we describe three instruments of social power in communities, and four approaches to community change that address each form of power. Fourth, we propose an "open systems" model of community change that involves empowered community organizations pursuing initiatives to enhance the quality of community life. Fifth, we illustrate these processes with three extended examples of community change initiatives. Sixth, we discuss overarching issues regarding the purposes and effectiveness of community change efforts.

## Psychology and Community Change

Let's begin with an exercise to illustrate the psychological aspects of community problems and community change.

- First, list at least five problems or challenges that your locality (e.g., city block, neighborhood, town, county) faces. These may include violence in various forms, health care, issues involving sexuality and/or pregnancy, drug abuse, poverty, quality of education, child abuse and neglect, crime, pollution or other environmental hazard, and many others.
- Second, list the age groups that are affected by each problem (e.g., young children, adolescents, adults, seniors, or more specific groups). This puts each problem in lifespan-developmental perspective.

- Third, list at least one negative psychological outcome or problem that is associated with each community problem.
- Finally, write briefly how each problem involves the community as a whole.

These community problems or challenges involve both psychological outcomes and community quality of life. For instance, poverty creates not only individual and family stressors but also is associated with less access to health care and with the costs of treating long-term health problems that could have been prevented with earlier care. As another example, drug abuse is not just an individual or family problem, but results in drunk driving, criminal acts to obtain money for drugs, costs for health care or imprisonment, and other emotional and material costs that are borne by the community and society.

How can communities address problems such as those you listed? Box 13.1 describes some examples of community change initiatives. Each of these involves both individual and community well-being. Each also involves citizen participation, empowerment, and community change.

## 13.1    *Community Change Initiatives*

Here are some examples of community change. As you read them, ask yourself "What qualities do these programs have in common?"

- Students are learning conflict mediation skills in many schools today. They are using them to settle disputes, thus reducing violence, harassment, and injuries among students (Lappe & DuBois, 1994, p. 6). An example: When a student new to a middle school squared off to fight another student, an onlooker defused the situation by asserting "Hey man, we don't do that in this school" (Comer, 1992).
- In four major areas of U.S. industry, worker-owned businesses have recently ranked in the top 10 firms. Stocks in worker-owned companies have outperformed major market averages (Lappe & DuBois, 1994, p. 7).
- In rural Bangladesh, the Grameen Bank network operates in 18,000 villages to provide small loans to more than a million landless poor women for their own small businesses. Loans are made to small groups of four to seven persons, who are responsible for repayment as a group and must have a business plan approved by the bank. The Grameen idea has spread internationally, in urban and rural settings, with women and men as borrowers, helping to create working businesses among the poor and typically enjoying very low default rates (Lappe & DuBois, 1994, pp. 99–100).
- In rural West Virginia, a coalition of churches and community groups provided the loan that began Wellspring, a crafts cooperative run by women in isolated communities with little access to jobs or transportation. Wellspring now markets handmade crafts through a shop and catalog (Kretzmann & McKnight, 1993, p. 308).
- Community Development Corporations (CDCs) in many U.S. localities provide funding and technical assistance, based on local and outside funding, for start-up and support of

*(continued)*

local businesses. Often these are created by or based in local churches, schools, or neighborhood associations (Kretzmann & McKnight, 1993; Schorr, 1997).

- A local chapter of the National Association of Black Accountants offered free accounting services to local community groups and businesses. They played a critical role in the start-up of local businesses and nonprofit groups (Kretzmann & McKnight, 1993, p. 133).
- In Birmingham, Alabama, neighborhood councils elected by citizens negotiate with city hall regarding city decisions. For the first time, African-American neighborhoods are getting their share of much-needed capital improvements (Lappe & DuBois, 1994, p. 7). Similar groups operate in many U.S. cities, with varying levels of power.
- In Chicago, an interfaith coalition of churches met with developers of a new professional sports stadium in their neighborhood. Backed by strong neighborhood support, they negotiated developer guarantees of replacement housing for everyone displaced by the stadium, a new public library, and access to parking (Kretzmann & McKnight, 1993, p. 149).
- In Minneapolis, a local man was troubled by the behavior of neighborhood young men. Talking with them, he found that they liked to make things. Together they decided to build wooden lawn furniture for the neighborhood. Without telling anyone, they produced 90 chairs. On a spring Sunday morning, they set the chairs out in the front yard of buildings in a two-block area. Area residents discovered the chairs with delight. Since then, more crews have made more chairs for the neighborhood. Another Minneapolis group created an association called the Youth Express, which set up youth-run enterprises, a skill bank identifying what individual youth can do, and a job-finding club (Kretzmann & McKnight, 1993, p. 135).
- In Los Angeles, police gather information about deteriorated buildings and provide it to city agencies for action. Then they start a clean-up campaign in those areas, with juvenile offenders performing community service. In San Diego, police work with local businesses and neighborhood associations to start clean-up campaigns and to coordinate responses to gang activities (Kretzmann & McKnight, 1993, pp. 246 and 248).
- In New York City, tenant-owned limited-equity cooperative housing provides secure, habitable, affordable housing for very-low-income persons and families who might otherwise be homeless. When the city seizes buildings from absentee landlords who have not paid taxes, it now has three options: manage them under city ownership, sell the buildings to new private landlords, or help to finance sale of the buildings to cooperatives of low-income tenants who manage the building. Cooperative housing has been shown to be higher in management quality, safety, freedom from drug activity, and resident satisfaction than buildings retained in city ownership or sold to new landlords (Saegert & Winkel, 1996, p. 520).
- Communities throughout the United States are forming coalitions of citizens and groups to address drug abuse. They write and implement action plans for community agencies, schools, religious congregations, media, and individual citizens to work together on addressing this community problem (Fawcett et al. 1995; Hawkins, Catalano, & Associates, 1992; B. McMillan et al., 1995).

## *Empowering Versus Empowered*

We must begin our discussion of empowerment and community change (see the examples in Box 13.1) with a conceptual distinction: communities and community organizations can be described as *empowering* or *empowered* (Zimmerman, 1995, 2000). Empowering organizations, as we discussed in chapter 12, provide experiences for their members that promote member participation in planning and implementing the activities of the group. This strengthens the sense of community within the group and promotes psychological empowerment. Empowered organizations, in contrast, are those that are able to influence the wider community in meaningful ways, helping to create community change and promote the quality of life for its citizens. Although community groups usually aim to become empowered (changing their community in some way), an important implicit goal of many is for the group to be empowering as well. Indeed, becoming an empowered organization often requires creating empowering opportunities for members and citizens (see B. McMillan et al., 1995).

Yet organizations and communities are not always both empowering and empowered. Organizations dominated by an elite, who exclude rank and file members from resources and from any real decision-making power, may nonetheless be powerful forces (for good or ill) in their communities. Organizations that operate with empowering, participatory methods may nonetheless lack influence in the wider community. In addition, focusing solely on empowering settings that promote individual well-being overlooks an important dimension of community life: how communities grapple with community problems, as illustrated by many examples in Box 13.1.

Speer (1997) proposed that empowerment research needs to have as much attention devoted to empowered community settings as has been devoted to studying empowering ones. Studying settings that empower individuals is important, yet so is identifying how organizations or communities acquire the social power necessary to create positive social and community change. Speer's perspective is consistent with several recent reviews that call for explicit attention to the relationship of empowerment to power (Riger, 1993), for more studies of empowerment at the organizational and community levels of analysis (D. D. Perkins, 1995), and for research on the actual impact of grassroots organizations (Zimmerman, 2000). Moreover, his view is also consistent with Rappaport's (1987) original emphasis on empowerment as occurring at multiple levels and in multiple contexts. To cover these issues, however, we first must discuss the role of power in community life.

# THREE INSTRUMENTS OF SOCIAL POWER

In this section, we describe the nature of power in communities. Power is often viewed with discomfort by students who imagine it only as an instrument of politics, conflict, or control over others. They are partly on the mark: In psychology, the concept of power often connotes control and mastery (Riger, 1993). Yet power can be used for constructive ends; for instance, to oppose injustice or to accomplish a community's shared goals. When balanced with principles of community, social justice, respect for diversity, and a concern for outgroups as well as ingroups, power has constructive potential for communities.

Gaventa (1980) described three "instruments of power" involved in community life (see also Speer & Hughey, 1995). The power to which Gaventa refers is *social power,* a relationship among members of a community or society. The first instrument is the *control of resources that can be used to bargain, reward, and punish* (Gaventa, 1980). This is the popular conception of power, and it fits most closely with a concept of power as the ability to compel or force others. In a community, economic or political power may be used for good or ill: for instance, to lay off workers or to boycott a corporation, to reward allies or to punish critics, to secure government services for a neighborhood, or to gain tax breaks for a corporation.

The second instrument of social power is the *control of channels for citizen participation* in community decisions (Gaventa, 1980; Rich et al., 1995). It refers to control of the forms or means for participation. Public hearings, signing petitions, and voting are traditional examples of such mechanisms. However, Gaventa also refers to subtler mechanisms, such as controlling meeting agendas to exclude citizen comments and debate or requiring citizens to hire attorneys to advocate for them. The second instrument of power often is used to limit citizen participation and empowerment. Consider the following example.

> A corporation filed for a permit to use sludge containing human waste on their farm site, which produced grass sod in a rural area in upstate New York. Under a temporary permit granted by the state without any local input, sludge dumping began. Local citizens discovered the stench without warning, and reacted with understandable anger. The state's Department of Environmental Conservation (DEC) held extensive public hearings on application for a permanent permit before an administrative law judge, which involved hours of testimony by technical experts and local citizens. In theory, all had full input into the DEC decision.
>
> In practice, however, this formal process was distinctly one-sided. The local citizens were assigned seats in rows behind attorneys involved in the case. They did not have the legal training or technical background of the corporation's hired experts, and knew neither the legal procedure nor the terminology used routinely during the hearings. They made a number of procedural errors until they hired their own attorney. When many of the local farmers became frustrated with their lack of real input, they used their tractors to block access to the sod farm. They were only temporarily successful.
>
> Perhaps most telling, local citizens' knowledge of local conditions was discounted. Years of accumulated practical experience had shaped their intuitive, practical understanding of processes such as the effects of rainwater runoff on local streams. Yet expert testimony, all of it by consultants who did not live or work in the community, primarily influenced the judge's decision. When that testimony revealed that the corporation's plans met all state regulations, the permit was granted.
>
> Within five years, virtually every negative outcome predicted by the local citizens had occurred. Wastes had flowed into a nearby river, groundwater was contaminated with toxic cadmium, and illegal hazardous wastes had been stored at the site. DEC had sued the operators of the site for repeated violations and finally had to classify the site as a hazardous waste site requiring further investigation and cleanup (adapted from Rich et al., 1995, pp. 660–662). Reprinted by permission of Kluwer Academic/Plenum Publishers.

In this example, legal procedures effectively prevented meaningful citizen participation in a decision affecting their health and livelihood. Yet a decision reflecting their views would have been wiser in the long run. A more participatory form of the second instrument of power would have allowed and respected citizen input.

The third instrument of power is often overlooked, because it is ground, not figure. It is the *ability to shape the definition of a public issue or conflict* (Gaventa, 1980). It is used to determine the "spin" or dominant public interpretation of a community issue, shaping the debate over that issue. For instance, in the sod farm case above, if local citizen objections are branded simply as "NIMBY (Not In My Back Yard) syndrome," they will be viewed as merely selfish and their substantive concerns about environmental hazards will be ignored. This instrument of power is also illustrated when discussions of urban neighborhoods are framed only in terms of problems and the strengths of such communities are ignored (Speer, 1997). It is easier to wield the other forms of power against a community when you think only of its limitations.

Gaventa (1980) especially focused on this instrument of power. He studied how local elites in the coalfields of Central Appalachia resisted community changes advocated by local citizens who were helped by a few "outsider" community organizers. Local leaders branded the organizers as outsiders, and succeeded in getting the community to frame the conflict as involving local, familiar neighbors versus "untrustworthy" outsiders. This obscured the economic exploitation of the community and environment by large corporations (also outsiders, but not mentioned) and local elites.

The media obviously play an influential role in defining community issues and debate, but the third instrument of power is not theirs alone. Behind the media are social institutions and interest groups with the money and perceived credibility to make their voices heard, and to create the spin through which controversies are interpreted by the media and public. Moreover, the defining myths, stories, rituals, and symbols of a community or society act to help define issues and preconceptions (Rappaport, 1995). We have often noted how individualism in the United States, reflected in its defining myths and rituals, can lead to ignoring the social, economic, or environmental aspects of public problems. (Recall the M. Levine and Levine, 1992, analysis of such forces in chap. 2.) Critical awareness (see chap. 12) involves becoming able to question these preconceptions.

Power, reflected in any of these three instruments, is a dynamic force that ebbs and flows over time. It is not simply the overt ability to compel. It includes the ability to influence the views and actual participation of citizens, even without their awareness. Power occurs in relationships between citizens, communities, and society, and its nature and strength change as those relationships change (Gaventa, 1980). As citizens gain critical awareness of the nature of power, especially the second and third instruments, and as they pursue their aims together, they gain power.

## FOUR APPROACHES TO COMMUNITY CHANGE

How can the three instruments of power be used for constructive community change? Successful struggles for social and community change have seldom been individual efforts, but have relied on collective efforts by groups or organizations. Pilisuk, McAllister, and Rothman (1996) identified three major approaches for grassroots social change organizations to create bottom-up community change. A fourth approach relies on the use of community research as a basis for advocacy. Table 13.1 summarizes the three instruments of social power and these four approaches to community and social change. You should understand that each approach actually represents a family of related strategies for change.

| TABLE 13.1 | INSTRUMENTS OF SOCIAL POWER AND APPROACHES TO COMMUNITY CHANGE |
|---|---|

| Instruments of Power | Corresponding Change Approaches |
|---|---|
| Use of resources to bargain, reward, and punish | Social action |
| Controlling forms of citizen participation | Community development, social action |
| Shaping the definition and understanding of a public issue | Consciousness raising, policy advocacy |

Note: Principal sources were Gaventa (1980) and Pilisuk et al. (1996). See text for full description.

## Social Action

Grassroots groups use social action to offset the power of money with the power of organized people (Alinsky, 1971). Social action identifies specific obstacles to empowerment of disadvantaged groups, and creates constructive conflict to remove these obstacles through direct, nonviolent action. This approach has a long history, with roots including the Boston Tea Party, labor movements in many countries, Gandhi's movement to free India, and the U.S. civil rights movement.

Saul Alinsky delineated social action principles in his classic *Rules for Radicals* (Alinsky, 1971). He argued that social power comes in two forms: organized money and organized people. The former can be opposed if adroit tactics are used by the latter. Citizens using social action must identify their capacities (the strengths of community group members and their potential to act together) and a situation that can be used to dramatize the need for community change. The social action approach relies mainly on use of the first instrument of social power, the ability to find and use rewards, punishments, and bargaining (e.g., a threatened action with potential for bad publicity) for cooperating with or opposing the group's aims. Social action methods illustrate how community change involves power and conflict. In addition, social action may also be necessary if the second and third instruments of power, control of opportunities for citizen participation and ability to shape public debate, are held by a powerful elite and used to limit citizen participation.

Social action is illustrated in the following example (adapted from Alinsky, 1971, pp. 146–148).

A large, prominent department store in a U.S. city traditionally hired African Americans only in very menial positions, and was more discriminatory in its hiring than its competitors. The store had resisted appeals to halt these practices. Boycotts called by African American community groups had failed, due to the prestige of the store. African American community groups met and decided to plan a "shop-in."

The plan called for busloads of African American customers to arrive at the store at its opening on a busy Saturday. In small groups they would shop every department in the store, carefully examining merchandise, asking sales clerks for help, doing nothing illegal yet occupying the store's space. These groups would rotate through the various departments in the store. Regular customers would arrive only to find the store crowded, and if they were hurried or uncomfortable with being in largely Black crowds they might go to another store. Finally, shortly before closing, customers would begin purchasing everything they could, to be delivered on Monday, with payment due on delivery. They planned to refuse these deliveries, causing even more expense for the store.

The community groups deliberately leaked these plans to the store, while going ahead with arrangements for buses, etc. The next day, officials of the store called to ask for an urgent meeting with African American groups to plan new hiring practices, to be held before the Saturday of the "shop-in." The "shop-in" never had to be carried out.

The "shop-in" had several elements that mark effective social action (Alinsky, 1971). First, the goal was clear and tangible. The protesters asked not for a global change in racial attitudes or a vague promise of good will; they insisted on specific changes in hiring policy and practices. Second, the actions required of the protesters were within their personal experience. Shopping was something they knew how to do; it would even be enjoyable. Social action that requires citizens to do things that are not within their experience will not generate widespread participation, and is ineffective (Alinsky, 1971). At the same time, the situation was outside the experience of their opponents: The store management had ignored boycotts and public appeals, but they had never faced a shop-in. Third, the tactic would cause disruption, potential bad publicity, and increased expenses for the store. Yet it was entirely legal; store security or police would have little recourse to stop it. Fourth, the threat was credible because the African American community was organized and willing to act. Fifth, the threat of competition from other retailers not being targeted increased the pressure on the targeted store. Finally, the tactic opposed economic power being used unjustly (through discriminatory hiring) with the power of numbers of committed citizens. The goal was just and the tactic shrewd; its power was revealed when the store quickly recognized the threat and sought a settlement (Alinsky, 1971).

Social action can address injustice and other community issues by constructive conflict and use of the power of people in numbers. However, effective social action requires an organized community, bringing out numbers of committed citizens to oppose powerful interests. Thus, it may require prior use of the two methods we discuss next.

## Community Development

A second approach focuses on localities, often neighborhoods. It emphasizes a gradual process of strengthening relationships among community members and on using that process to define community problems, resources, and strategies for solutions (Kaye & Wolff, 1997; Kretzmann & McKnight, 1993; Lappe & DuBois, 1994). Community development focuses on building consensus within a community (K. Heller et al., 1984). Its historical roots include the settlement house tradition described in chapter 2. The block associations studied in the Neighborhood Participation Project and the Block Booster Project, which we described in chapter 12, exemplify community development approaches. The community development approach attempts to broaden opportunities for participation and influence in community decision making. It principally involves the second instrument of power.

At the outset of Chapter 12, we quoted Louis Burgess describing his history of involvement with his block association in New York City. The association initiated crime watch patrols, improved street lighting, encouraged property cleanup, discouraged illegal drug sales, sponsored outdoor parties and recreational trips, and met regularly to discuss block activities and problems. These collective acts lowered crime, increased neighboring, and strengthened the sense of community.

Community development is an effective means of increasing citizen participation. A participatory, organized community can meet many challenges. Community development also builds personal connections and citizen sense of community that can sustain long-term commitment. However, its value may be limited unless it involves some form of shared values that go beyond the immediate neighborhood. That is the focus of the next approach.

## Consciousness Raising

A third approach to community and social change was outlined in the educational theory of Paulo Friere's (1970/1993) *Pedagogy of the Oppressed* and in many forms of feminist thought (Mulvey, 1988; see Pilisuk et al., 1996). It emphasizes increasing citizens' critical awareness of social conditions that affect them. For example, convincing women and men of the existence of sexism in the workplace and in the family raises their critical awareness, especially when this learning connects with their personal experiences. However, consciousness raising is not solely cognitive. New personal understanding is connected to actions for change. Those actions may be similar to the social action or community development approaches, but are distinctive because of the emphasis on critical awareness and understanding. That principally involves the third instrument of power, the ability to influence how community problems are defined and explained.

Consciousness raising is reflected in some of the changes experienced by the community activists interviewed by Kieffer (1984; recall this study from chap. 12). Kieffer's interviewees reported that the provocations that threatened their communities (e.g., violence, economic exploitation) led them to develop critical awareness. They questioned the credibility of the status quo, especially community and corporate leaders. This led them to assume greater responsibility in opposing the provocation and in insisting on citizen participation in decision making.

Kroeker (1995, 1996) reported on her experiences in working in an agricultural cooperative in Nicaragua that operated in part on Friere's (1970/1993) consciousness-raising principles. Farming coffee as a cooperative made it possible for the members to pool scarce material resources and labor and to obtain credit. They also were able to start a school for their children and to begin some adult education classes. Most importantly, they learned to make decisions cooperatively and to work together for shared goals and for mutual protection in a time of civil war. To outsiders, including both Kroeker and leaders of nearby communities, their decision making appeared chaotic at first, but it provided basic lessons in participation and building community. The residents used storytelling to make sense of their experiences and to strengthen their sense of unity. When some outsiders worked alongside cooperative members as partners, enacting a collaborative role of "accompaniment," both cooperative members and outsiders learned from each other and tangible benefits occurred (e.g., expansions in electrification, education, and health care; Kroeker, 1996, p. 134). Faced with very daunting obstacles and experiencing many setbacks, Nicaraguan cooperatives enabled extremely disadvantaged citizens to gain some power over their economic and social circumstances.

Consciousness raising creates change in the whole person, involving attitudes, behaviors, and interpersonal relationships. That can lead to committed, collective efforts for community and social change based on a transformed view of society (Friere, 1970/1993; Mulvey, 1988). Consciousness raising is usually a grassroots, bottom-up approach to change. Yet the critical awareness it generates can also lead to the next approach, the use of research in advocacy.

## Policy Research and Advocacy

Policy research and advocacy represents another approach to community and social change. It involves speaking out in some form to influence decisions (including judicial decisions), policies, or laws. It often involves seeking to persuade government officials, but may seek to influence or inform leaders in the private sector, journalists, or others. It principally involves the second and third instruments of power, participating in public decision making and influencing the ways in which an issue of conflict is defined or understood. This advocacy does not bargain or bring pressure based on threats, but seeks to persuade with information (especially research findings) and reasoned arguments.

Examples of policy advocacy by community psychologists include expert testimony in public interest lawsuits, filing amicus curiae ("friend of the court") briefs in court cases, interviews and other forms of providing information to the media, contacts with lawmakers or government officials, testimony in legislative hearings on proposed bills, working as a staff member for legislators or in other branches of government, and even serving as an elected official (from the local school board to wider office; D. D. Perkins, 1988; Rickel & Becker, 1997; Shinn, 1994; Toro, 1998; Vincent, 1990; Wurten & Sales, 1988).

Policy advocacy is often based on *policy research,* which is conducted to provide empirical information on social issues. An early instance of research-based public advocacy was the use of social science research findings in briefs filed in the 1954 Supreme Court case, *Brown vs. Board of Education of Topeka,* which outlawed segregationist policies in U.S. public schools. Policy research may generate findings that show the need for a new policy to address a social problem. Evaluation research studies the effectiveness of existing or innovative programs or policies, including their intended and unintended consequences (see chap. 14). Reviews of research literature offer strong implications for policy, because they are based on multiple studies in multiple contexts. For instance, meta-analyses of primary prevention and secondary prevention programs were described in chapter 10 (Durlak & Wells, 1997, 1998). The community research cited in prior chapters offers many examples of policy-relevant studies and findings. Community psychology's concern with the intersection of research and action equips it for policy research and advocacy (D. D. Perkins, 1988, 1995).

Yet advocacy is more than simply sharing results of research in an impartial way. It involves entering the public arena and allying with those on one side of a controversial issue. It demands clarity on one's value principles and wise choice of allies. Advocacy demands making the best case for the side one has chosen, with available evidence and reasoning. However, distortion of research findings is neither ethical nor wise advocacy. To

## 13.2    "Dr. Jason Goes to Washington": Advocacy Testimony

Below is an abridged version of an account by community psychologist Leonard Jason of his appearance in a Congressional committee hearing, during consideration by Congress of a national settlement of tobacco lawsuits. The full version appears in Jason (1998a). His team's research on youth access to tobacco appears in Jason, Berk, Schnopp-Wyatt and Talbot (1999).

• • •

On Tuesday, December 2nd, I was called by a staff member of the House Commerce Committee, Subcommittee on Health and Environment, and asked to testify about behavioral aspects of teenage tobacco use. The Congressional staff person asked me to address prevention strategies, and in particular issues involving youth access to tobacco products. He mentioned that I had 3 days to prepare my testimony, and I naively agreed to this request. I would have about 5 minutes to present my perspective on issues involving behavioral aspects of smoking and teenagers, and there would be two other presentations [one by a public health official and one by a consultant for the tobacco industry]. There would then be a question and answer period.

The issues involved in the tobacco settlement were varied, and they involved issues such as ways to restrict youth access to tobacco, smoking reduction targets, excise taxes, public education, advertising, international sales, and funding for science. The challenge was to be concise and focus on those pieces of information that might have the largest influence on the Congresspeople at the hearing. I religiously read dozens of new bills on the tobacco settlement being introduced into Congress and continued to seek consultation from [American Psychological Association (APA) staff]. During that week, I was also being called by Congressional staffers. I had written twenty pages of double spaced text, and I wasn't sure how to reduce this text to a few pages. I finally did write up a brief outline that summarized some of the issues I would cover in my testimony. By Monday morning, after spending the weekend with different drafts of the testimony, I finally had a document, although I continued to incorporate new ideas into it until I boarded the plane to Washington.

Pat from APA and I went to the Rayburn House Office Building on Tuesday morning. We were among the first people to enter the room where the testimony was to occur. There were television cameras from CSPAN and chairs for about 100 people. As people

---

be influential, an advocate must be credible to policy-makers, while also making clear recommendations for action. Box 13.2 presents an account of policy advocacy testimony.

Policy research and advocacy by community psychologists and other community researchers involves both research and action and provides a way to inform public debate with empirical evidence. The expertise of psychologists, particularly community psychologists, can be a powerful force in public decision making (Melton, 1995). Policy advocacy also involves persuasion rather than pressure tactics, and thus appeals to those with different skills than social activists.

began filtering in, the tension began to rise. Faithfully, I practiced my deep breathing exercises. Each of the speakers gave their testimony, and I was the last person to present my views. I had rehearsed my testimony about 5 times that morning. As the minutes [of my presentation] ticked away, my confidence gained. . . . My voice grew strong and clear.

I stressed that there was a considerable amount of behavioral data to indicate that it is possible to reduce the number of young people who smoke. Starting, continuing, and quitting smoking are fundamentally behavioral processes. I next indicated that it is possible to appreciably reduce the percent of vendors that sell to youth. I then mentioned that scientifically based, school prevention programs can effectively reduce the percentage of children who later smoke, and that the most exemplary programs include anti-smoking ads in the mass media and comprehensive school programs. I then talked about how even with the settlement, children will be exposed to imagery-laden tobacco advertisements, and that to deal with this we need a ratio of anti-smoking ads to cigarette ads to be 1:4 or greater. I would have preferred saying that all ads should be banned, but I knew that this would raise First Amendment rights issues. I then mentioned that while the federal government can provide leadership on initiatives to reduce tobacco-related disease and death, it should not manage state or local initiatives, and I added that we need to encourage grass roots efforts. In summing up my testimony, I mentioned that psychological research has led to a better understanding of the effects of tobacco advertisements, youth access laws, school and community prevention programs.

For the next hour and fifteen minutes, each of the Congress people had 5 minutes to ask us questions. They were attentive and rarely engaged in side conversations, and I was rather surprised at this high level of interest. Questions posed to me frequently involved issues of youth access to tobacco. One Congressperson asked me if I thought that smoking should be completely banned. In a set of subsequent questions, he kept using the terms "ban" and "restricting youth access to tobacco" interchangeably, and I had to constantly point out the differences in these two concepts. The time flew by, and the hour and a half of session ended.

So, what do I make of this experience? First, it is great fun to be able to testify in Congress, and actually have policymakers interested in your research and points of view. To do this type of work, one needs to be able to relatively quickly develop a position that addresses key points and reduces the cognitive complexity of a particular topic. Good stress management and public speaking skills are necessary but not sufficient. Working collaboratively with other organizations, in this case APA, are key attributes for reaching these types of audiences. Keeping a sense of humor, and being diplomatic, are prudent.

---

Yet advocacy is not effective unless policy-makers listen, and thus requires access to those in power. It is impossible if a group has been excluded from participation in community decision making; the other three approaches are then needed. Policy research and advocacy also is often a top-down method of social and community change; it may not reflect the actual life experiences and views of those affected by a policy. Wise policy advocates thus often find ways to ally themselves with grassroots community groups (see Toro, 1998). Participatory action research pursues policy research and advocacy with a bottom-up approach (Brydon-Miller, 1997).

In addition, policy advocacy requires awareness of the differences between public or judicial decision-making and scientific research. Clear recommendations for policy do not allow much room for the qualifications that careful scientists often make. Policy-makers or judges often demand a yes-or-no answer. The policy advocate must communicate recommendations clearly.

Like other forms of citizen participation, policy advocacy can be both exhilarating and demanding (Jason, 1998b; Rickel & Becker, 1997; Toro, 1998). It provides a pathway for participating in community and social change that differs from the approaches discussed above, yet can complement them.

How are these approaches to community and social change related to actual changes in community life? To answer this question, we must visualize the larger picture, a model of community change that we describe in the next section.

# AN "OPEN SYSTEMS" MODEL OF COMMUNITY CHANGE

In this section, we sketch a model of the principal elements of community change initiatives, based on open systems models of organizations (Katz & Kahn, 1978). The open systems approach has been extended to community organizations (Florin et al., 1992; Prestby & Wandersman, 1985; Wandersman, Goodman, & Butterfoss, 1997) and is similar to a model proposed by Fawcett et al. (1995). The open systems model we propose here also emphasizes community resources, interdependence, and ecological levels of analysis (recall these concepts from chap. 5). Finally, the model connects with the concepts of citizen participation and empowering settings from chapter 12. The model is illustrated in Figure 13.1.

An open systems model connects *input, throughput,* and *output.* Input refers to resources mobilized by the organization for its existence and work. These may be personal, social–cultural, or material. Throughput refers to building cohesion within the organization, to its performance of tasks, and to evaluation of that performance. Group cohesion and task functioning are classically recognized as the major domains of group functioning (McGrath, 1984). The qualities of empowering settings in chapter 12, for instance, concern throughput. Output refers to the actions that the organization takes in the community, and to their immediate and ultimate effects. It concerns whether the organization is empowered in its community.

## Input

Empowered community organizations cultivate many kinds of resources (Fawcett et al., 1995; Florin et al., 1992; Wandersman et al., 1997). Human resources include *stakeholders,* persons directly affected in some way by an issue. These may include influential community leaders, citizens representing the diversity of community viewpoints, and persons with knowledge and skills needed by the organization. A broad-based community coalition may even recruit potential opponents of a community initiative, in order to respond to their concerns and to identify common ground. Personal resources for the organization also include individuals' commitment to the organization's purposes and to the wider community. Funding is another resource, as are training, technical assistance, and staff time

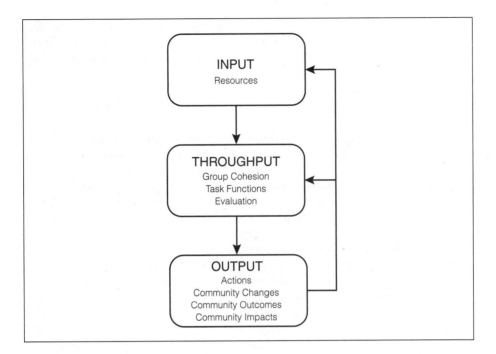

**FIGURE 13.1**

An open systems model of community change.

provided by other organizations. Finally, social and cultural resources include shared values and viewpoints, such as public support for improving children's health or addressing problems of substance abuse.

## *Throughput*

Community organizations use their resources for three purposes: carrying out *organizational tasks,* building *organizational cohesion* among members, and *evaluation* of their work. Empowered organizations have an explicit task focus: a clear mission, structured goals and objectives, and specific tasks for members (Fawcett et al., 1995; B. McMillan et al., 1995; Wandersman et al., 1997). That work can be energized by inclusive, democratic decision making that promotes member participation, and by small groups or work teams, each with a specific focus.

Organizational cohesion can be promoted by cultivating the qualities of empowering settings described in chapter 12. For instance, these include recognizing resources and interdependent relationships, creating opportunity role structures or participatory niches, facilitating mentoring relationships, and lowering obstacles to member participation (M. A. Bond & Keys, 1993; Kieffer, 1984; Maton & Salem, 1995; Prestby et al., 1990; Speer & Hughey, 1995). All of these provide roles for members and attract individual participation. They also promote a cohesive organizational climate that in itself represents a resource for pursuing the organization's work. That cohesion also is promoted by celebrating the organization's values and achievements, cultivating inspiring leaders, building peer support systems, and managing conflict constructively (M. A. Bond & Keys, 1993; Kaye & Wolff, 1997; Maton & Salem, 1995; Rappaport, 1995).

## Output

Movement from throughput to output occurs when a community organization undertakes *actions in the community;* for instance, using the community change approaches of social action, community development, consciousness raising, or policy advocacy. Actions represent intermediate steps in the direction of the organization's goals. Community actions may involve meetings with public officials, conducting a media campaign, organizing a shop-in, submitting a grant proposal to obtain staff for a new community program, or organizing a committee to plan an educational program in schools.

Output next involves *community changes.* These include actual implementing of new programs, changes in policies or laws, or alterations in the practices of community institutions (Fawcett et al., 1995). They are different from actions in that they are undertaken by the wider community or its institutions, not simply by the organization that advocates them. They represent one form of impact by the organization on the community. An organization becomes empowered when its actions lead to community changes. These involve at least one of Gaventa's (1980) three instruments of power: influencing decisions by community or institutional leaders, broadening forms of participation in community decision making, or changing public views on an issue.

Community changes facilitated by Project Freedom, a community coalition to reduce substance abuse in a Kansas community, included a new peer helper program on substance abuse at a local high school, a new radio station policy prohibiting disc jockey comments that glamorized drinking, and a training program for area ministers in substance abuse prevention strategies for their congregations (Fawcett et al., 1995, p. 690).

Community changes are effective if they result in *community outcomes and impacts.* Outcomes are more immediate effects of a community change, such as changes in knowledge or skills taught by an educational program in schools to reduce substance abuse. Impacts are longer term effects, such as a reduction in drug use, drunk driving, or hospital treatment for drug-related problems or accidents. As another example, a community coalition we describe later in this chapter measured its impact by increases in the proportion of children immunized against infectious disease by two years of age (Butterfoss et al., in press).

## Evaluation

Finally, as denoted in Figure 13.1, empowered organizations evaluate each stage of their functioning, from resource acquisition to community impact. This evaluation involves reviewing organizational task performance and cohesion, assessing the actual short-term and long-term effects of actions, and using this information to make future revisions. Evaluation "closes the circle" by using knowledge gained from community experiences to plan future initiatives (Fawcett et al., 1995; Speer & Hughey, 1995; Wandersman et al., 1997). In addition, evaluation can provide tangible evidence for celebrating an organization's successes and for sustaining member interest and participation. We have placed evaluation in the throughput stage to emphasize its role in the everyday functioning of the community organizations. Evaluation is the focus of chapter 14.

# EXAMPLES OF COMMUNITY CHANGE INITIATIVES

Can the concepts we have discussed describe changes in real-life communities? In this section, we describe three community organizations and their change initiatives.

## Block Booster: Capacity-Building in Community Organizations

The Block Booster Project (Florin et al., 1992) exemplifies a community development approach combined with concepts and methods of community psychology. Block Booster served 30 block associations in middle income and lower income neighborhoods of New York City, including the one involving Louis Burgess in chapter 12.

The Block Booster Project created a service to enhance the organizational strength of block associations; this is known in community development as "organizational capacity-building." Through the Citizens' Committee for New York City, a citywide umbrella organization, Block Booster provided step-by-step technical assistance to block associations (Florin et al., 1992, pp. 234–236). First, Block Booster staff conducted surveys of block residents regarding their attitudes about the block association, participation in block activities, and skills that might be useful for the neighborhood. Members of the block association were also surveyed about group cohesiveness, leader support, group order and organization, and related concepts drawn from the social climate scales developed by Moos and associates (Moos, 1994; see chap. 5). From these data, Block Booster Profiles were drawn up by staff to describe each block and block association.

Block Booster staff then conducted a workshop for block association leaders, explaining strengths and areas for improvement revealed in the Profiles, and outlining suggestions for improving the functioning of the block association. For instance, if member surveys indicated that an association was low on task focus and tangible problem solving, leaders could learn ways to hold more organized meetings and set group goals (Florin et al., 1992, p. 236). If residents indicated that lack of child care limited their participation, block association leaders were encouraged to provide child care at meetings. In the workshop, block association leaders also developed action plans for their groups. They put these into action over the next several months and evaluated the impact of their efforts.

Block Booster training and consultation helped block association leaders promote citizen participation, set clear organizational goals, plan actions in the community to pursue those goals, foster effective communication, and make decision making more inclusive. All these efforts helped make block associations more empowering settings. In the framework of the open systems model of Figure 13.1, Block Booster provided outside resources of technical assistance to block associations, promoting their cohesion, task functioning, and evaluation.

An experimental evaluation of the Block Booster Project (described in chap. 4) found that 10 months after the workshops, associations in the experimental condition, which received the workshop and active Block Booster consultation, were significantly more active than a comparison group (Florin et al., 1992). In essence, Block Booster provided an "enabling system" that strengthened block associations and promoted community development (Florin et al., 1992, p. 239).

## PICO: Community Organizing for Social Power

Speer, Hughey, and associates (Speer & Hughey, 1995; Speer et al., 1995) studied grassroots community organizations that are concerned with "community organizing for power," seeking direct, sociopolitical change in local communities. These researchers analyzed the organizing strategies of the Pacific Institute for Community Organizing (PICO), mainly studying groups using PICO methods in one Midwestern U.S. city. These organizations are empowered in their communities, initiating community change through social action, community development, and consciousness raising.

PICO assists local community organizations based in religious congregations in low-income communities. The PICO methods involve a "relationship-based" approach to build organizational capacity and a "pressure-group" approach to influence the wider community (Speer & Hughey, 1995, pp. 730–733). This proceeds through a *cycle of organizing* (Speer & Hughey, 1995, p. 734; Speer et al., 1995, p. 60). In the initial assessment phase, citizens meet in pairs to define community issues and to develop working partnerships that strengthen the group. This stage is similar to community development tactics and builds interdependence and sharing of support among members (Kelly, 1970; Maton & Salem, 1995). In the second phase, research, the most pressing community issue for the group as a whole is identified. Members then seek information on that issue. A key goal is to identify contradictions between stated policies and actual practices of community institutions. This phase involves development of critical awareness similar to consciousness raising approaches, and community identification of problems similar to community development approaches.

The third phase, mobilization/action, follows. Organization members meet to decide on an action plan and a person or office to be targeted for meetings to discuss community changes in the action plan. If preparatory meetings with an official do not succeed, a public community meeting is arranged with that official. The key function of the meeting is to confront the target official with the reality of the community problem and with actions that the community members demand to resolve it. Meetings often have brought together city officials with large groups of well-informed citizens making clear, focused demands (due to the extensive groundwork conducted by the organization). Meetings often result in commitments being made by the target official.

These meetings represent the social action tactics of organizing people and of creative conflict advocated by Alinsky (1971). Especially for a public official, facing a crowd of hundreds of citizens making clear demands is a potent experience of the first instrument of power, citizens' ability to reward or punish. Moreover, the citizen organization hosts the public meeting and carefully scripts its agenda, thus exercising the second instrument of power, channeling of participation.

The final reflection phase returns to the original pairs with whom the cycle began. It involves evaluation of the outcome of the organizing effort and of lessons learned, by all participants. The PICO organizations also use this time to monitor the keeping of promises made by the target officials and institutions. On the basis of conclusions reached in evaluation, the organization begins the cycle again with a new assessment phase.

Speer and Hughey (1995) and Speer et al. (1995) documented how groups in a Midwestern U.S. city influenced the wider community. These organizations were able to mobilize large numbers (often in the hundreds, sometimes in the thousands) of citizens for public meetings with officials of city government and private organizations, and to produce specific changes in policy and practices. Two such meetings are described in the following accounts.

> Members of one organization discovered in the research phase that a private social services agency was placing its immigrant clients in substandard housing owned by absentee landlords, in effect subsidizing the landlords' lack of property maintenance. This practice endangered not only the immigrants but also their neighbors, since the apartments did not meet health and fire codes. Officials of the social service agency refused to cooperate with members of the community organization in getting the landlords to comply with the codes. However, when confronted at a public meeting with 500 community residents, most of whom indicated their intent to write to the agency's funding sources about the problem, the agency "capitulated on the spot" (adapted from Speer & Hughey, 1995, p. 742).
>
> Members of 14 such organizations in the same city had worked independently on a variety of youth issues, including prevention of drug abuse and violence. They had learned that obtaining the resources needed for positive youth development was beyond the capacity of any one group. Working together, they discovered that because city schools, government, and recreation commission did not collaborate with each other, inner-city youth and families were denied access to gyms, pools, computers, and health facilities after school hours. After a year of research and planning, about 1,000 citizens met with the city mayor, school superintendent, various board members and representatives of civic groups, and citywide media. Testimony from adults and children documented the need for access to the facilities and the lack of collaboration among schools, government and recreation commission. The organizations presented their demands for a specific agreement for such collaboration. Officials signed the agreement at that meeting, and later collaborated to provide the demanded services (adapted from Speer & Hughey, 1995, p. 741).

Speer et al. (1995) compared the effectiveness of congregation-based organizations using the PICO model and neighborhood-based organizations. The latter brought together neighbors in specific areas, did not use existing social institutions such as churches, and did not spend as much time building the grassroots base of relationships among organization members. They used social action tactics such as picketing and sit-ins, but not planned public meetings with officials and large numbers of citizens. Over the 3-year period of the study, the congregation-based organizations had much higher attendance at community events. They also were able to articulate substantive ideas that were then covered in the local press and media at a much higher rate than the comparison neighborhood organizations. This coverage spread the impact of their ideas beyond their immediate communities.

Several psychological factors appear to contribute to the effectiveness of the PICO approach to empowerment. These include strong networks of interpersonal relationships among members of the organization, and their institutional base in religious congregations that help foster social support and a group-based belief system (Maton & Salem, 1995).

PICO organizations work to develop leaders by creating *participatory niches,* such as rotating offices and identifying tasks for emerging leaders (Speer & Hughey, 1995). These efforts make them empowering settings (see chap. 12). Targeting specific issues and institutions for change also increases the effectiveness of the community groups (Speer & Hughey, 1995). These factors enable organizations representing constituencies with few economic resources to struggle with powerful, well-funded private and public institutions.

## CINCH: A Community Coalition for Health

Health promotion is often understood in individual terms. For instance, it is easy to think in terms of encouraging exercise, a healthy diet, avoiding smoking, and other individual choices. Yet health is also a community issue. Access to affordable health care is limited or nonexistent for many, especially in urban and rural areas. Community problems such as youth and family violence, drug abuse, sexism, racism, poverty, and unemployment are linked to health outcomes, reflected in emergency rooms and clinics in terms of wounds and injuries, rape trauma, drug dependence, infectious diseases, lung cancer from smoking, prenatal and child health problems, and other outcomes. This often leaves community psychologists and others asking, "What happens when a community takes responsibility for improving its collective health?" and "What would a healthy community be like?"

Building healthy communities often involves coalitions among community organizations, a strategy increasingly used not only in health but to address other community issues. A *community coalition* is an organization composed of representatives of multiple community groups who bring together their resources to achieve a common goal not attainable by any of those groups alone (see Kaye & Wolff, 1997, pp. 14–15; Wandersman et al., 1997).

Child immunizations against infectious disease were the focus of Consortium for Immunization of Norfolk's Children (CINCH), a community coalition in Norfolk, Virginia. Despite its economic wealth, the United States has recently lagged behind other countries in this basic method of disease prevention. A measles epidemic in 1989–1991 and a nationwide resurgence of whooping cough prompted public health efforts to increase immunization rates. In Norfolk, only 48% of the city's children had been fully immunized by 2 years of age, a situation not unusual for urban areas. The CINCH coalition was Norfolk's response to this problem (Butterfoss et al., in press).

In 1993, representatives of several community organizations founded the coalition. For 6 months they gathered personal and material resources. They recruited 55 representatives of community organizations representing not only health care providers but also service organizations, civic groups, academic and religious institutions, and other community stakeholders. This group reflected the diversity of Norfolk in terms of age, occupation, race and ethnicity, and religion; it also included members with skills in planning, teaching, media presentations, and mobilizing volunteers. Coalition members also garnered grant monies, and local organizations provided services such as staff time and photocopying. This gathering of resources represents the input stage of the open systems model (see Figure 13.1).

CINCH members also devoted considerable effort to throughput. They developed a mission statement with five goals: increasing public awareness of childhood immunization in Norfolk, determining the causes of low immunization rates, forming and implementing plans to increase immunizations, evaluating and revising these strategies, and sharing what they learn with other communities. In addition, the coalition hired staff to provide training and support for coalition volunteers. They established procedures for meetings, criteria for membership and voting, and roles for members, leaders, and staff, in writing. These steps helped to overcome a common problem with community coalitions: lack of direction early in the coalition's existence, leading to loss of membership and effectiveness (Butterfoss et al., in press; Kaye & Wolff, 1997).

CINCH also built cohesion among members and commitment to the wider community. Members excluded titles from name tags and discussions and worked to recognize each others' skills and contribution to the coalition rather than organizational or personal status. They emphasized overarching, shared community goals. Leadership was decentralized by assigning much of CINCH's work to work groups dealing with specific tasks or issues. Members grew to appreciate interdependencies, such as the discovery that some were skilled planners, while others were skilled "doers" (Butterfoss et al., in press). This cohesion and commitment to overarching goals was important in resolving conflicts. Moreover, the processes of conflict, communication, and negotiation strengthened the ties among members in the long run.

The coalition conducted a needs assessment to learn about the problem of underimmunization in Norfolk. Focus groups with parents, patient interviews at clinics, and surveys of health care providers and households revealed that underimmunization existed at all socioeconomic levels. CINCH work groups then developed strategic plans for education of parents and health care providers, support for families at risk, and improvements in delivery of immunizations. Coalition leaders combined the various specific plans into an overall strategic plan with a budget.

Coalition members next proceeded to output. Member organizations implemented the coalition plans. CINCH evaluated this implementation, and revised plans when needed. Over 3 years, the coalition effectively implemented 77% of its strategies, many of which were adopted as routine practices of health institutions and community agencies. Community impact was measured by the overall immunization rate, which rose from 48% to 66% by the program's third year. Without experimental controls this cannot be attributed to CINCH alone, but its impact seems clear. Eventually, the coalition expanded to six nearby cities, led a statewide immunization coalition, broadened its mission to child health issues beyond immunization, and established a nationwide training institute (Butterfoss et al., in press).

CINCH represents a community development approach to community change, developing citywide ties among organizations rather than among residents in a smaller locality. It utilized the second and third instruments of social power, concerning citizen participation and public awareness of a health issue. CINCH benefited from its focus on children's health, a population and issue that have few public opponents. In addition, its effectiveness could be measured in easily understood terms, such as the immunization rate, providing a clear focus for planning. However, similar coalition-building methods have worked with more controversial and less easily measured objectives, such as curbing substance abuse, and in rural areas as well as urban ones (e.g., Fawcett et al., 1995; Goodman, Wandersman, Chinman, Imm, & Morrissey, 1996).

# OVERARCHING ISSUES FOR COMMUNITY CHANGE

Now that you have studied some examples of community change initiatives, we turn to some overarching issues concerning community change. Almost any community organization that seeks to improve the quality of community life must grapple with these. The first involves whether the goals and methods of the organization will focus on community betterment through top-down change or more bottom-up processes of community empowerment and citizen participation. The second concerns the common elements that usually mark effective community change initiatives.

## Community Betterment or Community Empowerment?

Efforts to promote community change, especially those based in coalitions or other linkages among citizen organizations, necessarily involve choices between the goals and methods of *community betterment* and *community empowerment* (Himmelman, cited in Kaye & Wolff, 1997).

Community betterment involves primarily top-down strategies. It is initiated by professionals or agencies who provide services in a community but who may not live there or be personally affected by community change. Community members or residents may be invited to join the process, but professionals retain primary influence. Betterment efforts often proceed by identifying needs or deficits in a community, then plan and implement new or improved services to meet those needs.

Community empowerment uses bottom-up strategies. Members or residents of a community are involved in initiating the effort, and they retain primary influence and control. Empowerment efforts assess community assets and resources, then define their goals based on these. Community changes may involve improved services similar to those in a betterment model or may involve other changes defined by the community. The crucial difference is that in the empowerment approach, community members retain control. Decisions are made by those whose lives will be most affected (Kaye & Wolff, 1997, chap. 2).

Kaye and Wolff (1997) described a community meeting in which members of a community coalition described their visions, ideas, and hopes for "their" community. When asked how many actually lived in this community, less than half raised their hands. That provided one indicator that a betterment rather than an empowerment approach was being taken. In another example, a community health center joined with a community organization of persons of color to obtain a minority health grant. When the grant was received, no members of the community organization were hired, and only a few were given positions on the advisory board for the project. Community members thus were largely excluded from influence (Kaye & Wolff, 1997). Both of these examples represent uses of the second instrument of power, controlling participation in community decision making (Gaventa, 1980).

In contrast, the CINCH coalition took steps to make its efforts empowering: involving citizens representing the diversity of Norfolk's population, eliminating titles on name tags, and emphasizing the value of contribution to coalition work rather than professional status (Butterfoss et al., in press). In Massachusetts, Healthy Communities coalitions using a community empowerment approach have begun a mobile health van program, started a shelter for the homeless, initiated a campaign to lessen sales of tobacco products to teens, hosted planning for economic development and for housing development, developed a health outreach program for a low-income neighborhood, and worked with schools and community agencies to develop a variety of health-related programs for children (Wolff, 1995). However, one must look to the methods by which the coalition works, not just its title, to determine whether it is pursuing community betterment or community empowerment.

As you learned in chapter 12, both bottom-up and top-down approaches have their advantages and drawbacks, and their effectiveness depends in part on contextual factors. A betterment approach may succeed in obtaining external resources not available in many urban and rural communities, and in improving services for community residents (Schorr, 1997, p. 356). However, the betterment process lessens community control, may overlook existing community resources, and requires a community to highlight its problems and deficits rather than its assets and resources (Kretzmann & McKnight, 1993). The strength of the empowerment approach is that community resources are fully used and control is retained locally.

## Elements of Effective Community Change Initiatives

Do effective community change efforts have any elements in common? The answer begins with a story.

In an undergraduate community psychology class, this chapter's primary author often shows a videotape profiling effective prevention programs (T. Levine, 1992). One segment describes a program that increased the socioemotional competence of students in a middle school (Comer, 1992; Weissberg et al., 1996). After seeing this video, a student once spoke up. "I worked this summer just down the street from that school. This program may affect those kids while they're in school, but as soon as they walk out the door, there are gangs, easily available drugs, lots of problems." Unspoken but implied in her comment was this question: "What good does a school-based program do for the community, or for students' lives outside the school?"

Of course, learning skills for resolving personal problems and interpersonal conflicts are important accomplishments, even if they involve only what happens inside school walls. In addition, many individuals will generalize their learning in some way outside those walls. But the questioning student is also right, that if community psychology interventions are to develop communities, they must go beyond a focus on one setting, such as a school, or one problem, such as child development. Her point illustrates several issues emphasized by Schorr (1997) in her review of community change initiatives. Schorr reviewed and visited a number of organizations seeking to improve neighborhood and community quality of life. She suggested seven generalized elements for effective community change (Schorr, 1997, pp. 360–368). These are listed in Table 13.2.

**Multiple Areas of Action**    Community problems seldom involve just education, or family problems, or crime, or economic development. Advocates for change often focus on a single problem, and assume that improvement in that one area will lead to improved community life in general. Yet the research evidence reviewed by Schorr, and the practical knowledge of community leaders she interviewed, indicated that change in one area seldom leads to wider community change on its own. Effective programs for community

| TABLE 13.2 | ELEMENTS OF EFFECTIVE COMMUNITY CHANGE INITIATIVES |
|---|---|

Multiple areas of action, linkages among programs

Local design of change initiatives

External linkages and resources

A plausible theory of community change

Effective intensity of intervention

Strengthening sense of community

Long-term perspective

Note. Adapted from Schorr (1997, pp. 360–368).

change address multiple issues: economic factors, human services, education, the physical environment, and community development.

It is not always possible for a community to address all these issues at once. Yet it is possible to develop what Schorr (1997, p. 361) calls a "comprehensive mind-set," in which linkages are recognized such as those between school and home, jobs and education, crime and sense of community, youth and the elderly. This can lead to community initiatives that tie successful changes in one setting to another, such as economic development to provide local jobs for graduates of job training programs, and finding senior citizens to volunteer in child care centers.

What are some examples of such linkages? The Dudley Street Neighborhood Initiative (DSNI) in Boston began when citizens of a low-income, multiracial neighborhood became incensed about their community's vacant land being illegally used for trash dumps by private trash haulers. They organized DSNI and successfully pressured city government to halt the dumping, then gained control of the vacant land. DSNI then moved to gain mass transit access for the neighborhood, a human services program, after-school programs, and housing construction and renovation (Schorr, 1997). DSNI is built on an explicit empowerment agenda involving local control of resources (Kretzmann & McKnight, 1993).

In Savannah, Georgia, the Youth Futures Authority (YFA) pursued community development in a low-income neighborhood. After an initial phase involving intensive case management services for at-risk children in middle school failed, the YFA took a broader perspective. It developed a family resource center providing preventive programs regarding health and nutrition, substance abuse, school readiness, and child development, as well as community activities such as scout groups, athletics, neighborhood murals, and conflict resolution classes. Because the center exists in a predominantly African-American neighborhood, many of these services are conducted in an Afrocentric format that emphasizes family and community ties, self-discipline, and constructive work. YFA initiatives have also included changes in policing and zoning (Schorr, 1997).

The New Community Corporation (NCC) in Newark, New Jersey, is often considered the most successful community development corporation in the United States. Begun by William Linder, a Catholic priest, the NCC now has spawned 30 organizations that own and manage housing, provide a variety of family services and programs for youth, run a credit union, provide home health care and a nursing home, administer a job-training program, and own a shopping center and other retail ventures in the center of Newark (Schorr, 1997).

***Local Design of Change Initiatives***  Schorr's (1997) second element of effective community initiatives concerns local control of planning. As often emphasized in our discussions of citizen participation and empowerment, local citizens often know best the resources, strengths, most pressing issues, and workable methods of change for their community. Of course, decisions need to be based on participation by a cross-section of a community, not just by powerful leaders pursuing only their own visions of community interest. Moreover, when citizens collectively determine their own goals, their talents are used and their commitment mobilized.

***External Linkages and Resources***  Few communities facing serious problems can make significant headway completely on their own. Thus, although community change is best initiated locally, at the grassroots level, it often requires resources from outside the community. These resources, Schorr (1997, p. 363) argued, come in three forms: funding, knowledge, and "clout."

External funding is required if change efforts exhaust local resources; thus it is especially important in less affluent communities. Knowledge or expertise is needed, not to define problems or dictate goals (these are best done within the community), but to provide technical assistance that can be used by citizens to design their own programs or changes (recall Block Booster and PICO). Knowledge of what has worked for other communities is also helpful, as long as it is recognized that alterations will probably be needed to meet local conditions. Finally, communities need connections to those with the political or economic power to influence decisions made elsewhere that affect the local community.

***A Plausible Theory of Community Change***  Schorr (1997, p. 364) asserted that successful community change needs to be guided by one or more theories of how change will occur. Such a theory needs to be based on evidence of some kind and needs to be evaluated continuously to ensure that it is working in practical terms. She was not advocating that such theory and evidence can be based only on social science research. Every citizen has some conception of how community change occurs, and evidence of whether an initiative is working is often available with simple measurement (as you will see in chap. 14). A plausible theory is one that is based on evidence that can be gathered by citizens, and based on their careful, shared reasoning about how their community can be improved. Such theorizing is not merely exchange of opinions, nor is it solely based on expert advice. In the PICO approach described earlier in this chapter, citizens conduct fact-finding research on the nature of community problems and meet after their community "actions" to evaluate their success and to plan further efforts (Speer & Hughey, 1995). That reflection on action builds a plausible, useful theory of change.

***Effective Intensity***  Initiatives for community change must involve specific changes that are strong enough to make detectable changes in the everyday lives of citizens. There is often a threshold of effective response to a community problem. Initiatives below that threshold will not be effective. Small businesses that create only a few jobs each will not clearly affect neighborhood unemployment. Educational innovations by a few dedicated teachers will make a difference in some students' lives but do little to change the overall climate of a school or improve overall education for a community. A crime prevention initiative will not be sustained if it makes little visible difference to citizens on the street.

"Intense" initiatives involve significant amounts of resources, chiefly funding and citizen involvement. In the United States, many community programs have never been funded at a sufficient level of intensity. Although these initiatives were effective in demonstration projects in specific communities, they were then applied more widely without sufficient resources to reach the threshold needed to create wider social change (Schorr, 1997). Thus, they have made little headway against entrenched social problems. Community change initiatives need to generate sufficient intensity through mobilization of sufficient resources, both monetary and human.

**Strengthening of Sense of Community**    A factor implicit in Schorr's (1997) discussion is the sense of community among residents or members of a community. Sense of community, as you learned in chapters 7 and 12, is a resource for community change. Effective community change initiatives both use and enhance this resource. Strengthening the following qualities creates community resources: individuals' sense of membership in a community, the mutual influence of individuals and the wider community, members' integration and support of each other, and a shared emotional connection among them. Do you recognize these ideas? They are the D. W. McMillan and Chavis (1986) elements of sense of community from chapter 7.

**Long-Term Perspective**    A final factor, also implicit in Schorr's (1997) discussion and examples, is the necessity for a long-term perspective. Community change does not occur overnight. The community initiatives described in this chapter are often the products of years of building a community organization and implementing actions in the community, before community outcomes occur. The work of coalitions such as CINCH usually is in its second or third year before measurable community outcomes occur (Fawcett et al. 1995; Butterfoss et al., in press). PICO organizations build their base of interpersonal relationships and commitment carefully for months (Speer et al., 1995). When decisions are made through widespread participation, time is a necessary resource. Yet initiatives that build slowly and steadily are likely to be sustained even if conditions change, because their participatory base is solid.

**Conclusions**    Describing these seven elements of effective community change initiatives may suggest that community change is something of a science. Yet there are no formulas for community change (Alinsky, 1971). The seven elements are best understood as rules of thumb, with many possible ways to apply them in practice. Each community, indeed each community issue, is contextual, involving a unique mix of resources, obstacles, allies and opponents, means and ends, and intended outcomes and unanticipated consequences. Community change initiatives are an art, but a collective art, involving personal relationships and shared successes and failures. They affect not only the community at large but also the quality of individual lives.

# CHAPTER SUMMARY

**1.** This chapter concerns two overarching questions: How do citizens, acting collectively, acquire and use power to promote positive changes in their communities? How can communities become empowered to address the problems and challenges they face? These questions concern psychologists because individual and community quality of life are intertwined.

**2.** Chapter 12 discussed *empowering* community settings. This chapter concerns *empowered* community settings that influence their communities to enhance the quality of life there.

**3.** Social power refers to relationships in communities and society. It is not just the ability to compel others to act, but has three instruments (Gaventa, 1980). These are the *control of resources that can be used to bargain, reward, and punish,* the *control of channels for citizen participation,* and the *ability to shape the definition of a public issue or conflict.*

**4.** Four approaches to community change address the instruments of power. Those are *social action, community development, consciousness raising,* and *policy advocacy.* These differ in their purposes, methods, and in which instruments of power they address or use. Table 13.1 summarizes the instruments of power and approaches to community change.

**5.** This chapter uses an open systems model of community change, involving how it proceeds through stages of *input, throughput,* and *output.* The model (illustrated in Figure 13.1) focuses on how an empowered community organization influences its community. Input involves the identification and mobilization of personal, social, and material *resources.* Community *stakeholders* are important resources and participants. Throughput involves the *organizational task functioning* of the organization, and the *cohesion* among members of the organization. Output involves the *actions* the organization takes in the community, *changes* in community programs, policies or practices that result, and the short-term *outcomes* and long-term *impacts* of those changes. *Evaluation* of the organization's work and the community effects helps the organization learn from its experiences and plan for the future.

**6.** We discussed three extended examples of community organizations involved in community change. The Block Booster Project trained leaders of block associations to enhance the functioning of their associations, which involves a community development approach. PICO-based organizations use community organizing for power, first using community development methods to build a community organization, then using social action techniques to influence community decision-making for social justice. CINCH, a city-wide health coalition, brought organizations, stakeholders, and citizens together to plan and implement initiatives to improve child health, specifically immunization.

**7.** One overarching issue concerning community change initiatives is whether they involve a top-down *community betterment* approach or a bottom-up *community empowerment* approach.

**8.** Seven elements of effective community change initiatives are listed in Table 13.2. They represent rules of thumb, not formulas, for planning community changes.

# BRIEF EXERCISES

**1.** Turn to Box 13.1. Can you identify examples of citizen participation? Of actions motivated by a sense of community or that promote a sense of community? Of empowerment of a group or community? Of any other concepts from this chapter or chapter 12?

**2.** Review the list you wrote of issues your community faces. Suggest how each of the four approaches to community and social change (social action, community development, consciousness raising, policy advocacy) could be applied to the issues you listed. How would each approach lead to community-wide change? How would each affect the lives of community members?

**3.** Identify a block association, neighborhood organization, homeowners' association, community coalition working on a specific problem, or similar group in your locality. Attend a meeting, and interview a member or leader. Identify the purposes of the group and the issues it addresses, some examples of its successes, who participates in the association, and other organizations to which it is related.

**4.** Write an action letter that advocates a policy change. Choose an issue with which you have personal experience or background knowledge and on which you have a viewpoint. Choose also a person or organization you want to address; the more specific the better. (Examples include a legislator, a city mayor, the president of your university or of your student organization, a newspaper editor, a private business, or employer.)

Your letter should include the following elements:

- Define the specific problem or issue you are addressing.
- Describe aspects of this issue that have gotten too little attention. This may include causes that have been overlooked. Cite sources of specific information.
- Advocate a specific, feasible course of action to address these aspects of the issue. Examples include a new policy, new practices or ways to carry out an existing policy, a new or modified community program, or research to analyze the issue further. Recognize that your ideas will probably cost resources (money, time, collaboration among groups). Advocate your course of action assertively.
- Remember that the likelihood of close reading by your addressee decreases with each page. Be as succinct as you can but cover all the elements above. A suggested length is two pages double-spaced.

It is your choice whether actually to send the letter or not.

# RECOMMENDED READINGS

Alinsky, S. (1971). *Rules for radicals: A practical primer for realistic radicals.* New York: Random House.

Fawcett, S., Paine-Andrews, A., Francisco, V., Schulz, J., Richter, K., Lewis, R., Williams, E., Harris, K., Berkley, J., Fisher, J., & Lopez, C. (1995). Using empowerment theory in collaborative partnership for community health and development. *American Journal of Community Psychology, 23,* 677–697.

Lappe, F., & DuBois, P. (1994). *The quickening of America: Rebuilding our nation, remaking our lives.* San Francisco: Jossey-Bass.

Pilisuk, M., McAllister, J., & Rothman, J. (1996). Coming together for action: The challenge of contemporary grassroots community organizing. *Journal of Social Issues, 52,* 15–37.

Schorr, L. (1997). *Common purpose: Strengthening families and neighborhoods to rebuild America.* New York; Doubleday.

### Empirical Reports on the Chapter's Extended Examples of Community Change Initiatives

Florin, P., Chavis, D., Wandersman, A., & Rich, R. (1992). A systems approach to understanding and enhancing grassroots organizations: The Block Booster Project. In R. Levine & H. Fitzgerald (Eds.), *Analysis of dynamic psychological systems: Methods and applications* (Vol. 2, pp. 215–243). New York: Plenum.

Speer P., & Hughey, J. (1995). Community organizing: An ecological route to empowerment and power. *American Journal of Community Psychology, 23,* 729–748.

Butterfoss, F., Goodman, R., & Wandersman, A. (in press). Citizen participation and health: Toward a psychology of improving health through individual, organizational and community involvement. In A. Baum, T. Revenson, & J. Singer (Eds.), *Handbook of health psychology.* Hillsdale, NJ: Erlbaum.

### Action Guidebooks for Community Change Initiatives

Kaye, G., & Wolff, T. (Eds.). (1997). *From the ground up: A workbook on coalition building and community development.* Amherst, MA: AHEC/Community Partners. Phone: 413-253-4283.

Kretzmann, J., & McKnight, J. (1993). *Building communities from the inside out: A path toward finding and mobilizing a community's assets.* Chicago: ACTA Publications. Phone: 800-397-0079.

(See also RECOMMENDED WEBSITES below and RECOMMENDED READINGS for chap. 12.)

# INFOTRAC KEYWORDS

*advocacy, citizen, citizen participation, coalition(s), community change, community development, community initiative(s), community organizing(ation), empowering(ed)(ment), participation(tory), power, sense of community, social action, social change.*

# RECOMMENDED WEBSITES

http://ctb.lsi.ukans.edu/
    The Community Tool Box (CTB) is an excellent site for learning about and planning community change. It is maintained by community psychologists and others in the Work Group on Health Promotion and Community Development. The CTB includes recommendations for planning, implementing, and evaluating community initiatives.

It also includes forums, chatrooms, links to related sites, a troubleshooting guide, and opportunities for partnerships with CTB staff.

http://www.livingdemocracy.org

The Center for Living Democracy focuses on ways in which communities can be organized to promote positive competencies and promote citizen participation and positive change at individual, organizational, locality, and macrosystem levels. This site includes many examples from practice.

# A COMMUNITY COALITION

The purpose of this exercise, which can be done alone or in a small group, is to use the concepts from chapters 12 and 13 to plan a community change initiative.

Choose a locality or neighborhood with which you are familiar. This can be your current or home town, neighborhood or urban block, or a rural area. If you do this exercise with classmates, it could be your university or its locality.

Imagine that residents of this community are troubled about ongoing drug use there, as most communities are. They are forming a community coalition to address the problem of abuse of legal (alcohol, tobacco) and illegal drugs and the problems that drug use creates for users, families, and community.

The coalition founders have invited you to join the coalition. Below are some questions for you to consider, based on chapters 12 and 13. Write and/or discuss with others your answers to each.

***Input: Resources***   The coalition founders have recruited representatives from the following segments of the community: a high school principal, a police officer, a juvenile probation officer, a professional counselor who treats persons with drug abuse problems, a local government official, and the president of the local chapter of Mothers Against Drunk Driving. They have not made an effort to recruit citizens or members of various population groups or other groups in the community. The coalition founders envision a final group of around 20 members.

- Who else should the coalition seek to recruit as members?
- From what groups, populations, and segments of the community would you suggest that they find representatives?
- Based on principles of citizen participation and empowerment, how could you include members of the community who would be most affected by coalition decisions and plans?
- Who else might be community resources to strengthen the work of this coalition in various ways?

***Throughput: Organizational Cohesion and Goals***   This concerns how you will strengthen group cohesion and determine the coalition's goals.

- Review the section in chapter 12 on empowering settings, and the section on Block Booster, PICO, and CINCH in chapter 13. Suggest steps the coalition could take to become an empowering setting for its members.
- Suggest ways to avoid domination of the group by professionals or existing community leaders, and some ways to get ordinary citizens fully involved.
- Does the coalition need to communicate its work in more than one language in your community?

Although in real life the coalition as a whole would make the following decisions, for this exercise make them yourself or with a few classmates.

- Describe the specific nature of problems in this community involving drugs, including types of drugs (including alcohol and tobacco) and the drug-related behaviors that are problems, and how these involve or challenge the whole community.
- Based on your current knowledge, suggest about five feasible goals for the initiative. How could these involve citizen participation and community empowerment?

***Output: Actions, changes, outcomes, and impacts***     Once the coalition's goals are determined, it needs to plan and carry out actions to pursue those goals.

- Suggest specific actions for the coalition members to take in the community to pursue each goal of the coalition you listed above.
- Indicate whether these actions involve social action, community development, consciousness raising, or policy advocacy strategies.
- Indicate the community changes you plan to obtain from the coalition's actions and whether each involves a new or existing program, policy, or practice.
- What other organizations in the community would be involved in each change?
- If you plan new programs, will they require paid staff? How might that be funded?
- Indicate short-term community outcomes, and long-term community impacts that you believe would result from these community changes. How are these related to your goals for the coalition?

# PROGRAM EVALUATION AND PROGRAM DEVELOPMENT

# IT SOUNDED LIKE A GOOD IDEA, BUT IS IT REALLY WORKING?

Each year billions of dollars in tax money, charitable contributions (e.g., United Way, American Cancer Society), and philanthropic foundation dollars (e.g., Kellogg Foundation, Ford Foundation) are spent to do good things in communities. Is that money making a difference? Picture yourself as a board member of a foundation who has to make funding decisions about community programs. You get many more requests for funding than you could possibly fund. It makes sense to ask grantees, "How can we know if your program, supported by our grant money, actually accomplishes its goals?"

Schorr (1997) described several types of answers to this question often given by nonprofit organizations and government agencies.

- *Trust and values.* "Trust us. What we do is so valuable, so complex, so hard to document, so hard to judge, and we are so well intentioned that the public should support us without demanding evidence of effectiveness. Don't let the bean counters who know the cost of everything and the value of nothing obstruct our valiant efforts to get the world's work done." (Schorr, 1997, p 116)

    Potential problem with this answer: We don't know the process of how the program works, and we don't know whether there are any results.
- *Process and outputs.* "Our agency sees 200 eligible clients yearly in the 20 parent education programs we offer with our 2 licensed staff who are funded by your grant." This is probably the most typical answer, with detailed documentation of programs or services provided and resources expended.

    Potential problem: In the past, parent education classes have been funded in the optimistic expectation that they would somehow reduce the incidence of child abuse. However, a few classroom sessions have never been shown to change parenting practices among parents at greatest risk of child abuse (Schorr, 1997, pp. 119–120). Similarly hopeful but undocumented expectations underlie many community programs.
- *Results-based accountability.* Using program evaluation, we can show that a specific program made a difference and achieved its intended effects, as desired by its stakeholders. We can also modify it to become even more effective. This is similar to the idea of continuous improvement discussed in chapter 11.

    Potential problems: Agency staff often are not trained to do evaluation. Also, what happens if the evaluation shows that the program does not have the intended results?

Government, nonprofit, and private sectors are being challenged to show results (e.g., U.S. General Accounting Office, 1990; United Way, 1996). At first, this can be a frightening prospect. Below are some common complaints and fears about program evaluation (compiled by the Northwest Regional Educational Laboratory, 1999).

- Evaluation can create anxiety among program staff.
- Staff may be unsure how to conduct evaluation.
- Evaluation can interfere with program activities, or compete with services for scarce resources.
- Evaluation results can be misused and misinterpreted, especially by program opponents.

Yet program evaluation does not have to be frightening. Results-based accountability requires us to understand program evaluation and how programs can be improved to achieve their goals. When done well, it can strengthen a program's quality as well as its ability to resist critics.

# WHAT ARE THE KEY POINTS OF THIS CHAPTER?

In this chapter, we address program accountability by describing both program evaluation and program development. Program evaluation refers to the collection of evidence to judge the effectiveness of community programs or other community interventions: deciding whether their "good ideas really work." Program development refers to the planning and implementing of a program: determining its purposes and setting goals, carrying out the program, improving it for the future. Our major theme is that well-designed, user-friendly evaluation generates feedback and ideas for promoting high-quality program development, through continuous program improvement.

To do this, first we describe the logic of program evaluation and the importance of program theory. Next, we describe a four-step model for evaluating community programs (the *Prevention Plus III* approach) that involves identifying program goals and outcomes, evaluating program process, and evaluating attainment of desired program outcomes and wider impacts. Then we apply this perspective to community programs, especially mentoring programs that bring together adult mentors and students. We emphasize how useful evaluation can be for continuous feedback and improvement of all programs.

Evaluation feedback for modifying an existing program can be extended to address the planning of a new program as well. That is the approach of *Comprehensive Quality Programming*, which uses nine accountability questions and corresponding strategies to incorporate a continuous improvement approach into all phases of program development. We apply this approach to two mentoring programs, one existing and one new one, and conclude by discussing how program development and evaluation can be intertwined.

# THE LOGIC OF PROGRAM EVALUATION

Project D.A.R.E. (Drug Abuse Resistance Education) is the most popular school-based drug-use prevention program in the United States, but there is limited evidence of its effectiveness. For instance, results from a longitudinal evaluation of the program in 36 schools in Illinois provide only limited evidence for D.A.R.E.'s impact on student's drug use immediately following the intervention, and no evidence of impact on drug use 1 or 2 years after receiving D.A.R.E. instruction. In addition, D.A.R.E. programs had only limited positive effects on psychological variables (e.g., self-esteem) and no effect on social skills variables (e.g., peer pressure resistance skills; Enett et al., 1994, p. 113).

How can we explain this lack of measurable outcomes in a popular intervention? Unfortunately, the cited study focused on outcomes for students who received D.A.R.E. and a comparison group who did not. Because of that outcome focus, the study was not able to tell us why the expected outcomes did not occur. There are at least two reasons why programs don't work: *theory failure* and *implementation failure.* Theory failure concerns program theory: the rationale for why a particular intervention is considered appropriate for a particular problem with a specific target population. Program theory also helps choose appropriate measurements or methods to study the effects of the program. Implementation failure concerns quality of program implementation. You may have an excellent program that has been demonstrated elsewhere to work with your target population, but the implementation in your location may be weak due to a lack of resources, inexperienced personnel, insufficient training, or other reasons (see chap. 11).

Since the 1960s, the field of program evaluation has developed concepts and methods for examining program theory and implementation based on the methods of the social sciences (see Patton, 1997; Rossi, Freeman, & Lipsey, 1999; Worthen, Sanders, & Fitzpatrick, 1997). Theory and implementation are often studied using process and outcome evaluations. This chapter uses many of the basic concepts in the program evaluation field. However, it relies heavily on approaches that make program evaluation user-friendly in order to make it accessible to a wider audience. Please see the references in this paragraph for a more detailed exposure to the program evaluation field.

Professional evaluators are trained to think causally. They recognize that an intervention or prevention activity is based on an underlying program theory or model of the causal factors contributing to the problem to be prevented. This model may be clearly stated by the prevention program's developers, or the program may only be based on implicit assumptions. Effects are not likely to occur if

- the underlying assumptions of program theory are incorrect,
- the program, even if implemented well, doesn't affect the variables specified by program theory,
- or the activity or program is not implemented adequately.

For social scientists, this type of thinking becomes so automatic that it is easy to forget it is not universal. Agency staff often need a "critical friend" to help them identify their underlying assumptions about their program theory, goals, and implementation.

For instance, a common community prevention activity is sponsoring a Red Ribbon Awareness Campaign. A local group wants to significantly reduce alcohol, tobacco, and other drug (ATOD) use by getting citizens to display red ribbons. Why would wearing a red ribbon lead to reductions in ATOD use? For example, the logic may be that a red ribbon stimulates awareness of the hazards of alcohol use which then either reduces one's own consumption of alcohol or at least stimulates a sober friend to drive. Questioning the connections between the display of red ribbons and the ultimate outcome of reduction of drunk driving requires critical thinking about cause and effect. It is important for school and community practitioners to use causal thinking and, as much as possible, to develop a causal model for a community program. That model then can indicate questions for evaluation of program process and outcome, which will help demonstrate program effectiveness.

The United Way, foundations, and other agencies have adopted and promoted the use of logic models for assessment (e.g., United Way, 1996). The logic model is also used to help assess several grant programs of the U.S. Federal Center for Substance Abuse Prevention. The principal purpose of a logic model is to show, on one piece of paper, the logical connections between the conditions that contribute to the need for a program in a community, the activities aimed at addressing these conditions, and the outcomes and impacts expected to result from the activities (Julian, Jones, & Dey, 1995; McEwan & Bigelow 1997).

The logic model is a graphic representation of the program. Figure 14.1 illustrates this format. Its top row consists of four circles, representing program conditions, activities, outcomes, and impacts. For a specific program, the logic model would have multiple examples in each circle, representing multiple conditions, activities, outcomes and impacts. The circles are linked together with lines that show the expected logical relationships among them, based on the program theory. These relationships among circles also show the sequence of intended events that occur as a result of program activities.

In the first circle, conditions include risk factors or processes, community problems, or organizational difficulties that the program seeks to address. The second circle includes the activities that address each condition; one or more activities can aim at solving each of the conditions. The third circle contains the immediate outcomes that result from the activity (e.g., changes in knowledge or attitudes of program participants, or changes in an organization or community) and intermediate outcomes (e.g., individual behavioral changes or changes in regulations, legislation, or relationships among community organizations). The fourth circle concerns the eventual impacts of the program on the community at large. For example, impacts in alcohol, tobacco, and other drugs (ATOD) have to do with lowering alcohol and other drug abuse in the community and related consequences of lowered substance use, such as lower crime and better health. Recall the distinction between outcomes and impacts also made in chapter 13.

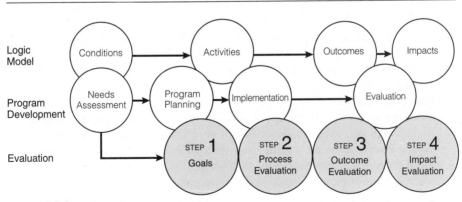

**FIGURE 14.1**

Four-step program evaluation.

Note: Adapted from *Prevention Plus III* (Linney & Wandersman, 1991, p. 9).

Row 2 of Figure 14.1 illustrates the steps in program development and their relationships to the logic model. A program developer assesses the need for a program (often with community surveys or interviews), plans a program to address the need, implements the program, and evaluates whether the program has been successful. Row 3 of Figure 14.1 shows how program evaluation relates to the logic model and to program development. That is the focus of the next section.

# A FOUR-STEP MODEL OF PROGRAM EVALUATION

Linney and Wandersman (1991) sought to design materials that would stimulate analytical thinking about the ways in which prevention programs might affect outcomes, realistic thinking about the effect of any one preventive effort, and careful planning for implementation. Their volume, *Prevention Plus III*, was developed to teach people at the local level the basics about evaluation and how to do elementary evaluations of their own programs. The book boils program evaluation down to four basic steps (goals and desired outcomes, process evaluation, outcome evaluation, and impact evaluation) that relate to the logic model (see Figure 14.1, row 3).

## Step 1: Identify Goals and Desired Outcomes

Starting with goals sets the project's sights. Goals represent what a project is striving for (e.g., children who have positive social relationships and are well-educated so that they will be productive members of society). Goals tend to be ambitious and set a framework for outcomes. Outcomes are more specific and represent what the project is accountable for. Goals can be general; outcomes must be specific and measurable (Schorr, 1997).

If a community program has prevention/promotion aims (see chaps. 9–11), goals and outcomes concern problems to be prevented or competencies and health outcomes to be promoted. Alternatively, if a community initiative addresses a wider community issue or problem (see chaps. 12 and 13), the changes it seeks to create indicate its goals and outcomes.

In Step 1, program developers describe

- The primary goals of the program, such as increasing parent involvement in the schools or reducing drug use.
- Target group(s) of the program. Whom does it try to reach (e.g., teachers, children of a specific age, parents, general public)? Target groups can be described by demographic characteristics (e.g., age, sex, race, socioeconomic status), developmental transitions (e.g., entering middle school, divorce, bereavement), risk processes (e.g., low grades, multiple conduct incidents in school), locality, or other criteria.
- What outcomes are desired. Examples include increases in attitudes rejecting smoking or decreases in school absences. Well-formulated outcomes are clearly defined and specific, realistic and attainable, and measurable.

Figure 14.2 illustrates the four-step evaluation method with worksheets adapted from *Prevention Plus III* (Linney & Wandersman, 1991). Step 1 in that figure shows the questions that program planners need to ask themselves to specify program goals, target groups, and desired outcomes.

## Step 1: Identify Goals and Desired Outcomes

**A. Make a list of the primary goals of the program.**

Ask yourself: "What were we trying to accomplish?"

1.

2.

3.

**B. What groups did you want to involve?**

Ask yourself: "Whom were we trying to reach?"

For each group, how many persons did you want to involve?

1.

2.

3.

**C. What outcomes did you desire?**

Ask yourself: "As a result of this program, how would we like participants to change? What would they learn? What attitudes, feelings, or behaviors would be different?"

1.

2.

3.

## Step 2: Process Evaluation

**A. What activities were implemented?**

Ask yourself: "What did we actually do to implement this program?" Form a chronology of events.

*Date      Description of Activity*

1.

2.

3.

For each activity above, indicate the following:

*Activity        Percentage of        Activity        Percentage of*
*length (hrs.)   time goal            attendance      attendance goal*

Total Duration of all activities (in hours) =

Total Attendance at all activities =

Other services delivered:

**FIGURE 14.2**

Four-step program evaluation: Specific questions.

**B. What can you learn from this experience?**

What topics or activities were planned but not delivered? What happened that these were not accomplished?

*Activity*                                     *Problem*

Who was missing that you had hoped to have participate in the program?

What explanations can you give for any discrepancy between the planned and actual participation?

What feedback can be used to improve the program in the future?

## Step 3: Outcome Evaluation

*Desired Outcome*                              *Measure*

1.                                             1.

2.                                             2.

3.                                             3.

## Step 4: Impact Evaluation

*Desired Impact*                               *Measure*

1.                                             1.

2.                                             2.

3.                                             3.

Note: Adapted from Linney & Wandersman (1991, pp. 44–51).

FIGURE **14.2** *(continued)*

## Step 2: Process Evaluation

In Step 2, the activities designed to reach the desired outcome are described. They answer the question, "What did the program actually do?"

***Purposes of Process Evaluation***   Process evaluation has several purposes. First, monitoring program activities helps organize program efforts. It helps ensure that all parts of the program are conducted as planned. It also helps the program use resources where they are needed; for example, not spending most of its money on only one activity or target group. Furthermore, it provides information to help manage the program and modify activities, leading to midcourse corrections that enhance the project's outcomes.

Second, information in a process evaluation provides accountability that the program is conducting the activities it promised to do. This can be furnished to administration, funding sources, boards of directors, or other stakeholders.

Third, after a later evaluation of outcomes and impacts, the process evaluation can provide information about why the program worked or did not work. By providing information on what was done and who was reached, program planners can identify reasons for achieving outcomes or not achieving them. Process evaluation information also can provide information for future improvements, and for sharing practical tips with others planning similar programs.

Fourth, process evaluation can help you decide whether or not you are ready to assess the effects of your program. For example, if a program has been in existence for only a short time and you have implemented only the first activity of a seven-activity program, then it is premature to assess program outcomes.

Fifth, sometimes conditions change and what was planned isn't what actually happens. Process evaluation helps keep track of such changes. Answering process evaluation questions before, during, and after the planned activities documents what actually happened.

***Conducting a Process Evaluation***    A process evaluation centers on two related questions: What were the intended and actual activities of the program? After it was implemented, what did program planners and staff learn from their experiences? (See Figure 14.2 Parts A and B, Step 2.)

Regarding activities, process evaluation asks: *Who* was supposed to do *what* with *whom* and *when* was it to be done? (See Figure 14.3.)

*Who* refers to the staff who deliver the services. How many staff? What kinds of qualifications and training do they need?

*What* refers to what the staff are asked to do (e.g., hold classes, show movies, model behavior).

*Whom* refers to the target groups for each activity.

*When* refers to the time and setting of the activity (e.g., during school assemblies, after school).

The more clearly the questions are answered, the more useful the process evaluation will be. (See Figure 14.2, Step 2, for specific questions.) All of the information gathered in the process evaluation can be used to improve (or discard) the activity in the future (see Figure 14.2, Part B of Step 2.)

## Step 3: Outcome Evaluation

Outcome evaluation assesses the immediate effects of a program. The "bottom line" of program evaluation concerns these immediate effects (see Figure 14.2, Step 3) and ultimate program impacts (Step 4). (Note that the field of program evaluation uses the terms *outcomes* and *impacts* as they are described in this chapter. The field of public health reverses these terms and uses the term *outcomes* to mean long-term indicators and *impacts* to mean short-term indicators.)

*Outcome evaluation,* as the term is used in program evaluation and community psychology, is concerned with measuring the short-term or immediate effects of a program on its participants or recipients. It attempts to determine the direct effects of the program, such as the degree to which a drug-use prevention program increased knowledge of drugs and the perceived risk of using drugs.

Basically, Step 3 looks at the desired outcomes defined in Step 1 and seeks evidence regarding the extent to which those outcomes were achieved (see Figure 14.2, Step 3). Evidence of program outcomes for a drug-abuse prevention program could include increased awareness of drug dangers, or improved scores on a measure of social skills for resisting pressure to use drugs. Planning how to collect this data or evidence is best begun along with planning program goals and outcomes.

**Outcome Measures**    These should be closely linked to goals, but more specific. There are several potential ways to measure outcomes.

Self-report questionnaires are commonly used to measure outcomes. As you probably know from prior methodology courses, they must be chosen with care; instrument reliability and validity should be considered. The test–retest reliability (stability) of a measure is a particular concern if it is to be given before and after an intervention. Construct validity, the extent to which a questionnaire measures what it claims to measure, also is an important concern. Does a particular measure of problem-solving skills actually measure those skills? Predictive validity is also a concern. Does a measure of attitudes about drug use predict actual drug use 1 year later? Program developers and evaluators need to consider these questions in light of their program theory. What measures of what constructs will best reflect the true outcomes of the program? A measure of self-esteem useful for adults may not work well for adolescents or for drug-related outcomes.

Self-report questionnaires are not the only means of collecting outcome data. For some purposes, it is useful to obtain information from other sources about a participant, such as ratings of a child by a parent or ratings of students by teachers. Persons completing questionnaires who are not reporting on themselves are termed *key informants.* Behavior observation ratings may be useful, although they are often cumbersome to collect.

## Step 4: Impact Evaluation

Impact evaluation is concerned with the ultimate effects desired by a program. In alcohol and other drug prevention programs, the ultimate effects might include reduction in overall drug use (prevalence), reduction in rate of new students starting drug use (incidence), decreases in drunk-driving arrests, and decreases in school disciplinary actions for drug or alcohol offenses (see Figure 14.2, Step 4).

Outcomes (Step 3) are immediate or short-term results of a program, whereas impacts (Step 4) are ultimate or longer-term effects of the program. Sound program theory and planning of goals and outcomes help delineate what are expected outcomes and impacts.

*Archival data,* based on records collected for other purposes, help assess impacts. Examples include medical records, juvenile court or police records, or school grades and attendance records.

## Summary Illustration of the Four-Step Evaluation Model

Suppose a coalition in your community implemented a prevention program to reduce adolescents' use of alcohol, tobacco and other drugs. The four-step *Prevention Plus III* evaluation model would be applied as follows. Figure 14.3 presents each step using adaptations of *Prevention Plus III* forms (Linney & Wandersman, 1991).

**Step 1: Identifying Goals**   This step involves specifying program goals, objectives, and target groups. The overall program goals are to reduce overall drug use and drug-related arrests, accidents, and illnesses among youth (and eventually, adults). Two specific program objectives are to increase citizen knowledge of drug-related issues, and their commitment to action on those issues. Additional objectives are to increase adolescents' skills in resisting pressure from peers and media to use drugs and to decrease local sales of tobacco to minors. Specific target groups include the community, parents of adolescents, students in Grades 7–9, and local stores that sell tobacco products (see Figure 14.3, Step 1).

**Step 2: Process Evaluation**   The program is to be implemented in several ways. A media campaign and public meetings will be conducted to raise public awareness of drug-related issues. School classes (Grades 7–9), including exercises and dramatic skits, and school assemblies will be conducted on drug-related issues, including skills for resisting drug use. A parent training course will focus on communications skills with adolescents. A behavioral intervention for testing stores' willingness to sell tobacco products to minors, and reinforcing their refusals to sell, will be implemented (see Biglan et al., 1996, discussed in chap. 4). To conduct the process evaluation, the following will be recorded: the number of meetings, classes, assemblies, and training workshops planned and actually held, the staff time spent on each, and attendance at each session. The time and persons involved in training of student testers and implementation of the behavioral intervention for testing stores would also be recorded (see Figure 14.3, Part A of Step 2). After each program component is implemented, the process evaluation also will include a discussion of what program staff and planners learned from the experience (see Figure 14.3, Part B of Step 2).

**Step 3: Outcome Evaluation**   Before and after public meetings, and in surveys of community members conducted before and after the media campaign, a questionnaire would assess changes in citizens' knowledge of drug abuse issues, and the number of volunteers for coalition activities. A questionnaire measuring parenting skills for communicating with adolescents would be given before and after the parent training course, to measure changes in these areas among course participants. In the schools, questionnaires completed by students and teachers would measure students' gains in skills for resisting drug use (measured before and after the classroom intervention). Student questionnaires could also be used to measure changes in attitudes and behavior regarding drug use. Finally, behavioral tests of store clerks' willingness or refusal to sell tobacco to minors would be conducted and recorded (see Figure 14.3, Step 3).

**Step 4: Impact Evaluation**   Long-term effects of the program could be measured, for example, by changes in drug-related school disciplinary actions, police arrest and accident records for youth, and hospital records of drug-related treatment (see Figure 14.3, Step 4).

## Step 1: Identify Goals and Desired Outcomes

### A. Make a list of the primary goals of the program.

Ask yourself: "What were we trying to accomplish?"

1. Decrease adolescent use of alcohol, tobacco, and other drugs
2. Decrease rates of accidents, illness, and other drug-related conditions, and drug-related arrests

### B. What groups did you want to involve?

Ask yourself: "Whom were we trying to reach?"
For each group, how many persons did you want to involve?

1. Local citizens (all residents of locality)
2. Parents in training course (20 families in first year)
3. Adolescents in grades 7-9 in school (500 in first year)
4. Local stores selling tobacco (25 stores)

### C. What outcomes did you desire?

Ask yourself: "As a result of this program, how would we like participants to change? What would they learn? What attitudes, feelings or behaviors would be different?"

1. Increase citizen knowledge of drug-related issues and problem
2. Increase citizen commitment to action on these issues
3. Increase parent skills in communicating with children about drug use
4. Increase teens' skills in resisting pressure to use drugs
5. Decrease local sales of tobacco to minors

## Step 2: Process Evaluation Worksheet

### A. What activities were implemented?

Ask yourself: "What did we actually do to implement this program?" Form a chronology of events.

| Date | Description of Activity |
|---|---|
| 1. | Public awareness campaign: TV, radio, newspapers (ads, letters, columns, brochures, interviews) |
| 2. | Public meetings: schools, religious congregations, etc. |
| 3. | Curriculum & materials in school health classes |
| 4. | Dramatic skits in schools by student team |
| 5. | Parent communication skills training (6 sessions) |
| 6. | Intervention to test and reduce store willingness to sell tobacco to teens, modeled on Biglan et al. (1996) |

For each activity above, indicate the following:

| Activity length (hrs.) | Percentage of time goal | Activity attendance | Percentage of attendance goal |
|---|---|---|---|
| 2. 46 hours | 92% | 250 | 50% |
| 3. 100 hours | 80% | 400 | 80% |
| 4. 10 hours | 100% | 400 | 80% |

FIGURE **14.3**

Four-step program evaluation: An example.

| Activity length (hrs.) | Percentage of time goal | Activity attendance | Percentage of attendance goal |
|---|---|---|---|
| 5. 12 hours | 100% | 18 | 90% |
| 6. 25 hours | 25% | 25 store visits | 25% |

Total duration of all activities (in hours) = 293 hours

Total attendance at all activities = 1,068 persons

Other services delivered:

1. 100 total actions to increase community awareness, involving media campaigns (Activity #1)
2. Guest lectures in community college classes

### B. What can you learn from this experience?

What topics or activities were planned but not delivered? What happened that these were not accomplished?

| Activity | Problem |
|---|---|
| Tobacco sales testing not completed | Training, logistics took longer than planned |

Who was missing that you had hoped to have participate in the program?

Youth, parents from high-risk family and neighborhood environments
Not enough business, civic and religious leaders

What explanations can you give for any discrepancy between the planned and actual participation?

Competing news events overshadowed some media campaigns
Courses, materials for youth need to be more appealing

What feedback can be used to improve the program in the future?

Improve "teen appeal" of course materials
Skits were a hit, use that format more
Identify potential student and community leaders, involve them
Involve youth, parents from high-risk environments in planning

## Step 3: Outcome Evaluation

| Desired Outcome | Measure |
|---|---|
| 1. Increased citizen knowledge of drug abuse issues | Scores on survey of knowledge |
| 2. Increased citizen commitment to action to prevent drug abuse | Number of volunteers for anti-drug activities |
| 3. Increased parent communication skills with teens re: drug use | Self-report survey of parent skills before and after training sessions |
| 4. Increased student resistance | Teacher ratings, student questionnaires on student resistance skills before and after training |
| 5. Decreased sales of tobacco | Number of times clerks were willing to sell when teen assessment teams attempted purchases before and after behavioral intervention |

## Step 4: Impact Evaluation

| *Desired Impact* | *Measure* |
|---|---|
| 1. Decreased drug-related traffic accidents, arrests | Police records: number of drug-related accidents, arrests; before and after program |
| 2. Decreased school disciplinary actions related to drug use | School records: number of drug-related disciplinary actions before and after program |
| 3. Decreased incidence of drug-related conditions, accidents | Hospital records: number of drug-related emergency room visits; number of admissions for drug-related conditions before and after program |

Note: Adapted from Linney & Wandersman (1991).

FIGURE **14.3** *(continued)*

Although the four-step program evaluation method in *Prevention Plus III* was initially developed for evaluation in the alcohol, tobacco, and other drug abuse domain, it is adaptable to any program area, such as community-based mental health prevention programs (McElhaney, 1995) and delinquency prevention (Morrissey, 1998).

# EXAMINING MENTORING FROM A PROGRAM EVALUATION PERSPECTIVE

In this section, we illustrate the program evaluation concepts by examining mentoring. First, we briefly describe the literature; second we present a *Prevention Plus III* mentoring case study.

In 1997, President Clinton, with the assistance of many others including General Colin Powell, launched a widely publicized volunteerism summit. A major goal of the summit was to establish many more mentoring relationships for high-risk youth (moving from 300,000 in 1997 to one million by 2000). Mentoring is viewed as a major strategy to help "high risk" youth (Powell's new war, 1997).

The term *mentoring* comes from Greek mythology where Mentor was a trusted friend of Odysseus and served as a guardian and tutor to Odysseus' son when Odysseus was away (Haskell, 1997). Mentoring relationships generally involve an older, more experienced person and a younger, less experienced person. The mentor helps develop the character and competence of the mentee or assists the mentee in reaching goals, while also displaying trust, confidence, and praise, modeling positive behavior and serving as an advocate for the mentee (Haensly & Parsons, 1993; Haskell, 1997; Rhodes, 1994, Slicker & Palmer, 1994). Yet consider the following summary of findings on mentoring programs.

> The evidence from the 10 available evaluations consistently indicates that noncontingent, supportive mentoring relationships do not have desired effects on outcomes

such as academic achievement, school attendance, dropout, various aspects of child behavior including misconduct, or employment. This lack of demonstrated effects has occurred whether mentors were paid or unpaid, and whether mentors were college undergraduates, community volunteers, members of the business community, or school personnel. However, when mentors used behavior management techniques in one small, short-term study, students' school attendance improved. This is consistent with the findings from studies of school behavior management interventions reported earlier. In another larger, longer-term experimental evaluation by the same researchers, unspecified mentoring relationships significantly increased delinquency for youth with no prior offenses but significantly decreased recidivism for youth with prior offenses. (Office of Juvenile Justice and Delinquency Prevention [OJJDP], 1995, p. 95)

This summary of findings of mentoring programs makes us want to know more about a specific program, since many programs did not have desired effects, but some did. Is it worth the necessary time, energy, and money to ensure that a mentoring program is having positive effects? An examination of mentoring programs in terms of stated goals, process, outcomes, and ultimate impacts is essential if we are to understand why some mentoring programs fail while others flourish. A case in point is the Big Brothers/Big Sisters (BB/S) mentoring program. Almost as the OJJDP report cited above was leaving the press, Public/Private Ventures (PPV) issued a report that concluded that the Big Brothers/Big Sisters mentoring program worked.[1]

> The most notable results are the deterrent effects on the initiation of drug and alcohol use, and the overall positive effects on academic performance that the mentoring experience produced. Improvement in grade-point average among Little Brothers and Little Sisters, while small in percentage terms, is still very encouraging, since non-academic interventions are rarely capable of producing effects in grade performance. (Sipe, 1996, p. 65)

The PPV study of BB/S followed 487 children with mentors in "noncontingent" mentoring relationships over a period of 18 months. Children in mentoring relationships were markedly less likely to use drugs or alcohol, engage in violence, or be truant from school. What can account for the contrast between the studies reviewed by OJJDP and those reported by PPV? There are several possibilities. Studies emphasized by OJJDP included programs that matched groups of children or adolescents to a single mentor. In fact, the negative effects attributed by OJJDP to mentoring were interpreted by the original researchers (Fox & O'Donnell, 1974) as stemming from negative peer influences from contact between students mentored in groups. This spreading of maladaptive behavior occurred between student group members, and does not seem applicable to individual student–mentor pairs (characteristic of BB/S and similar programs). Another prominent difference between the PPV study and those reviewed by OJJDP is the length of time the mentoring relationships were studied. Few of the programs reviewed by OJJDP examined mentoring relationships beyond 1 year. Finally, the OJJDP review summarized program evaluations of mentoring programs for both adolescents and children, without distinguishing between them.

---

[1] This analysis of the differences between the OJJDP summary and the PPV summary was written by Kevin Everhart.

Both the BB/S mentoring program and the programs reviewed by OJJDP began with similar goals and desired outcomes (prevention of delinquency, promotion of mental health and achievement). They differed, however, in the manner in which processes and activities were logically linked to desired outcomes. Consider the differences between a mentoring relationship at 6 months and again at 18 months. Or consider the same adult mentoring a 17-year-old adolescent, versus an 11-year-old. We can see how two simple procedural variables (duration of mentoring relationship and age of child to be matched with a mentor) may have profound influence on the kinds of outcomes we may expect. Thus, a program evaluation that carefully looks at process and outcomes is needed. Below, we describe an evaluation of a mentoring program that used the four-step method from *Prevention Plus III* as a guide.

## Mentoring: A Prevention Plus III Evaluation

The C.O.P.E. mentoring program in a rural county in South Carolina paired at-risk middle school students with adult volunteer mentors who met with their mentees during school hours. The targeted students were identified as at-risk by teachers and other school staff based on characteristics such as social withdrawal, aggression, academic failure, or truancy. When the evaluators became involved in the project, it had already been in ongoing implementation for 3 years. The mentoring program is described in more detail in Wandersman et al. (1998) and Davino, Wandersman, and Goodman (1995).

The first step in the evaluation was to work with the school staff in the clarification of the mentoring program's goals and desired outcomes (Step 1 of the four-step method). The broad goal of the mentoring program was to improve mentees' quality of life in three domains: relationships, self-esteem, and school-related problems. Next, this goal was developed into a more specific set of measurable outcomes for the program. Desired outcomes included high satisfaction with the program and with the mentoring relationship among mentees and mentors, high scores on a mentee self-esteem measure, increased school grades, increased school attendance, and decreased school behavioral problems (see Figure 14.4, Step 1).

In order to assess the degree to which the program was successfully achieving its goals and desired outcomes, both process and outcome evaluation components were conducted. Several different stakeholders in the program were surveyed in an attempt to get their feedback about satisfaction with the current program and suggestions for improvement. These stakeholders included mentors, mentees, teachers, and school staff who ran the program. In addition, work sheets were completed to document important program components (e.g., mentor recruitment, support meetings, luncheons) as well as components that were desired by participants but that had not yet been included as part of the program (e.g., mentor orientation sessions, group outings with mentors and mentees).

Process evaluation results also showed that 53% of the mentees had contact with their mentor once a week or more; 23% met at least once a month but less than once a week, and 24% less than once a month. On an open-ended question asking for suggested improvements, mentees had several ideas. Overwhelmingly, their responses to this question concerned wanting to see their mentor more often. Some of the responses may have been driven by ulterior motives, such as "we should get out of class every day." However,

## Step 1: Identify Goals and Desired Outcomes

### A. Make a list of the primary goals of the program.

Ask yourself: "What were we trying to accomplish?"

1. Build satisfying and consistent mentoring relationships
2. Improve mentee self-esteem
3. Decrease school problems

### B. What groups did you want to involve?

Ask yourself: "Whom were we trying to reach?"
For each group, how many persons did you want to involve?

1. At-risk middle school students: withdrawn, aggressive, academically failing, truant, pregnant, those with social problems
2. As many as possible (100 currently)

### C. What outcomes did you desire?

Ask yourself: "As a result of this program, how would we like participants to change? What would they learn? What attitudes, feelings, or behaviors would be different?"

1. Have high satisfaction with program and mentor relationship
2. Increased scores on self-esteem measures
3. Increased grades and school attendance
4. Decreased school behavior problems

Note: Adapted from Linney & Wandersman (1991).

FIGURE **14.4**

C.O.P.E. mentoring program goals and outcomes.

for other students there seemed to be a real concern about not being able to count on the mentor to come often or at the scheduled time. An example of this was the suggestion that "there should be a rule that mentors have to come every week."

Results of the C.O.P.E. mentoring program were mixed. The stakeholder surveys showed consistently positive responses among participants in all groups. For example, the majority of mentees and mentors saw the program as "helpful" or "very helpful" to the students. Both groups also rated the quality of their relationships as "good" or "great," saw their relationship as "improving," and reported the fit between mentor and mentee as "good" or "great." However, comparisons between mentees and a comparison group (children on a waiting list for mentors) on self-esteem, grades, school attendance, and decreased school behavior problems were not statistically significant.

Program participants felt good about the program, but measures of behavioral changes showed no effect of mentoring. Some reasons for this lack of behavioral changes may be that the program was not long enough or intensive enough to affect outcomes such as grades and self-esteem, the mentors were not sufficiently trained, the program needed to be conducted for more hours per week or in a different way, or the measures chosen (e.g., self-esteem) were affected by too many factors other than mentoring effects. Whatever the reasons, results such as these suggest that program planners need to step back and reexamine their goals and methods more closely. That is the topic of the next section.

# COMPREHENSIVE QUALITY PROGRAMMING: NINE ESSENTIAL STRATEGIES FOR IMPLEMENTING SUCCESSFUL PROGRAMS

The outcome results of the C.O.P.E. mentoring program were disappointing. The measured outcomes of many treatment, prevention, and educational programs are often disappointing. Yet, as with C.O.P.E., many participants and observers of a community program may believe that a program has the kernel of a good idea that will be effective, if the program is improved. Traditionally, program evaluation has been concerned with whether a program already developed is working, and why. However, this approach does not study how to develop an effective program in the first place.

As you learned in chapter 11, continuous improvement of programs relies on the use of evaluation data to plan and implement program modifications. Many barriers prevent program planners and staff from using such feedback well. First, programs may use an outside evaluator, a person with no stake in the success or failure of the program (thus presumably more objective). Such an approach sets up an "us versus them" relationship that can limit the quality and usefulness of the evaluation findings. (Recall from chap. 3 the importance of relationships between researchers and communities studied.) Yet program practitioners often believe that they do not have the time, resources, or expertise to conduct their own evaluation. Second, program evaluation usually provides evaluation feedback at the end of program implementation, without opportunities for midcourse corrections. Program staff thus often view evaluation as an intrusive process that results in a report card of success or failure, but no useful information for program improvement. A third, related barrier is the general perception of evaluation research and findings as too complex, theoretical, or not user-friendly.

To overcome the above barriers, there has been a growing discussion of new and evolving roles for evaluators that encourage the self-determination of program practitioners (e.g., Dugan, 1996; Fetterman, 1994, 1996; Fetterman, Kaftarian, & Wandersman, 1996; Linney & Wandersman, 1991; Stevenson, Mitchell, & Florin, 1996). This new approach to evaluation, termed *empowerment evaluation,* attempts to break down the above barriers inherent in traditional evaluation methods in favor of those which reflect an empowerment and/or citizen participation perspective (Fetterman, 1996). Empowerment evaluation is an evolving approach in which program planners and developers learn the basics of program evaluation so that they can more systematically plan and implement their programs, and thereby increase the probability of obtaining desired outcomes. Empowerment evaluators collaborate with community members and program practitioners to determine program goals and implementation strategies, serve as facilitators or coaches but not as outside experts, provide technical assistance to teach community members and program staff to do self-evaluation, and stress the importance of using information from the evaluation in ongoing program improvement. In sum, empowerment evaluation helps program developers and staff to achieve their program goals, by providing them with tools for assessing and improving the planning, implementation, and results of their programs.

Using the empowerment evaluation philosophy, Wandersman et al. (1998) presented eight specific strategies that can guide self-evaluation and continuous program improvement. Since then, a ninth strategy has been added (Step 1 from *Prevention Plus III*). The implementation of a quality prevention or community program requires the use of these nine essential planning and evaluation steps, as well as a commitment to use information from each to enhance program functioning continuously. The nine strategies are collectively termed *comprehensive quality programming* (CQP). CQP is a straightforward approach that demystifies the evaluation process and demonstrates to program practitioners the value of evaluation in implementing quality prevention programs. CQP addresses the widespread interest in accountability of programs and uses the four steps of *Prevention Plus III* as part of its process. Below, we describe accountability and how CQP can help practitioners demonstrate accountability. Then we define each of the nine strategies and discuss specific planning and evaluation tools for each.

## Basic Program Accountability Questions

When beginning a new program, or continuing an existing one, program practitioners can start thinking about program effectiveness and program improvement issues by answering the accountability questions below. Answering these questions can serve as a beginning guide to successful planning, implementation, and evaluation of programs.

1. Why is the intervention or program needed?
2. What are the program's goals, target population and desired outcomes?
3. How does your program use the scientific knowledge and "best practice" of what works?
4. How will this new program fit in with existing programs?
5. How will you carry out the program?
6. How well was the program carried out?
7. How well did the program work?
8. What can you do to improve the program the next time you do it?
9. If the program (or parts of the program) were effective, what are you doing to continue (institutionalize) the program?

## Linking the Accountability Questions to CQP Strategies

In this section, we address the accountability questions by providing strategies for answering them. The accountability questions can often serve as a useful teaching device to demonstrate to program practitioners and funders the relevance and importance of evaluation. The questions are understandable and often spark an interest and appreciation for the link between solid evaluation and continued funding. Table 14.1 is a chart of the accountability questions and the relevant strategic planning or evaluation focus for answering them. Wandersman et al. (1998) described the corresponding planning and evaluation tools needed to provide answers to the accountability questions.

In Table 14.1, we can see that CQP expands upon the 4 steps of *Prevention Plus III*. What Wandersman et al. (1998) realized was that *Prevention Plus III* (Strategies 2, 5, 6, and 7 in Table 14.1) can help program developers perform their programs better, but it did not help them ask whether they were doing the "right" program. Thus, using only *Prevention Plus III* would be like tuning up your engine and making it run better so that you

| TABLE 14.1 | ACCOUNTABILITY QUESTIONS AND CORRESPONDING CQP STRATEGIES |

| Accountability Questions | CQP Strategies |
| --- | --- |
| 1. Why is the program needed? | Needs and assets assessments |
| 2. What are the program goals, target population, and desired outcomes? | Identifying goals and desired outcomes |
| 3. How does your program use scientific knowledge and best practices? | Review research literature and best practices |
| 4. How will this new program fit with existing programs? | Community feedback and planning |
| 5. How will you carry out the program? | Planning, implementation |
| 6. How well was the program carried out? | Process evaluation |
| 7. How well did the program work? | Outcome and impact evaluations |
| 8. What can you do to improve the program for next time? | Continuous program improvement |
| 9. If the program was effective, what is being done to institutionalize it? | Institutionalization strategies |

could drive at 70 mph instead of 30, but you might just be going down the wrong road faster. Questions 1–4 in the CQP questions help the program developer choose the right program and the later questions help the program developer improve the program and keep it going.

***Question 1. Why Is an Intervention Needed?***　How do you know you need a program? Frequently, programs are selected because they are popular or have been implemented at other local sites, rather than because they have been demonstrated to effectively prevent a specified problem in your setting. For example, Kaskutas, Morgan, and Vaeth (1992) described the experience of a guidance counselor who was working on a project as part of an interagency collaboration who "discovered after two months of planning a drug group [for] the senior high school kids in the project who were non-working, that there were no senior high kids in the project who didn't have jobs!" (p. 179). Therefore, there was no need for the program.

In order to determine which types of programs are needed in a given community, school, or other agency, a planning strategy called a needs assessment is often used (Soriano, 1995; Witlein & Altschuld, 1995). This assessment is designed to gather information about the issues most in need of improvement or intervention in a community or organization (e.g., youth violence, alcohol, and drug abuse). A good needs assessment also includes a resource assessment and identification of community and organizational strengths. Kretzman and McKnight (1993) discussed the necessity of assessing a community's assets. This can lead to discovering community resources that can be used to develop programs that fit the culture of the community well. Assets may include individual talents, microsystems that can offer social support systems for persons involved in the program, or organizations that can provide funding, a meeting space, or a venue for public discussion of program goals. Assets assessment also provides a counterpoint to needs assessment. The identification of community problems involved in needs assessment is balanced by an assessment of community strengths. Assets assessment is consistent with the ideals of citizen participation and community empowerment discussed in chapters 12 and 13.

**Question 2. What Are the Goals, Target Population, and Desired Outcomes?** After the need for a program has been determined, it is essential to specify the goals of the program, the specific target group(s) of the program, and the desired outcomes. This is Step 1 of the four-step evaluation method covered earlier.

**Question 3. How Does Your Program Use Scientific Knowledge and Best Practices of What Works?** Once program personnel have decided that there is a need to address a specific program, how do they decide which program or intervention to use? For example, administrators of school and community programs are showered with glossy mailings advertising multimedia curriculum products for programs such as violence prevention, sex education, and substance abuse prevention. How does one decide which program to choose? This decision is frequently based on convenience or availability. Does one rely on the program used last year, regardless of success, or use the program that can be borrowed for free from another source, or maybe use the program advertised at the last convention? It is important to keep in mind that although convenience and availability are important, they do not ensure program effectiveness.

A goal of prevention science is to provide two kinds of information. One is empirical (usually quantitative) findings about the effectiveness of programs in attaining identified goals. Another is (usually qualitative) information about best practices, the elements and methods of programs that work best for a particular type of problem within a particular type of population (recall this idea from chap. 11). These types of knowledge are useful in answering the question of what program to select. To be effective, programs need to be based on a theory of the target problem and be tied to current and relevant research (Buford & Davis, 1995; Goodman & Wandersman, 1994; Green & Lewis, 1986; Leviton, 1994; Weiss, 1995). Best practices knowledge helps not only in program selection, but also in program planning and implementation.

**Question 4. How Will This New Program Fit in With Existing Programs?** Will this program enhance, interfere with, or be unrelated to other programs that are already offered? Will it be part of a comprehensive and coordinated package or just a new program in a long list of programs?

When designing a new program, it is important to be sure that it fits well with the community's needs as well as the available services already in place (Elias, 1995). To reduce duplication, practitioners should be familiar with the programs already existing in their school or community. In order to prevent overlap of programs or the implementation of a program that does not fit with overall agency or community goals, a process called program mapping can be used.

*Program mapping* is an assessment of how well a proposed program's goals and methods will fit with the broader goals or motivating philosophy of the sponsoring organization. Programs can fit into an organization in three basic ways. They can have an "add-on" effect (one program adds to another), a "synergistic" effect (one program multiplies the effect of another), or an "interference" effect (one program diminishes another).

*Question 5. How Will You Carry Out the Program?*    What are the steps that program personnel will take to carry it out? During this planning stage, program developers must identify how they will implement the program. Outlining how a program will be implemented includes determining specific steps to carry out the program, identifying and training persons to carry out each of these steps, and developing a timeline or schedule for this plan. Program staff should specify what will happen during scheduled program activities and where these activities will take place. All of these components must be clearly defined in order to plan and implement a program effectively.

*Question 6. How Well Was the Program Carried Out?*    Was the program actually implemented as planned? Was all of the program delivered? If not, which components were not delivered? What went right and what went wrong? Evaluating how a program was implemented is called process evaluation (Step 2 of the *Prevention Plus III* method discussed earlier).

*Question 7. How Well Did the Program Work?*    Did the program have the desired effects and proposed outcomes? Were there any unanticipated consequences? Evaluating outcomes and impacts comprised Steps 3 and 4 of the *Prevention Plus III* method discussed earlier.

*Question 8. What Can You Do to Improve the Program for Next Time?*    Many programs are repeated. Given that no program is perfect, what can be done to improve the program's effectiveness and efficiency in the future? If the process and outcome of a program are well-documented, the opportunity to learn from previous implementation efforts is enormous. Keeping track of program components that worked well ensures that such components will be included in the future. Assessing what program components did not work provides the opportunity for refinement and improvement. Lessons about what went well with a program and what areas can use improvement come from such informal sources as personal observations and verbal reports from participants and staff, or such formal sources as participant satisfaction measures and evaluations of the program process and outcome. However gathered, information for program improvement is obtained from the answers to Questions 1–7.

Program staff who are open to learning from the results of evaluation can continuously improve their programs. Instead of seeing evaluation as purely a documentation tool, it should be viewed as a feedback mechanism that can guide future planning and implementation. Recall our prior coverage of issues of action research and implementation in chapter 11.

*Question 9. What Is Being Done to Institutionalize the Program?*    After service providers have gone through the time, energy, and money to develop a successful program, what will they do to see it continued? Unfortunately, this is an often neglected question in prevention programming. Even when programs have successful outcomes, they often are not continued, due to a lack of funding, staff turnover, or loss of momentum. Lerner's (1995) review of prevention programs for youth development concluded that there are numerous effective programs to prevent risks and problem behaviors, but unfortunately, these programs were rarely sustained over time.

Goodman and Steckler (1987) defined institutionalization as developing community and organizational supports for health promotion and prevention programs so that they remain viable in the long term. They have identified factors related to successful institutionalization, such as identifying resources and making program components accessible and user-friendly to host organization staff. Chapter 11 covered similar issues of program implementation in host settings.

CQP never ends. Even for an effectively implemented, thoroughly institutionalized program, its staff start over again with Question 1.

# EXAMPLES OF CQP IN ACTION

Below, we describe two examples of using CQP to improve community programs.

## C.O.P.E.: Using the CQP Strategies in an Ongoing Program

CQP can be used to improve ongoing programs. Using the CQP strategies to continuously improve programs takes program evaluation beyond an accountability system that documents program effectiveness for funders, to a system of continuous program improvement, using evaluation data to continuously refine and enhance programs (Fetterman, 1996; Mark & Pines, 1995; Morrissey & Wandersman, 1995). A common goal of both practitioners and researchers is to ensure that programs are useful and effective. CQP provides a rationale and a means to meet this goal.

How can information from the evaluation of the C.O.P.E. mentoring program (described earlier in this chapter) be used for program improvement through CQP? During the process evaluation, feedback highlighting areas in need of improvement was gathered. For example, some mentees reported that their mentor was inconsistent in making contact on a weekly basis. Mentors, on the other hand, reported problems with scheduling and a feeling of being overburdened and overwhelmed with their many work, family and volunteer commitments. These are problems that need to be addressed.

The use of lessons learned to make midcourse corrections also indicated to program personnel some issues that had been overlooked when the original program plans were made. For example, both mentors and teachers expressed a desire to have more contact with each other and to work as a team in helping the mentee/student. However, no formal roles for teachers had been built into the program, and no formal process for connecting concerned mentors with their mentee's teacher had been established. Improvements in this area were implemented immediately because this information was obtained during ongoing process evaluation (Strategy 6 of CQP) instead of after the fact (Strategy 7 of CQP) as in traditional outcome evaluation.

Open-ended questions regarding suggestions for improvement also were valuable in that they allowed individuals with many different perspectives on the program to contribute valuable information to the process of making midcourse corrections. Mentors wanted more formal support and training in skills they needed to fulfill their role. Mentees wanted more formalized structures to maintain consistency of contact (rules), while teachers wanted contact with mentors as well as respect for the importance of academics and not missing class. These suggestions illuminated some current problems in the program as well as possible routes to correcting them.

Thus, the process evaluation allowed program staff to document generally high levels of satisfaction among different groups of participants, look at problems in the implementation of their plans (e.g., maintaining weekly contact), assess additional groups to include (e.g., teachers), and solicit suggestions for program improvement from diverse groups. Based on the feedback, school officials hired someone to coordinate more activities for mentors and mentees, check in with mentors each month and raise the mentor morale through such gestures as small gifts of appreciation. Mentors were even sent a roll of Lifesavers candy, with a note saying "You're a lifesaver."

## TROOPERS: Using the CQP Strategies at the Start of a Program

C.O.P.E. began using CQP strategies several years after the program's inception. It is best to develop programs using CQP strategies at the start of a program. Below, we describe an attempt to use CQP strategies, with an empowerment evaluation philosophy, at the beginning of a different mentoring initiative, called TROOPERS, in an elementary school in rural South Carolina (Everhart, Haskell, Wandersman, Laughlin, & Sullivan, 1998). The evaluation team worked with the mentoring program staff at the beginning of the program and used CQP strategies throughout.[2]

When the evaluation team initially asked the first accountability question (Why is an intervention needed?), the community agencies with whom we were consulting were somewhat vague in their response. They knew that they wanted a mentoring program, in large part because other communities within the state were receiving positive attention for mentoring initiatives. The coalition of agencies also recognized a deficit in their own approach to substance abuse prevention; other than D.A.R.E., there was an absence of prevention programs in the community targeting elementary school children.

The evaluation team thus conducted a series of meetings, during which the needs of children within the community were discussed. Community stakeholders voiced concern that children and adolescents in the community were faced with an absence of positive role models. Concern for the moral development of children in the community was also expressed, in light of conduct problems, drug and alcohol abuse, and poor school achievement. The stakeholders were convinced of the need for a program to address these concerns. They were further convinced of the need for character education within the community as a means of addressing their concerns.

Should a more systematic needs assessment have been conducted? Although this option was suggested by the evaluation team, the coalition of agencies was under pressure to meet a deadline for program initiation imposed by their funding source, and were operating within a time frame that did not permit completing a new needs assessment.

Having identified an area of need, the coalition of agencies was assisted in working through the second accountability question, "What are the goals, target population, and desired outcomes of the program?" This question defines the scope and mission of the program and provides the framework for evaluation. The goal of the TROOPERS program, broadly defined, was to "build character" (i.e., to increase the social and academic competence of child participants). All children in the third grade in one elementary school

---

[2] The CQP description on pp. 432–434 was written by Kevin Everhart.

were targeted for the intervention (see Question 3, page 433), with a subset of children demonstrating greatest risk for social and academic problems being selected for the more comprehensive mentoring intervention. Desired outcomes regarding improved peer social skills, increased adaptive classroom behavior, improved self-esteem, and improved class-room social climate were identified, as was methodology for measuring outcomes. These desired outcomes were linked to the desired impact of increased rates of high school completion, decreased crime and juvenile delinquency, and a decrease in the use of alcohol, tobacco, and other drugs.

In answering the third question, "How does your program use the scientific knowledge and best practices of what works?," the evaluation team assisted the community coalition with selecting and establishing procedures and assessment strategies that had been "road tested" through previous efforts. To address character development, the evaluation team recommended an empirically validated classroom-based moral reasoning development program (Schunke & Krogh, 1983). Complementary story books and videotapes were selected to reinforce this program, adding a skill development dimension focusing on social problem solving and conflict resolution skills. These would help third graders face critical transitions at school, including heavier academic demands and more complex peer relations.

Also, the selection of the third grade as a target for the program was based on considerations regarding cognitive and moral reasoning development during the latency stage and the salience of adult role models and positive adult attention in developing and solidifying attitudes. Thus, our model of the problem (academic demands, changes in peer relations, development of attitudes regarding moral behavior) was matched with approaches that could most readily harness the resources available to children at the targeted developmental level.

A model of the intervention was developed in which curriculum-guided mentorship, targeting third grade children, was proposed to produce small but sustainable changes in children's attitudes and behavior. These changes may, over time, permit the development of higher level coping strategies to counter risk factors for delinquency and substance abuse. Mentorship cannot alter all contextual risk factors in a child's life, of course, but it can provide important protective processes and nudge outcomes in positive directions.

The mentorship element was integrated into the developing program with the rationale that behavioral practice and modeling are central to promoting changes in moral conduct. Elements of the program (e.g., curriculum, materials, mentors, teachers) were combined into coordinated, synergistic initiatives. This addressed the fourth accountability question, "How will this new program link with existing programs?".

In addition, the intervention was designed to create changes at multiple levels: classroom environment and individual behavior. It addressed multiple targets: a curriculum-only condition was designed as a prevention effort for all students, whereas a curriculum-plus-mentoring component was designed as a secondary prevention initiative for at-risk children. The former represents primary or universal prevention, whereas the latter represents secondary and selected prevention (recall these terms from chap. 9).

In answer to the fifth accountability question ("How will you carry out the program?"), a plan for program implementation was developed in accordance with a flexible timeline. This plan included the "what" and "where" of program implementation. At the organizational level, planners developed a broad agenda for meeting program goals in the course of the school year. At the individual and microsystem levels, the roles and responsibilities of teachers, school personnel, mentors, stakeholders, and evaluators were delineated through comprehensive planning sessions. In addition, benchmarks for accountability were specified to ensure that teachers, mentors, and others adhered to plans and accomplished objectives. These benchmarks were integrated into a manual for service delivery, which provided clear instructions regarding responsibilities.

Careful attention to the what and where of carrying out the program provided the foundation for answering the sixth program accountability question, "How well was the program carried out?" Several mechanisms were instituted to promote the integrity of program implementation. Learning from the pitfalls of previous mentoring programs, which failed to promote close ties between volunteers and children, multiple safeguards were instituted to foster the development of a high-quality relationship and to remind mentors of their commitment. A feedback system was instituted in which mentors completed weekly logs documenting meetings with mentees and evaluated children's progress with regard to the character education curriculum. In addition to documenting time spent together, the log included questions related to relationship development and provided a mechanism for mentors to report problems or concerns. In addition, a checklist was designed to document the use of curriculum materials by teachers and to obtain their ratings of the materials' effectiveness and age-appropriateness. A paper trail of mentor logs and teacher ratings served two purposes. First, it promoted adherence to program design. Second, it permitted us to examine the degree to which the specified course of action was followed faithfully.

Ultimately, careful groundwork in addressing the first six accountability questions left the team well positioned to assess outcomes and impacts (Question 7: "How well did the program work?"). Measurement instruments representing outcomes were selected for reliability and validity, and other survey items were developed according to unique attributes of the program and desired outcomes.

Outcome and impact evaluations after implementation of the program indicated that it attained many of its goals. Based upon teacher ratings, grades, and self-report data, the results of the evaluation indicated improvement in several aspects of children's classroom behavior and academic performance compared to a comparison school which did not have the program. Further gains were evident among high-risk children matched with mentors. They evidenced significantly lower levels of acting-out behavior and higher levels of on-task behavior, and improved spelling and reading grades. Mentored children also had increased levels of self-esteem. Not all desired outcomes were obtained; no changes in frustration tolerance were evident, for example, and math grades did not improve. Still, the results were impressive in that they suggest a relationship between successful program development and use of the accountability questions and the CQP essential strategies and tools.

The next CQP question is "What can we do to improve the program next time?" In the second year of the program, the team used first-year survey feedback from children, mentors, teachers, and parents to make adjustments and improvements in the program. These included developing improved mechanisms for communication between parents, mentors, and teachers. The team increased efforts to attend to children's perceptions of the mentoring relationship as it unfolds, while providing for early detection of unpromising relationships. Guided by the research report from Public/Private Ventures (Sipe, 1996;

described earlier), the team included measurement of the types of strategies mentors use in developing relationships with mentees, and how these strategies develop over time. Having failed to find effects of the program with regard to social climate perceptions in the first year, the team selected and amended another measure of potentially greater sensitivity. In response to criticisms regarding the amount of paperwork, measures (surveys, logs, and checklists) were screened to eliminate redundant or unnecessary information. The team developed a more systematic method of determining members of the secondary prevention (mentoring) target group. The team also developed a mechanism for parents to provide early feedback regarding concerns or questions about mentors.

Finally, the team addressed the ninth program accountability question, "What can be done to continue and institutionalize this effective program?" This question is perhaps the ultimate evaluation of the evaluation team itself, involving issues such as "Have we been effective mentors ourselves for teaching continuous program improvement? How successful have we been at using empowerment evaluation principles? How well integrated is the program within the network of community services provided?" Every area of the development and evaluation process in which the evaluation team played a leadership role now represents a potential risk point for continuing it. As the program entered the final year of the grant, stakeholders were negotiating ownership of the program, pursuing funding, and weighing the resources against possible gains. Staff are turning over, and the original program coordinator will soon be replaced by someone who will not know program history on a personal level. The task of the evaluation team is to modify existing structures and measures to accommodate change. For instance, this may mean eliminating sophisticated measures requiring specialized knowledge to interpret, and replacing them with measures that can more readily be administered and utilized by existing school staff. Ultimately, this program can be streamlined for institutionalization by schools currently implementing it. For this to occur, it is essential that both process and outcome evaluation become integrated into the culture of participating schools.

## CONCLUSION

As citizens, consumers, or practitioners, we should be able to answer in detail the following question: "It sounds like a good idea, but is it really working?"

Program evaluation is necessary to find out whether or not our programs are working. As we have seen in this chapter, program evaluation concepts can be incorporated into program planning and program implementation. When this is done, the boundaries between program development and program evaluation are blurred for the sake of improving process and increasing the probability of successful results. CQP is an example of this approach. Although the CQP emphasis, so far, has been on the accountability of practitioners who receive money for prevention (or treatment or education), Wandersman (1999) noted that the accountability questions also apply to funders and researchers/evaluators. For example, when funders consider developing a new initiative, the questions of how do they know they need a new initiative, how will it use science and best practices, how does it fit with other initiatives, and so on, should be asked and answered. For evaluators, the same questions would concern whether a new or intensified evaluation process is needed or justified, how well it fits with existing evaluation procedures, and how best practices for program evaluation will be used in planning this evaluation.

As our society becomes more concerned about accountability and results for our schools and for our health and human services, evaluation can lead to fear and resistance or to openness, honesty, empowerment, and improvement. Evaluation and accountability need not be feared—if we work together for results.

## Chapter Summary

**1.** Program success depends upon having a good theory of why something works and implementing it with quality.

**2.** Logic models link community needs or conditions with activities, outcomes, and impacts. Program development and program evaluation have similar components.

**3.** A four-step program evaluation model (from *Prevention Plus III*) boils program evaluation down to identifying goals and desired outcomes, process evaluation, outcome evaluation, and evaluation of impacts.

**4.** Effective programs are linked to accountability using comprehensive quality programming (CQP) strategies. CQP asks and answers nine accountability questions, which are listed in Table 14.1. These concern not only program evaluation, but also development and institutionalization of effective programs.

## Recommended Readings

Fetterman, D., Kaftarian, S., & Wandersman, A. (Eds.). (1996). *Empowerment evaluation: Knowledge and tools for self-assessment and accountability*. Thousand Oaks, CA: Sage.

Linney, J. A., & Wandersman, A. (1996). Empowering community groups with evaluation skills: The Prevention Plus III Model. In D. Fetterman, S. Kaftarian, & A. Wandersman (Eds.), *Empowerment evaluation: Knowledge and tools for self-assessment and accountability* (pp. 259–276). Thousand Oaks, CA: Sage.

Patton, M. Q. (1997). *Utilization-focused evaluation* (3rd ed.). Thousand Oaks, CA: Sage.

Rossi, P. H., Freeman, H. E., & Lipsey, M. (1999). *Evaluation: A systematic approach* (6th ed.). Newbury Park, CA: Sage.

W. K. Kellogg Foundation. (1998). *Kellogg evaluation handbook*. Battle Creek, MI: Author.

Worthen, B. R., Sanders, J. R., Fitzpatrick, J. L. (1997). *Program evaluation: Alternative approaches and practical guidelines* (2nd ed.). White Plains, NY: Longman.

## InfoTrac Keywords

*evaluation* (or preceded by *impact, outcome, process,* or *program*), *program development, program planning.*

# RECOMMENDED WEBSITES

http://www.eval.org

> The American Evaluation Association Website has listings and links for a variety of program evaluations resources and networks. Their topical interest groups list information and resources for two topics especially relevant to this chapter: collaborative, participatory, and empowerment evaluation, and program theory in evaluation. Other interest groups include health programs, alcohol and drug abuse and mental health, crime and justice, minority issues, feminist issues, international and cross-cultural evaluation, qualitative issues, and quantitative methods.

http://www.stanford.edu/~davidf/empowermentevaluation.html

> This is the Website for empowerment evaluation approaches, tips and news, based on the Fetterman, Kaftarian, and Wandersman volume listed in RECOMMENDED READINGS and discussed in the chapter.

http://ctb.lsi.ukans.edu

> The Community Tool Box website, mentioned in previous chapters, has excellent sections on program planning and evaluation. These include a comprehensive conceptual framework as well as specific tools and resources for evaluation.

http://www.frca.org

> The Family Resource Coalition of America at this Website has published two assessment guides for programs related to family issues. Two of these are "How Are We Doing? A Program Self-Assessment Toolkit for the Family Support Field" and "Know Your Community: A Step-by-Step Guide to Community Needs and Resource Assessment" (suggested by Richard Jenkins).

# PLANNING AND EVALUATING A COMMUNITY PROGRAM

In this exercise, you will use the questions and strategies of Comprehensive Quality Programming (CQP) and *Prevention Plus III* to plan a prevention/promotion program, and simulate its evaluation.

Choose a community with which you are familiar, and a community problem which that community faces. Examples could include youth violence, school readiness of first-graders, adolescent pregnancy, drug abuse, and racism. (If you did the INTERCHAPTER EXERCISE following chap. 13, you may use the same community and problem, or choose a new one.) Imagine yourself as a member of a community coalition in this community, which has been created to prevent that problem or to promote competencies to prevent it. The other coalition members have heard that you read chapter 14, which makes you the "local expert" on program evaluation and how it can be used in program development! Indicate your answers to the CQP questions below, to prepare your recommendations to the coalition.

For a comprehensive learning experience, use all questions in this exercise. To focus on evaluation issues, answer Questions 2, 6, and 7. To focus on implementation issues, review Chapters 11 and 14 and answer Questions 2, 5, 8, and 9. To focus on planning a high-quality program that fits the context of a particular community, answer Questions 1–4 and use the TOURING THE PREVENTION/PROMOTION LITERATURE exercise following chapter 11. If time does not permit contacting a local informant or reviewing the literature, review chapter 10 for Question 3 and use your own knowledge for Question 4.

This exercise can be done in considerable depth, as a term project, or in briefer, perhaps outlined, form as an exercise. Your instructor can help you understand the appropriate depth and resources for your course. As indicated below, chapters in this textbook, sources in the research literature, and key informants from your chosen community are all potential resources for your thinking and planning.

**Question 1. Why Is an Intervention Needed?**   Give your own rationale for a prevention/promotion program addressing the community problem you chose. Where possible use research on this problem, as well as evidence such as local media accounts or personal experiences to show its existence in your community.

Outline a systematic community needs and assets assessment, using a survey of citizens and key informants. Who would you ask to complete this survey? What questions would you ask? How would you survey your community's resources or assets, not just its needs?

**Question 2. What Are the Goals, Target Population, and Desired Outcomes?**   Choose and describe these, being as specific as possible. For a target population, consider what age groups and settings (e.g., schools, senior centers) would be the focus of the program. Remember that goals are more general and ambitious, whereas desired outcomes are more specific, feasible, and measurable. Limit both to a list of about five or six. Use Figures 14.2, 14.3, and 14.4 here.

**Question 3. How Does Your Program Use Scientific Knowledge and Best Practices of What Works?**   Find at least one scholarly article or chapter on programs with similar goals, outcomes, and populations. (The *Touring the Literature* exercise following chapter 11 and recommended readings for chapters 10 and 11 are a good place to start.) Review these for effective approaches and for best practices on how to actually conduct such a program. Summarize your conclusions in terms useful for public discussion and planning.

Remember that a high-quality community intervention takes place over time, and becomes an ongoing part of the community, whereas a one-shot presentation has limited value.

**Question 4. How Will This New Program Fit in With Existing Programs?** Using your own community knowledge and at least one local informant in your community, identify similar or related programs already operating there. Explain how your program would complement them, not duplicate them.

**Question 5. How Will You Carry Out the Program?**   Describe how you would carry out the program. In what settings would it occur? How would you generate/recruit participants? Who would staff it, and would they be paid or volunteers? Does it involve elements of self-help or peer support, and how? How long would each session or component last, and how many of these would there be? What would be the goal or theme of each? How would participants be actively involved? Consider these and any other decisions necessary to plan a high-quality program. Chapters 11 and 13, and their RECOMMENDED WEBSITES, may help.

Next, list some resources needed to make this program a reality: for example, money, staff time and skills, community ideas, and support. What other community members would you want to help plan or carry out this program?

**Question 6. How Well Was the Program Carried Out?**   Indicate how you would document that the program was actually implemented with high quality. Consider that your documentation cannot involve too much paperwork for staff or participants. Use Figures 14.2 and 14.3 here.

**Question 7. How Well Did the Program Work?**   Indicate how you would assess, with qualitative or quantitative methods, the outcomes and impacts of your program. Use Figures 14.2 and 14.3 here. Chapter 4 on research methods, and the Chapter 14 RECOMMENDED WEBSITES, may help. Remember that *outcomes* refer to short-term results, particularly for program participants (e.g., knowledge and skills for resolving conflicts peacefully), whereas *impacts* refer to longer-term changes, particularly in the wider community (e.g., fewer arrests or school suspensions for fighting).

**Question 8. What Can You Do to Improve the Program for Next Time?**   If your program achieves all its desired outcomes, you are a talented and lucky planner! Anticipate three realistic ways in which your program may fall short of its goals, outcomes, and/or impacts. Describe one program improvement, based on process, outcome, or impact evaluation, to address each failure.

***Question 9. What Is Being Done to Institutionalize the Program?*** If your program is effective, what steps could your coalition take to institutionalize it within an existing community organization or setting? Remember that this involves carrying on the program with high quality, yet without its original founders and/or initial funding basis. Chapters 11 and 14 would be helpful here.

# Looking Back, Looking Ahead

We have four aims in this concluding chapter. All of them involve the book's title and major theme: linking individuals and communities. First, we "close the circle" by indicating how the concept of ecological levels and the core values of community psychology (covered in chap. 1) are related to the diverse issues discussed in the 14 chapters of this book. Second, we indicate some implications for the future of community psychology, particularly the seemingly contradictory ideas of "seizing the day" and "taking the long view". Third, we suggest some concluding thoughts and tell two brief stories of successful community change that illustrate community psychology themes. Finally, we issue a invitation to you, the reader.

# CLOSING THE CIRCLE:
# ECOLOGICAL LEVELS AND CORE VALUES

We can briefly review community psychology by looking at how our chapters have elaborated on concepts we introduced in chapter 1: ecological levels of analysis and the seven core value principles of community psychology.

*Ecological levels* have been an underlying theme in every chapter, as we have discussed the connections of individual life with microsystems, organizations, localities, and macrosystems. We especially emphasized ecological levels in chapter 5, in which we described ecological contexts and environments, and in chapters 3–4 in discussing community research. Chapters on human diversity (6), sense of community (7), prevention and promotion concepts (9), and community and social change (13) also applied ecological concepts to community and individual life.

Our chapter also reflected the values of community psychology. *Individual wellness* is a major goal or outcome of community psychologists' work. Wellness is the ultimate aim of prevention/promotion interventions (chaps. 9–11) and of efforts to promote ecological resources for coping, such as social support and self-help organizations (chaps. 7 and 8). In addition, our chapters on ecological concepts (5), human diversity (6), sense of community (7), citizen participation (12), and community change (13) concerned wellness indirectly, because the quality of individual lives and community life are intertwined.

*Sense of community*, the shared emotional connection among members of a community, is a powerful force linked with much of community psychologists' work. It was the explicit focus of chapter 7 and was emphasized along with citizen participation and psychological empowerment in chapter 12. Sense of community within the group was an underlying factor in empowering settings in chapter 12, and in empowered citizen organizations in chapter 13. Commitment to the wider community interest was also an important force in community coalitions and community development efforts in chapter 13.

*Respect for human diversity* was an explicit focus in chapter 6, where we described cultural oppression, and acculturation frameworks for understanding differences and similarities along dimensions of diversity important for community psychology. Human diversity also influenced our discussion of community research in chapters 3 and 4. In addition, throughout the text, beginning with the history of the field in chapter 2, we attempted wherever possible to frame issues of community life in the contexts of human diversity (Trickett, 1996).

The theme of *social justice* undergirds much of community psychologists' work. It concerns creating access to resources (material, social, personal) for all citizens. These resources promote individual coping and wellness as well as the quality of community life. We discussed social justice most explicitly while covering oppression concepts in chapter 6, citizen participation in chapter 12, and community change initiatives in chapter 13. Concepts of empowerment at multiple levels and of constructive use of the three instruments of social power (chapters 12 and 13) also reflect this principle.

In the community psychology perspective, social justice and empowerment are closely connected to the underlying value of *citizen participation*. Access to resources often involves participation in decision making, in organizations, neighborhoods, larger communities, and societies. That intertwining was reflected in chapters 12 and 13, especially in our discussions of community initiatives such as Block Booster, PICO community organizing, and coalitions such as CINCH in chapter 13. Principles of participation were also illustrated in chapter 11 on tailoring prevention/promotion initiatives to their host settings, and discussion of self-help organizations in chapters 7 and 8. Participation also is also intertwined with the sense of community, especially its elements of mutual influence and integration (chapters 7 and 12). In all of those contexts, we discussed how true community-based decision making usually involves decentralizing of power and participation.

A value for citizen participation applied to the conduct of community research yields the principle of *collaboration* between researchers and communities and recognition of community *strengths and resources*. This was a major theme of chapter 3 on community research, chapter 11 on implementing prevention/promotion interventions, and chapter 14 on program evaluation. Concepts of cultural competence and culturally sensitive research and intervention (chapters 3 and 6) connected the value of respect for diversity with those of citizen participation, collaboration with communities, and empowerment.

Finally, community psychology originated as a field of participant–conceptualizers, seeking to unite community action with community research. The principle that action is to be *grounded in empirical research,* and the corresponding idea that research is to be grounded in communities and connected somehow to action, is an underlying theme of the field and of this book. That was most explicit in the chapters about research issues and methods (3, 4, and 14), but also was reflected in every chapter.

# IMPLICATIONS FOR COMMUNITY PSYCHOLOGY AND COMMUNITY CHANGE

The history of social change, at least in the United States, illustrates the adaptive value of two seemingly contradictory ideas: "seizing the day," and "taking the long view." As Marris and Rein (1973) and K. Heller et al. (1984, p. 46) noted, democratic forms of government are designed to prevent the excessive influence of any one group, in the context of a number of diverse, competing interests. Systems of checks and balances, divided among branches and levels of government, maximize many individual freedoms and minimize the influence of government. This system affords appeals to utilitarian and expressive individualism, elevating "freedom from" government control, above the wider community interest (Bellah et al., 1991). The U.S. system of government is arguably the most decentralized in the developed world, yet these themes can be detected in other democracies as well.

While this decentralized structure has many advantages, a disadvantage is that it makes it difficult to muster sufficient agreement that a social problem exists, much less on how to respond. A social issue (e.g., homelessness, drug abuse, poverty, racism) must assume crisis proportions in order to be recognized as a sufficiently serious problem to merit society's attention. In the heat of that crisis, quick solutions will be preferred. Support for longer-term interventions becomes difficult to sustain (K. Heller et al., 1984; Marris & Rein, 1973), especially within short political election cycles. Thus, although community psychology and related fields have provided a number of effective interventions to address community problems, societies may not use these strategies effectively, in part because they require long-term action. That appears true at least in the United States (Riger, 1993; Schorr, 1997; Wachtel, 1999).

In this context, for community psychologists to seize the day means to apply its concepts, perspectives, research, and skills to today's social and community problems, and build coalitions with those who share their interests (K. Heller, 1989). It also involves calling attention to the views and experiences of those who are powerless and ignored (Price, 1989; Rappaport, 1981). Chapter 13 on community and social change, and chapter 12 on citizen participation, addressed issues of defining and responding to contemporary issues and problems. Our coverage of community research in chapters 3 and 4 also emphasized addressing the issues of the day in communities. We closed chapter 2 with a section on how community psychology can find common ground with citizens and communities, even in conservative times that usually promote individual-level views of social problems. These chapters especially concerned seizing the day.

Taking the long view means understanding swings of the historical pendulum for defining social and community issues (M. Levine & Levine, 1992). Moreover, it involves sustained commitment and involvement in the particular communities within which community psychologists work, perhaps for years (Elias, 1994; Kelly, 1990). Finally, it means devising, implementing, evaluating, and refining community interventions that can offer sound, scientific evidence of effectiveness in addressing clearly defined objectives. By doing that, we can provide empirically supported approaches that can, at least to some extent, weather the changes of social, political, and economic climate (K. Heller et al., 1984, p. 47). In these ways, community psychologists can continue to address community and social concerns despite changes in historical context.

Chapter 11's focus on implementing prevention/promotion programs, chapter 13's description of sustained, ongoing community initiatives, and chapter 14's focus on meshing program development, evaluation, and continuous improvement all addressed the long view of community action. Ultimately, efforts for constructive community change must be sustained by careful attention to their long-term consequences for communities. It is our view that such attention is best supported by empirical research conducted through collaborative partnerships with diverse groups of citizens, using a variety of methods to generate a rich tapestry of community knowledge.

Taking the long view thus involves knowing one's local context well, but also thinking beyond it. One of our themes in chapter 7 on sense of community concerned the value of thinking not only of the internal cohesion within a community, but also about the nature of its relations with outgroups and other communities. This perspective intersects with issues of understanding human diversity. Community psychology increasingly requires cultural competence and multicultural understanding beyond one's own community and culture. This perspective also applies to thinking of community psychology as an international discipline. Its international status affords contextual, historical study of cultural, national, and other macrosystem influences on community, microsystem, and individual quality of life.

## CONCLUSION

We intended to write this epilogue to bring some sense of closure to the diverse concerns of this book and of community psychology. Yet as one of its authors noted, we have opened the circle as much as closed it, especially by pointing out continuing and future challenges. Both the field of community psychology and today's communities are works in progress. In fact, at the outset of a new millennium, change in communities seems to be accelerating.

Yet many concerns of community psychology represent timeless issues for communities. These include, for instance, the intertwining of individual and community life, an understanding of human diversity, a concern with social justice, and the integration of knowledge and action. The study of community psychology yields concepts and tools for addressing such issues. The two stories that follow memorably illustrate enduring themes as well as constructive change in today's communities.

### The "Amesville Sixth-Grade Water Chemists"

Lappe and DuBois (1994, pp. 211–212) described a sixth-grade class in Amesville, Ohio, whose science lessons turned into a community initiative and lesson in citizen participation. After the class read a book in which the leading character tests the water in a nearby river, an oil company accident polluted their own town's creek. Although the Environmental Protection Agency managed the cleanup, the students decided to measure future water quality for themselves. Using their own money, and with consultation from experts, they bought a testing kit and began monitoring the creek.

This project involved learning some basic biology and chemistry, and how to collect and interpret quantitative data. It also involved cooperative teamwork, deciding how to plan and complete the work on an ongoing basis, speaking assertively and listening carefully, and negotiating and compromising among themselves. The students ultimately publicized their findings to the community, wrote letters, and formed a water testing service for community residents.

The initiative of Amesville's students revealed scientific and social competence among the students that surprised some of the community's adults. Yet it involved themes shared with community psychology: citizen participation, community advocacy and change, prevention and health promotion, and empirical grounding. Note, for instance, how their approach resembles the open-systems model of community action in chapter 13. Amesville's students linked themselves with their community, in ways that promoted their own learning while enriching community quality of life.

## The "Power of a Place": Altering the College Classroom

Stein, Ward, and Cislo (1992) developed a college course that integrated traditional college students with a group of community students: persons with serious mental illnesses. Their course was not like courses on many campuses in which students are helpers or companions for "patients," an approach that has value but that tends to create an unequal helper–patient role relationship. Instead, Stein et al. developed and led a course in social relationship skills, in which traditional and community students were defined as equals. Their study, entitled "The Power of a Place", illustrates the impact of altering social regularities (Seidman, 1988) to enhance student learning and interdependence.

The Stein et al. (1992) course had several distinctive elements. The class, a three-credit psychology course, met twice a week: once for didactic teaching and structured small-group cooperative learning exercises, and once for a group meeting patterned as a mutual help group, stressing mutual support and application of learning in everyday life. (This drew from the approach of GROW, a mutual help group described in chapter 7.) As much as possible, the instructors and assistants defined their roles as facilitators, not lecturers. Students drew names from a hat to form pairs of one traditional student and one community student. These pairs met for homework assignments and discussion outside of class. The instructors and course materials emphasized the idea that each person in the class has resources (unique life experiences and skills) for teaching others, as well as something to learn from classmates. All students were expected to participate actively and to abide by ground rules based on mutual help principles. In general, the class activities illustrated how mutual help and cooperative learning principles can be interwoven.

Evaluation findings were heartwarming. Informal observation indicated that the course methods provided equal access for all students to become fully involved. Observation and student journals also revealed that substantial interdependence and support developed between traditional and community students. Journals from both student groups described personal gains made during the course. Several members of each student group reported that they began the course with some stereotypes about the other group, but that those were dispelled by the course activities. In addition, both groups of students reported more positive changes in their personal relationships than did similar members of control groups.

The Stein et al. (1992) course clearly fostered development of interdependent, supportive relationships as equals between the two groups. Moreover, this occurred in a college classroom, "home ground" for the traditional students but not for community students. By blending methods of ecological analysis, cooperative learning, and mutual help, and through partnership of a university and mental health center, Stein et al. created an empowering setting (see chapter 12). Their class promoted personal development, fostered networks of social support, and undermined stereotypes about persons with mental illness. The class linked both groups of students with each other and with the wider community.

## An Invitation

We gleaned these two stories, and the others we have described in this text, from the literatures of community psychology and community change. Now that you are equipped with concepts and tools for understanding and changing communities, we invite you to engage yourself in your community, and create new stories of constructive change there. That is the real future of community psychology and community change.

# REFERENCES

Abdul-Adil, J. K., & Jason, L. A. (1991, Fall). Community psychology and Al-Islam: A religious framework for social change. *The Community Psychologist, 24*, 28–30.

Abraido-Lanza, A., Guier, C., & Colon, R. (1998). Psychological thriving among Latinas with chronic illness. *Journal of Social Issues, 54*, 405–424.

Adams, F., with Horton, M. (1975). *Unearthing seeds of fire: The idea of Highlander*. Winston-Salem, NC: Blair.

Albee, G. W. (1959). *Mental health manpower trends*. New York: Basic Books.

Albee, G. W. (1982). Preventing psychopathology and promoting human potential. *American Psychologist, 37*, 1043–1050.

Albee, G. W. (1995). [Untitled videotape interview]. In J. G. Kelly (Ed.), *The history of community psychology: A video presentation of context and exemplars*. Chicago: Society for Community Research and Action.

Albee, G. W., Bond, L., & Monsey, T. (1992). *Improving children's lives: Global perspectives on prevention* (Vol. 14 of the *Primary prevention of psychopathology* series). Thousand Oaks, CA: Sage.

Albee, G. W., & Gullotta, T. (Eds.). (1997). *Primary prevention works*. Thousand Oaks, CA: Sage.

Alderfer, C. (1994). A White man's perspective on the unconscious processes within Black-White relations in the United States. In E. J. Trickett, R. J. Watts, & D. Birman (Eds.), *Human diversity: Perspectives on people in context* (pp. 210–229). San Francisco: Jossey-Bass.

Alinsky, S. (1971). *Rules for radicals: A practical primer for realistic radicals*. New York: Random House.

Allison, K., Crawford, I., Leone, P., Trickett, E., Perez-Fables, A., Burton, L., & LeBlanc, R. (1999). Adolescent substance abuse: Preliminary examinations of school and neighborhood context. *American Journal of Community Psychology, 27*, 111–142.

Andersen, M., & Collins, P.H. (1998). *Race, class and gender: An anthology* (3rd ed.). Belmont, CA: Wadsworth.

Andresen, P. A., & Telleen, S. L. (1992). The relationship between social support and maternal behaviors and attitudes: A meta-analytical review. *American Journal of Community Psychology, 20*, 753–774.

Annie E. Casey Foundation. (1995). *The path of most resistance: Reflections on lessons learned from New Futures*. Baltimore, MD: Author.

Aronson, E. (1992). *The social animal* (6th ed.). San Francisco: W. H. Freeman.

Aronson, E., Stephan, C., Sikes, J., Blaney, N., & Snapp, M. (1978). *The jigsaw classroom*. Beverly Hills, CA: Sage.

Balcazar, F. (1999, Summer). Lessons from liberation theology. *The Community Psychologist, 32*, 19–24.

Balcazar, F., Seekins, T., Fawcett, S. B., & Hopkins, B. (1990). Empowering people with physical disabilities through advocacy skills training. *American Journal of Community Psychology, 18*, 281–296.

Bandura, A. (1982). Self-efficacy mechanisms in human agency. *American Psychologist, 37*, 122–147.

Bandura, A. (1986). *Social foundations of thought and action: A social cognitive theory*. Englewood Cliffs, NJ: Prentice-Hall.

Banyard, V. L. (1995). "Taking another route": Daily survival narratives from mothers who are homeless. *American Journal of Community Psychology, 23*, 871–892.

Barker, R. (1965). Explorations in ecological psychology. *American Psychologist, 20*, 1–14.

Barker, R. (1968). *Ecological psychology*. Stanford, CA: Stanford University Press.

Barker, R. (1978). Behavior settings. In R. Barker & Associates, *Habitats, environments, and human behavior* (pp. 29–35). San Francisco: Jossey-Bass.

Barker, R., & Associates. (1978). *Habitats, environments and human behavior*. San Francisco: Jossey-Bass.

Barker R., & Gump, P. (Eds.). (1964). *Big school, small school*. Stanford, CA: Stanford University Press.

Barker, R., & Schoggen, P. (1973). *Qualities of community life: Methods of measuring enviroment and bvehavior applied to an American and an English town*. San Francisco: Jossey-Bass.

Barker, R., & Wright, H. (1955). *Midwest and its children*. New York: Harper & Row.

Barker, R., & Wright, H. (1978). Standing patterns of behavior. In R. Barker & Associates, *Habitats, environments and human behavior* (pp. 24–28). San Francisco: Jossey-Bass. (Original work published 1955)

Barone, C., Aguirre-Deandreis, A., & Trickett, E. J. (1991). Means-ends problem-solving skills, life stress, and social support as mediators of adjustment in the normative transition to high school. *American Journal of Community Psychology, 19*, 207–226.

Barone, C., Iscoe, E., Trickett, E. J., & Schmid., K. D. (1998). An ecologically differentiated, multifactor model of adolescent network orientation. *American Journal of Community Psychology, 26*, 403–424.

Barrera, M. (1986). Distinctions between social support concepts, measures, and models. *American Journal of Community Psychology, 14*, 413–445.

Barrera, M., & Li, S. A. (1996). The relation of family support to adolescents' psychological distress and behavior problems. In G. R. Pierce, B. R. Sarason, & I. G. Sarason (Eds.), *Handbook of social support and the family* (pp. 313–344). New York: Plenum.

Barrera, M., Li, S. A., & Chassin, L. (1995). Effects of parental alcoholism and life stress on Hispanic and Non-Hispanic Caucasian adolescents: A prospective study. *American Journal of Community Psychology, 23*, 479–508.

Bartholomew, K., Cobb, R. J., & Poole, J. A. (1997). Adult attachment patterns and social support processes. In G. Pierce, B. Lakey, I. G. Sarason, & B. R. Sarason (Eds.), *Sourcebook of social support and personality* (pp. 359–378). New York: Plenum.

Barton, H., Hopkins, K., McElhaney, S., Heigel, J., & Salassi, A. (1995). *Getting started: The NMHA directory of model programs to prevent mental disorders and promote mental health*. Alexandria, VA: National Mental Health Association.

Bartunek, J. M., & Keys, C. B. (1979). Participation in school decision-making. *Urban Education, 14*, 52–75.

Bates, D. S., & Toro, P. A. (1999). Developing measures to assess social support among homeless and poor people. *Journal of Community Psychology, 26*, 137–156.

Battistich, V., Elias, M. J., & Branden-Muller, L. (1992). Two school-based approaches to promoting children's social competence. In G. W. Albee, L. A. Bond, & T. Monsey (Eds.), *Improving children's lives: Global perspectives on prevention* (Vol. 14 of the *Primary prevention of psychopathology* series; pp. 217–234). Thousand Oaks, CA: Sage.

Baum, A. (1987). Toxins, technology and natural disasters. In G. VandenBos & B. Bryant (Eds.), *Cataclysms, crises and catastrophes: Psychology in action* (pp. 5–54). Washington, DC: American Psychological Association.

Baum A., & Fleming, I. (1993). Implications of psychological research on stress and technological accidents. *American Psychologist, 48*, 665–672.

Bell, C., & Newby, H. (1971). *Community studies: An introduction to the sociology of the local community*. New York: Praeger.

Bellah, R., Madsen, R., Sullivan, W., Swidler, A., & Tipton, S. (1985). *Habits of the heart: Individualism and commitment in American life*. New York: Harper & Row.

Bellah, R., Madsen, R., Sullivan, W., Swidler, A., & Tipton, S. (1991). *The good society*. New York: Knopf.

Belenky, M., Clinchy, B., Goldberger, N., & Tarule, J. (1986). *Women's ways of knowing: The development of self, voice and mind*. New York: Basic Books.

Belsky, J. (1980). Child maltreatment: An ecological integration. *American Psychologist, 35*, 320–335.

Belsky, J. (1984). The determinants of parenting: A process model. *Child Development, 55*, 83–96.

Belsky, J. (1993). Etiology of child maltreatment: A developmental-ecological analysis. *Psychological Bulletin, 114*, 413–434.

Bennett, C., Anderson, L., Cooper, S., Hassol, L., Klein, D., & Rosenblum, G. (1966). *Community psychology: A report of the Boston Conference on the Education of Psychologists for Community Mental Health*. Boston: Boston University.

Berger, P., & Neuhaus, R. (1977). *To empower people*. Washington, DC: American Enterprise Institute.

Berkowitz, B. (1987). *Local heroes*. Lexington, MA: Lexington Books.

Berkowitz, B. (1990, Summer). Who is being empowered? *The Community Psychologist,* *23,* 10–11.

Berkowitz, B. (1996). Personal and community sustainability. *American Journal of Community Psychology, 24,* 441–460.

Bernal, G., & Enchautegui-de-Jesus, N. (1994). Latinos and Latinas in community psychology: A review of the literature. *American Journal of Community Psychology, 22,* 531–558.

Bernard, J. (1973). *The sociology of community.* Glenview, IL: Scott, Foresman.

Berrueta-Clement, J. R., Schweinhart, L. J., Barnett, W. S., Epstein, A. S., & Weikart, D. P. (1984). *Changed lives: The effects of the Perry preschool program on youths through age 19. (Monographs of the High/Scope Educational Research Foundation,* 8). Ypsilanti, MI: High/Scope Press.

Berry, J. W., & Sam, D. (1997). Acculturation and adaptation. In J. W. Berry, M. Segall, & C. Kagitçibasi (Eds.), *Handbook of cross-cultural psychology, Volume 3: Social behavior and applications* (pp. 291–325). Needham Heights, MA: Allyn & Bacon.

Betancourt, H., & Lopez, S. R. (1993). The study of culture, ethnicity, and race in American psychology. *American Psychologist, 48,* 629–637.

Bettencourt, B., Dillmann, G., & Wollman, N. (1996). The intragroup dynamics of maintaining a successful grassroots organization: A case study. *Journal of Social Issues, 52,* 169–186.

Bierman, K. (1997). Implementing a comprehensive program for the prevention of conduct problems in rural communities: The Fast Track experience. *American Journal of Community Psychology, 25,* 493–514.

Biglan, A., Ary, D., Koehn, V., Levings, D., Smith, S., Wright, Z., James, L., & Henderson, J. (1996). Mobilizing positive reinforcement in communities to reduce youth access to tobacco. *American Journal of Community Psychology, 24,* 625–638.

Biglan, A., Henderson, J., Humphreys, D., Yasui, M., Whisman, R., Black, C., & James, L. (1995). Mobilising positive reinforcement to reduce youth access to tobacco. *Tobacco Control, 4,* 42–48.

Birman, D. (1994). Acculturation and human diversity in a multicultural society. In E. J. Trickett, R. J. Watts, & D. Birman (Eds.), *Human diversity: Perspectives on people in context* (pp. 261–283). San Francisco: Jossey-Bass.

Birman, D. (1998). Biculturalism and perceived competence of Latino immigrant adolescents. *American Journal of Community Psychology, 26,* 335–354.

Bjorck, J., Lee, Y., & Cohen, L. (1997). Control beliefs and faith as stress moderation for Korean American versus Caucasian American Protestants. *American Journal of Community Psychology, 25,* 61–72.

Bloom, M. (1996). *Primary prevention practices: Issues in children's and families' lives (Vol. 5).* Thousand Oaks, CA: Sage.

Bond, G., Witheridge, T., Dincin, J., Wasmer, D., Webb, J., & De Graaf-Kaser, R. (1990). Assertive community treatment for frequent users of psychiatric hospitals in a large city: A controlled study. *American Journal of Community Psychology, 18,* 865–892.

Bond, L. A., & Compas, B. (Eds.). (1989). *Primary prevention and promotion in schools* (Vol. 12 of the *Primary prevention of psychopathology* series). Newbury Park, CA: Sage.

Bond, L. A., Cutler, S., & Grams, A. (Eds.). (1995). *Promoting successful and productive aging* (Vol. 16 of the *Primary prevention of psychopathology* series). Newbury Park, CA: Sage.

Bond, M. A. (1990). Defining the research relationship: Maximizing participation in an unequal world. In P. Tolan, C. Keys, F. Chertok, & L. Jason (Eds.), *Researching community psychology* (pp. 183–185). Washington, DC: American Psychological Association.

Bond, M. A. (1999). Gender, race and class in organizational contexts. *American Journal of Community Psychology, 27,* 327–356.

Bond, M. A., & Keys, C. B. (1993). Empowerment, diversity, and collaboration: Promoting synergy on community boards. *American Journal of Community Psychology, 21,* 37–58.

Borkman, T. (1990). Self-help groups at the turning point: Emerging egalitarian alliances with the formal health care systems? *American Journal of Community Psychology, 18,* 321–332.

Borkman, T. (1991a). Introduction to the special issue. *American Journal of Community Psychology, 19,* 643–650.

Borkman, T. (Ed.). (1991b). Self-help groups [Special issue]. *American Journal of Community Psychology, 19*(5).

Botvin, G., & Tortu, S. (1988). Preventing adolescent substance abuse through life skills training. In R. Price, E. Cowen, R. Lorion, & J. Ramos-McKay (Eds.), *Fourteen ounces of prevention* (pp. 98–110). Washington, DC: American Psychological Association.

Bower, E. (1972). Education as a humanizing process. In S. Golann & C. Eisdorfer (Eds.), *Handbook of community mental health* (pp. 37–50). New York: Appleton-Century-Crofts.

Bowlby, J. (1969). *Attachment and loss: Vol. 1. Attachment.* New York: Basic Books.

Bradford, L., Gibb, J., & Benne, K. (1964). *T-group theory and laboratory method: Innovation in re-education.* New York: Wiley.

Brendtro, L., Brokenleg, M., & Van Bockern, S. (1990). *Reclaiming youth at risk: Our hope for the future.* Bloomington, IN: National Educational Service.

Brewer, M. (1997). The social psychology of intergroup relations: Can research inform practice? *Journal of Social Issues, 53,* 197–211.

Brodsky, A. E. (1996). Resilient single mothers in risky neighborhoods: Negative psychological sense of community. *Journal of Community Psychology, 24,* 347–364.

Brodsky, A. E. (2000). The role of spirituality in the resilience of urban, African American, single mothers. *Journal of Community Psychology, 28,* 199–220.

Brodsky, A. E., O'Campo, P. J., & Aronson, R. E. (1999). PSOC in community context: Multi-level correlates of a measure of psychological sense of community in low-income, urban neighborhoods. *Journal of Community Psychology, 27,* 659–680.

Bronfenbrenner, U. (1979). *The ecology of human development: Experiments by nature and design.* Cambridge, MA: Harvard University Press.

Bronzaft, A., & McCarthy, D. (1975). The effects of elevated train noise on reading ability. *Environment and Behavior, 7,* 517–527.

Brooks, M., & Buckner, J. (1996). Work and welfare: Job histories, barriers to employment, and predictors of work among low-income single mothers. *American Journal of Orthopsychiatry, 66,* 526–537.

Bruene-Butler, L., Hampson, J., Elias, M. J., Clabby, J., & Schuyler, T. (1997). The Improving Social Awareness-Social Problem Solving Project. In G. Albee & T. Gullotta (Eds.), *Primary prevention works* (pp. 239–267). Thousand Oaks, CA: Sage.

Brydon-Miller, M. (1997). Participatory action research: Psychology and social change. *Journal of Social Issues, 53,* 657–666.

Brydon-Miller, M., & Tolman, D. (Eds.) (1997). Transforming psychology: Interpretive and participatory methods [Special issue]. *Journal of Social Issues, 53*(4).

Buckner, J. C. (1988). The development of an instrument to measure neighborhood cohesion. *American Journal of Community Psychology, 16,* 771–791.

Buford, B., & Davis, B. (1995). *Shining Stars: Prevention programs that work.* Louisville, KY: Southeast Regional Center for Drug-Free Schools and Communities.

Burgess, L. (1990). A block association president's perspective on citizen participation and research. *American Journal of Community Psychology, 18,* 159–162.

Burman, B., & Margolin, G. (1992). Analysis of the association between marital relationships and health problems: An interactional perspective. *Psychological Bulletin, 112,* 39–63.

Burman, E. (1997). Minding the gap: Positivism, psychology, and the politics of qualitative methods. *Journal of Social Issues, 53,* 785–802.

Buss, A. (1995). *Personality: Temperament, social behavior, and the self.* Boston: Allyn & Bacon.

Butler, J. (1992). Of kindred minds: The ties that bind. In M. Orlandi (Ed.), *Cultural competence for evaluators* (pp. 23–54). Rockville, MD: U. S. Department of Health and Human Services, Office for Substance Abuse Prevention.

Butterfoss, F., Goodman, R., & Wandersman, A. (in press). Citizen participation and health: Toward a psychology of improving health through individual, organizational and community involvement. In A. Baum, T. Revenson, & J. Singer (Eds.), *Handbook of health psychology.* Hillsdale, NJ: Erlbaum.

Campbell, D. T., & Stanley, J. (1963). *Experimental and quasi-experimental designs for research.* Chicago: Rand McNally.

Campbell, R. (1998). The community response to rape: Victim's experiences with the legal, medical, and mental health systems. *American Journal of Community Psychology, 26,* 355–380.

Canning, S. S. (1999, Winter). Stretching Procrusteus: True confessions on the road to cultural competence in community research and action. *The Community Psychologist, 32,* 30–32.

Caplan, G. (Ed.). (1961). *Prevention of mental disorders in children.* New York: Basic Books.

Caplan, G. (1964). *Principles of preventive psychiatry.* New York: Basic Books.

Caplan, G. (Ed.). (1974). *Support systems and community mental health.* New York: Human Sciences Press.

Caplan, R., Vinocur, A., & Price, R. (1997). From job loss to reemployment: Field experiments in prevention-focused coping. In G. Albee & T. Gullotta (Eds.), *Primary prevention works* (pp. 341–379). Thousand Oaks, CA: Sage.

Carels, R. A., Baucom, D. A., Leone, P., & Rigney, A. (1998). Psychosocial factors and psychological symptoms: HIV in a public health setting. *Journal of Community Psychology, 26,* 145–162.

Carnegie Corporation of New York. (1994). *Starting points: Meeting the needs of our youngest children*. New York: Author.

Cartledge, G., & Milburn, J. (Eds.). (1989). *Teaching social skills to children*. New York: Pergamon Press.

Carver, C. S. (1998). Resilience and thriving: Issues, models and linkages. *Journal of Social Issues, 54*, 245–266.

Carver, C. S., Scheier, M. F., & Weintraub, J. K. (1989). Assessing coping strategies: A theoretically-based approach. *Journal of Personality and Social Psychology, 56*, 267–283.

Cauce, A. M., Hannan, K., & Sargeant, M. (1992). Life stress, social support, and locus of control during early adolescence: Interactive effects. *American Journal of Community Psychology, 20*, 787–798.

Chataway, C. (1997). An examination of the constraints on mutual inquiry in a participatory action research project. *Journal of Social Issues, 53*, 747–766.

Chavis, D. M. (1993). A future for community psychology practice. *American Journal of Community Psychology, 21*, 171–184.

Chavis, D. M., Hogge, J., McMillan, D. W., & Wandersman, A. (1986). Sense of community through Brunswik's lens: A first look. *Journal of Community Psychology, 14*, 24–40.

Chavis, D. M., & Pretty, G. M. H. (Eds.). (1999). Sense of community II [Special issue]. *Journal of Community Psychology, 27*(6).

Chavis, D. M., Stucky, P., & Wandersman, A. (1983). Returning basic research to the community: A relationship between scientist and citizen. *American Psychologist, 38*, 424–434.

Chavis, D. M., & Wandersman, A. (1990). Sense of community in the urban environment: A catalyst for participation and community development. *American Journal of Community Psychology, 18*, 83–116.

Chen, S.-P. C., Telleen, S., & Chen E. H. (1995). Family and community support of urban pregnant students: Support person, function and parity. *Journal of Community Psychology, 23*, 28–33.

Chimienti, G., & Trivilas, S. (1994). Cognitive and behavioural effects of social skills training on Greek and Lebanese elementary school children. *International Journal of Mental Health, 23*, 53–68.

Chipuer, H. M., & Pretty, G. M. H. (1999). A review of the Sense of Community Index: Current uses, factor structure, reliability, and further development. *Journal of Community Psychology, 27*, 643–658.

Chung, H., & Elias, M. J. (1996). Patterns of adolescent involvement in problem behaviors:

Relationship to self-efficacy, social competence, and life events. *American Journal of Community Psychology, 24*, 771–810.

Coakes, S., & Bishop, B. (1996). The experience of moral community in a rural community. *Journal of Community Psychology, 24*, 108–117.

Cohen, L. H., Hettler, T. R., & Park, C. L. (1997). Social support, personality, and life stress adjustment. In G. Pierce, B. Lakey, I. G. Sarason, & B. R. Sarason (Eds.), *Sourcebook of social support and personality* (pp. 215–228). New York: Plenum.

Cohen, S., & Wills, T. A. (1985). Stress, social support, and the buffering hypothesis. *Psychological Bulletin, 98*, 310–357.

Coie, J., Watt, N., West, S., Hawkins, J. D., Asarnow, J., Markman, H., Ramey, S., Shure, M., & Long, B. (1993). The science of prevention: A conceptual framework and some directions for a national research program. *American Psychologist, 48*, 1013–1022.

Colby, A., & Damon, W. (1992). *Some do care: Contemporary lives of moral commitment*. New York: Free Press.

Comas-Diaz, L., Lykes, M. B., & Alarcon, R. (1998). Ethnic conflict and the psychology of liberation in Guatemala, Peru, and Puerto Rico. *American Psychologist, 53*, 778–792.

Comer, J. P. (1988). Educating poor minority children. *Scientific American, 259*, 42–48.

Comer, J. P. (1992). Video segment in *The world of abnormal psychology: An ounce of prevention* (T. Levine, Producer). New York: A. H. Perlmutter. (Available from Annenberg/CPB Collection, 1–800–LEARNER).

Comer, J. P., Haynes, N., Joyner, E., & Ben-Avie, M. (1996). *Rallying the whole village: The Comer process for reforming education*. New York: Teachers College Press.

Commins, W. & Elias, M. J. (1991). Institutionalization of mental health programs in organizational contexts: The case of elementary schools. *Journal of Community Psychology, 19*, 207–220.

Conger, R., Conger, K., Matthews, L., & Elder, G. (1999). Pathways of economic influence on adolescent adjustment. *American Journal of Community Psychology, 27*, 519–541.

Cook P., & Tauchen, G. (1982). The effect of liquor taxes on heavy drinking. *Bell Journal of Economics, 13*, 379–390.

Cook, T., & Campbell, D. (1979). *Quasi-experimentation: Design and analysis for field settings*. Chicago: Rand McNally.

Cortes, D. E., Rogler, L. H., & Malgady, R. G. (1994). Biculturality among Puerto Rican adults in the United States. *American Journal of Community Psychology, 22*, 707–721.

Cottrell, L. S. (1976). The competent community. In B. H. Kaplan, R. N. Wilson, & A. H. Leighton (Eds.), *Further explorations in social psychiatry* (pp. 195–209). New York: Basic Books.

Coudroglou, A. (1996). Violence as a social mutation. *American Journal of Orthopsychiatry, 66*, 323–328.

Cowen, E. L. (1973). Social and community interventions. *Annual Review of Psychology, 24*, 423–472.

Cowen, E. L. (1977). Baby steps toward primary prevention. *American Journal of Community Psychology, 5*, 1–22.

Cowen, E. L. (1991). In pursuit of wellness. *American Psychologist, 46*, 404–408.

Cowen, E. L. (1994). The enhancement of psychological wellness: Challenges and opportunities. *American Journal of Community Psychology, 22*, 149–180.

Cowen, E. L., Hightower, A. D., Pedro-Carroll, J., Work, W., Wyman, P., & Haffey, W. (1996). *School-based prevention for children at risk: The Primary Mental Health Project.* Washington, DC: American Psychological Association.

Cowen, E. L., McKim, B. J., & Weissberg, R. P. (1981). Bartenders as informal, interpersonal help-agents. *American Journal of Community Psychology, 9*, 715–729.

Coyne, J., Ellard, J., & Smith, D. (1990). Social support, interdependence, and the dilemmas of helping. In B. R. Sarason, I. G. Sarason, & G. Pierce (Eds.), *Social support: An interactional view* (pp. 129–148). New York: Wiley.

Cronan, T., Cruz, S., Arriaga, R., & Sarkin, A. (1996). The effects of a community-based literacy program on young children's language and conceptual development. *American Journal of Community Psychology, 24*, 251–271.

Cutrona, C. E. (1996). Social support as a determinant of marital quality: The interplay of negative and supportive behaviors. In G. R. Pierce, B. R. Sarason, & I. G. Sarason (Eds.), *Handbook of social support and the family* (pp. 173–194). New York: Plenum.

Cutrona, C. E., & Russell, D. (1990). Type of social support and specific stress: Toward a theory of optimal matching. In B. R. Sarason, I. G. Sarason, & G. Pierce (Eds.), *Social support: An interactional view* (pp. 319–365). New York: Wiley.

Davidson, W. B., & Cotter, P. (1986). Measurement of sense of community within the sphere of city. *Journal of Applied Social Psychology, 16*, 608–619.

Davidson, W. B., & Cotter, P. (1989). Sense of community and political participation. *Journal of Community Psychology, 17*, 119–125.

Davidson, W. B., & Cotter, P. (1993). Psychological sense of community and support for public school taxes. *American Journal of Community Psychology, 21*, 59–66.

Davidson, W. S., & Redner, R. (1988). The prevention of juvenile delinquency: Diversion from the juvenile justice system. In R. Price, E. Cowen, R. Lorion, & J. Ramos-McKay (Eds.), *Fourteen ounces of prevention* (pp. 123–138). Washington, DC: American Psychological Association.

Davino, K., Wandersman, A., & Goodman, R.M. (1995). *Cherokee County mentoring program evaluation interim report.* Unpublished manuscript, University of South Carolina.

Deaux, K. (1985). Sex and gender. *Annual Review of Psychology, 36*, 49–81.

Denzin, N., & Lincoln, Y. (Eds.). (1994). *Handbook of qualitative research.* Thousand Oaks, CA: Sage.

Dockett, K. H. (1999, June). Engaged Buddhism and community psychology: Partners in social change. In J. Kress (Chair), *Bringing together community psychology and religion/spirituality towards an action research agenda for SCRA.* Symposium conducted at the Biennial Meeting of the Society for Community Research and Action, New Haven, CT.

Doherty, W. (1995). *Soul searching: Why psychotherapy must promote moral responsibility.* New York: Basic Books.

Dohrenwend, B. S. (1978). Social stress and community psychology. *American Journal of Community Psychology, 6*, 1–14.

Dokecki, P. R., Newbrough, J. R., & O'Gorman, R. T. (in press). Toward a community-oriented action research framework for spirituality: Community psychological and theological perspectives. *Journal of Community Psychology.*

Dollard, J. (1937). *Caste and class in a Southern town.* Garden City, NY: Doubleday.

Dooley, D., & Prause, J. (1997). Effect of favorable employment change on alcohol abuse: One- and five-year follow-ups in the National Longitudinal Survey of Youth. *American Journal of Community Psychology, 25*, 787–808.

Douglass, F. (1995). *Narrative of the life of Frederick Douglass.* New York: Dover. (Original work published 1845)

Dovidio, J. F., Maruyama, G., & Alexander, M. G. (1997). A social psychology of national and international group relations. *Journal of Social Issues, 54*, 831–846.

DuBois, D. L., Felner, R. D., Sherman, M. D., & Bull, C. A. (1994). Socioenvironmental experiences, self-esteem, and emotional/behavioral problems in early adolescence. *American Journal of Community Psychology, 22,* 371–398.

DuBois, W. E. B. (1986). *The souls of black folk.* Republished in N. Huggins (Ed.), *W. E. B. DuBois: Writings* (pp. 357–548). New York: Library of America. (Original work published 1903)

Dugan, M.A. (1996). Participatory and empowerment evaluation: Lessons learned in training and technical assistance. In D. Fetterman, S., Kaftarian & A. Wandersman (Eds.), *Empowerment evaluation: Knowledge and tools for self-assessment and accountability* (pp. 277–303). Thousand Oaks, CA: Sage.

Dumka, L., Gonzales, N., Wood, J. & Formoso, D. (1998). Using qualitative methods to develop contextually relevant measures and preventive interventions: An illustration. *American Journal of Community Psychology, 26,* 605–637.

Dunham, P. J., Hursham, A., Litwin, E., Gusella, J., Ellsworth, C., & Dodd, P. W. D. (1998). Computer-mediated social support: Single young mothers as a model system. *American Journal of Community Psychology, 26,* 281–306.

Dunkel-Schetter, C., Sagrestano, L. M., Feldman, P., & Killingsworth, C. (1996). Social support and pregnancy: A comprehensive review focusing on ethnicity and culture. In G. R. Pierce, B. R. Sarason, & I. G. Sarason (Eds.), *Handbook of social support and the family* (pp. 375–412). New York: Plenum.

Durlak, J., & Wells, A. (1997). Primary prevention mental health programs for children and adolescents: A meta-analytic review. *American Journal of Community Psychology, 25,* 115–151.

Durlak, J., & Wells, A. (1998). Evaluation of indicated preventive intervention (secondary prevention) mental health programs for children and adolescents. *American Journal of Community Psychology, 26,* 775–802.

Elias, M. J. (1987). Establishing enduring prevention programs: Advancing the legacy of Swampscott. *American Journal of Community Psychology, 15,* 539–553.

Elias, M. J. (Ed.). (1993). *Social decision making and life skills development: Guidelines for middle school educators.* New Brunswick, NJ: Center for Applied Psychology, Rutgers University.

Elias, M. J. (1994). Capturing excellence in applied settings: A participant conceptualizer and praxis explicator role for community psychologists. *American Journal of Community Psychology, 22,* 293–318.

Elias, M. J. (1995). Primary prevention as health and social competence promotion. *Journal of Primary Prevention, 16,* 5–24.

Elias, M. J. (1997). Reinterpreting dissemination of prevention programs as widespread implementation with effectiveness and fidelity. In R. P. Weissberg (Ed.), *Health children 2010: Strategies to enhance social, emotional and physical wellness* (pp. 253–289). Newbury Park, CA: Sage.

Elias, M. J., & Bartz, K. (1995, June). *Talking with TJ: A corporate-led youth organization partnership for violence prevention and social competence promotion.* Presentation at the Biennial Meeting of the Society for Community Research and Action, Chicago.

Elias, M. J., & Clabby, J. (1992). *Building social problem-solving skills: Guidelines from a school-based program.* San Francisco: Jossey-Bass.

Elias, M. J., & Cohen, J. (1999). *Lessons for life: How smart schools build social, emotional, and academic intelligence.* Bloomington, IN: National Education Service/National Center for Innovation and Education (Available on World Wide Web at www.communitiesofhope. org)

Elias, M. J., Gager, P., & Hancock, M. (1993). *Prevention and social competence programs in use in New Jersey public schools: Findings from a statewide survey* (Working paper no. 3, School Intervention Implementation Study). New Brunswick, NJ: Rutgers University.

Elias, M. J., Gara, M. A., Schuyler, T. F., Branden-Muller, L. R., & Sayette, M. A. (1991). The promotion of social competence: Longitudinal study of a preventive school-based program. *American Journal of Orthopsychiatry, 61,* 409–417.

Elias, M. J., Gara, M. A., Ubriaco, M., Rothbaum, P., Clabby, J., & Schuyler, T. F. (1986). Impact of preventive social-problem-solving intervention on children's coping with middle school stressors. *American Journal of Community Psychology, 14,* 259–275.

Elias, M. J., Hoover, H. V. A., & Poedubicky, V. (1997). Computer-facilitated counseling for at-risk students in a social problem-solving "lab". *Elementary School Guidance and Counseling, 31,* 293–309.

Elias, M. J., & Tobias, S. E. (1996). *Social problem-solving interventions in the schools.* New York: Guilford.

Elias, M. J., Tobias, S. E., & Friedlander, B. S. (1994). Enhancing skills for everyday problem solving, decision making, and conflict resolution in special needs students with the support of computer-based technology. *Special Services in the Schools, 8*, 33–52.

Elias, M. J., Zins, J., Weissberg, R. P., Frey, K., Greenberg, M., Haynes, N., Kessler, R., Schwab-Stone, M., & Shriver, T. (1997). *Promoting social and emotional learning: Guidelines for educators.* Alexandria, VA: Association for Supervision and Curriculum Development.

Ellickson, P., & Bell, R. M. (1990). Drug prevention in junior high: A multi-site longitudinal test. *Science, 247*, 1299–1305.

Enett, S., Rosenbaum, D., Flewelling, R., Bieler, G., Ringwalt, C., & Bailey, S. (1994). Long-term evaluation of drug abuse resistance education. *Addictive Behaviors, 19*, 113–125.

Erikson, E. (1950). *Childhood and society.* New York: Norton.

Erikson, E. (1982). *The life cycle completed: A review.* New York: Norton.

Everhart, K., Haskell, I., Wandersman, A., Laughlin, J., & Sullivan, P. T. (1998). *Integrating adult-child mentorship and character development to promote social and academic competence: A report on the TROOPERS Project.* Manuscript in preparation.

Fairweather, G. W. (1967). *Methods for experimental social innovation.* New York: Wiley.

Fairweather, G. W. (1979). Experimental development and dissemination of an alternative to psychiatric hospitalization. In R. Munoz, L. Snowden, & J. G. Kelly (Eds.), *Social and psychological research in community settings* (pp. 305–342). San Francisco: Jossey-Bass.

Fairweather, G. W. (1994). [Untitled videotape interview]. In J. G. Kelly (Ed.), *The history of community psychology: A video presentation of context and exemplars.* Chicago, IL: Society for Community Research and Action.

Fairweather, G. W., Sanders, D., Cressler, D., & Maynard, H. (1969). *Community life for the mentally ill: An alternative to institutional care.* Chicago: Aldine.

Fawcett, S. B., Paine-Andrews, A., Francisco, V., Schulz, J., Richter, K., Lewis, R., Williams, E., Harris, K., Berkley, J., Fisher, J., & Lopez, C. (1995). Using empowerment theory in collaborative partnerships for community health and development. *American Journal of Community Psychology, 23*, 677–698.

Fawcett, S. B., White, G., Balcazar, F., Suarez-Balcazar, Y., Mathews, R., Paine-Andrews, A., Seekins, T., & Smith, J. (1994). A contextual-behavioral model of empowerment: Case studies involving people with physical disabilities. *American Journal of Community Psychology, 22*, 471–496.

Feagin, J., & Feagin, C. (1999). *Racial and ethnic relations* (6th ed.). Upper Saddle River, NJ: Prentice-Hall.

Felix, R. (1957). The role of psychology in the mental health effort. In C. Strother (Ed.), *Psychology and mental health* (pp. 4–20). Washington, DC: American Psychological Association.

Felner, R., & Adan, A. (1988). The School Transition Environment Project: An ecological intervention and evaluation. In R. Price, E. Cowen, R. Lorion, & J. Ramos-McKay (Eds.), *Fourteen ounces of prevention* (pp. 111–122). Washington, DC: American Psychological Association.

Felsinger, J., & Klein, D. (1957). A training program for clinical psychologists in community mental health theory and practice. In C. Strother (Ed.), *Psychology and mental health* (pp. 146–150). Washington, DC: American Psychological Association.

Felton, B., & Berry, C. (1992). Groups as social network members: Overlooked sources of social support. *American Journal of Community Psychology, 20*, 253–262.

Felton, B., & Shinn, M. (1992). Social integration and social support: Moving "social support" beyond the individual level. *Journal of Community Psychology, 20*, 103–115.

Festinger, L., Riecken, H., & Schacter, S. (1956). *When prophecy fails.* Minneapolis: University of Minnesota Press.

Fetterman, D. (1994). Steps of empowerment evaluation: From California to Cape Town. *Evaluation and Program Planning, 17*, 305–313.

Fetterman, D. (1996). Empowerment evaluation: An introduction to theory and practice. In D. Fetterman, S. Kaftarian, & A. Wandersman (Eds.), *Empowerment evaluation: Knowledge and tools for self-assessment and accountability* (pp. 3–46). Thousand Oaks, CA: Sage.

Fetterman, D., Kaftarian, S., & Wandersman, A. (Eds.). (1996). *Empowerment evaluation: Knowledge and tools for self-assessment and accountability.* Thousand Oaks, CA: Sage.

Fitzgerald, F. S. (1995). *The great Gatsby.* New York: Simon & Schuster. (Original work published 1925)

Flavell, J. H. (1963). *The developmental psychology of Jean Piaget.* New York: Van Nostrand.

Fleming, M. (1995). *Healthy youth 2000: A mid-decade review.* Chicago: American Medical Association.

Florin, P., Chavis, D., Wandersman, A., & Rich, R. (1992). A systems approach to understanding and enhancing grassroots organizations: The Block Booster Project. In R. Levine &

H. Fitzgerald (Eds.), *Analysis of dynamic psychological systems: Methods and applications* (Vol. 2, pp. 215–243). New York: Plenum.

Florin, P., & Wandersman, A. (1984). Cognitive social learning and participation in community development. *American Journal of Community Psychology, 12,* 689–708.

Florin, P., & Wandersman, A. (1990). An introduction to citizen participation, voluntary organizations, and community development: Insights for empowerment through research. *American Journal of Community Psychology, 18,* 41–54.

Fo, W. S., & O'Donnell, C. R. (1974). The Buddy System: Relationship and contingency conditions in a community intervention program for youth with nonprofessionals as behavior change agents. *Journal of Consulting and Clinical Psychology, 42,* 163–169.

Fondacaro, M., & Weinberg, D. (1999, June). Overview: Social justice concepts in community psychology. In M. Fondacaro (Chair), *Concepts of social justice in community psychology.* Symposium at the Biennial Meeting of the Society for Community Research and Action, New Haven, CT.

Foster-Fishman, P. G., & Keys, C. B. (1997). The person/environment dynamics of employee empowerment: An organizational culture analysis. *American Journal of Community Psychology, 25,* 345–370.

Foster-Fishman, P. G., Salem, D. A., Chibnall, S., Legler, R., & Yapchai, C. (1998). Empirical support for the critical assumptions of empowerment theory. *American Journal of Community Psychology, 26,* 507–536.

Frable, D. (1997). Gender, racial, ethnic, sexual and class identities. *Annual Review of Psychology, 48,* 139–162.

Frankl, V. (1984). *Man's search for meaning: An introduction to logotherapy* (3rd ed.). New York: Simon & Schuster. (Original work published 1959)

Friere, P. (1993). *Pedagogy of the oppressed* (Rev. ed.). New York: Continuum. (Original work published 1970)

Fullan, M. (1994). *Change forces: Probing the depths of educational reform.* Bristol, PA: Falmer Press.

Furtmuller, C. (1979). Alfred Adler: A biographical essay. In A. Adler, *Superiority and social interest* (H. Ansbacher & R. Ansbacher, Eds.), (pp. 311–393). New York: Norton.

Gager, P. J., & Elias, M. J. (1997). Implementing prevention programs in high-risk environments: Applications of the resiliency paradigm. *American Journal of Orthopsychiatry, 67,* 363–373.

Gaines, S., & Reed, E. (1995). Prejudice: From Allport to DuBois. *American Psychologist, 50,* 96–103.

Garbarino, J., & Kostelny, K. (1992). Child maltreatment as a community problem. *Child Abuse and Neglect, 16,* 455–464.

Garmezy, N. (1971). Vulnerability research and the issue of primary prevention. *American Journal of Orthopsychiatry, 41,* 101–116.

Garnets, L. D., & D'Augelli, A. R. (1994). Empowering lesbian and gay communities: A call for collaboration with community psychology. *American Journal of Community Psychology, 22,* 447–470.

Gatz, M., & Cotton, B. (1994). Age as a dimension of diversity: The experience of being old. In E. J. Trickett, R. J. Watts, & D. Birman (Eds.), *Human diversity: Perspectives on people in context* (pp. 334–355). San Francisco: Jossey-Bass.

Gaventa, J. (1980). *Power and powerlessness: Quiescence and rebellion in an Appalachian valley.* Urbana, IL: University of Illinois Press.

Gellman, M. (1997). *Always wear clean underwear.* New York: William Morrow.

Gergen, K. (1973). Social psychology as history. *Journal of Personality and Social Psychology, 26,* 309–320.

Gergen, K., Gulerce, A., Lock, A., & Misra, G. (1996). Psychological science in cultural context. *American Psychologist, 51,* 496–501.

Gesten, E., & Jason, L. (1987). Social and community interventions. *Annual Review of Psychology, 38,* 427–460.

Gidron, B., & Chesler, M. (1994). Universal and particular attributes of self-help: A framework for international and intranational analysis. *Prevention in Human Services, 11,* 1–44.

Gilens, M. (1996). Race and poverty in America: Public misperceptions and the American news media. *Public Opinion Quarterly, 60,* 515–541.

Gilligan, C. (1982). *In a different voice: Psychological theory and women's moral development.* Cambridge, MA: Harvard University Press.

Gillock, K. L., & Reyes, O. (1996). High school transition-related changes in urban minority students' academic performance and perceptions of self and school environment. *Journal of Community Psychology, 24,* 245–262.

Glidewell, J. (1977). Competence and conflict in community psychology. In I. Iscoe, B. Bloom, & C. Spielberger (Eds.), *Community psychology in transition: Proceedings of the national conference on training in community psychology* (pp. 71–76). Washington, DC: Hemisphere/John Wiley.

Glidewell, J. (Ed.). (1984). A tribute to Erich Lindemann [Special section]. *American Journal of Community Psychology, 12,* 511–536.

Glidewell, J. (1994). [Untitled videotape interview]. In J. G. Kelly (Ed.), *The history of community psychology: A video presentation of context and exemplars.* Chicago: Society for Community Research and Action.

Glidewell, J., Gildea, M., & Kaufman, M. (1973). The preventive and therapeutic effects of two school mental health programs. *American Journal of Community Psychology, 1,* 295–329.

Gloria, A. (1999, Winter). Creating and utilizing community with Chicana college students. *The Community Psychologist, 32,* 46–48.

Glynn, T. J. (1986). Neighborhood and sense of community. *Journal of Community Psychology, 14,* 341–352.

Goffman, E. (1959). *The presentation of self in everyday life.* Garden City, NY: Doubleday.

Golann, S., & Baker, J. (1975). *Current and future trends in community psychology.* New York: Human Sciences Press.

Goldston, S. (1994). [Untitled videotape interview]. In J. G. Kelly (Ed.), *The history of community psychology: A video presentation of context and exemplars.* Chicago: Society for Community Research and Action.

Goleman, D. (1995). *Emotional intelligence.* New York: Bantam.

Goleman, D. (1998). *Working with emotional intelligence.* New York: Bantam.

Gonsiorek, J. C., & Weinrich, J. D. (1991). The definition and scope of sexual orientation. In J. C. Gonsiorek & J. D. Weinrich (Eds.), *Homosexuality: Research implications for public policy* (pp. 1–12). Newbury Park, CA: Sage.

Gonzales, N. A., Cauce, A. M., Friedman, R. J., & Mason, C. A. (1996). Family, peer, and neighborhood influences on academic achievement among African-American adolescents: One-year prospective effects. *American Journal of Community Psychology, 24,* 365–388.

Goodman, R. M., & Steckler, A. (1987). A model for the institutionalization of health promotion programs. *Family and Community Health, 11,* 63–78.

Goodman, R. M., & Wandersman, A. (1994). FORECAST: A formative approach to evaluating community coalitions and community-based initiatives. In S. Kaftarian & W. Hansen (Eds.), *Journal of Community Psychology Monograph Series,* Center for Substance Abuse Prevention Special Issue, 6–25.

Goodman, R. M., Wandersman, A., Chinman, M., Imm, P., & Morrissey, E. (1996). An ecological assessment of community-based interventions for prevention and health promotion: Approaches to measuring community coalitions. *American Journal of Community Psychology, 24,* 33–61.

Goodstein, L., & Sandler, I. (1978). Using psychology to promote human welfare: A conceptual analysis of the role of community psychology. *American Psychologist, 33,* 882–891.

Goodwin, S., Operario, D., & Fiske, S. (1998). Situational power and interpersonal dominance facilitate bias and inequality. *Journal of Social Issues, 54,* 677–698.

Gore, S., & Aseltine, R. H. (1995). Protective processes in adolescence: Matching stressors with social resources. *American Journal of Community Psychology, 23,* 301–328.

Gould, S. J. (1981). *The mismeasure of man.* New York: Norton.

Granovetter, M. (1973). The strength of weak ties. *American Journal of Sociology, 78,* 1360–1380.

Green, L., & Lewis, M. (1986). *Measurement and evaluation in health education and health promotion.* Palo Alto: Mayfield.

Gruber, J., & Trickett, E. J. (1987). Can we empower others? The paradox of empowerment in the governing of an alternative public school. *American Journal of Community Psychology, 15,* 353–371.

Gurney, B. (1968). Alfred Adler and the current mental health revolution. *Journal of Individual Psychology, 26,* 124–134.

Hacker, A. (1992). *Two nations: Black and white, separate, hostile, unequal.* New York: Ballantine.

Haensly, P. A., & Parsons, J. L. (1993). Creative, intellectual, and psychosocial development through mentorship: Relationships and stages. *Youth and Society, 25,* 202–221.

Haggerty, R., Sherrod, L., Garmezy, N., & Rutter, M. (Eds.). (1994). *Stress, risk, and resilience in children and adolescents.* New York: Cambridge University Press.

Hall, C. C. I. (1997). Cultural malpractice: The growing obsolescence of psychology with the changing U.S. population. *American Psychologist, 52,* 642–651.

Hallmark Charitable Foundation. (1994). *Talking with TJ: A new educational resource to teach teamwork, cooperation, and conflict resolution.* Omaha, NE: Hallmark Inc.

Hancock, M. E. (1996). *Prediction of problem behavior in adolescence: The impact of stability and change in the number of risk and protective factors.* Unpublished doctoral dissertation, Rutgers University.

Hansen, W., & Graham, J. W. (1991). Preventing alcohol, marijuana, and cigarette use among adolescents: Peer resistance training versus establishing conservative norms. *Preventive Medicine, 20,* 414–430.

Harper, G., & Schneider, M. (Eds.). (1999, Spring). Interventions in lesbian, gay, bisexual and transgender communities [Special section]. *The Community Psychologist, 32,* 47–57.

Harrell, S. P. (1997, May). *Development and initial validation of scales to measure racism-related stress.* Poster presentation at the Biennial Conference of the Society for Community Research and Action, Columbia, SC.

Harrell, S. P. (2000). A multidimensional conceptualization of racism-related stress: Implications for the well-being of people of color. *American Journal of Orthopsychiatry, 70,* 1–16.

Harrell, S. P., Merchant, M. A., & Young, S. A. (1997, August). *Psychometric properties of the Racism and Life Experience Scales (RaLES).* Poster presentation at the Annual Convention of the American Psychological Association, Chicago.

Harrell, S., Taylor, S., & Burke, E. (Eds.). (1999, Winter). Cultural competence in community research and action [Special section]. *The Community Psychologist, 32,* 22–54.

Hartup, W. W., & Stevens, N. (1997). Friendships and adaptation in the life course. *Psychological Bulletin, 121,* 355–370.

Haskell, I. (1997). *The effectiveness of character education and mentoring: An evaluation of the Troopers school-based program.* Unpublished manuscript, University of South Carolina.

Hawkins, J. D., Catalano, R. F., & Associates. (1992). *Communities that care: Action for drug abuse prevention.* San Francisco: Jossey-Bass.

Hawkins, J. D., Catalano, R. F., Morrison, D., O'Donnell, J., Abbott, R., & Day, L. (1992). The Seattle Social Development Project: Effects of the first four years on protective factors and problem behaviors. In J. McCord & R. E. Tremblay (Eds.), *Preventing antisocial behavior: Interventions from birth through adolescence* (pp. 139–161). New York: Guilford.

Hawkins, J. D., & Lam, T. (1987). Teacher practices, social development, and delinquency. In J. D. Burchard & S. N. Burchard (Ed.) *Prevention of delinquent behavior* (pp. 241–274). Newbury Park, CA: Sage.

Hazel, K. L., & Mohatt, G. V. (in press). Cultural and spiritual pathways to sobriety: Informing substance abuse prevention and intervention for Native American communities. *Journal of Community Psychology.*

Heller, K. (1989). The return to community. *American Journal of Community Psychology, 17,* 1–16.

Heller. K. (1990). Social and community intervention. *Annual Review of Psychology, 41,* 141–168.

Heller, K., Price, R. H., Reinharz, S., Riger, S., & Wandersman, A. (1984). *Psychology and community change: Challenges of the future.* Homewood, IL: Dorsey Press/Pacific Grove, CA: Wadsworth.

Heller, M., & Firestone, W. (1995). Who's in charge here? Sources of leadership for change in eight schools. *Elementary School Journal, 96,* 65–86.

Helms, J. E. (1994). The conceptualizations of racial identity and other "racial" constructs. In E. J. Trickett, R. J. Watts, & D. Birman (Eds.), *Human diversity: Perspectives on people in context* (pp. 285–310). San Francisco: Jossey-Bass.

Henly, J. R. (1997). The complexity of support: The impact of family structure and provisional support on African American and White adolescent mothers' well-being. *American Journal of Community Psychology, 25,* 629–656.

Hermans, H., & Kempen, H. (1998). Moving cultures: The perilous problems of cultural dichotomies in a globalizing society. *American Psychologist, 53,* 1111–1120.

Herrnstein, R., & Murray, C. (1994). *The bell curve: Intelligence and class structure in American life.* New York: Free Press.

Hess, E. (1997, November). Class and me. *Friends Journal, 43,* 11.

Hill, H. M., & Madhere, S. (1996). Exposure to community violence and African American children: A multidimensional model of risks and resources. *Journal of Community Psychology, 24,* 44–65.

Hill, J. L. (1996). Psychological sense of community: Suggestions for future research. *Journal of Community Psychology, 24,* 431–438.

Hill, J. L. (2000). A rationale for the integration of spirituality into community psychology. *Journal of Community Psychology, 28,* 139–150.

Hirsch, B. J. (1980). Natural support systems and coping with life changes. *American Journal of Community Psychology, 8,* 159–172.

Hirsch, B. J., & DuBois, D. L. (1992). The relation of peer social support and psychological symptomatolgy during the transition to junior high school: A two-year longitudinal analysis. *American Journal of Community Psychology, 20,* 333–348.

Hirsch, B. J., Engel-Levy, A., DuBois, D. L., & Hardesty, P. (1990). The role of social environments in social support. In B. R. Sarason, I. G. Sarason, & G. Pierce (Eds.), *Social support: An interactional view* (pp. 367–393). New York: Wiley.

Hobfoll, S. E. (1988). *The ecology of stress.* New York: Hemisphere.

Hobfoll, S. E. (1998). *Stress, culture and community: The psychology and philosophy of stress.* New York: Plenum.

Hobfoll, S. E., Dunahoo, C. L., Ben-Porath, Y., & Monnier, J. (1994). Gender and coping: The dual-axis model of coping. *American Journal of Community Psychology, 22,* 49–82.

Hobfoll, S. E., & London, P. (1986). The relationship of self-concept and social support to emotional distress among women during war. *Journal of Social and Clinical Psychology, 4,* 189–203.

Hobfoll, S. E., & Vaux, A. (1993). Social support: Social resources and social context. In L. Goldberger & S. Breznitz (Eds.), *Handbook of stress: Theoretical and clinical aspects* (2nd ed.; pp. 685–705). New York: Free Press.

Hofstede, G. (1980). *Culture's consequences: International differences in work-related values.* Newbury Park, CA: Sage.

Hofstede, G. (1994). Foreword. In U. Kim, H. Triandis, C. Kagitcibiasi, S.-C. Choi, & G. Yoon (Eds.), *Individualism and collectivism: Theory, method, and applications* (pp. ix–xiii). Thousand Oaks, CA: Sage.

Holahan, C. J., & Moos, R. H. (1994). Life stressors and mental health: Advances in conceptualizing stress resistance. In W. Avison & I. Gotlib (Eds.), *Stress and mental health: Contemporary issues and prospects for the future* (pp. 213–238). New York: Plenum.

Holahan, C. J., Moos, R. H., & Bonin, L. (1997). Social support, coping, and psychological adjustment: A resources model. In G. Pierce, B. Lakey, I. G. Sarason, & B. R. Sarason (Eds.), *Sourcebook of social support and personality* (pp. 169–186). New York: Plenum.

Holahan, C. J., & Spearly, J. (1980). Coping and ecology: An integrative model for community psychology. *American Journal of Community Psychology, 8,* 671–685.

Hollingshead, A., & Redlich, F. (1958). *Social class and mental illness: A community study.* New York: Wiley.

Holmes, T. H., & Rahe, R. H. (1967). The social readjustment rating scale. *Journal of Psychosomatic Research, 11,* 213–218.

Hoyt-Meyers, L., Cowen, E. L., Work W. C., Wyman P. A., Magnus, K., Fagen, D. B., & Lotyczewski, B. S. (1995). Test correlates of resilient outcomes among highly stressed second- and third-grade urban children. *Journal of Community Psychology, 23,* 326–338.

Huggins, N. (Ed.) (1986). *W. E. B. Dubois: Writings.* [Notes and chronology]. New York: Library of America.

Hughes, D., & DuMont, K. (1993). Using focus groups to facilitate culturally anchored research. *American Journal of Community Psychology, 21,* 775–806.

Hughes, D., Seidman, E., & Williams, N. (1993). Cultural phenomena and the research enterprise: Toward a culturally anchored methodology. *American Journal of Community Psychology, 21,* 687–704.

Hughey, J., Speer, P. W., & Peterson, N. A. (1999). Sense of community in community organizations: Structure and evidence of validity. *Journal of Community Psychology, 27,* 97–113.

Humphreys, K. (1996). Clinical psychologists as psychotherapists: History, future, and alternatives. *American Psychologist, 51,* 190–197.

Humphreys, K. (1997, Spring). Individual and social benefits of mutual aid self-help groups. *Social Policy, 27,* 12–19.

Humphreys, K., Finney, J. W., & Moos, R. H. (1994). Applying a stress and coping framework to research on mutual help organizations. *Journal of Community Psychology, 22,* 312–327.

Humphreys, K., & Noke, J. M. (1997). The influence of posttreatment mutual help group participation on the friendship networks of substance abuse patients. *American Journal of Community Psychology, 25,* 1–16.

Humphreys, K., & Rappaport, J. (1993). From the community mental health movement to the war on drugs: A study in the definition of social problems. *American Psychologist, 48,* 892–901.

Humphreys, K., & Rappaport, J. (1994). Researching self-help/mutual aid groups and organizations: Many roads, one journey. *Applied and Preventive Psychology, 3,* 217–231.

Hunsberger, B. (1995). Religion and prejudice: The role of religious fundamentalism, quest and right -wing authoritarianism. *Journal of Social Issues, 51,* 113–130.

Hunter, A., & Riger, S. (1986). The meaning of community in community mental health. *Journal of Community Psychology, 14,* 55–70.

Hurtado, A. (1997). Understanding multiple group identities: Inserting women into cultural transformations. *Journal of Social Issues, 53,* 299–328.

Ickovics, J., & Park, C. (Eds.). (1998). Thriving: Broadening the paradigm beyond illness to health [Special issue]. *Journal of Social Issues, 54*(2).

Iscoe, I. (1974). Community psychology and the competent community. *American Psychologist, 29,* 607–613.

Iscoe, I., Bloom, B., & Spielberger, C. (Eds.). (1977). *Community psychology in transition: Proceedings of the national conference on training in community psychology.* Washington, DC: Hemisphere.

Jansen, M., & Johnson, E. (Eds.). (1993). Methodological issues in prevention research {Special issue]. *American Journal of Community Psychology, 21*(5).

Jason, L. A. (1991). Participating in social change: A fundamental value for our discipline. *American Journal of Community Psychology, 19,* 1–16.

Jason, L. A. (1997). *Community-building: Values for a sustainable future.* Westport, CT: Praeger.

Jason, L. A. (1998a). Tobacco, drug, and HIV prevention media interventions. *American Journal of Community Psychology, 26,* 151–188.

Jason, L. A. (1998b, February). Dr. Jason goes to Washington. *The Community Psychologist, 31*(1), 27–30.

Jason. L. A., Berk, M., Schnopp-Wyatt, D. L., & Talbot, B. (1999). Effects of enforcement of youth access laws on smoking prevalance. *American Journal of Community Psychology, 27,* 143–160.

Jason, L. A., & Hanaway, E. K. (1997). *Remote control: A sensible approach to kids, TV, and the new electronic media.* Sarasota, FL: Professional Resources Press.

Johnson, D. L., & Breckinridge, J. (1982). The Houston Parent-Child Development Center and the primary prevention of behavior problems in young children. *American Journal of Community Psychology, 10,* 305–316.

Johnston, J., Bauman, J., Milne, L., & Urdan, T. (1993). *Taking the measure of Talking With TJ: Series 1.* Ann Arbor: University of Michigan, Institute of Social Research.

Joint Commission on Mental Health and Mental Illness. (1961). *Action for Mental Health: Final Report.* New York: Basic Books.

Jones, J. M. (1991). The concept of race in social psychology. In R. L. Jones (Ed.), *Black psychology* (3rd ed.; pp. 441–467). Berkeley, CA: Cobb & Henry.

Jones, J. M. (1997a). *Prejudice and racism* (2nd ed.). New York: McGraw-Hill.

Jones, J. M. (1997b). Psychological knowledge and the new American dilemma of race. *Journal of Social Issues, 54,* 641–662.

Jones, R. L. (Ed.). (1991). *Black psychology* (3rd ed.). Berkeley, CA: Cobb & Henry.

Judd, C., & Kenny, D. (1981). *Estimating the effects of social interventions.* New York: Cambridge University Press.

Julian, J. A., Jones, A., & Dey, D. (1995). Open systems evaluation and the logic model: Program planning and evaluation tools. *Evaluation and Program Planning, 18,* 333–341.

Kabat-Zinn, J. (1993). Mindfulness meditation: Health benefits of an ancient Buddhist practice. In D. Goleman & J. Gurin (Eds.), *Mind-body medicine* (pp. 259–276.) New York: Consumer Reports Books/St. Martin's Press.

Kagan, J. (1994). *Galen's prophecy: Temperament in human nature.* New York: Basic Books.

Kagitçibasi, C. (1997). Individualism and collectivism. In J. W. Berry, M. Segall, & C. Kagitçibasi (Eds.), *Handbook of cross-cultural psychology, Volume 3: Social behavior and applications* (pp. 1–50). Needham Heights, MA: Allyn & Bacon.

Kamin, L. (1974). *The science and politics of IQ.* Potomac, MD: Erlbaum.

Kaniasty, K., & Norris, F. H. (1992). Social support and victims of crime: Matching event, support, and outcome. *American Journal of Community Psychology, 20,* 211–242.

Kaniasty, K., & Norris, F.H. (1995). In search of altruistic community: Patterns of social support mobilization following Hurricane Hugo. *American Journal of Community Psychology, 23,* 447–478.

Kanner, A., Coyne, J., Schaefer, C., & Lazarus, R. S. (1981). Comparison of two modes of stress measurement: Daily hassles and uplifts versus major life events. *Journal of Behavioral Medicine, 4,* 1–37.

Karakashian, M. (1998). Armenia: A country's history of challenges. *Journal of Social Issues, 54,* 381–392.

Kaskutas, L., Morgan, P., & Vaeth, P. (1992). Structural impediments in the development of community-based drug prevention programs for youth: Preliminary analysis from a qualitative formative evaluation study. *International Quarterly of Community Health Education, 12,* 169–182.

Katz, D., & Kahn, R. L. (1978). *The social psychology of organizations.* New York: Wiley.

Kaye, G., & Wolff, T. (Eds.). (1997). *From the ground up: A workbook on coalition building and community development.* Amherst, MA: AHEC/Community Partners.

Kelly, J. G. (1966). Ecological constraints on mental health services. *American Psychologist, 21,* 535–539.

Kelly, J. G. (1970). Toward an ecological conception of preventive interventions. In D. Adelson & B. Kalis ( Eds.), *Community psychology and mental health* (pp. 126–145). Scranton, PA: Chandler.

Kelly, J. G. (1977). Varied educational settings for community psychology. In I. Iscoe, B. Bloom, & C. Spielberger, (Eds.), *Community psychology in transition: Proceedings of the national conference on training in community psychology* (pp. 51–66). Washington, DC: Hemisphere/Wiley.

Kelly, J. G. (Ed.). (1979a). *Adolescent boys in high school: A psychological study of coping and adaptation.* Hillsdale, NJ: Erlbaum.

Kelly, J. G. (1979b). "Tain't what you do, it's the way you do it". *American Journal of Community Psychology, 7,* 244–258.

Kelly, J. G. (1984). In honor of Erich Lindemann. *American Journal of Community Psychology, 12,* 513–514.

Kelly, J. G. (1986). Context and process: An ecological view of the interdependence of practice and research. *American Journal of Community Psychology, 14,* 581–605.

Kelly, J. G. (1990). Changing contexts and the field of community psychology. *American Journal of Community Psychology, 18,* 769–792.

Kelly, J. G., Azelton, S., Burzette, R., & Mock, L. (1994). Creating social settings for diversity: An ecological thesis. In E. J. Trickett, R. J. Watts & D. Birman (Eds.), *Human diversity: Perspectives on people in context* (pp. 424–450). San Francisco: Jossey-Bass.

Kelly, J. G., Dassoff, N., Levin, I., Schreckengost, J., Stelzner, S., & Altman, B. (1988). *A guide to conducting prevention research in the community: First steps.* New York: Haworth.

W. K. Kellogg Foundation. (1998). *Kellogg evaluation handbook.* Battle Creek, MI: Author.

Kessler, R. C., Mickelson, K. D., & Zhao, S. (1997, Spring). Patterns and correlates of self-help groups membership in the United States. *Social Policy, 27,* 27–46.

Kessler, R. C., Price, R., & Wortman, C. (1985). Social factors in psychopathology: Stress, social support, and coping processes. *Annual Review of Psychology, 36,* 531–572.

Keys, C., & Frank, S. (1987). Community psychology and the study of organizations: A reciprocal relationship. *American Journal of Community Psychology, 15,* 239–251.

Kids Count. (1995). *Kids Count, America: An annual national survey of the status of children.* Westport, CT: Annie E. Casey Foundation.

Kieffer, C. (1984). Citizen empowerment: A developmental perspective. In J. Rappaport, C. Swift, & R. Hess (Eds.), *Studies in empowerment: Steps toward understanding and action* (pp. 9–36). New York: Haworth.

Kim, U., & Berry, J. (Eds.). (1993). *Indigenous psychologies: Research and experience in cultural context.* Newbury Park, CA: Sage.

Kim, U., Triandis, H., Kagitçibasi, C., Choi, S.-C., & Yoon, G. (Eds.) (1994). *Individualism and collectivism: Theory, method, and applications.* Thousand Oaks, CA: Sage.

King, M. L., Jr. (1968). The role of the behavioral scientist in the civil rights movement. *American Psychologist, 23,* 180–186.

Kingry-Westergaard, C., & Kelly, J. G. (1990). A contextualist epistemology for ecological research. In P. Tolan, C. Keys, F. Chertok & L. Jason (Eds.), *Researching community psychology* (pp. 23–32). Washington, DC: American Psychological Association.

Klein, D. (1984). Zen and the art of Erich Lindemann. *American Journal of Community Psychology, 12,* 515–517.

Klein, D. (1987). The context and times at Swampscott: My/story. *American Journal of Community Psychology, 12,* 515–517.

Klein, D. (1995). [Untitled videotape interview]. In J. G. Kelly (Ed.), *The history of community psychology: A video presentation of context and exemplars.* Chicago: Society for Community Research and Action.

Klein, D. C., & Goldston, S. E. (1977). Primary prevention: An idea whose time has come. *Proceedings of the Pilot Conference on Primary Prevention, April 24, 1976* (Department of Health, Education, and Welfare Pub. No. ADM 77–447). Washington, DC: U.S. Government Printing Office.

Klein, D., & Lindemann, E. (1961). Preventive intervention in individual and family crisis situations. In G. Caplan (Ed.), *Prevention of mental disorders in children* (pp. 283–306). New York: Basic Books.

Klicperova, M., Feierbend, I., & Hofstetter, C. (1997). In the search for a post-communist syndrome: A theoretical framework and empirical assessment. *Journal of Community and Applied Social Psychology, 7,* 39–52.

Kline, M., & Snow, D. (1994). Effects of a worksite coping skills intervention on the stress, social support, and health outcomes of working mothers. *Journal of Primary Prevention, 15,* 105–121.

Kloos, B., & Moore, T. (Eds.) (2000). Spirituality, religion, and community psychology [Special issue]. *Journal of Community Psychology, 28(2).*

Kloos, B., & Moore, T. (Eds.) (in press). Conceptualizing spirituality for community psychology: Resources, pathways, and perspectives [Special issue]. *Journal of Community Psychology.*

Kress, J. S., & Elias, M. J. (2000). Infusing community psychology and religion: Themes from an action-research project in Jewish identity. *Journal of Community Psychology, 28,* 187–198.

Kretzmann, J. P., & McKnight, J. L. (1993). *Building communities from the inside out: A path toward finding and mobilizing a community's assets.* Chicago, IL: ACTA Publications.

Kroeker, C. J. (1995). Individual, organizational and societal empowerment: A study of the processes in a Nicaraguan agricultural cooperative. *American Journal of Community Psychology, 23,* 749–764.

Kroeker, C. J. (1996). The cooperative movement in Nicaragua: Empowerment and accompaniment of severely disadvantaged persons. *Journal of Social Issues, 52,* 123–137.

Kuo, F. E., Sullivan, W. C., Coley, R. L., & Brunson, L. (1998). Fertile ground for community: Inner-city neighborhood common spaces. *American Journal of Community Psychology, 26,* 823–852.

LaFromboise, T., Coleman, H.L.K., & Gerton, J. (1993). Psychological impact of biculturalism: Evidence and theory. *Psychological Bulletin, 114,* 395–412.

Laird, M., Bradley, L., & Black, S. (1998). *The final evaluation of Quest International's Skills for Action.* Newark, OH: Lion's-Quest International.

Lamberth, J. (1998, August 24). DWB is not a crime: The numbers show that police unfairly and unconstitutionally pull over more cars driven by Blacks. *Washington Post National Weekly Edition,* p. 24.

Lappe, F. M., & DuBois, P. M. (1994). *The quickening of America: Rebuilding our nation, remaking our lives.* San Francisco, CA: Jossey-Bass.

Latkin, C. A., Mandell, W., Vlahov, D., Oziemkowska, M., & Celentano, D. D. (1996). The long-term outcome of a personal network-oriented HIV prevention intervention for injection drug users: The SAFE study. *American Journal of Community Psychology, 24,* 341–364.

LaVoie, F., Borkman, T., & Gidron, B. (Eds.). (1994). Self-help and mutual aid groups: International and multicultural perspectives [Special issue]. *Prevention in Human Services, 11*(1).

Lazarus, R. S. (1991). *Emotion and adaptation.* New York: Oxford University Press.

Lazarus, R. S. & Folkman, S. (1984). *Stress, appraisal, and coping.* New York: Springer.

Lazarus, S., & Prinsloo, R. (1995, Spring). Community psychology in South Africa. *The Community Psychologist, 28,* 24–27.

Leadbeater, B., Maton, K. I., & Schellenbach, C. (Moderators). (1999, June). *The Divison 27/37 policy advocacy initiative: Fostering resilient children, youth, families and communities: Strengths-based research and policy.* Symposium presented at the Biennial Meeting of the Society for Community Research and Action, New Haven, CT.

LeDoux, J. (1995). Emotion: Clues from the brain. *Annual Review of Psychology, 46,* 209–235.

Lerner, R. M. (1995). *America's youth in crisis: Challenges and options for programs and policies.* Thousand Oaks, CA: Sage.

Levine, A. (1982). *Love Canal: Science, politics, and people.* Lexington, MA: Heath.

Levine, I. S., & Zimmerman, J. D. (1996). Using qualitative data to inform public policy: Evaluating "Choose to De-Fuse." *American Journal of Orthopsychiatry, 66,* 363–377.

Levine, M. (1981). *The history and politics of community mental health.* New York: Oxford University Press.

Levine, M., & Levine, A. (1970). *A social history of helping services.* New York: Oxford University Press.

Levine, M., & Levine, A. (1992). *Helping children: A social history.* New York: Oxford University Press.

Levine, M., & Perkins, D. V. (1997). *Principles of community psychology: Perspectives and applications* (2nd ed.). New York: Oxford University Press.

Levine, T. (Producer). (1992). *The world of abnormal psychology: An ounce of prevention.* New York: A. H. Perlmutter. (Available from Annenberg/CPB Collection, 1–800–LEARNER)

Leviton, L. C. (1994). Program theory and evaluation theory in community-based programs. *Evaluation Practice, 15,* 89–92.

Lewin, K. (1935). *A dynamic theory of personality.* New York: McGraw-Hill.

Lewis, J. (1998). *Walking with the wind: A memoir of the movement.* New York: Simon & Schuster.

Liang, B. & Bogat, G. A. (1994). Culture, control, and coping: New perspective on social support. *American Journal of Community Psychology, 22,* 123–147.

Lindemann, E. (1944). Symptomatology and management of acute grief. *American Journal of Psychiatry, 101,* 141–148.

Lindemann, E. (1957). The nature of mental health work as a professional pursuit. In

C. Strother (Ed.), *Psychology and mental health* (pp. 136–145). Washington, DC: American Psychological Association.

Linney, J. A. (1986). Court-ordered school desegregation: Shuffling the deck or playing a different game. In E. Seidman & J. Rappaport (Eds.), *Redefining social problems* (pp. 259–274). New York: Plenum.

Linney, J. A. (1989). Optimizing research strategies in the schools. In L. A. Bond & B. E. Compas (Eds.), *Primary prevention in the schools* (pp. 50–76). Newbury Park, CA: Sage.

Linney, J. A. (1990). Community psychology into the 1990's: Capitalizing opportunity and promoting innovation. *American Journal of Community Psychology, 18*, 1–17.

Linney, J. A., & Reppucci, N. D. (1982). Research design and methods in community psychology. In P. Kendall & J. Butcher (Eds.), *Handbook of research methods in clinical psychology* (pp. 535–566). New York: Wiley.

Linney, J. A., & Wandersman, A. (1991). *Prevention plus III: Assessing alcohol and other drug prevention programs at the school and community level: A four-step guide to useful program assessment.* Rockville, MD: U.S. Department of Health and Human Services, Office for Substance Abuse Prevention.

Linney, J. A., & Wandersman, A. (1996). Empowering community groups with evaluation skills: The Prevention Plus III Model. In D. Fetterman, S. Kaftarian, & A. Wandersman (Eds.), *Empowerment evaluation: Knowledge and tools for self-assessment and accountability* (pp. 259–276). Thousand Oaks, CA: Sage.

Linney, J. A., Webb, D., & Rosenberg, M. (1985, April). *A time sampling procedure for behavior setting analysis in treatment facilities for juvenile offenders.* Poster presentation at Southeastern Psychological Association, Atlanta, GA.

Lipset, S. M. (1996). *American exceptionalism: A double-edged sword.* New York: Norton.

London, M., & MacDuffie, J. (1985). *Implementing managerial and technical innovations: Case examples and guidelines for practice.* Basking Ridge, NJ: AT&T Communications.

Lonner, W. (1994). Culture and human diversity. In E. J. Trickett, R. J. Watts, & D. Birman (Eds.), *Human diversity: Perspectives on people in context* (pp. 230–243). San Francisco: Jossey-Bass.

Loo, C., Fong, K., & Iwamasa, G. (1988). Ethnicity and cultural diversity: An analysis of work published in community psychology journals, 1965–1985. *Journal of Community Psychology, 16*, 332–349.

Lounsbury, J., Leader, D., Meares, E., & Cook, M. (1980). An analytic review of research in

community psychology. *American Journal of Community Psychology, 8*, 415–441.

Luke, D., Rappaport, J., & Seidman, E. (1991). Setting phenotypes in a mutual help organization: Expanding behavior setting theory. *American Journal of Community Psychology, 19*, 147–168.

Lustig, J., Wolchik, S., & Braver, S. (1992). Social support in chumships and adjustment in children of divorce. *American Journal of Community Psychology, 20*, 393–400.

Maccoby, N., & Altman, D. (1988). Disease prevention in communities: The Stanford Heart Disease Prevention Program. In R. Price, E. Cowen, R. Lorion, & J. Ramos-McKay (Eds.), *Fourteen ounces of prevention* (pp. 165–174). Washington, DC: American Psychological Association.

Madara, E. (1997, Spring). The mutual aid self-help online revolution. *Social Policy, 27*, 20–26.

Mann, P. (1998, April 22). Re: A sucker's bet. Message to the Society for Community Research and Action Listserve. [Online]. Available: <SCRA-L@LISTSERV.UIC.EDU>

Marecek, J., Fine, M., & Kidder, L. (1997). Working between worlds: Qualitative methods and social psychology. *Journal of Social Issues, 53*, 631–643.

Marin, G., Marin, B. V., Perez-Stable, E. J., Sabogal, F., & Otero-Sabogal, R. (1990). Changes in information as a function of a culturally appropriate smoking cessation community intervention for Hispanics. *American Journal of Community Psychology, 19*, 847–864.

Mark, M. M., & Pines, E. (1995). Implications of continuous quality improvement for program evaluation and evaluators. *Evaluation Practice, 16*, 131–139.

Markova, I. (Ed.). (1997). The individual and the community: A post-communist perspective [Special issue]. *Journal of Community and Applied Social Psychology, 7*(1).

Markus, H. T., & Kitayama, S. (1991). Culture and the self: Implications for cognition, emotion, and motivation. *Psychological Review, 98*, 224–253.

Marris, P., & Rein, M. (1973). *Dilemmas of social reform* (2nd. ed.). Chicago: Aldine.

Marrow, A. J. (1969). *The practical theorist.* New York: Basic Books.

Martin-Baro, I. (1990). Religion as an instrument of psychological warfare. *Journal of Social Issues, 46*, 93–107.

Mason, C., Chapman, D., & Scott, K. (1999). The identification of early risk factors for severe emotional disturbances and emotional handicaps: An epidemiological approach. *American*

*Journal of Community Psychology, 27,* 357–381.

Masterpasqua, F. (1981). Toward a synergism of developmental and community psychology. *American Psychologist, 36,* 782–786.

Maton, K. I. (1987). Patterns and psychological correlates of material support within a religious setting: The bidirectional support hypothesis. *American Journal of Community Psychology, 15,* 185–207.

Maton, K. I. (1988). Social support, organizational characteristics, psychological well-being, and group appraisal in three self-help group populations. *American Journal of Community Psychology, 16,* 53–77.

Maton, K. I. (1989). Community settings as buffers of life stress? Highly supportive churches, mutual help groups, and senior centers. *American Journal of Community Psychology, 17,* 203–232.

Maton, K. I. (1993). A bridge between cultures: Linked ethnographic empirical methodology for culture anchored research. *American Journal of Community Psychology, 21,* 747–774.

Maton, K. I., Hrabowski, R. A., & Greif, G. L. (1998). Preparing the way: A qualitative study of high achieving African American males and the role of the family. *American Journal of Community Psychology, 26,* 639–668.

Maton K. I., & Rappaport, J. (1984). Empowerment in a religious setting: A multivariate investigation. In J. Rappaport, C. Swift, & R. Hess (Eds.), *Studies in empowerment: Steps toward understanding and action* (pp. 37–71). New York: Haworth.

Maton, K. I., & Salem, D. A. (1995). Organizational characteristics of empowering community settings: A multiple case study approach. *American Journal of Community Psychology, 23,* 631–656.

Maton, K. I., Teti, D. M., Corns, K. M., Vieira-Baker, C. C., Lavine, J. R., Gouze, K. R., & Keating, D. P. (1996). Cultural specificity of support sources, correlates and contexts: Three studies of African-American and Caucasian youth. *American Journal of Community Psychology, 24,* 551–587.

Maton, K. I., & Wells, E. A. (1995). Religion as a community resource for well-being: Prevention, healing, and empowerment pathways. *Journal of Social Issues, 51,* 177–193.

McClure, L, Cannon, D., Allen, S., Belton, E., Connor, P., D'Ascoli, C., Stone, P., Sullivan, B., & McClure, G. (1980). Community psychology concepts and research base. *American Psychologist, 35,* 1000–1011.

McElhaney, S. (1995). *Getting started: NMHA guide to establishing community-based pre-*vention programs. Alexandria, VA: National Mental Health Association.

McEwan, K. L., & Bigelow, D. A. (1997). Using a logic model to focus health services on population health goals. *Canadian Journal of Program Evaluation, 12,* 167–174.

McGrath, J. A. (1984). *Groups: Interaction and performance.* Englewood Cliffs, NJ: Prentice-Hall.

McIntosh, P. (1998). White privilege and male privilege: A personal account of coming to see correspondences through work in women's studies. In M. Andersen & P. H. Collins (Eds.), *Race, class and gender: An anthology* (pp. 94–105). Belmont, CA: Wadsworth.

McMillan, B., Florin, P., Stevenson, J., Kerman, B., & Mitchell, R. E. (1995). Empowerment praxis in community coalitions. *American Journal of Community Psychology, 23,* 699–728.

McMillan, D. W. (1996). Sense of community. *Journal of Community Psychology, 24,* 315–326.

McMillan, D. W., & Chavis, D. M. (1986). Sense of community: Definition and theory. *Journal of Community Psychology, 14,* 6–23.

McQuancy, E. (1999). On track with Project TRAC. *Prevention Pipeline, 12,* 18–20.

Melton, G. B. (1991). Socialization in the global community: Respect for the dignity of children. *American Psychologist, 46,* 66–71.

Melton, G. B. (1995). Bringing psychology to Capitol Hill: Briefings on child and family policy. *American Psychologist, 50,* 766–770.

Miles, M., & Huberman, A. (1994). *Qualitative data analysis* (2d ed.). Thousand Oaks, CA: Sage.

Miller, J. B. (1976). *Toward a new psychology of women.* Boston: Beacon Press.

Miller, K., & Banyard, V. (Eds.) (1998). Qualitative research in community psychology [Special issue]. *American Journal of Community Psychology, 26*(4).

Mirowsky, J., & Ross, C. (1989). *Social causes of psychological distress.* New York: Aldine de Gruyter.

Mitchell, C., & Beals, J. (1997). The structure of problem and positive behavior among American Indian adolescents: Gender and community differences. *American Journal of Community Psychology, 25,* 257–287.

Mock, M. R. (1999, Winter). Cultural competency: Acts of justice in community mental health. *The Community Psychologist, 32,* 38–41.

Molock, S. D., & Douglas, K. B. (1999, Summer). Suicidality in the Black community: A collaborative response from a womanist theologian and a community psychologist. *The Community Psychologist, 32,* 32–36.

Montero, M. (1995, Spring). Community psychology in Venezuela. *The Community Psychologist, 28,* 27–30.

Montero, M. (1996). Parallel lives: Community psychology in Latin America and the United States. *American Journal of Community Psychology, 24,* 589–606.

Montero, M. (Ed.). (1998). Community psychology in Latin America [Special issue]. *Journal of Community Psychology, 26*(3).

Moodie, E., Markova, I., Farr, R., & Plichtova, J. (1997). The meanings of the community and of the individual in Slovakia and in Scotland. *Journal of Community and Applied Social Psychology, 7,* 19–38.

Moore, T. (1992). The African-American church: A source of empowerment, mutual help and social change. In K. I. Pargament, K. I. Maton, & R. Hess (Eds.), *Religion and prevention in mental health: Research, vision, and action* (pp. 237–257). New York: Haworth.

Moos, R. (1973). Conceptualizations of human environments. *American Psychologist, 28,* 652–665.

Moos, R. (1975). *Evaluating correctional and community settings.* New York: Wiley.

Moos, R. (1979). *Evaluating educational environments: Procedures, measures, findings and policy implications.* San Francisco: Jossey-Bass.

Moos, R. (1984). Context and coping: Toward a unifying conceptual framework. *American Journal of Community Psychology, 12,* 5–25.

Moos, R. (1994). *The social climate scales: A user's guide* (2nd. ed.). Palo Alto, CA: Consulting Psychologists Press.

Moos, R. (1996). Understanding environments: The key to improving social processes and program outcomes. *American Journal of Community Psychology, 24,* 193–201.

Moos, R., & Lemke, S. (1996). *Evaluating residential facilities: The Multiphasic Environmental Asessment Procedure.* Thousand Oaks, CA: Sage.

Moos, R., & Moos, B. (1986). *Family Environment Scale manual* (2nd ed.). Palo Alto, CA: Consulting Psychologists Press.

Moos, R., & Trickett, E. J. (1987). *Classroom Environment Scale manual* (2nd ed.). Palo Alto, CA: Consulting Psychologists Press.

Morrissey, E. (1998). *Evaluation of Camp Paupu Win.* Columbia, SC: South Carolina Department of Juvenile Justice.

Morrissey, E., & Wandersman, A. (1995). Total quality management in health care settings: A preliminary framework for successful implementation. In L. Ginsberg & P. Keys (Eds.), *New management in human services* (2nd ed; pp. 171–194). Washington, DC: National Association of Social Workers Press.

Moynihan, D. (1969). *Maximum feasible misunderstanding: Community action in the war on poverty.* New York: Free Press.

Mrazek, P., & Haggerty, R. (1994). *Reducing risks for mental disorders: Frontiers for preventive intervention research.* Washington, DC: National Academy Press.

Muehrer, P. (Ed.). (1997). Prevention research in rural settings [Special issue]. *American Journal of Community Psychology, 25*(4).

Mulvey, A. (1988). Community psychology and feminism: Tensions and commonalities. *Journal of Community Psychology, 16,* 70–83.

Mulvey, A., Gridley, H., & Gawith, L. (in press). Convent girls, feminism and community psychology. *Journal of Community Psychology.*

Munoz, M., Vasquez, C., Bermejo, M., & Vasquez, J. (1999). Stressful life events among homeless people: Quantity, types, timing, and perceived causality. *Journal of Community Psychology, 27,* 73–88.

Munoz, R. F. (1997). The San Francisco Depression Prevention Research Project. In G. Albee & T. Gullotta (Eds.), *Primary prevention works* (pp. 380–400). Thousand Oaks, CA: Sage.

Munoz, R. F., Snowden, L. R., Kelly, J. G., & Associates. (1979). *Social and psychological research in community settings.* San Francisco: Jossey-Bass.

Murray, H. (1938). *Explorations in personality.* New York: Oxford University Press.

Myers, J. K., & Bean, L. L. (1968). *A decade later: A follow-up of "Social class and mental illness".* New York: Wiley.

Myers, L. J., & Speight, S. (1994). Optimal theory and the psychology of human diversity. In E. J. Trickett, R. J. Watts, & D. Birman (Eds.), *Human diversity: Perspectives on people in context* (pp. 81–100). San Francisco: Jossey-Bass.

Naegele, K. (1955). A mental health project in a Boston suburb. In B. Paul (Ed.) *Health, culture and community* (pp. 295–323). New York: Russell Sage Foundation.

Newbrough, J. R. (1995). Toward community: A third position. *American Journal of Community Psychology, 23,* 9–38.

Newbrough, J. R. (Ed.). (1996). Sense of community [Special issue]. *Journal of Community Psychology, 24*(4).

Newbrough, J. R., & Chavis, D. M. (Eds.). (1986). Psychological sense of community: I. Theory and concepts [Special issue]. *Journal of Community Psychology, 14*(1).

Newbrough, J. R., & Chavis, D. M. (Eds.). (1986). Psychological sense of community: II. Research and applications [Special issue]. *Journal of Community Psychology, 14*(4).

Nigro, L. (1995). *The Social Problem Solving Lab: Re-referral intervention to enhance elementary students' critical thinking skills*. Unpublished dissertation, Graduate School of Applied and Professinal Psychology, Rutgers University.

Nobles, W. W. (1991). African philosophy: Foundations of Black psychology. In R. L. Jones (Ed.), *Black psychology* (3rd. ed.; pp. 47–64). Berkeley, CA: Cobb & Henry.

Norris, K. (1993). *Dakota: A spiritual geography*. Boston: Houghton Mifflin.

Northwest Regional Educational Laboratory (National Mentoring Center). (1999). *Making the case: Measuring the impact of your mentoring program* (p. 41). [Online]. Available on World Wide Web: *http://www.nwrel.org/mentoring/pdf/makingcase.pdf* .

Norton, J. R., & Fox, R. (1997). *The change equation: Capitalizing on diversity for effective organizational change*. Washington, DC: American Psychological Association.

Norton, S., Wandersman, A., & Goldman, C. (1993). Perceived costs and benefits of membership in a self-help group: Comparisons of members and nonmembers of the Alliance for the Mentally Ill. *Community Mental Health Journal, 29*, 143–160.

Novaco, R., & Monahan, J. (1980). Research in community psychology: An analysis of work published in the first six years of the *American Journal of Community Psychology. American Journal of Community Psychology, 8*, 131–145.

O'Donnell, C. R., Tharp, R. G., & Wilson, K. (1993). Activity settings as the unit of analysis: A theoretical basis for community intervention and development. *American Journal of Community Psychology, 21*, 501–520.

Office of Juvenile Justice and Delinquency Prevention. (1995). *Guide for implementing the comprehensive strategy for serious, violent, and chronic juvenile offenders*. Washington, DC: U. S. Department of Justice.

Olds, D. (1988). The Prenatal/Early Infancy Project. In R. Price, E. Cowen, R. Lorion, & J. Ramos-McKay (Eds.), *Fourteen ounces of prevention* (pp. 9–23). Washington, DC: American Psychological Association.

Olds, D. (1997). The Prenatal/Early Infancy Project: Fifteen years later. In G. Albee & T. Gullotta (Eds.), *Primary prevention works* (pp. 41–67). Thousand Oaks, CA: Sage.

O'Leary, V. (1998). Strength in the face of adversity: Individual and social thriving. *Journal of Social Issues, 54*, 425–446.

Olson, L. (1994, November 2). Learning their lessons: Scaling up; bringing good schools to every community. *Education Week, 14*(9), 43–46.

Olsson, J., Powell, B., & Stuehling, J. (1998). *Cultural bridges training manual* (Available from Cultural Bridges, 341 Ontelaunee Trail, Hamburg, PA 19526).

Olweus, D. (1991). Bully/victim problems among school children: Basic facts and effects of an intervention program. In D. Pepler & K. Rubin (Eds.), *The development and treatment of childhood aggression* (pp. 411–448).

O'Malley, P., & Wagenaar, A. (1991). Effects of minimum drinking age laws on alcohol use, related behaviors and traffic crash involvement among American youth: 1976–1987. *Journal of Studies on Alcohol, 52*, 478–491.

Orlandi, M. (Ed.). (1992). *Cultural competence for evaluators*. Rockville, MD: U.S. Department of Health and Human Services, Office for Substance Abuse Prevention.

Orley, J. (1996). *Life skills education in the schools*. Geneva, Switzerland: World Health Organization.

Oxley, D., & Barrera, M. (1984). Undermanning theory and the workplace: Implications of setting size for job satisfaction and social support. *Environment and Behavior, 16*, 211–234.

Ozer, E., Weinstein, R., Maslach, C., & Siegel, D. (1997). Adolescent AIDS prevention in context: The impact of peer educator qualities and classroom environments on intervention efficacy. *American Journal of Community Psychology, 25*, 289–323.

Paloutzian, R. F., & Kirkpatrick, L. A. (Eds.) (1995). Religious influences on personal and social well-being [Special issue]. *Journal of Social Issues, 51*(2).

Paquin, G. W., & Gambrill, E. (1994). The problem with neighbors. *Journal of Community Psychology, 22*, 21–32.

Pargament, K. I. (1997). *The psychology of religion and coping: Theory, research and practice*. New York: Guilford.

Pargament, K. I., & Maton, K. I. (2000). Religion in American life: A community psychology perspective. In J. Rappaport & E. Seidman (Eds.), *Handbook of community psychology* (pp. 495–522). New York: Plenum.

Pargament, K. I., Maton, K. I., & Hess, R. (Eds.). (1992). *Religion and prevention in mental health: Research, vision, and action*. New York: Haworth.

Patton, M. Q. (1997). *Utilization-focused evaluation* (3rd ed.). Thousand Oaks, CA: Sage.

Paul, B. (Ed.) (1955). *Health, culture and community.* New York: Russell Sage Foundation.

Payne, C. (1997). [Untitled videotape interview]. In J. G. Kelly (Ed.), *The history of community psychology: A video presentation of context and exemplars.* Chicago: Society for Community Research and Action.

Pedro-Carroll, J. (1997). The Children of Divorce Intervention Program: Fostering resilient outcomes for school-aged children. In G. W. Albee & T. Gullotta (Eds.), *Primary prevention works* (pp. 213–238). Thousand Oaks, CA: Sage.

Pepler, D., & Slaby, R. (1994). Theoretical and developmental perspectives on youth and violence. In L. Eron, J. Gentry, & P. Schlegel (Eds.), *Reason to hope: A psychosocial perspective on violence and youth* (pp. 27–58). Washington, DC: American Psychological Association.

Perkins, D. D. (1988). The use of social science in public interest litigation: A role for community psychologists. *American Journal of Community Psychology, 16,* 465–486.

Perkins, D. D. (1995). Speaking truth to power: Empowerment ideology as social intervention and policy. *American Journal of Community Psychology, 23,* 765–794.

Perkins, D. D., Brown, B. B., & Taylor, R. B. (1996). The ecology of empowerment: Predicting participation in community organizations. *Journal of Social Issues, 52,* 85–110.

Perkins, D. D., Florin, P., Rich, R., Wandersman, A., & Chavis, D. (1990). Participation and the social and physical environment of residential blocks: Crime and community context. *American Journal of Community Psychology, 18,* 83–116.

Perkins, D. D., & Taylor, R. (1996). Ecological assessments of community disorder: Their relationship to fear of crime and theoretical implications. *American Journal of Community Psychology, 24,* 63–108.

Perkins, D. D., & Zimmerman, M. (1995). Empowerment theory, research and application. *American Journal of Community Psychology, 23,* 569–580.

Perkins, D. V., Burns, T., Perry, J., & Nielsen, K. (1988). Behavior setting theory and community psychology: An analysis and critique. *Journal of Community Psychology, 16,* 355–372.

Perry, C. L., & Associates. (1989). WHO collaborative study on alcohol education and young people: Outcomes of a four-country study. *International Journal of the Addictions, 24,* 1145–1171.

Perry, C., & Jessor, R. (1985). The concept of health promotion and the prevention of adolescent drug abuse. *Health Education Quarterly, 12,* 169–184.

Peterson, J. (Ed.). (1998). HIV/AIDS prevention through community psychology [Special issue]. *American Journal of Community Psychology, 26*(1).

Peterson, J., Folkman, S., & Bakerman, R. (1996). Stress, coping, HIV status, psychosocial resources, and depressive mood in African American gay, bisexual, and heterosexual men. *American Journal of Community Psychology, 24,* 461–488.

Pettigrew, T. F. (1998). Intergroup contact theory. *Annual Review of Psychology, 49,* 65–85.

Phillips, K. (1993). *Looking backward: A critical reappraisal of communitarian thought.* Princeton, NJ: Princeton University Press.

Pierce, G., Lakey, B., Sarason, I. G., & Sarason, B. R. (Eds.). (1997). *Sourcebook of social support and personality.* New York: Plenum.

Pierce, G., Lakey, B., Sarason, I. G., Sarason, B. R., & Joseph, H. (1997). Personality and social support processes: A conceptual overview. In G. Pierce, B. Lakey, I. G. Sarason, & B. R. Sarason (Eds.), *Sourcebook of social support and personality* (pp. 3–18). New York: Plenum.

Pierce, G. R., Sarason, B. R., & Sarason, I. G. (Eds.). (1996). *Handbook of social support and the family.* New York: Plenum.

Pilisuk, M., McAllister, J., & Rothman, J. (1996). Coming together in action: The challenge of contemporary grassroots community organizing. *Journal of Social Issues, 52,* 15–37.

Pilkington, N., & D'Augelli, A. R. (1995). Victimization of lesbian, gay, and bisexual youth in community settings. *Journal of Community Psychology, 23,* 34–56.

Pistrang, N., & Barker, C. (1998). Partners and fellow patients: Two sources of emotional support for women with breast cancer. *American Journal of Community Psychology, 26,* 439–456.

Plas, J. M., & Lewis, S. E. (1996). Environmental factors and sense of community in a planned town. *American Journal of Community Psychology, 24,* 109–144.

Potts, R. (Ed.). (1999, Summer). The spirit of community psychology: Spirituality, religion, and community action [Special section]. *The Community Psychologist, 32*(3).

Powell's new war. (1997, April 28). *Newsweek,* pp. 28–37.

Pratkanis, A. R., & Turner, M. E. (1996). Persuasion and democracy: Strategies for increasing deliberative participation and enacting social change. *Journal of Social Issues, 52,* 187–206.

Prestby, J., & Wandersman, A. (1985). An empirical exploration of a framework of organizational viability: Maintaining block organizations. *Journal of Applied Behavioral Science, 21,* 287–305.

Prestby, J., Wandersman, A., Florin, P., Rich, R., & Chavis, D. (1990). Benefits, costs, incentive management and participation in vountary organizations: A means to understanding and promoting empowerment. *American Journal of Community Psychology, 18,* 117–150.

Pretty, G. M. H., Andrewes, L., & Collett, C. (1994). Exploring adolescents' sense of community and its relationship to loneliness. *Journal of Community Psychology, 22,* 346–358.

Pretty, G. M. H., Conroy, C., Dugay, J., Fowler, K., & Williams, D. (1996). Sense of community and its relevance to adolescents of all ages. *Journal of Community Psychology, 24,* 365–380.

Price, R. (1989). Bearing witness. *American Journal of Community Psychology, 17,* 151–167.

Price, R., & Cherniss, C. (1977). Training for a new profession: Research as social action. *Professional Psychology, 8,* 222–231.

Price, R., Cowen, E., Lorion, R., & Ramos-McKay, J. (Eds.). (1988). *Fourteen ounces of prevention: A casebook for practitioners.* Washington, DC: American Psychological Association.

Price, R., & Lorion, R. (1989). Prevention programming as organizational reinvention: From research to implementation. In D. Shaffer, I Phillips, & N. Enzer (Eds.), *Prevention of mental disorders, alcohol and other drug use in children and adolescents* (pp. 97–123). Office of Substance Abuse Prevention, Prevention Monograph No. 2 (Department of Health and Human Services Publication No. ADM 89–1646). Washington, DC: U.S. Government Printing Office.

Price, R., & Smith, S. (1985). A guide to evaluating prevention programs in mental health. (Department of Health and Human Services Publication No. ADM 85–144). Washington, DC: U.S. Government Printing Office.

Prilleltensky, I. (1997). Values, assumptions, and practices: Assessing the moral implications of psychological discourse and action. *American Psychologist, 52,* 517–535.

Prilleltensky, I. (1999, June). Critical psychology and social justice. In M. Fondacaro (Chair), *Concepts of social justice in community psychology.* Symposium at the Biennial Meeting of the Society for Community Research and Action, New Haven, CT.

Prilleltensky, I. & Gonick, L. (1994). The discourse of oppression in the social sciences: Past, present, and future. In E. J. Trickett, R. J. Watts, & D. Birman (Eds.), *Human diversity: Perspectives on people in context* (pp. 145–177). San Francisco: Jossey-Bass.

Prilleltensky, I., & Laurendeau, M. (Eds.). (1994). Prevention: Focus on children and youth [Special issue]. *Canadian Journal of Community Mental Health, 13*(2), 3–274.

Psychological Enterprises Incorporated. (1993). *The student conflict manager/personal problem-solving guide.* Cedar Knolls, NJ: Author.

Puddifoot, J. (1996). Some initial considerations in the measurement of community identity. *Journal of Community Psychology, 24,* 327–336.

Putnam, R. (1995). Bowling alone: America's declining social capital. *Journal of Democracy, 6,* 65–78.

Rabinowitz, C., & Weseen, S. (1997). Elu(ci)d(at)ing epistemological impasses: Reviewing the qualitative/quantitative debates in psychology. *Journal of Social Issues, 53,* 605–630.

Rapkin, B., & Mulvey, E. (1990). Toward excellence in quantitative community research. In P. Tolan, C. Keys, F. Chertok, & L. Jason (Eds.), *Researching community psychology* (pp. 147–152). Washington, DC: American Psychological Association.

Rappaport, J. (1977a). *Community psychology: Values, research, and action.* New York: Holt, Rinehart and Winston.

Rappaport, J. (1977b). From Noah to Babel: Relationships between conceptions, values, analysis levels, and social intervention strategies. In I. Iscoe, B. Bloom, & C. Spielberger (Eds.), *Community psychology in transition: Proceedings of the national conference on training in community psychology* (pp. 175–184). Washington, DC: Hemisphere/Wiley.

Rappaport, J. (1981). In praise of paradox: A social policy of empowerment over prevention. *American Journal of Community Psychology, 9,* 1–25.

Rappaport, J. (1987). Terms of empowerment/exemplars of prevention: Toward a theory for community psychology. *American Journal of Community Psychology, 15,* 121–144.

Rappaport, J. (1990). Research methods and the empowerment social agenda. In P. Tolan, C. Keys, F. Chertok, & L. Jason (Eds.), *Researching community psychology* (pp. 51–63). Washington, DC: American Psychological Association.

Rappaport, J. (1993). Narrative studies, personal stories, and identity transformation in the mutual help context. *Journal of Applied Behavioral Science, 29*, 239–256.

Rappaport, J. (1995). Empowerment meets narrative: Listening to stories and creating settings. *American Journal of Community Psychology, 23*, 795–808.

Rappaport, J. (1999, June). Comments on social justice. In M. Fondacaro (Chair), *Concepts of social justice in community psychology*. Symposium conducted at the Biennial Meeting of the Society for Community Research and Action, New Haven, CT.

Rappaport, J., & Seidman, E. (Eds.). (2000). *Handbook of community psychology*. New York: Plenum.

Rappaport, J., & Simkins, R. (1992). Healing and empowerment through community narrative. In K. I. Pargament, K. I. Maton, & R. Hess (Eds.), *Religion and prevention in mental health* (pp. 215–236). New York: Haworth.

Rapping, E. (1997, Spring). There's self-help and then there's self-help: Women and the recovery movement. *Social Policy*, 56–61.

Raviv, A., Raviv, A., & Reisel, E. (1990). Teachers and students: Two different perspectives? Measuring social climate in the classroom. *American Educational Research Journal, 27*, 141–157.

Reinharz, S. (1994). Toward an ethnography of "voice" and "silence". In E. J. Trickett, R. J. Watts, & D. Birman (Eds.), *Human diversity: Perspectives on people in context* (pp. 178–200). San Francisco: Jossey-Bass.

Repetti, R., & Cosmas, K. (1991). The quality of the social environment at work and job satisfaction. *Journal of Applied Social Psychology, 21*, 840–854.

Resnicow, K., Braithwaite, R., Ahluwalia, J., & Baranowski, T. (1999). Cultural sensitivity in public health: Defined and demystified. *Ethnicity and Disease, 9*, 10–21.

Reyes, O., Gillock, K., & Kobus, K. (1994). A longitudinal study of school adjustment in urban, minority adolescents: Effects of a high school transition program. *American Journal of Community Psychology, 22*, 341–370.

Rhodes, J. E. (1994). Older and wiser: Mentoring relationships in childhood and adolescence. *Journal of Primary Prevention, 14*, 187–196.

Rhodes, J. E., Contreras, J. M., & Mangelsdorf, S. C. (1994). Natural mentor relationships among Latina adolescent mothers: Psychological adjustment, moderating processes, and the role of early parental acceptance. *American Journal of Community Psychology, 22*, 211–228.

Rhodes, J. E., Ebert, L., & Fischer, K. (1992). Natural mentor: An overlooked resource in the social networks of young, African American mothers. *American Journal of Community Psychology, 20*, 445–462.

Rhodes, J. E., & Woods, M. (1995). Comfort and conflict in the relationships of pregnant, minority adolescents: Social support as moderator of social strain. *Journal of Community Psychology, 22*, 74–84.

Rich, R. C., Edelstein, M., Hallman, W., & Wandersman, A. (1995). Citizen participation and empowerment: The case of local environmental hazards. *American Journal of Community Psychology, 23*, 657–676.

Rickel, A. U., & Becker, E. (1997). *Keeping children from harm's way: How national policy affects psychological development*. Washington, DC: American Psychological Association.

Rieff, R. (1977). Ya gotta believe. In I. Iscoe, B. Bloom, & C. Spielberger, (Eds.), *Community psychology in transition: Proceedings of the National Conference on Training in Community Psychology* (pp. 45–50). Washington, DC: Hemisphere/Wiley.

Riessman, F. (1990). Restructuring help: A human services paradigm for the 1990's. *American Journal of Community Psychology, 18*, 221–230.

Riger, S. (1984). Vehicles for empowerment: The case of feminist movement organizations. In J. Rappaport, C. Swift & R. Hess (Eds.), *Studies in empowerment: Steps toward understanding and action* (pp. 99–118). New York: Haworth.

Riger, S. (1990). Ways of knowing and organizational approaches to community research. In P. Tolan, C. Keys, F. Chertok, & L. Jason (Eds.), *Researching community psychology* (pp. 42–50). Washington, DC: American Psychological Association.

Riger, S. (1993). What's wrong with empowerment? *American Journal of Community Psychology, 21*, 279–292.

Riger, S. (1999, June). Discussant presentation. In M. Fondacaro (Chair), *Concepts of social justice in community psychology*. Symposium at the Biennial Meeting of the Society for Community Research and Action, New Haven, CT, USA.

RMC Research Corporation. (1995). *National Diffusion Network schoolwide promising practices: Report of a pilot effort*. Portsmouth, NH: Author.

Roberts, B., & Thorsheim, H. (1992). Reciprocal ministry: A transforming vision of help and leadership. In K. I. Pargament, K. I. Maton, & R. Hess (Eds.), *Religion and prevention in mental health* (pp. 259–276). New York: Haworth.

Roberts, L., Luke, D., Rappaport, J., Seidman, E., Toro, P., & Reischl, T. (1991). Charting uncharted terrain: A behavioral observation system for mutual help groups. *American Journal of Community Psychology, 19,* 715–738.

Roberts, L., Salem, D., Rappaport, J., Toro, P. A., Luke, D., & Seidman, E. (1999). Giving and receiving help: Interpersonal transactions in mutual-help meetings and psychosocial adjustment of members. *American Journal of Community Psychology, 27,* 841–868.

Robinson, D., & Wilkinson, D. (1995). Sense of community in a remote mining town: Validating a neighborhood cohesion scale. *American Journal of Community Psychology, 23,* 137–148.

Robinson, W. L. (1990). Data feedback and communication to the host setting. In P. Tolan, C. Keys, F. Chertok, & L. Jason (Eds.), *Researching community psychology* (pp. 193–195). Washington, DC: American Psychological Association.

Rogers, T., Howard-Pitney, B., & Bruce, B. (1989). *What works? A guide to school-based alcohol and drug abuse prevention curricula.* Stanford, CA: Stanford Center for Research in Disease Prevention.

Roll, C. N., Toro, P. A., & Ortola, G. L. (1999). Characteristics and experiences of homeless adults: A comparison of single men, single women, and women with children. *Journal of Community Psychology, 27,* 189–198.

Roosa, M., Dumka, L., & Tein, J.-Y. (1996). Family characteristics as mediators of the influence of problem drinking and multiple risk status on child mental health. *American Journal of Community Psychology, 24,* 607–624.

Rosenhan, D. (1973). On being sane in insane places. *Science, 179,* 250–258.

Rossi, P. H. (1978). Issues in the evaluation of human services delivery. *Evaluation Quarterly, 2,* 573–599.

Rossi, P. H., Freeman, H. E., & Lipsey, M. (1999). *Evaluation: A systematic approach* (6th ed). Newbury Park, CA: Sage.

Rotheram-Borus, M. J. (1988). Assertiveness training with children. In R. Price, E. Cowen, R. Lorion, & J. Ramos-McKay (Eds.), *Fourteen ounces of prevention* (pp. 83–97). Washington, DC: Amer. Psychological Association.

Rotter, J. B. (1954). *Social learning and clinical psychology.* Englewood Cliffs, NJ: Prentice-Hall.

Rotter, J. B. (1966). Generalized expectancies for internal versus external contol of reinforcement. *Psychological Monographs, 80* (Whole No. 609).

Rotter, J. B. (1982). *The development and application of social learning theory.* New York: Praeger.

Runyan, W. (1982). *Life histories and psychobiography.* New York: Oxford University Press.

Russo, N. F., & Dabul, A. (1994). Feminism and psychology: A dynamic interaction. In E. J. Trickett, R. J. Watts, & D. Birman (Eds.), *Human diversity: Perspectives on people in context* (pp. 81–99). San Francisco: Jossey-Bass.

Ryan, W. (1971). *Blaming the victim.* New York: Random House.

Ryan, W. (1981). *Equality.* New York: Pantheon.

Ryan, W. (1994). Many cooks, brave men, apples, and oranges: How people think about equality. *American Journal of Community Psychology, 22,* 25–36.

Saegert, S. (1982). Environment and children's mental health: Residential density and low income children. In A. Baum & J. E. Singer (Eds.), *Handbook of psychology and health* (pp. 247–268). Hillsdale, NJ: Erlbaum.

Saegert, S., & Winkel, G. (1990). Environmental psychology. *Annual Review of Psychology, 41,* 441–477.

Saegert, S., & Winkel, G. (1996). Paths to community empowerment: Organizing at home. *American Journal of Community Psychology, 24,* 517–550.

Sagy, S., Stern, E., & Krakover, S. (1996). Macro- and microlevel factors related to sense of community: The case of temporary neighborhoods in Israel. *American Journal of Community Psychology, 24,* 657–676.

Salem, D. A., Bogat, G. A., & Reid, C. (1997). Mutual help goes on-line. *Journal of Community Psychology, 25,* 189–208.

Salovey, P., & Mayer, J. D. (1990). Emotional intelligence. *Imagination, Cognition and Personality, 9,* 185–211.

Salovey, P., & Sluyter, D. (Eds.). (1997). *Emotional development and emotional intelligence: Educational implications.* New York: Basic Books.

Sandler, I. N., & Lakey, B. (1982). Locus of control as a stress moderator: The role of control perceptions and social support. *American Journal of Community Psychology, 10,* 65–80.

Sandler, I. N., West, S. G., Baca, L., Pillow, D. R. Gersten, J. C., Rogosch, F., Virdin, L., Beals, J., Reynolds, K. D., Kallgren, C., Tein, J., Kriege, G., Cole, E., & Cislo, D. A. (1992). Linking empirically based theory and evaluation: The family bereavement program. *American Journal of Community Psychology, 20,* 491–522.

Santiago-Rivera, A., Morse, G.S., Hunt, A., & Lickers, H. (1998). Building a community-based research partnership: Lessons from the Mohawk Nation of Akwesasne. *Journal of Community Psychology, 26*, 163–174.

Sarason, B. R., Pierce, G., & Sarason, I. G. (1990). Social support: The sense of acceptance and the role of relationships. In B. R. Sarason, I. G. Sarason, & G. Pierce (Eds.), *Social support: An interactional view* (pp. 95–128). New York: Wiley.

Sarason, B. R., Sarason, I. G., & Pierce, G. (1990a). Traditional views of social support and their impact on assessment. In B. R. Sarason, I. G. Sarason, & G. Pierce (Eds.), *Social support: An interactional view* (pp. 9–25). New York: Wiley.

Sarason, B. R., Sarason, I. G., & Pierce, G. (Eds.). (1990b). *Social support: An interactional view.* New York: Wiley.

Sarason, S. B. (1972). *The creation of settings and the future societies.* San Francisco: Jossey-Bass.

Sarason, S. B. (1974). *The psychological sense of community: Prospects for a community psychology.* San Fransisco: Jossey-Bass.

Sarason, S. B. (1976). Community psychology and the anarchist insight. *American Journal of Community Psychology, 4*, 243–261.

Sarason, S. B. (1977). Community psychology, networks, and Mr. Everyman. In I. Iscoe, B. Bloom, & C. Spielberger (Eds.), *Community psychology in transition: Proceedings of the national conference on training in community psychology* (pp. 25–44). Washington, DC: Hemisphere/Wiley.

Sarason, S. B. (1978). The nature of problem-solving in social action. *American Psychologist, 33*, 370–380.

Sarason, S. B. (1982). *The culture of the school and the problem of change* (2nd ed.). Boston: Allyn & Bacon.

Sarason, S. B. (1986). Commentary: The emergence of a conceptual center. *Journal of Community Psychology, 14*, 405–407.

Sarason, S. B. (1988). *The making of an American psychologist: An autobiography.* San Francisco: Jossey-Bass.

Sarason, S. B. (1993). American psychology and the needs for the transcendence and community. *American Journal of Community Psychology, 21*, 185–202.

Sarason, S. B. (1994). The American worldview. In S. B. Sarason, *Psychoanalysis, General Custer, and the verdicts of history, and other essays on psychology in the social scene* (pp. 100–118). San Francisco: Jossey-Bass.

Sarason, S. B. (1995). [Untitled videotape interview]. In J. G. Kelly (Ed.), *The history of community psychology: A video presentation of context and exemplars.* Chicago: Society for Community Research and Action.

Sarbin, T. (1970). A role-theory perspective for community psychology: The structure of social identity. In D. Adelson & B. Kalis (Eds.), *Community psychology and mental health* (pp. 89–113). Scranton, PA: Chandler.

Sasao, T. (1999, Winter). Cultural competence promotion as a general prevention strategy in urban settings: Some lessons learned from working with Asian American adolescents. *The Community Psychologist, 32*, 41–43.

Sasao, T., & Sue, S. (1993). Toward a culturally anchored ecological framework of research in ethnic-cultural communities. *American Journal of Community Psychology, 21*, 705–728.

Schoggen, P. (1988). Commentary on Perkins, Burns, Perry & Nielsen's "Behavior setting theory and community psychology: An analysis and critique". *Journal of Community Psychology, 16*, 373–386.

Schoggen, P. (1989). *Behavior settings.* Stanford, CA: Stanford University Press.

Schoggen, P., & Schoggen, M. (1988). Student voluntary participation and high school size. *Journal of Educational Research, 81*, 288–293.

Schorr, L. (1988). *Within our reach: Breaking the cycle of disadvantage.* New York: Doubleday.

Schorr, L. (1997). *Common purpose: Strengthening families and neighborhoods to rebuild America.* New York: Anchor Books.

Schubert, M., & Borkman, T. (1991). An organizational typology for self-help groups. *American Journal of Community Psychology, 19*, 769–788.

Schuncke, G., & Krogh, S. (1983). *Helping children choose: Resources, strategies, and activities for teachers of young children.* Glenview, IL: Scott, Foresman & Company.

Schwarzer, R., Hahn, A., & Schroder, H. (1994). Social integration and social support in a life crisis: Effects of macrosocial change in East Germany. *American Journal of Community Psychology, 22*, 685–706.

Schweinhart, L., & Weikart, D. (1988). The High/Scope Perry Preschool Program. In R. Price, E. Cowen, R. Lorion, & J. Ramos-McKay (Eds.), *Fourteen ounces of prevention* (pp. 53–65). Washington, DC: American Psychological Association.

Sefa-Dedeh, A. (1992). Improving children's lives: The case for primary prevention in Ghana. In G. W. Albee, L. A. Bond, & T. Monsey (Eds.), *Improving children's lives: Global perspectives on prevention* (Vol. 14 of the *Primary prevention of psychopathology* series; pp. 63–72). Thousand Oaks, CA: Sage.

Seidman, E. (1988). Back to the future, community psychology: Unfolding a theory of social intervention. *American Journal of Community Psychology, 16,* 3–24.

Seidman, E. (1990). Pursuing the meaning and utility of social regularities for community psychology. In P. Tolan, C. Keys, F. Chertok, & L. Jason (Eds.), *Researching community psychology* (pp. 91–100). Washington, DC: American Psychological Association.

Seidman, E. (1991). Growing up the hard way: Pathways of urban adolescents. *American Journal of Community Psychology, 19,* 173–206.

Seidman, E., Aber, J. L., Allen, L., & French, S. E. (1996). The impact of the transition to high school on the self-system and perceived social context of poor urban youth. *American Journal of Community Psychology, 24,* 489–516.

Seidman, E., Allen, L., Aber, J. L., Mitchell, C., & Feinman, J. (1994). The impact of school transitions in early adolescence on the self-system and perceived social context of poor urban youth. *Child Development, 65,* 507–522.

Seidman, E., Allen, L., Aber, J. L., Mitchell, C., Feinman, J., Yoshikawa, H., Comtois, K. A., Goltz, J., Miller, R. L., Oritz-Torres, B., & Roper, C. (1995). Development and validtion of adolescent-perceived microsystem scales: Social support, daily hassles, and involvement. *American Journal of Community Psychology, 23,* 335–388.

Seidman, E., Hughes, D., & Williams, N. (Eds.). (1993). Culturally anchored methodology [Special issue]. *American Journal of Community Psychology, 21*(6).

Seidman, E., & Rappaport, J. (Eds.). (1986). *Redefining social problems.* New York: Plenum.

Sellers, R. M., Kuperminc, G. P., & Damas, A. (1997). The college life experience of African American women athletes. *American Journal of Community Psychology, 25,* 699–720.

Serrano-Garcia, I. (1984). The illusion of empowerment: Community development within a colonial context. In J. Rappaport, C. Swift, & R. Hess (Eds.), *Studies in empowerment: Steps toward understanding and action* (pp. 173–200). New York: Haworth.

Serrano-Garcia, I. (1990). Implementing research: Putting our values to work. In P. Tolan, C. Keys, F. Chertok, & L. Jason (Eds.), *Researching community psychology* (pp. 171–182). Washington, DC: American Psychological Association.

Serrano-Garcia, I., & Bond, M. (Eds.). (1994). Empowering the silent ranks [Special issue].

*American Journal of Community Psychology, 22*(4).

Shapiro, D. H., Schwartz, C. E., & Astin J. (1996). Controlling ourselves, controlling our world: Psychology's role in understanding positive and negative consequences of seeking and gaining control. *American Psychologist, 51,* 1213–1230.

Shinn, M. (1987). Expanding community psychology's domain. *American Journal of Community Psychology, 15,* 555–573.

Shinn, M. (1990). Mixing and matching: Levels of conceptualization, measurement, and statistical analysis in community research. In P. Tolan, C. Keys, F. Chertok, & L. Jason (Eds.), *Researching community psychology* (pp. 111–126). Washington, DC: American Psychological Association.

Shinn, M. (1992). Homelessness: What is a psychologist to do? *American Journal of Community Psychology, 20,* 1–24.

Shinn, M. (1994, Fall). A community psychologist's involvement in the legal system. *The Community Psychologist, 28,* 35–36.

Shinn, M. (1996a). Ecological assessment: Introduction to the special issue. *American Journal of Community Psychology, 24,* 1–4.

Shinn, M. (Ed.). (1996b). Ecological assessment. *American Journal of Community Psychology* [Special issue], *24*(1).

Shriver, T. (1992). Video segment in *The world of abnormal psychology: An ounce of prevention* (T. Levine, Producer). New York: A. H. Perlmutter. (Available from Annenberg/CPB Collection, 1–800–LEARNER).

Shulman, S., Kedem, P., Kaplan, K., Server, I., & Braja, M. (1998). Latchkey children: Potential sources of support. *Journal of Community Psychology, 26,* 185–197.

Shure, M. B. (1997). Interpersonal Cognitive Problem-Solving: Primary prevention of early high-risk behaviors in the preschool and primary years. In G. Albee & T. Gullotta (Eds.), *Primary prevention works* (pp. 167–188). Thousand Oaks, CA: Sage.

Shure, M. B., & Spivack, G. (1988). Interpersonal Cognitive Problem-Solving. In R. Price, E. Cowen, R. Lorion, & J. Ramos-McKay (Eds.), *Fourteen ounces of prevention* (pp. 69–82). Washington, DC: American Psychological Association.

Siegel, K., Raveis, V. H., & Karus, D. (1997). Illness-related support and negative network interactions: Effects on HIV-infected men's depressive symptomatology. *American Journal of Community Psychology, 25,* 395.420.

Silka, L., & Tip, J. (1994). Empowering the silent ranks: The Southeast Asian experience.

*American Journal of Community Psychology,* 22, 497–530.

Silver, E. J., Ireys, H., Bauman, L. J., & Stein, R. E. K. (1997). Psychological outcomes of a support intervention in mothers of children with ongoing health conditions: The Parent-to-Parent Network. *Journal of Community Psychology*, 25, 249–264.

Silverman, P. (1988). Widow-to-Widow: A mutual help program for the widowed. In R. Price, E. Cowen, R. Lorion, & J. Ramos-McKay (Eds.), *Fourteen ounces of prevention* (pp. 175–186). Washington, DC: American Psychological Association.

Simons, R., Johnson, C., Beaman, J., Conger, R., & Whitbeck, L. (1996). Parents and peer group as mediators of the effect of community structure on adolescent problem behavior. *American Journal of Community Psychology,* 24, 145–172.

Sipe, C. L. (1996). *Mentoring: A synthesis of P/PV's Research: 1988–1995.* Philadelphia, PA: Public/Private Ventures.

Skjaeveland, O., Garling, T., & Maeland, J. (1996). A multidimensional measure of neighboring. *American Journal of Community Psychology,* 24, 413–436.

Slicker, E., & Palmer, D. (1994). Mentoring at-risk high school students: Evaluation of a school-based program. *School Counselor*, 40, 327–334.

Smith, B. K. (1992). Austin Groups for the Elderly. Video segment in *The world of abnormal psychology: An ounce of prevention* (T. Levine, Producer). New York: A. H. Perlmutter. (Available from Annenberg/CPB Collection, 1–800–LEARNER).

Snowden, L. R. (1987). The peculiar successes of community psychology: Service delivery to ethnic minorities and the poor. *American Journal of Community Psychology*, 15, 575–586.

Solomon, D., Watson, M., Battistich, V., Schaps, E., & Delucchi, K. (1996). Creating classrooms that students experience as communities. *American Journal of Community Psychology*, 24, 719–748.

Sonn, C., & Fisher, A. (1996). Psychological sense of community in a politically constructed group. *Journal of Community Psychology*, 24, 417–430.

Sonn, C., & Fisher, A. (1998). Sense of community: Community resilient responses to oppression and change. *Journal of Community Psychology*, 26, 457–472.

Soriano, F. (1995). *Conducting needs assessments: A multidisciplinary approach*. Thousand Oaks, CA: Sage.

Sparks, M. (1998). Neighborhood revitalization in Vallejo. *Prevention Pipeline, 11*(5), 5–7.

Spaulding, J., & Balch, P. (1983). A brief history of primary prevention in the twentieth century: 1908 to 1980. *American Journal of Community Psychology, 11,* 59–80.

Speer, P. (1997). *Social power and forms of change: Implications for empowerment theory.* Manuscript in preparation, Rutgers University.

Speer, P., Dey, S., Griggs, P., Gibson, C., Lubin, L., & Hughey, J. (1992). In search of community: An analysis of community psychology research from 1984–1988. *American Journal of Community Psychology*, 20, 195–210.

Speer P., & Hughey, J. (1995). Community organizing: An ecological route to empowerment and power. *American Journal of Community Psychology*, 23, 729–748.

Speer, P., Hughey, J., Gensheimer, L., & Adams-Leavitt, W. (1995). Organizing for power: A comparative case study. *Journal of Community Psychology*, 23, 57–73.

Spoth, R., Redmond, C., Hockaday, C., & Yoo, S. (1996). Protective factors and young adolescent tendency in problem behaviors: Relationship to self-efficacy, social competence, and life events. *American Journal of Community Psychology*, 24, 749–770.

Stack, C. (1974). *All our kin: Strategies for survival in a Black community.* New York: Harper.

Stanton, A., & Schwartz, M. (1954). *The mental hospital.* New York: Basic Books.

Steele, C. (1997). A threat in the air: How stereotypes shape intellectual identity and performance. *American Psychologist*, 52, 613–629.

Stein, C. H., Ward, M., & Cislo, D. A. (1992). The power of a place: Opening the college classroom to people with serious mental illness. *American Journal of Community Psychology*, 20, 523–548.

Stevenson, J., Mitchell, R. E., & Florin, P. (1996). Evaluation and self-direction in community prevention coalitions. In D. Fetterman, S. Kaftarian, & A. Wandersman (Eds.), *Empowerment evaluation: Knowledge and tools for self-assessment and accountability* (pp. 208–233). Thousand Oaks, CA: Sage.

Stewart, M., Banks, S., Crossman, D., & Poel, D. (1994). Partnerships between health professionals and self-help groups: Meanings and mechanisms. *Prevention in Human Services, 11,* 199–240.

Stokols, D. & Altman, I. (Eds.). (1987). *Handbook of environmental psychology.* New York: Wiley.

Stolz, S. B. (1984). Preventive models: Implications for a technology of practice. In M. Roberts & L. Peterson (Eds.), *Prevention of problems in childhood* (pp. 391–413). New York: Wiley.

Stone, R. A., & Levine, A. G. (1985). Reactions to collective stress: Correlates of active citizen participation at Love Canal. *Prevention in Human Services, 4*, 153–177.

Strauss, A. (1987). *Qualitative analysis for social scientists.* Cambridge, England: Cambridge University Press.

Strother, C. (Ed.) (1957). *Psychology and mental health.* Washington, DC: American Psychological Association.

Strother, C. (1987). Reflections on the Stanford Conference and subsequent events. *American Journal of Community Psychology, 15*, 519–522.

Suarez-Balcazar, Y. (1998, July). Are we addressing the racial divide? *The Community Psychologist, 31*, 12–13.

Suarez-Balcazar, Y., Durlak, J. A., & Smith, C. (1994). Multicultural training practices in community psychology programs. *American Journal of Community Psychology, 22*, 785–798.

Sundberg, N., Hadiyono, J., Latkin, C., & Padilla, J. (1995). Cross-cultural prevention program transfer: Questions regarding developing countries. *Journal of Primary Prevention, 15*, 361–376.

Sundstrom, E., Bell, P., Busby, P., & Asmus, C. (1996). Environmental psychology, 1989–1994. *Annual Review of Psychology, 47*, 485–512.

Swift, C. (1990). Research as intervention. In P. Tolan, C. Keys, F. Chertok, & L. Jason (Eds.), *Researching community psychology* (pp. 196–198). Washington, DC: American Psychological Association.

Sylvestre, J., Pancer, M., Brophy, K., & Cameron, G. (1994). The planning and implementation of government-sponsored community-based primary prevention: A case study. *Canadian Journal of Community Mental Health, 13*, 189–196.

Sylwester, R. (1995). *A celebration of neurons: An educator's guide to the human brain.* Alexandria, VA: ASCD.

Szendre, E. N., & Jose, P. E. (1996). Telephone support by elderly volunteers to inner-city children. *Journal of Community Psychology, 24*, 87–96.

Tandon, S. D., Azelton, L. S., Kelly, J. G., & Strickland, D. A. (1998). Constructing a tree for community leaders: Contexts and processes in collaborative inquiry. *American Journal of Community Psychology, 26*, 669–696.

Tappan, M. (1997). Interpretive psychology: Stories, circles, and understanding lived experience. *Journal of Social Issues, 53*, 645–656.

Tatum, B. (1997). *Why are all the Black kids sitting together in the cafeteria?* New York: Basic Books.

Tausig, M. (1992). Caregiver network structure, support, and caregiver distress. *American Journal of Community Psychology, 20*, 81–96.

Taylor, R.B., & Perkins, D.D. (1989). Mental health: Stress and coping with urban crime and fear. Final report to the National Institute of Mental Health. Philadelphia: Dept. of Criminal Justice, Temple University. (Available from Douglas D. Perkins, FCS Dept., University of Utah, 225 S. 1400 E., Salt Lake City, UT, 84112; or electronic mail address: Perkins@FCS.Utah.Edu

Taylor, S., & Brinkley-Kennedy, R. (1999, Winter). Cultural competence through community action: The South Central Training Consortium, Inc. *The Community Psychologist, 32*, 43–44.

Thoits, P. A. (1983). Multiple identities and psychological well-being: A reformulation and test of the social hypothesis. *American Sociological Review, 48*, 174–187.

Timko, C. (1996). Physical characteristics of residential psychiatric and substance abuse programs: Organizational determinants and patient outcomes. *American Journal of Community Psychology, 24*, 173–192.

Tocqueville, A. de. (1945). *Democracy in America* (2 vols.; H. Reeve and P. Bowen, Eds.). New York: Vintage. (Original work published 1835)

Tocqueville, A. de. (1987). Of individualism in democracies. [Excerpt from *Democracy in America*]. In R. Bellah, R. Madsen, W. Sullivan, A. Swidler, & S. Tipton (Eds.), *Individualism and commitment in American life: Readings on the themes of Habits of the Heart* (pp. 11–13). New York: Harper & Row. (Original work published 1835)

Todd, D. M. (1979). Appendix: Social network mapping. In W. R. Curtis, (Ed.), *The future use of social networks in mental health.* Boston: Social Matrix Research, Inc.

Tolan, P., Keys, C., Chertok, F., & Jason, L. (Eds.). (1990). *Researching community psychology: Issues of theory and methods.* Washington, DC: American Psychological Association.

Tornatzky, L. & Fleischer, M. (1986, October). *Dissemination and/or implementation: The problem of complex socio-technical systems.* Paper presented at the meeting of the American Evaluation Association, Kansas City, MO.

Toro, P. (1990). Evaluating professionally operated and self-help programs for the seriously mentally ill. *American Journal of Community Psychology, 18*, 903–908.

Toro, P. (1998, February). A community psychologist's role in policy on homelessness in two cities. *The Community Psychologist, 31*, 25–26.

Toro, P., Rappaport, J., & Seidman E. (1987). Social climate comparison of mutual help and psychotherapy groups. *Journal of Consulting and Clinical Psychology, 55*, 430–431.

Toro, P., Reischl, T., Zimmerman, M., Rappaport, J., Seidman, E., Luke, D., & Roberts, L. (1988). Professionals in mutual help groups: Impact on social climate and members' behavior. *Journal of Consulting and Clinical Psychology, 56*, 631–632.

Toro, P., & Rojansky, A. (1990, Fall). Homelessness: Some thoughts from an international perspective. *The Community Psychologist, 24*, 8–11.

Trafimow, D., Triandis, H. C., & Goto, S. G. (1991). Some tests of the distinction between the private self and the collective self. *Journal of Personality and Social Psychology, 60*, 649–655.

Triandis, H. C. (1994). *Culture and social behavior*. New York: McGraw-Hill.

Trickett, E. J. (1984). Toward a distinctive community psychology: An ecological metaphor for the conduct of community research and the nature of training. *American Journal of Community Psychology, 12*, 261–279.

Trickett, E. J. (1996). A future for community psychology: The contexts of diversity and the diversity of contexts. *American Journal of Community Psychology, 24*, 209–234.

Trickett, E. J. (1997). Ecology and primary prevention: Reflections on a meta-analysis. *American Journal of Community Psychology, 25*, 197–206.

Trickett, E. J., Kelly, J. G., & Todd, D. M. (1972). The social environment of the school: Guidelines for individual change and organizational redevelopment. In S. Golann & C. Eisdorfer (Eds.), *Handbook of community mental health* (pp. 331–406). New York: Appleton-Century-Crofts.

Trickett, E. J., Kelly, J. G., & Vincent, T. (1985). The spirit of ecological inquiry in community research. In E. Susskind & D. Klein (Eds.), *Community research: Methods, paradigms, and applications* (pp. 283–333). New York: Praeger.

Trickett, E. J., Trickett, P., Castro, J., & Schaffner, P. (1982). The independent school experience: Aspects of the normative environments of single sex and coed secondary schools. *Journal of Educational Psychology, 74*, 374–381.

Trickett, E. J., Watts, R. J., & Birman, D. (Eds.). (1994). *Human diversity: Perspectives on people in context*. San Francisco: Jossey-Bass.

Turner, H. A., & Catania, J. A. (1997). Informal caregiving to persons with AIDS in the United States: Caregiver burden among central cities residents eighteen to forty-nine years old. *American Journal of Community Psychology, 25*, 35–60.

Tyler, F., Pargament, K., & Gatz, M. (1983). The resource collaborator role: A model for interactions involving psychologists. *American Psychologist, 38*, 388–398.

Uchino, B. N., Cacioppo, J. T., & Kiecolt-Glaser, J. K. (1996). The relationship between social support and physiological processes: A review with emphasis on underlying mechanisms and implications for health. *Psychological Bulletin, 119*, 488–531.

Unger, D. G., & Wandersman, A. (1983). Neighboring and its role in block organizations: An exploratory report. *American Journal of Community Psychology, 11*, 291–300.

Unger, D. G., & Wandersman, A. (1985). The importance of neighbors: The social, cognitive and affective components of neighboring. *American Journal of Community Psychology, 13*, 139–170.

Unger, J., Kipke, M., Simon, T., Montgomery, S., & Johnson, C. (1997). Homeless youths and young adults in Los Angeles: Prevalence of mental health problems and the relationship between mental health and substance abuse disorders. *American Journal of Community Psychology, 25*, 289–323.

Unger, R. K., & Crawford, M. (1992). *Women and gender: A feminist psychology*. Philadelphia: Temple University Press.

United Way of America. (1996). *Measuring program outcomes: A practical approach: Effective practices and measuring impact*. Alexandria, VA: Author.

U.S. General Accounting Office. (1990). *Drug education: School-based programs seen as useful but impact unknown* [GAO/HRD-91-27]. Washington, DC: Author.

Van de Ven, A. (1986). Central problems in the management of innovation. *Management Science, 32*, 590–608.

Vega, W. A. (1992). Theoretical and pragmatic implications of cultural diversity for community research. *American Journal of Community Psychology, 20*, 375–392.

Ventis, W. L. (1995). The relationships between religion and mental health. *Journal of Social Issues, 51*, 33–48.

Verburg, H., Janssen, H., Rikken, M., Hoefnagels, C., & van Willenswaard, E. (1992). The Dutch way of prevention. In G. W. Albee, L. A. Bond, & T. Monsey (Eds.), *Improving children's lives: Global perspectives on prevention*

(Vol. 14 of the *Primary prevention of psychopathology* series; pp. 177–190). Thousand Oaks, CA: Sage.

Vincent, T. (1990). A view from the Hill: The human element in policy making on Capitol Hill. *American Psychologist, 45,* 61–64.

Vincent, T., & Trickett, E. (1983). Preventive intervention intervention and the human context: Ecological approaches to environmental assessment and change. In R. Felner, L. Jason, J. Moritsugu, & S. Farber (Eds.), *Preventive psychology: Theory, research, and practice* (pp. 67–86). New York: Pergamon.

Vinokur, A. D., & Selzer, M. L. (1975). Desirable vs. undesirable life events: Their relationship to stress and mental distress. *Journal of Personality and Social Psychology, 32,* 329–337.

Wachtel, P. (1999). *Race in the mind of America.* New York: Routledge.

Wager, C. (1993). Toward a shared ethical culture. *Educational Leadership, 50*(4), 19–23.

Waldo, C. R., Hesson-McInnis, M. S., & D'Augelli, A. R. (1998). Antecedents and consequences of victimization of lesbian, gay, and bisexual young people: A structural model comparing rural university and urban samples. *American Journal of Community Psychology, 26,* 307–334.

Wallach, M. & Wallach, L. (1983). *Psychology's sanction for selfishness: The error of egoism in theory and therapy.* San Francisco: Freeman.

Walsh, R. (1987). A social historical note on the formal emergence of community psychology. *American Journal of Community Psychology, 15,* 523–529.

Walsh-Bowers, R. (2000). A personal sojourn to spiritualize community psychology. *Journal of Community Psychology, 28,* 221–236.

Wandersman, A. (1999). *Community interventions and effective prevention: Bringing evaluators/researchers, funders and practitioners together to promote accountability.* Manuscript in preparation.

Wandersman, A., & Florin, P. (1990). Citizen participation, voluntary organizations and community development: Insights for empowerment and research [Special section]. *American Journal of Community Psychology, 18*(1), 41–177.

Wandersman, A., & Florin, P. (2000). Citizen participation and community organizations. In J. Rappaport & E. Seidman (Eds.), *Handbook of community psychology* (pp. 247–272). New York: Plenum.

Wandersman, A., Goodman, R. M., & Butterfoss, F. D. (1997). Understanding coalitions and how they operate: An "open systems" organizational framework. In M. Minkler (Ed.), *Community organizing and community building for health* (pp. 261–277). New Brunswick, NJ: Rutgers University Press.

Wandersman, A., & Hallman W. (1993). Are people acting irrationally? Understanding public concerns about environmental threats. *American Psychologist, 48,* 681–686.

Wandersman, A., Morrissey, E., Davino, K., Seybolt, D., Crusto, C., Nation, M., Goodman, R., & Imm, P. (1998). Comprehensive quality programming and accountability: Eight essential strategies for implementing successful prevention programs. *Journal of Primary Prevention, 19,* 3–30.

Wandersman, A., & Nation, M. (1998). Urban neighborhoods and mental health: Psychological contributions to understanding toxicity, resilience and interventions. *American Psychologist, 53,* 647–656.

Warren, R. B., & Warren, D. I. (1977). *The neighborhood organizer's handbook.* Notre Dame, IN: University of Notre Dame Press.

Watts, R. J. (1993). Community action through manhood development: A look at concepts and concerns from the frontline. *American Journal of Community Psychology, 21,* 333–360.

Watts, R. J. (1994). Paradigms of diversity. In E. J. Trickett, R. J. Watts, & D. Birman (Eds.), *Human diversity: Perspectives on people in context* (pp. 49–79). San Francisco: Jossey-Bass.

Watts, R. J., Griffith, D. M., & Abdul-Adil, J. (1999). Sociopolitical development as an antidote for oppression: Theory and action. *American Journal of Community Psychology, 27,* 255–272.

Watzlawick, P., Weakland, J., & Fisch, R. (1974). *Change: Principles of problem formation and problem resolution.* New York: Norton.

Weick, K. (1984). Small wins: Redefining the scale of social issues. *American Psychologist, 39,* 40–49.

Weikart, D., & Schweinhart, L. (1997). High/Scope Perry Preschool Program. In G. Albee & T. Gullotta (Eds.), *Primary prevention works* (pp. 146–166). Thousand Oaks, CA: Sage.

Weiss, C. H. (1995). Nothing as practical as good theory: Exploring theory-based evaluation for comprehensive community initiatives for children and families. In J. P. Connell, A. Kubisch, L. Schorr, & C. H. Weiss (Eds.), *New approaches to evaluating community initiatives: Concepts, methods, and contexts* (pp. 65–92). Washington, DC: Aspen Institute.

Weissberg, R. P., Barton, H. A., & Shriver, T. P. (1997). The Social-Competence Promotion Program for young adolescents. In G. Albee &

T. Gullotta (Eds.), *Primary prevention works* (pp. 268–289). Thousand Oaks, CA: Sage.

Weissberg, R. P., & Bell, D. N. (1997). A meta-analytic review of primary prevention programs for children and adolescents: Contributions and caveats. *American Journal of Community Psychology, 25,* 207–214.

Weissberg, R. P., & Greenberg, M. T. (1997). School and community competence-enhancement and prevention programs. In I. Sigel & K. Renniger (Eds.), *Handbook of child psychology, Vol. 4: Child psychology in practice* (5th Ed.; pp. 877–954). New York: Wiley.

Weissberg, R. P., Gullotta, T., Hampton, R., Ryan, B., & Adams, G. (Eds.). (1997a). *Enhancing children's wellness.* Thousand Oaks, CA: Sage.

Weissberg, R. P., Gullotta, T., Hampton, R., Ryan, B., & Adams, G. (Eds.). (1997b). *Establishing preventive services.* Thousand Oaks, CA: Sage.

Werner, E. E., & Smith, R. (1992). *Overcoming the odds: High risk children from birth to adulthood.* New York: Cornell University Press.

West-Olatunji, C. A., & Watson, Z. E. P. (1999, Winter). Community-as-client mental health needs assessment: Use of culture-centered theory and research. *The Community Psychologist, 32,* 36–38.

Wicker, A. (1969). Size of church membership and members' support of church behavior settings. *Journal of Personality and Social Psychology, 13,* 278–288.

Wicker, A. (1973). Undermanning theory and research: Implications for the study of psychological and behavioral effects of excess populations. *Representative Research in Social Psychology, 4,* 185–206.

Wicker, A. (1979). Ecological psychology: Some recent and prospective developments. *American Psychologist, 34,* 755–765.

Wicker, A. (1987). Behavior settings reconsidered: Temporal stages, resources, internal dynamics, and context. In D. Stokols & I. Altman (Eds.), *Handbook of environmental psychology* (Vol. 1; pp. 613–653). New York: Wiley.

Wicker, A., & Sommer, R. (1993). The resident researcher: An alternative career model centered on community. *American Journal of Community Psychology, 21,* 469–482.

Wiesenfeld, E. (1996). The concept of "we": A community social psychology myth? *Journal of Community Psychology, 24,* 337–346.

Wilcox, B. L. (1981). Social support in adjusting to marital disruption: A network analysis. In B. Gottlieb (Ed.), *Social networks and social support* (pp. 97–116). Beverly Hills, CA: Sage.

Wilcox, B. L. (1993). Deterring risky behavior: Policy perspectives on adolescent risk-taking. In N. Bell & R. Bell (Eds.), *Adolescent risk taking* (pp. 148–164). Newbury Park, CA: Sage.

Wills, T. A., Vaccaro, D., & McNamara, G. (1992). The role of life event, family support, and competence in adolescent substance use: A test of vulnerablity and protective factors. *American Journal of Community Psychology, 20,* 349–374.

Wilson, M. (Ed.). (1997). Women of color: Social challenges of dual minority status and competing community contexts [Special issue]. *American Journal of Community Psychology, 25*(5).

Winerip, M. (1999, May 23). Bedlam on the streets: Increasingly, the mentally ill have nowhere to go. That's their problem — and ours. *New York Times Magazine,* pp. 42–49, 56, 65–66, 70.

Wink, P. (1997). Beyond ethnic differences: Contextualizing the influence of ethnicity on individualism and collectivism. *Journal of Social Issues, 53,* 299–328.

Witlein, B., & Altschuld, J. (1995). *Planning and conducting needs assessments.* Thousand Oaks, CA: Sage.

Wittig, M. A., & Bettencourt, B. A. (Eds.). (1996). Social psychological perspectives on grassroots organizing [Special issue]. *Journal of Social Issues, 52*(1).

Wolchik, S. A., West, S. G., Westover, S., Sandler, I. N., Martin, A., Lustig, J., Tein, J., & Fisher, J. (1993). The children of divorce parenting intervention: Outcome evaluation of an empirically based program. *American Journal of Community Psychology, 21,* 293–332.

Wolff, T. (1987). Community psychology and empowerment: An activist's insights. *American Journal of Community Psychology, 15,* 151–166.

Wolff, T. (1994, Summer). Keynote address given at the fourth biennial conference. *The Community Psychologist, 27,* 20–26.

Wolff, T. (1995, Spring). Healthy Communities Massachusetts: One vision of civic democracy. *Municipal Advocate* (Massachusetts Municipal Association), pp. 22–24. (Available from AHEC/Community Partners, 24 S. Prospect St., Amherst, MA 01002.)

Wolff, T., & Lee, P. (1997, June). *The Healthy Communities movement: An exciting new area for research and action by community psychologists.* Workshop presented at the meeting of the Society for Community Research and Action, Columbia, SC.

Wood, P. A., Hurlburt, M., Hough, R., & Hofstetter, G. R. (1998). Longitudinal assessment of family support among homeless mentally ill participants in a supported housing program. *Journal of Community Psychology, 26,* 327–344.

World Health Organization, Division of Mental Health. *"Skills for Life" Newsletter.* Geneva, Switzerland: Author. (Available from: WHO Division of Mental Health, CH-1211 Geneva 27, Switzerland).

Worthen, B., Sanders, J., & Fitzpatrick, J. (1997). *Program evaluation: Alternative approaches and practical guidelines* (2nd ed). White Plains, NY: Longman.

Wursten, A. & Sales, B. (1988). Community psychology in state legislative decision-making. *American Journal of Community Psychology, 16,* 487–502.

Wuthnow, R. (1994). *Sharing the journey: Support groups and America's new quest for community.* New York: Free Press.

Wyman, P., Cowen, E., Work, W., & Parker, G. (1991). Developmental and family milieu correlates of resilience in urban children who have experienced major life stress. *American Journal of Community Psychology, 19,* 405–425.

Yeich, S. (1996). Grassroots organizing with homeless people: A participatory research approach. *Journal of Social Issues, 52,* 111–122.

Ying, Y. (1995). Cultural orientation and psychological well-being in Chinese Americans. *American Journal of Community Psychology, 23,* 893–912.

Zander, A. (1995). [Untitled videotape interview]. In J. G. Kelly (Ed.), *The history of community psychology: A video presentation of context and exemplars.* Chicago: Society for Community Research and Action.

Zane, N., & Sue, S. (1986). Reappraisal of ethnic minority issues: Research alternatives. In E.

Seidman & J. Rappaport (Eds.), *Redefining social problems* (pp. 289–304). New York: Plenum.

Zea, M. C., Jarama, S. L., & Bianchi, F. T. (1995). Social support and psychological competence: Explaining the adaptation to college of ethnically diverse students. *American Journal of Community Psychology, 23,* 509–532.

Zigler, E. (1994). Reshaping early childhood intervention to be a more effective weapon against poverty. *American Journal of Community Psychology, 22,* 37–48.

Zimmerman, M. A. (1995). Psychological empowerment: Issues and illustrations. *American Journal of Community Psychology, 23,* 581–600.

Zimmerman, M. A. (2000). Empowerment theory: psychological, organizational and community levels of analysis. In J. Rappaport & E. Seidman (Eds.), *Handbook of community psychology* (pp. 43–63). New York: Plenum.

Zimmerman, M. A., Israel, B. A., Schulz, A. & Checkoway, B. (1992). Further explorations in empowerment theory: An empirical analysis of psychological empowerment. *American Journal of Community Psychology, 20,* 707–728.

Zimmerman, M. A., & Perkins, D. (Eds.). (1995). Empowerment theory, research and application [Special issue]. *American Journal of Community Psychology, 23*(5).

Zimmerman, M. A., & Rappaport, J. (1988). Citizen participation, perceived control and psychological empowerment. *American Journal of Community Psychology, 16,* 725–750.

Zimmerman, M. A., Reischl, T. M., Seidman, E., Rappaport, J., Toro, P. A., & Salem, D. A. (1991). Expansion strategies of a mutual help organization. *American Journal of Community Psychology, 19,* 251–278.

Zuckerman, M. (1990). Some dubious premises in research and theory on racial differences: Social, scientific and ethical issues. *American Psychologist, 45,* 1297–1303.

# NAME INDEX

# SUBJECT INDEX